Advance Praise for *Head First Python*,

"A Python book should be as much fun as the language is. With Head First Python, master teach Barry delivers a quick-paced, entertaining and engaging guide to the language that will leave you well prepared to write real-world Python code."

— **Dr. Eric Freeman, computer scientist, technology educator, and former CTO of Disney Online**

"*Head First Python* is a great introduction to both the language and how to use Python in the real world. It's full of practical advice on coding for the web and databases, and it doesn't shy away from difficult subjects like collections and immutability. If you're looking for a great introduction to Python, then this is the place to start."

— **David Griffiths, author and Agile coach**

"With major changes and updates from the first edition, this edition of Head First Python is sure to become a favourite in the rapidly growing collection of great Python guides. The content is structured to deliver high impact to the reader, and is heavily focused on being productive as soon as possible. All the necessary topics are covered with great clarity, and the entertaining delivery makes this book a delight to read."

— **Caleb Hattingh, author of** *20 Python Libraries You Aren't Using (But Should)* **and** *Learning Cython*

"Here's a clear and clean entry into the Python pool. No bellyflops, and you'll go deeper than you expected to."

— **Bill Lubanovic, author of Introducing Python**

Praise for the first edition

"*Head First Python* is a great introduction to not just the Python language, but Python as it's used in the real world. The book goes beyond the syntax to teach you how to create applications for Android phones, Google's App Engine, and more."

— **David Griffiths, author and Agile coach**

"Where other books start with theory and progress to examples, *Head First Python* jumps right in with code and explains the theory as you read along. This is a much more effective learning environment, because it engages the reader to *do* from the very beginning. It was also just a joy to read. It was fun without being flippant and informative without being condescending. The breadth of examples and explanation covered the majority of what you'll use in your job every day. I'll recommend this book to anyone starting out on Python."

— **Jeremy Jones, coauthor of** *Python for Unix and Linux System Administration*

Praise for other Head First books

"Kathy and Bert's *Head First Java* transforms the printed page into the closest thing to a GUI you've ever seen. In a wry, hip manner, the authors make learning Java an engaging 'what're they gonna do next?' experience."

— **Warren Keuffel, *Software Development Magazine***

"Beyond the engaging style that drags you forward from know-nothing into exalted Java warrior status, *Head First Java* covers a huge amount of practical matters that other texts leave as the dreaded 'exercise for the reader....' It's clever, wry, hip and practical—there aren't a lot of textbooks that can make that claim and live up to it while also teaching you about object serialization and network launch protocols."

— **Dr. Dan Russell, Director of User Sciences and Experience Research IBM Almaden Research Center (and teaches Artificial Intelligence at Stanford University)**

"It's fast, irreverent, fun, and engaging. Be careful—you might actually learn something!"

— **Ken Arnold, former Senior Engineer at Sun Microsystems Coauthor (with James Gosling, creator of Java), *The Java Programming Language***

"I feel like a thousand pounds of books have just been lifted off of my head."

— **Ward Cunningham, inventor of the Wiki and founder of the Hillside Group**

"Just the right tone for the geeked-out, casual-cool guru coder in all of us. The right reference for practical development strategies—gets my brain going without having to slog through a bunch of tired, stale professor-speak."

— **Travis Kalanick, cofounder and CEO of Uber**

"There are books you buy, books you keep, books you keep on your desk, and thanks to O'Reilly and the Head First crew, there is the penultimate category, Head First books. They're the ones that are dog-eared, mangled, and carried everywhere. *Head First SQL* is at the top of my stack. Heck, even the PDF I have for review is tattered and torn."

— **Bill Sawyer, ATG Curriculum Manager, Oracle**

"This book's admirable clarity, humor and substantial doses of clever make it the sort of book that helps even nonprogrammers think well about problem-solving."

— **Cory Doctorow, co-editor of Boing Boing Author, *Down and Out in the Magic Kingdom* and *Someone Comes to Town, Someone Leaves Town***

"I received the book yesterday and started to read it…and I couldn't stop. This is definitely très 'cool.' It is fun, but they cover a lot of ground and they are right to the point. I'm really impressed."

— **Erich Gamma, IBM Distinguished Engineer, and coauthor of *Design Patterns***

"One of the funniest and smartest books on software design I've ever read."

— **Aaron LaBerge, VP Technology, ESPN.com**

"What used to be a long trial and error learning process has now been reduced neatly into an engaging paperback."

— **Mike Davidson, CEO, Newsvine, Inc.**

"Elegant design is at the core of every chapter here, each concept conveyed with equal doses of pragmatism and wit."

— **Ken Goldstein, Executive Vice President, Disney Online**

"I ♥ *Head First HTML with CSS & XHTML*—it teaches you everything you need to learn in a 'fun-coated' format."

— **Sally Applin, UI Designer and Artist**

"Usually when reading through a book or article on design patterns, I'd have to occasionally stick myself in the eye with something just to make sure I was paying attention. Not with this book. Odd as it may sound, this book makes learning about design patterns fun.

"While other books on design patterns are saying 'Bueller…Bueller…Bueller…' this book is on the float belting out 'Shake it up, baby!'"

— **Eric Wuehler**

"I literally love this book. In fact, I kissed this book in front of my wife."

— **Satish Kumar**

Other related books from O'Reilly

Learning Python

Programming Python

Python in a Nutshell

Python Cookbook

Fluent Python

Other books in O'Reilly's Head First series

Head First Ajax

Head First Android Development

Head First C

Head First C#, Third Edition

Head First Data Analysis

Head First HTML and CSS, Second Edition

Head First HTML5 Programming

Head First iPhone and iPad Development, Third Edition

Head First JavaScript Programming

Head First jQuery

Head First Networking

Head First PHP & MySQL

Head First PMP, Third Edition

Head First Programming

Head First Python, Second Edition

Head First Ruby

Head First Servlets and JSP, Second Edition

Head First Software Development

Head First SQL

Head First Statistics

Head First Web Design

Head First WordPress

For a full list of titles, go to *headfirstlabs.com/books.php*.

Head First **Python**

Second Edition

Wouldn't it be dreamy if there were a Python book that didn't make you wish you were anywhere other than stuck in front of your computer writing code? I guess it's just a fantasy...

Paul Barry

Beijing • Boston • Farnham • Sebastopol • Tokyo

Head First Python, Second Edition

by Paul Barry

Published by O'Reilly Media, Inc., 1005 Gravenstein Highway North, Sebastopol, CA 95472.

O'Reilly Media books may be purchased for educational, business, or sales promotional use. Online editions are also available for most titles (*http://safaribooksonline.com*). For more information, contact our corporate/institutional sales department: (800) 998-9938 or *corporate@oreilly.com*.

Series Creators:	Kathy Sierra, Bert Bates
Editor:	Dawn Schanafelt
Cover Designer:	Randy Comer
Production Editor:	Melanie Yarbrough
Proofreader:	Rachel Monaghan
Indexer:	Lucie Haskins
Page Viewers:	Deirdre, Joseph, Aaron, and Aideen

Deirdre

Aaron

Aideen

Joseph

Printing History:

November 2010: First edition.
November 2016: Second edition.

No weblogs were inappropriately searched in the making of this book, and the photos on this page (as well as the one on the author page) were supplied by *Aideen Barry*.

ISBN: 978-1-491-91953-8

[M]

I continue to dedicate this book to all those generous people in the Python community who continue to help make Python what it is today.

And to all those that made learning Python and its technologies just complex enough that people need a book like *this* to learn it.

Author of Head First Python, 2nd Edition

While out walking, Paul pauses to discuss the correct pronunciation of the word "tuple" with his long-suffering wife.

This is Deirdre's usual reaction. ☺

Paul Barry lives and works in *Carlow, Ireland*, which is a small town of 35,000 people or so, located just over 80km southwest of the nation's capital: *Dublin*.

Paul has a *B.Sc. in Information Systems*, as well as an *M.Sc. in Computing*. He also has a postgraduate qualification in *Learning and Teaching*.

Paul has worked at *The Institute of Technology, Carlow* since 1995, and lectured there since 1997. Prior to becoming involved in teaching, Paul spent a decade in the IT industry working in Ireland and Canada, with the majority of his work within a healthcare setting. Paul is married to Deirdre, and they have three children (two of whom are now in college).

The Python programming language (and its related technologies) has formed an integral part of Paul's undergraduate courses since the 2007 academic year.

Paul is the author (or coauthor) of four other technical books: two on Python and two on *Perl*. In the past, he's written a heap of material for *Linux Journal Magazine*, where he was a contributing editor.

Paul was raised in *Belfast, Northern Ireland*, which may go some of the way toward explaining his take on things as well as his funny accent (unless, of course, you're also from "The North," in which case Paul's outlook and accent are *perfectly normal*).

Find Paul on *Twitter* (*@barrypj*), as well as at his home on the Web: *http://paulbarry.itcarlow.ie*.

Table of Contents (Summary)

Table of Contents (the real thing)

Intro

Your brain on Python.
Here *you* are trying to *learn* something, while here your *brain* is, doing you a favor by making sure the learning doesn't *stick*. Your brain's thinking, "Better leave room for more important things, like which wild animals to avoid and whether naked snowboarding is a bad idea." So how *do* you trick your brain into thinking that your life depends on knowing how to program in Python?

the basics

1 Getting Started Quickly

Get going with Python programming as quickly as possible.

In this chapter, we introduce the basics of programming in Python, and we do this in typical *Head First* style: by jumping right in. After just a few pages, you'll have run your first sample program. By the end of the chapter, you'll not only be able to run the sample program, but you'll understand its code too (and more besides). Along the way, you'll learn about a few of the things that make **Python** the programming language it is.

list data

2 Working with Data

All programs process data, and Python programs are no exception.

In fact, take a look around: *data is everywhere*. A lot of, if not most, programming is all about data: *acquiring* data, *processing* data, *understanding* data. To work with data effectively, you need somewhere to *put* your data when processing it. Python shines in this regard, thanks (in no small part) to its inclusion of a handful of *widely applicable* data structures: **lists**, **dictionaries**, **tuples**, and **sets**. In this chapter, we'll preview all four, before spending the majority of this chapter digging deeper into **lists** (and we'll deep-dive into the other three in the next chapter). We're covering these data structures early, as most of what you'll likely do with Python will revolve around working with data.

structured data

3

Working with Structured Data

Python's list data structure is great, but it isn't a data

panacea. When you have *truly* structured data (and using a list to store it may not be the best choice), Python comes to your rescue with its built-in **dictionary**. Out of the box, the dictionary lets you store and manipulate any collection of *key/value pairs*. We look long and hard at Python's dictionary in this chapter, and—along the way—meet **set** and **tuple**, too. Together with the **list** (which we met in the previous chapter), the dictionary, set, and tuple data structures provide a set of built-in data tools that help to make Python and data a powerful combination.

Name: Ford Prefect
Gender: Male
Occupation: Researcher
Home Planet: Betelgeuse Seven

code reuse

4

Functions and Modules

Reusing code is key to building a maintainable system.

And when it comes to reusing code in Python, it all starts and ends with the humble **function**. Take some lines of code, give them a name, and you've got a function (which can be reused). Take a collection of functions and package them as a file, and you've got a **module** (which can also be reused). It's true what they say: *it's good to share*, and by the end of this chapter, you'll be well on your way to **sharing** and **reusing** your code, thanks to an understanding of how Python's functions and modules work.

module

building a webapp

5

Getting Real

At this stage, you know enough Python to be dangerous.

With this book's first four chapters behind you, you're now in a position to productively use Python within any number of application areas (even though there's still lots of Python to learn). Rather than explore the long list of what these application areas are, in this and subsequent chapters, we're going to structure our learning around the development of a web-hosted application, which is an area where Python is especially strong. Along the way, you'll learn a bit more about Python.

storing and manipulating data

Where to Put Your Data

6

Sooner or later, you'll need to safely store your data somewhere.

And when it comes to **storing data**, Python has you covered. In this chapter, you'll learn about storing and retrieving data from *text files*, which—as storage mechanisms go—may feel a bit simplistic, but is nevertheless used in many problem areas. As well as storing and retrieving your data from files, you'll also learn some tricks of the trade when it comes to manipulating data. We're saving the "serious stuff" (storing data in a database) until the next chapter, but there's plenty to keep us busy for now when working with files.

Form Data	Remote_addr	User_agent	Results
ImmutableMultiDict([('phrase', 'hitch-hiker'), ('letters', 'aeiou')])	127.0.0.1	Mozilla/5.0 (Macintosh; Intel Mac OS X 10_11_2) AppleWebKit/537.36 (KHTML, like Gecko) Chrome/47.0.2526 .106 Safari/537.36	{'e', 'i'}

using a database

7

Putting Python's DB-API to Use

Storing data in a relational database system is handy. In this chapter, you'll learn how to write code that interacts with the popular **MySQL** database technology, using a generic database API called **DB-API**. The DB-API (which comes standard with every Python install) allows you to write code that is easily transferred from one database product to the next... assuming your database talks SQL. Although we'll be using MySQL, there's nothing stopping you from using your DB-API code with your favorite relational database, whatever it may be. Let's see what's involved in using a relational database with Python. There's not a lot of new Python in this chapter, but using Python to talk to databases is a **big deal**, so it's well worth learning.

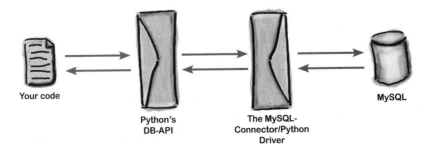

Your code   Python's DB-API   The MySQL-Connector/Python Driver   MySQL

a little bit of class

Abstracting Behavior and State

Classes let you bundle code behavior and state together.

In this chapter, you're setting your webapp aside while you learn about creating Python **classes**. You're doing this in order to get to the point where you can create a context manager with the help of a Python class. As creating and using classes is such a useful thing to know about anyway, we're dedicating this chapter to them. We won't cover everything about classes, but we'll touch on all the bits you'll need to understand in order to confidently create the context manager your webapp is waiting for.

```
● ● ●    countfromby.py - /Users/paul/Desktop/_NewBook/ch07/countfromby.py (3.5.1)

class CountFromBy:

    def __init__(self, v: int, i: int) -> None:
        self.val = v
        self.incr = i

    def increase(self) -> None:
        self.val += self.incr

                                                      Ln: 2  Col: 0
```

the context management protocol

Hooking into Python's with Statements

It's time to take what you've just learned and put it to work.

Chapter 7 discussed using a **relational database** with Python, while Chapter 8 provided an introduction to using **classes** in your Python code. In this chapter, both of these techniques are combined to produce a **context manager** that lets us extend the with statement to work with relational database systems. In this chapter, you'll hook into the with statement by creating a new class, which conforms to Python's **context management protocol**.

```
File Edit Window Help  Checking our log DB
$ mysql -u vsearch -p vsearchlogDB
Enter password:

Welcome to MySQL monitor...


mysql> select * from log;
+----+---------------------+---------------------+---------+-----------+---------------+------------------------+
| id | ts                  | phrase              | letters | ip        | browser_string| results                |
+----+---------------------+---------------------+---------+-----------+---------------+------------------------+
|  1 | 2016-03-09 13:40:46 | life, the uni ... ything | aeiou   | 127.0.0.1 | firefox       | {'u', 'e', 'i', 'a'}   |
|  2 | 2016-03-09 13:42:07 | hitch-hiker         | aeiou   | 127.0.0.1 | safari        | {'i', 'e'}             |
|  3 | 2016-03-09 13:42:15 | galaxy              | xyz     | 127.0.0.1 | chrome        | {'y', 'x'}             |
|  4 | 2016-03-09 13:43:07 | hitch-hiker         | xyz     | 127.0.0.1 | firefox       | set()                  |
+----+---------------------+---------------------+---------+-----------+---------------+------------------------+
4 rows in set (0.0 sec)


mysql> quit
Bye
```

10

function decorators

Wrapping Functions

When it comes to augmenting your code, Chapter 9's context management protocol is not the only game in town. Python also lets you use function **decorators**, a technique whereby you can add code to an existing function *without* having to change any of the existing function's code. If you think this sounds like some sort of black art, don't despair: it's nothing of the sort. However, as coding techniques go, creating a function decorator is often considered to be on the harder side by many Python programmers, and thus is not used as often as it should be. In this chapter, our plan is to show you that, despite being an advanced technique, creating and using your own decorators is not that hard.

checker.py - /Users/paul/Desktop/_NewBook/ch10/checker.py (3.5.1)

```
from flask import session
from functools import wraps
def check_logged_in(func):
    @wraps(func)
    def wrapper(*args, **kwargs):
        if 'logged_in' in session:
            return func(*args, **kwargs)
        return 'You are NOT logged in.'
    return wrapper
```

Ln: 13 Col: 0

exception handling

11 What to Do When Things Go Wrong
Things go wrong, all the time—no matter how good your code is.

You've successfully executed all of the examples in this book, and you're likely confident all of the code presented thus far works. But does this mean the code is robust? Probably not. Writing code based on the assumption that nothing bad ever happens is (at best) naive. At worst, it's dangerous, as unforeseen things do (and will) happen. It's much better if you're wary while coding, as opposed to trusting. Care is needed to ensure your code does what you want it to, as well as reacts properly when things go south.

```
    ...
Exception
   +-- StopIteration
   +-- StopAsyncIteration
   +-- ArithmeticError
   |    +-- FloatingPointError
   |    +-- OverflowError
   |    +-- ZeroDivisionError
   +-- AssertionError
   +-- AttributeError
   +-- BufferError
   +-- EOFError
    ...
```

a little bit of threading

$11\ ^{3}/_{4}$

Dealing with Waiting

Your code can sometimes take a long time to execute.

Depending on who notices, this may or may not be an issue. If some code takes 30 seconds to do its thing "behind the scenes," the wait may not be an issue. However, if your user is waiting for your application to respond, and it takes 30 seconds, everyone notices. What you should do to fix this problem depends on what you're trying to do (and who's doing the waiting). In this short chapter, we'll briefly discuss some options, then look at one solution to the issue at hand: *what happens if something takes too long?*

Wait!

advanced iteration

12

Looking Like Crazy

It's often amazing how much time our programs spend in loops.

This isn't a surprise, as most programs exist to perform something quickly a whole heap of times. When it comes to optimizing loops, there are two approaches: (1) improve the loop syntax (to make it easier to specify a loop), and (2) improve how loops execute (to make them go faster). Early in the lifetime of Python 2 (that is, a *long, long* time ago), the language designers added a single language feature that implements both approaches, and it goes by a rather strange name: **comprehension**.

installation

a

Installing Python

First things first: let's get Python installed on your computer.

Whether you're running on *Windows*, *Mac OS X*, or *Linux*, Python's got you covered. How you install it on each of these platforms is specific to how things work on each of these operating systems (we know...a shocker, eh?), and the Python community works hard to provide installers that target all the popular systems. In this short appendix, you'll be guided through installing Python on your computer.

pythonanywhere

b

Deploying Your Webapp

At the end of Chapter 5, we claimed that deploying your webapp to the cloud was only 10 minutes away. It's now time to make good on that promise.

In this appendix, we are going to take you through the process of deploying your webapp on *PythonAnywhere*, going from zero to deployed in about 10 minutes. *PythonAnywhere* is a favorite among the Python programming community, and it's not hard to see why: it works exactly as you'd expect it to, has great support for Python (and Flask), and—best of all—you can get started hosting your webapp at no cost.

top ten things we didn't cover

There's Always More to Learn

It was never our intention to try to cover everything. This book's goal was always to show you enough Python to get you up to speed as quickly as possible. There's a lot more we could've covered, but didn't. In this appendix, we discuss the top 10 things that—given another 600 pages or so—we would've eventually gotten around to. Not all of the 10 things will interest you, but quickly flip through them just in case we've hit on your sweet spot, or provided an answer to that nagging question. All the programming technologies in this appendix come baked in to Python and its interpreter.

d top ten projects not covered

Even More Tools, Libraries, and Modules

We know what you're thinking as you read this appendix's title.

Why on Earth didn't they make the title of the last appendix: *The Top Twenty Things We Didn't Cover*? Why *another* 10? In the last appendix, we limited our discussion to stuff that comes baked in to Python (part of the language's "batteries included"). In this appendix, we cast the net much further afield, discussing a whole host of technologies that are available to you *because* Python exists. There's lots of good stuff here and—just like with the last appendix—a quick perusal won't hurt you *one single bit*.

getting involved

The Python Community

Python is much more than a great programming language.

It's a great community, too. The Python Community is welcoming, diverse, open, friendly, sharing, and giving. We're just amazed that no one, to date, has thought to put that on a greeting card! Seriously, though, there's more to programming in Python than the language. An entire ecosystem has grown up around Python, in the form of excellent books, blogs, websites, conferences, meetups, user groups, and personalities. In this appendix, we take a survey of the Python community and see what it has to offer. Don't just sit around programming on your own: **get involved!**

how to use this book

Intro

In this section, we answer the burning question: "So why DID they put that in a Python book?"

Who Is This Book For?

If you can answer "yes" to all of these:

 Do you already know how to program in another programming language?

 Do you wish you had the know-how to program Python, add it to your list of tools, and make it do new things?

 Do you prefer actually doing things and applying the stuff you learn over listening to someone in a lecture rattle on for hours on end?

this book is for you.

Who should probably back away from this book?

If you can answer "yes" to any of these:

 Do you already know most of what you need to know to program with Python?

 Are you looking for a reference book to Python, one that covers all the details in excruciating detail?

 Would you rather have your toenails pulled out by 15 screaming monkeys than learn something new? Do you believe a Python book should cover *everything* and if it bores the reader to tears in the process, then so much the better?

this book is **not** for you.

This is NOT a reference book, and we assume you've programmed before.

[Note from marketing: this book is for anyone with a credit card... we'll accept a check, too.]

We Know What You're Thinking

"How can *this* be a serious Python book?"

"What's with all the graphics?"

"Can I actually *learn* it this way?"

We know what your *brain* is thinking

Your brain craves novelty. It's always searching, scanning, *waiting* for something unusual. It was built that way, and it helps you stay alive.

So what does your brain do with all the routine, ordinary, normal things you encounter? Everything it *can* to stop them from interfering with the brain's *real* job—recording things that *matter*. It doesn't bother saving the boring things; they never make it past the "this is obviously not important" filter.

How does your brain *know* what's important? Suppose you're out for a day hike and a tiger jumps in front of you, what happens inside your head and body?

Neurons fire. Emotions crank up. *Chemicals surge.*

And that's how your brain knows…

This must be important! Don't forget it!

But imagine you're at home, or in a library. It's a safe, warm, tiger-free zone. You're studying. Getting ready for an exam. Or trying to learn some tough technical topic your boss thinks will take a week, 10 days at the most.

Just one problem. Your brain's trying to do you a big favor. It's trying to make sure that this *obviously* nonimportant content doesn't clutter up scarce resources. Resources that are better spent storing the really *big* things. Like tigers. Like the danger of fire. Like how you should never have posted those "party" photos on your Facebook page. And there's no simple way to tell your brain, "Hey brain, thank you very much, but no matter how dull this book is, and how little I'm registering on the emotional Richter scale right now, I really *do* want you to keep this stuff around."

Your brain thinks THIS is important.

Great. Only 450 more dull, dry, boring pages.

Your brain thinks THIS isn't worth saving.

We think of a "Head First" reader as a <u>learner</u>.

So what does it take to *learn* something? First, you have to *get* it, then make sure you don't *forget* it. It's not about pushing facts into your head. Based on the latest research in cognitive science, neurobiology, and educational psychology, *learning* takes a lot more than text on a page. We know what turns your brain on.

Some of the Head First learning principles:

Make it visual. Images are far more memorable than words alone, and make learning much more effective (up to 89% improvement in recall and transfer studies). It also makes things more understandable. **Put the words within or near the graphics** they relate to, rather than on the bottom or on another page, and learners will be up to *twice* as likely to solve problems related to the content.

Use a conversational and personalized style. In recent studies, students performed up to 40% better on post-learning tests if the content spoke directly to the reader, using a first-person, conversational style rather than taking a formal tone. Tell stories instead of lecturing. Use casual language. Don't take yourself too seriously. Which would *you* pay more attention to: a stimulating dinner party companion or a lecture?

Get the learner to think more deeply. In other words, unless you actively flex your neurons, nothing much happens in your head. A reader has to be motivated, engaged, curious, and inspired to solve problems, draw conclusions, and generate new knowledge. And for that, you need challenges, exercises, and thought-provoking questions, and activities that involve both sides of the brain and multiple senses.

Get—and keep—the reader's attention. We've all had the "I really want to learn this, but I can't stay awake past page one" experience. Your brain pays attention to things that are out of the ordinary, interesting, strange, eye-catching, unexpected. Learning a new, tough, technical topic doesn't have to be boring. Your brain will learn much more quickly if it's not.

Touch their emotions. We now know that your ability to remember something is largely dependent on its emotional content. You remember what you care about. You remember when you *feel* something. No, we're not talking heart-wrenching stories about a boy and his dog. We're talking emotions like surprise, curiosity, fun, "what the...?", and the feeling of "I rule!" that comes when you solve a puzzle, learn something everybody else thinks is hard, or realize you know something that "I'm more technical than thou" Bob from engineering *doesn't*.

Metacognition: Thinking About Thinking

If you really want to learn, and you want to learn more quickly and more deeply, pay attention to how you pay attention. Think about how you think. Learn how you learn.

Most of us did not take courses on metacognition or learning theory when we were growing up. We were *expected* to learn, but rarely *taught* to learn.

I wonder how I can trick my brain into remembering this stuff...

But we assume that if you're holding this book, you really want to learn how to solve programming problems with Python. And you probably don't want to spend a lot of time. If you want to use what you read in this book, you need to *remember* what you read. And for that, you've got to *understand* it. To get the most from this book, or *any* book or learning experience, take responsibility for your brain. Your brain on *this* content.

The trick is to get your brain to see the new material you're learning as Really Important. Crucial to your well-being. As important as a tiger. Otherwise, you're in for a constant battle, with your brain doing its best to keep the new content from sticking.

So just how *DO* you get your brain to treat programming like it was a hungry tiger?

There's the slow, tedious way, or the faster, more effective way. The slow way is about sheer repetition. You obviously know that you *are* able to learn and remember even the dullest of topics if you keep pounding the same thing into your brain. With enough repetition, your brain says, "This doesn't *feel* important to him, but he keeps looking at the same thing *over* and *over* and *over*, so I suppose it must be."

The faster way is to do **anything that increases brain activity,** especially different *types* of brain activity. The things on the previous page are a big part of the solution, and they're all things that have been proven to help your brain work in your favor. For example, studies show that putting words *within* the pictures they describe (as opposed to somewhere else in the page, like a caption or in the body text) causes your brain to try to makes sense of how the words and picture relate, and this causes more neurons to fire. More neurons firing = more chances for your brain to *get* that this is something worth paying attention to, and possibly recording.

A conversational style helps because people tend to pay more attention when they perceive that they're in a conversation, since they're expected to follow along and hold up their end. The amazing thing is, your brain doesn't necessarily *care* that the "conversation" is between you and a book! On the other hand, if the writing style is formal and dry, your brain perceives it the same way you experience being lectured to while sitting in a roomful of passive attendees. No need to stay awake.

But pictures and conversational style are just the beginning…

Here's What WE Did:

We used *pictures*, because your brain is tuned for visuals, not text. As far as your brain's concerned, a picture really *is* worth a thousand words. And when text and pictures work together, we embedded the text *in* the pictures because your brain works more effectively when the text is *within* the thing the text refers to, as opposed to in a caption or buried in the text somewhere.

We used *redundancy*, saying the same thing in *different* ways and with different media types, and *multiple senses*, to increase the chance that the content gets coded into more than one area of your brain.

We used concepts and pictures in *unexpected* ways because your brain is tuned for novelty, and we used pictures and ideas with at least *some emotional* content, because your brain is tuned to pay attention to the biochemistry of emotions. That which causes you to *feel* something is more likely to be remembered, even if that feeling is nothing more than a little *humor*, *surprise*, or *interest*.

We used a personalized, *conversational style*, because your brain is tuned to pay more attention when it believes you're in a conversation than if it thinks you're passively listening to a presentation. Your brain does this even when you're *reading*.

We included more than 80 *activities*, because your brain is tuned to learn and remember more when you *do* things than when you *read* about things. And we made the exercises challenging-yet-doable, because that's what most people prefer.

We used *multiple learning styles*, because *you* might prefer step-by-step procedures, while someone else wants to understand the big picture first, and someone else just wants to see an example. But regardless of your own learning preference, *everyone* benefits from seeing the same content represented in multiple ways.

We include content for *both sides of your brain*, because the more of your brain you engage, the more likely you are to learn and remember, and the longer you can stay focused. Since working one side of the brain often means giving the other side a chance to rest, you can be more productive at learning for a longer period of time.

And we included *stories* and exercises that present *more than one point of view,* because your brain is tuned to learn more deeply when it's forced to make evaluations and judgments.

We included *challenges*, with exercises, and asked *questions* that don't always have a straight answer, because your brain is tuned to learn and remember when it has to *work* at something. Think about it—you can't get your *body* in shape just by *watching* people at the gym. But we did our best to make sure that when you're working hard, it's on the *right* things. That *you're not spending one extra dendrite* processing a hard-to-understand example, or parsing difficult, jargon-laden, or overly terse text.

We used *people*. In stories, examples, pictures, and so on, because, well, *you're* a person. And your brain pays more attention to *people* than it does to *things*.

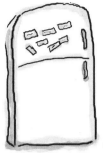

Here's what YOU can do to bend your brain into submission

So, we did our part. The rest is up to you. These tips are a starting point; listen to your brain and figure out what works for you and what doesn't. Try new things.

Cut this out and stick it on your refrigerator.

---

1 **Slow down. The more you understand, the less you have to memorize.**

Don't just *read*. Stop and think. When the book asks you a question, don't just skip to the answer. Imagine that someone really *is* asking the question. The more deeply you force your brain to think, the better chance you have of learning and remembering.

2 **Do the exercises. Write your own notes.**

We put them in, but if we did them for you, that would be like having someone else do your workouts for you. And don't just *look* at the exercises. **Use a pencil.** There's plenty of evidence that physical activity *while* learning can increase the learning.

3 **Read the "There Are No Dumb Questions" sections.**

That means all of them. They're not optional sidebars, ***they're part of the core content!*** Don't skip them.

4 **Make this the last thing you read before bed. Or at least the last challenging thing.**

Part of the learning (especially the transfer to long-term memory) happens *after* you put the book down. Your brain needs time on its own, to do more processing. If you put in something new during that processing time, some of what you just learned will be lost.

5 **Talk about it. Out loud.**

Speaking activates a different part of the brain. If you're trying to understand something or increase your chance of remembering it later, say it out loud. Better still, try to explain it out loud to someone else. You'll learn more quickly, and you might uncover ideas you hadn't known were there when you were reading about it.

6 **Drink water. Lots of it.**

Your brain works best in a nice bath of fluid. Dehydration (which can happen before you ever feel thirsty) decreases cognitive function.

7 **Listen to your brain.**

Pay attention to whether your brain is getting overloaded. If you find yourself starting to skim the surface or forget what you just read, it's time for a break. Once you go past a certain point, you won't learn faster by trying to shove more in, and you might even hurt the process.

8 **Feel something.**

Your brain needs to know that this *matters*. Get involved with the stories. Make up your own captions for the photos. Groaning over a bad joke is *still* better than feeling nothing at all.

9 **Write a lot of code!**

There's only one way to learn to program in Python: **write a lot of code**. And that's what you're going to do throughout this book. Coding is a skill, and the only way to get good at it is to practice. We're going to give you a lot of practice: every chapter has exercises that pose a problem for you to solve. Don't just skip over them—a lot of the learning happens when you solve the exercises. We included a solution to each exercise—don't be afraid to **peek at the solution** if you get stuck! (It's easy to get snagged on something small.) But try to solve the problem before you look at the solution. And definitely get it working before you move on to the next part of the book.

Read Me, 1 of 2

This is a learning experience, not a reference book. We deliberately stripped out everything that might get in the way of learning whatever it is we're working on at that point in the book. And the first time through, you need to begin at the beginning, because the book makes assumptions about what you've already seen and learned.

This book is designed to get you up to speed as quickly as possible.

As you need to know stuff, we teach it. So you won't find long lists of technical material, no tables of Python's operators, nor its operator precedence rules. We don't cover *everything*, but we've worked really hard to cover the essential material as well as we can, so that you can get Python into your brain *quickly* and have it stay there. The only assumption we make is that you already know how to program in some other programming language.

This book targets Python 3

We use Release 3 of the Python programming language in this book, and we cover how to get and install Python 3 in *Appendix A*. This book does **not** use Python 2.

We put Python to work for you right away.

We get you doing useful stuff in Chapter 1 and build from there. There's no hanging around, because we want you to be *productive* with Python right away.

The activities are NOT optional—you have to do the work.

The exercises and activities are not add-ons; they're part of the core content of the book. Some of them are to help with memory, some are for understanding, and some will help you apply what you've learned. ***Don't skip the exercises.***

The redundancy is intentional and important.

One distinct difference in a Head First book is that we want you to *really* get it. And we want you to finish the book remembering what you've learned. Most reference books don't have retention and recall as a goal, but this book is about *learning*, so you'll see some of the same concepts come up more than once.

The examples are as lean as possible.

Our readers tell us that it's frustrating to wade through 200 lines of an example looking for the two lines they need to understand. Most examples in this book are shown within the smallest possible context, so that the part you're trying to learn is clear and simple. Don't expect all of the examples to be robust, or even complete—they are written specifically for learning, and aren't always fully functional (although we've tried to ensure as much as possible that they are).

Read Me, 2 of 2

Yes, there's more...

This second edition is NOT at all like the first.

This is an update to the first edition of *Head First Python*, which published late in 2010. Although that book and this one share the same author, he's now older and (hopefully) wiser, and thus, decided to completely rewrite the first edition's content for this edition. So...*everything* is new: the order is different, the content has been updated, the examples are better, and the stories are either gone or have been replaced. We kept the cover—with minor amendments—as we figured we didn't want to rock the boat too much. It's been a long six years...we hope you enjoy what we've come up with.

Where's the code?

We've placed the code examples on the Web so you can copy and paste them as needed (although we do recommend that you type in the code *as you follow along*). You'll find the code at these locations:

> *http://bit.ly/head-first-python-2e*
>
> *http://python.itcarlow.ie*

The Technical Review Team

Bill Lubanovic has been a developer and admin for forty years. He's also written for O'Reilly: chapters for two Linux security books, co-authored a Linux admin book, and solo "Introducing Python". He lives by a frozen lake in the Sangre de Sasquatch mountains of Minnesota with one lovely wife, two lovely children, and three fur-laden cats.

Bill

Edward

Adrienne

Edward Yue Shung Wong has been hooked on coding since he wrote his first line of Haskell in 2006. Currently he works on event driven tradeprocessing in the heart of the City of London. He enjoys sharing his passion for development with the London Java Community and Software Craftsmanship Community. Away from the keyboard, find Edward in his element on a football pitch or gaming on YouTube (@arkangelofkaos).

Adrienne Lowe is a former personal chef from Atlanta turned Python developer who shares stories, conference recaps, and recipes at her cooking and coding blog Coding with Knives (http://codingwithknives.com). She organizes PyLadiesATL and Django Girls Atlanta and runs the weekly Django Girls "Your Django Story" interview series for women in Python. Adrienne works as a Support Engineer at Emma Inc., as Director of Advancement of the Django Software Foundation, and is on the core team of Write the Docs. She prefers a handwritten letter to email and has been building out her stamp collection since childhood.

Monte Milanuk provided valuable feedback.

Acknowledgments and Thanks

Dawn

My editor: This edition's editor is **Dawn Schanafelt**, and this book is much, much better for Dawn's involvement. Not only is Dawn a great editor, but her eye for detail and the right way to express things has greatly improved what's written here. *O'Reilly Media* make a habit of hiring bright, friendly, capable people, and Dawn is the very personification of these attributes.

The O'Reilly Media team: This edition of *Head First Python* took four years to write (it's a long story). It's only natural, then, that a lot of people from the *O'Reilly Media* team were involved. **Courtney Nash** talked me into doing "a quick rewrite" in 2012, then was on hand as the project's scope ballooned. Courtney was this edition's first editor, and was on hand when disaster struck and it looked like this book was doomed. As things *slowly* got back on track, Courtney headed off to bigger and better things within *O'Reilly Media*, handing over the editing reins in 2014 to the very busy **Meghan Blanchette**, who watched (I'm guessing, with mounting horror) as delay piled upon delay, and this book went on and off the tracks at regular intervals. Things were only just getting back to normal when Meghan went off to pastures new, and Dawn took over as this book's editor. That was one year ago, and the bulk of this book's 12¾ chapters were written under Dawn's ever-watchful eye. As I mentioned above, *O'Reilly Media* hires good people, and Courtney and Meghan's editing contributions and support are gratefully acknowledged. Elsewhere, thanks are due to **Maureen Spencer**, **Heather Scherer**, **Karen Shaner**, and **Chris Pappas** for working away "behind the scenes." Thanks, also, to the invisible unsung heroes known as **Production**, who took my *InDesign* chapters and turned them into this finished product. They did a great job.

A shout-out to **Bert Bates** who, together with **Kathy Sierra**, created this series of books with their wonderful *Head First Java*. Bert spent a lot of time working with me to ensure this edition was firmly pointed in the right direction.

Friends and colleagues: My thanks again to **Nigel Whyte** (Head of the *Department of Computing* at the *Institute of Technology, Carlow*) for supporting my involvement in this rewrite. Many of my students had a lot of this material thrust upon them as part of their studies, and I hope they get a chuckle out of seeing one (or more) of their classroom examples on the printed page.

Thanks once again to **David Griffiths** (my partner-in-crime on *Head First Programming*) for telling me at one particularly low point to stop agonizing over everything and just *write the damned thing!* It was perfect advice, and it's great to know that David, together with Dawn (his wife and Head First coauthor), is only ever an email away. Be sure to check out David and Dawn's great Head First books.

Family: My family (wife **Deirdre**, and children **Joseph**, **Aaron,** and **Aideen**) had to endure four years of ups-and-downs, fits-and-starts, huffs-and-puffs, and a life-changing experience from which we all managed to come through with our wits, thankfully, still intact. This book survived, I survived, and our family survived. I'm very thankful and love them all, and I know I don't need to say this, but will: *I do this for you guys.*

The without-whom list: My technical review team did an excellent job: check out their mini-profiles on the previous page. I considered all of the feedback they gave me, fixed all the errors they found, and was always rather chuffed when any of them took the time to tell me what a great job I was doing. I'm very grateful to them all.

Safari® Books Online

Safari Books Online is an on-demand digital library that delivers expert content in both book and video form from the world's leading authors in technology and business.

Technology professionals, software developers, web designers, and business and creative professionals use Safari Books Online as their primary resource for research, problem solving, learning, and certification training.

Safari Books Online offers a range of plans and pricing for enterprise, government, education, and individuals.

Members have access to thousands of books, training videos, and prepublication manuscripts in one fully searchable database from publishers like O'Reilly Media, Prentice Hall Professional, Addison-Wesley Professional, Microsoft Press, Sams, Que, Peachpit Press, Focal Press, Cisco Press, John Wiley & Sons, Syngress, Morgan Kaufmann, IBM Redbooks, Packt, Adobe Press, FT Press, Apress, Manning, New Riders, McGraw-Hill, Jones & Bartlett, Course Technology, and hundreds more. For more information about Safari Books Online, please visit us online.

1 the basics

✳ *Getting Started Quickly* ✳

> What's Python? A nonvenomous snake? A late 1960s comedy troupe? A programming language? Gosh! It's all of these things!

> Somebody's obviously spent far too many days at sea...

Get going with Python programming as quickly as possible.

In this chapter, we introduce the basics of programming in Python, and we do this in typical *Head First* style: by jumping right in. After just a few pages, you'll have run your first sample program. By the end of the chapter, you'll not only be able to run the sample program, but you'll understand its code too (and more besides). Along the way, you'll learn about a few of the things that make **Python** the programming language it is. So, let's not waste any more time. Flip the page and let's get going!

Breaking with Tradition

Pick up almost any book on a programming language, and the first thing you'll see is the *Hello World* example.

I knew it—you're starting with "Hello, World!", aren't you?

No, we aren't.

This is a *Head First* book, and we do things differently 'round here. With other books, there is a tradition to start by showing you how to write the *Hello World* program in the language under consideration. However, with Python, what you end up with is a single statement that invokes Python's built-in `print` function, which displays the traditional "Hello, World!" message on screen. It's almost too exciting...and it teaches you next to nothing.

So, no, we aren't going to show you the *Hello World* program in Python, as there's really nothing to learn from it. We're going to take a different path...

Starting with a meatier example

Our plan for this chapter is to start with an example that's somewhat larger and, consequently, more useful than *Hello World*.

We'll be right up front and tell you that the example we have is somewhat *contrived*: it does do something, but may not be entirely useful in the long run. That said, we've chosen it to provide a vehicle with which to cover a lot of Python in as short a timespan as possible. And we promise by the time you've worked through the first example program, you'll know enough to write *Hello World* in Python without our help.

Jump Right In

If you haven't already installed a version of Python 3 on your computer, pause now and head on over to Appendix A for some step-by-step installation instructions (it'll only take a couple minutes, promise).

With the latest Python 3 installed, you're ready to start programming Python, and to help with this—for now—we're going to use Python's built-in integrated development environment (IDE).

Python's IDLE is all you need to get going

When you install Python 3 on your computer, you also get a very simple yet usable IDE called IDLE. Although there are many different ways in which to run Python code (and you'll meet a lot of them throughout this book), IDLE is all you need when starting out.

Start IDLE on your computer, then use the *File...→New File...* menu option to open a new editing window. When we did this on our computer, we ended up with two windows: one called the Python Shell and another called Untitled:

This window pops up first. Think of it as the "first window."

After you select File...→New File..., this window appears. Think of this as the "second window."

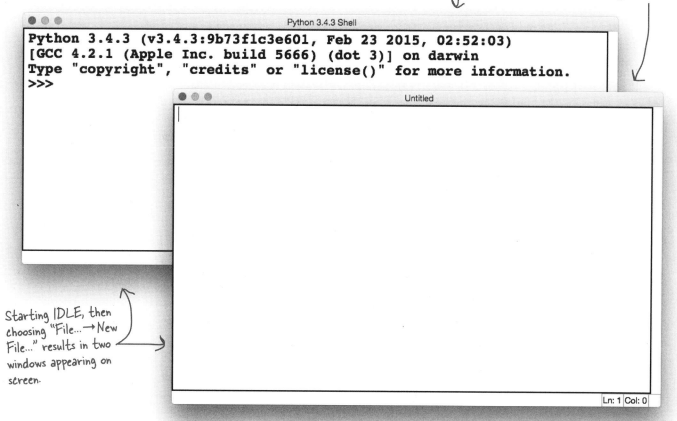

Starting IDLE, then choosing "File...→New File..." results in two windows appearing on screen.

Understanding IDLE's Windows

Both of these IDLE windows are important.

The first window, the Python Shell, is a REPL environment used to run snippets of Python code, typically a single statement at a time. The more you work with Python, the more you'll come to love the Python Shell, and you'll be using it a lot as you progress through this book. For now, though, we are more interested in the second window.

The second window, Untitled, is a text editing window that can be used to write complete Python programs. It's not the greatest editor in the world (as that honor goes to *<insert your favorite text editor's name here>*), but IDLE's editor is quite usable, and has a bunch of modern features built right in, including color-syntax handling and the like.

As we are jumping right in, let's go ahead and enter a small Python program into this window. When you are done typing in the code below, use the *File...*→*Save...* menu option to save your program under the name odd.py.

Be sure to enter the code *exactly* as shown here:

> Geek Bits
>
> What does REPL mean?
>
> It's geek shorthand for "read-eval-print-loop," and describes an interactive programming tool that lets you experiment with snippets of code to your heart's desire. Find out way more than you need to know by visiting *http://en.wikipedia.org/wiki/Read-eval-print_loop*.

odd.py - /Users/Paul/Desktop/_NewBook/ch01/odd.py (3.4.3)

```python
from datetime import datetime

odds = [ 1,  3,  5,  7,  9, 11, 13, 15, 17, 19,
        21, 23, 25, 27, 29, 31, 33, 35, 37, 39,
        41, 43, 45, 47, 49, 51, 53, 55, 57, 59 ]

right_this_minute = datetime.today().minute

if right_this_minute in odds:
    print("This minute seems a little odd.")
else:
    print("Not an odd minute.")
```

Ln: 15 Col: 0

Don't worry about what this code does for now. Just type it into the editing window. Be sure to save it as "odd.py" before continuing.

So...*now what?* If you're anything like us, you can't wait to run this code, right? Let's do this now. With your code in the edit window (as shown above), press the F5 key on your keyboard. A number of things can happen...

What Happens Next...

If your code ran without error, flip over to the next page, and *keep going*.

If you forgot to save your code *before* you tried to run it, IDLE complains, as you have to save any new code to a file *first*. You'll see a message similar to this one if you didn't save your code:

> **Source Must Be Saved**
> **OK to Save?**
>
> Cancel   OK

By default, IDLE won't run code that hasn't been saved.

Click the OK button, then provide a name for your file. We've chosen `odd` as the name for our file, and we've added a `.py` extension (which is a Python convention well worth adhering to):

> Save As: `odd.py`   ⌄
> Tags:
> Where: ch01   ⌄
>
>   Cancel   Save

You are free to use whatever name you like for your program, but it's probably best—if you're following along—to stick to the same name as us.

If your code now runs (having been saved), flip over to the next page, and *keep going*. If, however, you have a syntax error somewhere in your code, you'll see this message:

> **invalid syntax**
>
>   OK

As you can no doubt tell, IDLE isn't great at stating what the syntax error is. But click OK, and a large red block indicates where IDLE thinks the problem is.

Click the OK button, then note where IDLE thinks the syntax error is: look for the large red block in the edit window. Make sure your code matches ours exactly, save your file again, and then press F5 to ask IDLE to execute your code once more.

Press F5 to Run Your Code

Pressing F5 executes the code in the currently selected IDLE text-editing window—assuming, of course, that your code doesn't contain a runtime error. If you have a runtime error, you'll see a **Traceback** error message (in red). Read the message, then return to the edit window to make sure the code you entered is exactly the same as ours. Save your amended code, then press F5 again. When we pressed F5, the Python Shell became the active window, and here's what we saw:

From this point on, we'll refer to "the IDLE text-editing window" simply as "the edit window."

```
● ● ●                              Python 3.4.3 Shell
Python 3.4.3 (v3.4.3:9b73f1c3e601, Feb 23 2015, 02:52:03)
[GCC 4.2.1 (Apple Inc. build 5666) (dot 3)] on darwin
Type "copyright", "credits" or "license()" for more information.
>>> ============================== RESTART ==============================
>>>
This minute seems a little odd.
>>> |
```
Ln: 7 Col: 4

Don't worry if you see a different message. Read on to learn why this is.

Depending on what time of day it is, you may have seen the *Not an odd minute* message instead. Don't worry if you did, as this program displays one or the other message depending on whether your computer's current time contains a minute value that's an odd number (we did say this example was *contrived*, didn't we?). If you wait a minute, then click the edit window to select it, then press F5 again, your code runs again. You'll see the other message this time (assuming you waited the required minute). Feel free to run this code as often as you like. Here is what we saw when we (very patiently) waited the required minute:

Pressing F5 while in the edit window runs your code, then displays the resulting output in the Python Shell.

```
● ● ●                              Python 3.4.3 Shell
Python 3.4.3 (v3.4.3:9b73f1c3e601, Feb 23 2015, 02:52:03)
[GCC 4.2.1 (Apple Inc. build 5666) (dot 3)] on darwin
Type "copyright", "credits" or "license()" for more information.
>>> ============================== RESTART ==============================
>>>
This minute seems a little odd.
>>> ============================== RESTART ==============================
>>>
Not an odd minute.
>>> |
```
Ln: 10 Col: 4

Let's spend some time learning how this code runs.

Code Runs Immediately

When IDLE asks Python to run the code in the edit window, Python starts at the top of the file and begins executing code straightaway.

For those of you coming to Python from one of the C-like languages, note that there is no notion of a `main()` function or method in Python. There's also no notion of the familiar edit-compile-link-run process. With Python, you edit your code and save it, and run it *immediately*.

> Hang on a second. You said "IDLE asks Python to run the code"...but isn't Python the programming language and IDLE the IDE? If so, what's actually doing the running here?!?

Oh, good catch. That is confusing.

Here's what you need to know: "Python" is the name given to the programming language and "IDLE" is the name given to the built-in Python IDE.

That said, when you install Python 3 on your computer, an **interpreter** is installed, too. This is the technology that runs your Python code. Rather confusingly, this interpreter is also known by the name "Python." By right, everyone should use the more correct name when referring to this technology, which is to call it "the Python interpreter." But, alas, nobody ever does.

Starting this very second, in this book, we'll use the word "Python" to refer to the language, and the word "interpreter" to refer to the technology that runs your Python code. "IDLE" refers to the IDE, which takes your Python code and runs it through the interpreter. It's the interpreter that does all the actual work here.

there are no Dumb Questions

Q: Is the Python interpreter something like the Java VM?

A: Yes and no. Yes, in that the interpreter runs your code. But no, in how it does it. In Python, there's no real notion of your source code being compiled into an "executable." Unlike the Java VM, the interpreter doesn't run `.class` files, it just runs your code.

Q: But, surely, compilation has to happen at some stage?

A: Yes, it does, but the interpreter does not expose this process to the Python programmer (you). All of the details are taken care of for you. All you see is your code running as IDLE does all the heavy lifting, interacting with the interpreter on your behalf. We'll talk more about this process as this book progresses.

Executing Code, One Statement at a Time

Here is the program code from page 4 again:

```
from datetime import datetime

odds = [ 1,   3,   5,   7,   9, 11, 13, 15, 17, 19,
        21, 23, 25, 27, 29, 31, 33, 35, 37, 39,
        41, 43, 45, 47, 49, 51, 53, 55, 57, 59 ]


right_this_minute = datetime.today().minute


if right_this_minute in odds:
    print("This minute seems a little odd.")
else:
    print("Not an odd minute.")
```

Let's be the Python interpreter

Let's take some time to run through this code in much the same way that the interpreter does, line by line, from the *top* of the file to the *bottom*.

The first line of code **imports** some preexisting functionality from Python's **standard library,** which is a large stock of software modules providing lots of prebuilt (and high-quality) reusable code.

In our code, we specifically request one submodule from the standard library's datetime module. The fact that the submodule is also called datetime is confusing, but that's how this works. The datetime submodule provides a mechanism to work out the time, as you'll see over the next few pages.

Think of modules as a collection of related functions.

This is the name of the submodule.

```
from datetime import datetime

odds = [ 1,   3,   5,   7,   9, 11, 13, 15, 17, 19,
        21, 23, 25, 27, 29, 31, 33, 35, 37, 39,
        41, 43, 45, 47, 49, 51, 53, 55, 57, 59 ]
        ...
```

This is the name of the standard library module to import the reusable code from.

Remember: the interpreter starts at the top of the file and works down toward the bottom, executing each line of Python code as it goes.

In this book, when we want you to pay particular attention to a line of code, we highlight it (just like we did here).

Functions + Modules = The Standard Library

Python's **standard library** is very *rich*, and provides a lot of reusable code.

Let's look at another module, called os, which provides a platform-independent way to interact with your underlying operating system (we'll return to the datetime module in a moment). Let's concentrate on just one provided function, getcwd, which—when invoked—returns your *current working directory*.

Here's how you'd typically *import*, then *invoke*, this function within a Python program:

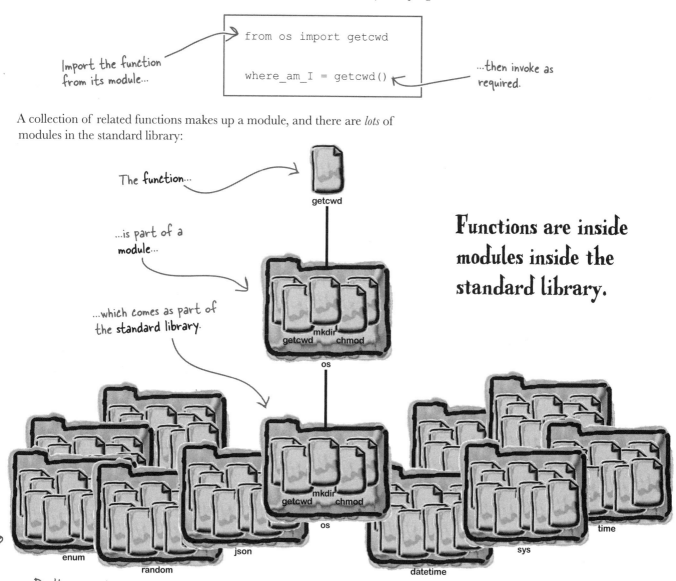

Import the function from its module...

```
from os import getcwd

where_am_I = getcwd()
```

...then invoke as required.

A collection of related functions makes up a module, and there are *lots* of modules in the standard library:

The function...

getcwd

...is part of a module...

getcwd mkdir chmod

os

...which comes as part of the standard library.

Functions are inside modules inside the standard library.

getcwd mkdir chmod

os

enum

random

json

datetime

sys

time

— Don't worry about what each of these modules does at this stage. We have a quick preview of some of them over the page, and will see more of the rest later in this book.

Up Close with the Standard Library

The **standard library** is the jewel in Python's crown, supplying reusable modules that help you with everything from, for example, working with data, through manipulating ZIP archives, to sending emails, to working with HTML. The standard library even includes a web server, as well as the popular *SQLite* database technology. In this *Up Close*, we'll present an overview of just a few of the most commonly used modules in the standard library. To follow along, you can enter these examples as shown at your >>> prompt (in IDLE). If you are currently looking at IDLE's edit window, choose *Run...→Python Shell* from the menu to access the >>> prompt.

Let's start by learning a little about the system your interpreter is running on. Although Python prides itself on being cross-platform, in that code written on one platform can be executed (generally unaltered) on another, there are times when it's important to know that you are running on, say, *Mac OS X*. The sys module exists to help you learn more about your interpreter's system. Here's how to determine the identity of your underlying operating system, by first importing the sys module, then accessing the platform attribute:

```
>>> import sys
>>> sys.platform
'darwin'
```

Import the module you need, then access the attribute of interest. It looks like we are running "darwin", which is the Mac OS X kernel name.

The sys module is a good example of a reusable module that primarily provides access to preset attributes (such as platform). As another example, here's how to determine which version of Python is running, which we pass to the print function to display on screen:

```
>>> print(sys.version)
3.4.3 (v3.4.3:9b73f1c3e601, Feb 23 2015, 02:52:03)
[GCC 4.2.1 (Apple Inc. build 5666) (dot 3)]
```

There's a lot of information about the Python version we're running, including that it's 3.4.3.

The os module is a good example of a reusable module that primarily yields functionality, as well as providing a system-independent way for your Python code to interact with the underlying operating system, regardless of exactly which operating system that is.

For example, here's how to work out the name of the folder your code is operating within using the getcwd function. As with any module, you begin by importing the module before invoking the function:

```
>>> import os
>>> os.getcwd()
'/Users/HeadFirst/CodeExamples'
```

Import the module, then invoke the functionality you need.

You can access your system's environment variables, as a whole (using the environ attribute) or individually (using the getenv function):

```
>>> os.environ
'environ({'XPC_FLAGS': '0x0', 'HOME': '/Users/HeadFirst', 'TMPDIR': '/var/
folders/18/t93gmhc546b7b2cngfhz10100000gn/T/', ... 'PYTHONPATH': '/Applications/
Python 3.4/IDLE.app/Contents/Resources', ... 'SHELL': '/bin/bash', 'USER':
'HeadFirst'})'
>>> os.getenv('HOME')
'/Users/HeadFirst'
```

The "environ" attribute contains lots of data.

You can access a specifically named attribute (from the data contained in "environ") using "getenv".

Up Close with the Standard Library, Continued

Working with dates (and times) comes up a lot, and the standard library provides the `datetime` module to help when you're working with this type of data. The `date.today` function provides today's date:

```
>>> import datetime
>>> datetime.date.today()
datetime.date(2015, 5, 31)
```
← Today's date

That's certainly a strange way to display today's date, though, isn't it? You can access the day, month, and year values separately by appending an attribute access onto the call to `date.today`:

```
>>> datetime.date.today().day
31
>>> datetime.date.today().month
5
>>> datetime.date.today().year
2015
```
← The component parts of today's date

You can also invoke the `date.isoformat` function and pass in today's date to display a much more user-friendly version of today's date, which is converted to a string by `isoformat`:

```
>>> datetime.date.isoformat(datetime.date.today())
'2015-05-31'
```
← Today's date as a string

And then there's time, which none of us seem to have enough of. Can the *standard library* tell us what time it is? Yes. After importing the `time` module, call the `strftime` function and specify how you want the time displayed. In this case, we are interested in the current time's hours (`%H`) and minutes (`%M`) values in 24-hour format:

```
>>> import time
>>> time.strftime("%H:%M")
'23:55'
```
← Good heavens! Is that the time?

How about working out the day of the week, and whether or not it's before noon? Using the `%A %p` specification with `strftime` does just that:

```
>>> time.strftime("%A %p")
'Sunday PM'
```
We've now worked out that it's five minutes to midnight on Sunday evening...time for bed, perhaps?

As a final example of the type of reusable functionality the *standard library* provides, imagine you have some HTML that you are worried might contain some potentially dangerous `<script>` tags. Rather than parsing the HTML to detect and remove the tags, why not encode all those troublesome angle brackets using the `escape` function from the `html` module? Or maybe you have some encoded HTML that you'd like to return to its original form? The `unescape` function can do that. Here are examples of both:

```
>>> import html
>>> html.escape("This HTML fragment contains a <script>script</script> tag.")
'This HTML fragment contains a &lt;script&gt;script&lt;/script&gt; tag.'
>>> html.unescape("I &hearts; Python's &lt;standard library&gt;.")
"I ♥ Python's <standard library>."
```
Converting to and from HTML encoded text

Batteries Included

I guess this is what people mean by the term "Python comes with batteries included," right?

Yes. That's what they mean.

As the *standard library* is *so* rich, the thinking is all you need to be **immediately productive** with the language is to have Python installed.

Unlike Christmas morning, when you open your new toy only to discover that it doesn't come with batteries, Python doesn't disappoint; it comes with everything you need to get going. And it's not just the modules in the *standard library* that this thinking applies to: don't forget the inclusion of IDLE, which provides a small, yet usable, IDE right out of the box.

All you have to do is code.

---

there are no Dumb Questions

Q: How am I supposed to work out what any particular module from the standard library does?

A: The Python documentation has all the answers on the standard library. Here's the kicking-off point: *https://docs.python.org/3/library/index.html*.

Geek Bits

The standard library isn't the only place you'll find excellent importable modules to use with your code. The Python community also supports a thriving collection of third-party modules, some of which we'll explore later in this book. If you want a preview, check out the community-run repository: *http://pypi.python.org*.

Data Structures Come Built-in

As well as coming with a top-notch *standard library*, Python also has some powerful built-in **data structures**. One of these is the **list**, which can be thought of as a very powerful *array*. Like arrays in many other languages, lists in Python are enclosed within square brackets ([]).

The next three lines of code in our program (shown below) assign a *literal* list of odd numbers to a variable called odds. In this code, odds is *a list of integers*, but lists in Python can contain *any* data of *any* type, and you can even mix the types of data in a list (if that's what you're into). Note how the odds list extends over three lines, despite being a single statement. This is OK, as the interpreter won't decide a single statement has come to an end until it finds the closing bracket (]) that matches the opening one ([). Typically, **the end of the line marks the end of a statement in Python**, but there can be exceptions to this general rule, and multiline lists are just one of them (we'll meet the others later).

> **Like arrays, lists can hold data of any type.**

```
from datetime import datetime

odds = [ 1,  3,  5,  7,  9, 11, 13, 15, 17, 19,
        21, 23, 25, 27, 29, 31, 33, 35, 37, 39,
        41, 43, 45, 47, 49, 51, 53, 55, 57, 59 ]
                    . . .
```

This is a new variable, called "odds", which is assigned a list of odd numbers.

This is the list of odd numbers, enclosed in square brackets. This single statement extends over three lines, which is OK.

There are lots of things that can be done with lists, but we're going to defer any further discussion until a later chapter. All you need to know now is that this list now *exists*, has been *assigned* to the odds variable (thanks to the use of the **assignment operator**, =), and *contains* the numbers shown.

Python variables are dynamically assigned

Before getting to the next line of code, perhaps a few words are needed about variables, especially if you are one of those programmers who might be used to predeclaring variables with type information *before* using them (as is the case in statically typed programming languages).

In Python, variables pop into existence the first time you use them, and **their type does not need to be predeclared**. Python variables take their type information from the type of the object they're assigned. In our program, the odds variable is assigned a list of numbers, so odds is a list in this case.

Let's look at another variable assignment statement. As luck would have it, this just so happens to also be the next line of code in our program.

> **Python comes with all the usual operators, including <, >, <=, >=, ==, !=, as well as the = assignment operator.**

Invoking Methods Obtains Results

The third line of code in our program is another **assignment statement**.

Unlike the last one, this one doesn't assign a data structure to a variable, but instead assigns the **result** of a method call to another new variable, called `right_this_minute`. Take another look at the third line of code:

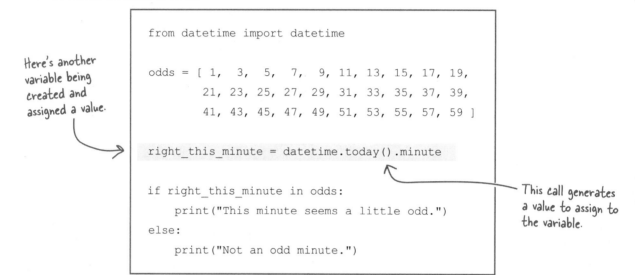

Here's another variable being created and assigned a value.

```
from datetime import datetime

odds = [ 1,  3,  5,  7,  9, 11, 13, 15, 17, 19,
        21, 23, 25, 27, 29, 31, 33, 35, 37, 39,
        41, 43, 45, 47, 49, 51, 53, 55, 57, 59 ]

right_this_minute = datetime.today().minute

if right_this_minute in odds:
    print("This minute seems a little odd.")
else:
    print("Not an odd minute.")
```

This call generates a value to assign to the variable.

Invoking built-in module functionality

The third line of code invokes a method called `today` that comes with the `datetime` submodule, which is *itself* part of the `datetime` module (we did say this naming strategy *was* a little confusing). You can tell `today` is being invoked due to the standard postfix parentheses: `()`.

When `today` is invoked, it returns a "time object," which contains many pieces of information about the current time. These are the current time's **attributes**, which you can access via the customary **dot-notation** syntax. In this program, we are interested in the minute attribute, which we can access by appending `.minute` to the method invocation, as shown above. The resulting value is then assigned to the `right_this_minute` variable. You can think of this line of code as saying: *create an object that represents today's time, then extract the value of the minute attribute before assigning it to a variable.* It is tempting to *split* this single line of code into two lines to make it "easier to understand," as follows:

You'll see more of the dot-notation syntax later in this book.

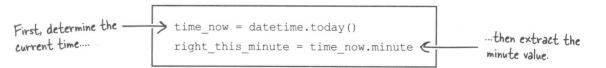

First, determine the current time.....

```
time_now = datetime.today()
right_this_minute = time_now.minute
```

...then extract the minute value.

You can do this (if you like), but most Python programmers prefer **not** to create the temporary variable (`time_now` in this example) *unless* it's needed at some point later in the program.

Deciding When to Run Blocks of Code

At this stage we have a list of numbers called odds. We also have a minute value called `right_this_minute`. In order to work out whether the current minute value stored in `right_this_minute` is an odd number, we need some way of determining if it is in the odds list. But how do we do this?

It turns out that Python makes this type of thing very straightforward. As well as including all the usual comparison operators that you'd expect to find in any programming language (such as >, <, >=, <=, and so on), Python comes with a few "super" operators of its own, one of which is in.

The in operator checks if one thing is *inside* another. Take a look at the next line of code in our program, which uses the in operator to check whether `right_this_minute` is *inside* the odds list:

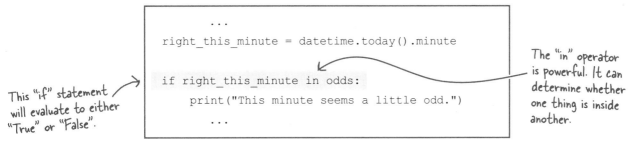

This "if" statement will evaluate to either "True" or "False".

The "in" operator is powerful. It can determine whether one thing is inside another.

The in operator returns either `True` or `False`. As you'd expect, if the value in `right_this_minute` is in odds, the if statement evaluates to `True`, and the block of code associated with the if statement executes.

Blocks in Python are easy to spot, as they are always indented.

In our program there are two blocks, which each contain a single call to the print function. This function can display messages on screen (and we'll see lots of uses of it throughout this book). When you enter this program code into the edit window, you may have noticed that IDLE helps keep you straight by indenting automatically. This is very useful, but do be sure to check that IDLE's indentation is what you want:

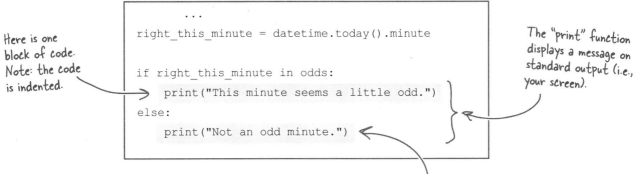

Here is one block of code. Note: the code is indented.

The "print" function displays a message on standard output (i.e., your screen).

Did you notice that there are no curly braces here?

And here is another block of code. Note: it's indented, too.

What Happened to My Curly Braces?

If you are used to a programming language that uses curly braces ({ and }) to delimit blocks of code, encountering blocks in Python for the first time can be disorienting, as Python doesn't use curly braces for this purpose. Python uses **indentation** to demarcate a block of code, which Python programmers prefer to call **suite** as opposed to *block* (just to mix things up a little).

It's not that curly braces don't have a use in Python. They do, but—as we'll see in Chapter 3—curly braces have more to do with delimiting data than they have to do with delimiting suites (i.e., *blocks*) of code.

Suites within any Python program are easy to spot, as they are always indented. This helps your brain quickly identify suites when reading code. The other visual clue for you to look out for is the colon character (:), which is used to introduce a suite that's associated with any of Python's control statements (such as if, else, for, and the like). You'll see lots of examples of this usage as you progress through this book.

> Instead of referring to a code "block," Python programmers use the word "suite." Both names are used in practice, but the Python docs prefer "suite."

A colon introduces an indented suite of code

The colon (:) is important, in that it introduces a new suite of code that must be indented to the right. If you forget to indent your code after a colon, the interpreter raises an error.

Not only does the if statement in our example have a colon, the else has one, too. Here's all the code again:

```
from datetime import datetime

odds = [ 1,  3,  5,  7,  9, 11, 13, 15, 17, 19,
        21, 23, 25, 27, 29, 31, 33, 35, 37, 39,
        41, 43, 45, 47, 49, 51, 53, 55, 57, 59 ]

right_this_minute = datetime.today().minute

if right_this_minute in odds:          ←——— Colons introduce
    print("This minute seems a little odd.")        indented suites.
else:   ←
    print("Not an odd minute.")
```

We're nearly done. There's just one final statement to discuss.

What "else" Can You Have with "if"?

We are nearly done with the code for our example program, in that there is only one line of code left to discuss. It is not a very big line of code, but it's an important one: the else statement that identifies the block of code that executes when the matching if statement returns a False value.

Take a closer look at the else statement from our program code, which we need to unindent to align with the if part of this statement:

```
if right_this_minute in odds:
    print("This minute seems a little odd.")
else:
    print("Not an odd minute.")
```

See the colon? →

Did you spot that the "else" is unindented to align with the "if"?

I guess if there's an "else", there must also be an "else if", or does Python spell it "elseif"?

It is a very common slip-up for Python newbies to forget the colon when first writing code.

Neither. Python spells it elif.

If you have a number of conditions that you need to check as part of an if statement, Python provides elif as well as else. You can have as many elif statements (each with its own suite) as needed.

Here's a small example that assumes a variable called today is previously assigned a string representing whatever today is:

```
if today == 'Saturday':
    print('Party!!')
elif today == 'Sunday':
    print('Recover.')
else:
    print('Work, work, work.')
```

Three individual suites: one for the "if", another for the "elif", and the final catch-all for the "else".

Suites Can Contain Embedded Suites

Any suite can contain any number of embedded suites, which also have to be indented. When Python programmers talk about embedded suites, they tend to talk about **levels of indentation**.

The initial level of indentation for any program is generally referred to as the *first* or (as is so common when it comes to counting with many programming languages) indentation level *zero*. Subsequent levels are referred to as the second, third, fourth, and so on (or level one, level two, level three, and so on).

Here's a variation on the today example code from the last page. Note how an embedded if/else has been added to the if statement that executes when today is set to 'Sunday'. We're also assuming another variable called condition exists and is set to a value that expresses how you're currently feeling. We've indicated where each of the suites is, as well as at which level of indentation it appears:

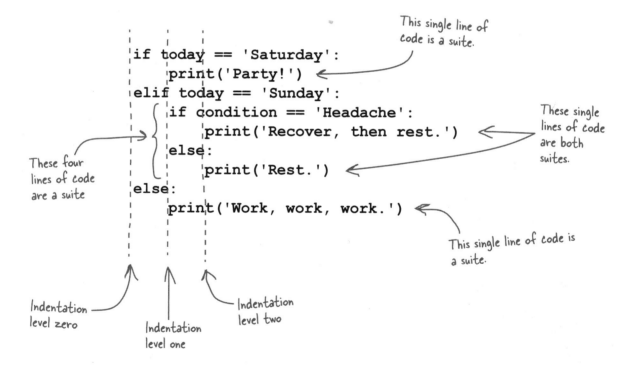

This single line of code is a suite.

These single lines of code are both suites.

These four lines of code are a suite

This single line of code is a suite.

Indentation level zero

Indentation level one

Indentation level two

```python
if today == 'Saturday':
    print('Party!')
elif today == 'Sunday':
    if condition == 'Headache':
        print('Recover, then rest.')
    else:
        print('Rest.')
else:
    print('Work, work, work.')
```

It is important to note that code at the same level of indentation is only related to other code at the same level of indentation if all the code appears *within the same suite*. Otherwise, they are in separate suites, and it does not matter that they share a level of indentation. The key point is that indentation is used to demarcate suites of code in Python.

What We Already Know

With the final few lines of code discussed, let's pause to review what
the `odd.py` program has told us about Python:

BULLET POINTS

- Python comes with a built-in IDE called IDLE, which lets you create, edit, and run your Python code—all you need to do is type in your code, save it, and then press F5.

- IDLE interacts with the Python interpreter, which automates the compile-link-run process for you. This lets you concentrate on writing your code.

- The interpreter runs your code (stored in a file) from top to bottom, one line at a time. There is no notion of a `main()` function/method in Python.

- Python comes with a powerful standard library, which provides access to lots of reusable modules (of which `datetime` is just one example).

- There is a collection of standard data structures available to you when you're writing Python programs. The list is one of them, and is very similar in notion to an array.

- The type of a variable does not need to be declared. When you assign a value to a variable in Python, it dynamically takes on the type of the data it refers to.

- You make decisions with the `if`/`elif`/`else` statement. The `if`, `elif`, and `else` keywords precede blocks of code, which are known in the Python world as "suites."

- It is easy to spot suites of code, as they are always indented. Indentation is the only code grouping mechanism provided by Python.

- In addition to indentation, suites of code are also preceded by a colon (`:`). This is a syntactical requirement of the language.

> That's a long list for such a short program! So...what's the plan for the rest of this chapter?

Let's extend this program to do more.

It's true that we needed more lines to describe what this short program does than we actually needed to write the code. But this is one of the great strengths of Python: *you can get a lot done with a few lines of code.*

Review the list above once more, and then turn the page to make a start on seeing what our program's extensions will be.

Extending Our Program to Do More

Let's extend our program in order to learn a bit more Python.

At the moment, the program runs once, then terminates. Imagine that we want this program to execute more than once; let's say five times. Specifically, let's execute the "minute checking code" and the `if/else` statement five times, pausing for a random number of seconds between each message display (just to keep things interesting). When the program terminates, five messages should be on screen, as opposed to one.

Here's the code again, with the code we want to run multiple times circled:

Let's tweak the program to run this code a number of times.

```
from datetime import datetime

odds = [ 1,  3,  5,  7,  9, 11, 13, 15, 17, 19,
        21, 23, 25, 27, 29, 31, 33, 35, 37, 39,
        41, 43, 45, 47, 49, 51, 53, 55, 57, 59 ]

right_this_minute = datetime.today().minute

if right_this_minute in odds:
    print("This minute seems a little odd.")
else:
    print("Not an odd minute.")
```

What we need to do:

 Loop over the encircled code.
A loop lets us iterate over any suite, and Python provides a number of ways to do just that. In this case (and without getting into why), we'll use Python's `for` loop to iterate.

 Pause execution.
Python's standard `time` module provides a function called `sleep` that can pause execution for an indicated number of seconds.

 Generate a random number.
Happily, another Python module, `random`, provides a function called `randint` that we can use to generate a random number. Let's use `randint` to generate a number between 1 and 60, then use that number to pause the execution of our program on each iteration.

We now know what we want to do. But is there a preferred way of going about making these changes?

What's the Best Approach to Solving This Problem?

You know what you need to do: put your head down, read the docs, and work out the Python code you need to solve this problem. When you've done this, you're ready to change your program as needed...

That approach works, but I'm more of an experimenter myself. I like to try out small snippets of code before I commit to making changes to my working program. I'm happy to read the docs, but like to experiment too...

Bob →

← Laura

Both approaches work with Python

You can follow *both* of these approaches when working with Python, but most Python programmers favor **experimentation** when trying to work out what code they need for a particular situation.

Don't get us wrong: we are not suggesting that Bob's approach is wrong and Laura's is right. It's just that Python programmers have both options available to them, and the Python Shell (which we met briefly at the start of this chapter) makes experimentation a natural choice for Python programmers.

Let's determine the code we need in order to extend our program, by experimenting at the >>> prompt.

Experimenting at the >>> prompt helps you work out the code you need.

Returning to the Python Shell

Here's how the Python Shell looked the last time we interacted with it (yours might look a little different, as your messages may have appeared in an alternate order):

```
●●●                          Python 3.4.3 Shell
Python 3.4.3 (v3.4.3:9b73f1c3e601, Feb 23 2015, 02:52:03)
[GCC 4.2.1 (Apple Inc. build 5666) (dot 3)] on darwin
Type "copyright", "credits" or "license()" for more information.
>>> ============================ RESTART ================================
>>>
This minute seems a little odd.
>>> ============================ RESTART ================================
>>>
Not an odd minute.
>>> |
                                                              Ln: 10 Col: 4
```

The Python Shell (or just "shell" for short) has displayed our program's messages, but it can do so much more than this. The >>> prompt allows you to enter any Python code statement and have it execute *immediately*. If the statement produces output, the shell displays it. If the statement results in a value, the shell displays the calculated value. If, however, you create a new variable and assign it a value, you need to enter the variable's name at the >>> prompt to see what value it contains.

Check out the example interactions, shown below. It is even better if you follow along and try out these examples at *your* shell. Just be sure to press the *Enter* key to terminate each program statement, which also tells the shell to execute it *now*:

```
●●●                          Python 3.4.3 Shell
Python 3.4.3 (v3.4.3:9b73f1c3e601, Feb 23 2015, 02:52:03)
[GCC 4.2.1 (Apple Inc. build 5666) (dot 3)] on darwin
Type "copyright", "credits" or "license()" for more information.
>>> ============================ RESTART ================================
>>>
This minute seems a little odd.
>>> ============================ RESTART ================================
>>>
Not an odd minute.
>>>
>>> print('Hello Mum!')          The shell displays a message on screen as a result of this
Hello Mum!                        code statement executing (don't forget to press Enter).
>>>
>>> 21+21              If you perform a calculation, the shell displays the
42                      resulting value (after you press Enter).
>>>
>>> ultimate_answer = 21+21       Assigning a value to a variable does not display the
>>> ultimate_answer               variable's value. You have to specifically ask the
42                                shell to do so.
>>> |
                                                              Ln: 20 Col: 4
```

Experimenting at the Shell

Now that you know you can type a single Python statement into the >>> prompt and have it execute immediately, you can start to work out the code you need to extend your program.

Here's what you need your new code to do:

 Loop a specified number of times. We've already decided to use Python's for loop here.

 Pause the program for a specified number of seconds. The sleep function from the standard library's time module can do this.

 Generate a random number between two provided values. The randint function from the random module will do the trick.

Rather than continuing to show you complete IDLE screenshots, we're only going to show you the >>> prompt and any displayed output. Specifically, from this point onward, you'll see something like the following instead of the earlier screenshots:

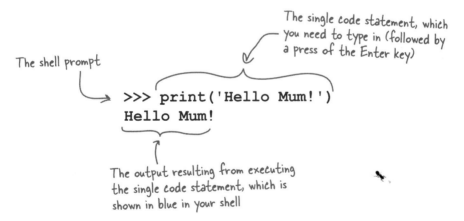

The shell prompt

The single code statement, which you need to type in (followed by a press of the Enter key)

```
>>> print('Hello Mum!')
Hello Mum!
```

The output resulting from executing the single code statement, which is shown in blue in your shell

Over the next few pages, we're going to experiment to figure out how to add the three features listed above. We'll *play* with code at the >>> prompt until we determine exactly the statements we need to add to our program. Leave the odd. py code as is for now, then make sure the shell window is active by selecting it. The cursor should be blinking away to the right of the >>> , waiting for you to type some code.

Flip the page when you're ready. Let the experiments begin.

Iterating Over a Sequence of Objects

We said earlier that we were going to employ Python's `for` loop here. The `for` loop is *perfect* for controlling looping when you know ahead of time how many iterations you need. (When you don't know, we recommend the `while` loop, but we'll save discussing the details of this alternate looping construct until we actually need it). At this stage, all we need is `for`, so let's see it in action at the >>> prompt.

We present three typical uses of `for`. Let's see which one best fits our needs.

Usage example 1. This `for` loop, below, takes a list of numbers and iterates once for each number in the list, displaying the current number on screen. As it does so, the `for` loop assigns each number in turn to a *loop iteration variable*, which is given the name `i` in this code.

As this code is more than a single line, the shell indents automatically for you when you press Enter after the colon. To signal to the shell that you are done entering code, press Enter *twice* at the end of the loop's suite:

> **Use "for" when looping a known number of times.**

```
>>> for i in [1, 2, 3]:
        print(i)

1
2
3
```

> *We used "i" as the loop iteration variable in this example, but we could've called it just about anything. Having said that, "i", "j", and "k" are incredibly popular among most programmers in this situation.*

> *As this is a suite, you need to press the Enter key TWICE after typing in this code in order to terminate the statement and see it execute.*

Note the *indentation* and *colon*. Like `if` statements, the code associated with a `for` statement needs to be **indented**.

Usage example 2. This `for` loop, below, iterates over a string, with each character in the string being processed during each iteration. This works because a string in Python is a **sequence**. A sequence is an ordered collection of objects (and we'll see lots of examples of sequences in this book), and every sequence in Python can be iterated over by the interpreter.

> **A sequence is an ordered collection of objects.**

```
>>> for ch in "Hi!":
        print(ch)

H
i
!
```

> *Python is smart enough to work out that this string should be iterated over one-character at a time (and that's why we used "ch" as the loop variable name here).*

Nowhere did you have to tell the `for` loop *how big the string is*. Python is smart enough to work out when the string *ends*, and arranges to terminate (i.e., end) the `for` loop on your behalf when it exhausts all the objects in the sequence.

Iterating a Specific Number of Times

In addition to using `for` to iterate over a sequence, you can be more exact and specify a number of iterations, thanks to the built-in function called `range`.

Let's look at another usage example that showcases using `range`.

Usage example 3. In its most basic form, `range` accepts a single integer argument that dictates how many times the `for` loop runs (we'll see other uses of `range` later in this book). In this loop, we use `range` to generate a list of numbers that are assigned one at a time to the `num` variable:

```
>>> for num in range(5):
        print('Head First Rocks!')

Head First Rocks!
Head First Rocks!
Head First Rocks!
Head First Rocks!
Head First Rocks!
```

We asked for a range of five numbers, so we iterated five times, which results in five messages. Remember: press Enter twice to run code that has a suite.

The `for` loop *didn't use* the `num` loop iteration variable *anywhere* in the loop's suite. This did not raise an error, which is OK, as it is up to you (the programmer) to decide whether or not `num` needs to be processed further in the suite. In this case, doing nothing with `num` is fine.

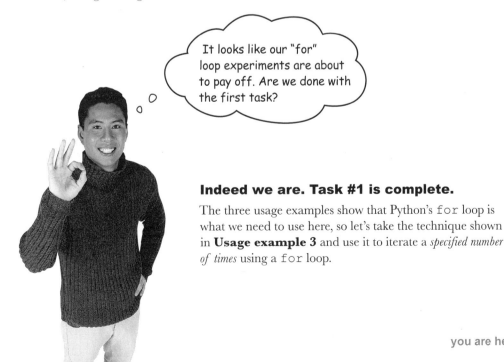

It looks like our "for" loop experiments are about to pay off. Are we done with the first task?

Indeed we are. Task #1 is complete.

The three usage examples show that Python's `for` loop is what we need to use here, so let's take the technique shown in **Usage example 3** and use it to iterate a *specified number of times* using a `for` loop.

Applying the Outcome of Task #1 to Our Code

Here's how our code looked in IDLE's edit window *before* we worked on Task #1:

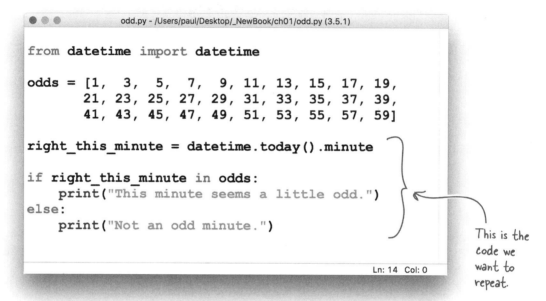

This is the code we want to repeat.

You now know that you can use a `for` loop to repeat the five lines of code at the bottom of this program five times. The five lines will need to be **indented** under the `for` loop, as they are going to form the loop's suite. Specifically, each line of code needs to be indented *once*. However, don't be tempted to perform this action on each individual line. Instead, let IDLE indent the entire suite for you *in one go*.

Begin by using your mouse to select the lines of code you want to indent:

```
odd.py - /Users/paul/Desktop/_NewBook/ch01/odd.py (3.5.1)

from datetime import datetime

odds = [1,  3,  5,  7,  9, 11, 13, 15, 17, 19,
        21, 23, 25, 27, 29, 31, 33, 35, 37, 39,
        41, 43, 45, 47, 49, 51, 53, 55, 57, 59]

right_this_minute = datetime.today().minute

if right_this_minute in odds:
    print("This minute seems a little odd.")
else:
    print("Not an odd minute.")

                                          Ln: 14  Col: 0
```

Use your mouse to select the lines of code you want to indent.

Indent Suites with Format...Indent Region

With the five lines of code selected, choose *Indent Region* from the *Format* menu in IDLE's edit window. The entire suite moves to the right by one indentation level:

```
*odd.py - /Users/paul/Desktop/_NewBook/ch01/odd.py (3.5.1)*

from datetime import datetime

odds = [1,   3,   5,   7,   9, 11, 13, 15, 17, 19,
        21, 23, 25, 27, 29, 31, 33, 35, 37, 39,
        41, 43, 45, 47, 49, 51, 53, 55, 57, 59]

        right_this_minute = datetime.today().minute

        if right_this_minute in odds:
            print("This minute seems a little odd.")
        else:
            print("Not an odd minute.")

                                            Ln: 14  Col: 0
```

The Indent Region option from the Format menu indents all of the selected lines of code in one go.

Note that IDLE also has a *Dedent Region* menu option, which unindents suites, and that both the *Indent* and *Dedent* menu commands have keyboard shortcuts, which differ slightly based on the operating system you are running. Take the time to learn the keyboard shortcuts that your system uses *now* (as you'll use them all the time). With the suite indented, it's time to add the `for` loop:

Add the "for" loop line.

The "for" loop's suite is properly indented.

```
odd.py - /Users/paul/Desktop/_NewBook/ch01/odd.py (3.5.1)

from datetime import datetime

odds = [1,   3,   5,   7,   9, 11, 13, 15, 17, 19,
        21, 23, 25, 27, 29, 31, 33, 35, 37, 39,
        41, 43, 45, 47, 49, 51, 53, 55, 57, 59]

for i in range(5):
    right_this_minute = datetime.today().minute

    if right_this_minute in odds:
        print("This minute seems a little odd.")
    else:
        print("Not an odd minute.")

                                            Ln: 15  Col: 0
```

Arranging to Pause Execution

Let's remind ourselves of what we need this code to do:

 Loop a specified number of times.

 Pause the program for a specified number of seconds.

☐ **Generate** a random number between two provided values.

We're now ready to return to the shell and try out some more code to help with the second task: *pause the program for a specified number of seconds*.

However, before we do that, recall the opening line of our program, which imported a specifically named function from a specifically named module:

```
from datetime import datetime
```

This usage of "import" brings in the named function to your program. You can then invoke it without using the dot-notation syntax.

This is one way to import a function into your program. Another equally common technique is to import a module *without* being specific about the function you want to use. Let's use this second technique here, as it will appear in many Python programs you'll come across.

As mentioned earlier in this chapter, the `sleep` function can pause execution for a specified number of seconds, and is provided by the standard library's `time` module. Let's **import** the module *first*, without mentioning `sleep` just yet:

```
>>> import time
>>>
```

This tells the shell to import the "time" module.

When the `import` statement is used as it is with the `time` module above, you get access to the facilities provided by the module without anything expressly *named* being imported into your program's code. To access a function provided by a module imported in this way, use the dot-notation syntax to name it, as shown here:

This is the number of seconds to sleep for.

Name the module first (before the period).

```
>>> time.sleep(5)
>>>
```

Specify the function you want to invoke (after the period).

Note that when you invoke `sleep` in this way, the shell pauses for five seconds before the >>> prompt reappears. Go ahead, and *try it now.*

Importation Confusion

> Hang on a second...Python supports two importation mechanisms? Doesn't that get kind of confusing?

That's a great question.

Just to be clear, there aren't *two* importation mechanisms in Python, as there is only *one* `import` statement. However, the `import` statement can be used *in two ways*.

The first, which we initially saw in our example program, imports a named function into our program's **namespace**, which then allows us to invoke the function as necessary without having to *link* the function back to the imported module. (The notion of a namespace is important in Python, as it defines the context within which your code runs. That said, we're going to wait until a later chapter to explore namespaces in detail).

In our example program, we use the first importation technique, then invoke the `datetime` function as `datetime()`, *not* as `datetime.datetime()`.

The second way to use `import` is to just import the module, as we did when experimenting with the `time` module. When we import this way, we have to use the dot-notation syntax to access the module's functionality, as we did with `time.sleep()`.

there are no
Dumb Questions

Q: **Is there a correct way to use** `import`**?**

A: It can often come down to personal preference, as some programmers like to be very specific, while others don't. However, there is a situation that occurs when two modules (we'll call them A and B) have a function of the same name, which we'll call F. If you put `from A import F` and `from B import F` in your code, how is Python to know which F to invoke when you call `F()`? The only way you can be sure is to use the nonspecific `import` statement (that is, put `import A` and `import B` in your code), then invoke the specific F you want using either `A.F()` or `B.F()` as needed. Doing so negates any confusion.

Generating Random Integers with Python

Although it is tempting to add `import time` to the top of our program, then call `time.sleep(5)` in the `for` loop's suite, we aren't going to do this right now. We aren't done with our experimentations. Pausing for five seconds isn't enough; we need to be able to pause for a *random amount of time*. With that in mind, let's remind ourselves of what we've done, and what remains:

 ✓ **Loop** a specified number of times.

✓ **Pause** the program for a specified number of seconds.

☐ **Generate** a random number between two provided values.

Once we have this last task completed, we can get back to confidently changing our program to incorporate all that we've learned from our experimentations. But we're not there yet—let's look at the last task, which is to generate a random number.

As with sleeping, the *standard library* can help here, as it includes a module called `random`. With just this piece of information to guide us, let's experiment at the shell:

```
>>> import random
>>>
```

Use "dir" to query an object.

Now what? We could look at the Python docs or consult a Python reference book...but that involves taking our attention away from the shell, even though it might only take a few moments. As it happens, the shell provides some additional functions that can help here. These functions aren't meant to be used within your program code; they are designed for use at the >>> prompt. The first is called `dir`, and it displays all the **attributes** associated with anything in Python, including modules:

Buried in the middle of this long list is the name of the function we need.

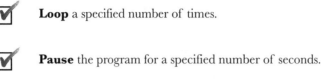

```
>>> dir(random)
['BPF', 'LOG4', 'NV_MAGICCONST', 'RECIP_BPF',
'Random',    ...   'randint', 'random', 'randrange',
'sample', 'seed', 'setstate', 'shuffle', 'triangular',
'uniform', 'vonmisesvariate', 'weibullvariate']
```

This list has a lot in it. Of interest is the `randint()` function. To learn more about `randint`, let's ask the shell for some **help**.

This is an abridged list. What you'll see on your screen is much longer.

Asking the Interpreter for Help

Once you know the name of something, you can ask the shell for **help**. When you do, the shell displays the section from the Python docs related to the name you're interested in.

Let's see this mechanism in action at the >>> prompt by asking for **help** with the `randint` function from the `random` module:

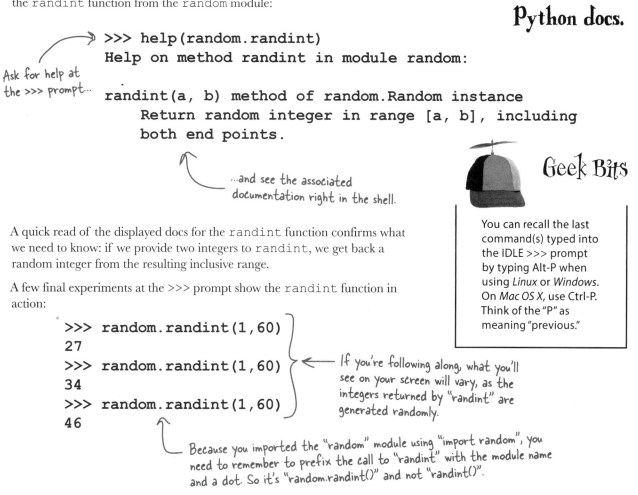

Ask for help at the >>> prompt...

```
>>> help(random.randint)
Help on method randint in module random:

randint(a, b) method of random.Random instance
    Return random integer in range [a, b], including
    both end points.
```

...and see the associated documentation right in the shell.

Geek Bits

You can recall the last command(s) typed into the IDLE >>> prompt by typing Alt-P when using *Linux* or *Windows*. On *Mac OS X*, use Ctrl-P. Think of the "P" as meaning "previous."

A quick read of the displayed docs for the `randint` function confirms what we need to know: if we provide two integers to `randint`, we get back a random integer from the resulting inclusive range.

A few final experiments at the >>> prompt show the `randint` function in action:

```
>>> random.randint(1,60)
27
>>> random.randint(1,60)
34
>>> random.randint(1,60)
46
```

If you're following along, what you'll see on your screen will vary, as the integers returned by "randint" are generated randomly.

Because you imported the "random" module using "import random", you need to remember to prefix the call to "randint" with the module name and a dot. So it's "random.randint()" and not "randint()".

With this, you are now in a position to place a satisfying check mark against the last of our tasks, as you now know enough to generate a random number between two provided values:

   Generate a random number between two provided values.

It's time to return to our program and make our changes.

Reviewing Our Experiments

Before you forge ahead and change your program, let's quickly review the outcome of our shell experiments.

We started by writing a `for` loop, which iterated five times:

```
>>> for num in range(5):
        print('Head First Rocks!')
```

```
Head First Rocks!
Head First Rocks!
Head First Rocks!
Head First Rocks!
Head First Rocks!
```

We asked for a range of five numbers, so we iterated five times, which results in five messages.

Then we used the `sleep` function from the `time` module to pause execution of our code for a specified number of seconds:

```
>>> import time
>>> time.sleep(5)
```

The shell imports the "time" module, letting us invoke the "sleep" function.

And then we experimented with the `randint` function (from the `random` module) to generate a random integer from a provided range:

```
>>> import random
>>> random.randint(1,60)
12
>>> random.randint(1,60)
42
>>> random.randint(1,60)
17
```

Note: different integers are generated once more, as "randint" returns a different random integer each time it's invoked.

We can now put all of this together and change our program.

Let's remind ourselves of what we decided to do earlier in this chapter: have our program iterate, executing the "minute checking code" and the `if/else` statement five times, and pausing for a random number of seconds between each iteration. This should result in five messages appearing on screen before the program terminates.

Code Experiments Magnets

Based on the specification at the bottom of the last page, as well as the results of our experimentations, we went ahead and did some of the required work for you. But, as we were arranging our code magnets on the fridge (don't ask) someone slammed the door, and now some of our code's all over the floor.

Your job is to put everything back together, so that we can run the new version of our program and confirm that it's working as required.

```
from datetime import datetime
```

Decide which code magnet goes in each of the dashed-line locations.

```
..................................................
..................................................

odds = [ 1,   3,   5,   7,   9, 11, 13, 15, 17, 19,
        21, 23, 25, 27, 29, 31, 33, 35, 37, 39,
        41, 43, 45, 47, 49, 51, 53, 55, 57, 59 ]


..................................................
    right_this_minute = datetime.today().minute
    if right_this_minute in odds:
        print("This minute seems a little odd.")
    else:
        print("Not an odd minute.")
    wait_time = ..................................................
        ..................................  ( .................................. )
```

Where do all these go?

```
time.sleep
```

```
import time
```

```
wait_time
```

```
import random
```

```
for i in range(5):
```

```
random.randint(1, 60)
```

Code Experiments Magnets Solution

Based on the specification from earlier, as well as the results of our experimentations, we went ahead and did some of the required work for you. But, as we were arranging our code magnets on the fridge (don't ask) someone slammed the door, and now some of our code's all over the floor.

Your job was to put everything back together, so that we could run the new version of our program and confirm that it's working as required.

You don't have to put your imports at the top of your code, but it is a well-established convention among Python programmers to do so.

The "for" loop iterates EXACTLY five times.

The "randint" function provides a random integer that is assigned to a new variable called "wait_time", which...

...is then used in the call to "sleep" to pause the program's execution for a random number of seconds.

All of this code is indented under the "for" statement, as it is all part of the "for" statement's suite. Remember: Python does not use curly braces to delimit suites; it uses indentation instead.

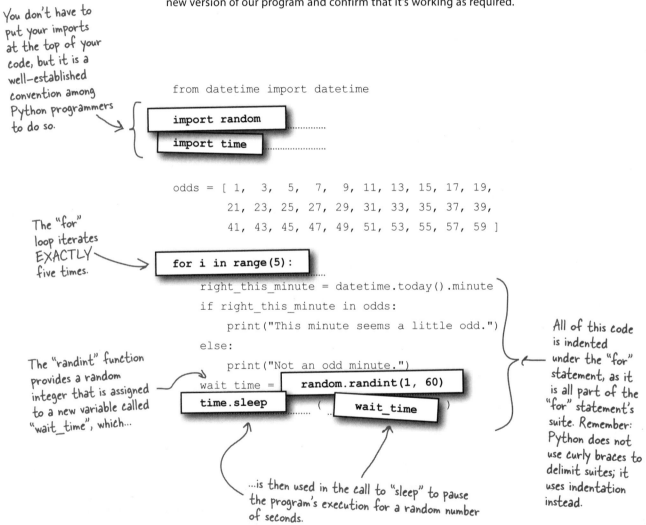

```python
from datetime import datetime
import random
import time

odds = [ 1,  3,  5,  7,  9, 11, 13, 15, 17, 19,
        21, 23, 25, 27, 29, 31, 33, 35, 37, 39,
        41, 43, 45, 47, 49, 51, 53, 55, 57, 59 ]

for i in range(5):
    right_this_minute = datetime.today().minute
    if right_this_minute in odds:
        print("This minute seems a little odd.")
    else:
        print("Not an odd minute.")
    wait_time = random.randint(1, 60)
    time.sleep(wait_time)
```

TEST DRIVE

Let's try running our upgraded program in IDLE to see what happens. Change your version of `odd.py` as needed, then save a copy of your new program as `odd2.py`. When you're ready, press F5 to execute your code.

When you press F5 to run this code...

```
odd2.py - /Users/Paul/Desktop/_NewBook/ch01/odd2.py (3.4.3)

from datetime import datetime

import random
import time

odds = [ 1,  3,  5,  7,  9, 11, 13, 15, 17, 19,
        21, 23, 25, 27, 29, 31, 33, 35, 37, 39,
        41, 43, 45, 47, 49, 51, 53, 55, 57, 59 ]

for i in range(5):
    right_this_minute = datetime.today().minute
    if right_this_minute in odds:
        print("This minute seems a little odd.")
    else:
        print("Not an odd minute.")
    wait_time = random.randint(1, 60)
    time.sleep(wait_time)

                                          Ln: 19 Col: 0
```

...you should see output similar to this. Just remember that your output will differ, as the random numbers your program generates most likely won't match ours.

```
Python 3.4.3 Shell

>>> ================================ RESTART ================================
>>>
This minute seems a little odd.
This minute seems a little odd.
Not an odd minute.
Not an odd minute.
Not an odd minute.
>>>
                                                          Ln: 25 Col: 4
```

Don't worry if you see a different list of messages than those shown here. You should see five messages, as that's how many times the loop code runs.

Updating What We Already Know

With `odd2.py` working, let's pause once more to review the new things we're learned about Python from these last 15 pages:

BULLET POINTS

- When trying to determine the code that they need to solve a particular problem, Python programmers often favor experimenting with code snippets at the shell.

- If you're looking at the >>> prompt, you're at the Python Shell. Go ahead: type in a single Python statement and see what happens when it runs.

- The shell takes your line of code and sends it to the interpreter, which then executes it. Any results are returned to the shell and are then displayed on screen.

- The `for` loop can be used to iterate a fixed number of times. If you know ahead of time how many times you need to loop, use `for`.

- When you don't know ahead of time how often you're going to iterate, use Python's `while` loop (which we have yet to see, but—don't worry—we will see it in action later).

- The `for` loop can iterate over any sequence (like a list or a string), as well as execute a fixed number of times (thanks to the `range` function).

- If you need to pause the execution of your program for a specified number of seconds, use the `sleep` function provided by the standard library's `time` module.

- You can import a specific function from a module. For example, `from time import sleep` imports the `sleep` function, letting you invoke it without qualification.

- If you simply import a module—for example, `import time`—you then need to qualify the usage of any of the module's functions with the module name, like so: `time.sleep()`.

- The `random` module has a very useful function called `randint` that generates a random integer within a specified range.

- The shell provides two interactive functions that work at the >>> prompt. The `dir` function lists an object's attributes, whereas `help` provides access to the Python docs.

---

there are no Dumb Questions

Q: Do I have to remember all this stuff?

A: No, and don't freak out if your brain is resisting the insertion of everything seen so far. This is only the first chapter, and we've designed it to be a quick introduction to the world of Python programming. If you're getting the gist of what's going on with this code, then you're doing fine.

A Few Lines of Code Do a Lot

Phew! That's another big list...

It is, but we are on a roll here.

It's true we've only touched on a small amount of the Python language so far. But what we've looked at has been very useful.

What we've seen so far helps to demonstrate one of Python's big selling points: *a few lines of code do a lot*. Another of the language's claims to fame is this: *Python code is easy to read*.

In an attempt to prove just how easy, we present on the next page a completely different program that you already know enough about Python to understand.

Who's in the mood for a nice, cold beer?

Coding a Serious Business Application

With a tip of the hat to *Head First Java*, let's take a look at the Python version of that classic's first serious application: the beer song.

Shown below is a screenshot of the Python version of the beer song code. Other than a slight variation on the usage of the `range` function (which we'll discuss in a bit), most of this code should make sense. The IDLE edit window contains the code, while the tail end of the program's output appears in a shell window:

```
beersong.py - /Users/Paul/Desktop/_NewBook/ch01/beersong.py (3.4.3)

word = "bottles"
for beer_num in range(99, 0, -1):
    print(beer_num, word, "of beer on the wall.")
    print(beer_num, word, "of beer.")
    print("Take one down.")
    print("Pass it around.")
    if beer_num == 1:
        print("No more bottles of beer on the wall.")
    else:
        new_num = beer_num - 1
        if new_num == 1:
            word = "bottle"
        print(new_num, word, "of beer on the wall.")
    print()
```

Running this code produces this output in the shell.

Dealing with all that beer...

With the code shown above typed into an IDLE edit window and saved, pressing F5 produces a lot of output in the shell. We've only shown a little bit of the resulting output in the window on the right, as the beer song starts with 99 bottles of beer on the wall and counts down until there's no more beer. In fact, the only real twist in this code is how it handles this "counting down," so let's take a look at how that works before looking at the program's code in detail.

```
Python 3.4.3 Shell

3 bottles of beer on the wall.
3 bottles of beer.
Take one down.
Pass it around.
2 bottles of| beer on the wall.

2 bottles of beer on the wall.
2 bottles of beer.
Take one down.
Pass it around.
1 bottle of beer on the wall.

1 bottle of beer on the wall.
1 bottle of beer.
Take one down.
Pass it around.
No more bottles of beer on the wall.

>>>

Ln: 660  Col: 12
```

Python Code Is Easy to Read

That code really is easy to read. But what's the catch?

There isn't one!

When most programmers new to Python first encounter code like that of the beer song, they assume that something's got to give somewhere else.

There has to be a catch, doesn't there?

No, there doesn't. It's not by accident that Python code is easy to read: the language was designed with that specific goal in mind. *Guido van Rossum*, the language's creator, wanted to create a powerful programming tool that produced code that was easy to maintain, which meant code created in Python has to be easy to read, too.

Is Indentation Driving You Crazy?

Hang on a second. All this indentation is driving me crazy. Surely that's the catch?

Indentation takes time to get used to.

Don't worry. Everyone coming to Python from a "curly-braced language" struggles with indentation *at first*. But it does get better. After a day or two of working with Python, you'll hardly notice you're indenting your suites.

One problem that some programmers do have with indentation occurs when they mix *tabs* with *spaces*. Due to the way the interpreter counts **whitespace**, this can lead to problems, in that the code "looks fine" but refuses to run. This is frustrating when you're starting out with Python.

Our advice: *don't mix tabs with spaces in your Python code*.

In fact, we'd go even further and advise you to configure your editor to replace a tap of the *Tab* key with *four spaces* (and while you're at it, automatically remove any trailing whitespace, too). This is the well-established convention among many Python programmers, and you should follow it, too. We'll have more to say about dealing with indentation at the end of this chapter.

Getting back to the beer song code

If you take a look at the invocation of `range` in the beer song, you'll notice that it takes *three* arguments as opposed to just one (as in our first example program).

Take a closer look, and without looking at the explanation on the next page, see if you can work out what's going on with this call to `range`:

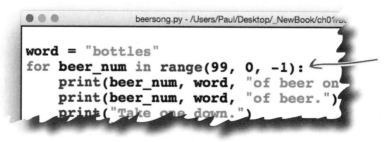

```
beersong.py - /Users/Paul/Desktop/_NewBook/ch01...

word = "bottles"
for beer_num in range(99, 0, -1):
    print(beer_num, word, "of beer on
    print(beer_num, word, "of beer.")
    print("Take one down.")
```

This is new: the call to "range" takes three arguments, not one.

Asking the Interpreter for Help on a Function

Recall that you can use the shell to ask for **help** with anything to do with Python, so let's ask for some help with the range function.

When you do this in IDLE, the resulting documentation is more than a screen's worth and it quickly scrolls off the screen. All you need to do is scroll back in the window to where you asked the shell for help (as that's where the interesting stuff about range is):

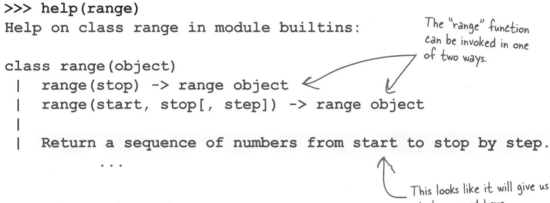

```
>>> help(range)
Help on class range in module builtins:

class range(object)
 |   range(stop) -> range object
 |   range(start, stop[, step]) -> range object
 |
 |   Return a sequence of numbers from start to stop by step.
        . . .
```

The "range" function can be invoked in one of two ways.

This looks like it will give us what we need here.

Starting, stopping, and stepping

As range is not the only place you'll come across **start**, **stop**, and **step**, let's take a moment to describe what each of these means, before looking at some representative examples (on the next page):

 The START value lets you control from WHERE the range begins.
So far, we've used the single-argument version of range, which—from the documentation—expects a value for **stop** to be provided. When no other value is provided, range defaults to using 0 as the **start** value, but you can set it to a value of your choosing. When you do, you *must* provide a value for **stop**. In this way, range becomes a multi-argument invocation.

 The STOP value lets you control WHEN the range ends.
We've already seen this in use when we invoked range(5) in our code. Note that the range that's generated *never* contains the **stop** value, so it's a case of up-to-but-not-including **stop**.

 The STEP value lets you control HOW the range is generated.
When specifying **start** and **stop** values, you can also (optionally) specify a value for **step**. By default, the **step** value is 1, and this tells range to generate each value with a *stride* of 1; that is, 0, 1, 2, 3, 4, and so on. You can set **step** to any value to adjust the stride taken. You can also set **step** to a negative value to adjust the *direction* of the generated range.

Experimenting with Ranges

Now that you know a little bit about **start**, **stop**, and **step**, let's experiment at the shell to learn how we can use the range function to produce many different ranges of integers.

To help see what's going on, we use another function, list, to transform range's output into a human-readable list that we can see on screen:

```
>>> range(5)
range(0, 5)
```
This is how we used "range" in our first program.

```
>>> list(range(5))
[0, 1, 2, 3, 4]
```
Feeding the output from "range" to "list" produces a list.

```
>>> list(range(5, 10))
[5, 6, 7, 8, 9]
```
We can adjust the START and STOP values for "range".

```
>>> list(range(0, 10, 2))
[0, 2, 4, 6, 8]
```
It is also possible to adjust the STEP value.

```
>>> list(range(10, 0, -2))
[10, 8, 6, 4, 2]
```
Things get really interesting when you adjust the range's direction by negating the STEP value.

```
>>> list(range(10, 0, 2))
[]
```
Python won't stop you from being silly. If your START value is bigger than your STOP value, and STEP is positive, you get back nothing (in this case, an empty list).

```
>>> list(range(99, 0, -1))
[99, 98, 97, 96, 95, 94, 93, 92,  ...  5, 4, 3, 2, 1]
```

After all of our experimentations, we arrive at a range invocation (shown last, above) that produces a list of values from 99 down to 1, which is exactly what the beer song's for loop does:

```
beersong.py - /Users/Paul/Desktop/_NewBook/ch0...

word = "bottles"
for beer_num in range(99, 0, -1):
    print(beer_num, word, "of beer on
    print(beer_num, word, "of beer.")
    print("Take one down.")
```
The call to "range" takes three arguments: start, stop, and step.

Sharpen your pencil

Here again is the beer code, which has been spread out over the entire page so that you can **concentrate** on each line of code that makes up this "serious business application."

Grab your pencil and, in the spaces provided, write in what you thought each line of code does. Be sure to attempt this yourself *before* looking at what we came up with on the next page. We've got you started by doing the first line of code for you.

```python
word = "bottles"

for beer_num in range(99, 0, -1):

    print(beer_num, word, "of beer on the wall.")

    print(beer_num, word, "of beer.")

    print("Take one down.")

    print("Pass it around.")

    if beer_num == 1:

        print("No more bottles of beer on the wall.")

    else:

        new_num = beer_num - 1

        if new_num == 1:

            word = "bottle"

        print(new_num, word, "of beer on the wall.")

    print()
```

Assign the value "bottles" (a string) to a new variable called "word".

Sharpen your pencil
Solution

Here again is the beer code, which has been spread out over the entire page so that you can **concentrate** on each line of code that makes up this "serious business application."

You were to grab your pencil and then, in the spaces provided, write in what you thought each line of code does. We did the first line of code for you to get you started.

How did you get on? Are your explanations similar to ours?

```
word = "bottles"
```
Assign the value "bottles" (a string) to a new variable called "word".

```
for beer_num in range(99, 0, -1):
```
Loop a specified number of times, from 99 down to none. Use "beer_num" as the loop iteration variable.

```
    print(beer_num, word, "of beer on the wall.")
```

```
    print(beer_num, word, "of beer.")
```

```
    print("Take one down.")
```

```
    print("Pass it around.")
```
The four calls to the print function display the current iteration's song lyrics, "99 bottles of beer on the wall. 99 bottles of beer. Take one down. Pass it around.", and so on with each iteration.

```
    if beer_num == 1:
```
Check to see if we are on the last passed-around beer...

```
        print("No more bottles of beer on the wall.")
```
And if we are, end the song lyrics.

```
    else:
```
Otherwise...

```
        new_num = beer_num - 1
```
Remember the number of the next beer in another variable called "new_num".

```
        if new_num == 1:
```
If we're about to drink our last beer...

```
            word = "bottle"
```
Change the value of the "word" variable so the last lines of the lyric make sense.

```
        print(new_num, word, "of beer on the wall.")
```
Complete this iteration's song lyrics.

```
    print()
```
At the end of this iteration, print a blank line. When all the iterations are complete, terminate the program.

Don't Forget to Try the Beer Song Code

If you haven't done so already, type the beer song code into IDLE, save it as `beersong.py`, and then press F5 to take it for a spin. *Do not move on to the next chapter until you have a working beer song.*

there are no Dumb Questions

Q: I keep getting errors when I try to run my beer song code. But my code looks fine to me, so I'm a little frustrated. Any suggestions?

A: The first thing to check is that you have your indentation right. If you do, then check to see if you have mixed tabs with spaces in your code. Remember: the code will look fine (to you), but the interpreter refuses to run it. If you suspect this, a quick fix is to bring your code into an IDLE edit window, then choose *Edit...→Select All* from the menu system, before choosing *Format...→Untabify Region*. If you've mixed tabs with spaces, this will convert all your tabs to spaces in one go (and fix any indentation issues).

You can then save your code and press F5 to try running it again. If it still refuses to run, check that your code is *exactly* the same as we presented in this chapter. Be very careful of any spelling mistakes you may have made with your variable names.

Q: The Python interpreter won't warn me if I misspell `new_num` **as** `nwe_num`?

A: No, it won't. As long as a variable is assigned a value, Python assumes you know what you're doing, and continues to execute your code. It is something to watch for, though, so be vigilant.

Wrapping up what you already know

Here are some new things you learned as a result of working through (and running) the beer song code:

BULLET POINTS

- Indentation takes a little time to get used to. Every programmer new to Python complains about indentation at some point, but don't worry: soon you'll not even notice you're doing it.

- If there's one thing that you should never, ever do, it's mix tabs with spaces when indenting your Python code. Save yourself some future heartache, and don't do this.

- The `range` function can take more than one argument when invoked. These arguments let you control the start and stop values of the generated range, as well as the step value.

- The `range` function's step value can also be specified with a negative value, which changes the direction of the generated range

With all the beer gone, what's next?

That's it for Chapter 1. In the next chapter, you are going to learn a bit more about how Python handles data. We only just touched on **lists** in this chapter, and it's time to dive in a little deeper.

Chapter 1's Code

```
from datetime import datetime

odds = [ 1,  3,  5,  7,  9, 11, 13, 15, 17, 19,
        21, 23, 25, 27, 29, 31, 33, 35, 37, 39,
        41, 43, 45, 47, 49, 51, 53, 55, 57, 59 ]

right_this_minute = datetime.today().minute

if right_this_minute in odds:
    print("This minute seems a little odd.")
else:
    print("Not an odd minute.")
```

We started with
the "odd.py"
program, then...

```
from datetime import datetime

import random
import time

odds = [ 1,  3,  5,  7,  9, 11, 13, 15, 17, 19,
        21, 23, 25, 27, 29, 31, 33, 35, 37, 39,
        41, 43, 45, 47, 49, 51, 53, 55, 57, 59 ]

for i in range(5):
    right_this_minute = datetime.today().minute
    if right_this_minute in odds:
        print("This minute seems a little odd.")
    else:
        print("Not an odd minute.")
    wait_time = random.randint(1, 60)
    time.sleep(wait_time)
```

... extended the code to
create "odd2.py", which ran
the "minute checking code"
five times (thanks to the use
of Python's "for" loop).

```
word = "bottles"
for beer_num in range(99, 0, -1):
    print(beer_num, word, "of beer on the wall.")
    print(beer_num, word, "of beer.")
    print("Take one down.")
    print("Pass it around.")
    if beer_num == 1:
        print("No more bottles of beer on the wall.")
    else:
        new_num = beer_num - 1
        if new_num == 1:
            word = "bottle"
        print(new_num, word, "of beer on the wall.")
    print()
```

We concluded this
chapter with the Python
version of the Head
First classic "beer song."
And, yes, we know: it's
hard not to work on
this code without singing
along... ☺

2 list data
✳ Working with Ordered Data ✳

This data would be sooooo much easier to work with...if only I'd arranged it as a list.

All programs process data, and Python programs are no exception.

In fact, take a look around: *data is everywhere*. A lot of, if not most, programming is all about data: *acquiring* data, *processing* data, *understanding* data. To work with data effectively, you need somewhere to *put* your data when processing it. Python shines in this regard, thanks (in no small part) to its inclusion of a handful of *widely applicable* data structures: **lists**, **dictionaries**, **tuples**, and **sets**. In this chapter, we'll preview all four, before spending the majority of this chapter digging deeper into **lists** (and we'll deep-dive into the other three in the next chapter). We're covering these data structures early, as most of what you'll likely do with Python will revolve around working with data.

Numbers, Strings...and Objects

Working with a *single* data value in Python works just like you'd expect it to. Assign a value to a variable, and you're all set. With help from the shell, let's look at some examples to recall what we learned in the last chapter.

Numbers

Let's assume that this example has already imported the `random` module. We then call the `random.randint` function to generate a random number between 1 and 60, which is then assigned to the `wait_time` variable. As the generated number is an **integer**, that's what type `wait_time` is in this instance:

```
>>> wait_time = random.randint(1, 60)
>>> wait_time
26
```

Note how you didn't have to tell the interpreter that `wait_time` is going to contain an integer. We *assigned* an integer to the variable, and the interpreter took care of the details (note: not all programming languages work this way).

A variable takes on the type of the value assigned.

Strings

If you assign a string to a variable, the same thing happens: the interpreter takes care of the details. Again, we do not need to declare ahead of time that the `word` variable in this example is going to contain a **string**:

```
>>> word = "bottles"
>>> word
'bottles'
```

This ability to *dynamically* assign a value to a variable is central to Python's notion of variables and type. In fact, things are more general than this in that you can assign *anything* to a variable in Python.

Objects

In Python everything is an object. The means that numbers, strings, functions, modules—*everything*—is an object. A direct consequence of this is that all objects can be assigned to variables. This has some interesting ramifications, which we'll start learning about on the next page.

Everything is an object in Python, and any object can be assigned to a variable.

"Everything Is an Object"

Any object can be dynamically assigned to any variable in Python. Which begs the question: *what's an object in Python?* The answer: **everything is an object**.

All data values in Python are objects, even though—on the face of things—"Don't panic!" is a string and 42 is a number. To Python programmers, "Don't panic!" is a *string object* and 42 is a *number object*. Like in other programming languages, objects can have **state** (attributes or values) and **behavior** (methods).

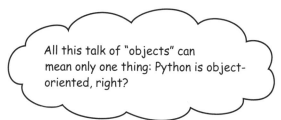

All this talk of "objects" can mean only one thing: Python is object-oriented, right?

Sort of.

You can certainly program Python in an object-oriented way using classes, objects, instances, and so on (more on all of this later in this book), but you don't have to. Recall the programs from the last chapter...none of them needed classes. Those programs just contained code, and they worked fine.

Unlike some other programming languages (most notably, *Java*), you do not need to start with a class when first creating code in Python: you just write the code you need.

Now, having said all that (and just to keep you on your toes), everything in Python *behaves* as if it is an object *derived from* some class. In this way, you can think of Python as being more **object-based** as opposed to purely object-oriented, which means that object-oriented programming is optional in Python.

But...what does all this actually mean?

As everything is an object in Python, any "thing" can be assigned to any variable, and variables can be assigned *anything* (regardless of what the thing is: a number, a string, a function, a widget...any object). Tuck this away in the back of your brain for now; we'll return to this theme many times throughout this book.

There's really not a lot more to storing single data values in variables. Let's now take a look at Python's built-in support for storing a **collection** of values.

Meet the Four Built-in Data Structures

Python comes with **four** built-in *data structures* that you can use to hold any *collection* of objects, and they are **list**, **tuple**, **dictionary**, and **set**.

Note that by "built-in" we mean that lists, tuples, dictionaries, and sets are always available to your code and *they do not need to be imported prior to use*: each of these data structures is part of the language.

Over the next few pages, we present an overview of all four of these built-in data structures. You may be tempted to skip over this overview, but please don't.

If you think you have a pretty good idea what a **list** is, think again. Python's list is more similar to what you might think of as an *array*, as opposed to a *linked-list*, which is what often comes to mind when programmers hear the word "list." (If you're lucky enough not to know what a linked-list is, sit back and be thankful).

Python's list is the first of two ordered-collection data structures:

 List: an ordered mutable collection of objects

A list in Python is very similar to the notion of an **array** in other programming languages, in that you can think of a list as being an indexed collection of related objects, with each slot in the list numbered from zero upward.

Unlike arrays in a lot of other programming languages, though, lists are **dynamic** in Python, in that they can grow (and shrink) on demand. There is no need to predeclare the size of a list prior to using it to store any objects.

Lists are also heterogeneous, in that you do not need to predeclare the type of the object you're storing—you can mix'n'match objects of different types in the one list if you like.

Lists are **mutable**, in that you can change a list at any time by adding, removing, or changing objects.

> **A list is like an array— the objects it stores are ordered sequentially in slots.**

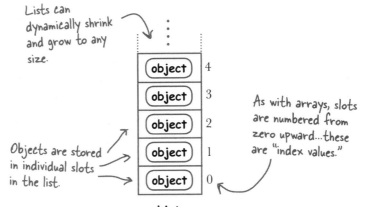

List

Ordered Collections Are Mutable/Immutable

Python's list is an example of a **mutable** data structure, in that it can change (or mutate) at runtime. You can grow and shrink a list by adding and removing objects as needed. It's also possible to change any object stored in any slot. We'll have lots more to say about lists in a few pages' time as the remainder of this chapter is devoted to providing a comprehensive introduction to using lists.

When an ordered list-like collection is **immutable** (that is, it cannot change), it's called a **tuple**:

 Tuple: an ordered immutable collection of objects

A tuple is an immutable list. This means that once you assign objects to a tuple, the tuple cannot be changed under any circumstance.

It is often useful to think of a tuple as a constant list.

Most new Python programmers scratch their head in bemusement when they first encounter tuples, as it can be hard to work out their purpose. After all, what use is a list that cannot change? It turns out that there are plenty of use cases where you'll want to ensure that your objects can't be changed by your (or anyone else's) code. We'll return to tuples in the next chapter (as well as later in this book) when we talk about them in a bit more detail, as well as use them.

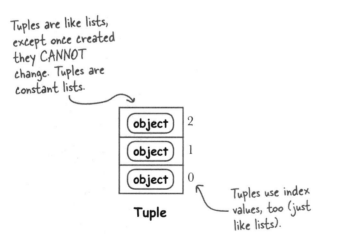

Tuples are like lists, except once created they CANNOT change. Tuples are constant lists.

Tuple

Tuples use index values, too (just like lists).

A tuple is an immutable list.

Lists and tuples are great when you want to present data in an ordered way (such as a list of destinations on a travel itinerary, where the order of destinations *is* important). But sometimes the order in which you present the data *isn't* important. For instance, you might want to store some user's details (such as their *id* and *password*), but you may not care in what order they're stored (just that they are). With data like this, an alternative to Python's list/tuple is needed.

An Unordered Data Structure: Dictionary

If keeping your data in a specific order isn't important to you, but structure is, Python comes with a choice of two unordered data structures: **dictionary** and **set**. Let's look at each in turn, starting with Python's dictionary.

 Dictionary: an unordered set of key/value pairs

Depending on your programming background, you may already know what a **dictionary** is, but you may know it by another name, such as associative array, map, symbol table, or hash.

Like those other data structures in those other languages, Python's dictionary allows you to store a collection of key/value pairs. Each unique **key** has a **value** associated with it in the dictionary, and dictionaries can have any number of pairs. The values associated with a key can be any object.

Dictionaries are unordered and mutable. It can be useful to think of Python's dictionary as a two-columned, multirow data structure. Like lists, dictionaries can grow (and shrink) on demand.

Dictionaries associate keys with values, and (like lists) can dynamically shrink and grow to any size.

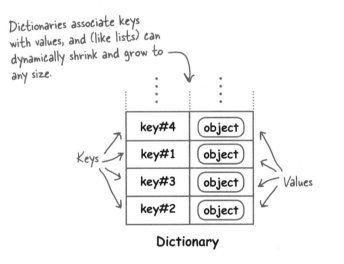

Dictionary

A dictionary stores key/ value pairs.

Something to watch out for when using a dictionary is that you cannot rely upon the internal ordering used by the interpreter. Specifically, the order in which you add key/value pairs to a dictionary is not maintained by the interpreter, and has no meaning (to Python). This can stump programmers when they first encounter it, so we're making you aware of it now so that when we meet it again—and in detail—in the next chapter, you'll get less of a shock. Rest assured: it is possible to display your dictionary data in a specific order if need be, and we'll show you how to do that in the next chapter, too.

A Data Structure That Avoids Duplicates: Set

The final built-in data structure is the **set**, which is great to have at hand when you want to remove duplicates quickly from any other collection. And don't worry if the mention of sets has you recalling high school math class and breaking out in a cold sweat. Python's implementation of sets can be used in lots of places.

 Set: an unordered set of unique objects

In Python, a **set** is a handy data structure for remembering a collection of related objects while ensuring none of the objects are duplicated.

The fact that sets let you perform unions, intersections, and differences is an added bonus (especially if you are a math type who loves set theory).

Sets, like lists and dictionaries, can grow (and shrink) as needed. Like dictionaries, sets are unordered, so you cannot make assumptions about the order of the objects in your set. As with tuples and dictionaries, you'll get to see sets in action in the next chapter.

Think of a set as a collection of unordered unique items—no duplicates allowed.

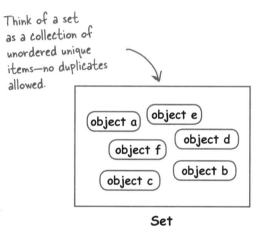

Set

A set does not allow duplicate objects.

The 80/20 data structure rule of thumb

The four built-in data structures are useful, but they don't cover every possible data need. However, they do cover a lot of them. It's the usual story with technologies designed to be generally useful: about 80% of what you need to do is covered, while the other, highly specific, 20% requires you to do more work. Later in this book, you'll learn how to extend Python to support any bespoke data requirements you may have. However, for now, in the remainder of this chapter and the next, we're going to concentrate on the 80% of your data needs.

The rest of this chapter is dedicated to exploring how to work with the first of our four built-in data structures: the **list**. We'll get to know the remaining three data structures, **dictionary**, **set**, and **tuple**, in the next chapter.

A List Is an Ordered Collection of Objects

When you have a bunch of related objects and you need to put them somewhere in your code, think **list**. For instance, imagine you have a month's worth of daily temperature readings; storing these readings in a list makes perfect sense.

Whereas arrays tend to be homogeneous affairs in other programming languages, in that you can have an array of integers, or an array of strings, or an array of temperature readings, Python's **list** is less restrictive. You can have a list of *objects*, and each object can be of a differing type. In addition to being **heterogeneous**, lists are **dynamic**: they can grow and shrink as needed.

Before learning how to work with lists, let's spend some time learning how to spot lists in Python code.

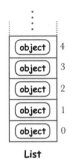

List

How to spot a list in code

Lists are always enclosed in **square brackets**, and the objects contained within the list are always separated by a **comma**.

Recall the `odds` list from the last chapter, which contained the odd numbers from 0 through 60, as follows:

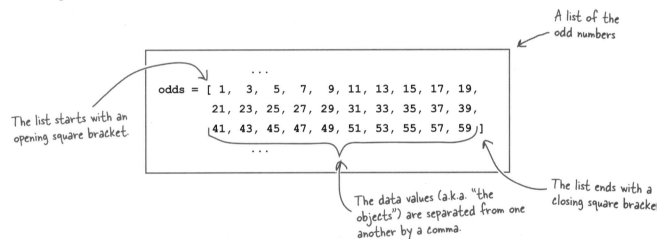

The list starts with an opening square bracket.

A list of the odd numbers

```
odds = [ 1,   3,   5,   7,   9, 11, 13, 15, 17, 19,
        21, 23, 25, 27, 29, 31, 33, 35, 37, 39,
        41, 43, 45, 47, 49, 51, 53, 55, 57, 59 ]
```

The data values (a.k.a. "the objects") are separated from one another by a comma.

The list ends with a closing square bracket.

When a list is created where the objects are assigned to a new list directly in your code (as shown above), Python programmers refer to this as a **literal list**, in that the list is created *and* populated in one go.

The other way to create and populate a list is to "grow" the list in code, appending objects to the list as the code executes. We'll see an example of this method later in this chapter.

Let's look at some literal list examples.

Lists can be created literally or "grown" in code.

Creating Lists Literally

Our first example creates an **empty** list by assigning [ ] to a variable called `prices`:

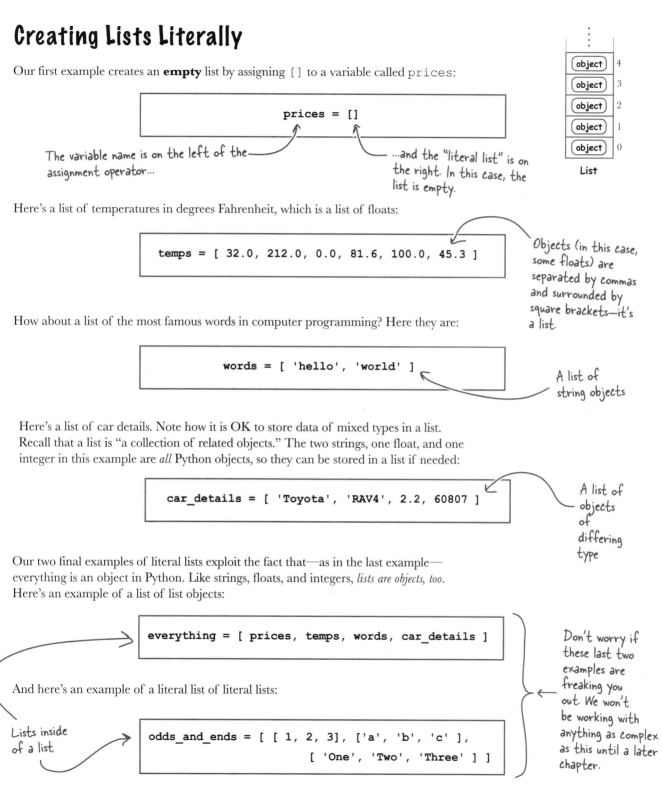

```
prices = []
```

The variable name is on the left of the assignment operator...

...and the "literal list" is on the right. In this case, the list is empty.

object 4
object 3
object 2
object 1
object 0

List

Here's a list of temperatures in degrees Fahrenheit, which is a list of floats:

```
temps = [ 32.0, 212.0, 0.0, 81.6, 100.0, 45.3 ]
```

Objects (in this case, some floats) are separated by commas and surrounded by square brackets—it's a list.

How about a list of the most famous words in computer programming? Here they are:

```
words = [ 'hello', 'world' ]
```

A list of string objects

Here's a list of car details. Note how it is OK to store data of mixed types in a list. Recall that a list is "a collection of related objects." The two strings, one float, and one integer in this example are *all* Python objects, so they can be stored in a list if needed:

```
car_details = [ 'Toyota', 'RAV4', 2.2, 60807 ]
```

A list of objects of differing type

Our two final examples of literal lists exploit the fact that—as in the last example—everything is an object in Python. Like strings, floats, and integers, *lists are objects, too.* Here's an example of a list of list objects:

```
everything = [ prices, temps, words, car_details ]
```

And here's an example of a literal list of literal lists:

Lists inside of a list

```
odds_and_ends = [ [ 1, 2, 3], ['a', 'b', 'c' ],
                  [ 'One', 'Two', 'Three' ] ]
```

Don't worry if these last two examples are freaking you out. We won't be working with anything as complex as this until a later chapter.

Putting Lists to Work

The literal lists on the last page demonstrate how quickly lists can be created and populated in code. Type in the data, and you're off and running.

In a page or two, we'll cover the mechanism that allows you to grow (or shrink) a list while your program executes. After all, there are many situations where you don't know ahead of time what data you need to store, nor how many objects you're going to need. In this case, your code has to grow (or "generate") the list as needed. You'll learn how to do that in a few pages' time.

For now, imagine you have a requirement to determine whether a given word contains any of the vowels (that is, the letters *a*, *e*, *i*, *o*, or *u*). Can we use Python's list to help code up a solution to this problem? Let's see whether we can come up with a solution by experimenting at the shell.

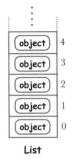

List

Working with lists

We'll use the shell to first define a list called `vowels`, then check to see if each letter in a word is in the `vowels` list. Let's define a list of vowels:

A list of the
five vowels

```
>>> vowels = ['a', 'e', 'i', 'o', 'u']
```

With `vowels` defined, we now need a word to check, so let's create a variable called `word` and set it to `"Milliways"`:

Here's a word
to check.

```
>>> word = "Milliways"
```

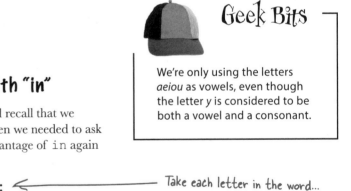

Geek Bits

We're only using the letters *aeiou* as vowels, even though the letter *y* is considered to be both a vowel and a consonant.

Is one object inside another? Check with "in"

If you remember the programs from Chapter 1, you will recall that we used Python's `in` operator to check for membership when we needed to ask whether one object was inside another. We can take advantage of `in` again here:

```
>>> for letter in word:
        if letter in vowels:
            print(letter)
```

Take each letter in the word...

...and if it is in the "vowels" list...

...display the letter on screen.

```
i
i
a
```

The output from this code confirms the identity
of the vowels in the word "Milliways".

Let's use this code as the basis for our working with lists.

Use Your Editor When Working on More Than a Few Lines of Code

In order to learn a bit more about how lists work, let's take this code and extend it to display each found vowel only once. At the moment, the code displays each vowel more than once on output if the word being searched contains more than one instance of the vowel.

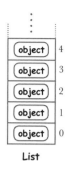

List

First, let's copy and paste the code you've just typed from the shell into a new IDLE edit window (select *File...→New File...* from IDLE's menu). We're going to be making a series of changes to this code, so moving it into the editor makes perfect sense. As a general rule, when the code we're experimenting with at the >>> prompt starts to run to more than a few lines, we find it more convenient to use the editor. Save your five lines of code as vowels.py.

When copying code from the shell into the editor, **be careful** *not* to include the >>> prompt in the copy, as your code won't run if you do (the interpreter will throw a syntax error when it encounters >>>).

When you've copied your code and saved your file, your IDLE edit window should look like this:

Your list example code saved as "vowels.py" inside an IDLE edit window.

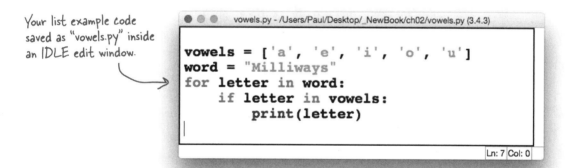

Don't forget: press F5 to run your program

With the code in the edit window, press F5 and then watch as IDLE jumps to a restarted shell window, then displays the program's output:

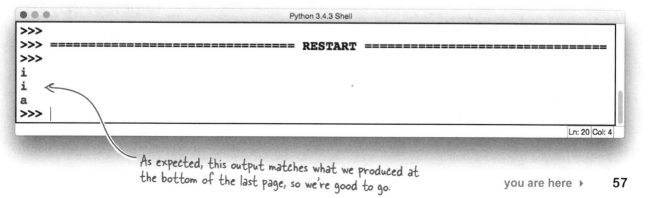

As expected, this output matches what we produced at the bottom of the last page, so we're good to go.

"Growing" a List at Runtime

Our current program *displays* each found vowel on screen, including any duplicates found. In order to list each unique vowel found (and avoid displaying duplicates), we need to remember any unique vowels that we find, before displaying them on screen. To do this, we need to use a second data structure.

We can't use the existing vowels list because it exists to let us quickly determine whether the letter we're currently processing is a vowel. We need a second list that starts out empty, as we're going to populate it at runtime with any vowels we find.

As we did in the last chapter, let's experiment at the shell *before* making any changes to our program code. To create a new, empty list, decide on a new variable name, then assign an empty list to it. Let's call our second list found. Here we assign an empty list ([]) to found, then use Python's built-in function len to check how many objects are in a collection:

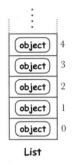

List

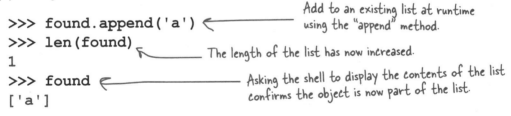

```
>>> found = []
>>> len(found)
0
```

An empty list...

...which the interpreter (thanks to "len") confirms has no objects.

> The "len" built-in function reports on the size of an object.

Lists come with a collection of built-in **methods** that you can use to manipulate the list's objects. To invoke a method use the *dot-notation syntax*: postfix the list's name with a dot and the method invocation. We'll meet more methods later in this chapter. For now, let's use the append method to add an object to the end of the empty list we just created:

```
>>> found.append('a')
>>> len(found)
1
>>> found
['a']
```

Add to an existing list at runtime using the "append" method.

The length of the list has now increased.

Asking the shell to display the contents of the list confirms the object is now part of the list.

Repeated calls to the append method add more objects onto the end of the list:

> Lists come with a bunch of built-in methods.

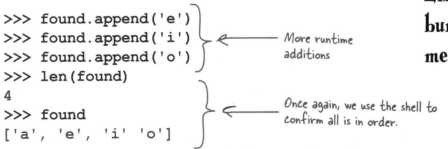

```
>>> found.append('e')
>>> found.append('i')
>>> found.append('o')
>>> len(found)
4
>>> found
['a', 'e', 'i' 'o']
```

More runtime additions

Once again, we use the shell to confirm all is in order.

Let's now look at what's involved in checking whether a list contains an object.

Checking for Membership with "in"

We already know how to do this. Recall the "Millyways" example from a few pages ago, as well as the odds.py code from the previous chapter, which checked to see whether a calculated minute value was in the odds list:

The "in" operator checks for membership.

```
        ...
    if right_this_minute in odds:
        print("This minute seems a little odd.")
        ...
```

Is the object "in" or "not in"?

As well as using the in operator to check whether an object is contained within a collection, it is also possible to check whether an object *does not exist within a collection* using the not in operator combination.

Using not in allows you to append to an existing list *only* when you know that the object to be added isn't already part of the list:

```
>>> if 'u' not in found:
        found.append('u')

>>> found
['a', 'e', 'i' 'o', 'u']
>>>
>>> if 'u' not in found:
        found.append('u')

>>> found
['a', 'e', 'i' 'o', 'u']
```

This first invocation of "append" works, as "u" does not currently exist within the "found" list (as you saw on the previous page, the list contained ['a', 'e', 'i', 'o']).

This next invocation of "append" does not execute, as "u" already exists in "found" so does not need to be added again.

> Would it not be better to use a set here? Isn't a set a better choice when you're trying to avoid duplicates?

Good catch. A set might be better here.

But, we're going to hold off on using a set until the next chapter. We'll return to this example when we do. For now, concentrate on learning how a list can be generated at runtime with the append method.

It's Time to Update Our Code

Now that we know about `not in` and `append`, we can change our code with some confidence. Here's the original code from `vowels.py` again:

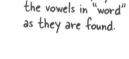

The original
"vowels.py"
code

```
vowels = ['a', 'e', 'i', 'o', 'u']
word = "Milliways"
for letter in word:
    if letter in vowels:
        print(letter)
```

This code displays
the vowels in "word"
as they are found.

Save a copy of this code as `vowels2.py` so that we can make our changes to this new version while leaving the original code intact.

We need to add in the creation of an empty `found` list. Then we need some extra code to populate `found` at runtime. As we no longer display the found vowels as we find them, another `for` loop is required to process the letters in `found`, and this second `for` loop needs to execute *after* the first loop (note how the indentation of both loops is *aligned* below). The new code you need is highlighted:

This is
"vowels2.py".

Start with
an empty list.

```
vowels = ['a', 'e', 'i', 'o', 'u']
word = "Milliways"
found = []
for letter in word:
    if letter in vowels:
        if letter not in found:
            found.append(letter)
for vowel in found:
    print(vowel)
```

Include the code that
decides whether to
update the list of
found vowels.

When this first "for" loop terminates, this
second one gets to run, and it displays the
vowels found in "word".

Let's make a final tweak to this code to change the line that sets `word` to "Milliways" to be more *generic* and more *interactive*.

Changing the line of code that reads:

```
        word = "Milliways"
```

to:

```
        word = input("Provide a word to search for vowels: ")
```

instructs the interpreter to *prompt* your user for a word to search for vowels. The `input` function is another piece of built-in goodness provided by Python.

Do this!

Make the change as suggested
on the left, then save your
updated code as `vowels3.py`.

Test Drive

With the change at the bottom of the last page applied, and this latest version of your program saved as `vowels3.py`, let's take this program for a few spins within IDLE. Remember: to run your program multiple times, you need to return to the IDLE edit window *before* pressing the F5 key.

Here's our version of "vowels3.py" with the "input" edit applied.

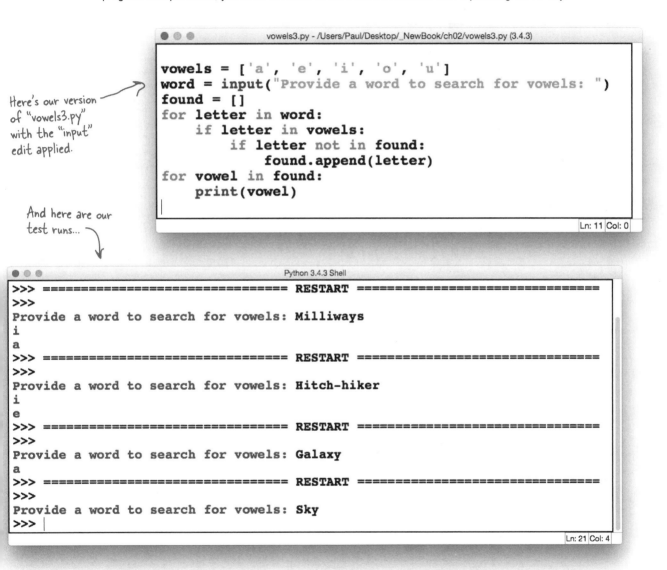

```
vowels = ['a', 'e', 'i', 'o', 'u']
word = input("Provide a word to search for vowels: ")
found = []
for letter in word:
    if letter in vowels:
        if letter not in found:
            found.append(letter)
for vowel in found:
    print(vowel)
```

And here are our test runs...

```
>>> ================================ RESTART ================================
>>>
Provide a word to search for vowels: Milliways
i
a
>>> ================================ RESTART ================================
>>>
Provide a word to search for vowels: Hitch-hiker
i
e
>>> ================================ RESTART ================================
>>>
Provide a word to search for vowels: Galaxy
a
>>> ================================ RESTART ================================
>>>
Provide a word to search for vowels: Sky
>>>
```

Our output confirms that this small program is working as expected, and it even *does the right thing* when the word contains no vowels. How did you get on when you ran your program in IDLE?

Removing Objects from a List

Lists in Python are just like arrays in other languages, and then some.

The fact that lists can grow dynamically when more space is needed (thanks to the append method) is a huge productivity boon. Like a lot of other things in Python, the interpreter takes care of the details for you. If the list needs more memory, the interpreter dynamically *allocates* as much memory as needed. Likewise, when a list shrinks, the interpreter dynamically *reclaims* memory no longer needed by the list.

Other methods exist to help you manipulate lists. Over the next four pages we introduce four of the most useful methods: remove, pop, extend, and insert:

List

1   remove: takes an object's value as its sole argument
The remove method removes the first occurrence of a specified data value from a list. If the data value is found in the list, the object that contains it is removed from the list (and the list shrinks in size by one). If the data value is *not* in the list, the interpreter will *raise an error* (more on this later):

```
>>> nums = [1, 2, 3, 4]
>>> nums
[1, 2, 3, 4]
```

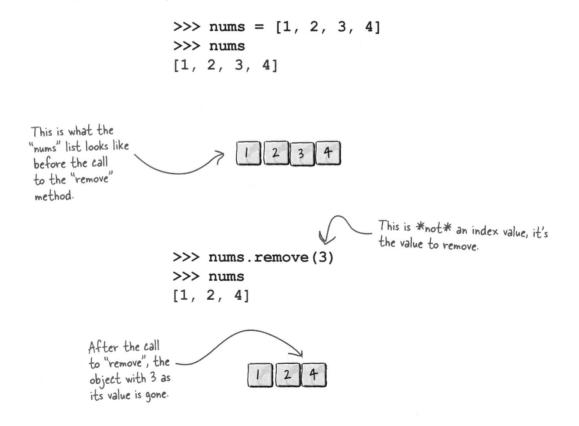

This is what the "nums" list looks like before the call to the "remove" method.

This is *not* an index value, it's the value to remove.

```
>>> nums.remove(3)
>>> nums
[1, 2, 4]
```

After the call to "remove", the object with 3 as its value is gone.

Popping Objects Off a List

The `remove` method is great for when you know the value of the object you want to remove. But often it is the case that you want to remove an object from a specific index slot.

For this, Python provides the `pop` method:

 pop: takes an optional index value as its argument
The `pop` method removes *and returns* an object from an existing list based on the object's index value. If you invoke `pop` without specifying an index value, the last object in the list is removed and returned. If you specify an index value, the object in that location is removed and returned. If a list is empty or you invoke `pop` with a nonexistent index value, the interpreter *raises an error* (more on this later).

Objects returned by `pop` can be assigned to a variable if you so wish, in which case they are retained. However, if the popped object is not assigned to a variable, its memory is reclaimed and the object disappears.

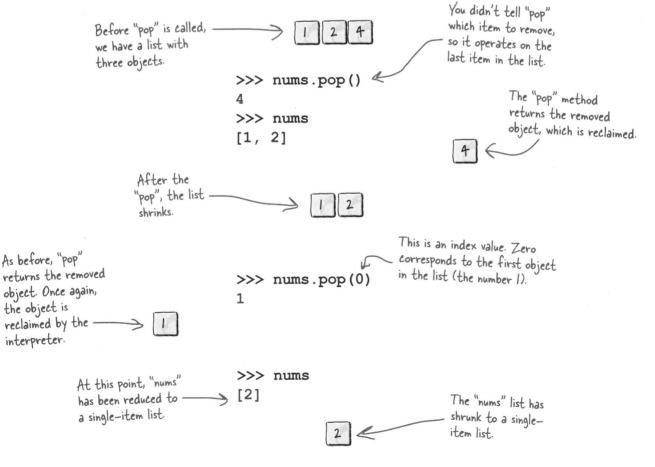

Before "pop" is called, we have a list with three objects.

```
>>> nums.pop()
4
>>> nums
[1, 2]
```

You didn't tell "pop" which item to remove, so it operates on the last item in the list.

The "pop" method returns the removed object, which is reclaimed.

After the "pop", the list shrinks.

As before, "pop" returns the removed object. Once again, the object is reclaimed by the interpreter.

```
>>> nums.pop(0)
1
```

This is an index value. Zero corresponds to the first object in the list (the number 1).

At this point, "nums" has been reduced to a single-item list.

```
>>> nums
[2]
```

The "nums" list has shrunk to a single-item list.

Extending a List with Objects

You already know that `append` can be used to add a single object to an existing list. Other methods can dynamically add data to a list, too:

3 **extend: takes a list of objects as its sole argument**
The `extend` method takes a second list and adds each of its objects to an existing list. This method is very useful for combining two lists into one:

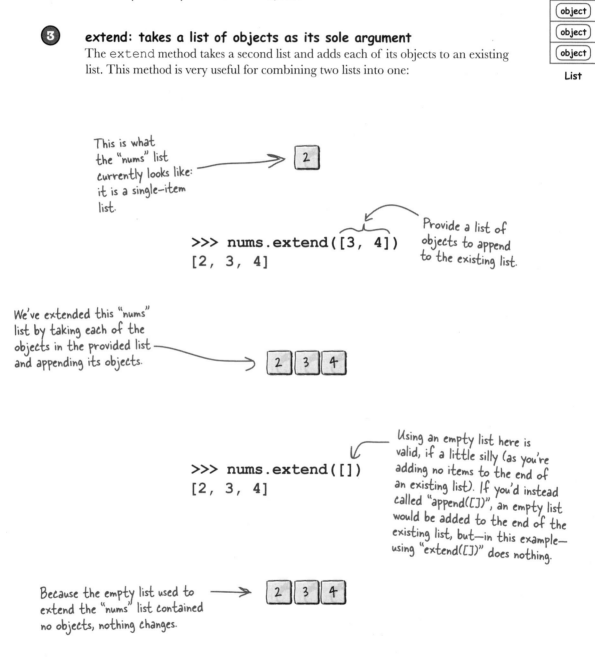

This is what the "nums" list currently looks like: it is a single-item list.

```
>>> nums.extend([3, 4])
[2, 3, 4]
```

Provide a list of objects to append to the existing list.

We've extended this "nums" list by taking each of the objects in the provided list and appending its objects.

```
>>> nums.extend([])
[2, 3, 4]
```

Using an empty list here is valid, if a little silly (as you're adding no items to the end of an existing list). If you'd instead called "append([])", an empty list would be added to the end of the existing list, but—in this example—using "extend([])" does nothing.

Because the empty list used to extend the "nums" list contained no objects, nothing changes.

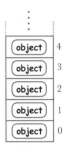

List

Inserting an Object into a List

The `append` and `extend` methods get a lot of use, but they are restricted to adding objects onto the end (the righthand side) of an existing list. Sometimes, you'll want to add to the beginning (the lefthand side) of a list. When this is the case, you'll want to use the `insert` method.

④ **`insert`: takes an index value and an object as its arguments**

The `insert` method inserts an object into an existing list *before* a specified index value. This lets you insert the object at the start of an existing list or anywhere within the list. It is not possible to insert at the end of the list, as that's what the `append` method does:

Here's how the "nums" list looked after all that extending from the → previous page.

    2 3 4

```
>>> nums.insert(0, 1)
>>> nums
[1, 2, 3, 4]
```

The value (aka "object") to insert

The index of the object to insert *before*

    1 2 3 4 ⟵── Back to where we started

After all that removing, popping, extending, and inserting, we've ended up with the same list we started with a few pages ago: [1, 2, 3, 4].

Note how it's also possible to use `insert` to add an object into any slot in an existing list. In the example above, we decided to add an object (the number 1) to the start of the list, but we could just as easily have used any slot number to insert *into* the list. Let's look at one final example, which—just for fun—adds a string into the middle of the `nums` list, thanks to the use of the value 2 as the first argument to `insert`:

The first argument to "insert" indicates the index value to insert *before*.

```
>>> nums.insert(2, "two-and-a-half")
>>> nums
[1, 2, 'two-and-a-half', 3, 4]
```

    1 2 two-and-a-half 3 4

And there it is—the final "nums" list, which has five objects: four numbers and one string.

Let's now gain some experience using these list methods.

What About Using Square Brackets?

I'm a little confused. You keep telling me that lists are "just like arrays in other programming languages," but you've yet to say anything about the square bracket notation I use with arrays in my other favorite programming language. What gives?

Don't worry, we're going to get to that in a bit.

The familiar square bracket notation that you know and love from working with arrays in other programming languages does indeed work with Python's lists. However, before we get around to discussing how, let's have a bit of fun with some of the list methods that you now know about.

there are no Dumb Questions

Q: How do I find out more about these and any other list methods?

A: You ask for help. At the >>> prompt, type **help(list)** to access Python's list documentation (which provides a few pages of material) or type **help(list.append)** to request just the documentation for the append method. Replace append with any other list method name to access that method's documentation.

Sharpen your pencil

Time for a challenge.

Before you do anything else, take the seven lines of code shown below and type them into a new IDLE edit window. Save the code as `panic.py`, and execute it (by pressing F5).

Study the messages that appear on screen. Note how the first four lines of code take a string (in `phrase`), and turn it into a list (in `plist`), before displaying both `phrase` and `plist` on screen.

The other three lines of code take `plist` and transform it back into a string (in `new_phrase`) before displaying `plist` and `new_phrase` on screen.

Your challenge is to *transform* the string `"Don't panic!"` into the string `"on tap"` using only the list methods shown thus far in this book. (There's no hidden meaning in the choice of these two strings: it's merely a matter of the letters in "on tap" appearing in `"Don't panic!"`). At the moment, `panic.py` displays `"Don't panic!"` *twice*.

Hint: use a `for` loop when performing any operation multiple times.

We are starting with a string.

```
phrase = "Don't panic!"
```

We turn the string into a list.

```
plist = list(phrase)
print(phrase)
print(plist)
```

We display the string and the list on screen.

....
....
....
....

Add your list manipulation code here.

....
....
....
....
....

```
new_phrase = ''.join(plist)
print(plist)
print(new_phrase)
```

We display the transformed list and the new string on screen.

This line takes the list and turns it back into a string.

Sharpen your pencil
Solution

It was time for a challenge.

Before you did anything else, you were to take the seven lines of code shown on the previous page and type them into a new IDLE edit window, save the code as `panic.py`, and execute it (by pressing F5).

Your challenge was to *transform* the string `"Don't panic!"` into the string `"on tap"` using only the list methods shown thus far in this book. Before your changes, `panic.py` displayed "Don't panic!" *twice*.

The new string (displaying "on tap") is to be stored in the `new_phrase` variable.

You were to add your list manipulation code here. This is what we came up with—don't worry if yours is very different from ours. There's more than one way to perform the necessary transformations using the list methods.

```
phrase = "Don't panic!"
plist = list(phrase)
print(phrase)
print(plist)
```

```
for i in range(4):
    plist.pop()
```

This small loop pops the last four objects from "plist". No more "nic!".

Get rid of the 'D' at the start of the list.

```
plist.pop(0)
plist.remove(" ' ")
```

Find, then remove, the apostrophe from the list.

```
plist.extend([plist.pop(), plist.pop()])
plist.insert(2, plist.pop(3))
```

Swap the two objects at the end of the list by first popping each object from the list, then using the popped objects to extend the list. This is a line of code that you'll need to think about for a little bit. Key point: the pops occur *first* (in the order shown), then the extend happens.

```
new_phrase = ''.join(plist)
print(plist)
print(new_phrase)
```

This line of code pops the space from the list, then inserts it back into the list at index location 2. Just like the last line of code, the pop occurs *first*, before the insert happens. And, remember: spaces are characters, too.

As there's a lot going on in this exercise solution, the next two pages explain this code in detail.

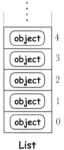

List

What Happened to "plist"?

Let's pause to consider what actually happened to plist as the code in panic.py executed.

On the left of this page (and the next) is the code from panic.py, which, like every other Python program, is executed from top to bottom. On the right of this page is a visual representation of plist together with some notes about what's happening. Note how plist dynamically shrinks and grows as the code executes:

The Code   **The State of plist**

```
phrase = "Don't panic!"
```

At this point in the code, plist does not yet exist. The second line of code *transforms* the phrase string into a new list, which is assigned to the plist variable:

```
plist = list(phrase)
```

```
print(phrase)
print(plist)
```
↙ These calls to "print" display the current state of the variables (before we start our manipulations).

Each time the for loop iterates, plist shrinks by one object until the last four objects are gone:

```
for i in range(4):
    plist.pop()
```

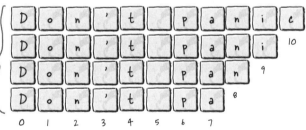

The loop terminates, and plist has shrunk until eight objects remain. It's now time to get rid of some other unwanted objects. Another call to pop removes the first item on the list (which is at index number 0):

```
plist.pop(0)
```

With the letter D popped off the front of the list, a call to remove dispatches with the apostrophe:

```
plist.remove("'")
```

What Happened to "plist", Continued

We've been pausing for a moment to consider what actually happened to `plist` as the code in `panic.py` executed.

Based on the execution of the code from the last page, we now have a six-item list with the characters o, n, t, space, p, and a available to us. Let's keep executing our code:

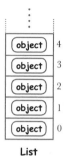

List

The Code   **The State of `plist`**

This is what `plist` looks like as a result of the code on the previous page executing:

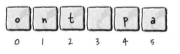

The next line of code contains **three** method invocations: two calls to `pop` and one to `extend`. The calls to `pop` happen first (from left to right):

```
plist.extend([plist.pop(), plist.pop()])
```

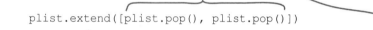

The call to `extend` takes the popped objects and adds them to the end of `plist`. It can be useful to think of `extend` as shorthand for multiple calls to the `append` method:

All that's left to do (to `plist`) is to swap the t character at location 2 with the space character at index location 3. The next line of code contains **two** method invocations. The first uses `pop` to extract the space character:

```
plist.insert(2, plist.pop(3))
```

Turn "plist" back into a string.

```
new_phrase = ''.join(plist)
print(plist)
print(new_phrase)
```

These calls to "print" display the state of the variables (after we've performed our manipulations).

Then the call to `insert` slots the space character into the correct place (*before* index location 2):

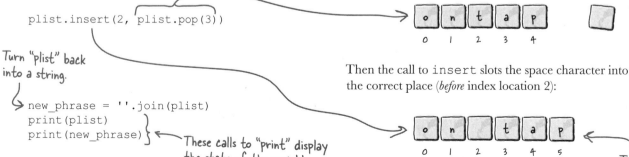

Ta da!

Lists: What We Know

We're 20 pages in, so let's take a little break and review what we've learned about lists so far:

BULLET POINTS

- Lists are great for storing a collection of related objects. If you have a bunch of similar things that you'd like to treat as one, a list is a great place to put them.

- List are similar to arrays in other languages. However, unlike arrays in other languages (which tend to be fixed in size), Python's lists can grow and shrink dynamically as needed.

- In code, a list of objects is enclosed in square brackets, and the list objects are separated from each other by a comma.

- An empty list is represented like this: `[]`.

- The fastest way to check whether an object is in a list is to use Python's `in` operator, which checks for membership.

- Growing a list at runtime is possible due to the inclusion of a handful of list methods, which include `append`, `extend`, and `insert`.

- Shrinking a list at runtime is possible due to the inclusion of the `remove` and `pop` methods.

That's all fine by me, but is there anything I need to watch out for when manipulating lists?

Yes. Care is always needed.

As working with and manipulating lists in Python is often very convenient, care needs to be taken to ensure the interpreter is doing exactly what you want it to.

A case in point is copying one list to another list. Are you copying the list, or are you copying the objects in the list? Depending on your answer and on what you are trying to do, the interpreter will behave differently. Flip the page to learn what we mean by this.

What Looks Like a Copy, But Isn't

When to comes to copying an existing list to another one, it's tempting to use the assignment operator:

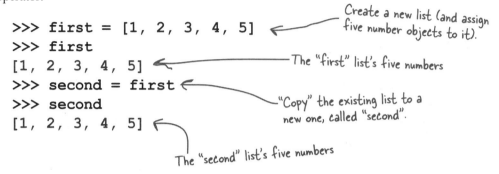

```
>>> first = [1, 2, 3, 4, 5]
>>> first
[1, 2, 3, 4, 5]
>>> second = first
>>> second
[1, 2, 3, 4, 5]
```

Create a new list (and assign five number objects to it).

The "first" list's five numbers

"Copy" the existing list to a new one, called "second".

The "second" list's five numbers

So far, so good. That looks like it worked, as the five number objects from `first` have been copied to `second`:

Or, have they? Let's see what happens when we `append` a new number to `second`, which seems like a reasonable thing to do, but leads to a problem:

```
>>> second.append(6)
>>> second
[1, 2, 3, 4, 5, 6]
```

This seems OK, but isn't.

Again, so far, so good—but there's a **bug** here. Look what happens when we ask the shell to display the contents of `first`—the new object is appended to `first` too!

```
>>> first
[1, 2, 3, 4, 5, 6]
```

Whoops! The new object is appended to "first" too.

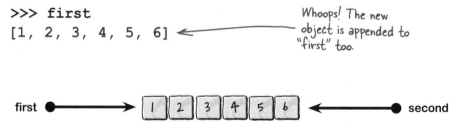

This is a problem, in that both `first` and `second` are pointing to the same data. If you change one list, the other changes, too. This is not good.

How to Copy a Data Structure

If using the assignment operator isn't the way to copy one list to another, what is? What's happening is that a **reference** to the list is *shared* among first and second.

To solve this problem, lists come with a copy method, which does the right thing. Take a look at how copy works:

```
>>> third = second.copy()
>>> third
[1, 2, 3, 4, 5, 6]
```

With third created (thanks to the copy method), let's append an object to it, then see what happens:

```
>>> third.append(7)
>>> third
[1, 2, 3, 4, 5, 6, 7]
>>> second
[1, 2, 3, 4, 5, 6]
```

The "third" list is grown by one object.

Much better. The existing list is unchanged.

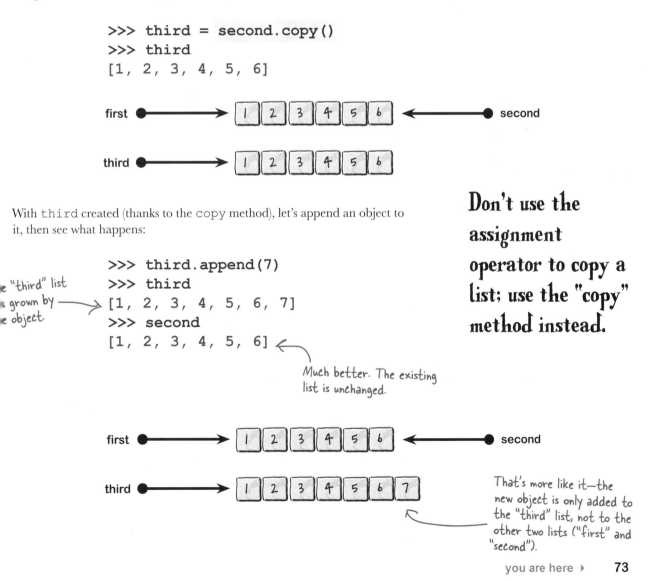

That's more like it—the new object is only added to the "third" list, not to the other two lists ("first" and "second").

Don't use the assignment operator to copy a list; use the "copy" method instead.

Square Brackets Are Everywhere

I can't believe how many square brackets are on that last page...yet I still haven't seen how they can be used to select and access data in my Python list.

Python supports the square bracket notation, and then some.

Everyone who has used square brackets with an array in almost any other programming language knows that they can access the first value in an array called names using names[0]. The next value is in names[1], the next in names[2], and so on. Python works this way, too, when it comes to accessing objects in any list.

However, Python extends the notation to improve upon this standardized behavior by supporting **negative index values** (-1, -2, -3, and so on) as well as a notation to select a **range** of objects from a list.

Lists: Updating What We Already Know

Before we dive into a description of how Python extends the square bracket notation, let's add to our list of bullet points:

BULLET POINTS

- Take care when copying one list to another. If you want to have another variable reference an existing list, use the assignment operator (=). If you want to make a copy of the objects in an existing list and use them to initialize a new list, be sure to use the copy method instead.

Lists Extend the Square Bracket Notation

All our talk of Python's lists being like arrays in other programming languages wasn't just idle talk. Like other languages, Python starts counting from zero when it comes to numbering index locations, and uses the well-known **square bracket notation** to access objects in a list.

Unlike a lot of other programming languages, Python lets you access the list relative to each end: positive index values count from left to right, whereas negative index values count from right to left:

object 4
object 3
object 2
object 1
object 0
List

Python's lists understand positive index values, which start from 0...

```
 0   1   2   3   4   5   6   7   8   9  10  11
 D   o   n   '   t       p   a   n   i   c   !
-12 -11 -10 -9  -8  -7  -6  -5  -4  -3  -2  -1
```

...as well as negative index values, which start from −1.

Let's see some examples while working at the shell:

Create a list of letters.

```
>>> saying = "Don't panic!"
>>> letters = list(saying)
>>> letters
['D', 'o', 'n', "'", 't', ' ', 'p', 'a', 'n', 'i', 'c', '!']
>>> letters[0]
'D'
>>> letters[3]
"'"
>>> letters[6]
'p'
>>> letters[-1]
'!'
>>> letters[-3]
'i'
>>> letters[-6]
'p'
```

Using positive index values counts from left to right...

...whereas negative index values count right to left.

As lists grow and shrink while your Python code executes, being able to index into the list using a negative index value is often useful. For instance, using −1 as the index value is always guaranteed to return the last object in the list *no matter how big the list is*, just as using 0 always returns the first object.

Python's extensions to the square bracket notation don't stop with support for negative index values. Lists understand **start**, **stop**, and **step**, too.

It's easy to get at the first and last objects in any list.

```
>>> first = letters[0]
>>> last = letters[-1]
>>> first
'D'
>>> last
'!'
```

Lists Understand Start, Stop, and Step

We first met **start**, **stop**, and **step** in the previous chapter when discussing the three-argument version of the range function:

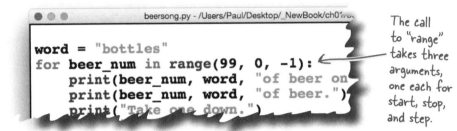

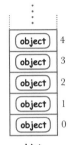

The call to "range" takes three arguments, one each for start, stop, and step.

List

Recall what **start**, **stop**, and **step** mean when it comes to specifying ranges (and let's relate them to lists):

 The START value lets you control WHERE the range begins.
When used with lists, the **start** value indicates the starting index value.

 The STOP value lets you control WHEN the range ends.
When used with lists, the **stop** value indicates the index value to stop at, **but not include**.

 The STEP value lets you control HOW the range is generated.
When used with lists, the **step** value refers to the *stride* to take.

You can put start, stop, and step inside square brackets

When used with lists, **start**, **stop**, and **step** are specified *within* the square brackets and are separated from one another by the colon (:) character:

<code>letters[start:stop:step]</code>

The square bracket notation is extended to work with start, stop, and step.

It might seem somewhat counterintuitive, but all three values are *optional* when used together:

When **start** is missing, it has a default value of 0.

When **stop** is missing, it takes on the maximum value allowable for the list.

When **step** is missing, it has a default value of 1.

List Slices in Action

Given the existing list `letters` from a few pages back, you can specify
values for **start**, **stop**, and **step** in any number of ways.

Let's look at some examples:

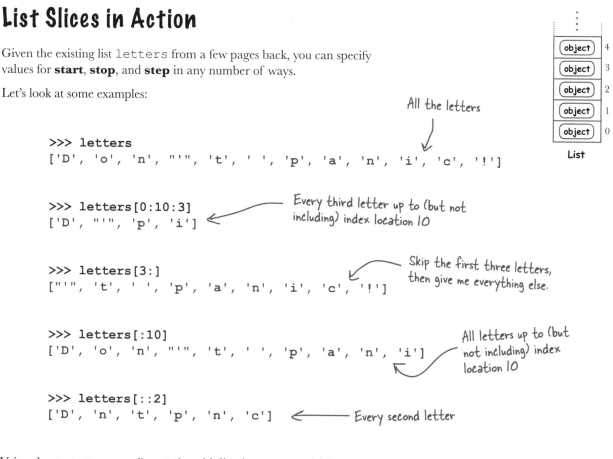

All the letters

```
>>> letters
['D', 'o', 'n', "'", 't', ' ', 'p', 'a', 'n', 'i', 'c', '!']
```

```
>>> letters[0:10:3]
['D', "'", 'p', 'i']
```
Every third letter up to (but not including) index location 10

```
>>> letters[3:]
["'", 't', ' ', 'p', 'a', 'n', 'i', 'c', '!']
```
Skip the first three letters, then give me everything else.

```
>>> letters[:10]
['D', 'o', 'n', "'", 't', ' ', 'p', 'a', 'n', 'i']
```
All letters up to (but not including) index location 10

```
>>> letters[::2]
['D', 'n', 't', 'p', 'n', 'c']
```
Every second letter

Using the start, stop, step *slice notation* with lists is very powerful (not to
mention handy), and you are advised to take some time to understand how
these examples work. Be sure to follow along at your >>> prompt, and feel
free to experiment with this notation, too.

---

there are no
Dumb Questions

Q: **I notice that some of the characters on this page are surrounded by single quotes and others by double quotes. Is there some sort of standard I should follow?**

A: No, there's no standard, as Python lets you use either single or double quotes around strings of any length, including strings that contain only a single character (like the ones shown on this page; technically, they are single-character strings, not letters). Most Python programmers use single quotes to delimit their strings (but that's a preference, not a rule). If a string contains a single quote, double quotes can be used to avoid the requirement to escape characters with a backslash (\). as most programmers find it's easier to read " ' " than ' \ ' '. You'll see more examples of both quotes being used on the next two pages.

Starting and Stopping with Lists

Follow along with the examples on this page (and the next) at your >>> prompt and make sure you get the same output as we do.

We start by turning a string into a list of letters:

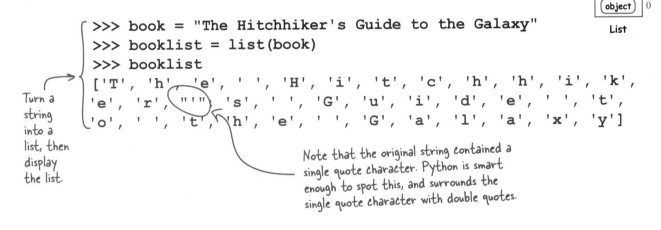

Turn a string into a list, then display the list.

```
>>> book = "The Hitchhiker's Guide to the Galaxy"
>>> booklist = list(book)
>>> booklist
['T', 'h', 'e', ' ', 'H', 'i', 't', 'c', 'h', 'h', 'i', 'k',
'e', 'r', '"'"', 's', ' ', 'G', 'u', 'i', 'd', 'e', ' ', 't',
'o', ' ', 't', 'h', 'e', ' ', 'G', 'a', 'l', 'a', 'x', 'y']
```

Note that the original string contained a single quote character. Python is smart enough to spot this, and surrounds the single quote character with double quotes.

The newly created list (called booklist above) is then used to select a range of letters from within the list:

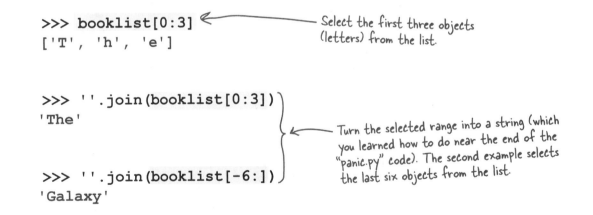

```
>>> booklist[0:3]
['T', 'h', 'e']
```

Select the first three objects (letters) from the list.

```
>>> ''.join(booklist[0:3])
'The'
```

```
>>> ''.join(booklist[-6:])
'Galaxy'
```

Turn the selected range into a string (which you learned how to do near the end of the "panic.py" code). The second example selects the last six objects from the list.

Be sure to take time to study this page (and the next) until you're confident you understand how each example works, and be sure to try out each example within IDLE.

With the last example above, note how the interpreter is happy to use any of the default values for **start**, **stop**, and **step**.

Stepping with Lists

Here are two more examples, which show off the use of **step** with lists.

The first example selects all the letters, starting from the end of the list (that is, it is selecting *in reverse*), whereas the second selects every other letter in the list. Note how the **step** value controls this behavior:

```
>>> backwards = booklist[::-1]
>>> ''.join(backwards)
"yxalaG eht ot ediuG s'rekihhctiH ehT"
```

Looks like gobbledegook, doesn't it? But it is actually the original string reversed.

```
>>> every_other = booklist[::2]
>>> ''.join(every_other)
"TeHthie' ud oteGlx"
```

And this looks like gibberish! But "every_other" is a list made up from every second object (letter) starting from the first and going to the last. Note: "start" and "stop" are defaulted.

Two final examples confirm that it is possible to start and stop anywhere within the list and select objects. When you do this, the returned data is referred to as a **slice**. Think of a slice as a *fragment* of an existing list.

Both of these examples select the letters from `booklist` that spell the word `'Hitchhiker'`. The first selection is joined to show the word `'Hitchhiker'`, whereas the second displays `'Hitchhiker'` in reverse:

```
>>> ''.join(booklist[4:14])
'Hitchhiker'
```
Slice out the word "Hitchhiker".

A "slice" is a fragment of a list.

```
>>> ''.join(booklist[13:3:-1])
'rekihhctiH'
```
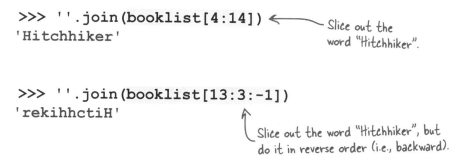
Slice out the word "Hitchhiker", but do it in reverse order (i.e., backward).

Slices are everywhere

The slice notation doesn't just work with lists. In fact, you'll find that you can slice any sequence in Python, accessing it with **[start:stop:step]**.

Putting Slices to Work on Lists

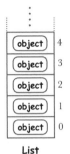

object 4
object 3
object 2
object 1
object 0

List

Python's slice notation is a useful extension to the square bracket notation, and it is used in many places throughout the language. You'll see lots of uses of slices as you continue to work your way through this book.

For now, let's see Python's square bracket notation (including the use of slices) in action. We are going to take the panic.py program from earlier and refactor it to use the square bracket notation and slices to achieve what was previously accomplished with list methods.

Before doing the actual work, here's a quick reminder of what panic.py does.

Converting "Don't panic!" to "on tap"

This is "panic.py".

This code transforms one string into another by manipulating an existing list using the list methods. Starting with the string "Don't panic!", this code produced "on tap" after the manipulations:

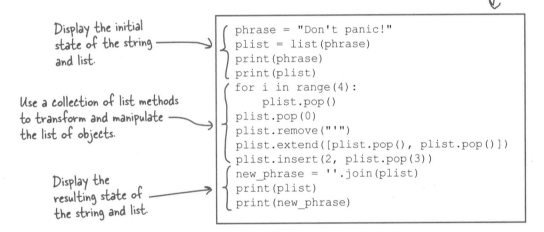

Display the initial state of the string and list.

```
phrase = "Don't panic!"
plist = list(phrase)
print(phrase)
print(plist)
```

Use a collection of list methods to transform and manipulate the list of objects.

```
for i in range(4):
    plist.pop()
plist.pop(0)
plist.remove("'")
plist.extend([plist.pop(), plist.pop()])
plist.insert(2, plist.pop(3))
```

Display the resulting state of the string and list.

```
new_phrase = ''.join(plist)
print(plist)
print(new_phrase)
```

Here's the output produced by this program when it runs within IDLE:

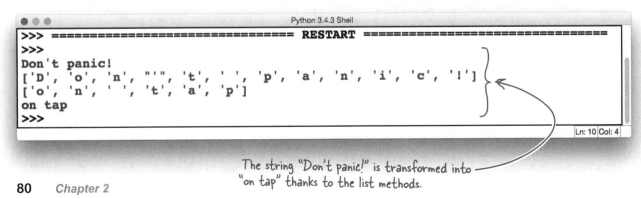

```
Python 3.4.3 Shell
>>> ============================== RESTART ==============================
>>>
Don't panic!
['D', 'o', 'n', "'", 't', ' ', 'p', 'a', 'n', 'i', 'c', '!']
['o', 'n', ' ', 't', 'a', 'p']
on tap
>>>
                                                              Ln: 10 Col: 4
```

The string "Don't panic!" is transformed into "on tap" thanks to the list methods.

Putting Slices to Work on Lists, Continued

It's time for the actual work. Here's the `panic.py` code again, with the code you need to change highlighted:

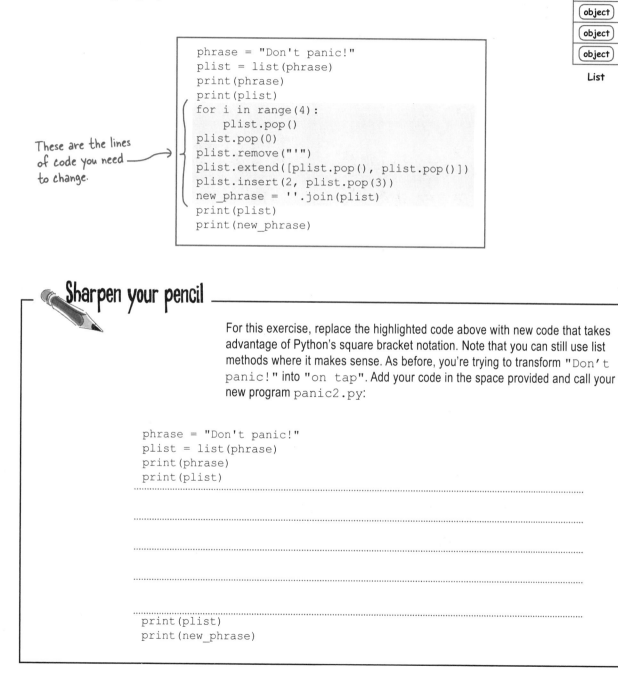

```
phrase = "Don't panic!"
plist = list(phrase)
print(phrase)
print(plist)
for i in range(4):
    plist.pop()
plist.pop(0)
plist.remove("'")
plist.extend([plist.pop(), plist.pop()])
plist.insert(2, plist.pop(3))
new_phrase = ''.join(plist)
print(plist)
print(new_phrase)
```

These are the lines of code you need to change.

Sharpen your pencil

For this exercise, replace the highlighted code above with new code that takes advantage of Python's square bracket notation. Note that you can still use list methods where it makes sense. As before, you're trying to transform `"Don't panic!"` into `"on tap"`. Add your code in the space provided and call your new program `panic2.py`:

```
phrase = "Don't panic!"
plist = list(phrase)
print(phrase)
print(plist)
```

....

....

....

....

....

```
print(plist)
print(new_phrase)
```

Sharpen your pencil
Solution

For this exercise, you were to replace the highlighted code on the previous page with new code that takes advantage of Python's square bracket notation. Note that you can still use list methods where it makes sense. As before, you're trying to transform "Don't panic!" into "on tap". You were to call your new program panic2.py:

```
phrase = "Don't panic!"
plist = list(phrase)
print(phrase)
print(plist)
```

new_phrase = ''.join(plist[1:3]) ← We started by slicing out the word "on" from "plist"...

new_phrase = new_phrase + ''.join([plist[5], plist[4], plist[7], plist[6]])

...then picked out each additional letter that we needed: space, "t", "a", and "p".

```
print(plist)
print(new_phrase)
```

I wonder which of these two programs—"panic.py" or "panic2.py"—is better?

That's a great question.

Some programmers will look at the code in panic2.py and, when comparing it to the code in panic.py, conclude that two lines of code is always better than seven, especially when the output from both programs is the same. Which is a fine measurement of "betterness," but not really useful in this case.

To see what we mean by this, let's take a look at the output produced by both programs.

TEST DRIVE

Use IDLE to open `panic.py` and `panic2.py` in separate edit windows. Select the `panic.py` window first, then press F5. Next select the `panic2.py` window, then press F5. Compare the results from both programs in your shell.

"panic.py"

panic.py - /Users/Paul/Desktop/_NewBook/ch02/panic.py (3.4.3)

```
phrase = "Don't panic!"
plist = list(phrase)
print(phrase)
print(plist)

for i in range(4):
    plist.pop()
plist.pop(0)
plist.remove("'")
plist.extend([plist.pop(), plist.pop()])
plist.insert(2, plist.pop(3))

new_phrase = ''.join(plist)
print(plist)
print(new_phrase)
```

Ln: 17 Col: 0

"panic2.py"

panic2.py

```
phrase = "Don't panic!"
plist = list(phrase)
print(phrase)
print(plist)

new_phrase = ''.join(plist[1:3])
new_phrase = new_phrase + ''.join([plist[5], plist[4], plist[7], plist[6]])

print(plist)
print(new_phrase)
```

Python 3.4.3 Shell

```
>>> ================================ RESTART ================================
>>>
Don't panic!
['D', 'o', 'n', "'", 't', ' ', 'p', 'a', 'n', 'i', 'c', '!']
['o', 'n', ' ', 't', 'a', 'p']
on tap
>>> ================================ RESTART ================================
>>>
Don't panic!
['D', 'o', 'n', "'", 't', ' ', 'p', 'a', 'n', 'i', 'c', '!']
['D', 'o', 'n', "'", 't', ' ', 'p', 'a', 'n', 'i', 'c', '!']
on tap
>>>
```

output produced
running the "panic.py"
gram

e output produced by
ning the "panic2.py"
gram

Notice how different these outputs are.

Which Is Better? It Depends...

We executed both `panic.py` and `panic2.py` in IDLE to help us determine which of these two programs is "better."

Take a look at the second-to-last line of output from both programs:

This is the output produced by "panic.py"...

```
>>>
Don't panic!
['D', 'o', 'n', "'", 't', ' ', 'p', 'a', 'n', 'i', 'c', '!']
['o', 'n', ' ', 't', 'a', 'p']
on tap
>>> ========================= RESTART =========================
>>>
Don't panic!
['D', 'o', 'n', "'", 't', ' ', 'p', 'a', 'n', 'i', 'c', '!']
['D', 'o', 'n', "'", 't', ' ', 'p', 'a', 'n', 'i', 'c', '!']
on tap
>>>
```

...whereas this output is produced by "panic2.py".

Although both programs conclude by displaying the string `"on tap"` (having first started with the string `"Don't panic!"`), `panic2.py` does not change `plist` in any way, whereas `panic.py` does.

It is worth pausing for a moment to consider this.

Recall our discussion from earlier in this chapter called *"What happened to 'plist'?"*. That discussion detailed the steps that converted this list:

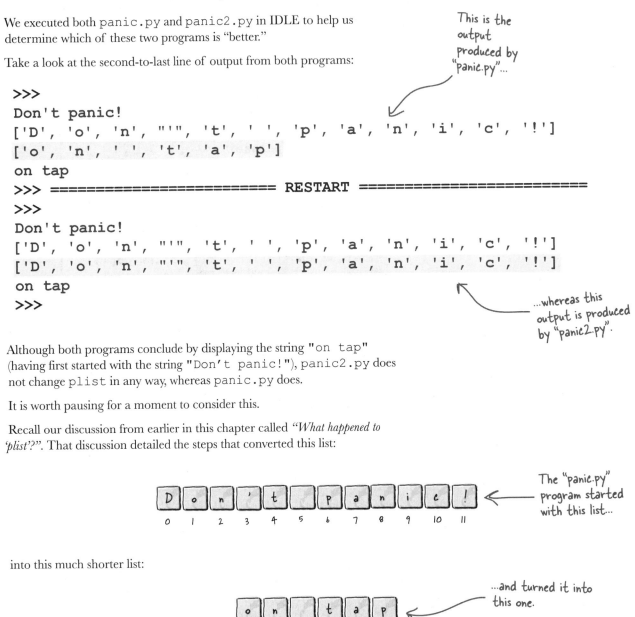

The "panic.py" program started with this list...

into this much shorter list:

...and turned it into this one.

All those list manipulations using the `pop`, `remove`, `extend`, and `insert` methods changed the list, which is fine, as that's primarily what the list methods are designed to do: change the list. But what about `panic2.py`?

Slicing a List Is Nondestructive

The list methods used by the `panic.py` program to convert one string into another were **destructive**, in that the original state of the list was altered by the code. Slicing a list is **nondestructive**, as extracting objects from an existing list does not alter it; the original data remains intact.

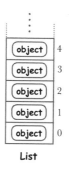

The "panic2.py" program started with this list.

The slices used by `panic2.py` are shown here. Note that each extracts data from the list, but does not change it. Here are the two lines of code that do all the heavy lifting, together with a representation of the data each slice extracts:

The code

```
new_phrase = ''.join(plist[1:3])
new_phrase = new_phrase + ''.join([plist[5], plist[4], plist[7], plist[6]])
```

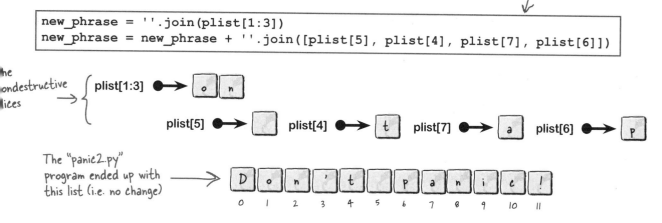

The nondestructive slices

The "panic2.py" program ended up with this list (i.e. no change)

So...which is better?

Using list methods to manipulate and transform an existing list does just that: it manipulates *and* transforms the list. The original state of the list is no longer available to your program. Depending on what you're doing, this may (or may not) be an issue. Using Python's square bracket notation generally does *not* alter an existing list, unless you decide to assign a new value to an existing index location. Using slices also results in no changes to the list: the original data remains as it was.

Which of these two approaches you decide is "better" depends on what you are trying to do (and it's perfectly OK not to like either). There is always more than one way to perform a computation, and Python lists are flexible enough to support many ways of interacting with the data you store in them.

We are nearly done with our initial tour of lists. There's just one more topic to introduce you to at this stage: *list iteration*.

List methods change the state of a list, whereas using square brackets and slices (typically) does not.

Python's "for" Loop Understands Lists

Python's `for` loop knows all about lists and, when provided with *any* list, knows where the start of the list is, how many objects the list contains, and where the end of the list is. You never have to tell the `for` loop any of this, as it works it out for itself.

An example helps to illustrate. Follow along by opening up a new edit window in IDLE and typing in the code shown below. Save this new program as `marvin.py`, then press F5 to take it for a spin:

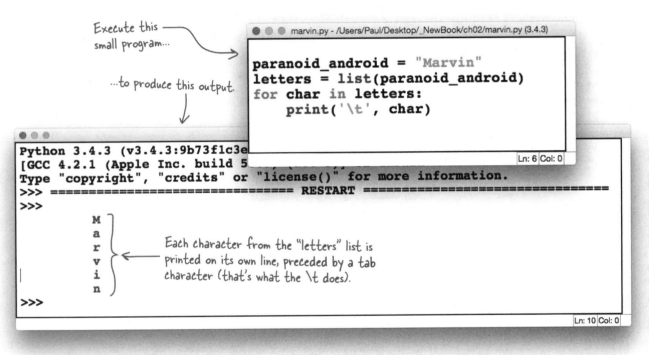

Execute this small program...

...to produce this output.

marvin.py - /Users/Paul/Desktop/_NewBook/ch02/marvin.py (3.4.3)

```python
paranoid_android = "Marvin"
letters = list(paranoid_android)
for char in letters:
    print('\t', char)
```

Ln: 6 Col: 0

```
Python 3.4.3 (v3.4.3:9b73f1c3e
[GCC 4.2.1 (Apple Inc. build 5
Type "copyright", "credits" or "license()" for more information.
>>> ============================= RESTART =============================
>>>
        M
        a
        r
        v
        i
        n
>>>
```

Ln: 10 Col: 0

Each character from the "letters" list is printed on its own line, preceded by a tab character (that's what the \t does).

Understanding marvin.py's code

The first two lines of `marvin.py` are familiar: assign a string to a variable (called `paranoid_android`), then turn the string into a list of character objects (assigned to a new variable called `letters`).

It's the next statement—the `for` loop—that we want you to concentrate on.

On each iteration, the `for` loop arranges to take each object in the `letters` list and assign them one at a time to another variable, called `char`. Within the indented loop body `char` takes on the current value of the object being processed by the `for` loop. Note that the `for` loop knows when to *start* iterating, when to *stop* iterating, as well as *how many* objects are in the `letters` list. You don't need to worry about any of this: that's the interpreter's job.

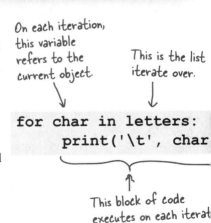

On each iteration, this variable refers to the current object.

This is the list iterate over.

```python
for char in letters:
    print('\t', char
```

This block of code executes on each iterat

Python's "for" Loop Understands Slices

If you use the square bracket notation to select a slice from a list, the `for` loop "does the right thing" and only iterates over the sliced objects. An update to our most recent program shows this in action. Save a new version of `marvin.py` as `marvin2.py`, then change the code to look like that shown below.

Of interest is our use of Python's **multiplication operator** (`*`), which is used to control how many tab characters are printed before each object in the second and third `for` loop. We use `*` here to "multiply" how many times we want tab to appear:

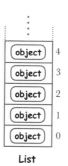

List

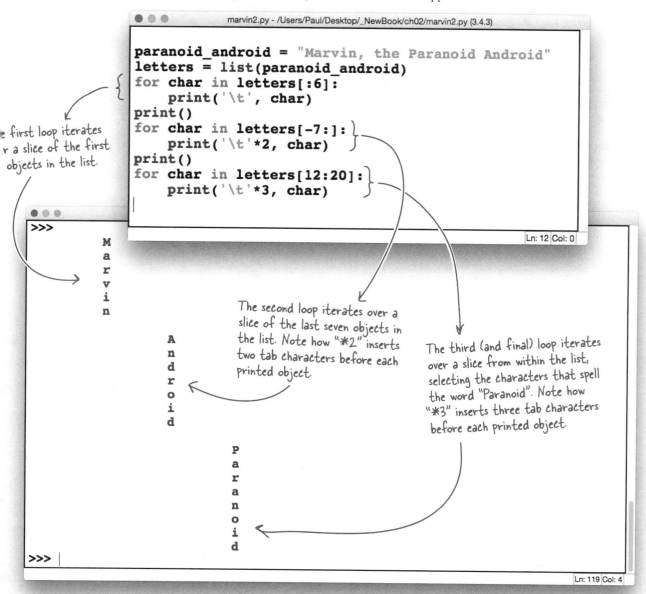

```
paranoid_android = "Marvin, the Paranoid Android"
letters = list(paranoid_android)
for char in letters[:6]:
    print('\t', char)
print()
for char in letters[-7:]:
    print('\t'*2, char)
print()
for char in letters[12:20]:
    print('\t'*3, char)
```

marvin2.py - /Users/Paul/Desktop/_NewBook/ch02/marvin2.py (3.4.3)

Ln: 12 Col: 0

The first loop iterates over a slice of the first objects in the list.

The second loop iterates over a slice of the last seven objects in the list. Note how "*2" inserts two tab characters before each printed object.

The third (and final) loop iterates over a slice from within the list, selecting the characters that spell the word "Paranoid". Note how "*3" inserts three tab characters before each printed object.

```
M
a
r
v
i
n

        A
        n
        d
        r
        o
        i
        d

                P
                a
                r
                a
                n
                o
                i
                d
```

Ln: 119 Col: 4

Marvin's Slices in Detail

Let's take a look at each of the slices in the last program in detail, as this technique appears a lot in Python programs. Below, each line of slice code is presented once more, together with a graphical representation of what's going on.

Before looking at the three slices, note that the program begins by assigning a string to a variable (called `paranoid_android`) and converting it to a list (called `letters`):

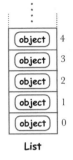

```
paranoid_android = "Marvin, the Paranoid Android"
letters = list(paranoid_android)
```

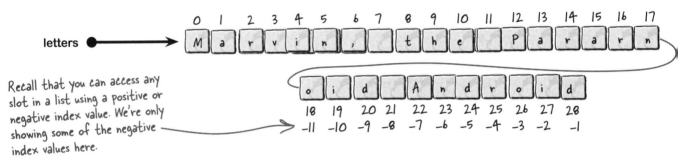

Recall that you can access any slot in a list using a positive or negative index value. We're only showing some of the negative index values here.

We'll look at each of the slices from the `marvin2.py` program and see what they produce. When the interpreter sees the slice specification, it extracts the sliced objects from `letters` and returns a copy of the objects to the `for` loop. The original `letters` list is unaffected by these slices.

The first slice extracts from the start of the list and ends (but doesn't include) the object in slot 6:

```
for char in letters[:6]:
    print('\t', char)
```

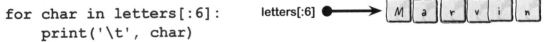

The second slice extracts from the end of the `letters` list, starting at slot −7 and going to the end of `letters`:

```
for char in letters[-7:]:
    print('\t'*2, char)
```

And finally, the third slice extracts from the middle of the list, starting at slot 12 and including everything up to but not including slot 20:

```
for char in letters[12:20]:
    print('\t'*3, char)
```

Lists: Updating What We Know

Now that you've seen how lists and `for` loops interact, let's quickly review
what you've learned over the last few pages:

BULLET POINTS

- Lists understand the square bracket notation, which can be used to select individual objects from any list.

- Like a lot of other programming languages, Python starts counting from zero, so the first object in any list is at index location 0, the second at 1, and so on.

- Unlike a lot of other programming languages, Python lets you index into a list from either end. Using –1 selects the last item in the list, –2 the second last, and so on.

- Lists also provide slices (or fragments) of a list by supporting the specification of start, stop, and step as part of the square bracket notation.

> I can see myself putting lists to lots of uses in my Python programs. But is there anything lists aren't good at?

Lists are used a lot, but...

They are *not* a data structure panacea. Lists can be used in lots of places; if you have a collection of similar objects that you need to store in a data structure, lists are the perfect choice.

However—and perhaps somewhat counterintuitively—if the data you're working with exhibits some *structure*, lists can be a **bad choice**. We'll start exploring this problem (and what you can do about it) on the next page.

there are no Dumb Questions

Q: Surely there's a lot more to lists than this?

A: Yes, there is. Think of the material in this chapter as a quick introduction to Python's built-in data structures, together with what they can do for you. We are by no means done with lists, and will be returning to them throughout the remainder of this book.

Q: But what about sorting lists? Isn't that important?

A: Yes, it is, but let's not worry about stuff like that until we actually need to. For now, if you have a good grasp of the basics, that's all you need at this stage. And don't worry: we'll get to sorting soon.

What's Wrong with Lists?

When Python programmers find themselves in a situation where they need to store a collection of similar objects, using a list is often the natural choice. After all, we've used nothing but lists in this chapter so far.

Recall how lists are great at storing a collection of related letters, such as with the `vowels` list:

```
vowels = ['a', 'e', 'i', 'o', 'u']
```

And if the data is a collection of numbers, lists are a great choice, too:

```
nums = [1, 2, 3, 4, 5]
```

In fact, lists are a great choice when you have a collection of related *anythings*.

But imagine you need to store data about a person, and the sample data you've been given looks something like this:

Name: Ford Prefect
Gender: Male
Occupation: Researcher
Home Planet: Betelgeuse Seven

Some data for you to play with

On the face of things, this data does indeed conform to a structure, in that there's *tags* on the left and *associated data values* on the right. So, why not put this data in a list? After all, this data is related to the person, right?

To see why we shouldn't, let's look at two ways to store this data using lists (starting on the next page). We are going to be totally upfront here: *both* of our attempts exhibit problems that make using lists less than ideal for data like this. But, as the journey is often half the fun of getting there, we're going to try lists anyway.

Our first attempt concentrates on the data values on the right of the napkin, whereas our second attempt uses the tags on the left as well as the associated data values. Have a think about how you'd handle this type of structured data using lists, then flip to the next page to see how our two attempts fared. ·

When Not to Use Lists

We have our sample data (on the back of a napkin) and we've decided to store the data in a list (as that's all we know at this point in our Python travels).

Our first attempt takes the data values and puts them in a list:

```
>>> person1 = ['Ford Prefect', 'Male',
'Researcher', 'Betelgeuse Seven']
>>> person1
['Ford Prefect', 'Male', 'Researcher',
'Betelgeuse Seven']
```

This results in a list of string objects, which works. As shown above, the shell confirms that the data values are now in a list called `person1`.

But we have a problem, in that we have to remember that the first index location (at index value 0) is the person's name, the next is the person's gender (at index value 1), and so on. For a small number of data items, this is not a big deal, but imagine if this data expanded to include many more data values (perhaps to support a profile page on that Facebook-killer you've been meaning to build). With data like this, using index values to refer to the data in the `person1` list is brittle, and best avoided.

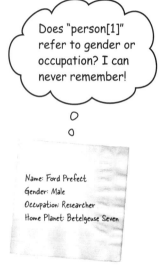

Our second attempt adds the tags into the list, so that each data value is preceded by its associated tag. Meet the `person2` list:

```
>>> person2 = ['Name', 'Ford Prefect', 'Gender',
'Male', 'Occupation', 'Researcher', 'Home Planet',
'Betelgeuse Seven']
>>> person2
['Name', 'Ford Prefect', 'Gender', 'Male',
'Occupation', 'Researcher', 'Home Planet',
'Betelgeuse Seven']
```

This clearly works, but now we no longer have one problem; we have two. Not only do we still have to remember what's at each index location, but we now have to remember that index values 0, 2, 4, 6, and so on are tags, while index values 1, 3, 5, 7, and so on are data values.

Surely there has to be a better way to handle data with a structure like this?

There is, and it involves foregoing the use of lists for structured data like this. We need to use something else, and in Python, that something else is called a **dictionary**, which we get to in the next chapter.

> **If the data you want to store has an identifiable structure, consider using something other than a list.**

Chapter 2's Code, 1 of 2

```
vowels = ['a', 'e', 'i', 'o', 'u']
word = "Milliways"
for letter in word:
    if letter in vowels:
        print(letter)
```

The first version of the vowels program that displays *all* the vowels found in the word "Milliways" (including any duplicates).

The "vowels2.py" program added code that used a list to avoid duplicates. This program displays the list of unique vowels found in the word "Milliways".

```
vowels = ['a', 'e', 'i', 'o', 'u']
word = "Milliways"
found = []
for letter in word:
    if letter in vowels:
        if letter not in found:
            found.append(letter)
for vowel in found:
    print(vowel)
```

```
vowels = ['a', 'e', 'i', 'o', 'u']
word = input("Provide a word to search for vowels: ")
found = []
for letter in word:
    if letter in vowels:
        if letter not in found:
            found.append(letter)
for vowel in found:
    print(vowel)
```

The third (and final) version of the vowels program for this chapter, "vowels3.py", displays the unique vowels found in a word entered by our user.

It's the best advice in the universe: "Don't panic!" This program, called "panic.py", takes a string containing this advice and, using a bunch of list methods, transforms the string into another string that describes how the Head First editors prefer their beer: "on tap".

```
phrase = "Don't panic!"
plist = list(phrase)
print(phrase)
print(plist)

for i in range(4):
    plist.pop()
plist.pop(0)
plist.remove("'")
plist.extend([plist.pop(), plist.pop()])
plist.insert(2, plist.pop(3))

new_phrase = ''.join(plist)
print(plist)
print(new_phrase)
```

Chapter 2's Code, 2 of 2

```
phrase = "Don't panic!"
plist = list(phrase)
print(phrase)
print(plist)

new_phrase = ''.join(plist[1:3])
new_phrase = new_phrase + ''.join([plist[5], plist[4], plist[7], plist[6]])

print(plist)
print(new_phrase)
```

When it comes to manipulating lists, using methods isn't the only game in town. The "panic2.py" program achieved the same end using Python's square bracket notation.

```
paranoid_android = "Marvin"
letters = list(paranoid_android)
for char in letters:
    print('\t', char)
```

The shortest program in this chapter, "marvin.py", demonstrated how well lists play with Python's "for" loop. (Just don't tell Marvin...if he hears that his program is the shortest in this chapter, it'll make him even more paranoid than he already is).

The "marvin2.py" program showed off Python's square bracket notation by using three slices to extract and display fragments from a list of letters.

```
paranoid_android = "Marvin, the Paranoid Android"
letters = list(paranoid_android)
for char in letters[:6]:
    print('\t', char)
print()
for char in letters[-7:]:
    print('\t'*2, char)
print()
for char in letters[12:20]:
    print('\t'*3, char)
```

3 structured data

Working with Structured Data

Lists are great, but I sometimes need more structure in my life...

Python's list data structure is great, but it isn't a data panacea.

When you have *truly* structured data (and using a list to store it may not be the best choice), Python comes to your rescue with its built-in **dictionary**. Out of the box, the dictionary lets you store and manipulate any collection of *key/value pairs*. We look long and hard at Python's dictionary in this chapter, and—along the way—meet **set** and **tuple**, too. Together with the **list** (which we met in the previous chapter), the dictionary, set, and tuple data structures provide a set of built-in data tools that help to make Python and data a powerful combination.

A Dictionary Stores Key/Value Pairs

Unlike a list, which is a collection of related objects, the **dictionary** is used to hold a collection of **key/value pairs**, where each unique *key* has a *value* associated with it. The dictionary is often referred to as an *associative array* by computer scientists, and other programming languages often use other names for dictionary (such as map, hash, and table).

The key part of a Python dictionary is typically a string, whereas the associated value part can be any Python object.

Data that conforms to the dictionary model is easy to spot: there are **two columns**, with potentially **multiple rows** of data. With this in mind, take another look at our "data napkin" from the end of the last chapter:

key#4	object
key#1	object
key#3	object
key#2	object

Dictionary

...and here's the second column of data.

Here's one column of data...

Name: Ford Prefect
Gender: Male
Occupation: Researcher
Home Planet: Betelgeuse Seven

There are multiple rows of two-columned data on this napkin.

In C++ and Java, a dictionary is known as "map," whereas Perl and Ruby use the name "hash."

It looks like the data on this napkin is a perfect fit for Python's dictionary.

Let's return to the >>> shell to see how to create a dictionary using our napkin data. It's tempting to try to enter the dictionary as a single line of code, but we're not going to do this. As we want our dictionary code to be easy to read, we're purposely entering each row of data (i.e., each key/value pair) on its own line instead. Take a look:

The name of the dictionary. (Recall that we met "person1" and "person2" at the end of the last chapter.)

The key

The associated data value

```
>>> person3 = { 'Name': 'Ford Prefect',
                'Gender': 'Male',
                'Occupation': 'Researcher',
                'Home Planet': 'Betelgeuse Seven' }
```

Key

Value

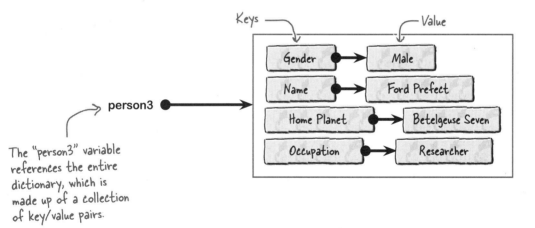

Make Dictionaries Easy to Read

It's tempting to take the four lines of code from the bottom of the last page and type them into the shell like this:

```
>>> person3 = { 'Name': 'Ford Prefect', 'Gender':
'Male', 'Occupation': 'Researcher', 'Home Planet':
'Betelgeuse Seven' }
```

Although the interpreter doesn't care which approach you use, entering a dictionary as one long line of code is hard to read, and should be avoided whenever possible.

If you litter your code with dictionaries that are hard to read, other programmers (which includes *you* in six months' time) will get upset...so take the time to align your dictionary code so that it *is* easy to read.

Here's a visual representation of how the dictionary appears in Python's memory after either of these dictionary-assigning statements executes:

The "person3" variable references the entire dictionary, which is made up of a collection of key/value pairs.

This is a more complicated structure than the array-like list. If the idea behind Python's dictionary is new to you, it's often useful to think of it as a **lookup table**. The key on the left is used to *look up* the value on the right (just like you look up a word in a paper dictionary).

Let's spend some time getting to know Python's dictionary in more detail. We'll begin with a detailed explanation of how to spot a Python dictionary in your code, before talking about some of this data structure's unique characteristics and uses.

How to Spot a Dictionary in Code

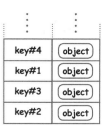

Dictionary

Take a closer look at how we defined the `person3` dictionary at the >>> shell. For starters, the *entire* dictionary is enclosed in curly braces. Each **key** is enclosed in quotes, as they are strings, as is each **value,** which are also strings in this example. (Keys and values don't have to be strings, however.) Each key is separated from its associated value by a **colon** character (`:`), and each key/value pair (a.k.a. "row") is separated from the next by a **comma**:

An opening curly brace starts each dictionary.

In this dictionary, the values are all string objects, so they are enclosed in quotes.

Each key/value pair is separated from the next by a comma.

```
{ 'Name': 'Ford Prefect',
  'Gender': 'Male',
  'Occupation': 'Researcher',
  'Home Planet': 'Betelgeuse Seven' }
```

Each key is enclosed in quotes.

A colon associates each key with its value.

A closing curly brace ends each dictionary.

As stated earlier, the data on this napkin maps nicely to a Python dictionary. In fact, any data that exhibits a similar structure—multiple two-columned rows—is as perfect a fit as you're likely to find. Which is great, but it does come at a price. Let's return to the >>> prompt to learn what this price is:

Ask the shell to display the contents of the dictionary...

```
>>> person3
{'Gender': 'Male', 'Name': 'Ford Prefect', 'Home
Planet': 'Betelgeuse Seven', 'Occupation': 'Researcher'}
```

...and there it is. All the key/value pairs are shown.

What happened to the insertion order?

Take a long hard look at the dictionary displayed by the interpreter. Did you notice that the ordering is different from what was used on input? When you created the dictionary, you inserted the rows in name, gender, occupation, and home planet order, but the shell is displaying them in gender, name, home planet, and occupation order. The ordering has changed.

What's going on here? Why did the ordering change?

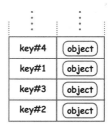

Dictionary

Insertion Order Is NOT Maintained

Unlike lists, which keep your objects arranged in the order in which you inserted them, Python's dictionary does **not**. This means you cannot assume that the rows in any dictionary are in any particular order; for all intents and purposes, they are **unordered**.

Take another look at the `person3` dictionary and compare the ordering on input to that shown by the interpreter at the >>> prompt:

You insert your data into a dictionary in one order...

...but the interpreter uses another ordering.

```
>>> person3 = { 'Name': 'Ford Prefect',
                'Gender': 'Male',
                'Occupation': 'Researcher',
                'Home Planet': 'Betelgeuse Seven' }
>>> person3
{'Gender': 'Male', 'Name': 'Ford Prefect', 'Home Planet':
'Betelgeuse Seven', 'Occupation': 'Researcher'}
```

If you're scratching your head and wondering why you'd want to trust your precious data to such an unordered data structure, don't worry, as the ordering rarely makes a difference. When you select data stored in a dictionary, it has nothing to do with the dictionary's order, and everything to do with the key you used. Remember: a key is used to look up a value.

Dictionaries understand square brackets

Like lists, dictionaries understand the square bracket notation. However, unlike lists, which use numeric index values to access data, dictionaries use keys to access their associated data values. Let's see this in action at the interpreter's >>> prompt:

Use keys to access data in a dictionary.

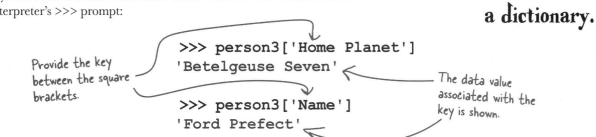

Provide the key between the square brackets.

```
>>> person3['Home Planet']
'Betelgeuse Seven'
>>> person3['Name']
'Ford Prefect'
```

The data value associated with the key is shown.

When you consider you can access your data in this way, it becomes apparent that it does not matter in what order the interpreter stores your data.

Value Lookup with Square Brackets

Using square brackets with dictionaries works the same as with lists. However, instead of accessing your data in a specified slot using an index value, with Python's dictionary you access your data via the key associated with it.

As we saw at the bottom of the last page, when you place a key inside a dictionary's square brackets, the interpreter returns the value associated with the key. Let's consider those examples again to help cement this idea in your brain:

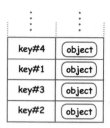

Dictionary

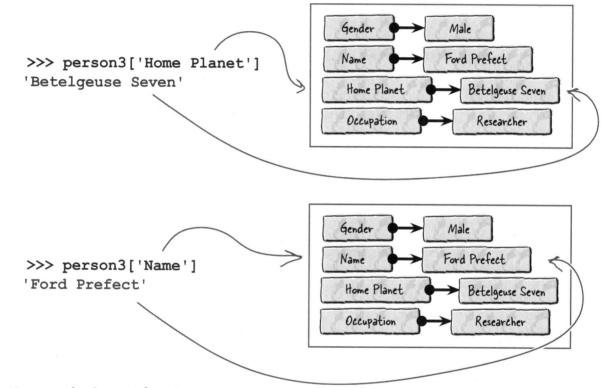

```
>>> person3['Home Planet']
'Betelgeuse Seven'
```

```
>>> person3['Name']
'Ford Prefect'
```

Dictionary lookup is fast!

This ability to extract any value from a dictionary using its associated key is what makes Python's dictionary so useful, as there are lots of occasions when doing so is needed—for instance, looking up user details in a profile, which is essentially what we're doing here with the `person3` dictionary.

It does not matter in what order the dictionary is stored. All that matters is that the interpreter can access the value associated with a key *quickly* (no matter how big your dictionary gets). The good news is that the interpreter does just that, thanks to the employment of a highly optimized *hashing algorithm*. As with a lot of Python's internals, you can safely leave the interpreter to handle all the details here, while you get on with taking advantage of what Python's dictionary has to offer.

Geek Bits

Python's dictionary is implemented as a resizeable hash table, which has been heavily optimized for lots of special cases. As a result, dictionaries perform lookups very quickly.

Working with Dictionaries at Runtime

Knowing how the square bracket notation works with dictionaries is central to understanding how dictionaries grow at runtime. If you have an existing dictionary, you can add a new key/value pair to it by assigning an object to a new key, which you provide within square brackets.

For instance, here we display the current state of the `person3` dictionary, then add a new key/value pair that associates 33 with a key called Age. We then display the `person3` dictionary again to confirm the new row of data is successfully added:

Before the new
row is added

```
>>> person3
{'Name': 'Ford Prefect', 'Gender': 'Male',
'Home Planet': 'Betelgeuse Seven',
'Occupation': 'Researcher'}
```

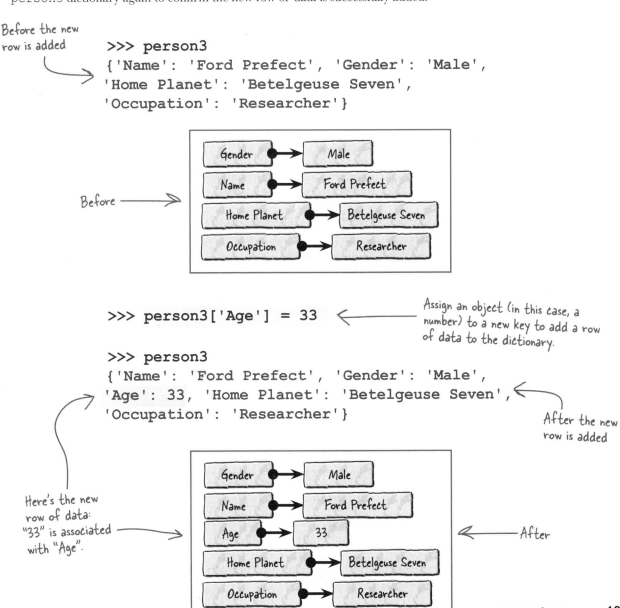

Before

```
>>> person3['Age'] = 33
```

Assign an object (in this case, a number) to a new key to add a row of data to the dictionary.

```
>>> person3
{'Name': 'Ford Prefect', 'Gender': 'Male',
'Age': 33, 'Home Planet': 'Betelgeuse Seven',
'Occupation': 'Researcher'}
```

After the new
row is added

Here's the new
row of data:
"33" is associated
with "Age".

After

Recap: Displaying Found Vowels (Lists)

As shown on the last page, growing a dictionary in this way can be used
in many different situations. One very common application is to perform
a *frequency count*: processing some data and maintaining a count of what
you find. Before demonstrating how to perform a frequency count using a
dictionary, let's return to our vowel counting example from the last chapter.

Recall that vowels3.py determines a unique list of vowels found in a word.
Imagine you've now been asked to extend this program to produce output
that details how many times each vowel appears in the word.

Here's the code from Chapter 2, which, given a word, displays a unique list of
found vowels:

This is "vowels3.py",
which reports on
the unique vowels
found in a word.

```
vowels = ['a', 'e', 'i', 'o', 'u']
word = input("Provide a word to search for vowels: ")
found = []
for letter in word:
    if letter in vowels:
        if letter not in found:
            found.append(letter)
for vowel in found:
    print(vowel)
```

vowels3.py - /Users/Paul/Desktop/_NewBook/ch02/vowels3.py (3.4.3)

Ln: 11 Col: 0

Recall that we ran this code through IDLE a number of times:

```
Python 3.4.3 Shell
>>> ============================= RESTART =============================
>>>
Provide a word to search for vowels: Milliways
i
a
>>> ============================= RESTART =============================
>>>
Provide a word to search for vowels: Hitch-hiker
i
e
>>> ============================= RESTART =============================
>>>
Provide a word to search for vowels: Galaxy
a
>>> ============================= RESTART =============================
>>>
Provide a word to search for vowels: Sky
>>>
```

Ln: 21 Col: 4

How Can a Dictionary Help Here?

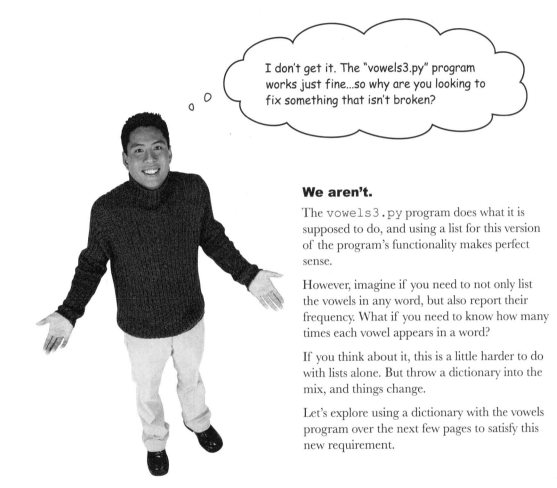

> I don't get it. The "vowels3.py" program works just fine...so why are you looking to fix something that isn't broken?

We aren't.

The `vowels3.py` program does what it is supposed to do, and using a list for this version of the program's functionality makes perfect sense.

However, imagine if you need to not only list the vowels in any word, but also report their frequency. What if you need to know how many times each vowel appears in a word?

If you think about it, this is a little harder to do with lists alone. But throw a dictionary into the mix, and things change.

Let's explore using a dictionary with the vowels program over the next few pages to satisfy this new requirement.

---
there are no
Dumb Questions

Q: Is it just me, or is the word "dictionary" a strange name for something that's basically a table?

A: No, it's not just you. The word "dictionary" is what the Python documentation uses. In fact, most Python programmers use the shorter "dict" as opposed to the full word. In its most basic form, a dictionary is a table that has exactly two columns and any number of rows.

Selecting a Frequency Count Data Structure

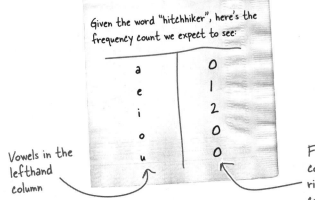

We want to adjust the vowels3.py program to maintain a count of how often each vowel is present in a word; that is, what is each vowel's frequency? Let's sketch out what we expect to see as output from this program:

Given the word "hitchhiker", here's the frequency count we expect to see:

a	0
e	1
i	2
o	0
u	0

Vowels in the lefthand column

Frequency counts in the righthand column

Dictionary

This output is a perfect match with how the interpreter regards a dictionary. Rather than using a list to store the found vowels (as is the case in vowels3.py), let's use a dictionary instead. We can continue to call the collection found, but we need to initialize it to an empty dictionary as opposed to an empty list.

As always, let's experiment and work out what we need to do at the >>> prompt, before committing any changes to the vowels3.py code. To create an empty dictionary, assign { } to a variable:

```
>>> found = {}
>>> found
{}
```

Curly braces on their own mean the dictionary starts out empty.

Let's record the fact that we haven't found any vowels yet by creating a row for each vowel and initializing its associated value to 0. Each vowel is used as a key:

```
>>> found['a'] = 0
>>> found['e'] = 0
>>> found['i'] = 0
>>> found['o'] = 0
>>> found['u'] = 0
>>> found
{'o': 0, 'u': 0, 'a': 0, 'i': 0, 'e': 0}
```

We've initialized all the vowel counts to 0. Note how insertion order is not maintained (but that doesn't matter here).

All we need to do now is find a vowel in a given word, then update these frequency counts as required.

Updating a Frequency Counter

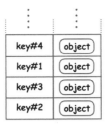

Dictionary

Before getting to the code that updates the frequency counts, consider how the interpreter sees the found dictionary in memory after the dictionary initialization code executes:

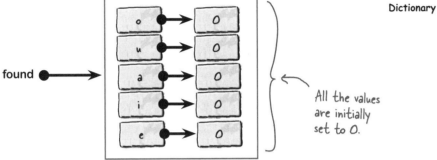

All the values
are initially
set to 0.

With the frequency counts initialized to 0, it's not difficult to increment any particular value, as needed. For instance, here's how to increment e's frequency count:

Everything
is 0.

```
>>> found
{'o': 0, 'u': 0, 'a': 0, 'i': 0, 'e': 0}
>>> found['e'] = found['e'] + 1
>>> found
{'o': 0, 'i': 0, 'a': 0, 'u': 0, 'e': 1}
```

Increment e's
count.

The dictionary has been
updated. The value
associated with "e" has
been incremented.

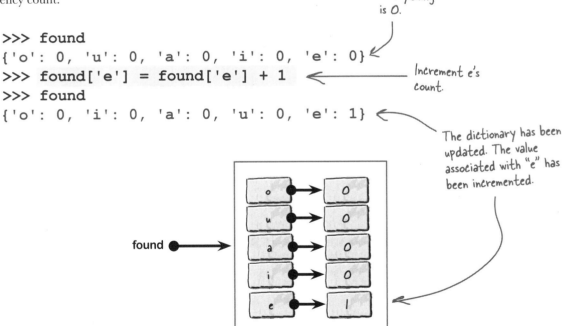

Code like that highlighted above certainly works, but having to repeat found['e'] on either side of the assignment operator gets very old, very quickly. So, let's look at a shortcut for this operation (on the next page).

Updating a Frequency Counter, v2.0

Having to put found['e'] on either side of the assignment operator (=) quickly becomes tiresome, so Python supports the familiar += operator, which does the same thing, but in a more succinct way:

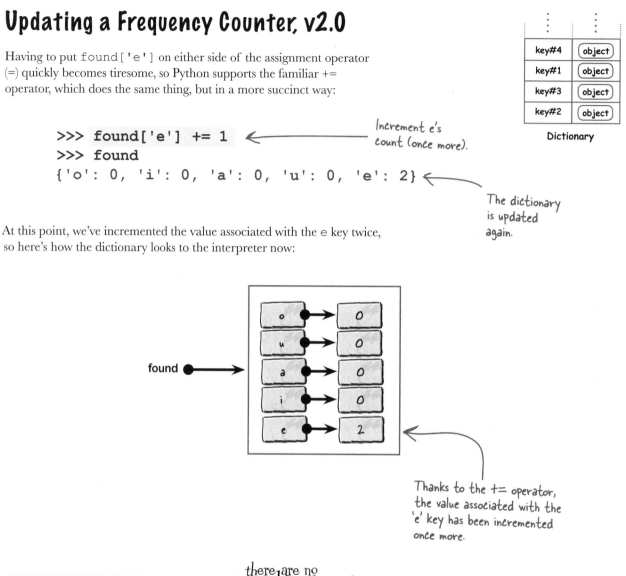

```
>>> found['e'] += 1
>>> found
{'o': 0, 'i': 0, 'a': 0, 'u': 0, 'e': 2}
```

Increment e's count (once more).

The dictionary is updated again.

Dictionary

key#4	object
key#1	object
key#3	object
key#2	object

At this point, we've incremented the value associated with the e key twice, so here's how the dictionary looks to the interpreter now:

found →

o → 0
u → 0
a → 0
i → 0
e → 2

Thanks to the += operator, the value associated with the 'e' key has been incremented once more.

---

there are no Dumb Questions

Q: Does Python have ++?

A: No...which is a bummer. If you're a fan of the ++ increment operator in other programming languages, you'll just have to get used to using += instead. Same goes for the -- decrement operator: Python doesn't have it. You need to use -= instead.

Q: Is there a handy list of operators?

A: Yes. Head over to *https://docs.python.org/3/reference/lexical_analysis.html#operators* for a list, and then see *https://docs.python.org/3/library/stdtypes.html* for a detailed explanation of their usage in relation to Python's built-in types.

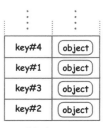

Dictionary

Iterating Over a Dictionary

At this point, we've shown you how to initialize a dictionary with zeroed data, as well as update a dictionary by incrementing a value associated with a key. We're nearly ready to update the `vowels3.py` program to perform a frequency count based on vowels found in a word. However, before doing so, let's determine what happens when we iterate over a dictionary, as once we have the dictionary populated with data, we'll need a way to display our frequency counts on screen.

You'd be forgiven for thinking that all we need to do here is use the dictionary with a `for` loop, but doing so produces unexpected results:

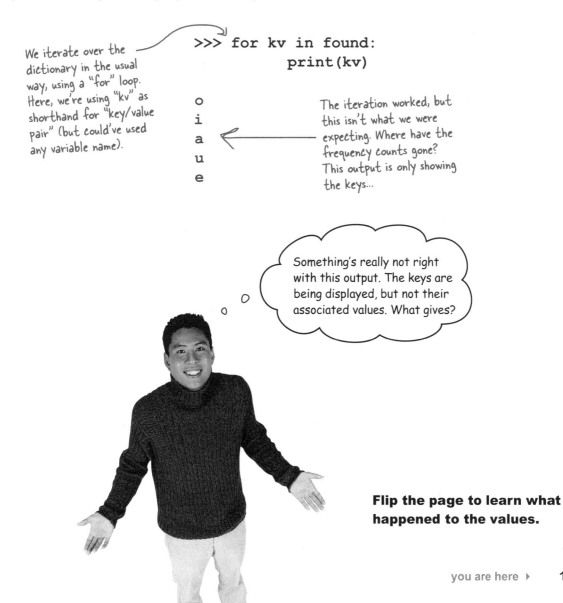

We iterate over the dictionary in the usual way, using a "for" loop. Here, we're using "kv" as shorthand for "key/value pair" (but could've used any variable name).

```
>>> for kv in found:
        print(kv)
```

```
o
i
a
u
e
```

The iteration worked, but this isn't what we were expecting. Where have the frequency counts gone? This output is only showing the keys...

Something's really not right with this output. The keys are being displayed, but not their associated values. What gives?

Flip the page to learn what happened to the values.

Iterating Over Keys and Values

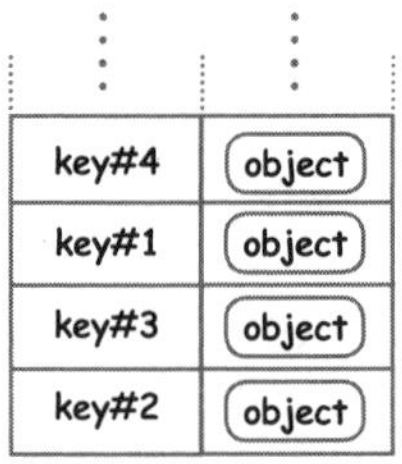

When you iterated over a dictionary with your `for` loop, the interpreter only processed the dictionary's keys.

To access the associated data values, you need to put each key within square brackets and use it together with the dictionary name to gain access to the values associated with the key.

The version of the loop shown below does just that, providing not just the keys, but also their associated data values. We've changed the suite to access each value based on each key provided to the `for` loop.

As the `for` loop iterates over each key/value pair in the dictionary, the current row's key is assigned to k, then `found[k]` is used to access its associated value. We've also produced more human-friendly output by passing two strings to the call to the `print` function:

> *We're using "k" to represent the key, and "found[k]" to access the value.*

```
>>> for k in found:
        print(k, 'was found', found[k], 'time(s).')
```

```
o was found 0 time(s).
i was found 0 time(s).
a was found 0 time(s).
u was found 0 time(s).
e was found 2 time(s).
```

> *This is more like it. The keys and the values are being processed by the loop and displayed on screen.*

key#4 object
key#1 object
key#3 object
key#2 object

Dictionary

If you are following along at your >>> prompt and your output is ordered differently from ours, don't worry: the interpreter uses a random internal ordering as you're using a dictionary here, and there are no guarantees regarding ordering when one is used. Your ordering will likely differ from ours, but don't be alarmed. Our primary concern is that the data is safely stored in the dictionary, which it is.

The above loop *obviously* works. However, there are two points that we'd like to make.

Firstly: it would be nice if the output was ordered a, e, i, o, u, as opposed to randomly, wouldn't it?

Secondly: even though this loop clearly works, coding a dictionary iteration in this way is not the preferred approach—most Python programmers code this differently.

Let's explore these two points in a bit more detail (after a quick review).

Dictionaries: What We Already Know

Here's what we know about Python's dictionary data structure so far:

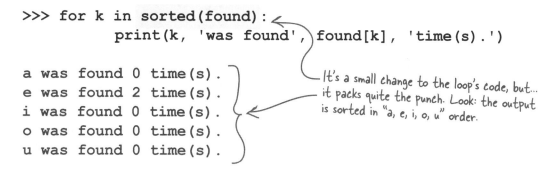

BULLET POINTS

- Think of a dictionary as a collection of rows, with each row containing exactly two columns. The first column stores a **key**, while the second contains a **value**.

- Each row is known as a **key/value pair**, and a dictionary can grow to contain any number of key/value pairs. Like lists, dictionaries grow and shrink on demand.

- A dictionary is easy to spot: it's enclosed in curly braces, with each key/value pair separated from the next by a comma, and each key separated from its value by a colon.

- Insertion order is *not* maintained by a dictionary. The order in which rows are inserted has nothing to do with how they are stored.

- Accessing data in a dictionary uses the **square bracket notation**. Put a key inside square brackets to access its associated value.

- Python's `for` loop can be used to iterate over a dictionary. On each iteration, the key is assigned to the loop variable, which is used to access the data value.

Specifying the ordering of a dictionary on output

We want to be able to produce output from the `for` loop in a, e, i, o, u order as opposed to randomly. Python makes this trivial thanks to the inclusion of the `sorted` built-in function. Simply pass the `found` dictionary to the `sorted` function as part of the `for` loop to arrange the output alphabetically:

```
>>> for k in sorted(found):
        print(k, 'was found', found[k], 'time(s).')

a was found 0 time(s).
e was found 2 time(s).
i was found 0 time(s).
o was found 0 time(s).
u was found 0 time(s).
```

It's a small change to the loop's code, but... it packs quite the punch. Look: the output is sorted in "a, e, i, o, u" order.

That's point one of two dealt with. Next up is learning about the approach that most Python programmers *prefer* over the above code (although the approach shown on this page is often used, so you still need to know about it).

Iterating Over a Dictionary with "items"

We've seen that it's possible to iterate over the rows of data in a dictionary using this code:

```
>>> for k in sorted(found):
        print(k, 'was found', found[k], 'time(s).')

a was found 0 time(s).
e was found 2 time(s).
i was found 0 time(s).
o was found 0 time(s).
u was found 0 time(s).
```

Like lists, dictionaries have a bunch of built-in methods, and one of these is the items method, which returns a list of the key/value pairs. Using items with for is often the preferred technique for iterating over a dictionary, as it gives you access to the key *and* the value as loop variables, which you can then use in your suite. The resulting suite is easier on the eye, which makes it easier to read.

Here is the items equivalent of the above loop code. Note how there are now *two* loop variables in this version of the code (k and v), and that we continue to use the sorted function to control the output ordering:

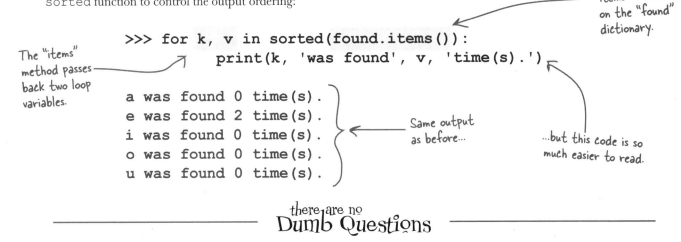

The "items" method passes back two loop variables.

We invoke the "items" method on the "found" dictionary.

```
>>> for k, v in sorted(found.items()):
        print(k, 'was found', v, 'time(s).')

a was found 0 time(s).
e was found 2 time(s).
i was found 0 time(s).
o was found 0 time(s).
u was found 0 time(s).
```

Same output as before...

...but this code is so much easier to read.

---

there are no
Dumb Questions

Q: Why are we calling sorted again in the second loop? The first loop arranged the dictionary in the ordering we want, so this must mean we don't have to sort it a second time, right?

A: No, not quite. The sorted built-in function doesn't change the ordering of the data you provide to it, but instead returns an **ordered copy** of the data. In the case of the found dictionary, this is an ordered copy of each key/value pair, with the key being used to determine the ordering (alphabetical, from A through Z). The original ordering of the dictionary remains intact, which means every time we need to iterate over the key/value pairs in some specific order, we need to call sorted, as the random ordering still exists in the dictionary.

Frequency Count Magnets

Having concluded our experimentation at the >>> prompt, it's now time to make changes to the vowels3.py program. Below are all of the code snippets we think you might need. Your job is to rearrange the magnets to produce a working program that, when given a word, produces a frequency count for each vowel found.

```
vowels = ['a', 'e', 'i', 'o', 'u']
word = input("Provide a word to search for vowels: ")
```

Decide which code magnet goes in each of the dashed-line locations to create "vowels4.py".

```
.........................................
.........................................
.........................................
.........................................
.........................................
.........................................
.........................................

for letter in word:
    if letter in vowels:

        .........................  ...................

for ..............  in sorted( .................................... ):

    print( ........ , 'was found', ........ , 'time(s).')
```

Where do all these go? Be careful: not all these magnets are needed.

```
found = {}
```
```
found[letter]
```
```
k, v
```
```
k
```
```
found['a'] = 0
found['e'] = 0
found['i'] = 0
found['o'] = 0
found['u'] = 0
```
```
value
```
```
+= 1
```
```
key
```
```
found
```
```
v
```
```
found.items()
```
```
found = []
```

Once you've placed the magnets where you think they should go, bring vowels3.py into IDLE's edit window, rename it vowels4.py, and then apply your code changes to the new version of this program.

Frequency Count Magnets Solution

Having concluded our experimentation at the >>> prompt, it was time to make changes to the vowels3.py program. Your job was to rearrange the magnets to produce a working program that, when given a word, produces a frequency count for each vowel found.

Once you'd placed the magnets where you thought they should go, you were to bring vowels3.py into an IDLE's edit window, rename it vowels4.py, and then apply your code changes to the new version of this program.

This is the "vowels4.py" program.

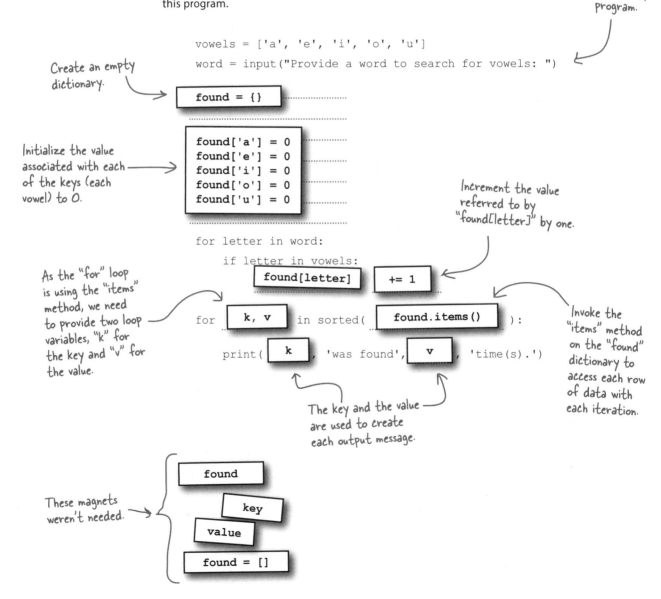

```
vowels = ['a', 'e', 'i', 'o', 'u']
word = input("Provide a word to search for vowels: ")
```

Create an empty dictionary.

```
found = {}
```

Initialize the value associated with each of the keys (each vowel) to 0.

```
found['a'] = 0
found['e'] = 0
found['i'] = 0
found['o'] = 0
found['u'] = 0
```

Increment the value referred to by "found[letter]" by one.

```
for letter in word:
    if letter in vowels:
        found[letter]   += 1
```

As the "for" loop is using the "items" method, we need to provide two loop variables, "k" for the key and "v" for the value.

```
for   k, v   in sorted(   found.items()   ):
    print(   k   , 'was found',   v   , 'time(s).')
```

Invoke the "items" method on the "found" dictionary to access each row of data with each iteration.

The key and the value are used to create each output message.

These magnets weren't needed.

```
found
        key
value
found = []
```

TEST DRIVE

Let's take `vowels4.py` for a spin. With your code in an IDLE edit window, press F5 to see how it performs:

● ● ●   vowels4.py - /Users/Paul/Desktop/_NewBook/ch02/vowels4.py (3.4.3)

```
vowels = ['a', 'e', 'i', 'o', 'u']
word = input("Provide a word to search for vowels: ")

found = {}

found['a'] = 0
found['e'] = 0
found['i'] = 0
found['o'] = 0
found['u'] = 0

for letter in word:
    if letter in vowels:
        found[letter] += 1

for k, v in sorted(found.items()):
    print(k, 'was found', v, 'time(s).')
```

The "vowels4.py" →
code

We ran the code three
times to see how well it
performs.

● ● ●   Python 3.4.3 Shell

```
>>> ============================ RESTART ============================
>>>
Provide a word to search for vowels: hitch-hiker
a was found 0 time(s).
e was found 1 time(s).
i was found 2 time(s).
o was found 0 time(s).
u was found 0 time(s).
>>> ============================ RESTART ============================
>>>
Provide a word to search for vowels: life, the universe, and everything
a was found 1 time(s).
e was found 6 time(s).
i was found 3 time(s).
o was found 0 time(s).
u was found 1 time(s).
>>> ============================ RESTART ============================
>>>
Provide a word to search for vowels: sky
a was found 0 time(s).
e was found 0 time(s).
i was found 0 time(s).
o was found 0 time(s).
u was found 0 time(s).
>>>
```

These three "runs"
produce the output we
expect them to.

I like where this is going. But do I really need to be told when a vowel isn't found?

Just How Dynamic Are Dictionaries?

The `vowels4.py` program reports on all the found vowels, even when they aren't found. This may not bother you, but let's imagine that it does and you want this code to only display results when results are *actually* found. That is, you don't want to see any of those "found 0 time(s)" messages.

How might you go about solving this problem?

Python's dictionary is dynamic, right? So, all we have to do is remove those five lines that initialize each vowel's frequency count? With those lines gone, only found vowels will be counted, right?

That sounds like it might work.

We currently have five lines of code near the start of the `vowels4.py` program that we've included in order to *initially* set each vowel's frequency count to 0. This creates a key/value pair for each vowel, even though some may never be used. If we take those five lines away, we should end up only recording frequency counts for found vowels, and ignore the rest.

Let's give this idea a try.

This is the "vowels5.py" code with the initializa[tion] code removed.

Do this!

Take the code in `vowels4.py` and save it as `vowels5.py`. Then remove the five lines of initialization code. Your IDLE edit window should look like that on the right of this page.

```
vowels5.py - /Users/Paul/Desktop/_NewBook/ch03/vowels5.py (3.4.3)

vowels = ['a', 'e', 'i', 'o', 'u']
word = input("Provide a word to search for vowels:

found = {}

for letter in word:
    if letter in vowels:
        found[letter] += 1

for k, v in sorted(found.items()):
    print(k, 'was found', v, 'time(s).')
```

Ln: 13

Test Drive

You know the drill. Make sure `vowels5.py` is in an IDLE edit window, then press F5 to run your program. You'll be confronted by a runtime error message:

```
Python 3.4.3 Shell
>>> ============================== RESTART ==============================
>>>
Provide a word to search for vowels: hitchhiker
Traceback (most recent call last):
  File "/Users/Paul/Desktop/_NewBook/ch03/vowels5.py", line 9, in <module>
    found[letter] += 1
KeyError: 'i'
>>>
                                                              Ln: 11 Col: 0
```

— This can't be good.

It's clear that removing the five lines of initialization code wasn't the way to go here. But why has this happened? The fact that Python's dictionary grows dynamically at runtime should mean that this code *cannot* crash, but it does. Why are we getting this error?

Dictionary keys must be initialized

Removing the initialization code has resulted in a runtime error, specifically a `KeyError`, which is raised when you try to access a value associated with a nonexistent key. Because the key can't be found, the value associated with it can't be found either, and you get an error.

Does this mean that we have to put the initialization code back in? After all, it is only five short lines of code, so what's the harm? We can certainly do this, but let's think about doing so for a moment.

Imagine that, instead of five frequency counts, you have a requirement to track a thousand (or more). Suddenly, we have *lots* of initialization code. We could "automate" the initialization with a loop, but we'd still be creating a large dictionary with lots of rows, many of which may end up never being used.

If only there were a way to create a key/value pair on the fly, just as soon as we realize we need it.

Geek Bits

An alternative approach to handling this issue is to deal with the run-time exception raised here (which is a "KeyError" in this example). We're holding off talking about how Python handles run-time exceptions until a later chapter, so bear with us for now.

I wonder does the "in" operator work with dictionaries?

That's a great question.

We first met `in` when checking lists for a value. Maybe `in` works with dictionaries, too?

Let's experiment at the `>>>` prompt to find out.

Avoiding KeyErrors at Runtime

As with lists, it is possible to use the `in` operator to check whether a key exists in a dictionary; the interpreter returns `True` or `False` depending on what's found.

Let's use this fact to avoid that `KeyError` exception, because it can be annoying when your code stops as a result of this error being raised during an attempt to populate a dictionary at runtime.

To demonstrate this technique, we're going to create a dictionary called `fruits`, then use the `in` operator to avoid raising a `KeyError` when accessing a nonexistent key. We start by creating an empty dictionary; then we assign a key/value pair that associates the value `10` with the key `apples`. With the row of data in the dictionary, we can use the `in` operator to confirm that the key `apples` now exists:

```
>>> fruits = {}
>>> fruits
{}
>>> fruits['apples'] = 10
>>> fruits
{'apples': 10}
>>> 'apples' in fruits
True
```

This is all as expected. The value is associated with the key, and there's no runtime error when we use the "in" operator to check for the key's existence.

Before we do anything else, let's consider how the interpreter views the `fruits` dictionary in memory after executing the above code:

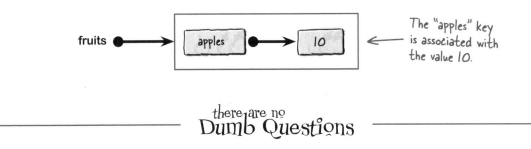

The "apples" key is associated with the value 10.

fruits

apples → 10

---

there are no
Dumb Questions

Q: I take it from the example on this page that Python uses the constant value *True* for *true*? Is there a `False`, too, and does case matter when using either of these values?

A: Yes, to all those questions. When you need to specify a boolean in Python, you can use either `True` or `False`. These are constant values provided by the interpreter, and must be specified with a leading uppercase letter, as the interpreter treats `true` and `false` as variable names, *not* boolean values, so care is needed here.

Checking for Membership with "in"

Let's add in another row of data to the `fruits` dictionary for `bananas` and see what happens. However, instead of a straight assignment to `bananas`, (as was the case with `apples`), let's increment the value associated with `bananas` by 1 if it already exists in the `fruits` dictionary or, if it doesn't exist, let's initialize `bananas` to 1. This is a very common activity, especially when you're performing frequency counts using a dictionary, and the logic we employ should hopefully help us avoid a `KeyError`.

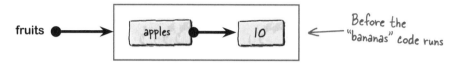

key#4	object
key#1	object
key#3	object
key#2	object

Dictionary

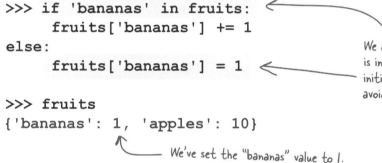

fruits → apples → 10

← Before the "bananas" code runs

In the code that follows, the `in` operator in conjunction with an `if` statement avoids any slip-ups with `bananas`, which—as wordplays go—is pretty bad (even for us):

```
>>> if 'bananas' in fruits:
        fruits['bananas'] += 1
else:
        fruits['bananas'] = 1

>>> fruits
{'bananas': 1, 'apples': 10}
```

We check to see if the "bananas" key is in the dictionary, and as it isn't, we initialize its value to 1. Critically, we avoid any possibility of a "KeyError".

We've set the "bananas" value to 1.

The above code changes the state of the `fruits` dictionary within the interpreter's memory, as shown here:

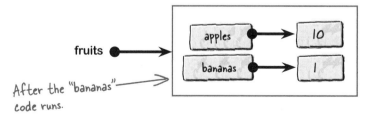

fruits → apples → 10 / bananas → 1

After the "bananas" code runs.

As expected, the `fruits` dictionary has grown by one key/value pair, and the `bananas` value has been initialized to 1. This happened because the condition associated with the `if` statement evaluated to `False` (as the key wasn't found), so the second suite (that is, the one associated with `else`) executed instead. Let's see what happens when this code runs again.

Geek Bits

If you are familiar with the **?:** **ternary operator** from other languages, note that Python supports a similar construct. You can say this:

```
x = 10 if y > 3 else 20
```

to set **x** to either **10** or **20** depending on whether or not the value of **y** is greater than **3**. That said, most Python programmers frown on its use, as the equivalent **if... else...** statements are considered easier to read.

Ensuring Initialization Before Use

If we execute the code again, the value associated with `bananas` should now be increased by 1, as the `if` suite executes this time due to the fact that the `bananas` key already exists in the `fruits` dictionary:

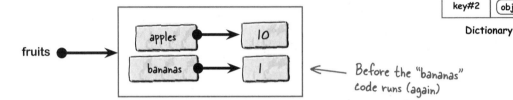

Dictionary

fruits

apples → 10

bananas → 1

← Before the "bananas" code runs (again)

To run this code again, press *Ctrl-P* (on a Mac) or *Alt-P* (on Linux/Windows) to cycle back through your previously entered code statements while at IDLE's >>> prompt (as using the up arrow to recall input doesn't work at IDLE's >>> prompt). Remember to press Enter *twice* to execute the code once more:

```
>>> if 'bananas' in fruits:
        fruits['bananas'] += 1
else:
        fruits['bananas'] = 1

>>> fruits
{'bananas': 2, 'apples': 10}
```

This time around, the "bananas" key does exist in the dictionary, so we increment its value by 1. As before, our use of "if" and "in" together stop a "KeyError" exception from crashing this code.

We've increased the "bananas" value by 1.

As the code associated with the `if` statement now executes, the value associated with `bananas` is incremented within the interpreter's memory:

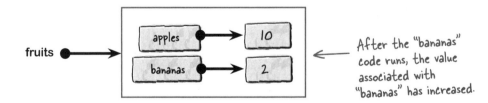

fruits

apples → 10

bananas → 2

← After the "bananas" code runs, the value associated with "bananas" has increased.

This mechanism is so common that many Python programmers shorten these four lines of code by inverting the condition. Instead of checking with `in`, they use `not in`. This allows you to initialize the key to a starter value (usually 0) if it isn't found, then perform the increment right after.

Let's take a look at how this mechanism works.

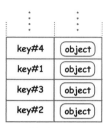

Substituting "not in" for "in"

At the bottom of the last page, we stated that most Python programmers refactor the original four lines of code to use not in instead of in. Let's see this in action by using this mechanism to ensure the pears key is set to 0 before we try to increment its value:

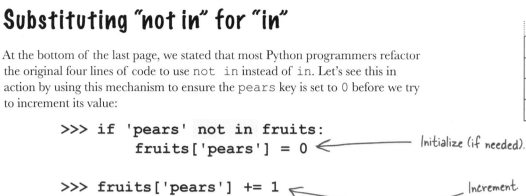

```
>>> if 'pears' not in fruits:
        fruits['pears'] = 0
```
Initialize (if needed).

```
>>> fruits['pears'] += 1
>>> fruits
{'bananas': 2, 'pears': 1, 'apples': 10}
```
Increment.

These three lines of code have grown the dictionary once more. There are now three key/value pairs in the fruits dictionary:

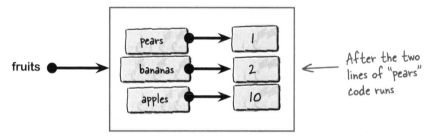

After the two lines of "pears" code runs

The above three lines of code are so common in Python that the language provides a dictionary method that makes this if/not in combination more convenient and less error prone. The setdefault method does what the two-line if/not in statements do, but uses only a *single* line of code.

Here's the equivalent of the pears code from the top of the page rewritten to use setdefault:

```
>>> fruits.setdefault('pears', 0)
>>> fruits['pears'] += 1
>>> fruits
{'bananas': 2, 'pears': 2, 'apples': 10}
```
Initialize (if needed).

Increment.

The single call to setdetfault has replaced the two-line if/not in statement, and its usage guarantees that a key is always initialized to a starter value before it's used. Any possibility of a KeyError exception is negated. The current state of the fruits dictionary is shown here (on the right) to confirm that invoking setdefault after a key already exists has no effect (as is the case with pears), which is exactly what we want in this case.

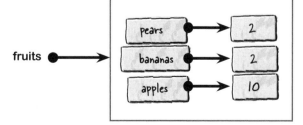

Putting the "setdefault" Method to Work

Recall that our current version of vowels5.py results in a runtime error, specifically a KeyError, which is raised due to our code trying to access the value of a nonexistent key:

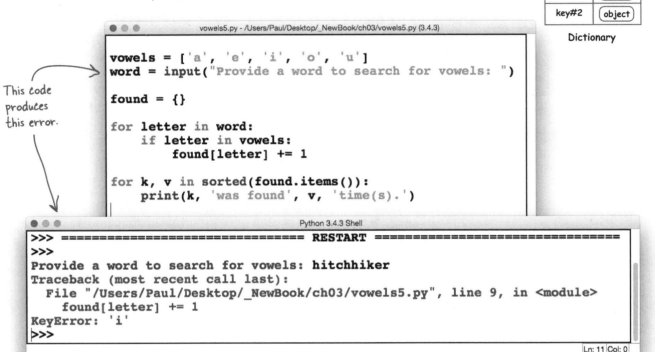

This code produces this error.

```
vowels5.py - /Users/Paul/Desktop/_NewBook/ch03/vowels5.py (3.4.3)

vowels = ['a', 'e', 'i', 'o', 'u']
word = input("Provide a word to search for vowels: ")

found = {}

for letter in word:
    if letter in vowels:
        found[letter] += 1

for k, v in sorted(found.items()):
    print(k, 'was found', v, 'time(s).')
```

```
Python 3.4.3 Shell

>>> ============================= RESTART =============================
>>>
Provide a word to search for vowels: hitchhiker
Traceback (most recent call last):
  File "/Users/Paul/Desktop/_NewBook/ch03/vowels5.py", line 9, in <module>
    found[letter] += 1
KeyError: 'i'
>>>
                                                          Ln: 11 Col: 0
```

Dictionary

```
   key#4   object
   key#1   object
   key#3   object
   key#2   object
```

From our experiments with fruits, we know we can call setdefault as often as we like without having to worry about any nasty errors. We know setdefault's behavior is guaranteed to initialize a nonexistent key to a supplied default value, or to do nothing (that is, to leave any existing value associated with any existing key alone). If we invoke setdefault immediately before we try to use a key in our vowels5.py code, we are guaranteed to avoid a KeyError, as the key will either exist or it won't. Either way, our program keeps running and no longer crashes (thanks to our use of setdefault).

Within your IDLE edit window, change the first of the vowels5.py program's for loops to look like this (by adding the call to setdefault), then save your new version as vowels6.py:

Use "setdefault" to help avoid the "KeyError" exception.

```
for letter in word:
    if letter in vowels:
        found.setdefault(letter, 0)
        found[letter] += 1
```

A single line of code can often make all the difference.

TEST DRIVE

With the most recent `vowels6.py` program in your IDLE edit window, press F5. Run this version a few times to confirm the nasty `KeyError` exception no longer appears.

```
●●●                        Python 3.4.3 Shell
>>> ============================== RESTART ==============================
>>>
Provide a word to search for vowels: hitch-hiker
e was found 1 time(s).
i was found 2 time(s).
>>> ============================== RESTART ==============================
>>>
Provide a word to search for vowels: life, the universe, and everything
a was found 1 time(s).
e was found 6 time(s).
i was found 3 time(s).
u was found 1 time(s).
>>>
                                                              Ln: 23 Col: 4
```

The use of the `setdefault` method has solved the `KeyError` problem we had with our code. Using this technique allows you to dynamically grow a dictionary at runtime, safe in the knowledge that you'll only ever create a new key/value pair when you actually need one.

This is looking good. The "KeyError" is gone.

When you use `setdefault` in this way, you **never** need to spend time initializing all your rows of dictionary data ahead of time.

Dictionaries: updating what we already know

Let's add to the list of things you now know about Python's dictionary:

BULLET POINTS

- By default, every dictionary is unordered, as insertion order is not maintained. If you need to sort a dictionary on output, use the `sorted` built-in function.

- The `items` method allows you to iterate over a dictionary by row—that is, by key/value pair. On each iteration, the `items` method returns the next key and its associated value to your `for` loop.

- Trying to access a nonexistent key in an existing dictionary results in a `KeyError`. When a `KeyError` occurs, your program crashes with a runtime error.

- You can avoid a `KeyError` by ensuring every key in your dictionary has a value associated with it before you try to access it. Although the `in` and `not in` operators can help here, the established technique is to use the `setdefault` method instead.

Aren't Dictionaries (and Lists) Enough?

> We've been talking about data structures for ages...how much more of this is there? Surely dictionaries—together with lists—are all I'll need most of the time?

Dictionaries (and lists) are great.

But they are not the only show in town.

Granted, you can do a lot with dictionaries and lists, and many Python programmers rarely need anything more. But, if truth be told, these programmers are missing out, as the two remaining built-in data structures—**set** and **tuple**—are useful in *specific circumstances*, and using them can greatly simplify your code, again in specific circumstances.

The trick is spotting when the specific circumstances *occur*. To help with this, let's look at typical examples for both set and tuple, starting with set.

there are no
Dumb Questions

Q: Is that it for dictionaries? Surely it's common for the value part of a dictionary to be, for instance, a list or another dictionary?

A: Yes, that is a common usage. But we're going to hang on until the end of this chapter to show you how to do this. In the meantime, let what you already know about dictionaries sink in...

Sets Don't Allow Duplicates

Python's **set** data structure is just like the sets you learned about in school: it has certain mathematical properties that always hold, the key characteristic being that *duplicate values are forbidden*.

Imagine you are provided with a long list of all the first names for everyone in a large organization, but you are only interested in the (much smaller) list of unique first names. You need a quick and foolproof way to remove any duplicates from your long list of names. Sets are great at solving this type of problem: simply convert the long list of names to a set (which removes the duplicates), then convert the set back to a list and—ta da!—you have a list of unique first names.

Python's set data structure is optimized for very speedy lookup, which makes using a set much faster than its equivalent list when lookup is the primary requirement. As lists always perform slow sequential searches, sets should always be preferred for lookup.

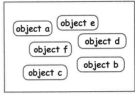

Set

Spotting sets in your code

Sets are easy to spot in code: a collection of objects are separated from one another by commas and surrounded by curly braces.

For example, here's a set of vowels:

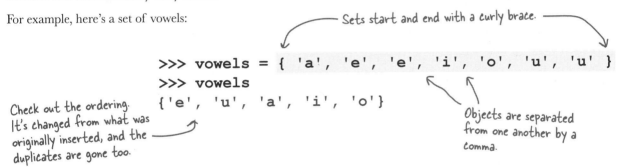

— Sets start and end with a curly brace. —

```
>>> vowels = { 'a', 'e', 'e', 'i', 'o', 'u', 'u' }
>>> vowels
{'e', 'u', 'a', 'i', 'o'}
```

Check out the ordering. It's changed from what was originally inserted, and the duplicates are gone too.

Objects are separated from one another by a comma.

The fact that a set is enclosed in curly braces can often result in your brain mistaking a set for a dictionary, which is *also* enclosed in curly braces. The key difference is the use of the colon character (:) in dictionaries to separate keys from values. The colon never appears in a set, only commas.

In addition to forbidding duplicates, note that—as in a dictionary—insertion order is *not* maintained by the interpreter when a set is used. However, like all other data structures, sets can be ordered on output with the sorted function. And, like lists and dictionaries, sets can also grow and shrink as needed.

Being a set, this data structure can perform set-like operations, such as *difference*, *intersection*, and *union*. To demonstrate sets in action, we are going to revisit our vowel counting program from earlier in this chapter once more. We made a promise when we were first developing vowels3.py (in the last chapter) that we'd consider a set over a list as the primary data structure for that program. Let's make good on that promise now.

Creating Sets Efficiently

Let's take yet another look at `vowels3.py`, which uses a list to work out which vowels appear in any word.

Here's the code once more. Note how we have logic in this program to ensure we only remember each found vowel once. That is, we are very deliberately ensuring that no duplicate vowels are *ever* added to the found list:

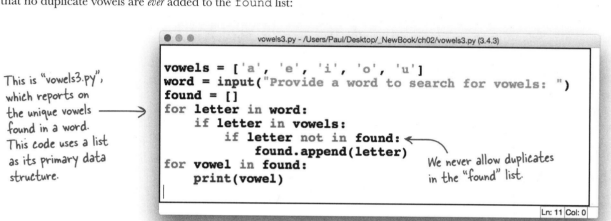

This is "vowels3.py", which reports on the unique vowels found in a word. This code uses a list as its primary data structure.

```
vowels = ['a', 'e', 'i', 'o', 'u']
word = input("Provide a word to search for vowels: ")
found = []
for letter in word:
    if letter in vowels:
        if letter not in found:
            found.append(letter)
for vowel in found:
    print(vowel)
```

We never allow duplicates in the "found" list.

`Ln: 11 Col: 0`

Before continuing, use IDLE to save this code as `vowels7.py` so that we can make changes without having to worry about breaking our list-based solution (which we know works). As is becoming our standard practice, let's experiment at the >>> prompt first before adjusting the `vowels7.py` code. We'll edit the code in the IDLE edit window once we've worked out the code we need.

Creating sets from sequences

We start by creating a set of vowels using the code from the middle of the last page (you can skip this step if you've already typed that code into your >>> prompt):

```
>>> vowels = { 'a', 'e', 'e', 'i', 'o', 'u', 'u' }
>>> vowels
{'e', 'u', 'a', 'i', 'o'}
```

These two lines of code do the same thing: both assign a new set object to a variable.

Below is a useful shorthand that allows you to pass any sequence (such as a string) to the set function to quickly generate a set. Here's how to create the set of vowels using the set function:

```
>>> vowels2 = set('aeeiouu')
>>> vowels2
{'e', 'u', 'a', 'i', 'o'}
```

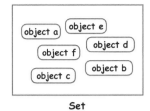

Set

Taking Advantage of Set Methods

Now that we have our vowels in a set, our next step is to take a word and determine whether any of the letters in the word are vowels. We could do this by checking whether each letter in the word is in the set, as the `in` operator works with sets in much the same way as it does with dictionaries and lists. That is, we could use `in` to determine whether a set contains any letter, and then cycle through the letters in the word using a `for` loop.

However, let's not follow that strategy here, as the set methods can do a lot of this looping work for us.

There's a much better way to perform this type of operation when using sets. It involves taking advantage of the methods that come with every set, and that allow you to perform operations such as union, difference, and intersection. Prior to changing the code in `vowels7.py`, let's learn how these methods work by experimenting at the `>>>` prompt and considering how the interpreter sees the set data. Be sure to follow along on your computer. Let's start by creating a set of vowels, then assigning a value to the `word` variable:

```
>>> vowels = set('aeiou')
>>> word = 'hello'
```

The interpreter creates two objects: one set and one string. Here's what the `vowels` set looks like in the interpreter's memory:

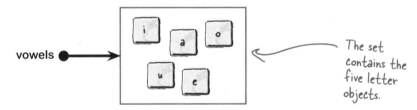

The set contains the five letter objects.

Let's see what happens when we perform a union of the `vowels` set and the set of letters created from the value in the `word` variable. We'll create a second set on-the-fly by passing the `word` variable to the `set` function, which is then passed to the `union` method provided by `vowels`. The result of this call is another set, which we assign to another variable (called u here). This new variable is a *combination* of the objects in both sets (a union):

Python conversts the value in "word" into a set of letter objects (removing any duplicates as it does so).

```
>>> u = vowels.union(set(word))
```

The "union" method combines one set with another, which is then assigned to a new variable called "u" (which is another set).

After this call to the union **method, what do the** *vowels* **and** u **sets look like?**

union Works by Combining Sets

At the bottom of the previous page we used the union method to create a
new set called u, which was a combination of the letters in the vowels set
together with the set of unique letters in word. The act of creating this new
set has no impact on vowels, which remains as it was before the union.
However, the u set is new, as it is created as a result of the union.

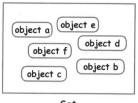

Set

Here's what happens:

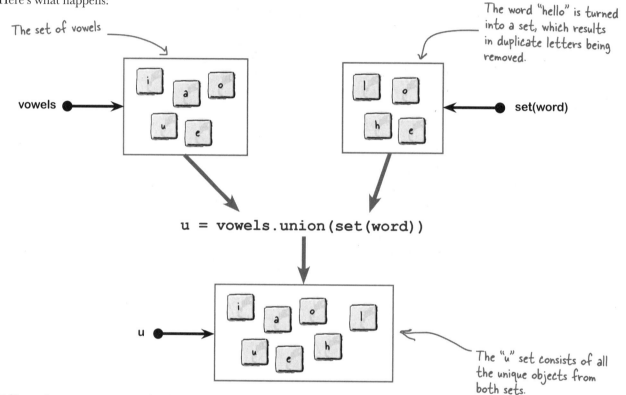

The set of vowels

The word "hello" is turned
into a set, which results
in duplicate letters being
removed.

vowels

set(word)

u = vowels.union(set(word))

u

The "u" set consists of all
the unique objects from
both sets.

What happened to the loop code?

That single line of code packs a lot of punch. Note that you haven't
specifically instructed the interpreter to perform a loop. Instead, you told the
interpreter *what* you wanted done—not *how* you wanted it done—and the
interpreter has obliged by creating a new set containing the objects you're
after.

A common requirement (now that we've created the union) is to turn the
resulting set into a sorted list. Doing so is trivial, thanks to the sorted and
list functions:

A sorted list of
unique letters

```
>>> u_list = sorted(list(u))
>>> u_list
['a', 'e', 'h', 'i', 'l', 'o', 'u']
```

difference Tells You What's Not Shared

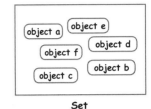

Set

Another set method is difference, which, given two sets, can tell you what's in one set but not the other. Let's use difference in much the same way as we did with union and see what we end up with:

```
>>> d = vowels.difference(set(word))
>>> d
{'u', 'i', 'a'}
```

The difference function compares the objects in vowels against the objects in set(word), then returns a new set of objects (called d here) which are in the vowels set but *not* in set(word).

Here's what happens:

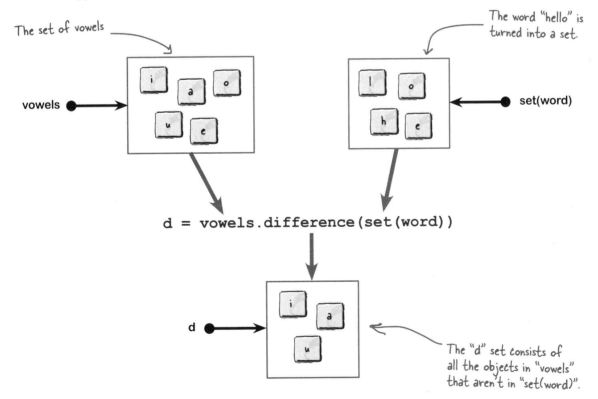

We once again draw your attention to the fact that this outcome has been accomplished *without* using a for loop. The difference function does all the grunt work here; all we did was state what was required.

Flip over to the next page to look at one final set method: intersection.

intersection Reports on Commonality

The third set method that we'll look at is `intersection`, which takes the objects in one set and compares them to those in another, then reports on any common objects found.

In relation to the requirements that we have with `vowels7.py`, what the `intersection` method does sounds very promising, as we want to know which of the letters in the user's word are vowels.

Recall that we have the string `"hello"` in the `word` variable, and our vowels in the `vowels` set. Here's the `intersection` method in action:

```
>>> i = vowels.intersection(set(word))
>>> i
{'e', 'o'}
```

The `intersection` method confirms the vowels e and o are in the `word` variable. Here's what happens:

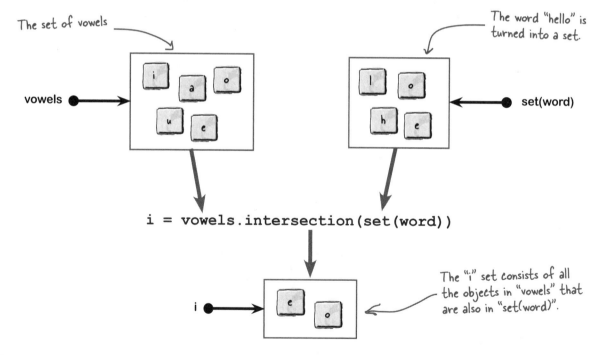

The set of vowels

The word "hello" is turned into a set.

vowels

set(word)

i = vowels.intersection(set(word))

The "i" set consists of all the objects in "vowels" that are also in "set(word)".

i

There are more set methods than the three we've looked at over these last few pages, but of the three, `intersection` is of most interest to us here. In a single line of code, we've solved the problem we posed near the start of the last chapter: *identify the vowels in any string*. And all without having to use any loop code. Let's return to the `vowels7.py` program and apply what we know now.

Sets: What You Already Know

Here's a quick rundown of what you already know about Python's set data structure:

BULLET POINTS

- Sets in Python do not allow duplicates.

- Like dictionaries, sets are enclosed in curly braces, but sets do not identify key/value pairs. Instead, each unique object in the set is separated from the next by a comma.

- Also like dictionaries, sets do not maintain insertion order (but can be ordered with the `sorted` function).

- You can pass any sequence to the `set` function to create a set of elements from the objects in the sequence (minus any duplicates).

- Sets come pre-packaged with lots of built-in functionality, including methods to perform union, difference, and intersection.

Sharpen your pencil

Here is the code to the `vowels3.py` program once more.

Based on what you now know about sets, grab your pencil and strike out the code you no longer need. In the space provided on the right, provide the code you'd add to convert this list-using program to take advantage of a set.

Hint: you'll end up with a lot less code.

```
vowels = ['a', 'e', 'i', 'o', 'u']
word = input("Provide a word to search for vowels: ")
found = []
for letter in word:
    if letter in vowels:
        if letter not in found:
            found.append(letter)
for vowel in found:
    print(vowel)
```

When you're done, be sure to rename your file `vowels7.py`.

Sharpen your pencil
Solution

Here is the code to the `vowels3.py` program once more.

Based on what you now know about sets, you were to grab your pencil and strike out the code you no longer needed. In the space provided on the right, you were to provide the code you'd add to convert this list-using program to take advantage of a set.

Hint: you'll end up with a lot less code.

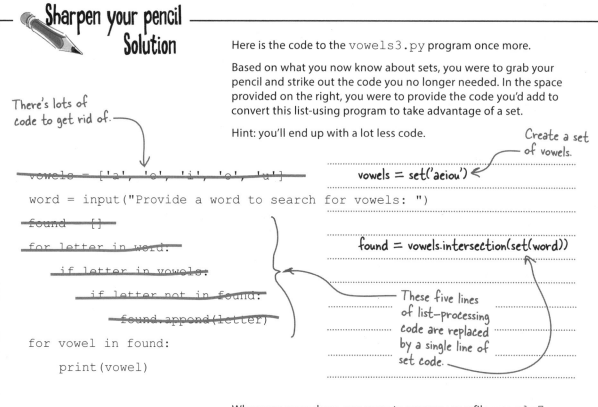

There's lots of code to get rid of.

Create a set of vowels.

```
vowels = ['a', 'e', 'i', 'o', 'u']
word = input("Provide a word to search for vowels: ")
found = []
for letter in word:
    if letter in vowels:
        if letter not in found:
            found.append(letter)
for vowel in found:
    print(vowel)
```

```
vowels = set('aeiou')
```

```
found = vowels.intersection(set(word))
```

These five lines of list-processing code are replaced by a single line of set code.

When you were done, you were to rename your file `vowels7.py`.

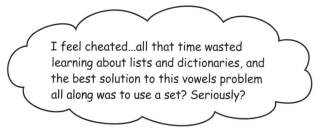

I feel cheated...all that time wasted learning about lists and dictionaries, and the best solution to this vowels problem all along was to use a set? Seriously?

It wasn't a waste of time.

Being able to spot when to use one built-in data structure over another is important (as you'll want to be sure you're picking the right one). The only way you can do this is to get experience using *all* of them. None of the built-in data structures qualify as a "one size fits all" technology, as they all have their strengths and weaknesses. Once you understand what these are, you'll be better equipped to select the correct data structure based on your application's specific data requirements.

TEST DRIVE

Let's take `vowels7.py` for a spin to confirm that the set-based version of our program runs as expected:

Our latest code →

```
vowels7.py - /Users/Paul/Desktop/_NewBook/ch03/vowels7.py (3.4.3)

vowels = set('aeiou')
word = input("Provide a word to search for vowels: ")
found = vowels.intersection(set(word))
for vowel in found:
    print(vowel)
```

```
Python 3.4.3 Shell

>>> ================================ RESTART ================================
>>>
Provide a word to search for vowels: hitch-hiker
e
i
>>> ================================ RESTART ================================
>>>
Provide a word to search for vowels: Galaxy
a
>>> ================================ RESTART ================================
>>>
Provide a word to search for vowels: life, the universe, and everything
i
a
u
e
>>> ================================ RESTART ================================
>>>
Provide a word to search for vowels: sky
>>>
                                                                    Ln: 23 Col: 4
```

Everything is working as expected.

Using a set was the perfect choice here...

But that's not to say that the two other data structures don't have their uses. For instance, if you need to perform, say, a frequency count, Python's dictionary works best. However, if you are more concerned with maintaining insertion order, then only a list will do...which is almost true. There's one other built-in data structure that maintains insertion order, and which we've yet to discuss: the **tuple**.

Let's spend the remainder of this chapter in the company of Python's tuple.

why?

Making the Case for Tuples

When most programmers new to Python first come across the **tuple**, they question why such a data structure even exists. After all, a tuple is like a list that cannot be changed once it's created (and populated with data). Tuples are immutable: *they cannot change*. So, why do we need them?

It turns out that having an immutable data structure can often be useful. Imagine that you need to guard against side effects by ensuring some data in your program never changes. Or perhaps you have a large constant list (which you know won't change) and you're worried about performance. Why incur the cost of all that extra (mutable) list processing code if you're never going to need it? Using a tuple in these cases avoids unnecessary overhead and guards against nasty data side effects (were they to occur).

How to spot a tuple in code

As tuples are closely related to lists, it's no surprise that they look similar (and behave in a similar way). Tuples are surrounded by parentheses, whereas lists use square brackets. A quick visit to the >>> prompt lets us compare tuples with lists. Note how we're using the type built-in function to confirm the type of each object created:

There's nothing new here. A list of vowels is created.

The "type" built-in function reports the type of any object.

```
>>> vowels = [ 'a', 'e', 'i', 'o', 'u' ]
>>> type(vowels)
<class 'list'>
>>> vowels2 = ( 'a', 'e', 'i', 'o', 'u' )
>>> type(vowels2)
<class 'tuple'>
```

This tuple looks like a list, but isn't. Tuples are surrounded by parentheses (not square brackets).

Now that vowels and vowels2 exist (and are populated with data), we can ask the shell to display what they contain. Doing so confirms that the tuple is not quite the same as the list:

```
>>> vowels
['a', 'e', 'i', 'o', 'u']
>>> vowels2
('a', 'e', 'i', 'o', 'u')
```

The parentheses indicate that this is a tuple.

But what happens if we try to change a tuple?

there are no
Dumb Questions

Q: **Where does the name "tuple" come from?**

A: It depends whom you ask, but the name has its origin in mathematics. Find out more than you'd ever want to know by visiting *https://en.wikipedia.org/wiki/Tuple*.

Tuples Are Immutable

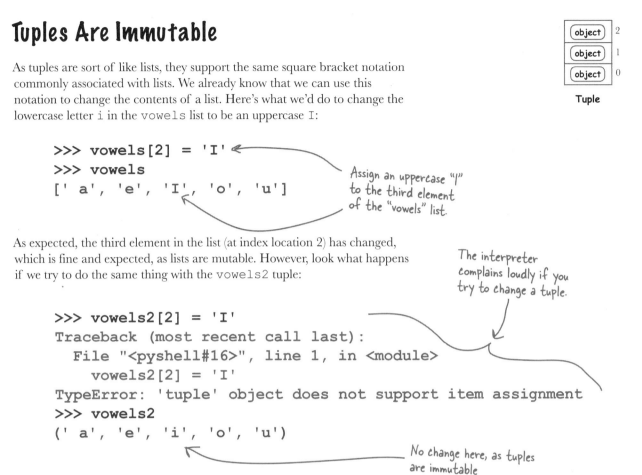

As tuples are sort of like lists, they support the same square bracket notation commonly associated with lists. We already know that we can use this notation to change the contents of a list. Here's what we'd do to change the lowercase letter i in the vowels list to be an uppercase I:

```
>>> vowels[2] = 'I'
>>> vowels
['a', 'e', 'I', 'o', 'u']
```

Assign an uppercase "I" to the third element of the "vowels" list.

As expected, the third element in the list (at index location 2) has changed, which is fine and expected, as lists are mutable. However, look what happens if we try to do the same thing with the vowels2 tuple:

The interpreter complains loudly if you try to change a tuple.

```
>>> vowels2[2] = 'I'
Traceback (most recent call last):
  File "<pyshell#16>", line 1, in <module>
    vowels2[2] = 'I'
TypeError: 'tuple' object does not support item assignment
>>> vowels2
('a', 'e', 'i', 'o', 'u')
```

No change here, as tuples are immutable

Tuples are immutable, so we can't complain when the interpreter protests at our trying to change the objects stored in the tuple. After all, that's the whole point of a tuple: once created and populated with data, a tuple cannot change.

Make no mistake: this behavior is useful, especially when you need to ensure that some data can't change. The only way to ensure this is to put the data in a tuple, which then instructs the interpreter to stop any code from trying to change the tuple's data.

As we work our way through the rest of this book, we'll always use tuples when it makes sense to do so. With reference to the vowel-processing code, it should now be clear that the vowels data structure should always be stored in a tuple as opposed to a list, as it makes no sense to use a mutable data structure in this instance (as the five vowels *never* need to change).

There's not much else to tuples—think of them as immutable lists, nothing more. However, there is one usage that trips up many a programmer, so let's learn what this is so that you can avoid it.

If the data in your structure never changes, put it in a tuple.

Watch Out for Single-Object Tuples

Tuple

Let's imagine you want to store a single string in a tuple. It's tempting to put the string inside parentheses, and then assign it to a variable name...but doing so does not produce the expected outcome.

Take a look at this interaction with the >>> prompt, which demonstrates what happens when you do this:

```
>>> t = ('Python')
>>> type(t)
<class 'str'>
>>> t
'Python'
```

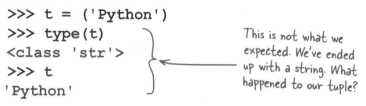

This is not what we expected. We've ended up with a string. What happened to our tuple?

What looks like a single-object tuple isn't; it's a string. This has happened due to a syntactical quirk in the Python language. The rule is that, in order for a tuple to be a tuple, every tuple needs to include at least one comma between the parentheses, even when the tuple contains a single object. This rule means that in order to assign a single object to a tuple (we're assigning a string object in this instance), we need to include the trailing comma, like so:

```
>>> t2 = ('Python',)
```

That trailing comma makes all the difference, as it tells the interpreter that this is a tuple.

This looks a little weird, but don't let that worry you. Just remember this rule and you'll be fine: *every tuple needs to include at least one comma between the parentheses*. When you now ask the interpreter to tell you what type t2 is (as well as display its value), you learn that t2 is a tuple, which is what is expected:

```
>>> type(t2)
<class 'tuple'>
>>> t2
('Python',)
```

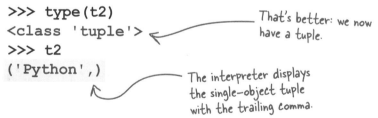

That's better: we now have a tuple.

The interpreter displays the single-object tuple with the trailing comma.

It is quite common for functions to both accept and return their arguments as a tuple, even when they accept or return a single object. Consequently, you'll come across this syntax often when working with functions. We'll have more to say about the relationship between functions and tuples in a little bit; in fact, we'll devote the next chapter to functions (so you won't have long to wait).

Now that you know about the four data structure built-ins, and before we get to the chapter on functions, let's take a little detour and squeeze in a short—and fun!—example of a more complex data structure.

Combining the Built-in Data Structures

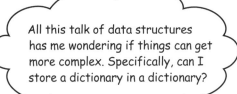

All this talk of data structures has me wondering if things can get more complex. Specifically, can I store a dictionary in a dictionary?

This question gets asked a lot.

Once programmers become used to storing numbers, strings, and booleans in lists and dictionaries, they very quickly graduate to wondering whether the built-ins support storing more complex data. That is, can the built-in data structures themselves store built-in data structures?

The answer is **yes**, and the reason this is so is due to the fact that *everything is an object in Python*.

Everything we've stored so far in each of the built-ins has been an object. The fact they've been "simple objects" (like numbers and strings) does not matter, as the built-ins can store *any* object. All of the built-ins (despite being "complex") are objects, too, so you can mix-and-match in whatever way you choose. Simply assign the built-in data structure as you would a simple object, and you're golden.

Let's look at an example that uses a dictionary of dictionaries.

there are no
Dumb Questions

Q: Does what you're about to do only work with dictionaries? Can I have a list of lists, or a set of lists, or a tuple of dictionaries?

A: Yes, you can. We'll demonstrate how a dictionary of dictionaries works, but you can combine the built-ins in whichever way you choose.

Storing a Table of Data

As everything is an object, any of the built-in data structures can be stored in any other built-in data structure, enabling the construction of arbitrarily complex data structures...subject to your brain's ability to actually visualize what's going on. For instance, although *a dictionary of lists containing tuples that contain sets of dictionaries* might sound like a good idea, it may not be, as its complexity is off the scale.

A complex structure that comes up a lot is a dictionary of dictionaries. This structure can be used to create a *mutable table*. To illustrate, imagine we have this table describing a motley collection of characters:

Name	Gender	Occupation	Home Planet
Ford Prefect	Male	Researcher	Betelgeuse Seven
Arthur Dent	Male	Sandwich-Maker	Earth
Tricia McMillan	Female	Mathematician	Earth
Marvin	Unknown	Paranoid Android	Unknown

Recall how, at the start of this chapter, we created a dictionary called `person3` to store Ford Prefect's data:

```
person3 = { 'Name': 'Ford Prefect',
            'Gender': 'Male',
            'Occupation': 'Researcher',
            'Home Planet': 'Betelgeuse Seven' }
```

Rather than create (and then grapple with) four individual dictionary variables for each line of data in our table, let's create a single dictionary variable, called `people`. We'll then use `people` to store any number of other dictionaries.

To get going, we first create an empty `people` dictionary, then assign Ford Prefect's data to a key:

```
>>> people = {}
>>> people['Ford'] = { 'Name': 'Ford Prefect',
                       'Gender': 'Male',
                       'Occupation': 'Researcher',
                       'Home Planet': 'Betelgeuse Seven' }
```

Start with a new, empty dictionary.

The key is "Ford", and the value is another dictionary.

A Dictionary Containing a Dictionary

A dictionary embedded in a dictionary—note the extra curly braces.

With the `people` dictionary created and one row of data added (Ford's), we can ask the interpreter to display the `people` dictionary at the >>> prompt. The resulting output looks a little confusing, but all of our data is there:

```
>>> people
{'Ford': {'Occupation': 'Researcher', 'Gender': 'Male',
'Home Planet': 'Betelgeuse Seven', 'Name': 'Ford Prefect'}}
```

There is only one embedded dictionary in `people` (at the moment), so calling this a "dictionary of dictionaries" is a bit of a stretch, as `people` contains just the one right now. Here's what `people` looks like to the interpreter:

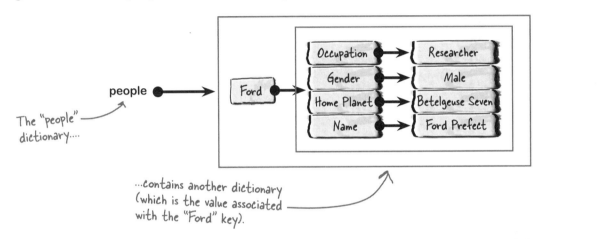

The "people" dictionary....

...contains another dictionary (which is the value associated with the "Ford" key).

We can now proceed to add in the data from the other three rows in our table:

Arthur's data

```
>>> people['Arthur'] = { 'Name': 'Arthur Dent',
                         'Gender': 'Male',
                         'Occupation': 'Sandwich-Maker',
                         'Home Planet': 'Earth' }
>>> people['Trillian'] = { 'Name': 'Tricia McMillan',
                           'Gender': 'Female',
                           'Occupation': 'Mathematician',
                           'Home Planet': 'Earth' }
>>> people['Robot'] = { 'Name': 'Marvin',
                        'Gender': 'Unknown',
                        'Occupation': 'Paranoid Android',
                        'Home Planet': 'Unknown' }
```

Tricia's data is associated with the "Trillian" key.

Marvin's data is associated with the "Robot" key.

A Dictionary of Dictionaries (a.k.a. a Table)

With the `people` dictionary populated with four embedded dictionaries, we can ask the interpreter to display the `people` dictionary at the `>>>` prompt.

Doing so results in an unholy mess of data on screen (see below).

Despite the mess, all of our data is there. Note that each opening curly brace starts a new dictionary, while a closing curly brace terminates a dictionary. Go ahead and count them (there are five of each):

It's a little hard to read, but all the data is there.

```
>>> people
{'Ford': {'Occupation': 'Researcher', 'Gender': 'Male',
'Home Planet': 'Betelgeuse Seven', 'Name': 'Ford Prefect'},
'Trillian': {'Occupation': 'Mathematician', 'Gender':
'Female', 'Home Planet': 'Earth', 'Name': 'Tricia
McMillan'}, 'Robot': {'Occupation': 'Paranoid Android',
'Gender': 'Unknown', 'Home Planet': 'Unknown', 'Name':
'Marvin'}, 'Arthur': {'Occupation': 'Sandwich-Maker',
'Gender': 'Male', 'Home Planet': 'Earth', 'Name': 'Arthur
Dent'}}
```

The interpreter just dumps the data to the screen. Any chance we can make this more presentable?

Yes, we can make this easier to read.

We could pop over to the >>> prompt and code up a quick `for` loop that could iterate over each of the keys in the `people` dictionary. As we did this, a nested `for` loop could process each of the embedded dictionaries, being sure to output something easier to read on screen.

We could...but we aren't going to, as someone else has already done this work for us.

Pretty-Printing Complex Data Structures

The standard library includes a module called `pprint` that can take any data structure and display it in a easier-to-read format. The name `pprint` is a shorthand for "pretty print."

Let's use the `pprint` module with our `people` dictionary (of dictionaries). Below, we once more display the data "in the raw" at the >>> prompt, and then we import the `pprint` module before invoking its `pprint` function to produce the output we need:

```
>>> people
{'Ford': {'Occupation': 'Researcher', 'Gender': 'Male',
'Home Planet': 'Betelgeuse Seven', 'Name': 'Ford Prefect'},
'Trillian': {'Occupation': 'Mathematician', 'Gender':
'Female', 'Home Planet': 'Earth', 'Name': 'Tricia
McMillan'}, 'Robot': {'Occupation': 'Paranoid Android',
'Gender': 'Unknown', 'Home Planet': 'Unknown', 'Name':
'Marvin'}, 'Arthur': {'Occupation': 'Sandwich-Maker',
'Gender': 'Male', 'Home Planet': 'Earth', 'Name': 'Arthur
Dent'}}
>>>
>>> import pprint
>>>
>>> pprint.pprint(people)
{'Arthur': {'Gender': 'Male',
            'Home Planet': 'Earth',
            'Name': 'Arthur Dent',
            'Occupation': 'Sandwich-Maker'},
 'Ford': {'Gender': 'Male',
          'Home Planet': 'Betelgeuse Seven',
          'Name': 'Ford Prefect',
          'Occupation': 'Researcher'},
 'Robot': {'Gender': 'Unknown',
           'Home Planet': 'Unknown',
           'Name': 'Marvin',
           'Occupation': 'Paranoid Android'},
 'Trillian': {'Gender': 'Female',
              'Home Planet': 'Earth',
              'Name': 'Tricia McMillan',
              'Occupation': 'Mathematician'}}
```

Our dictionary of dictionaries is hard to read.

Import the "pprint" module, then invoke the "pprint" function to do the work.

This output is much easier on the eye. Note that we still have five opening and five closing curly braces. It's just that—thanks to "pprint"—they are now so much easier to see (and count).

Visualizing Complex Data Structures

Let's update our diagram depicting what the interpreter now "sees" when the `people` dictionary of dictionaries is populated with data:

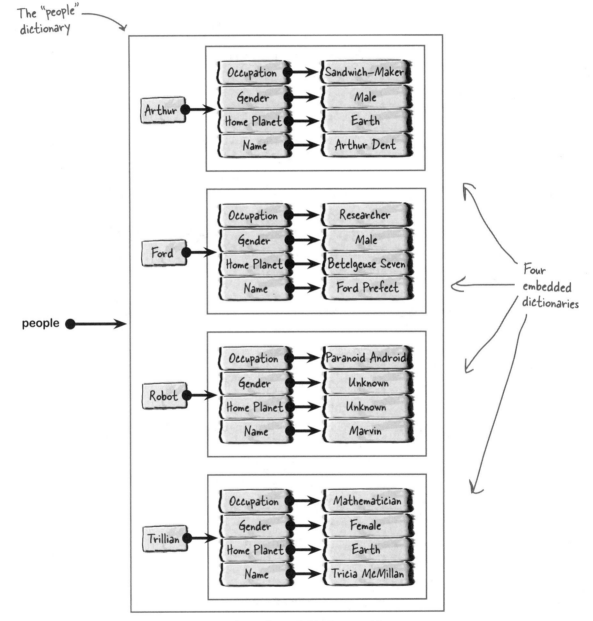

At this point, a reasonable question to ask is: *Now that we have all this data stored in a dictionary of dictionaries, how do we get at it?* Let's answer this question on the next page.

Accessing a Complex Data Structure's Data

We now have our table of data stored in the `people` dictionary. Let's remind ourselves of what the original table of data looked like:

Name	Gender	Occupation	Home Planet
Ford Prefect	Male	Researcher	Betelgeuse Seven
Arthur Dent	Male	Sandwich-Maker	Earth
Tricia McMillan	Female	Mathematician	Earth
Marvin	Unknown	Paranoid Android	Unknown

If we were asked to work out what Arthur does, we'd start by looking down the **Name** column for Arthur's name, and then we'd look across the row of data until we arrived at the **Occupation** column, where we'd be able to read "Sandwich-Maker."

When it comes to accessing data in a complex data structure (such as our `people` dictionary of dictionaries), we can follow a similar process, which we're now going to demonstrate at the >>> prompt.

We start by finding Arthur's data in the `people` dictionary, which we can do by putting Arthur's key between square brackets:

Ask for Arthur's row of data.

```
>>> people['Arthur']
{'Occupation': 'Sandwich-Maker', 'Home Planet': 'Earth',
'Gender': 'Male', 'Name': 'Arthur Dent'}
```

The row of dictionary data associated with the "Arthur" key

Having found Arthur's row of data, we can now ask for the value associated with the `Occupation` key. To do this, we employ a **second** pair of square brackets to index into Arthur's dictionary and access the data we're looking for:

Identify the row.   Identify the column.

```
>>> people['Arthur']['Occupation']
'Sandwich-Maker'
```

Using double square brackets lets you access any data value from a table by identifying the row and column you are interested in. The row corresponds to a key used by the enclosing dictionary (`people`, in our example), while the column corresponds to any of the keys used by an embedded dictionary.

Data Is As Complex As You Make It

Whether you have a small amount of data (a simple list) or something more complex (a dictionary of dictionaries), it's nice to know that Python's four built-in data structures can accommodate your data needs. What's especially nice is the dynamic nature of the data structures you build; other than tuples, each of the data structures can grow and shrink as needed, with Python's interpreter taking care of any memory allocation/deallocation details for you.

We are not done with data yet, and we'll come back to this topic again later in this book. For now, though, you know enough to be getting on with things.

In the next chapter, we start to talk about techniques to effectively reuse code with Python, by learning about the most basic of the code reuse technologies: functions.

Chapter 3's Code, 1 of 2

```
vowels = ['a', 'e', 'i', 'o', 'u']
word = input("Provide a word to search for vowels: ")

found = {}

found['a'] = 0
found['e'] = 0
found['i'] = 0
found['o'] = 0
found['u'] = 0

for letter in word:
    if letter in vowels:
        found[letter] += 1

for k, v in sorted(found.items()):
    print(k, 'was found', v, 'time(s).')
```

This is the code for "vowels4.py", which performed a frequency count. This code was (loosely) based on "vowels3.py", which we first saw in Chapter 2.

In an attempt to remove the dictionary initialization code, we created "vowels5.py", which crashed with a runtime error (due to us failing to initialize the frequency counts).

```
vowels = ['a', 'e', 'i', 'o', 'u']
word = input("Provide a word to search for vowels: ")

found = {}

for letter in word:
    if letter in vowels:
        found[letter] += 1

for k, v in sorted(found.items()):
    print(k, 'was found', v, 'time(s).')
```

```
vowels = ['a', 'e', 'i', 'o', 'u']
word = input("Provide a word to search for vowels: ")

found = {}

for letter in word:
    if letter in vowels:
        found.setdefault(letter, 0)
        found[letter] += 1

for k, v in sorted(found.items()):
    print(k, 'was found', v, 'time(s).')
```

"vowels6.py" fixed the runtime error thanks to the use of the "setdefault" method, which comes with every dictionary (and assigns a default value to a key if a value isn't already set).

Chapter 3's Code, 2 of 2

```
vowels = set('aeiou')
word = input("Provide a word to search for vowels: ")
found = vowels.intersection(set(word))
for vowel in found:
    print(vowel)
```

The final version of the vowels program, "vowels7.py", took advantage of Python's set data structure to considerably shrink the list–based "vowels3.py" code while still providing the same functionality.

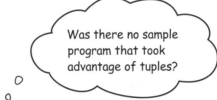

Was there no sample program that took advantage of tuples?

No, there wasn't. But that's OK.

We didn't exploit tuples in this chapter with an example program, as tuples don't come into their own until discussed in relation to functions. As we have already stated, we'll see tuples again when we meet functions (in the next chapter), as well as elsewhere in this book. Each time we see them, we'll be sure to point out each tuple usage. As you continue with your Python travels, you'll see tuples pop up all over the place.

4 code reuse

*Functions and Modules

No matter how much code I write, things just become totally unmanageable after a while...

Reusing code is key to building a maintainable system.

And when it comes to reusing code in Python, it all starts and ends with the humble **function**. Take some lines of code, give them a name, and you've got a function (which can be reused). Take a collection of functions and package them as a file, and you've got a **module** (which can also be reused). It's true what they say: *it's good to share*, and by the end of this chapter, you'll be well on your way to **sharing** and **reusing** your code, thanks to an understanding of how Python's functions and modules work.

Reusing Code with Functions

Although a few lines of code can accomplish a lot in Python, sooner or later you're going to find your program's codebase is growing...and, when it does, things quickly become harder to manage. What started out as 20 lines of Python code has somehow ballooned to 500 lines or more! When this happens, it's time to start thinking about what strategies you can use to reduce the complexity of your codebase.

Like many other programming languages, Python supports **modularity**, in that you can break large chunks of code into smaller, more manageable pieces. You do this by creating **functions**, which you can think of as named chunks of code. Recall this diagram from Chapter 1, which shows the relationship between functions, modules, and the standard library:

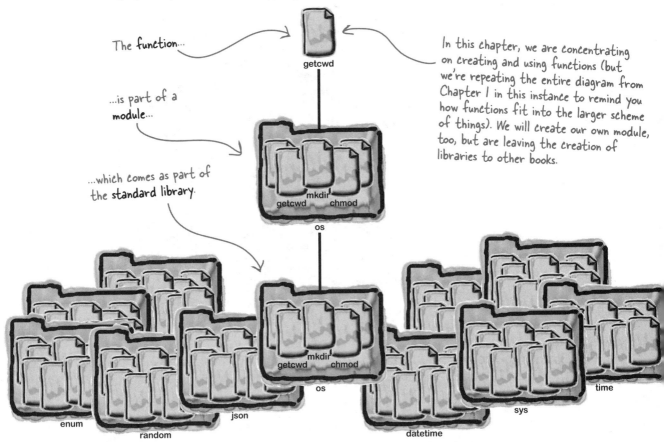

The function...

...is part of a module...

...which comes as part of the standard library.

getcwd

mkdir getcwd chmod

os

In this chapter, we are concentrating on creating and using functions (but we're repeating the entire diagram from Chapter 1 in this instance to remind you how functions fit into the larger scheme of things). We will create our own module, too, but are leaving the creation of libraries to other books.

enum

random

json

mkdir getcwd chmod

os

datetime

sys

time

In this chapter, we're going to concentrate on what's involved in creating your own functions, shown at the very top of the diagram. Once you're happily creating functions, we'll also show you how to create a module.

Introducing Functions

Before we get to turning some of our existing code into a function, let's spend a moment looking at the anatomy of *any* function in Python. Once this introduction is complete, we'll look at some of our existing code and go through the steps required to turn it into a function that you can reuse.

Don't sweat the details just yet. All you need to do here is get a feel for what functions look like in Python, as described on this and the next page. We'll delve into the details of all you need to know as this chapter progresses. The IDLE window on this page presents a template you can use when creating any function. As you are looking at it, consider the following:

1 **Functions introduce two new keywords: `def` and `return`**
Both of these keywords are colored orange in IDLE. The `def` keyword names the function (shown in blue), and details any arguments the function may have. The use of the `return` keyword is optional, and is used to pass back a value to the code that invoked the function.

2 **Functions can accept argument data**
A function can accept argument data (i.e., input to the function). You can specify a list of arguments between the parentheses on the `def` line, following the function's name.

3 **Functions contain code and (usually) documentation**
Code is indented one level beneath the `def` line, and should include comments where it makes sense. We demonstrate two ways to add comments to code: using a triple-quoted string (shown in green in the template and known as a **docstring**), and using a single-line comment, which is prefixed by the # symbol (and shown in red, below).

A handy function template

The "def" line names the function and lists any arguments.

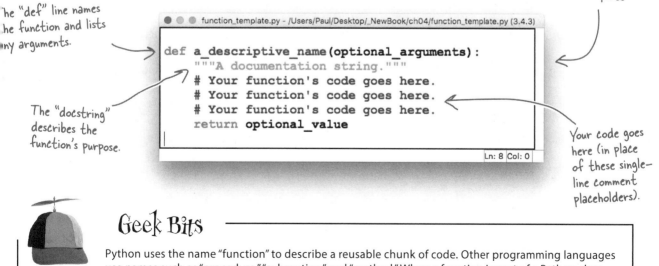

```
function_template.py - /Users/Paul/Desktop/_NewBook/ch04/function_template.py (3.4.3)

def a_descriptive_name(optional_arguments):
    """A documentation string."""
    # Your function's code goes here.
    # Your function's code goes here.
    # Your function's code goes here.
    return optional_value
```
Ln: 8 Col: 0

The "docstring" describes the function's purpose.

Your code goes here (in place of these single-line comment placeholders).

Geek Bits

Python uses the name "function" to describe a reusable chunk of code. Other programming languages use names such as "procedure," "subroutine," and "method." When a function is part of a Python class, it's known as a "method." You'll learn all about Python's classes and methods in a later chapter.

What About Type Information?

Take another look at our function template. Other than some code to execute, do you think there's anything missing? Is there anything you'd expect to be specified, but isn't? Take another look:

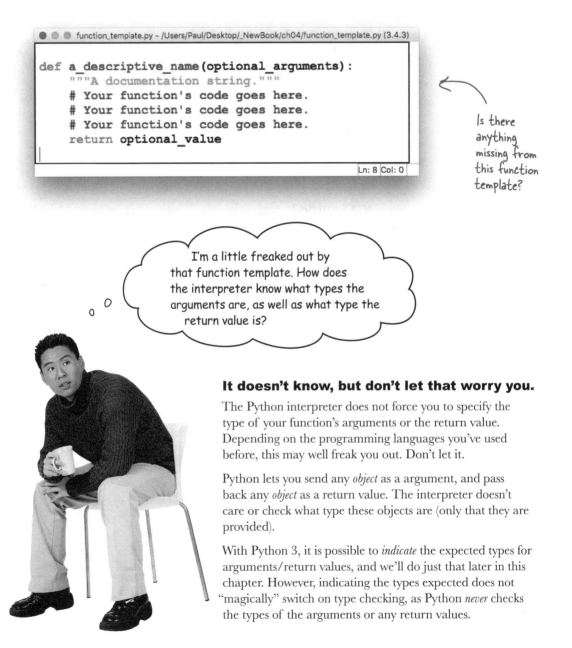

```
● ● ●   function_template.py - /Users/Paul/Desktop/_NewBook/ch04/function_template.py (3.4.3)

def a_descriptive_name(optional_arguments):
    """A documentation string."""
    # Your function's code goes here.
    # Your function's code goes here.
    # Your function's code goes here.
    return optional_value
                                                            Ln: 8 Col: 0
```

Is there anything missing from this function template?

I'm a little freaked out by that function template. How does the interpreter know what types the arguments are, as well as what type the return value is?

It doesn't know, but don't let that worry you.

The Python interpreter does not force you to specify the type of your function's arguments or the return value. Depending on the programming languages you've used before, this may well freak you out. Don't let it.

Python lets you send any *object* as a argument, and pass back any *object* as a return value. The interpreter doesn't care or check what type these objects are (only that they are provided).

With Python 3, it is possible to *indicate* the expected types for arguments/return values, and we'll do just that later in this chapter. However, indicating the types expected does not "magically" switch on type checking, as Python *never* checks the types of the arguments or any return values.

Naming a Chunk of Code with "def"

Once you've identified a chunk of your Python code you want to reuse, it's time to create a function. You create a function using the `def` keyword (which is short for *define*). The `def` keyword is followed by the function's name, an optionally empty list of arguments (enclosed in parentheses), a colon, and then one or more lines of indented code.

Recall the `vowels7.py` program from the end of the last chapter, which, given a word, prints the vowels contained in that word:

Take a set of vowels...

...and a word...

...then perform an intersection.

```
vowels = set('aeiou')
word = input("Provide a word to search for vowels: ")
found = vowels.intersection(set(word))
for vowel in found:
    print(vowel)
```
Display any results.

This is "vowels7.py" from the end of Chapter 3.

Let's imagine you plan to use these five lines of code many times in a much larger program. The last thing you'll want to do is copy and paste this code everywhere it's needed...so, to keep things manageable and to ensure you only need to maintain **one copy** of this code, let's create a function.

We'll demonstrate how at the Python Shell (for now). To turn the above five lines of code into a function, use the `def` keyword to indicate that a function is starting; give the function a descriptive name (*always* a good idea); provide an optionally empty list of arguments in parentheses, followed by a colon; and then indent the lines of code relative to the `def` keyword, as follows:

Take the time to choose a good descriptive name for your function.

Give your function a nice, descriptive name.

Provide an optional list of arguments—in this case, this function has no arguments, so the list is empty.

Start with the "def" keyword.

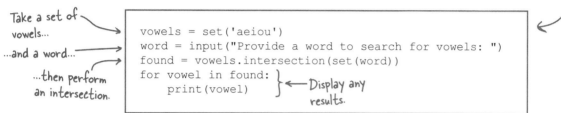

```
>>> def search4vowels():
        vowels = set('aeiou')
        word = input("Provide a word to search for vowels: ")
        found = vowels.intersection(set(word))
        for vowel in found:
            print(vowel)
```

Don't forget the colon.

The fives lines of code from the "vowels7.py" program, suitably indented

As this is the shell, remember to press the Enter key TWICE to confirm that the indented code has concluded.

Now that the function exists, let's invoke it to see if it is working the way we expect it to.

Invoking Your Function

To invoke functions in Python, provide the function name together with
values for any arguments the function expects. As the `search4vowels`
function (currently) takes no arguments, we can invoke it with an empty
argument list, like so:

```
>>> search4vowels()
Provide a word to search for vowels: hitch-hiker
e
i
```

Invoking the function again runs it again:

```
>>> search4vowels()
Provide a word to search for vowels: galaxy
a
```

There are no surprises here: invoking the function executes its code.

Edit your function in an editor, not at the prompt

At the moment, the code for the `search4vowels` function has been
entered into the >>> prompt, and it looks like this:

```
>>> def search4vowels():
        vowels = set('aeiou')
        word = input("Provide a word to search for vowels: ")
        found = vowels.intersection(set(word))
        for vowel in found:
            print(vowel)
```

*Our function
as entered
at the shell
prompt.*

In order to work further with this code, you can recall it at the >>> prompt
and edit it, but this becomes very unwieldy, very quickly. Recall that once the
code you're working with at the >>> prompt is more than a few lines long,
you're better off copying the code into an IDLE edit window. You can edit it
much more easily there. So, let's do that before continuing.

Create a new, empty IDLE edit window, then copy the function's code from
the >>> prompt (being sure *not* to copy the >>> characters), and paste it into
the edit window. Once you're satisfied that the formatting and indentation are
correct, save your file as `vsearch.py` before continuing.

**Be sure you've
saved your code
as "vsearch.py"
after copying the
function's code
from the shell.**

Use IDLE's Editor to Make Changes

The function's code is now in an IDLE edit window, and has been saved as "vsearch.py".

Here's what the `vsearch.py` file looks like in IDLE:

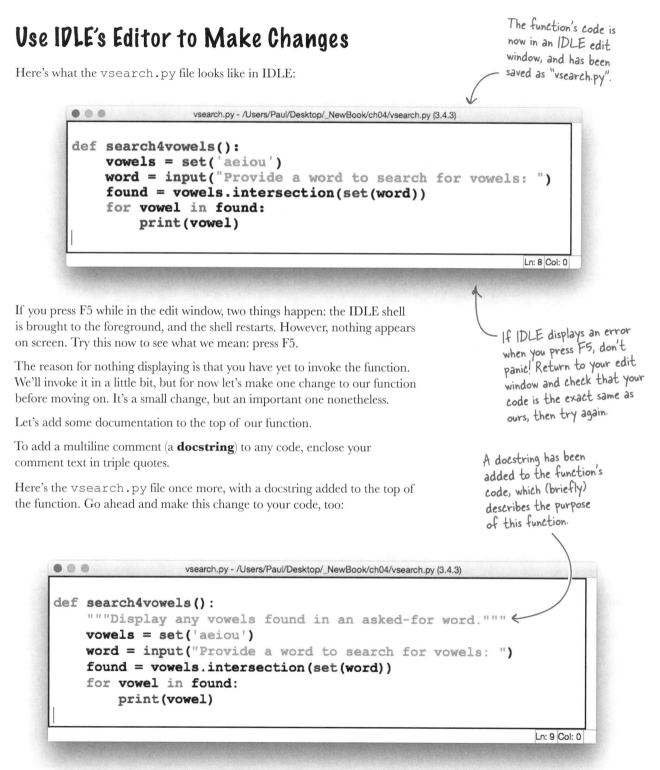

```
vsearch.py - /Users/Paul/Desktop/_NewBook/ch04/vsearch.py (3.4.3)

def search4vowels():
    vowels = set('aeiou')
    word = input("Provide a word to search for vowels: ")
    found = vowels.intersection(set(word))
    for vowel in found:
        print(vowel)

Ln: 8 Col: 0
```

If you press F5 while in the edit window, two things happen: the IDLE shell is brought to the foreground, and the shell restarts. However, nothing appears on screen. Try this now to see what we mean: press F5.

The reason for nothing displaying is that you have yet to invoke the function. We'll invoke it in a little bit, but for now let's make one change to our function before moving on. It's a small change, but an important one nonetheless.

Let's add some documentation to the top of our function.

To add a multiline comment (a **docstring**) to any code, enclose your comment text in triple quotes.

Here's the `vsearch.py` file once more, with a docstring added to the top of the function. Go ahead and make this change to your code, too:

If IDLE displays an error when you press F5, don't panic! Return to your edit window and check that your code is the exact same as ours, then try again.

A docstring has been added to the function's code, which (briefly) describes the purpose of this function.

```
vsearch.py - /Users/Paul/Desktop/_NewBook/ch04/vsearch.py (3.4.3)

def search4vowels():
    """Display any vowels found in an asked-for word."""
    vowels = set('aeiou')
    word = input("Provide a word to search for vowels: ")
    found = vowels.intersection(set(word))
    for vowel in found:
        print(vowel)

Ln: 9 Col: 0
```

What's the Deal with All Those Strings?

Take another look at the function as it currently stands. Pay particular attention to the three strings in this code, which are all colored green by IDLE:

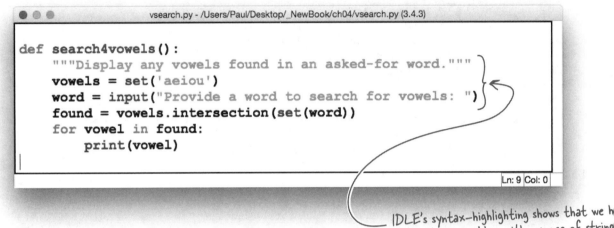

IDLE's syntax-highlighting shows that we h
a consistency problem with our use of string
quotes. When do we use which style?

Understanding the string quote characters

In Python, strings can be enclosed in a single quote character ('), a double quote character ("), or what's known as triple quotes (""" or ''').

As mentioned earlier, triple quotes around strings are known as **docstrings**, because they are mainly used to document a function's purpose (as shown above). Even though you can use """ or ''' to surround your docstrings, most Python programmers prefer to use """. Docstrings have an interesting characteristic in that they can span multiple lines (other programming languages use the name "heredoc" for the same concept).

Strings enclosed by a single quote character (') or a double quote character (") **cannot** span multiple lines: you must terminate the string with a matching quote character on the same line (as Python uses the end of the line as a statement terminator).

Which character you use to enclose your strings is up to you, although using the single quote character is very popular with the majority of Python programmers. That said, and above all else, your usage should be consistent.

The code shown at the top of this page (despite being only a handful of lines of code) is *not* consistent in its use of string quote characters. Note that the code runs fine (as the interpreter doesn't care which style you use), but mixing and matching styles can make the code harder to read than it needs to be (which is a shame).

Be consistent in your use of string quote characters. If possible, use single quotes.

Follow Best Practice As Per the PEPs

When it comes to formatting your code (not just strings), the Python programming community has spent a long time establishing and documenting best practice. This best practice is known as **PEP 8**. PEP is shorthand for "Python Enhancement Protocol."

There are a large number of PEP documents in existence, and they primarily detail proposed and implemented enhancements to the Python programming language, but can also document advice (on what to do and what not to do), as well as describe various Python processes. The details of the PEP documents can be very technical and (often) esoteric. Thus, the vast majority of Python programmers are aware of their existence but rarely interact with PEPs in detail. This is true of most PEPs *except* for PEP 8.

PEP 8 is *the* style guide for Python code. It is recommended reading for all Python programmers, and it is the document that suggests the "be consistent" advice for string quotes described on the last page. Take the time to read PEP 8 at least once. Another document, PEP 257, offers conventions on how to format docstrings, and it's worth reading, too.

Here is the search4vowels function once more in its PEP 8– and PEP 257– compliant form. The changes aren't extensive, but standardizing on single quote characters around our strings (but not around our docstrings) does look a bit better:

> Find the list of PEPs here: https://www. python.org/ dev/peps/.

> This is a PEP 257–compliant docstring.

```
vsearch.py - /Users/Paul/Desktop/_NewBook/ch04/vsearch.py (3.4.3)

def search4vowels():
    """Display any vowels found in an asked-for word."""
    vowels = set('aeiou')
    word = input('Provide a word to search for vowels: ')
    found = vowels.intersection(set(word))
    for vowel in found:
        print(vowel)

                                                        Ln: 9  Col: 0
```

> We've heeded PEP 8's advice on being consistent with the single quote character we use to surround our strings.

Of course, you don't have to write code that conforms *exactly* to PEP 8. For example, our function name, search4vowels, does not conform to the guidelines, which suggests that words in a function's name should be separated by an underscore: a more compliant name is search_for_vowels. Note that PEP 8 is a set of guidelines, not rules. You don't have to comply, only consider, and we like the name search4vowels.

That said, the vast majority of Python programmers will thank you for writing code that conforms to PEP 8, as it is often easier to read than code that doesn't.

Let's now return to enhancing the search4vowels function to accept arguments.

Functions Can Accept Arguments

Rather than having the function prompt the user for a word to search, let's change the `search4vowels` function so we can pass it the word as input to an argument.

Adding an argument is straightforward: you simply insert the argument's name between the parentheses on the `def` line. This argument name then becomes a variable in the function's suite. This is an easy edit.

Let's also remove the line of code that prompts the user to supply a word to search, which is another easy edit.

Let's remind ourselves of the current state of our code:

Remember: "suite" is Python-speak for "block."

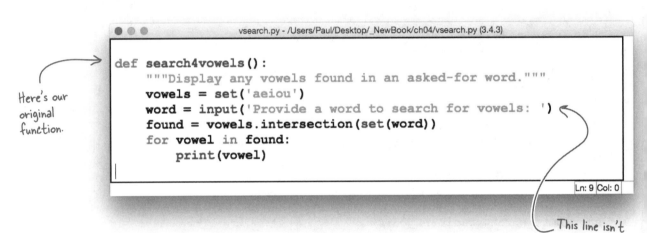

Here's our original function.

```python
def search4vowels():
    """Display any vowels found in an asked-for word."""
    vowels = set('aeiou')
    word = input('Provide a word to search for vowels: ')
    found = vowels.intersection(set(word))
    for vowel in found:
        print(vowel)
```

This line isn't needed anymore.

Applying the two suggested edits (from above) to our function results in the IDLE edit window looking like this (note: we've updated our docstring, too, which is *always* a good idea):

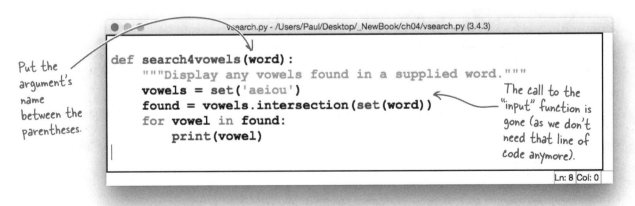

Put the argument's name between the parentheses.

```python
def search4vowels(word):
    """Display any vowels found in a supplied word."""
    vowels = set('aeiou')
    found = vowels.intersection(set(word))
    for vowel in found:
        print(vowel)
```

The call to the "input" function is gone (as we don't need that line of code anymore).

Be sure to save your file after each code change, before pressing F5 to take the new version of your function for a spin.

TEST DRIVE

With your code loaded into IDLE's edit window (and saved), press F5, then invoke the function a few times and see what happens:

```
vsearch.py - /Users/Paul/Desktop/_NewBook/ch04/vsearch.py (3.4.3)

def search4vowels(word):
    """Display any vowels found in a supplied word."""
    vowels = set('aeiou')
    found = vowels.intersection(set(word))
    for vowel in found:
        print(vowel)
```

The current "search4vowels" code

```
Python 3.4.3 Shell

>>> ================================ RESTART ================================
>>>
>>> search4vowels()
Traceback (most recent call last):
  File "<pyshell#3>", line 1, in <module>
    search4vowels()
TypeError: search4vowels() missing 1 required positional argument: 'word'
>>> search4vowels('hitch-hiker')
e
i
>>> search4vowels('hitch-hiker', 'galaxy')
Traceback (most recent call last):
  File "<pyshell#5>", line 1, in <module>
    search4vowels('hitch-hiker', 'galaxy')
TypeError: search4vowels() takes 1 positional argument but 2 were given
>>> |
                                                                    Ln: 12 Col: 4
```

Although we've invoked the "search4vowels" function three times in this Test Drive, the only invocation that ran successfully was the one that passed in a single, stringed argument. The other two failed. Take a moment to read the error messages produced by the interpreter to learn why each of the incorrect calls failed.

there are no Dumb Questions

Q: Am I restricted to only a single argument when creating functions in Python?

A: No, you can have as many arguments as you want, depending on the service your function is providing. We are deliberately starting off with a straightforward example, and we'll get to more involved examples as this chapter progresses. You can do a lot with arguments to functions in Python, and we plan to discuss most of what's possible over the next dozen pages or so.

Functions Return a Result

As well as using a function to abstract some code and give it a name, programmers typically want functions to return some calculated value, which the code that called the function can then work with. To support returning a value (or values) from a function, Python provides the `return` statement.

When the interpreter encounters a `return` statement in your function's suite, two things happen: the function terminates at the `return` statement, and any value provided to the `return` statement is passed back to your calling code. This behavior mimics how `return` works in the majority of other programming languages.

Let's start with a straightforward example of returning a single value from our `search4vowels` function. Specifically, let's return either `True` or `False` depending on whether the `word` supplied as an argument contains any vowels.

This *is* a bit of a departure from our function's existing functionality, but bear with us, as we are going to build up to something more complex (and useful) in a bit. Starting with a simple example ensures we have the basics in place first, before moving on.

> That sounds like a plan I can live with. The only question I have is how do I know whether something is true or false?

The truth is...

Python comes with a built-in function called `bool` that, when provided with any value, tells you whether the value evaluates to `True` or `False`.

Not only does `bool` work with any value, it works with any Python object. The effect of this is that Python's notion of truth extends far beyond the `1` for `True` and the `0` for `False` that other programming languages employ.

Let's pause and take a brief look at `True` and `False` before getting back to our discussion of `return`.

Truth Up Close

Every object in Python has a truth value associated with it, in that the object evaluates to either True or False.

Something is False if it evaluates to 0, the value None, an empty string, or an empty built-in data structure. This means all of these examples are False:

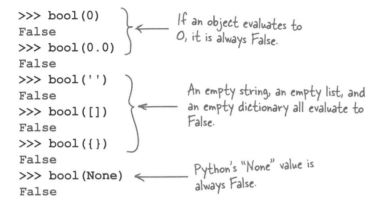

```
>>> bool(0)
False
>>> bool(0.0)
False
```
If an object evaluates to 0, it is always False.

```
>>> bool('')
False
>>> bool([])
False
>>> bool({})
False
```
An empty string, an empty list, and an empty dictionary all evaluate to False.

```
>>> bool(None)
False
```
Python's "None" value is always False.

Every other object in Python evaluates to True. Here are some examples of objects that are True:

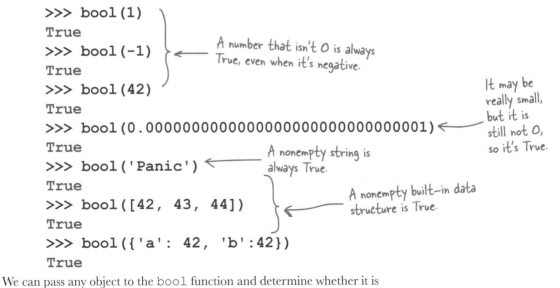

```
>>> bool(1)
True
>>> bool(-1)
True
>>> bool(42)
True
```
A number that isn't 0 is always True, even when it's negative.

```
>>> bool(0.00000000000000000000000000001)
True
```
It may be really small, but it is still not 0, so it's True.

```
>>> bool('Panic')
True
```
A nonempty string is always True.

```
>>> bool([42, 43, 44])
True
>>> bool({'a': 42, 'b':42})
True
```
A nonempty built-in data structure is True.

We can pass any object to the bool function and determine whether it is True or False.

Critically, any nonempty data structure evaluates to True.

Returning One Value

Take another look at our function's code, which currently accepts any value as an argument, searches the supplied value for vowels, and then displays the found vowels on screen:

```
def search4vowels(word):
    """Display any vowels found in a supplied word."""
    vowels = set('aeiou')
    found = vowels.intersection(set(word))
    for vowel in found:
        print(vowel)
```

We'll change these two lines.

Changing this function to return either `True` or `False`, based on whether any vowels were found, is straightforward. Simply replace the last two lines of code (the `for` loop) with this line of code:

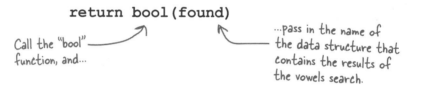

return bool(found)

Call the "bool" function, and...

...pass in the name of the data structure that contains the results of the vowels search.

If nothing is found, the function returns `False`; otherwise, it returns `True`. With this change made, you can now test this new version of your function at the Python Shell and see what happens:

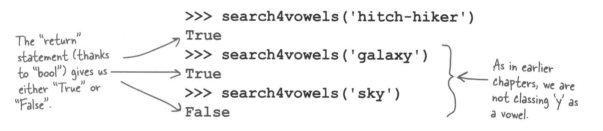

```
>>> search4vowels('hitch-hiker')
True
>>> search4vowels('galaxy')
True
>>> search4vowels('sky')
False
```

The "return" statement (thanks to "bool") gives us either "True" or "False".

As in earlier chapters, we are not classing 'y' as a vowel.

If you continue to see the previous version's behavior, ensure you've saved the new version of your function, as well as pressed F5 from the edit window.

Geek Bits

Don't be tempted to put parentheses around the object that `return` passes back to the calling code. You don't need to. The `return` statement is not a function call, so the use of parentheses isn't a syntactical requirement. You can use them (if you *really* want to), but most Python programmers don't.

Returning More Than One Value

Functions are designed to return a single value, but it is sometimes necessary to return more than one value. The only way to do this is to package the multiple values in a single data structure, then return that. Thus, you're still returning one thing, even though it potentially contains many individual pieces of data.

Here's our current function, which returns a boolean value (i.e., one thing):

Note: we've updated the comment.

```
def search4vowels(word):
    """Return a boolean based on any vowels found."""
    vowels = set('aeiou')
    found = vowels.intersection(set(word))
    return bool(found)
```

It's a trivial edit to have the function return multiple values (in one set) as opposed to a boolean. All we need to do is drop the call to `bool`:

```
def search4vowels(word):
    """Return any vowels found in a supplied word."""
    vowels = set('aeiou')
    found = vowels.intersection(set(word))
    return found
```

Return the results as a data structure (a set).

We've updated the comment again.

We can further reduce the last two lines of code in the above version of our function to one line by removing the unnecessary use of the `found` variable. Rather than assigning the results of the `intersection` to the `found` variable and returning that, just return the `intersection`:

```
def search4vowels(word):
    """Return any vowels found in a supplied word."""
    vowels = set('aeiou')
    return vowels.intersection(set(word))
```

Return the data without the use of the unnecessary "found" variable.

Our function now returns a set of vowels found in a word, which is exactly what we set out to do.

However, when we tested it, one of our results has us scratching our head...

TEST DRIVE

Let's take this latest version of the `search4vowels` function for a spin and see how it behaves. With the latest code loaded into an IDLE edit window, press F5 to import the function into the Python Shell, and then invoke the function a few times:

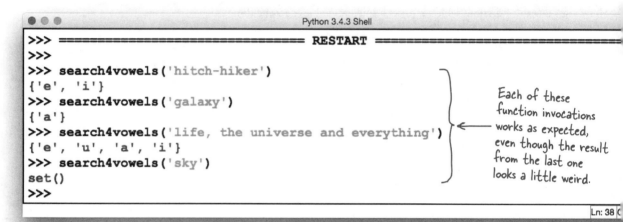

```
●  ●  ●                              Python 3.4.3 Shell
>>> ============================== RESTART ==============================
>>>
>>> search4vowels('hitch-hiker')
{'e', 'i'}
>>> search4vowels('galaxy')
{'a'}
>>> search4vowels('life, the universe and everything')
{'e', 'u', 'a', 'i'}
>>> search4vowels('sky')
set()
>>>
```

Each of these function invocations works as expected, even though the result from the last one looks a little weird.

Ln: 38 (

What's the deal with "set()"?

Each example in the above *Test Drive* works fine, in that the function takes a single string value as an argument, then returns the set of vowels found. The one result, the set, contains many values. However, the last response looks a little weird, doesn't it? Let's have a closer look:

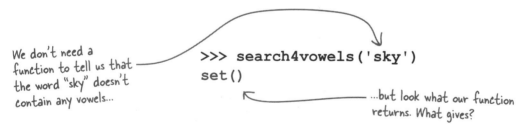

We don't need a function to tell us that the word "sky" doesn't contain any vowels...

```
>>> search4vowels('sky')
set()
```

...but look what our function returns. What gives?

You may have expected the function to return { } to represent an empty set, but that's a common misunderstanding, as { } represents an empty dictionary, *not* an empty set.

An empty set is represented as `set()` by the interpreter.

This may well look a little weird, but it's just the way things work in Python. Let's take a moment to recall the four built-in data structures, with a eye to seeing how each empty data structure is represented by the interpreter.

Recalling the Built-in Data Structures

Let's remind ourselves of the four built-in data structures available to us. We'll take each data structure in turn, working through list, dictionary, set, and finally tuple.

Working at the shell, let's create an empty data structure using the data structure built-in functions (BIFs for short), then assign a small amount of data to each. We'll then display the contents of each data structure after each assignment:

BIF is short-hand for "built-in function."

```
>>> l = list()          Use the "list" BIF to
>>> l                    define an empty list,
[]                       then assign some data.
>>> l = [ 1, 2, 3 ]
>>> l
[1, 2, 3]
```

An empty list

```
>>> d = dict()          Use the "dict" BIF to
>>> d                    define an empty dictionary,
{}                       then assign some data.
>>> d = { 'first': 1, 'second': 2, 'third': 3 }
>>> d
{'second': 2, 'third': 3, 'first': 1}
```

An empty dictionary

```
>>> s = set()           Use the "set" BIF to
>>> s                   define an empty set,
set()                   then assign some data.
>>> s = {1, 2, 3}
>>> s
{1, 2, 3}
```

An empty set

Even though sets are enclosed in curly braces, so too are dictionaries. An empty dictionary is already using the double curly braces, so an empty set has to be represented as "set()".

```
>>> t = tuple()         Use the "tuple" BIF to
>>> t                   define an empty tuple,
()                      then assign some data.
>>> t = (1, 2, 3)
>>> t
(1, 2, 3)
```

An empty tuple

Before moving on, take a moment to review how the interpreter represents each of the empty data structures as shown on this page.

Use Annotations to Improve Your Docs

Our review of the four data structures confirms that the `search4vowels` function returns a set. But, other than calling the function and checking the return type, how can users of our function know this ahead of time? How do they know what to expect?

A solution is to add this information to the docstring. This assumes that you very clearly indicate in your docstring what the arguments and return value are going to be and that this information is easy to find. Getting programmers to agree on a standard for documenting functions is problematic (PEP 257 only suggests the *format* of docstrings), so Python 3 now supports a notation called **annotations** (also known as *type hints*). When used, annotations document—in a standard way—the return type, as well as the types of any arguments. Keep these points in mind:

 Function annotations are optional
It's OK not to use them. In fact, a lot of existing Python code doesn't (as they were only made available to programmers in the most recent versions of Python 3).

 Function annotations are informational
They provide details about your function, but they do not imply any other behavior (such as type checking).

Let's annotate the `search4vowels` function's arguments. The first annotation states that the function expects a string as the type of the `word` argument (`:str`), while the second annotation states that the function returns a set to its caller (`-> set`):

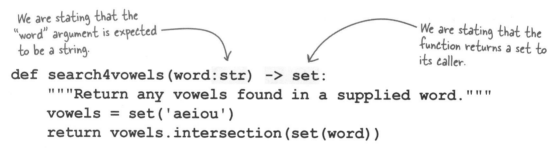

We are stating that the "word" argument is expected to be a string.

We are stating that the function returns a set to its caller.

```python
def search4vowels(word:str) -> set:
    """Return any vowels found in a supplied word."""
    vowels = set('aeiou')
    return vowels.intersection(set(word))
```

Annotation syntax is straightforward. Each function argument has a colon appended to it, together with the type that is expected. In our example, `:str` specifies that the function expects a string. The return type is provided after the argument list, and is indicated by an arrow symbol, which is itself followed by the return type, then the colon. Here `-> set:` indicates that the function is going to return a set.

So far, so good.

We've now annotated our function in a standard way. Because of this, programmers using our function now know what's expected of them, as well as what to expect from the function. However, the interpreter **won't** check that the function is always called with a string, nor will it check that the function always returns a set. Which begs a rather obvious question...

For more details on annotations, see PEP 3107 at https://www. python.org/dev/ peps/pep-3107/.

Why Use Function Annotations?

If the Python interpreter isn't going to use your annotations to check the types of your function's arguments and its return type, why bother with annotations at all?

The goal of annotations is *not* to make life easier for the interpreter; it's to make life easier for the user of your function. Annotations are a **documentation standard**, *not* a type enforcement mechanism.

In fact, the interpreter does not care what type your arguments are, nor does it care what type of data your function returns. The interpreter calls your function with whatever arguments are provided to it (no matter their type), executes your function's code, and then returns to the caller whatever value it is given by the `return` statement. The type of the data being passed back and forth is not considered by the interpreter.

What annotations do for programmers using your function is rid them of the need to read your function's code to learn what types are expected by, and returned from, your function. This is what they'll have to do if annotations aren't used. Even the most beautifully written docstring will still have to be read if it doesn't include annotations.

Which leads to another question: how do we view the annotations without reading the function's code? From IDLE's editor, press F5, then use the `help` BIF at the >>> prompt.

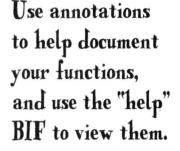

Use annotations to help document your functions, and use the "help" BIF to view them.

Test Drive

If you haven't done so already, use IDLE's editor to annotate your copy of search4vowels, save your code, and then press the F5 key. The Python Shell will restart and the >>> prompt will be waiting for you to do something. Ask the `help` BIF to display search4vowels documentation, like so:

```
Python 3.4.3 Shell
>>> ================================ RESTART ================================
>>>
>>> help(search4vowels)
Help on function search4vowels in module __main__:

search4vowels(word:str) -> set
    Return any vowels found in a supplied word.

>>> |
                                                                    Ln: 51 Col: 4
```

Not only does "help" display the annotations, but it shows the docstring too.

Functions: What We Know Already

Let's pause for a moment and review what we know (so far) about Python functions.

🔫 BULLET POINTS

- Functions are named chunks of code.

- The `def` keyword is used to name a function, with the function's code indented under (and relative to) the `def` keyword.

- Python's triple-quoted strings can be used to add multiline comments to a function. When they are used in this way, they are known as *docstrings*.

- Functions can accept any number of named arguments, including none.

- The `return` statement lets your functions return any number of values (including none).

- Function annotations can be used to document the type of your function's arguments, as well as its return type.

Let's take a moment to once more review the code for the `search4vowels` function. Now that it accepts an argument and returns a set, it is more useful than the very first version of the function from the start of this chapter, as we can now use it in many more places:

The most recent version of our function

```
def search4vowels(word:str) -> set:
    """Return any vowels found in a supplied word."""
    vowels = set('aeiou')
    return vowels.intersection(set(word))
```

This function would be even more useful if, in addition to accepting an argument for the word to search, it also accepted a second argument detailing what to search for. This would allow us to look for any set of letters, not just the five vowels.

Additionally, the use of the name `word` as an argument name is OK, but not great, as this function clearly accepts *any* string as an argument, as opposed to a single word. A better variable name might be `phrase`, as it more closely matches what it is we expect to receive from the users of our function.

Let's change our function now to reflect this last suggestion.

Making a Generically Useful Function

Here's a version of the `search4vowels` function (as it appears in IDLE) after it has been changed to reflect the second of the two suggestions from the bottom of the last page. Namely, we've changed the name of the `word` variable to the more appropriate `phrase`:

The "word" variable is now called "phrase".

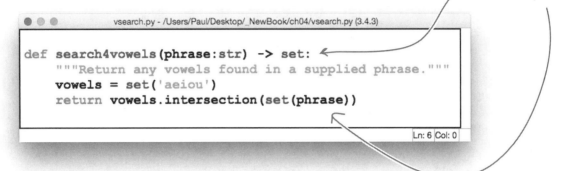

```
vsearch.py - /Users/Paul/Desktop/_NewBook/ch04/vsearch.py (3.4.3)

def search4vowels(phrase:str) -> set:
    """Return any vowels found in a supplied phrase."""
    vowels = set('aeiou')
    return vowels.intersection(set(phrase))

                                                    Ln: 6  Col: 0
```

The other suggestion from the bottom of the last page was to allow users to specify the set of letters to search for, as opposed to always using the five vowels. To do this we can add a second argument to the function that specifies the letters to search `phrase` for. This is an easy change to make. However, once we make it, the function (as it stands) will be incorrectly named, as we'll no longer be searching for vowels, we'll be searching for any set of letters. Rather than change the current function, let's create a second one that is based on the first. Here's what we propose to do:

 Give the new function a more generic name
Rather than continuing to adjust `search4vowels`, let's create a new function called `search4letters`, which is a name that better reflects the new function's purpose.

 Add a second argument
Adding a second argument allows us to specify the set of letters to search the string for. Let's call the second argument `letters`. And let's not forget to annotate `letters`, too.

 Remove the `vowels` variable
The use of the name `vowels` in the function's suite no longer makes any sense, as we are now looking for a user-specified set of letters.

 Update the docstring
There's no point copying, then changing, the code if we don't also adjust the docstring. Our documentation needs be updated to reflect what the new function does.

We are going to work through these four tasks together. As each task is discussed, be sure to edit your `vsearch.py` file to reflect the presented changes.

Creating Another Function, 1 of 3

If you haven't done so already, open the `vsearch.py` file in an IDLE edit window.

Step 1 involves creating a new function, which we'll call `search4letters`. Be aware that PEP 8 suggests that all top-level functions are surrounded by two blank lines. All of this book's downloads conform to this guideline, but the code we show on the printed page doesn't (as space is at a premium here).

At the bottom of the file, type **def** followed by the name of your new function:

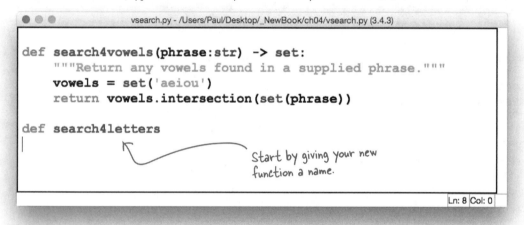

Start by giving your new function a name.

For **Step 2** we're completing the function's `def` line by adding in the names of the two required arguments, `phrase` and `letters`. Remember to enclose the list of arguments within parentheses, and don't forget to include the trailing colon (and the annotations):

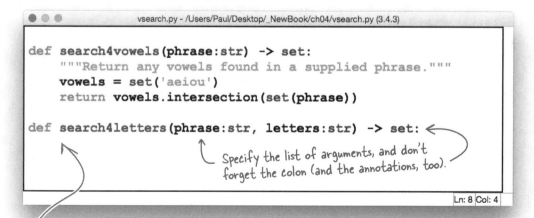

Specify the list of arguments, and don't forget the colon (and the annotations, too).

Did you notice how IDLE's editor has anticipated that the next line of code needs to be indented (and automatically positioned the cursor)?

With Steps 1 and 2 complete, we're now ready to write the function's code. This code is going to be similar to that in the `search4vowels` function, except that we plan to remove our reliance on the `vowels` variable.

Creating Another Function, 2 of 3

On to **Step 3**, which is to write the code for the function in such a way as to remove the need for the `vowels` variable. We could continue to use the variable, but give it a new name (as `vowels` no longer represents what the variable does), but a temporary variable is not needed here, for much the same reason as why we no longer needed the `found` variable earlier. Take a look at the new line of code in `search4letters`, which does the same job as the two lines in `search4vowels`:

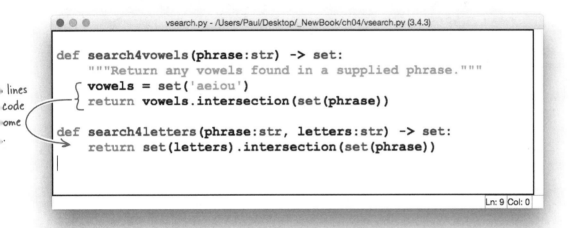

```
vsearch.py - /Users/Paul/Desktop/_NewBook/ch04/vsearch.py (3.4.3)

def search4vowels(phrase:str) -> set:
    """Return any vowels found in a supplied phrase."""
    vowels = set('aeiou')
    return vowels.intersection(set(phrase))

def search4letters(phrase:str, letters:str) -> set:
    return set(letters).intersection(set(phrase))

                                                    Ln: 9  Col: 0
```

lines
code
ome

If that single line of code in `search4letters` has you scratching your head, don't despair. It looks more complex than it is. Let's go through this line of code in detail to work out exactly what it does. It starts when the value of the `letters` argument is turned into a set:

set(letters) ⟵   Create a set object from "letters".

This call to the `set` BIF creates a set object from the characters in the `letters` variable. We don't need to assign this set object to a variable, as we are more interested in using the set of letters right away than in storing the set in a variable for later use. To use the just-created set object, append a dot, then specify the method you want to invoke, as even objects that aren't assigned to variables have methods. As we know from using sets in the last chapter, the `intersection` method takes the set of characters contained in its argument (`phrase`) and intersects them with an existing set object (`letters`):

Perform a set intersection on the set object made from "letters" with the set object made from "phrase".

set(letters).intersection(set(phrase))

And, finally, the result of the intersection is returned to the calling code, thanks to the `return` statement:

return set(letters).intersection(set(phrase))

nd the results
ck to the
lling code.

Creating Another Function, 3 of 3

All that remains is **Step 4**, where we add a docstring to our newly created function. To do this, add a triple-quoted string right after your new function's `def` line. Here's what we used (as comments go it's terse, but effective):

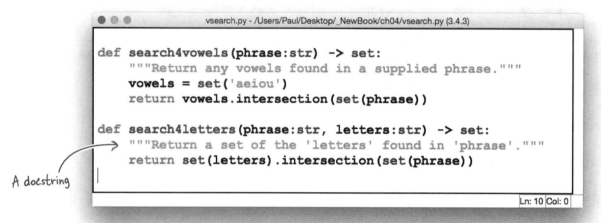

```
def search4vowels(phrase:str) -> set:
    """Return any vowels found in a supplied phrase."""
    vowels = set('aeiou')
    return vowels.intersection(set(phrase))

def search4letters(phrase:str, letters:str) -> set:
    """Return a set of the 'letters' found in 'phrase'."""
    return set(letters).intersection(set(phrase))
```

A docstring

And with that, our four steps are complete and `search4letters` is ready to be tested.

Why go to all the trouble of creating a one-line function? Isn't it better to just copy and paste that line of code whenever you need it?

Functions can hide complexity, too.

It *is* correct to observe that we've just created a one-line function, which may not feel like much of a "savings." However, note that our function contains a complex single line of code, which we are hiding from the users of this function, and this can be a very worthwhile practice (not to mention, way better than all that copying and pasting).

For instance, most programmers would be able to guess what `search4letters` does if they were to come across an invocation of it in a program. However, if they came across that complex single line of code in a program, they may well scratch their heads and wonder what it does. So, even though `search4letters` is "short," it's still a good idea to abstract this type of complexity inside a function.

TEST DRIVE

Save the `vsearch.py` file once more, and then press F5 to try out the `search4letters` function:

```
●  ●  ●                          Python 3.4.3 Shell
>>> =============================== RESTART ===============================
>>>
>>> help(search4letters)                                    Use the "help" BIF
Help on function search4letters in module __main__:  ←     to learn how to use
                                                           "search4letters".
search4letters(phrase:str, letters:str) -> set
    Return a set of the 'letters' found in 'phrase'.

>>> search4letters('hitch-hiker', 'aeiou')
{'e', 'i'}                                                 All of these
>>> search4letters('galaxy', 'xyz')               ←─       examples
{'x', 'y'}                                                 produce what
>>> search4letters('life, the universe, and everything', 'o')  we expect them
set()                                                      to.
>>> |
                                                        Ln: 78  Col: 4
```

The `search4letters` function is now more generic than `search4vowels`, in that it takes *any* set of letters and searches a given phrase for them, rather than just searching for the letters a, e, i, o, and u. This makes our new function much more useful than `search4vowels`. Let's now imagine that we have a large, existing codebase that has used `search4vowels` extensively. A decision has been made to retire `search4vowels` and replace it with `search4letters`, as the "powers that be" don't see the need for both functions, now that `search4letters` can do what `search4vowels` does. A global search-and-replace of your codebase for the name "search4vowels" with "search4letters" won't work here, as you'll need to add in that second argument value, which is always going to be `aeiou` when simulating the behavior of `search4vowels` with `search4letters`. So, for instance, this single-argument call:

> `search4vowels("Don't panic!")`

now needs to be replaced with this dual-argument one (which is a much harder edit to automate):

> `search4letters("Don't panic!", 'aeiou')`

It would be nice if we could somehow specify a *default value* for `search4letters`'s second argument, then have the function use it if no alternative value is provided. If we could arrange to set the default to `aeiou`, we'd then be able to apply a global search-and-replace (which is an easy edit).

> Wouldn't it be dreamy if Python let me specify default values? But I know it's just a fantasy...

169

Specifying Default Values for Arguments

Any argument to a Python function can be assigned a default value, which can then be automatically used if the code calling the function fails to supply an alternate value. The mechanism for assigning a default value to an argument is straightforward: include the default value as an assignment in the function's `def` line.

Here's `search4letters`'s current `def` line:

```
def search4letters(phrase:str, letters:str) -> set:
```

This version of our function's `def` line (above) expects *exactly* two arguments, one for `phrase` and another for `letters`. However, if we assign a default value to `letters`, the function's `def` line changes to look like this:

```
def search4letters(phrase:str, letters:str='aeiou') -> set:
```

We can continue to use the `search4letters` function in the same way as before: providing both arguments with values as needed. However, if we forget to supply the second argument (`letters`), the interpreter will substitute in the value `aeiou` on our behalf.

A default value has been assigned to the "letters" argument and will be used whenever the calling code doesn't provide an alterr value.

If we were to make this change to our code in the `vsearch.py` file (and save it), we could then invoke our functions as follows:

```
>>> search4letters('life, the universe, and everything')
{'a', 'e', 'i', 'u'}
>>> search4letters('life, the universe, and everything', 'aeio
{'a', 'e', 'i', 'u'}
>>> search4vowels('life, the universe, and everything')
{'a', 'e', 'i', 'u'}
```

These three function calls all produce the same results.

In this invocation, we are calling "search4vowels", not "search4letters".

Not only do these function calls produce the same output, they also demonstrate that the `search4vowels` function is no longer needed now that the `letters` argument to `search4letters` supports a default value (compare the first and last invocations above).

Now, if we are asked to retire the `search4vowels` function and replace all invocations of it within our codebase with `search4letters`, our exploitation of the default value mechanism for function arguments lets us do so with a simple global search-and-replace. And we don't have to use `search4letters` to only search for vowels. That second argument allows us to specify *any* set of characters to look for. As a consequence, `search4letters` is now more generic, *and* more useful.

Positional Versus Keyword Assignment

As we've just seen, the search4letters function can be invoked with either one or two arguments, the second argument being optional. If you provide only one argument, the letters argument defaults to a string of vowels. Take another look at the function's def line:

Our function's "def" line ——

```
def search4letters(phrase:str, letters:str='aeiou') -> set:
```

As well as supporting default arguments, the Python interpreter also lets you invoke a function using **keyword arguments**. To understand what a keyword argument is, consider how we've invoked search4letters up until now, for example:

```
search4letters('galaxy', 'xyz')
```

```
def search4letters(phrase:str, letters:str='aeiou') -> set:
```

In the above invocation, the two strings are assigned to the phrase and letters arguments based on their position. That is, the first string is assigned to phrase, while the second is assigned to letters. This is known as **positional assignment**, as it's based on the order of the arguments.

In Python, it is also possible to refer to arguments by their argument name, and when you do, positional ordering no longer applies. This is known as **keyword assignment**. To use keywords, assign each string *in any order* to its correct argument name when invoking the function, as shown here:

The ordering of the arguments isn't important when keyword arguments are used during invocation.

```
search4letters(letters='xyz', phrase='galaxy')
```

```
def search4letters(phrase:str, letters:str='aeiou') -> set:
```

Both invocations of the search4letters function on this page produce the same result: a set containing the letters y and z. Although it may be hard to appreciate the benefit of using keyword arguments with our small search4letters function, the flexibility this feature gives you becomes clear when you invoke a function that accepts many arguments. We'll see an example of one such function (provided by the standard library) before the end of this chapter.

Updating What We Know About Functions

Let's update what you know about functions now that you've spent some time exploring how function arguments work:

 **BULLET POINTS**

- As well as supporting code reuse, functions can hide complexity. If you have a complex line of code you intend to use a lot, abstract it behind a simple function call.

- Any function argument can be assigned a default value in the function's `def` line. When this happens, the specification of a value for that argument during a function's invocation is optional.

- As well as assigning arguments by position, you can use keywords, too. When you do, any ordering is acceptable (as any possibility of ambiguity is removed by the use of keywords and position doesn't matter anymore).

These functions really hit the mark for me. How do I go about using and sharing them?

There's more than one way to do it.

Now that you have some code that's worth sharing, it is reasonable to ask how best to use and share these functions. As with most things, there's more than one answer to that question. However, on the next pages, you'll learn how best to package and distribute your functions to ensure it's easy for you and others to benefit from your work.

module

Functions Beget Modules

Having gone to all the trouble of creating a reusable function (or two, as is the case with the functions currently in our `vsearch.py` file), it is reasonable to ask: *what's the best way to share functions?*

It is possible to share any function by copying and pasting it throughout your codebase where needed, but as that's such a wasteful and bad idea, we aren't going to consider it for very much longer. Having multiple copies of the same function littering your codebase is a sure-fire recipe for disaster (should you ever decide to change how your function works). It's much better to create a **module** that contains a single, canonical copy of any functions you want to share. Which raises another question: *how are modules created in Python?*

The answer couldn't be simpler: a module is any file that contains functions. Happily, this means that `vsearch.py` is *already* a module. Here it is again, in all its module glory:

Share your functions in modules.

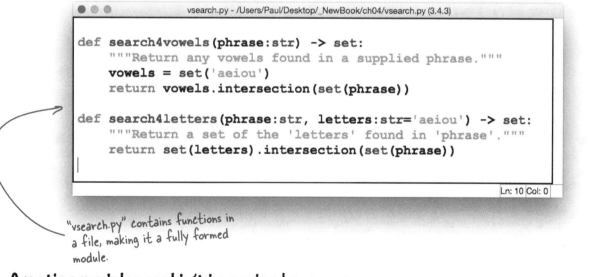

```
vsearch.py - /Users/Paul/Desktop/_NewBook/ch04/vsearch.py (3.4.3)

def search4vowels(phrase:str) -> set:
    """Return any vowels found in a supplied phrase."""
    vowels = set('aeiou')
    return vowels.intersection(set(phrase))

def search4letters(phrase:str, letters:str='aeiou') -> set:
    """Return a set of the 'letters' found in 'phrase'."""
    return set(letters).intersection(set(phrase))

                                                        Ln: 10 Col: 0
```

"vsearch.py" contains functions in a file, making it a fully formed module.

Creating modules couldn't be easier, however...

Creating modules is a piece of cake: simply create a file of the functions you want to share.

Once your module exists, making its contents available to your programs is also straightforward: all you have to do is import the module using Python's `import` statement.

This in itself is not complex. However, the interpreter makes the assumption that the module in question is in the **search path**, and ensuring this is the case can be tricky. Let's explore the ins and outs of module importation over the next few pages.

How Are Modules Found?

Recall from this book's first chapter how we imported and then used the
`randint` function from the `random` module, which comes included as part
of Python's standard library. Here's what we did at the shell:

module

```
>>> import random
>>> random.randint(0, 255)
42
```

Identify the module to import, then...

...invoke one of the module's functions.

What happens during module importation is described in great detail in the
Python documentation, which you are free to go and explore if the nitty-
gritty details float your boat. However, all you really need to know are the
three main locations the interpreter searches when looking for a module.
These are:

 Your current working directory
This is the folder that the interpreter thinks you are currently
working in.

 Your interpreter's site-packages locations
These are the directories that contain any third-party Python
modules you may have installed (including any written by you).

 The standard library locations
These are the directories that contains all the modules that make up
the standard library.

The order in which locations 2 and 3 are searched by the interpreter can vary
depending on many factors. But don't worry: it is not important that you
know how this searching mechanism works. What *is* important to understand
is that the interpreter always searches your current working directory *first*,
which is what can cause trouble when you're working with your own custom
modules.

To demonstrate what can go wrong, let's run though a small exercise that is
designed to highlight the issue. Here's what you need to do before we begin:

Geek Bits

Depending on the operating
system you're running, the
name given to a location
that holds files may be either
directory or **folder**. We'll use
"folder" in this book, except
when we discuss the *current
working directory* (which is a
well-established term).

☐ Create a folder called `mymodules`, which we'll use to store your modules. It
doesn't matter where in your filesystem you create this folder; just make sure it
is somewhere where you have read/write access.

☐ Move your `vsearch.py` file into your newly created `mymodules` folder.
This file should be the only copy of the `vsearch.py` file on your computer.

module

Running Python from the Command Line

We're going to run the Python interpreter from your operating system's command line (or terminal) to demonstrate what can go wrong here (even though the problem we are about to discuss also manifests in IDLE).

If you are running any version of *Windows*, open up a command prompt and follow along with this session. If you are not on *Windows*, we discuss your platform halfway down the next page (but read on for now anyway). You can invoke the Python interpreter (outside of IDLE) by typing **py -3** at the *Windows* C:\> prompt. Note below how prior to invoking the interpreter, we use the cd command to make the mymodules folder our current working directory. Also, observe that we can exit the interpreter at any time by typing quit() at the >>> prompt:

Change into the "mymodules" folder.

Start Python 3.

Import the module.

Use the module's functions.

the Python reter and return ur operating n's command prompt.

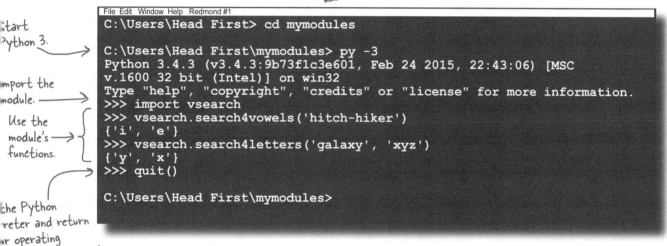

```
File  Edit  Window  Help  Redmond #1
C:\Users\Head First> cd mymodules

C:\Users\Head First\mymodules> py -3
Python 3.4.3 (v3.4.3:9b73f1c3e601, Feb 24 2015, 22:43:06) [MSC
v.1600 32 bit (Intel)] on win32
Type "help", "copyright", "credits" or "license" for more information.
>>> import vsearch
>>> vsearch.search4vowels('hitch-hiker')
{'i', 'e'}
>>> vsearch.search4letters('galaxy', 'xyz')
{'y', 'x'}
>>> quit()

C:\Users\Head First\mymodules>
```

This works as expected: we successfully import the vsearch module, then use each of its functions by prefixing the function name with the name of its module and a dot. Note how the behavior of the >>> prompt at the command line is identical to the behavior within IDLE (the only difference is the lack of syntax highlighting). It's the same Python interpreter, after all.

Although this interaction with the interpreter was successful, it only worked because we started off in a folder that contained the vsearch.py file. Doing this makes this folder the current working directory. Based on how the interpreter searches for modules, we know that the current working directory is searched first, so it shouldn't surprise us that this interaction worked and that the interpreter found our module.

But what happens if our module isn't in the current working directory?

Not Found Modules Produce ImportErrors

module

Repeat the exercise from the last page, after moving out of the folder that contains our module. Let's see what happens when we try to import our module now. Here is another interaction with the *Windows* command prompt:

> Change to another folder (in this case, we are moving to the top-level folder).

> Start Python 3 again.

> Try to import the module...

> ...but this time we get an error!

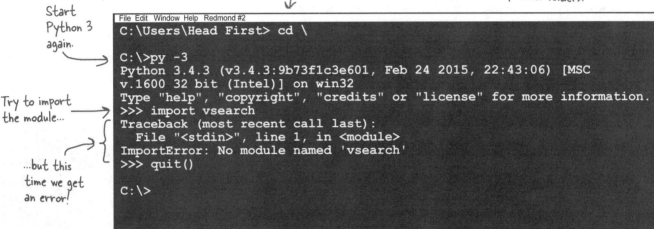

```
File Edit  Window Help  Redmond #2
C:\Users\Head First> cd \

C:\>py -3
Python 3.4.3 (v3.4.3:9b73f1c3e601, Feb 24 2015, 22:43:06) [MSC
v.1600 32 bit (Intel)] on win32
Type "help", "copyright", "credits" or "license" for more information.
>>> import vsearch
Traceback (most recent call last):
  File "<stdin>", line 1, in <module>
ImportError: No module named 'vsearch'
>>> quit()

C:\>
```

The vsearch.py file is no longer in the interpreter's current working directory, as we are now working in a folder other than mymodules. This means our module file can't be found, which in turn means we can't import it—hence the ImportError from the interpreter.

If we try the same exercise on a platform other than *Windows*, we get the same results (whether we're on *Linux*, *Unix*, or *Mac OS X*). Here's the above interaction with the interpreter from within the mymodules folder on *OS X*:

> Change into the folder and then type "python3" to start the interpreter.

> Import the module.

> It works: we can use the module's functions.

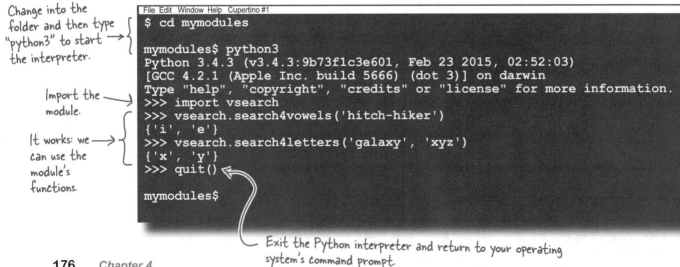

```
File Edit  Window Help  Cupertino #1
$ cd mymodules

mymodules$ python3
Python 3.4.3 (v3.4.3:9b73f1c3e601, Feb 23 2015, 02:52:03)
[GCC 4.2.1 (Apple Inc. build 5666) (dot 3)] on darwin
Type "help", "copyright", "credits" or "license" for more information.
>>> import vsearch
>>> vsearch.search4vowels('hitch-hiker')
{'i', 'e'}
>>> vsearch.search4letters('galaxy', 'xyz')
{'x', 'y'}
>>> quit()

mymodules$
```

> Exit the Python interpreter and return to your operating system's command prompt.

ImportErrors Occur No Matter the Platform

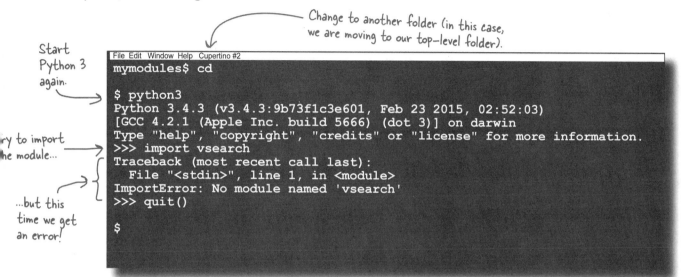

module

If you think running on a non-*Windows* platform will somehow fix this import issue we saw on that platform, think again: the same `ImportError` occurs on UNIX-like systems, once we change to another folder:

Change to another folder (in this case, we are moving to our top-level folder).

Start Python 3 again.

try to import the module...

...but this time we get an error!

```
File  Edit  Window  Help  Cupertino #2
mymodules$ cd

$ python3
Python 3.4.3 (v3.4.3:9b73f1c3e601, Feb 23 2015, 02:52:03)
[GCC 4.2.1 (Apple Inc. build 5666) (dot 3)] on darwin
Type "help", "copyright", "credits" or "license" for more information.
>>> import vsearch
Traceback (most recent call last):
  File "<stdin>", line 1, in <module>
ImportError: No module named 'vsearch'
>>> quit()

$
```

As was the case when we were working on *Windows*, the `vsearch.py` file is no longer in the interpreter's current working directory, as we are now working in a folder other than `mymodules`. This means our module file can't be found, which in turn means we can't import it—hence the `ImportError` from the interpreter. This problem presents no matter which platform you're running Python on.

there are no Dumb Questions

Q: Can't we be location specific and say something like `import C:\mymodules\vsearch` on Windows platforms, or perhaps `import /mymodules/vsearch` on UNIX-like systems?

A: No, you can't. Granted, doing something like that does sound tempting, but ultimately won't work, as you can't use paths in this way with Python's `import` statement. And, anyway, the last thing you'll want to do is put hardcoded paths into any of your programs, as paths can often change (for a whole host of reasons). It is best to avoid hardcoding paths in your code, if at all possible.

Q: If I can't use paths, how can I arrange for the interpreter to find my modules?

A: If the interpreter can't find your module in the current working directory, it looks in the **site-packages** locations as well as in the standard library (and there's more about site-packages on the next page). If you can arrange to add your module to one of the **site-packages** locations, the interpreter can then find it there (no matter its path).

Getting a Module into Site-packages

module

Recall what we had to say about **site-packages** a few pages back when we introduced them as the second of three locations searched by the interpreter's import mechanism:

 Your interpreter's site-packages locations
These are the directories that contain any third-party Python modules which you may have installed (including any written by you).

As the provision and support of third-party modules is central to Python's code reuse strategy, it should come as no surprise that the interpreter comes with the built-in ability to add modules to your Python setup.

Note that the set of modules included with the standard library is managed by the Python core developers, and this large collection of modules has been designed to be widely used, but not tampered with. Specifically, don't add or remove your own modules to/from the standard library. However, adding or removing modules to your site-packages locations is positively encouraged, so much so that Python comes with some tools to make it straightforward.

Using "setuptools" to install into site-packages

As of release 3.4 of Python, the standard library includes a module called `setuptools`, which can be used to add any module into site-packages. Although the details of module distribution can—initially—appear complex, all we want to do here is install `vsearch` into site-packages, which is something `setuptools` is more than capable of doing in three steps:

> **Python 3.4 (or newer) makes using setuptools a breeze. If you aren't running 3.4 (or newer), consider upgrading.**

 Create a distribution description
This identifies the module we want `setuptools` to install.

 Generate a distribution file
Using Python at the command line, we'll create a shareable distribution file to contain our module's code.

 Install the distribution file
Again, using Python at the command line, install the distribution file (which includes our module) into site-packages.

Step 1 requires us to create (at a minimum) two descriptive files for our module: `setup.py` and `README.txt`. Let's see what's involved.

Creating the Required Setup Files

If we follow the three steps shown at the bottom of the last page, we'll end up creating a **distribution package** for our module. This package is a single compressed file that contains everything required to install our module into site-packages.

For Step 1, *Create a distribution description*, we need to create two files that we'll place in the same folder as our vsearch.py file. We'll do this no matter what platform we're running on. The first file, which must be called setup. py, describes our module in some detail.

Find below the setup.py file we created to describe the module in the vsearch.py file. It contains two lines of Python code: the first line imports the setup function from the setuptools module, while the second invokes the setup function.

The setup function accepts a large number of arguments, many of which are optional. Note how, for readability purposes, our call to setup is spread over nine lines. We're taking advantage of Python's support for keyword arguments to clearly indicate which value is being assigned to which argument in this call. The most important arguments are highlighted; the first names the distribution, while the second lists the .py files to include when creating the distribution package:

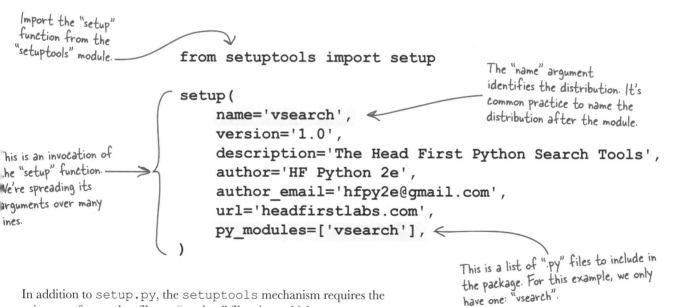

Import the "setup" function from the "setuptools" module.

```
from setuptools import setup

setup(
    name='vsearch',
    version='1.0',
    description='The Head First Python Search Tools',
    author='HF Python 2e',
    author_email='hfpy2e@gmail.com',
    url='headfirstlabs.com',
    py_modules=['vsearch'],
)
```

This is an invocation of the "setup" function. We're spreading its arguments over many lines.

The "name" argument identifies the distribution. It's common practice to name the distribution after the module.

This is a list of ".py" files to include in the package. For this example, we only have one: "vsearch".

In addition to setup.py, the setuptools mechanism requires the existence of one other file—a "readme" file—into which you can put a textual description of your package. Although having this file is required, its contents are optional, so (for now) you can create an empty file called README.txt in the same folder as the setup.py file. This is enough to satisfy the requirement for a second file in Step 1.

Create a distribution description.

Generate a distribution file.

Install the distribution file.

We'll check off each completed step as we work through this material.

Creating the Distribution File

At this stage, you should have three files, which we have put in our mymodules folder: vsearch.py, setup.py, and README.txt.

We're now ready to create a distribution package from these files. This is Step 2 from our earlier list: *Generate a distribution file*. We'll do this at the command line. Although doing so is straightforward, this step requires that different commands be entered based on whether you are on *Windows* or on one of the UNIX-like operating systems (*Linux*, *Unix*, or *Mac OS X*).

> ☑ Create a distribution description.
> ☐ Generate a distribution file.
> ☐ Install the distribution file.

Creating a distribution file on Windows

If you are running on *Windows*, open a command prompt in the folder that contains your three files, then enter this command:

Run Python 3 on Windows.

```
C:\Users\Head First\mymodules> py -3 setup.py sdist
```

Execute the code in "setup.py"...

... and pass "sdist" as an argument.

The Python interpreter goes to work immediately after you issue this command. A large number of messages appear on screen (which we show here in an abridged form):

```
running sdist
running egg_info
creating vsearch.egg-info
    . . .
creating dist
creating 'dist\vsearch-1.0.zip' and adding 'vsearch-1.0' to it
adding 'vsearch-1.0\PKG-INFO'
adding 'vsearch-1.0\README.txt'
    . . .
adding 'vsearch-1.0\vsearch.egg-info\top_level.txt'
removing 'vsearch-1.0' (and everything under it)
```

If you see this message, all is well. If you get errors, check that you're running at least Python 3.4, and also make sure your "setup.py" file is identical to ours.

When the *Windows* command prompt reappears, your three files have been combined into a single **distribution file**. This is an installable file that contains the source code for your module and, in this case, is called vsearch-1.0.zip.

You'll find your newly created ZIP file in a folder called dist, which has also been created by setuptools under the folder you are working in (which is mymodules in our case).

Distribution Files on UNIX-like OSes

☑ Create a distribution description.

☐ Generate a distribution file.

☐ Install the distribution file.

If you are not working on *Windows*, you can create a distribution file in much the same way as on the previous page. With the three files (`setup.py`, `README.txt`, and `vsearch.py`) in a folder, issue this command at your operating system's command line:

Run Python 3.

```
mymodules$ python3 setup.py sdist
```

Execute the code in "setup.py"...

...and pass "sdist" as an argument.

Like on *Windows*, this command produces a slew of messages on screen:

```
running sdist
running egg_info
creating vsearch.egg-info
        . . .
running check
creating vsearch-1.0
creating vsearch-1.0/vsearch.egg-info
        . . .
creating dist
Creating tar archive
removing 'vsearch-1.0' (and everything under it)
```

The messages differ slightly from those produced on Windows. If you see this message, all is well. If not (as with Windows) double-check everything.

When your operating system's command line reappears, your three files have been combined into a **source distribution** file (hence the `sdist` argument above). This is an installable file that contains the source code for your module and, in this case, is called `vsearch-1.0.tar.gz`.

You'll find your newly created archive file in a folder called `dist`, which has also been created by `setuptools` under the folder you are working in (which is `mymodules` in our case).

With your source distribution file created (as a ZIP or as a compressed tar archive), you're now ready to install your module into site-packages.

Installing Packages with "pip"

☑	Create a distribution description.
☑	Generate a distribution file.
☐	Install the distribution file.

Now that your distribution file exists as a ZIP or a tarred archive (depending on your platform), it's time for Step 3: *Install the distribution file*. As with many such things, Python comes with the tools to make this straightforward. In particular, Python 3.4 (and newer) includes a tool called pip, which is *the* **P**ackage **I**nstaller for **P**ython.

Step 3 on Windows

Locate your newly created ZIP file under the dist folder (recall that the file is called vsearch-1.0.zip). While in the *Windows Explorer*, hold down the Shift key, then right-click your mouse to bring up a context-sensitive menu. Select *Open command window here* from this menu. A new *Windows* command prompt opens. At this command prompt, type this line to complete Step 3:

Run Python 3 with the module pip, and then ask pip to install the identified ZIP file.

```
C:\Users\...\dist> py -3 -m pip install vsearch-1.0.zip
```

If this command fails with a permissions error, you may need to restart the command prompt as the *Windows* administrator, then try again.

When the above command succeeds, the following messages appear on screen:

```
Processing c:\users\...\dist\vsearch-1.0.zip
Installing collected packages: vsearch
  Running setup.py install for vsearch
Successfully installed vsearch-1.0
```

Success!

Step 3 on UNIX-like OSes

Run Python 3 with the module pip, and then ask pip to install the identified compressed tar file.

On *Linux*, *Unix*, or *Mac OS X*, open a terminal within the newly created dict folder, and then issue this command at the prompt:

```
.../dist$ sudo python3 -m pip install vsearch-1.0.tar.gz
```

When the above command succeeds, the following messages appear on screen:

```
Processing ./vsearch-1.0.tar.gz
Installing collected packages: vsearch
  Running setup.py install for vsearch
Successfully installed vsearch-1.0
```

Success!

We are using the "sudo" command here to ensure we install with the correct permissions.

The vsearch module is now installed as part of site-packages.

Modules: What We Know Already

Now that our `vsearch` module has been installed, we can use `import vsearch` in any of our programs, safe in the knowledge that the interpreter can now find the module's functions when needed.

If we later decide to update any of the module's code, we can repeat these three steps to install any update into site-packages. If you do produce a new version of your module, be sure to assign a new version number within the `setup.py` file.

Let's take a moment to summarize what we now know about modules:

- ☑ Create a distribution description.
- ☑ Generate a distribution file.
- ☑ Install the distribution file.

All done!

> ### BULLET POINTS
>
> - A module is one or more functions saved in a file.
>
> - You can share a module by ensuring it is always available with the interpreter's *current working directory* (which is possible, but brittle) or within the interpreter's *site-packages locations* (by far the better choice).
>
> - Following the `setuptools` three-step process ensures that your module is installed into *site-packages*, which allows you to `import` the module and use its functions no matter what your *current working directory* happens to be.

Giving your code away (a.k.a. sharing)

Now that you have a distribution file created, you can share this file with other Python programmers, allowing them to install your module using `pip`, too. You can share your file in one of two ways: informally, or formally.

To share your module informally, simply distribute it in whatever way you wish and to whomever you wish (perhaps using email, a USB stick, or via a download from your personal website). It's up to you, really.

To share your module formally, you can upload your distribution file to Python's centrally managed web-based software repository, called PyPI (pronounced "pie-pee-eye," and short for the *Python Package Index*). This site exists to allow all manner of Python programmers to share all manner of third-party Python modules. To learn more about what's on offer, visit the PyPI site at: ***https://pypi.python.org/pypi***. To learn more about the process of uploading and sharing your distribution files through PyPI, read the online guide maintained by the *Python Packaging Authority*, which you'll find here: ***https://www.pypa.io***. (There's not much to it, but the details are beyond the scope of this book.)

We are nearly done with our introduction to functions and modules. There's just a small mystery that needs our attention (for not more than five minutes). Flip the page when you're ready.

Any Python programmer can also use pip to install your module.

The case of the misbehaving function arguments

Tom and Sarah have just worked through this chapter, and are now arguing over the behavior of function arguments.

Tom is convinced that when arguments are passed into a function, the data is passed **by value**, and he's written a small function called `double` to help make his case. Tom's `double` function works with any type of data provided to it.

Here's Tom's code:

Five Minute Mystery

```
def double(arg):
    print('Before: ', arg)
    arg = arg * 2
    print('After:  ', arg)
```

Sarah, on the other hand, is convinced that when arguments are passed into a function, the data is passed **by reference**. Sarah has also written a small function, called `change`, which works with lists and helps to prove her point.

Here's a copy of Sarah's code:

```
def change(arg):
    print('Before: ', arg)
    arg.append('More data')
    print('After:  ', arg)
```

We'd rather nobody was arguing about this type of thing, as—until now— Tom and Sarah have been the best of programming buddies. To help resolve this, let's experiment at the >>> prompt in an attempt to see who is right: "by value" Tom, or "by reference" Sarah. They can't both be right, can they? It's certainly a bit of a mystery that needs solving, which leads to this often-asked question:

Do function arguments support by-value or by-reference call semantics in Python?

Geek Bits

In case you need a quick refresher, note that **by-value argument passing** refers to the practice of using the value of a variable in place of a function's argument. If the value changes in the function's suite, it has no effect on the value of the variable in the code that called the function. Think of the argument as a *copy* of the original variable's value. **By-reference argument passing** (sometimes referred to as **by-address argument passing**) maintains a link to the variable in the code that called the function. If the variable in the function's suite is changed, the value in the code that called the function changes, too. Think of the argument as an *alias* to the original variable.

Demonstrating Call-by-Value Semantics

To work out what Tom and Sarah are arguing about, let's put their functions into their very own module, which we'll call `mystery.py`. Here's the module in an IDLE edit window:

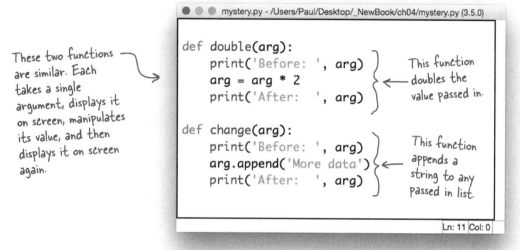

These two functions are similar. Each takes a single argument, displays it on screen, manipulates its value, and then displays it on screen again.

```
mystery.py - /Users/Paul/Desktop/_NewBook/ch04/mystery.py (3.5.0)

def double(arg):
    print('Before: ', arg)
    arg = arg * 2
    print('After:  ', arg)

def change(arg):
    print('Before: ', arg)
    arg.append('More data')
    print('After:  ', arg)
```

This function doubles the value passed in.

This function appends a string to any passed in list.

Ln: 11 Col: 0

As soon as Tom sees this module on screen, he sits down, takes control of the keyboard, presses F5, and then types the following into IDLE's >>> prompt. Once done, Tom leans back in his chair, crosses his arms, and says: "See? I told you it's call-by-value." Take a look at Tom's shell interactions with his function:

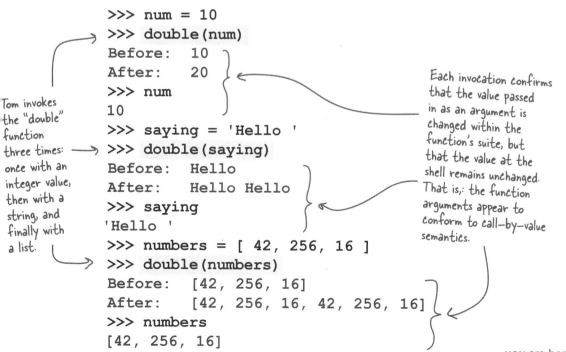

```
>>> num = 10
>>> double(num)
Before:   10
After:    20
>>> num
10
>>> saying = 'Hello '
>>> double(saying)
Before:   Hello
After:    Hello Hello
>>> saying
'Hello '
>>> numbers = [ 42, 256, 16 ]
>>> double(numbers)
Before:   [42, 256, 16]
After:    [42, 256, 16, 42, 256, 16]
>>> numbers
[42, 256, 16]
```

Tom invokes the "double" function three times: once with an integer value, then with a string, and finally with a list.

Each invocation confirms that the value passed in as an argument is changed within the function's suite, but that the value at the shell remains unchanged. That is,: the function arguments appear to conform to call–by–value semantics.

Demonstrating Call-by-Reference Semantics

Undeterred by Tom's apparent slam-dunk, Sarah sits down and takes control of the keyboard in preparation for interacting with the shell. Here's the code in the IDLE edit window once more, with Sarah's `change` function ready for action:

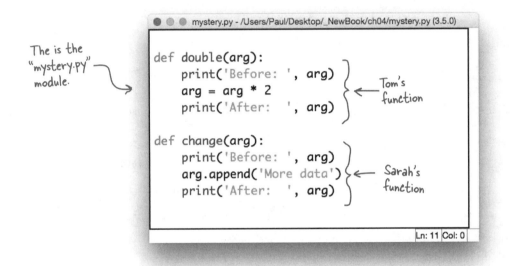

The is the "mystery.py" module.

```python
def double(arg):
    print('Before: ', arg)
    arg = arg * 2
    print('After:  ', arg)
```
Tom's function

```python
def change(arg):
    print('Before: ', arg)
    arg.append('More data')
    print('After:  ', arg)
```
Sarah's function

Ln: 11 Col: 0

Sarah types a few lines of code into the >>> prompt, then leans back in her chair, crosses her arms, and says to Tom: "Well, if Python only supports call-by-value, how do you explain this behavior?" Tom is speechless.

Take a look at Sarah's interaction with the shell:

```
>>> numbers = [ 42, 256, 16 ]
>>> change(numbers)
Before:  [42, 256, 16]
After:   [42, 256, 16, 'More data']
>>> numbers
[42, 256, 16, 'More data']
```

Using the same list data as Tom, Sarah invokes her "change" function.

Look what's happened! This time the argument's value has been changed in the function as well as at the shell. This would seem to suggest that Python functions *also* support call-by-reference semantics.

This *is* strange behavior.

Tom's function clearly shows call-by-value argument semantics, whereas Sarah's function demonstrates call-by-reference.

How can this be? What's going on here? Does Python support *both*?

Solved: the case of the misbehaving function arguments

Do Python function arguments support by-value or by-reference call semantics?

Here's the kicker: both Tom *and* Sarah are right. Depending on the situation, Python's function argument semantics support **both** call-by-value *and* call-by-reference.

Recall once again that variables in Python aren't variables as we are used to thinking about them in other programming languages; variables are **object references**. It is useful to think of the value stored in the variable as being the memory address of the value, not its actual value. It's this memory address that's passed into a function, not the actual value. This means that Python's functions support what's more correctly called *by-object-reference call semantics*.

Based on the type of the object referred to, the actual call semantics that apply at any point in time can differ. So, how come in Tom's and Sarah's functions the arguments appeared to conform to by-value and by-reference call semantics? First off, they didn't—they only appeared to. What actually happens is that the interpreter looks at the type of the value referred to by the object reference (the memory address) and, if the variable refers to a **mutable** value, call-by-reference semantics apply. If the type of the data referred to is **immutable**, call-by-value semantics kick in. Consider now what this means for our data.

Lists, dictionaries, and sets (being mutable) are always passed into a function by reference—any changes made to the variable's data structure within the function's suite are reflected in the calling code. The data is mutable, after all.

Strings, integers, and tuples (being immutable) are always passed into a function by value—any changes to the variable within the function are private to the function and are not reflected in the calling code. As the data is immutable, it cannot change.

Which all makes sense until you consider this line of code:

```
arg = arg * 2
```

How come this line of code appeared to change a passed-in list within the function's suite, but when the list was displayed in the shell after invocation, the list hadn't changed (leading Tom to believe—incorrectly—that all argument passing conformed to call-by-value)? On the face of things, this looks like a bug in the interpreter, as we've just stated that changes to a mutable value are reflected back in the calling code, but they aren't here. That is, Tom's function *didn't* change the numbers list in the calling code, even though lists are mutable. So, what gives?

To understand what has happened here, consider that the above line of code is an **assignment statement**. Here's what happens during assignment: the code to the right of the = symbol is executed *first*, and then whatever value is created has its object reference assigned to the variable on the left of the = symbol. Executing the code arg * 2 creates a *new* value, which is assigned a *new* object reference, which is then assigned to the arg variable, overwriting the previous object reference stored in arg in the function's suite. However, the "old" object reference still exists in the calling code and its value hasn't changed, so the shell still sees the original list, not the new doubled list created in Tom's code. Contrast this behavior to Sarah's code, which calls the append method on an existing list. As there's no assignment here, there's no overwriting of object references, so Sarah's code changes the list in the shell, too, as both the list referred to in the functions' suite and the list referred to in the calling code have the *same* object reference.

With our mystery solved, we're nearly ready for Chapter 5. There's just one outstanding issue.

Can I Test for PEP 8 Compliance?

I have a quick question before we move on. I like the idea of writing PEP 8 compliant code...is there any way I can automatically check my code for compliance?

Yes. It is possible.

But not with Python alone, as the Python interpreter does not provide any way to check code for PEP 8 compliance. However, there are a number of third-party tools that do.

Before jumping into Chapter 5, let's take a little detour and look at one tool that can help you stay on the right side of PEP 8 compliance.

Getting Ready to Check PEP 8 Compliance

Let's detour for just a moment to check our code for PEP 8 compliance.

The Python programming community at large has spent a great deal of time creating developer tools to make the lives of Python programmers a little bit better. One such tool is **pytest**, which is a *testing framework* that is primarily designed to make the testing of Python programs easier. No matter what type of tests you're writing, **pytest** can help. And you can add plug-ins to **pytest** to extend its capabilities.

One such plug-in is **pep8**, which uses the **pytest** testing framework to check your code for violations of the PEP 8 guidelines.

Recalling our code

Let's remind ourselves of our `vsearch.py` code once more, before feeding it to the **pytest/pep8** combination to find out how PEP 8–compliant it is. Note that we'll need to install both of these developer tools, as they do not come installed with Python (we'll do that over the page).

One more, here is the code to the `vsearch.py` module, which is going to be checked for compliance to the PEP 8 guidelines:

Learn more about pytest from http://doc.pytest. org/en/latest/.

```python
def search4vowels(phrase:str) -> set:
    """Return any vowels found in a supplied phrase."""
    vowels = set('aeiou')
    return vowels.intersection(set(phrase))

def search4letters(phrase:str, letters:str='aeiou') -> set:
    """Return a set of the 'letters' found in 'phrase'."""
    return set(letters).intersection(set(phrase))
```

This code is in "vsearch.py".

Installing pytest and the pep8 plug-in

Earlier in this chapter, you used the `pip` tool to install your `vsearch.py` module into the Python interpreter on your computer. The `pip` tool can also be used to install third-party code into your interpreter.

To do so, you need to operate at your operating system's command prompt (and be connected to the Internet). You'll use `pip` in the next chapter to install a third-party library. For now, though, let's use `pip` to install the **pytest** testing framework and the **pep8** plug-in.

Install the Testing Developer Tools

In the example screens that follow, we are showing the messages that appear when you are running on the *Windows* platform. On *Windows*, you invoke Python 3 using the `py -3` command. If you are on *Linux* or *Mac OS X*, replace the *Windows* command with `sudo python3`. To install **pytest** using `pip` on *Windows*, issue this command from the command prompt while running as administrator (search for `cmd.exe`, then right-click on it, and choose *Run as Administrator* from the pop-up menu):

> **DETOUR**

`py  -3  -m  pip  install  pytest`

Start in
Administrator
mode...

...then issue the
"pip" command to
install "pytest"...

...then check
whether it
installed
successfully.

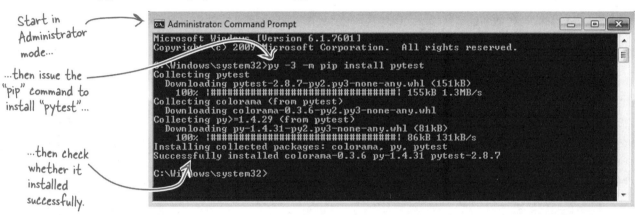

If you examine the messages produced by `pip`, you'll notice that two of **pytest**'s dependencies were also installed (**colorama** and **py**). The same thing happens when you use `pip` to install the **pep8** plug-in: it also installs a host of dependencies. Here's the command to install the plug-in:

Remember: if you aren't
running Windows, replace
"py -3" with "sudo python3".

`py  -3  -m  pip  install  pytest-pep8`

While still in
Administrator mode,
issue this command,
which installs the
"pep8" plug-in.

This command
succeeded too, and
also installed the
required dependencies.

How PEP 8-Compliant Is Our Code?

With **pytest** and **pep8** installed, you're now ready to test your code for PEP 8 compliance. Regardless of the operating system you're using, you'll issue the same command (as only the installation instructions differ on each platform).

The **pytest** installation process has installed a new program on your computer called `py.test`. Let's run this program now to check our `vsearch.py` code for PEP 8 compliance. Make sure you are in the same folder as the one that contains the `vsearch.py` file, then issue this command:

```
py.test --pep8 vsearch.py
```

Here's the output produced when we did this on our *Windows* computer:

Uh, oh. The red output can't be good, can it?

```
C:\Windows\system32\cmd.exe

E:\_NewBook\ch04>py.test --pep8 vsearch.py
=========================== test session starts ===========================
platform win32 -- Python 3.5.0, pytest-2.8.7, py-1.4.31, pluggy-0.3.1
rootdir: E:\_NewBook\ch04, inifile:
plugins: pep8-1.0.6
collected 1 items

vsearch.py F

================================ FAILURES ================================
_____ PEP8-check _____
E:\_NewBook\ch04\vsearch.py:2:25: E231 missing whitespace after ':'
def search4vowels(phrase:str) -> set:
                        ^
E:\_NewBook\ch04\vsearch.py:3:56: W291 trailing whitespace
    """Return any vowels found in a supplied phrase."""
                                                       ^
E:\_NewBook\ch04\vsearch.py:7:1: E302 expected 2 blank lines, found 1
def search4letters(phrase:str, letters:str='aeiou') -> set:
^
E:\_NewBook\ch04\vsearch.py:7:26: E231 missing whitespace after ':'
def search4letters(phrase:str, letters:str='aeiou') -> set:
                         ^
E:\_NewBook\ch04\vsearch.py:7:39: E231 missing whitespace after ':'
def search4letters(phrase:str, letters:str='aeiou') -> set:
                         ^
===================== 1 failed in 0.05 seconds =====================

E:\_NewBook\ch04>
```

Whoops! It looks like we have **failures**, which means this code is not as compliant with the PEP 8 guidelines as it could be.

Take a moment to read the messages shown here (or on your screen, if you are following along). All of the "failures" appear to refer—in some way—to *whitespace* (for instance, spaces, tabs, newlines, and the like). Let's take a look at each of them in a little more detail.

Understanding the Failure Messages

Together, **pytest** and the **pep8** plug-in have highlighted *five* issues with our vsearch.py code.

The first issue has to do with the fact that we haven't inserted a space after the : character when annotating our function's arguments, and we've done this in three places. Look at the first message, noting **pytest**'s use of the *caret* character (^) to indicate exactly where the problem is:

```
                    ...:2:25: E231 missing whitespace after ':'
        def search4vowels(phrase:str) -> set:
                                ^
```

Here's what's wrong.

Here's where it's wrong.

If you look at the two issues at the bottom of **pytest**'s output, you'll see that we've repeated this mistake in three locations: once on line 2, and twice on line 7. There's an easy fix: *add a single space character after the colon.*

The next issue may not seem like a big deal, but is raised as a failure because the line of code in question (line 3) does break a PEP 8 guideline that says not to include extra spaces at the end of lines:

```
                    ...:3:56: W291 trailing whitespace
        """Return any vowels found in a supplied phrase."""
                                        ^
```

What's wrong

Where it's wrong

Dealing with this issue on line 3 is another easy fix: *remove all trailing whitespace.*

The last issue (at the start of line 7) is this:

```
                    ...7:1: E302 expected 2 blank lines, found 1
        def search4letters(phrase:str, letters:str='aeiou') -> set:
        ^
```

This issue presents at the start of line 7.

Here's what's wrong.

There is a PEP 8 guideline that offers this advice for creating functions in a module: *Surround top-level function and class definitions with two blank lines.* In our code, the search4vowels and search4letters functions are both at the "top level" of the vsearch.py file, and are separated from each other by a single blank line. To be PEP 8–compliant, there should be *two* blank lines here.

Again, it's an easy fix: *insert an extra blank line between the two functions.* Let's apply these fixes now, then retest our amended code.

BTW: Check out http://pep8.org/ for a beautifully rendered version of Python's style guidelines.

Confirming PEP 8 Compliance

With the amendments made to the Python code in `vsearch.py`, the file's contents now look like this:

```python
def search4vowels(phrase: str) -> set:
    """Return any vowels found in a supplied phrase."""
    vowels = set('aeiou')
    return vowels.intersection(set(phrase))


def search4letters(phrase: str, letters: str='aeiou') -> set:
    """Return a set of the 'letters' found in 'phrase'."""
    return set(letters).intersection(set(phrase))
```

The PEP 8-compliant version of "vsearch.py".

When this version of the code is run through **pytest**'s **pep8** plug-in, the output confirms we no longer have any issues with PEP 8 compliance. Here's what we saw on our computer (again, running on *Windows*):

Green is good—this code has no PEP 8 issues. ☺

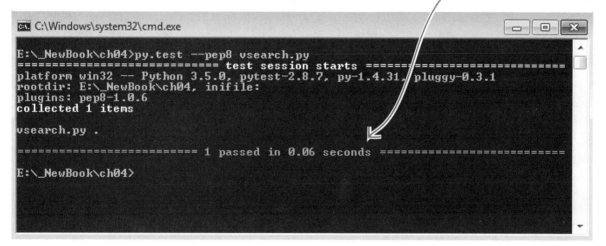

```
C:\Windows\system32\cmd.exe

E:\_NewBook\ch04>py.test --pep8 vsearch.py
============================ test session starts =============================
platform win32 -- Python 3.5.0, pytest-2.8.7, py-1.4.31, pluggy-0.3.1
rootdir: E:\_NewBook\ch04, inifile:
plugins: pep8-1.0.6
collected 1 items

vsearch.py .

========================= 1 passed in 0.06 seconds ==========================

E:\_NewBook\ch04>
```

Conformance to PEP 8 is a good thing

If you're looking at all of this wondering what all the fuss is about (especially over a little bit of whitespace), think carefully about why you'd want to comply to PEP 8. The PEP 8 documentation states that *readability counts*, and that code is *read much more often than it is written*. If your code conforms to a standard coding style, it follows that reading it is easier, as it "looks like" everything else the programmer has seen. Consistency is a very good thing.

From this point forward (and as much as is practical), all of the code in this book will conform to the PEP 8 guidelines. You should try to ensure your code does too.

This is the end of the pytest detour. See you in Chapter 5.

Chapter 4's Code

```python
def search4vowels(phrase: str) -> set:
    """Returns the set of vowels found in 'phrase'."""
    return set('aeiou').intersection(set(phrase))


def search4letters(phrase: str, letters: str='aeiou') -> set:
    """Returns the set of 'letters' found in 'phrase'."""
    return set(letters).intersection(set(phrase))
```

This is the code from the "vsearch.py" module, which contains our two functions: "search4vowels" and "search4letters".

This is the "setup.py" file, which allowed us to turn our module into an installable distribution.

```python
from setuptools import setup

setup(
    name='vsearch',
    version='1.0',
    description='The Head First Python Search Tools',
    author='HF Python 2e',
    author_email='hfpy2e@gmail.com',
    url='headfirstlabs.com',
    py_modules=['vsearch'],
)
```

```python
def double(arg):
    print('Before: ', arg)
    arg = arg * 2
    print('After:  ', arg)


def change(arg: list):
    print('Before: ', arg)
    arg.append('More data')
    print('After:  ', arg)
```

And this is the "mystery.py" module, which had Tom and Sarah upset at each other. Thankfully, now that the mystery is solved, they are back to being programming buddies once more. ☺

5 building a webapp

Getting Real

See? I told you getting Python into your brain wouldn't hurt a bit.

At this stage, you know enough Python to be dangerous.

With this book's first four chapters behind you, you're now in a position to productively use Python within any number of application areas (even though there's still lots of Python to learn). Rather than explore the long list of what these application areas are, in this and subsequent chapters, we're going to structure our learning around the development of a web-hosted application, which is an area where Python is especially strong. Along the way, you'll learn a bit more about Python. Before we get going, however, let's have a quick recap of the Python you already know.

Python: What You Already Know

Now that you've got four chapters under your belt, let's pause for a moment
and review the Python material presented so far.

BULLET POINTS

- IDLE, Python's built-in IDE, is used to experiment with and execute Python code, either as single-statement snippets or as larger multistatement programs written within IDLE's text editor. As well as using IDLE, you ran a file of Python code directly from your operating system's command line, using the `py -3` command (on Windows) or `python3` (on everything else).

- You've learned how Python supports single-value data items, such as integers and strings, as well as the booleans `True` and `False`.

- You've explored use cases for the four built-in data structures: lists, dictionaries, sets, and tuples. You know that you can create complex data structures by combining these four built-ins in any number of ways.

- You've used a collection of Python statements, including `if`, `elif`, `else`, `return`, `for`, `from`, and `import`.

- You know that Python provides a rich standard library, and you've seen the following modules in action: `datetime`, `random`, `sys`, `os`, `time`, `html`, `pprint`, `setuptools`, and `pip`.

- As well as the standard library, Python comes with a handy collection of built-in functions, known as the BIFs. Here are some of the BIFs you've worked with: `print`, `dir`, `help`, `range`, `list`, `len`, `input`, `sorted`, `dict`, `set`, `tuple`, and `type`.

- Python supports all the usual operators, and then some. Those you've already seen include: `in`, `not in`, `+`, `-`, `=` (assignment), `==` (equality), `+=`, and `*`.

- As well as supporting the square bracket notation for working with items in a sequence (i.e., `[ ]`), Python extends the notation to support **slices**, which allow you to specify **start**, **stop**, and **step** values.

- You've learned how to create your own custom functions in Python, using the `def` statement. Python functions can optionally accept any number of arguments as well as return a value.

- Although it's possible to enclose strings in either single or double quotes, the Python conventions (documented in **PEP 8**) suggest picking one style and sticking to it. For this book, we've decided to enclose all of our strings within single quotes, unless the string we're quoting itself contains a single quote character, in which case we'll use double quotes (as a one-off, special case).

- Triple-quoted strings are also supported, and you've seen how they are used to add docstrings to your custom functions.

- You learned that you can group related functions into modules. Modules form the basis of the code reuse mechanism in Python, and you've seen how the `pip` module (included in the standard library) lets you consistently manage your module installations.

- Speaking of things working in a consistent manner, you learned that in Python **everything is an object**, which ensures—as much as possible—that everything works just as you expect it to. This concept really pays off when you start to define your own custom objects using classes, which we'll show you how to do in a later chapter.

Let's Build Something

> OK. I'm convinced...I already know a bit about Python. That said, what's the plan? What are we going to do now?

Let's build a webapp.

Specifically, let's take our `search4letters` function and make it accessible over the Web, enabling anyone with a web browser to access the service provided by our function.

We could build any type of application, but building a working web application lets us explore a number of Python features while building something that's generally useful, as well as being a whole heap *meatier* than the code snippets you've seen so far in this book.

Python is particularly strong on the server side of the Web, which is where we're going to build and deploy our webapp in this chapter.

But, before we get going, let's make sure everyone is on the same page by reviewing how the Web works.

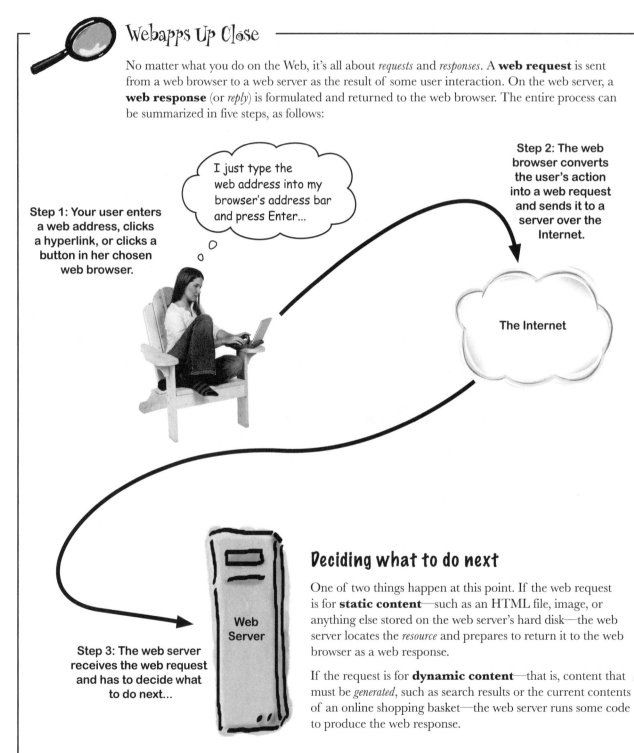

Webapps Up Close

No matter what you do on the Web, it's all about *requests* and *responses*. A **web request** is sent from a web browser to a web server as the result of some user interaction. On the web server, a **web response** (or *reply*) is formulated and returned to the web browser. The entire process can be summarized in five steps, as follows:

I just type the web address into my browser's address bar and press Enter...

Step 1: Your user enters a web address, clicks a hyperlink, or clicks a button in her chosen web browser.

Step 2: The web browser converts the user's action into a web request and sends it to a server over the Internet.

The Internet

Web Server

Step 3: The web server receives the web request and has to decide what to do next...

Deciding what to do next

One of two things happen at this point. If the web request is for **static content**—such as an HTML file, image, or anything else stored on the web server's hard disk—the web server locates the *resource* and prepares to return it to the web browser as a web response.

If the request is for **dynamic content**—that is, content that must be *generated*, such as search results or the current contents of an online shopping basket—the web server runs some code to produce the web response.

The (potentially) many substeps of Step 3

In practice, Step 3 can involve multiple substeps, depending on what the web server has to do to produce the response. Obviously, if all the server has to do is locate static content and return it to the browser, the substeps aren't too taxing, as it's just a matter of reading from the web server's disk drive.

However, when dynamic content must be generated, the substeps involve the web server running code and then capturing the output from the program as a web response, before sending the response back to the waiting web browser.

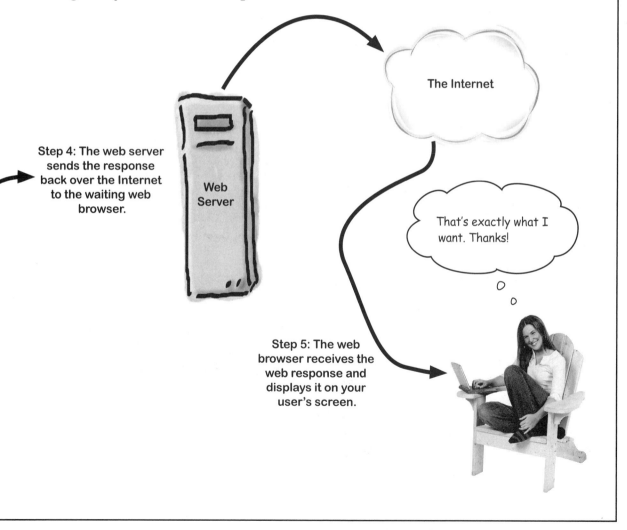

The Internet

Step 4: The web server sends the response back over the Internet to the waiting web browser.

Web Server

That's exactly what I want. Thanks!

Step 5: The web browser receives the web response and displays it on your user's screen.

What Do We Want Our Webapp to Do?

As tempting as it always is to *just start coding*, let's first think about how our webapp is going to work.

Users interact with our webapp using their favorite web browser. All they have to do is enter the URL for the webapp into their browser's address bar to access its services. A web page then appears in the browser asking the user to provide arguments to the search4letters function. Once these are entered, the user clicks on a button to see their results.

Recall the def line for our most recent version of search4letters, which shows the function expecting at least one—but no more than two—arguments: a phrase to search, together with the letters to search for. Remember, the letters argument is optional (defaulting to aeiou):

> *The "def" line for the "search4letters" function, which takes one, but no more than two, arguments*

```
def search4letters(phrase:str, letters:str='aeiou') -> set:
```

Let's grab a paper napkin and sketch out how we want our web page to appear. Here's what we came up with:

Welcome to search4letters on the Web!

> *Our web page has a title and some descriptive text.*

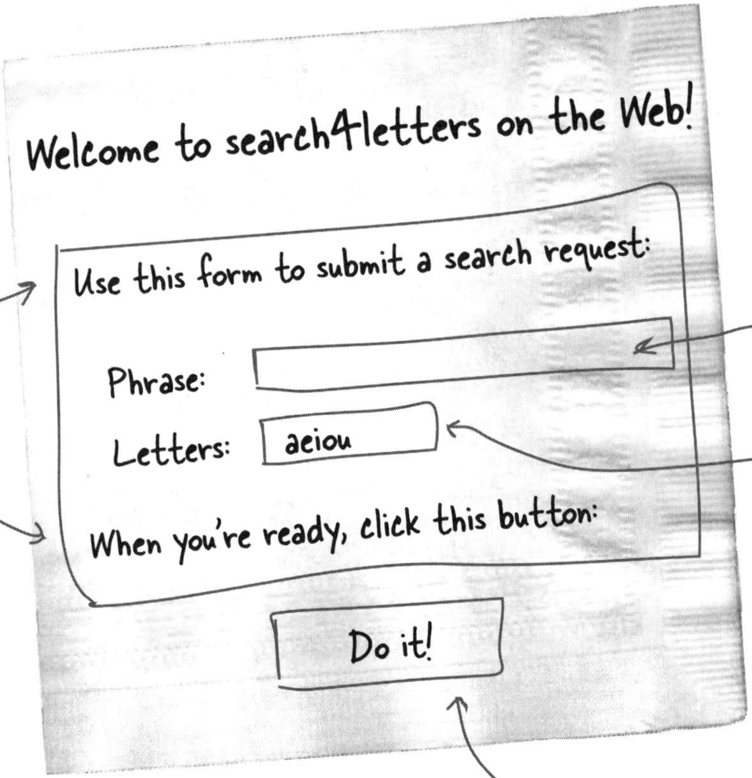

Use this form to submit a search request:

Phrase: [   ]

Letters: [aeiou]

> *One input box has room for the "phrase", while another allows the "letters" to be entered (note the default).*

When you're ready, click this button:

[Do it!]

> *Clicking on this button sends the user's data to our waiting web server.*

What Happens on the Web Server?

When the user clicks on the **Do it!** button, the browser sends the data to the waiting web server, which extracts the `phrase` and `letters` values, before calling the `search4letters` function on behalf of the now-waiting user.

Any results from the function are returned to the user's browser as another web page, which we again sketch out on a paper napkin (shown below). For now, let's assume the user entered "hitch-hiker" as the `phrase` and left the `letters` value defaulted to `aeiou`. Here's what the results web page might look like:

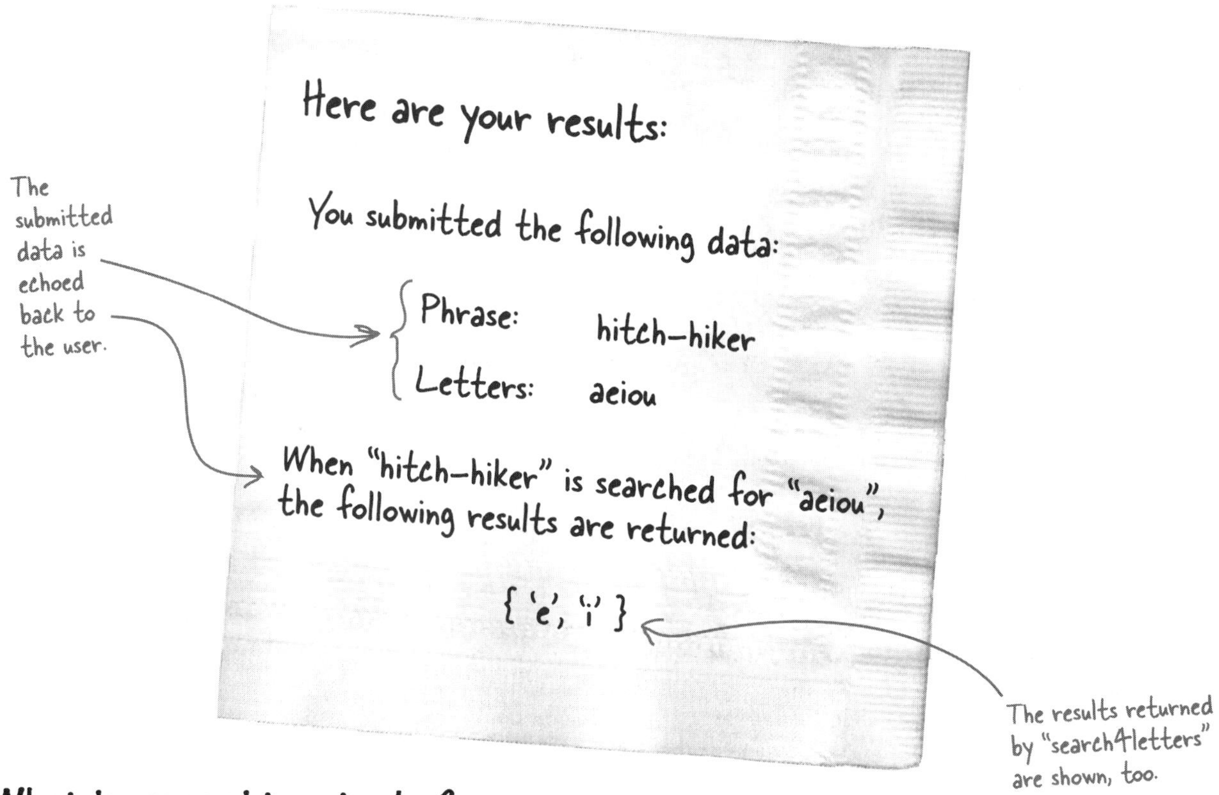

The submitted data is echoed back to the user.

Here are your results:

You submitted the following data:

Phrase: hitch-hiker

Letters: aeiou

When "hitch-hiker" is searched for "aeiou", the following results are returned:

{ 'e', 'i' }

The results returned by "search4letters" are shown, too.

What do we need to get going?

Other than the knowledge you already have about Python, the only thing you need to build a working server-side web application is a **web application framework**, which provides a set of general foundational technologies upon which you can build your webapp.

Although it's more than possible to use Python to build everything you need from scratch, it would be madness to contemplate doing so. Other programmers have already taken the time to build these web frameworks for you. Python has many choices here. However, we're not going to agonize over which framework to choose, and are instead just going to pick a popular one called *Flask* and move on.

Let's Install Flask

We know from Chapter 1 that Python's standard library comes with lots of *batteries included*. However, there are times when we need to use an application-specific third-party module, which is *not* part of the standard library. Third-party modules are imported into your Python program as needed. However, unlike the standard library modules, third-party modules need to be installed *before* they are imported and used. Flask is one such third-party module.

As mentioned in the previous chapter, the Python community maintains a centrally managed website for third-party modules called **PyPI** (short for *the Python Package Index*), which hosts the latest version of Flask (as well as many other projects).

Recall how we used `pip` to install our `vsearch` module into Python earlier in this book. `pip` also works with PyPI. If you know the name of the module you want, you can use `pip` to install any PyPI-hosted module directly into your Python environment.

Find PyPI at pypi.python.org.

Install Flask from the command-line with pip

If you are running on *Linux* or *Mac OS X*, type the following command into a terminal window:

```
$ sudo -H python3 -m pip install flask
```

Use this command on Mac OS X and Linux.

If you are running on *Windows*, open up a command prompt—being sure to *Run as Administrator* (by right-clicking on the option and choosing from the pop-up menu)—and then issue this command:

```
C:\> py -3 -m pip install flask
```

Note: case is important here. That's a lowercase "f" for "flask".

Use this command on Windows.

This command (regardless of your operating system) connects to the PyPI website, then downloads and installs the **Flask** module and four other modules Flask depends on: **Werkzeug**, **MarkupSafe**, **Jinja2**, and **itsdangerous**. Don't worry (for now) about what these extra modules do; just make sure they install correctly. If all is well, you'll see a message similar to the following at the bottom of the output generated by `pip`. Note that the output runs to over a dozen lines or so:

```
    . . .
Successfully installed Jinja2-2.8 MarkupSafe-0.23 Werkzeug-0.11 flask-0.10.1
itsdangerous-0.24
```

At the time of writing, these are the current version numbers associated with these modules.

If you don't see the "`Successfully installed...`" message, make sure you're connected to the Internet, and that you've entered the command for your operating system *exactly* as shown above. And don't be too alarmed if the version numbers for the modules installed into your Python differ from ours (as modules are constantly being updated, and dependencies can change, too). As long as the versions you install are *at least* as current as those shown above, everything is fine.

How Does Flask Work?

Flask provides a collection of modules that help you build server-side web applications. It's technically a *micro* web framework, in that it provides the minimum set of technologies needed for this task. This means Flask is not as feature-full as some of its competitors—such as **Django**, the mother of all Python web frameworks—but it is small, lightweight, and easy to use.

As our requirements aren't heavy (we only have two web pages), Flask is more than enough web framework for us at this time.

Check that Flask is installed and working

Here's the code for the most basic of Flask webapps, which we are going to use to test that Flask is set up and ready to go.

Use your favorite text editor to create a new file, and type the code shown below into the file, saving it is as `hello_flask.py` (you can save the file in its own folder, too, if you like—we called our folder `webapp`):

Geek Bits

Django is a hugely popular web application framework within the Python community. It has an especially strong, prebuilt administration facility that can make working with large webapps very manageable. It's overkill for what we're doing here, so we've opted for the much simpler, but more lightweight, **Flask**.

This is "hello_flask.py".

Ready Bake Code

```
from flask import Flask

app = Flask(__name__)

@app.route('/')
def hello() -> str:
    return 'Hello world from Flask!'

app.run()
```

Type this code in exactly as shown here... we'll get to what it means in a moment.

Run Flask from your OS command line

Don't be tempted to run this Flask code within IDLE, as IDLE wasn't really designed to do this sort of thing well. IDLE is great for experimenting with small snippets of code, but when it comes to running applications, you are much better off running your code directly via the interpreter, at your operating system's command line. Let's do that now and see what happens.

Don't use IDLE to run this code.

Running Your Flask Webapp for the First Time

If you are running on *Windows*, open a command prompt in the folder that contains your `hello_flask.py` program file. (Hint: if you have your folder open within the *File Explorer*, press the Shift key together with the right mouse button to bring up a context-sensitive menu from which you can choose *Open command window here*). With the Windows command line ready, type in this command to start your Flask app:

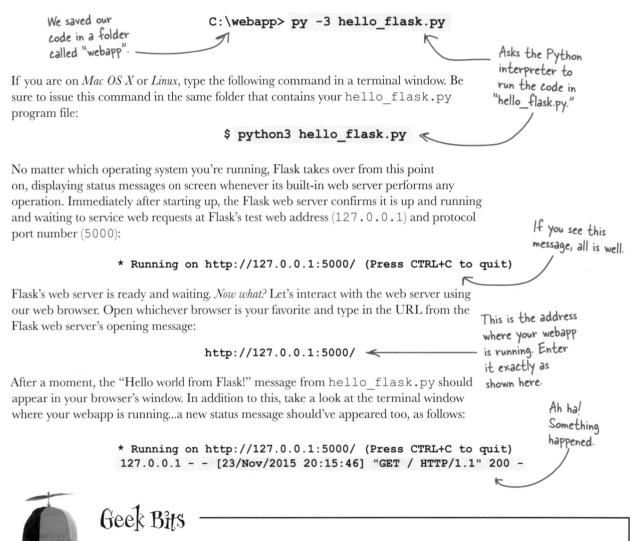

We saved our code in a folder called "webapp".

`C:\webapp> py -3 hello_flask.py`

Asks the Python interpreter to run the code in "hello_flask.py."

If you are on *Mac OS X* or *Linux*, type the following command in a terminal window. Be sure to issue this command in the same folder that contains your `hello_flask.py` program file:

`$ python3 hello_flask.py`

No matter which operating system you're running, Flask takes over from this point on, displaying status messages on screen whenever its built-in web server performs any operation. Immediately after starting up, the Flask web server confirms it is up and running and waiting to service web requests at Flask's test web address (`127.0.0.1`) and protocol port number (`5000`):

If you see this message, all is well.

`* Running on http://127.0.0.1:5000/ (Press CTRL+C to quit)`

Flask's web server is ready and waiting. *Now what?* Let's interact with the web server using our web browser. Open whichever browser is your favorite and type in the URL from the Flask web server's opening message:

`http://127.0.0.1:5000/`

This is the address where your webapp is running. Enter it exactly as shown here.

After a moment, the "Hello world from Flask!" message from `hello_flask.py` should appear in your browser's window. In addition to this, take a look at the terminal window where your webapp is running...a new status message should've appeared too, as follows:

Ah ha! Something happened.

`* Running on http://127.0.0.1:5000/ (Press CTRL+C to quit)`
`127.0.0.1 - - [23/Nov/2015 20:15:46] "GET / HTTP/1.1" 200 -`

Geek Bits

Getting into the specifics of what constitutes a **protocol port number** is beyond the scope of this book. However, if you'd like to know more, start reading here:

https://en.wikipedia.org/wiki/Port_(computer_networking)

Here's What Happened (Line by Line)

In addition to Flask updating the terminal with a status line, your web browser now displays the web server's response. Here's how our browser now looks (this is *Safari* on *Mac OS X*):

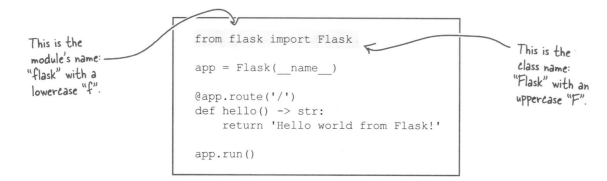

There's the message returned from the Flask web server.

127.0.0.1:5000

Hello world from Flask!

By using our browser to visit the URL listed in our webapp's opening status message, the server has responded with the "Hello world from Flask!" message.

Although our webapp has only six lines of code, there's a lot going on here, so let's review the code to see how all of this happened, taking each line in turn. Everything else we plan to do builds on these six lines of code.

The first line imports the `Flask` class from the `flask` module:

This is the module's name: "flask" with a lowercase "f".

```
from flask import Flask

app = Flask(__name__)

@app.route('/')
def hello() -> str:
    return 'Hello world from Flask!'

app.run()
```

This is the class name: "Flask" with an uppercase "F".

Remember when we discussed alternate ways of importing?

You could have written `import flask` here, then referred to the `Flask` class as `flask.Flask`, but using the `from` version of the `import` statement in this instance is preferred, as the `flask.Flask` usage is not as easy to read.

Creating a Flask Webapp Object

The second line of code creates an object of type `Flask`, assigning it to the `app` variable. This looks straightforward, but for the use of the strange argument to `Flask`, namely `__name__`:

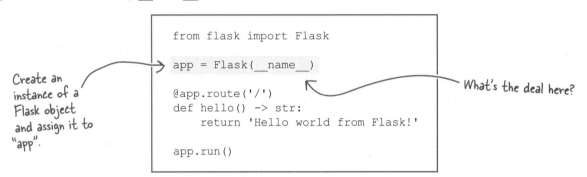

Create an instance of a Flask object and assign it to "app".

```
from flask import Flask

app = Flask(__name__)

@app.route('/')
def hello() -> str:
    return 'Hello world from Flask!'

app.run()
```

What's the deal here?

The `__name__` value is maintained by the Python interpreter and, when used anywhere within your program's code, is set to the name of the currently active module. It turns out that the `Flask` class needs to know the current value of `__name__` when creating a new `Flask` object, so it must be passed as an argument, which is why we've used it here (even though its usage does look *strange*).

This single line of code, despite being short, does an awful lot for you, as the Flask framework abstracts away many web development details, allowing you to concentrate on defining what you want to happen when a web request arrives at your waiting web server. We do just that starting on the very next line of code.

Geek Bits

Note that `__name__` is two underscore characters followed by the word "name" followed by another two underscore characters, which are referred to as "double underscores" when used to prefix and suffix a name in Python code. You'll see this naming convention a lot in your Python travels, and rather than use the long-winded: "double underscore, name, double underscore" phrase, savvy Python programmers say: "dunder name," which is **shorthand for the same thing**. As there's a lot of double underscore usages in Python, they are collectively known as "the dunders," and you'll see lots of examples of other dunders and their usages throughout the rest of this book.

As well as the dunders, there is also a convention to use a single underscore character to prefix certain variable names. Some Python programmers refer to single-underscore-prefixed names by the groan-inducing name "wonder" (shorthand for "one underscore").

Decorating a Function with a URL

The next line of code introduces a new piece of Python syntax: **decorators**. A function decorator, which is what we have in this code, adjusts the behavior of an existing function *without* you having to change that function's code (that is, the function being decorated).

You might want to read that last sentence a few times.

In essence, decorators allow you to take some existing code and augment it with additional behavior as needed. Although decorators can also be applied to classes as well as functions, they are mainly applied to functions, which results in most Python programmers referring to them as **function decorators**.

Let's take a look at the function decorator in our webapp's code, which is easy to spot, as it starts with the @ symbol:

Geek Bits

Python's decorator syntax take inspiration from Java's annotation syntax, as well as the world of functional programming.

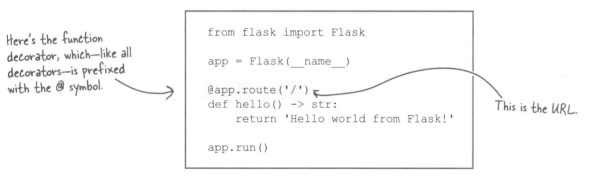

Here's the function decorator, which—like all decorators—is prefixed with the @ symbol.

```
from flask import Flask

app = Flask(__name__)

@app.route('/')
def hello() -> str:
    return 'Hello world from Flask!'

app.run()
```

This is the URL.

Although it is possible to create your own function decorators (coming up in a later chapter), for now let's concentrate on just using them. There are a bunch of decorators built in to Python, and many third-party modules (such as Flask) provide decorators for specific purposes (`route` being one of them).

Flask's `route` decorator is available to your webapp's code via the `app` variable, which was created on the previous line of code.

The `route` decorator lets you associate a URL web path with an existing Python function. In this case, the URL "/" is associated with the function defined on the very next line of code, which is called `hello`. The `route` decorator arranges for the Flask web server to call the function when a request for the "/" URL arrives at the server. The `route` decorator then waits for any output produced by the decorated function before returning the output to the server, which then returns it to the waiting web browser.

It's not important to know how Flask (and the `route` decorator) does all of the above "magic." What is important is that Flask does all of this for you, and all you have to do is write a function that produces the output you require. Flask and the `route` decorator then take care of the details.

A function decorator adjusts the behavior of an existing function (without changing the function's code).

Running Your Webapp's Behavior(s)

With the `route` decorator line written, the function decorated by it starts on the next line. In our webapp, this is the `hello` function, which does only one thing: returns the message "Hello world from Flask!" when invoked:

This is just a regular Python function which, when invoked, returns a string to its caller (note the '-> str' annotation).

```
from flask import Flask

app = Flask(__name__)

@app.route('/')
def hello() -> str:
    return 'Hello world from Flask!'

app.run()
```

The final line of code takes the Flask object assigned to the `app` variable and asks Flask to start running its web server. It does this by invoking `run`:

```
from flask import Flask

app = Flask(__name__)

@app.route('/')
def hello() -> str:
    return 'Hello world from Flask!'

app.run()
```

Asks the webapp to start running

At this point, Flask starts up its included web server and runs your webapp code within it. Any requests received by the web server for the "/" URL are responded to with the "Hello world from Flask!" message, whereas a request for any other URL results in a 404 "Resource not found" error message. To see the error handling in action, type this URL into your browser's address bar:

`http://127.0.0.1:5000/doesthiswork.html`

Your browser displays a "Not Found" message, and your webapp running within its terminal window updates its status with an appropriate message:

That URL does not exist: 404!

```
* Running on http://127.0.0.1:5000/ (Press CTRL+C to quit)
127.0.0.1 - - [23/Nov/2015 20:15:46] "GET / HTTP/1.1" 200 -
127.0.0.1 - - [23/Nov/2015 21:30:26] "GET /doesthiswork.html HTTP/1.1" 404 -
```

The messages you see may differ slightly. Don't let this worry you.

Exposing Functionality to the Web

Putting to one side the fact that you've just built a working webapp in a mere six lines of code, consider what Flask is doing for you here: it's providing a mechanism whereby you can take any existing Python function and display its output within a web browser.

To add more functionality to your webapp, all you have to do is decide on the URL you want to associate your functionality with, then write an appropriate `@app.route` decorator line above a function that does the actual work. Let's do this now, using our `search4letters` functionality from the last chapter.

✏️ Sharpen your pencil

Let's amend `hello_flask.py` to include a second URL: `/search4`. Write the code that associates this URL with a function called `do_search`, which calls the `search4letters` function (from our `vsearch` module). Then arrange for the `do_search` function to return the results determined when searching the phrase: "life, the universe, and everything!" for this string of characters: `'eiru,!'`.

Shown below is our existing code, with space reserved for the new code you need to write. Your job is to provide the missing code.

Hint: the results returned from `search4letters` are a Python set. Be sure to cast the results to a string by calling the `str` BIF *before* returning anything to the waiting web browser, as it's expecting textual data, not a Python set. (Remember: "BIF" is Python-speak for *built-in function*.)

Do you need to import anything?

```
from flask import Flask

.................................................

.................................................

app = Flask(__name__)

@app.route('/')
def hello() -> str:
    return 'Hello world from Flask!'
```

Add in a second decorator.

```
.................................................

.................................................

.................................................

.................................................

app.run()
```

Add code for the "do_search" function here.

Sharpen your pencil
Solution

You were to amend `hello_flask.py` to include a second URL, */search4*, writing the code that associates the URL with a function called `do_search`, which itself calls the `search4letters` function (from our `vsearch` module). You were to arrange for the `do_search` function to return the results determined when searching the phrase: "life, the universe, and everything!" for the string of characters: `'eiru,!'`.

Shown below is our existing code, with space reserved for the new code you need to write. Your job was to provide the missing code.

How does your code compare to ours?

You need to import the "search4letters" function from the "vsearch" module before you call it.

```python
from flask import Flask

from vsearch import search4letters

app = Flask(__name__)

@app.route('/')
def hello() -> str:
    return 'Hello world from Flask!'

@app.route('/search4')

def do_search() -> str:
    return str(search4letters('life, the universe, and everything', 'eiru,!'))

app.run()
```

A second decorator sets up the "/search4" URL.

The "do_search" function invokes "search4letters", then returns any results as a string.

To test this new functionality, you'll need to restart your Flask webapp, as it is currently running the older version of your code. To stop the webapp, return to your terminal window, then press Ctrl and C together. Your webapp will terminate, and you'll be returned to your operating system's prompt. Press the up arrow to recall the previous command (the one that previously started `hello_flask.py`) and then press the Enter key. The initial Flask status message reappears to confirm your updated webapp is waiting for requests:

Stop the webapp...

```
$ python3 hello_flask.py
 * Running on http://127.0.0.1:5000/ (Press CTRL+C to quit)
127.0.0.1 - - [23/Nov/2015 20:15:46] "GET / HTTP/1.1" 200 -
127.0.0.1 - - [23/Nov/2015 21:30:26] "GET /doesthiswork.html HTTP/1.1" 404 -
^C
```

...then restart it.

```
$ python3 hello_flask.py
 * Running on http://127.0.0.1:5000/ (Press CTRL+C to quit)
```

We are up and running again.

TEST DRIVE

As you haven't changed the code associated with the default '/' URL, that functionality still works, displaying the "Hello world from Flask!" message.

However, if you enter ***http://127.0.0.1:5000/search4*** into your browser's address bar, you'll see the results from the call to search4letters:

There are the results from the call to "search4letters". Granted, this output is nothing to get excited about, but it does prove that using the "/search4" URL invokes the function and returns the results.

```
● ● ●   <  >   □   🌐 127.0.0.1:5000/search4        ⟳        ↑   ⬜   +

{'u', 'i', ',', 'e', 'r'}
```

there are no Dumb Questions

Q: I'm a little confused by the 127.0.0.1 and :5000 parts of the URL used to access the webapp. What's the deal with those?

A: At the moment, you're testing your webapp on your computer, which—because it's connected to the Internet—has its own unique IP address. Despite this fact, Flask doesn't use your IP address and instead connects its test web server to the Internet's **loopback address**: 127.0.0.1, also commonly known as localhost. Both are shorthand for "my computer, no matter what its actual IP address is." For your web browser (also on your computer) to communicate with your Flask web server, you need to specify the address that is running your webapp, namely:127.0.0.1. This is a standard IP address reserved for this exact purpose.

The :5000 part of the URL identifies the **protocol port number** your web server is running on.

Typically, web servers run on protocol port 80, which is an Internet standard, and as such, doesn't need to be specified. You could type oreilly.com:80 into your browser's address bar and it would work, but nobody does, as oreilly.com alone is sufficient (as the :80 is assumed).

When you're building a webapp, it's very rare to test on protocol port 80 (as that's reserved for production servers), so most web frameworks choose another port to run on. 8080 is a popular choice for this, but Flask uses 5000 as its test protocol port.

Q: Can I use some protocol port other than 5000 when I test and run my Flask webapp?

A: Yes, app.run() allows you to specify a value for port that can be set to any value. But, unless you have a very good reason to change, stick with Flask's default of 5000 for now.

Recall What We're Trying to Build

Our webapp needs a web page which accepts input, and another which displays the results of feeding the input to the search4letters function. Our current webapp code is nowhere near doing all of this, but what we have does provide a basis upon which to build what *is* required.

Shown below on the left is a copy of our current code, while on the right, we have copies of the "napkin specifications" from earlier in this chapter. We have indicated where we think the functionality for each napkin can be provided in the code:

```python
from flask import Flask
from vsearch import search4letters


app = Flask(__name__)


@app.route('/')
def hello() -> str:
    return 'Hello world from Flask!'


@app.route('/search4')
def do_search() -> str:
    return str(search4letters( ... ))


app.run()
```

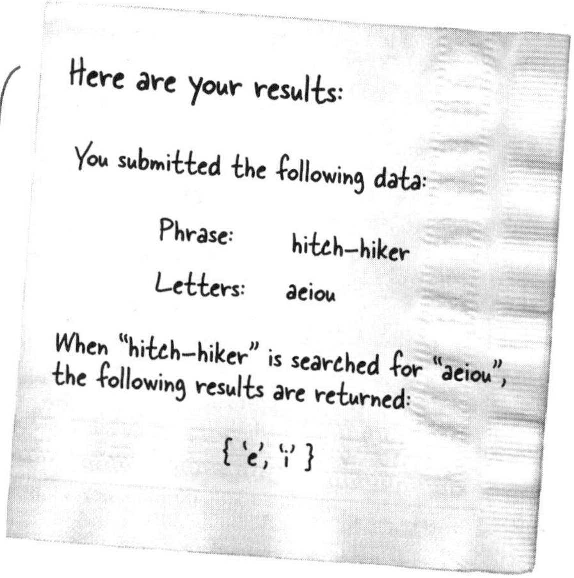

> Note: to make everything fit, we aren't showing the entire line of code here.

Welcome to search4letters on the Web!

Use this form to submit a search request:

Phrase:

Letters: aeiou

When you're ready, click this button:

Do it!

Here are your results:

You submitted the following data:

Phrase: hitch-hiker

Letters: aeiou

When "hitch-hiker" is searched for "aeiou", the following results are returned:

{ 'e', 'i' }

Here's the plan

Let's change the hello function to return the HTML form. Then we'll change the do_search function to accept the form's input, before calling the search4letters function. The results are then returned by do_search as another web page.

Building the HTML Form

The required HTML form isn't all that complicated. Other than the descriptive text, the form is made up of two input boxes and a button.

But...what if you're new to all this HTML stuff?

Don't panic if all this talk of HTML forms, input boxes, and buttons has you in a tizzy. Fear not, we have what you're looking for: the second edition of *Head First HTML and CSS* provides the best introduction to these technologies should you require a quick primer (or a speedy refresher).

Even if the thought of setting aside this book in order to bone up on HTML feels like too much work, note that we provide all the HTML you need to work with the examples in the book, and we do this without you having to be an HTML expert. A little exposure to HTML helps, but it's not a absolute requirement (after all, this is a book about Python, not HTML).

Note from Marketing: This is the book we wholeheartedly recommend for quickly getting up to speed with HTML...not that we're biased or anything. ☺

Create the HTML, then send it to the browser

There's always more than one way to do things, and when it comes to creating HTML text from within your Flask webapp, you have choices:

> I like to put my HTML inside **large strings**, which I then embed in my Python code, returning the strings as needed. That way, everything I need is right there in my code, and I have complete control... which is how I roll. What's not to like, Laura?

> Well, Bob, putting all the HTML in your code works, but it doesn't scale. As your webapp gets bigger, all that embedded HTML gets kinda messy... and it's hard to hand off your HTML to a web designer to beautify. Nor is it easy to reuse chunks of HTML. Therefore, I always use a **template engine** with my webapps. It's a bit more work to begin with, but over time I find using templates really pays off...

Laura's right—templates make HTML much easier to maintain than Bob's approach. We'll dive into templates on the next page.

Templates Up Close

Template engines let programmers apply the object-oriented notions of inheritance and reuse to the production of textual data, such as web pages.

A website's look and feel can be defined in a top-level HTML template, known as the **base template**, which is then inherited from by other HTML pages. If you make a change to the base template, the change is then reflected in *all* the HTML pages that inherit from it.

The template engine shipped with Flask is called *Jinja2*, and it is both easy to use and powerful. It is not this book's intention to teach you all you need to know about Jinja2, so what appears on these two pages is—by necessity—both brief and to the point. For more details on what's possible with Jinja2, see:

http://jinja.pocoo.org/docs/dev/

Here's the base template we'll use for our webapp. In this file, called `base.html`, we put the HTML markup that we want all of our web pages to share. We also use some Jinja2-specific markup to indicate content that will be supplied when HTML pages inheriting from this one are rendered (i.e., prepared prior to delivery to a waiting web browser). Note that markup appearing between `{{` and `}}`, as well as markup enclosed between `{%` and `%}`, is meant for the Jinja2 template engine: we've highlighted these cases to make them easy to spot:

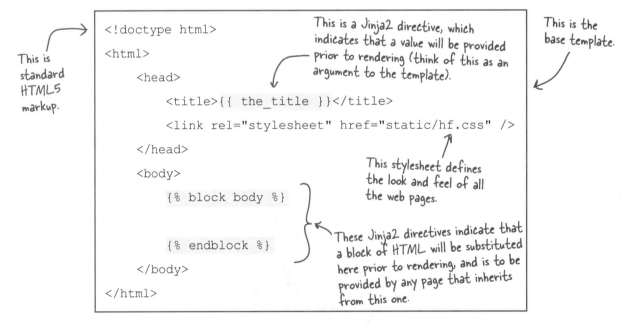

This is standard HTML5 markup.

```
<!doctype html>

<html>

    <head>

        <title>{{ the_title }}</title>

        <link rel="stylesheet" href="static/hf.css" />

    </head>

    <body>
        {% block body %}


        {% endblock %}
    </body>
</html>
```

This is a Jinja2 directive, which indicates that a value will be provided prior to rendering (think of this as an argument to the template).

This is the base template.

This stylesheet defines the look and feel of all the web pages.

These Jinja2 directives indicate that a block of HTML will be substituted here prior to rendering, and is to be provided by any page that inherits from this one.

With the base template ready, we can inherit from it using Jinja2's `extends` directive. When we do, the HTML files that inherit need only provide the HTML for any named blocks in the base. In our case, we have only one named block: `body`.

Here's the markup for the first of our pages, which we are calling entry.html. This is markup for a HTML form that users can interact with in order to provide the value for phrase and letters expected by our webapp.

Note how the "boilerplate" HTML in the base template is not repeated in this file, as the extends directive includes this markup for us. All we need to do is provide the HTML that is specific to this file, and we do this by providing the markup within the Jinja2 block called body:

```
{% extends 'base.html' %}

{% block body %}

<h2>{{ the_title }}</h2>

<form method='POST' action='/search4'>
<table>
<p>Use this form to submit a search request:</p>
<tr><td>Phrase:</td><td><input name='phrase' type='TEXT' width='60'></td></tr>
<tr><td>Letters:</td><td><input name='letters' type='TEXT' value='aeiou'></td></tr>
</table>
<p>When you're ready, click this button:</p>
<p><input value='Do it!' type='SUBMIT'></p>
</form>

{% endblock %}
```

This template inherits from the base, and provides a replacement for the block called "body".

And, finally, here's the markup for the results.html file, which is used to render the results of our search. This template inherits from the base template, too:

```
{% extends 'base.html' %}

{% block body %}

<h2>{{ the_title }}</h2>

<p>You submitted the following data:</p>
<table>
<tr><td>Phrase:</td><td>{{ the_phrase }}</td></tr>
<tr><td>Letters:</td><td>{{ the_letters }}</td></tr>
</table>

<p>When "{{the_phrase }}" is search for "{{ the_letters }}", the following
results are returned:</p>
<h3>{{ the_results }}</h3>

{% endblock %}
```

As with "entry.html", this template also inherits from the base, and also provides a replacement for the block called "body".

Note these additional argument values, which you need to provide values for prior to rendering.

Templates Relate to Web Pages

Our webapp needs to render two web pages, and now we have two templates that can help with this. Both templates inherit from the base template and thus inherit the base template's look and feel. Now all we need to do is render the pages.

Before we see how Flask (together with Jinja2) renders, let's take another look at our "napkin specifications" alongside our template markup. Note how the HTML enclosed within the Jinja2 `{% block %}` directive closely matches the hand-drawn specifications. The main omission is each page's title, which we'll provide in place of the `{{ the_title }}` directive during rendering. Think of each name enclosed in double curly braces as an argument to the template:

Download these templates (and the CSS) from here: *http://python.itcarlow.ie/ed2/.*

Welcome to search4letters on the Web!

Use this form to submit a search request:

Phrase:

Letters: aeiou

When you're ready, click this button:

Do it!

```
{% extends 'base.html' %}

{% block body %}

<h2>{{ the_title }}</h2>

<form method='POST' action='/search4'>
<table>
<p>Use this form to submit a search request:</p>
<tr><td>Phrase:</td><td><input name='phrase' type='TEXT'
width='60'></td></tr>
<tr><td>Letters:</td><td><input name='letters' type='TEXT'
value='aeiou'></td></tr>
</table>
<p>When you're ready, click this button:</p>
<p><input value='Do it!' type='SUBMIT'></p>
</form>

{% endblock %}
```

Here are your results:

You submitted the following data:

Phrase: hitch-hiker

Letters: aeiou

When "hitch-hiker" is searched for "aeiou", the following results are returned:

{ 'e', 'i' }

```
{% extends 'base.html' %}

{% block body %}

<h2>{{ the_title }}</h2>

<p>You submitted the following data:</p>
<table>
<tr><td>Phrase:</td><td>{{ the_phrase }}</td></tr>
<tr><td>Letters:</td><td>{{ the_letters }}</td></tr>
</table>

<p>When "{{the_phrase }}" is search for "{{ the_letters }}",
the following results are returned:</p>
<h3>{{ the_results }}</h3>

{% endblock %}
```

Don't forget those additional arguments.

Rendering Templates from Flask

Flask comes with a function called `render_template`, which, when provided with the name of a template and any required arguments, returns a string of HTML when invoked. To use `render_template`, add its name to the list of imports from the `flask` module (at the top of your code), then invoke the function as needed.

Before doing so, however, let's rename the file containing our webapp's code (currently called `hello_flask.py`) to something more appropriate. You can use any name you wish for your webapp, but we're renaming our file `vsearch4web.py`. Here's the code currently in this file:

```python
from flask import Flask
from vsearch import search4letters

app = Flask(__name__)

@app.route('/')
def hello() -> str:
    return 'Hello world from Flask!'

@app.route('/search4')
def do_search() -> str:
    return str(search4letters('life, the universe, and everything', 'eiru,!'))

app.run()
```

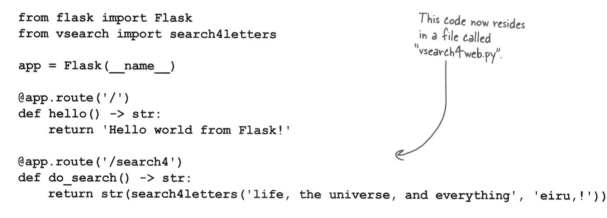

This code now resides in a file called "vsearch4web.py".

To render the HTML form in the `entry.html` template, we need to make a number of changes to the above code:

 Import the `render_template` function
Add `render_template` to the import list on the `from flask` line at the top of the code.

 Create a new URL—in this case, `/entry`
Every time you need a new URL in your Flask webapp, you need to add a new `@app.route` line, too. We'll do this before the `app.run()` line of code.

 Create a function that returns the correctly rendered HTML
With the `@app.route` line written, you can associate code with it by creating a function that does the actual work (and makes your webapp more useful to your users). The function calls (and returns the output from) the `render_template` function, passing in the name of the template file (`entry.html` in this case), as well as any argument values that are required by the template (in the case, we need a value for `the_title`).

Let's make these changes to our existing code.

Displaying the Webapp's HTML Form

Let's add the code to enable the three changes detailed at the bottom of the last page. Follow along by making the same changes to your code:

① **Import the `render_template` function**

```
from flask import Flask, render_template
```

Add "render_template" to the list of technologies imported from the "flask" module.

② **Create a new URL—in this case, /entry**

```
@app.route('/entry')
```

Underneath the "do_search" function, but before the "app.run()" line, insert this line to add a new URL to the webapp.

③ **Create a function that returns the correctly rendered HTML**

Provide the name of the template to render.

```
@app.route('/entry')
def entry_page() -> 'html':
        return render_template('entry.html',
                    the_title='Welcome to search4letters on the web!')
```

Add this function directly underneath the new "@app.route" line.

Provide a value to associate with the "the_title" argument.

With these changes made, the code to our webapp—with the additions highlighted—now looks like this:

```
from flask import Flask, render_template
from vsearch import search4letters

app = Flask(__name__)

@app.route('/')
def hello() -> str:
    return 'Hello world from Flask!'

@app.route('/search4')
def do_search() -> str:
    return str(search4letters('life, the universe, and everything', 'eiru,!'))

@app.route('/entry')
def entry_page() -> 'html':
    return render_template('entry.html',
                    the_title='Welcome to search4letters on the web!')

app.run()
```

We're leaving the rest of this code as is for now.

Preparing to Run the Template Code

It's tempting to open a command prompt, then run the latest version of our code. However, for a number of reasons, this won't immediately work.

For starters, the base template refers to a stylesheet called `hf.css`, and this needs to exist in a folder called `static` (which is relative to the folder that contains your code). Here's a snippet of the base template that shows this:

If you haven't done so already, download the templates and the CSS from here: *http://python.itcarlow.ie/ed2/.*

```
    . . .
    <title>{{ the_title }}</title>
    <link rel="stylesheet" href="static/hf.css" />
</head>
    . . .
```

The "hf.css" file needs to exist (in the "static" folder).

Feel free to grab a copy of the CSS file from this book's support website (see the URL at the side of this page). Just be sure to put the downloaded stylesheet in a folder called `static`.

In addition to this, Flask requires that your templates be stored in a folder called `templates`, which—like `static`—needs to be relative to the folder that contains your code. The download for this chapter also contains all three templates...so you can avoid typing in all that HTML!

Assuming that you've put your webapp's code file in a folder called `webapp`, here's the structure you should have in place prior to attempting to run the most recent version of `vsearch4web.py`:

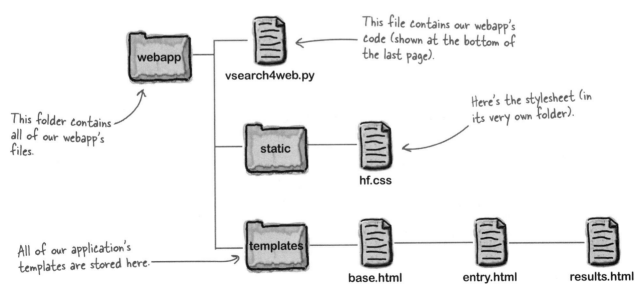

This file contains our webapp's code (shown at the bottom of the last page).

vsearch4web.py

This folder contains all of our webapp's files.

webapp

Here's the stylesheet (in its very own folder).

static

hf.css

All of our application's templates are stored here.

templates

base.html   **entry.html**   **results.html**

We're Ready for a Test Run

If you have everything ready—the stylesheet and templates downloaded, and the code updated—you're now ready to take your Flask webapp for another spin.

The previous version of your code is likely still running at your command prompt.

Return to that window now and press *Ctrl* and *C* together to stop the previous webapp's execution. Then press the *up arrow* key to recall the last command line, edit the name of the file to run, and then press *Enter*. Your new version of your code should now run, displaying the usual status messages:

```
    . . .
 * Running on http://127.0.0.1:5000/ (Press CTRL+C to quit)
127.0.0.1 - - [23/Nov/2015 21:51:38] "GET / HTTP/1.1" 200 -
127.0.0.1 - - [23/Nov/2015 21:51:48] "GET /search4 HTTP/1.1" 200 -
^C
$ python3 vsearch4web.py
 * Running on http://127.0.0.1:5000/ (Press CTRL+C to quit)
```

Stop the webapp again...

Start up your new code (which is in the "vsearch4web.py" file).

The new code is up and running, and waiting to service requests.

Recall that this new version of our code still supports the / and /search4 URLs, so if you use a browser to request those, the responses will be the same as shown earlier in this chapter. However, if you use this URL:

http://127.0.0.1:5000/entry

the response displayed in your browser should be the rendered HTML form (shown at the top of the next page). The command-prompt should display two additional status lines: one for the /entry request and another related to your browser's request for the hf.css stylesheet:

You request the HTML form....

...and your browser also requests the stylesheet.

```
    . . .
127.0.0.1 - - [23/Nov/2015 21:55:59] "GET /entry HTTP/1.1" 200 -
127.0.0.1 - - [23/Nov/2015 21:55:59] "GET /static/hf.css HTTP/1.1" 304 -
```

Test Drive

Here's what appears on screen when we type `http://127.0.0.1:5000/entry` into our browser:

> **Welcome to search4letters on the web!**
>
> Use this form to submit a search request:
>
> | Phrase: | |
> |---------|---|
> | Letters: | aeiou |
>
> When you're ready, click this button:
>
> Do it!

Looking good

We aren't going to win any web design awards for this page, but it looks OK, and resembles what we had on the back of our napkin. Unfortunately, when you type in a phrase and (optionally) adjust the Letters value to suit, clicking the *Do it!* button produces this error page:

> **Method Not Allowed**
>
> The method is not allowed for the requested URL.

Whoops! That can't be good.

This is a bit of a bummer, isn't it? Let's see what's going on.

Understanding HTTP Status Codes

When something goes wrong with your webapp, the web server responds with a HTTP status code (which it sends to your browser). HTTP is the communications protocol that lets web browsers and servers communicate. The meaning of the status codes is well established (see the *Geek Bits* on the right). In fact, every web *request* generates an HTTP status code *response*.

To see which status code was sent to your browser from your webapp, review the status messages appearing at your command prompt. Here's what we saw:

```
    . . .
127.0.0.1 - - [23/Nov/2015 21:55:59] "GET /entry HTTP/1.1" 200 -
127.0.0.1 - - [23/Nov/2015 21:55:59] "GET /static/hf.css HTTP/1.1" 304 -
127.0.0.1 - - [23/Nov/2015 21:56:54] "POST /search4 HTTP/1.1" 405 -
```

Uh-oh. Something has gone wrong, and the server has generated a client-error status code.

The 405 status code indicates that the client (your browser) sent a request using a HTTP method that this server doesn't allow. There are a handful of HTTP methods, but for our purposes, you only need to be aware of two of them: *GET* and *POST*.

 The GET method
Browsers typically use this method to request a resource from the web server, and this method is by far the most used. (We say "typically" here as it is possible to—rather confusingly—use GET to *send* data from your browser to the server, but we're not focusing on that option here.) All of the URLs in our webapp currently support GET, which is Flask's default HTTP method.

 The POST method
This method allows a web browser to send data to the server over HTTP, and is closely associated with the HTML <form> tag. You can tell your Flask webapp to accept posted data from a browser by providing an extra argument on the @app.route line.

Let's adjust the @app.route line paired with our webapp's */search4* URL to accept posted data. To do this, return to your editor and edit the vsearch4web.py file once more.

Geek Bits

Here's a quick and dirty explanation of the various HTTP status codes that can be sent from a web server (e.g., your Flask webapp) to a web client (e.g., your web browser).

There are five main categories of status code: 100s, 200s, 300s, 400s, and 500s.

Codes in the **100–199** range are **informational** messages: all is OK, and the server is providing details related to the client's request.

Codes in the **200–299** range are **success** messages: the server has received, understood, and processed the client's request. All is good.

Codes in the **300–399** range are **redirection** messages: the server is informing the client that the request can be handled elsewhere.

Codes in the **400–499** range are **client error** messages: the server received a request from the client that it does not understand and can't process. Typically, the client is at fault here.

Codes in the **500–599** range are **server error** messages: the server received a request from the client, but the server failed while trying to process it. Typically, the server is at fault here.

For more details, please see: *https://en.wikipedia.org/wiki/ List_of_HTTP_status_codes*.

Handling Posted Data

As well as accepting the URL as its first argument, the @app.route decorator accepts other, optional arguments.

One of these is the methods argument, which lists the HTTP method(s) that the URL supports. By default, Flask supports GET for all URLs. However, if the methods argument is assigned a list of HTTP methods to support, this default behavior is overridden. Here's what the @app.route line currently looks like:

`@app.route('/search4')`

We have not specified an HTTP method to support here, so Flask defaults to GET.

To have the */search4* URL support POST, add the methods argument to the decorator and assign the list of HTTP methods you want the URL to support. This line of code, below, states that the */search4* URL now only supports the POST method (meaning GET requests are no longer supported):

`@app.route('/search4', methods=['POST'])`

The "/search4" URL now supports only the POST method.

This small change is enough to rid your webapp of the "Method Not Allowed" message, as the POST associated with the HTML form matches up with the POST on the @app.route line:

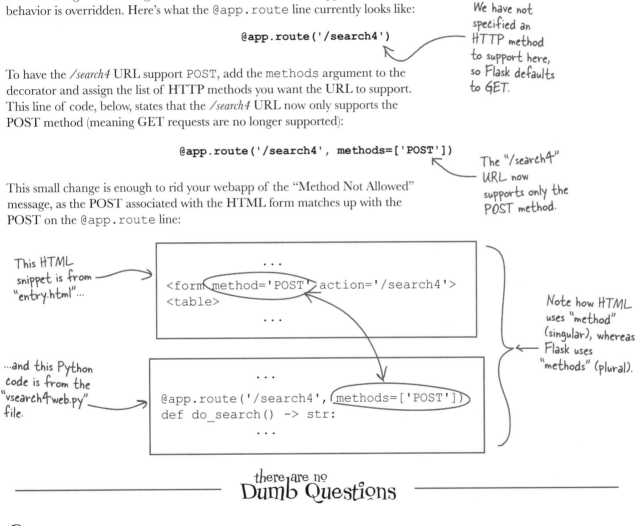

This HTML snippet is from "entry.html"...

```
            . . .
<form method='POST' action='/search4'>
<table>
            . . .
```

...and this Python code is from the "vsearch4web.py" file.

```
            . . .
@app.route('/search4', methods=['POST'])
def do_search() -> str:
            . . .
```

Note how HTML uses "method" (singular), whereas Flask uses "methods" (plural).

---

there are no Dumb Questions

Q: What if I need my URL to support both the GET method as well as POST? Is that possible?

A: Yes, all you need to do is add the name of the HTTP method you need to support to the list assigned to the methods arguments. For example, if you wanted to add GET support to the */search4* URL, you need only change the @app.route line of code to look like this: @app.route('/search4', methods=['GET', 'POST']). For more on this, see the Flask docs, which are available here *http://flask.pocoo.org*.

Refining the Edit/Stop/Start/Test Cycle

At this point, having saved our amended code, it's a reasonable course of action to stop the webapp at the command prompt, then restart it to test our new code. This edit/stop/start/test cycle works, but becomes tedious after a while (especially if you end up making a long series of small changes to your webapp's code).

To improve the efficiency of this process, Flask allows you to run your webapp in *debugging mode*, which, among other things, automatically restarts your webapp every time Flask notices your code has changed (typically as a result of you making and saving a change). This is worth doing, so let's switch on debugging by changing the last line of code in `vsearch4web.py` to look like this:

```
app.run(debug=True)   ⟵————— Switches on debugging
```

Your program code should now look like this:

```python
from flask import Flask, render_template
from vsearch import search4letters

app = Flask(__name__)

@app.route('/')
def hello() -> str:
    return 'Hello world from Flask!'

@app.route('/search4', methods=['POST'])
def do_search() -> str:
    return str(search4letters('life, the universe, and everything', 'eiru,!'))

@app.route('/entry')
def entry_page() -> 'html':
    return render_template('entry.html',
                           the_title='Welcome to search4letters on the web!')

app.run(debug=True)
```

We are now ready to take this code for a test run. To do so, stop your currently running webapp (for the last time) by pressing *Ctrl-C*, then restart it at your command prompt by pressing the *up arrow* and *Enter*.

Rather than showing the usual "`Running on http://127...`" message, Flask spits out three new status lines, which is its way of telling you debugging mode is now active. Here's what we saw on our computer:

```
$ python3 vsearch4web.py
 * Running on http://127.0.0.1:5000/ (Press CTRL+C to quit)
 * Restarting with stat      ⟵
 * Debugger is active!
 * Debugger pin code: 228-903-465
```

This is Flask's way of telling you that your webapp will automatically restart if your code changes. Also: don't worry if your debugger pin code is different from ours (that's OK). We won't use this pin.

Now that we are up and running again, let's interact with our webapp once more and see what's changed.

Test Drive

Return to the entry form by typing **http://127.0.0.1:5000/entry** into your browser:

Still looking good

The "Method Not Allowed" error has gone, but things still aren't working right. You can type any phrase into this form, then click the *Do it!* button without the error appearing. If you try it a few times, you'll notice that the results returned are always the same (no matter what phrase or letters you use). Let's investigate what's going on here.

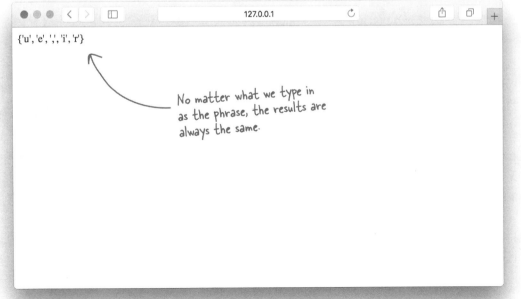

No matter what we type in as the phrase, the results are always the same.

Accessing HTML Form Data with Flask

Our webapp no longer fails with a "Method Not Allowed" error. Instead, it always returns the same set of characters: *u, e, comma, i,* and *r*. If you take a quick look at the code that executes when the */search4* URL is posted to, you'll see why this is: the values for phrase and letters are *hardcoded* into the function:

```
        . . .
@app.route('/search4', methods=['POST'])
def do_search() -> str:
    return str(search4letters('life, the universe, and everything', 'eiru,!'))
        . . .
```

> No matter what we type into the HTML form, our code is always going to use these hardcoded values.

Our HTML form posts its data to the web server, but in order to do something with the data, we need to amend our webapp's code to accept the data, then perform some operation on it.

Flask comes with a built-in object called request that provides easy access to posted data. The request object contains a dictionary attribute called form that provides access to a HTML form's data posted from the browser. As form is like any other Python dictionary, it supports the same square bracket notation you first saw in Chapter 3. To access a piece of data from the form, put the form element's name inside square brackets:

> The data from this form element is available in our webapp's code as "request.form['phrase']". —

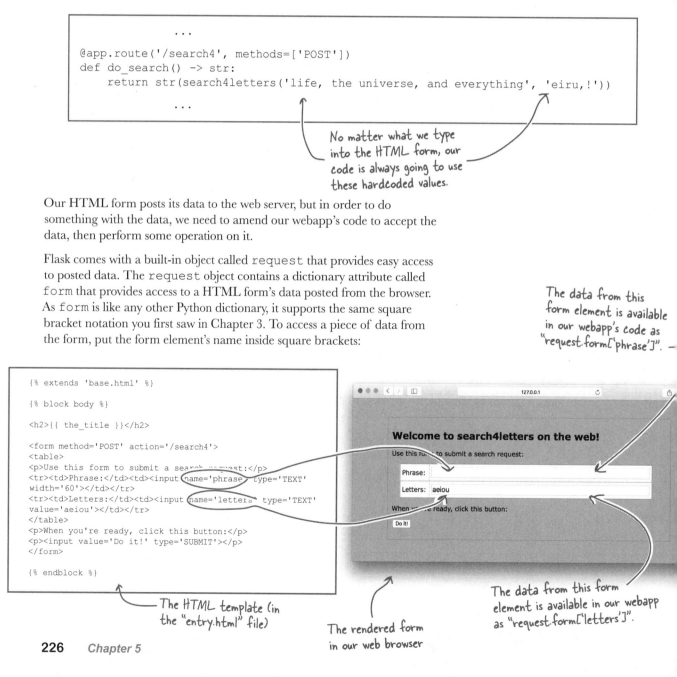

```
{% extends 'base.html' %}

{% block body %}

<h2>{{ the_title }}</h2>

<form method='POST' action='/search4'>
<table>
<p>Use this form to submit a search request:</p>
<tr><td>Phrase:</td><td><input name='phrase' type='TEXT'
width='60'></td></tr>
<tr><td>Letters:</td><td><input name='letters' type='TEXT'
value='aeiou'></td></tr>
</table>
<p>When you're ready, click this button:</p>
<p><input value='Do it!' type='SUBMIT'></p>
</form>

{% endblock %}
```

> The HTML template (in the "entry.html" file)

Welcome to search4letters on the web!

Use this form to submit a search request:

Phrase:

Letters: aeiou

When you're ready, click this button:

Do it!

> The rendered form in our web browser

> The data from this form element is available in our webapp as "request.form['letters']".

Using Request Data in Your Webapp

To use the `request` object, import it on the `from flask` line at the top of your program code, then access the data from `request.form` as needed. For our purposes, we want to replace the hardcoded data value in our `do_search` function with the data from the form. Doing so ensures that every time the HTML form is used with different values for `phrase` and `letters`, the results returned from our webapp adjust accordingly.

Let's make these changes to our program code. Start by adding the `request` object to the list of imports from Flask. To do that, change the first line of `vsearch4web.py` to look like this:

```python
from flask import Flask, render_template, request
```

Add "request" to the list of imports.

We know from the information on the last page that we can access the `phrase` entered into the HTML form within our code as `request.form['phrase']`, whereas the entered `letters` is available to us as `request.form['letters']`. Let's adjust the `do_search` function to use these values (and remove the hardcoded strings):

Create two new variables...

```python
@app.route('/search4', methods=['POST'])
def do_search() -> str:
    phrase = request.form['phrase']
    letters = request.form['letters']
    return str(search4letters(phrase, letters))
```

...and assign the HTML form's data to the newly created variables...

...then, use the variables in the call to "search4letters".

Automatic Reloads

Now...before you do anything else (having made the changes to your program code above) save your `vsearch4web.py` file, then flip over to your command prompt and take a look at the status messages produced by your webapp. Here's what we saw (you should see something similar):

```
$ python3 vsearch4web.py
 * Restarting with stat
 * Debugger is active!
 * Debugger pin code: 228-903-465
127.0.0.1 - - [23/Nov/2015 22:39:11] "GET /entry HTTP/1.1" 200 -
127.0.0.1 - - [23/Nov/2015 22:39:11] "GET /static/hf.css HTTP/1.1" 200 -
127.0.0.1 - - [23/Nov/2015 22:17:58] "POST /search4 HTTP/1.1" 200 -
 * Detected change in 'vsearch4web.py', reloading
 * Restarting with stat
 * Debugger is active!
 * Debugger pin code: 228-903-465
```

The Flask debugger has spotted the code changes, and restarted your webapp for you. Pretty handy, eh?

Don't panic if you see something other than what's shown here. Automatic reloading only works if the code changes you make are correct. If your code has errors, the webapp bombs out to your command prompt. To get going again, fix your coding errors, then restart your webapp manually (by pressing the *up arrow*, then *Enter*).

TEST DRIVE

Now that we've changed our webapp to accept (and process) the data from our HTML form, we can throw different phrases and letters at it, and it should do the right thing:

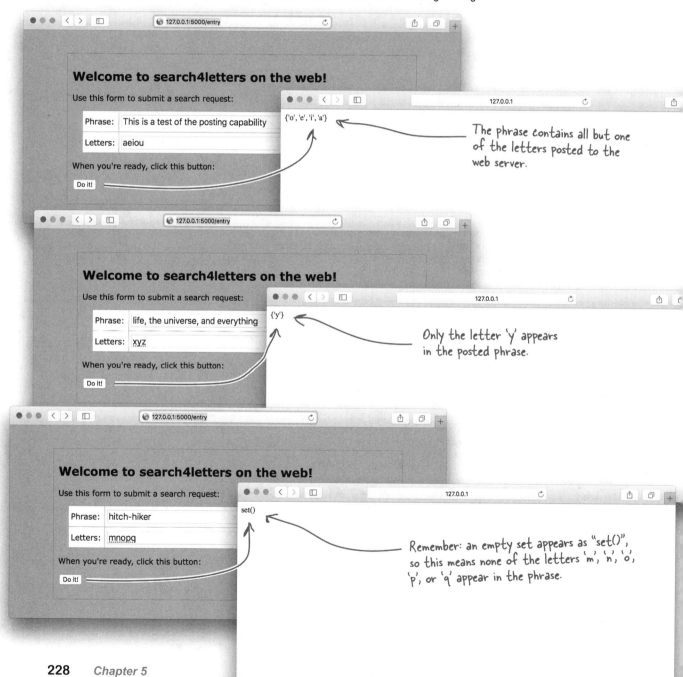

The phrase contains all but one of the letters posted to the web server.

Only the letter 'y' appears in the posted phrase.

Remember: an empty set appears as "set()", so this means none of the letters 'm', 'n', 'o', 'p', or 'q' appear in the phrase.

Producing the Results As HTML

At this point, the functionality associated with our webapp is working: any web browser can submit a `phrase`/`letters` combination, and our webapp invokes `search4letters` on our behalf, returning any results. However, the output produced isn't really a HTML webpage—it's just the raw data returned as text to the waiting browser (which displays it on screen).

Recall the back-of-the-napkin specifications from earlier in this chapter. This is what we were hoping to produce:

This part is done. The "entry.html" template produces an approximation of this form for us.

Welcome to search4letters on the Web!

Use this form to submit a search request:

Phrase:

Letters: aeiou

When you're ready, click this button:

Do it!

Here are your results:

You submitted the following data:

Phrase: hitch-hiker

Letters: aeiou

When "hitch-hiker" is searched for "aeiou", the following results are returned:

{ 'e', 'i' }

This part remains to be done. At the moment, we're only displaying the results as raw data.

When we learned about Jinja2's template technology, we presented two HTML templates. The first, `entry.html`, is used to produce the form. The second, `results.html`, is used to display the results. Let's use it now to take our raw data output and turn it into HTML.

there are no
Dumb Questions

Q: It is possible to use Jinja2 to template textual data other than HTML?

A: Yes. Jinja2 is a text template engine that can be put to many uses. That said, its typical use case is with web development projects (as used here with Flask), but there's nothing stopping you from using it with other textual data if you really want to.

Calculating the Data We Need

Let's remind ourselves of the contents of the `results.html` template as presented earlier in this chapter. The Jinja2-specific markup is highlighted:

This is "results.html".

```
{% extends 'base.html' %}

{% block body %}

<h2>{{ the_title }}</h2>

<p>You submitted the following data:</p>
<table>
<tr><td>Phrase:</td><td>{{ the_phrase }}</td></tr>
<tr><td>Letters:</td><td>{{ the_letters }}</td></tr>
</table>

<p>When "{{the_phrase }}" is search for "{{ the_letters }}", the following
results are returned:</p>
<h3>{{ the_results }}</h3>

{% endblock %}
```

The highlighted names enclosed in double curly braces are Jinja2 variables that take their value from corresponding variables in your Python code. There are four of these variables: `the_title`, `the_phrase`, `the_letters`, and `the_results`. Take another look at the `do_search` function's code (below), which we are going to adjust in just a moment to render the HTML template shown above. As you can see, this function already contains two of the four variables we need to render the template (and to keep things as simple as possible, we've used variable names in our Python code that are similar to those used in the Jinja2 template):

Here are two of the four values we need.

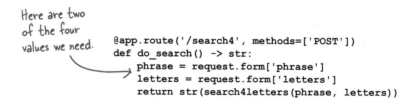

```
@app.route('/search4', methods=['POST'])
def do_search() -> str:
    phrase = request.form['phrase']
    letters = request.form['letters']
    return str(search4letters(phrase, letters))
```

The two remaining required template arguments (`the_title` and `the_results`) still need to be created from variables in this function and assigned values.

We can assign the "`Here are your results:`" string to `the_title`, and then assign the call to `search4letters` to `the_results`. All four variables can then be passed into the `results.html` template as arguments prior to rendering.

Template Magnets

The *Head First* authors got together and, based on the requirements for the updated `do_search` function outlined at the bottom of the last page, wrote the code required. In true *Head First* style, they did so with the help of some coding magnets...and a fridge (best if you don't ask). Upon their success, the resulting celebrations got so rowdy that a certain *series editor* bumped into the fridge (while singing the *beer song*) and now the magnets are all over the floor. Your job is to stick the magnets back in their correct locations in the code.

```python
from flask import Flask, render_template, request
from vsearch import search4letters

app = Flask(__name__)

@app.route('/')
def hello() -> str:
    return 'Hello world from Flask!'

@app.route('/search4', methods=['POST'])

def do_search() -> ..............:
    phrase = request.form['phrase']
    letters = request.form['letters']

    .........................................................

    .........................................................
    return .......................................................
                    ...........................................
                    ...........................................
                    ...........................................
                    ...........................................

@app.route('/entry')
def entry_page() -> 'html':
    return render_template('entry.html',
                    the_title='Welcome to search4letters on the web!')

app.run(debug=True)
```

Decide which code magnet goes in each of the dashed-line locations.

Here are the magnets you have to work with:

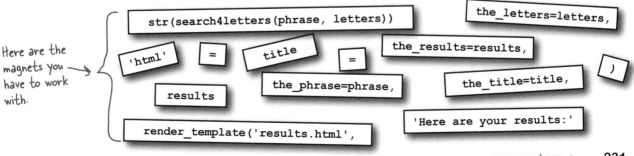

- `str(search4letters(phrase, letters))`
- `the_letters=letters,`
- `'html'`
- `=`
- `title`
- `=`
- `the_results=results,`
- `)`
- `results`
- `the_phrase=phrase,`
- `the_title=title,`
- `render_template('results.html',`
- `'Here are your results:'`

Template Magnets Solution

Having made a note to keep a future eye on a certain series editor's beer consumption, you set to work restoring all of the code magnets for the updated `do_search` function. Your job was to stick the magnets back in their correct locations in the code.

Here's what we came up with when we performed this task:

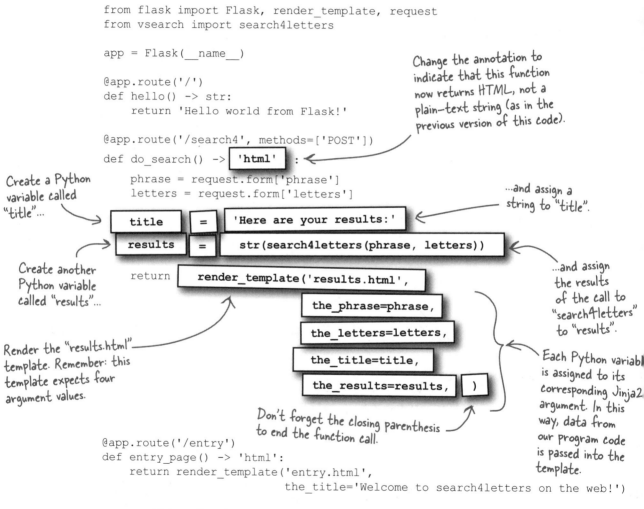

```python
from flask import Flask, render_template, request
from vsearch import search4letters

app = Flask(__name__)

@app.route('/')
def hello() -> str:
    return 'Hello world from Flask!'

@app.route('/search4', methods=['POST'])
def do_search() -> 'html' :
    phrase = request.form['phrase']
    letters = request.form['letters']
    title = 'Here are your results:'
    results = str(search4letters(phrase, letters))
    return render_template('results.html',
            the_phrase=phrase,
            the_letters=letters,
            the_title=title,
            the_results=results, )

@app.route('/entry')
def entry_page() -> 'html':
    return render_template('entry.html',
                    the_title='Welcome to search4letters on the web!')

app.run(debug=True)
```

Change the annotation to indicate that this function now returns HTML, not a plain-text string (as in the previous version of this code).

Create a Python variable called "title"...

...and assign a string to "title".

Create another Python variable called "results"...

...and assign the results of the call to "search4letters" to "results".

Render the "results.html" template. Remember: this template expects four argument values.

Don't forget the closing parenthesis to end the function call.

Each Python variable is assigned to its corresponding Jinja2 argument. In this way, data from our program code is passed into the template.

Now that the magnets are back in their correct locations, make these code changes to your copy of `vsearch4web.py`. Be sure to save your file to ensure that Flask automatically reloads your webapp. We're now ready for another test.

Test Drive

Let's test the new version of our webapp using the same examples from earlier in this chapter. Note that Flask restarted your webapp the moment you saved your code.

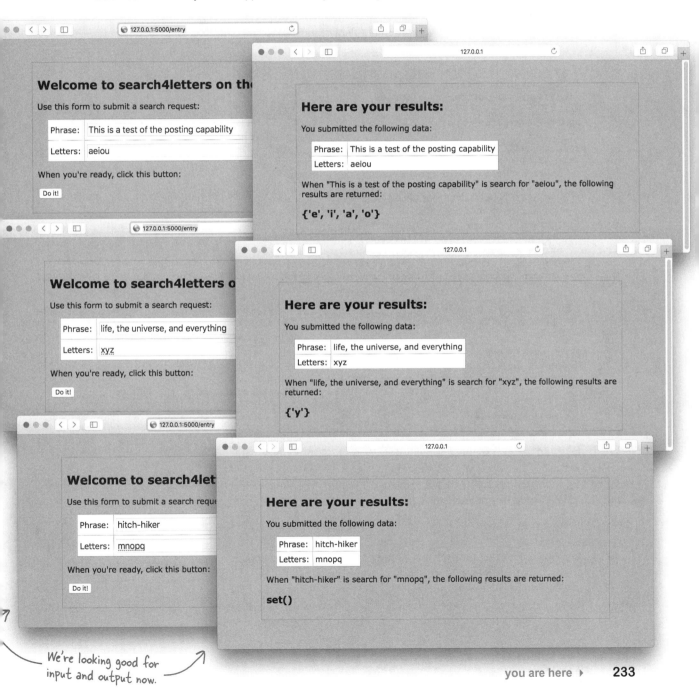

We're looking good for input and output now.

Adding a Finishing Touch

Let's take another look at the code that currently makes up `vsearch4web.py`. Hopefully, by now, all this code should make sense to you. One small syntactical element that often confuses programmers moving to Python is the inclusion of the final comma in the call to `render_template`, as most programmers feel this should be a syntax error and shouldn't be allowed. Although it does look somewhat strange (at first), Python allows it—but does not require it—so we can safely move on and not worry about it:

```python
from flask import Flask, render_template, request
from vsearch import search4letters

app = Flask(__name__)

@app.route('/')
def hello() -> str:
    return 'Hello world from Flask!'

@app.route('/search4', methods=['POST'])
def do_search() -> 'html':
    phrase = request.form['phrase']
    letters = request.form['letters']
    title = 'Here are your results:'
    results = str(search4letters(phrase, letters))
    return render_template('results.html',
                           the_title=title,
                           the_phrase=phrase,
                           the_letters=letters,
                           the_results=results,)

@app.route('/entry')
def entry_page() -> 'html':
    return render_template('entry.html',
                           the_title='Welcome to search4letters on the web!')

app.run(debug=True)
```

This extra comma looks a little strange, but is perfectly fine (though optional) Python syntax.

This version of our webapp supports three URLs: /, */search4*, and */entry*, with some dating back to the very first Flask webapp we created (right at the start of this chapter). At the moment, the / URL displays the friendly, but somewhat unhelpful, "Hello world from Flask!" message.

We could remove this URL and its associated `hello` function from our code (as we no longer need either), but doing so would result in a 404 "Not Found" error in any web browser contacting our webapp on the / URL, which is the default URL for most webapps and websites. To avoid this annoying error message, let's ask Flask to redirect any request for the / URL to the */entry* URL. We do this by adjusting the `hello` function to return a HTML `redirect` to any web browser that requests the / URL, effectively substituting the */entry* URL for any request made for /.

Redirect to Avoid Unwanted Errors

To use Flask's redirection technology, add `redirect` to the `from flask` import line (at the top of your code), then change the `hello` function's code to look like this:

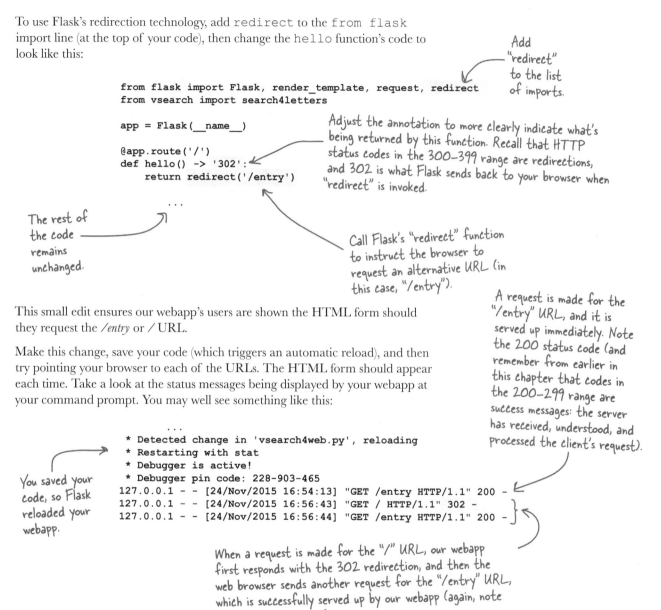

Add "redirect" to the list of imports.

```
from flask import Flask, render_template, request, redirect
from vsearch import search4letters

app = Flask(__name__)

@app.route('/')
def hello() -> '302':
    return redirect('/entry')

        . . .
```

Adjust the annotation to more clearly indicate what's being returned by this function. Recall that HTTP status codes in the 300–399 range are redirections, and 302 is what Flask sends back to your browser when "redirect" is invoked.

The rest of the code remains unchanged.

Call Flask's "redirect" function to instruct the browser to request an alternative URL (in this case, "/entry").

This small edit ensures our webapp's users are shown the HTML form should they request the */entry* or */* URL.

Make this change, save your code (which triggers an automatic reload), and then try pointing your browser to each of the URLs. The HTML form should appear each time. Take a look at the status messages being displayed by your webapp at your command prompt. You may well see something like this:

A request is made for the "/entry" URL, and it is served up immediately. Note the 200 status code (and remember from earlier in this chapter that codes in the 200–299 range are success messages: the server has received, understood, and processed the client's request).

```
        . . .
* Detected change in 'vsearch4web.py', reloading
* Restarting with stat
* Debugger is active!
* Debugger pin code: 228-903-465
127.0.0.1 - - [24/Nov/2015 16:54:13] "GET /entry HTTP/1.1" 200 -
127.0.0.1 - - [24/Nov/2015 16:56:43] "GET / HTTP/1.1" 302 -
127.0.0.1 - - [24/Nov/2015 16:56:44] "GET /entry HTTP/1.1" 200 -
```

You saved your code, so Flask reloaded your webapp.

When a request is made for the "/" URL, our webapp first responds with the 302 redirection, and then the web browser sends another request for the "/entry" URL, which is successfully served up by our webapp (again, note the 200 status code).

As a strategy, our use of redirection here works, but it is somewhat wasteful—a single request for the / URL turns into two requests every time (although client-side caching can help, this is still not optimal). If only Flask could somehow associate more than one URL with a given function, effectively removing the need for the redirection altogether. That would be nice, wouldn't it?

Functions Can Have Multiple URLs

It's not hard to guess where we are going with this, is it?

It turns out that Flask can indeed associate more than one URL with a given function, which can reduce the need for redirections like the one demonstrated on the last page. When a function has more than one URL associated with it, Flask tries to match each of the URLs in turn, and if it finds a match, the function is executed.

It's not hard to take advantage of this Flask feature. To begin, remove `redirect` from the `from flask` import line at the top of your program code; we no longer need it, so let's not import code we don't intend to use. Next, using your editor, cut the `@app.route('/')` line of code and then paste it above the `@app.route('/entry')` line near the bottom of your file. Finally, delete the two lines of code that make up the `hello` function, as our webapp no longer needs them.

When you're done making these changes, your program code should look like this:

```
from flask import Flask, render_template, request
from vsearch import search4letters

app = Flask(__name__)

@app.route('/search4', methods=['POST'])
def do_search() -> 'html':
    phrase = request.form['phrase']
    letters = request.form['letters']
    title = 'Here are your results:'
    results = str(search4letters(phrase, letters))
    return render_template('results.html',
                           the_title=title,
                           the_phrase=phrase,
                           the_letters=letters,
                           the_results=results,)

@app.route('/')
@app.route('/entry')
def entry_page() -> 'html':
    return render_template('entry.html',
                           the_title='Welcome to search4letters on the web!')

app.run(debug=True)
```

We no longer need to import "redirect", so we've removed it from this import line.

The "hello" function has been removed.

The "entry_page" function now has two URLs associated with it.

Saving this code (which triggers a reload) allows us to test this new functionality. If you visit the / URL, the HTML form appears. A quick look at your webapp's status messages confirms that processing / now results in one request, as opposed to two (as was previously the case):

```
  . . .
 * Detected change in 'vsearch4web.py', reloading
 * Restarting with stat
 * Debugger is active!
 * Debugger pin code: 228-903-465
127.0.0.1 - - [24/Nov/2015 16:59:10] "GET / HTTP/1.1" 200 -
```

As always, the new version of our webapp reloads.

One request, one response. That's more like it. ☺

Updating What We Know

We've just spent the last 40 pages creating a small webapp that exposes the functionality provided by our `search4letters` function to the World Wide Web (via a simple two-page website). At the moment, the webapp runs locally on your computer. In a bit, we'll discuss deploying your webapp to the cloud, but for now let's update what you know:

BULLET POINTS

- You learned about the Python Package Index (**PyPI**), which is a centralized repository for third-party Python modules. When connected to the Internet, you can automatically install packages from PyPI using `pip`.

- You used `pip` to install the **Flask** micro-web framework, which you then used to build your webapp.

- The `__name__` value (maintained by the interpreter) identifies the currently active namespace (more on this later).

- The `@` symbol before a function's name identifies it as a **decorator**. Decorators let you change the behavior of an existing function without having to change the function's code. In your webapp, you used Flask's `@app.route` decorator to associate URLs with Python functions. A function can be decorated more than once (as you saw with the `do_search` function).

- You learned how to use the **Jinja2** text template engine to render HTML pages from within your webapp.

Is that all there is to this chapter?

You'd be forgiven for thinking this chapter doesn't introduce much new Python. It doesn't. However, one of the points of this chapter was to show you just how few lines of Python code you need to produce something that's generally useful on the Web, thanks in no small part to our use of Flask. Using a template technology helps a lot, too, as it allows you to keep your Python code (your webapp's logic) separate from your HTML pages (your webapp's user interface).

It's not an awful lot of work to extend this webapp to do more. In fact, you could have an HTML whiz-kid produce more pages for you while you concentrate on writing the Python code that ties everything together. As your webapp scales, this separation of duties really starts to pay off. You get to concentrate on the Python code (as you're the programmer on the project), whereas the HTML whiz-kid concentrates on the markup (as that's their bailiwick). Of course, you both have to learn a little bit about Jinja2 templates, but that's not too difficult, is it?

Preparing Your Webapp for the Cloud

With your webapp working to specification locally on your computer, it's time to think about deploying it for use by a wider audience. There are lots of options here, with many different web-based hosting setups available to you as a Python programmer. One popular service is cloud-based, hosted on AWS, and is called *PythonAnywhere*. We love it over at *Head First Labs*.

Like nearly every other cloud-hosted deployment solution, *PythonAnywhere* likes to control how your webapp starts. For you, this means *PythonAnywhere* assumes responsibility for calling `app.run()` on your behalf, which means you no longer need to call `app.run()` in your code. In fact, if you try to execute that line of code, *PythonAnywhere* simply refuses to run your webapp.

A simple solution to this problem would be to remove that last line of code from your file *before* deploying to the cloud. This certainly works, but means you need to put that line of code back in again whenever you run your webapp locally. If you're writing and testing new code, you should do so locally (not on *PythonAnywhere*), as you use the cloud for deployment only, not for development. Also, removing the offending line of code effectively amounts to you having to maintain two versions of the same webapp, one with and one without that line of code. This is never a good idea (and gets harder to manage as you make more changes).

It would be nice if there were a way to selectively execute code based on whether you're running your webapp locally on your computer or remotely on *PythonAnywhere*...

> I've looked at an awful lot of Python programs online, and many of them contain a suite near the bottom that starts with: `if __name__ == '__main__':` Would something like that help here?

Yes, that's a great suggestion.

That particular line of code *is* used in lots of Python programs. It's affectionately referred to as "dunder name dunder main." To understand why it's so useful (and why we can take advantage of it with *PythonAnywhere*), let's take a closer look at what it does, and how it works.

Dunder Name Dunder Main Up Close

To understand the programming construct suggested at the bottom of the last page, let's look at a small program that uses it, called dunder.py. This three-line program begins by displaying a message on screen that prints the currently active namespace, stored in the __name__ variable. An if statement then checks to see whether the value of __name__ is set to __main__, and—if it is—another message is displayed confirming the value of __name__ (i.e., the code associated with the if suite executes):

The "dunder.py" program code—all three lines of it.

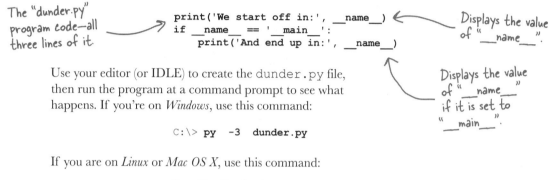

```
print('We start off in:', __name__)
if __name__ == '__main__':
    print('And end up in:', __name__)
```

Displays the value of "__name__".

Displays the value of "__name__" if it is set to "__main__".

Use your editor (or IDLE) to create the dunder.py file, then run the program at a command prompt to see what happens. If you're on *Windows*, use this command:

```
C:\> py -3 dunder.py
```

If you are on *Linux* or *Mac OS X*, use this command:

```
$ python3 dunder.py
```

No matter which operating system you're running, the dunder.py program—when executed *directly* by Python—produces this output on screen:

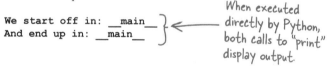

```
We start off in: __main__
And end up in: __main__
```

When executed directly by Python, both calls to "print" display output.

So far, so good.

Now, look what happens when we import the dunder.py file (which, remember, is *also* a module) into the >>> prompt. We're showing the output on *Linux/Mac OS X* here. To do the same thing on *Windows*, replace python3 (below) with py -3:

```
$ python3
Python 3.5.1 ...
Type "help", "copyright", "credits" or "license" for more information.
>>> import dunder
We start off in: dunder
```

Look at this: there's only a single line displayed (as opposed to two), as "__name__" has been set to "dunder" (which is the name of the imported module).

Here's the bit you need to understand: if your program code is executed *directly* by Python, an if statement like the one in dunder.py returns True, as the active namespace is __main__. If, however, your program code is imported as a module (as in the Python Shell prompt example above), the if statement always returns False, as the value of __name__ is not __main__, but the name of the imported module (dunder in this case).

Exploiting Dunder Name Dunder Main

Now that you know what *dunder name dunder main* does, let's exploit it to solve the problem we have with *PythonAnywhere* wanting to execute `app.run()` on our behalf.

It turns out that when *PythonAnywhere* executes our webapp code, it does so by importing the file that contains our code, treating it like any other module. If the import is successful, *PythonAnywhere* then calls `app.run()`. This explains why leaving `app.run()` at the bottom of our code is such a problem for *PythonAnywhere*, as it assumes the `app.run()` call has not been made, and fails to start our webapp when the `app.run()` call has been made.

To get around this problem, wrap the `app.run()` call in a *dunder name dunder main* `if` statement (which ensures `app.run()` is never executed when the webapp code is imported).

Edit `vsearch4web.py` one last time (in this chapter, anyway) and change the final line of code to this:

```
if __name__ == '__main__':
    app.run(debug=True)
```

The "app.run()" line of code now only runs when executed directly by Python.

This small change lets you continue to execute your webapp locally (where the `app.run()` line *will* execute) as well as deploy your webapp to *PythonAnywhere* (where the `app.run()` line *won't* execute). No matter where your webapp runs, you've now got one version of your code that does the right thing.

Deploying to PythonAnywhere (well... almost)

All that remains is for you to perform that actual deployment to *PythonAnywhere's* cloud-hosted environment.

Note that, for the purposes of this book, deploying your webapp to the cloud is *not* an absolute requirement. Despite the fact that we intend to extend `vsearch4web.py` with additional functionality in the next chapter, you do not need to deploy to *PythonAnywhere* to follow along. You can happily continue to edit/run/test your webapp locally as we extend it in the next chapter (and beyond).

However, if you really do want to deploy to the cloud, see *Appendix B*, which provides step-by-step instructions on how to complete the deployment on *PythonAnywhere*. It's not hard, and won't take more than 10 minutes.

Whether you're deploying to the cloud or not, we'll see you in the next chapter, where we'll start to look at some of the options available for saving data from within your Python programs.

Chapter 5's Code

```
from flask import Flask
from vsearch import search4letters

app = Flask(__name__)

@app.route('/')
def hello() -> str:
    return 'Hello world from Flask!'

@app.route('/search4')
def do_search() -> str:
    return str(search4letters('life, the universe, and everything', 'eiru,!'))

app.run()
```

This is "hello_flask.
py", our first webapp
based on Flask (one of
Python's micro-web
framework technologies).

This is "vsearch4web.py".
This webapp exposed the
functionality provided by our
"search4letters" function to
the World Wide Web. In addition
to Flask, this code exploited
the Jinja2 template engine.

```
from flask import Flask, render_template, request
from vsearch import search4letters

app = Flask(__name__)

@app.route('/search4', methods=['POST'])
def do_search() -> 'html':
    phrase = request.form['phrase']
    letters = request.form['letters']
    title = 'Here are your results:'
    results = str(search4letters(phrase, letters))
    return render_template('results.html',
                            the_title=title,
                            the_phrase=phrase,
                            the_letters=letters,
                            the_results=results,)

@app.route('/')
@app.route('/entry')
def entry_page() -> 'html':
    return render_template('entry.html',
                            the_title='Welcome to... web!')

if __name__ == '__main__':
    app.run(debug=True)
```

This is "dunder.py", which
helped us understand the very
handy "dunder name dunder main"
mechanism.

```
print('We start off in:', __name__)
if __name__ == '__main__':
    print('And end up in:', __name__)
```

6 storing and manipulating data

Where to Put Your Data

Yes, yes...your data is safely stored. In fact, I'm writing down everything as we speak.

Sooner or later, you'll need to safely store your data somewhere.

And when it comes to **storing data**, Python has you covered. In this chapter, you'll learn about storing and retrieving data from *text files*, which—as storage mechanisms go—may feel a bit simplistic, but is nevertheless used in many problem areas. As well as storing and retrieving your data from files, you'll also learn some tricks of the trade when it comes to manipulating data. We're saving the "serious stuff" (storing data in a database) until the next chapter, but there's plenty to keep us busy for now when working with files.

Doing Something with Your Webapp's Data

At the moment, your webapp (developed in Chapter 5) accepts input from any web browser (in the form of a `phrase` and some `letters`), performs a `search4letters` call, and then returns any results to the waiting web browser. Once done, your webapp discards any data it has.

There are a bunch of questions that we could ask of the data our webapp uses. For instance: *How many requests have been responded to? What's the most common list of letters? Which IP addresses are the requests coming from? Which browser is being used the most?* and so on, and so forth.

In order to begin answering these (and other) questions, we need to save the webapp's data as opposed to simply throwing it away. The suggestion above makes perfect sense: let's log data about each web request, then—once we have the logging mechanism in place—go about answering any questions we have.

Python Supports Open, Process, Close

No matter the programming language, the easiest way to store data is to save it to a text file. Consequently, Python comes with built-in support for *open, process, close*. This common technique lets you **open** a file, **process** its data in some way (reading, writing, and/or appending data), and then **close** the file when you're done (which saves your changes).

Here's how to use Python's *open, process, close* technique to open a file, process it by appending some short strings to it, and then close the file. As we're only experimenting for now, let's run our code at the Python >>> shell.

We start by calling open on a file called todos.txt, using *append mode*, as our plan is to add data to this file. If the call to open succeeds, the interpreter returns an object (known as a *file stream*) which is an alias for the actual file. The object is assigned to a variable and given the name todos (although you could use whichever name you wish here):

Geek Bits

To access the >>> prompt:

- run IDLE on your computer;

- run the python3 command in a *Linux* or *Mac OS X* terminal; or

- use py -3 at a *Windows* command line.

Open a file...   ...which has this
                                  filename...

```
>>> todos = open('todos.txt', 'a')
```

...and open the file in "append-mode".

If all is OK, "open" returns a file stream, which we've assigned to this variable.

The todos variable lets you refer to your file in your code (other programming languages refer to this as a *file handle*). Now that the file is open, let's write to it using print. Note how, below, print takes an extra argument (file), which identifies the file stream to write to. We have three things to remember to do (it's never-ending, really), so we call print three times:

We print a message...   ...to the file stream.

```
>>> print('Put out the trash.', file=todos)
>>> print('Feed the cat.', file=todos)
>>> print('Prepare tax return.', file=todos)
```

As we have nothing else to add to our to-do list, let's close the file by calling the close method, which is made available by the interpreter to every file stream:

```
>>> todos.close()
```

We're done, so let's tidy up after ourselves by closing the file stream.

If you forget to call close, you could *potentially* lose data. Remembering to always call close is important.

Reading Data from an Existing File

Now that you've added some lines of data to the `todos.txt` file, let's look at the *open, process, close* code needed to read the saved data from the file and display it on screen.

Rather than opening the file in append mode, this time you are only interested in reading from the file. As reading is `open`'s **default mode**, you don't need to provide a mode argument; the name of the file is all you need here. We're not using `todos` as the alias for the file in this code; instead, we'll refer to the open file by the name `tasks` (as before, you can use whichever variable name you want to here):

"Reading" is the "open" function's default mode.

Open a file...

...which has this filename.

```
>>> tasks = open('todos.txt')
```

If all is OK, "open" returns a file stream, which we've assigned to this variable.

Let's now use `tasks` with a `for` loop to read each individual line from the file. When we do this, the `for` loop's iteration variable (`chore`) is assigned the current line of data as read from the file. Each iteration assigns a line of data to `chore`. When you use a file stream with Python's `for` loop, the interpreter is smart enough to read a line of data from the file each time the loop iterates. It's also smart enough to terminate the loop when there's no more data to read:

The "tasks" variable is the file stream.

```
>>> for chore in tasks:
...     print(chore)
...
Put out the trash.

Feed the cat.

File tax return.
```

Think of "chore" as an alias for the line in the file.

The output shows the data from the "todos.txt" file. Note how the loop ends when we run out of lines to read.

As you are merely reading from an already written-to file, calling `close` is less critical here than when you are writing data. But it's always a good idea to close a file when it is no longer needed, so call the `close` method when you're done:

```
>>> tasks.close()
```

We're done, so let's tidy up after ourselves by closing the file stream.

there are no
Dumb Questions

Q: **What's the deal with the extra newlines on output? The data in the file is three lines long, but the** `for` **loop produced six lines of output on my display. What gives?**

A: Yes, the `for` loop's output does look strange, doesn't it? To understand what's happening, consider that the `print` function appends a newline to everything it displays on screen *as its default behavior*. When you combine this with the fact that each line in the file ends in a newline character (and the newline is read in as part of the line), you end up printing two newlines: the one from the file together with the one from `print`. To instruct `print` not to include the second newline, change `print(chore)` to `print(chore, end='')`. This has the effect of suppressing `print`'s newline-appending behavior, so the extra newlines no longer appear on screen.

Q: **What other modes are available to me when I'm working with data in files?**

A: There are a few, which we've summarized in the following *Geek Bits* box. (That's a great question, BTW.)

Geek Bits

The first argument to `open` is the name of the file to process. The second argument is **optional**. It can be set to a number of different values, and dictates the **mode** the file is opened in. Modes include "reading," "writing," and "appending." Here are the most common mode values, where each (except for `'r'`) creates a new empty file if the file named in the first argument doesn't already exist:

- `'r'` Open a file for **reading**. This is the default mode and, as such, is optional. When no second argument is provided, `'r'` is assumed. It is also assumed that the file being read from already exists.
- `'w'` Open a file for **writing**. If the file already contains data, empty the file of its data before continuing.
- `'a'` Open a file for **appending**. Preserve the file's contents, adding any new data to the end of the file (compare this behavior to `'w'`).
- `'x'` Open a **new file** for writing. Fail if the file already exists (compare this behavior to `'w'` and to `'a'`).

By default, files open in **text** mode, where the file is assumed to contain lines of textual data (e.g., ASCII or UTF-8). If you are working with nontextual data (e.g., an image file or an MP3), you can specify **binary** mode by adding "b" to any of the modes (e.g., `'wb'` means "write to a binary data"). If you include "+" as part of the second argument, the file is opened for reading *and* writing (e.g., `'x+b'` means "read from and write to a new binary file"). Refer to the Python docs for more details on `open` (including information on its other optional arguments).

> I've looked at a bunch of Python projects on GitHub, and most of them use a "with" statement when opening files. What's the deal with that?

The `with` statement is more convenient.

Although using the `open` function together with the `close` method (with a bit of processing in the middle) works fine, most Python programmers shun *open, process, close* in favor of the `with` statement. Let's take some time to find out why.

247

A Better Open, Process, Close: "with"

Before we describe why `with` is so popular, let's take a look at some code that uses `with`. Here is the code we wrote (two pages ago) to read in and display the current contents of our `todos.txt` file. Note that we've adjusted the `print` function call to suppress the extra newline on output:

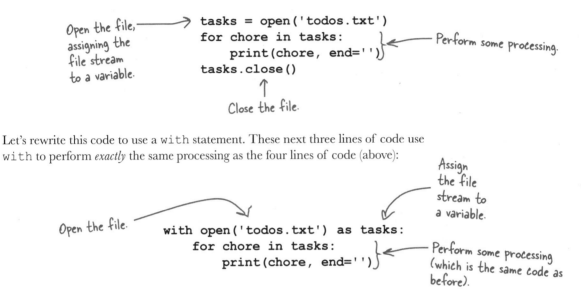

```
Open the file,
assigning the
file stream
to a variable.          tasks = open('todos.txt')
                        for chore in tasks:
                            print(chore, end='')      Perform some processing.
                        tasks.close()
                             ↑
                        Close the file.
```

Let's rewrite this code to use a `with` statement. These next three lines of code use `with` to perform *exactly* the same processing as the four lines of code (above):

```
                                                    Assign
                                                    the file
                                                    stream to
                                                    a variable.
Open the file.   with open('todos.txt') as tasks:
                     for chore in tasks:
                         print(chore, end='')        Perform some processing
                                                     (which is the same code as
                                                     before).
```

Notice anything missing? The call to `close` does not make an appearance. The `with` statement is smart enough to remember to call `close` *on your behalf* whenever its suite of code ends.

This is actually much more useful than it initially sounds, as lots of programmers often forget to call `close` when they're done processing a file. This is not such a big deal when all you're doing is reading from a file, but when you're writing to a file, forgetting to call close can potentially cause *data loss* or *data corruption*. By relieving you of the need to remember to always call `close`, the `with` statement lets you concentrate on what it is you're actually doing with the data in the open file.

The "with" statement manages context

The `with` statement conforms to a coding convention built into Python called the **context management protocol**. We're deferring a detailed discussion of this protocol until later in this book. For now, all you have to concern yourself with is the fact that when you use `with` when working with files, you can forget about calling `close`. The `with` statement is managing the context within which its suite runs, and when you use `with` and `open` together, the interpreter cleans up after you, calling `close` as and when required.

> **Python supports "open, process, close." But most Python programmers prefer to use the "with" statement.**

Exercise

Let's put what you now know about working with files to use. Here is the current code for your webapp. Give it another read before we tell you what you have to do:

```
from flask import Flask, render_template, request
from vsearch import search4letters

app = Flask(__name__)

@app.route('/search4', methods=['POST'])
def do_search() -> 'html':
    phrase = request.form['phrase']
    letters = request.form['letters']
    title = 'Here are your results:'
    results = str(search4letters(phrase, letters))
    return render_template('results.html',
                            the_title=title,
                            the_phrase=phrase,
                            the_letters=letters,
                            the_results=results,)

@app.route('/')
@app.route('/entry')
def entry_page() -> 'html':
    return render_template('entry.html',
                            the_title='Welcome to search4letters on the web!')

if __name__ == '__main__':
    app.run(debug=True)
```

This is the "vsearch4web.py" code from Chapter 5.

Your job is to write a new function, called `log_request`, which takes two arguments: `req` and `res`. When invoked, the `req` argument is assigned the current Flask request object, while the `res` argument is assigned the results from calling `search4letters`. The `log_request` function's suite should append the value of `req` and `res` (as one line) to a file called `vsearch.log`. We've got you started by providing the function's `def` line. You are to provide the missing code (hint: use `with`):

Write this function's suite here.

```
def log_request(req: 'flask_request', res: str) -> None:
```

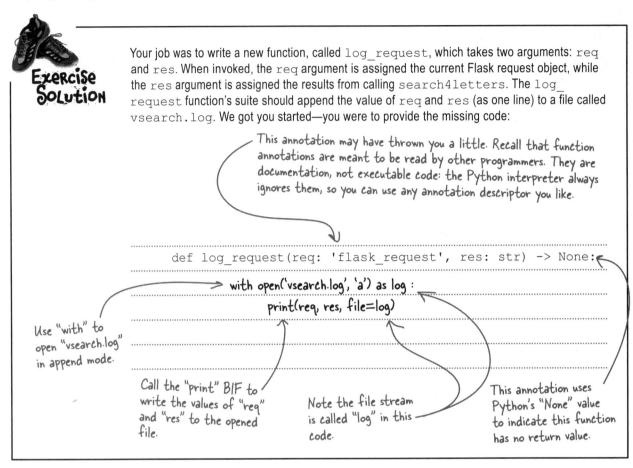

Exercise Solution

Your job was to write a new function, called `log_request`, which takes two arguments: `req` and `res`. When invoked, the `req` argument is assigned the current Flask request object, while the `res` argument is assigned the results from calling `search4letters`. The `log_request` function's suite should append the value of `req` and `res` (as one line) to a file called `vsearch.log`. We got you started—you were to provide the missing code:

This annotation may have thrown you a little. Recall that function annotations are meant to be read by other programmers. They are documentation, not executable code: the Python interpreter always ignores them, so you can use any annotation descriptor you like.

```
def log_request(req: 'flask_request', res: str) -> None:
    with open('vsearch.log', 'a') as log :
        print(req, res, file=log)
```

Use "with" to open "vsearch.log" in append mode.

Call the "print" BIF to write the values of "req" and "res" to the opened file.

Note the file stream is called "log" in this code.

This annotation uses Python's "None" value to indicate this function has no return value.

Invoking the logging function

Now that the `log_request` function exists, when do we invoke it?

Well, for starters, let's add the `log_request` code into the `vsearch4web.py` file. You can put it anywhere in this file, but we inserted it directly above the `do_search` function and its associated `@app.route` decorator. We did this because we're going to invoke it from within the `do_search` function, and putting it above the calling function seems like a good idea.

We need to be sure to call `log_request` before the `do_search` function ends, but after the `results` have been returned from the call to `search4letters`. Here's a snippet of `do_search`'s code showing the inserted call:

Call the "log_request" function here.

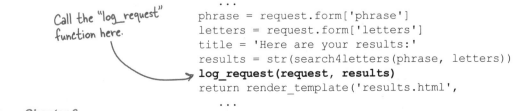

```
    ...
    phrase = request.form['phrase']
    letters = request.form['letters']
    title = 'Here are your results:'
    results = str(search4letters(phrase, letters))
    log_request(request, results)
    return render_template('results.html',
    ...
```

A Quick Review

Before taking this latest version of `vsearch4web.py` for a spin, let's check that your code is the same as ours. Here's the entire file, with the latest additions highlighted:

```python
from flask import Flask, render_template, request
from vsearch import search4letters

app = Flask(__name__)

def log_request(req: 'flask_request', res: str) -> None:
    with open('vsearch.log', 'a') as log:
        print(req, res, file=log)

@app.route('/search4', methods=['POST'])
def do_search() -> 'html':
    phrase = request.form['phrase']
    letters = request.form['letters']
    title = 'Here are your results:'
    results = str(search4letters(phrase, letters))
    log_request(request, results)
    return render_template('results.html',
                           the_title=title,
                           the_phrase=phrase,
                           the_letters=letters,
                           the_results=results,)

@app.route('/')
@app.route('/entry')
def entry_page() -> 'html':
    return render_template('entry.html',
                           the_title='Welcome to search4letters on the web!')

if __name__ == '__main__':
    app.run(debug=True)
```

Here are the latest additions, which arrange to log each web request to a file called "vsearch.log".

Take your webapp for a spin...

Start up this version of your webapp (if required) at a command prompt. On *Windows*, use this command:

```
C:\webapps> py -3 vsearch4web.py
```

While on *Linux* or *Mac OS X*, use this command:

```
$ python3 vsearch4web.py
```

With your webapp up and running, let's log some data via the HTML form.

You may have noticed that none of our webapp's functions contain comments. This is a deliberate omission on our part (as there's only so much room on these pages, and something had to give). Note that any code you download from this book's support website always includes comments.

Test Drive

Use your web browser to submit data to it via the webapp's HTML form. If you want to follow along with what we're doing, submit three searches using the following values for `phrase` and `letters`:

> `hitch-hiker` with `aeiou`.

> `life, the universe, and everything` with `aeiou`.

> `galaxy` with `xyz`.

Before you begin, note that the `vsearch.log` file does not yet exist.

The first search

Welcome to search4l

Use this form to submit a search re

Phrase:	hitch-hiker
Letters:	aeiou

When you're ready, click this button

Do it!

Here are your results:

You submitted the following data:

Phrase:	hitch-hiker
Letters:	aeiou

When "hitch-hiker" is search for "aeiou", the following results are returned:

{'e', 'i'}

Welcome to search4letters on t

Use this form to submit a search request:

Phrase:	life, the universe, and everything
Letters:	aeiou

When you're ready, click this button:

Do it!

Here are your results:

You submitted the following data:

Phrase:	life, the universe, and everything
Letters:	aeiou

When "life, the universe, and everything" is search for "aeiou", the following results are returned:

{'e', 'u', 'a', 'i'}

The second search

The browser windows:

Welcome to search4letters on the web!

Use this form to submit a search request:

Phrase:	galaxy
Letters:	xyz

When you're ready, click this button:

Do it!

The third (and final) search

Here are your results:

You submitted the following data:

Phrase:	galaxy
Letters:	xyz

When "galaxy" is search for "xyz", the following results are returned:

{'y', 'x'}

Data is logged (behind the scenes)

Each time the HTML form is used to submit data to the webapp, the `log_request` function saves details of the web request and writes the results to the log file. Immediately after the first search, the `vsearch.log` file is created in the same folder as your webapp's code:

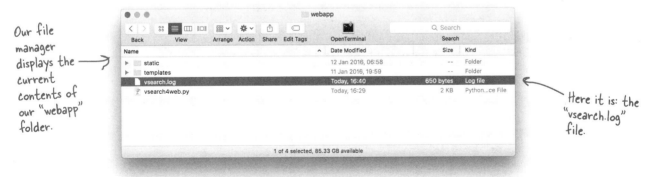

Our file manager displays the current contents of our "webapp" folder.

Here it is: the "vsearch.log" file.

It's tempting to consider using your text editor to view the `vsearch.log` file's contents. But where's the *fun* in that? As this is a webapp, let's provide access to the logged data via the webapp itself. That way, you'll never have to move away from your web browser when interacting with your webapp's data. Let's create a new URL, called */viewlog*, which displays the log's contents on demand.

View the Log Through Your Webapp

You're going to add support for the */viewlog* URL to your webapp. When your webapp receives a request for */viewlog*, it should open the `vsearch.log` file, read in all of its data, and then send the data to the waiting browser.

Most of what you need to do you already know. Start by creating a new `@app.route` line (we're adding this code near the bottom of `vsearch4web.py`, just above the *dunder name dunder main* line):

```
@app.route('/viewlog')
```

We have a brand new URL.

Having decided on the URL, next we'll write a function to go with it. Let's call our new function `view_the_log`. This function won't take any arguments, and will return a string to its caller; the string will be concatenation of all of the lines of data from the `vsearch.log` file. Here's the function's `def` line:

```
def view_the_log() -> str:
```

And we have a brand new function, which (according to the annotation) returns a string.

Now to write the function's suite. You have to open the file *for reading*. This is the `open` function's default mode, so you only need the name of the file as an argument to `open`. Let's manage the context within which our file processing code executes using a `with` statement:

```
with open('vsearch.log') as log:
```

Open the log file for reading.

Within the `with` statement's suite, we need to read all the lines from the file. Your first thought might be to loop through the file, reading each line as you go. However, the interpreter provides a `read` method, which, when invoked, returns the *entire* contents of the file "in one go." Here's the single line of code that does just that, creating a new string called `contents`:

```
contents = log.read()
```

Read the entire file "in one go" and assign it to a variable (which we've called "contents").

With the file read, the `with` statement's suite ends (closing the file), and you are now ready to send the data back to the waiting web browser. This is straightforward:

```
return contents
```

Take the list of lines in "contents" and return them.

With everything put together, you now have all the code you need to respond to the */viewlog* request; it looks like this:

This is all of the code you need to support the "/viewlog" URL. →

```
@app.route('/viewlog')
def view_the_log() -> str:
    with open('vsearch.log') as log:
        contents = log.read()
    return contents
```

TEST DRIVE

With the new code added and saved, your webapp should automatically reload. You can enter some new searches if you like, but the ones you ran a few pages ago are already logged. Any new searches you perform will be appended to the log file. Let's use the */viewlog* URL to take a look at what's been saved. Type ***http://127.0.0.1:5000/viewlog*** into your browser's address bar.

Here's what we saw when we used *Safari* on *Mac OS X* (we also checked *Firefox* and *Chrome*, and got the same output):

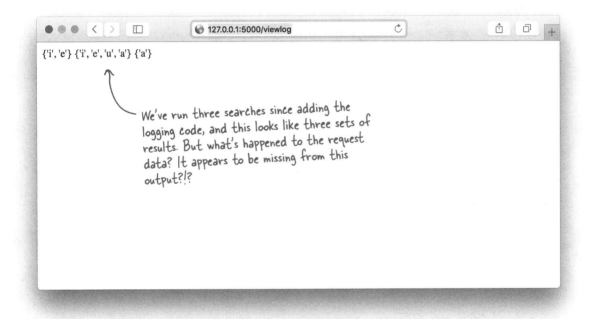

We've run three searches since adding the logging code, and this looks like three sets of results. But what's happened to the request data? It appears to be missing from this output?!?

Where to start when things go wrong with your output

When your output doesn't quite match what you were expecting (which *is* the case above), it's best to start by checking exactly what data the webapp sent you. It's important to note that what's just appeared on screen is a *rendering* (or interpretation) of the webapp's data as performed by your web browser. All the major browsers allow you to view the raw data received with no rendering applied. This is known as the **source** of the page, and viewing it can be a useful debugging aid, as well as a great first step toward understanding what's going on here.

If you are using *Firefox* or *Chrome*, right-click on your browser window and select **View Page Source** from the pop-up menu to see the raw data as sent by your webapp. If you are running *Safari*, you'll first need to enable the developer options: open up Safari's preferences, then switch on the *Show Develop menu in the menu bar* option at the bottom of the *Advanced* tab. Once you do this, you can return to your browser window, right-click, and then select **Show Page Source** from the pop-up menu. Go ahead and view the raw data now, then compare it to what we got (on the next page).

Examine the Raw Data with View Source

Remember, the `log_request` function saves two pieces of data for each web request it logs: the request object as well as the results of the call to `search4letters`. But when you view the log (with */viewlog*), you're only seeing the results data. Does viewing the source (i.e., the raw data returned from the webapp) offer any clue as to what happened to the request object?

Here's what we saw when we used *Firefox* to view the raw data. The fact that each request object's output is colored red is another clue that something is amiss with our log data:

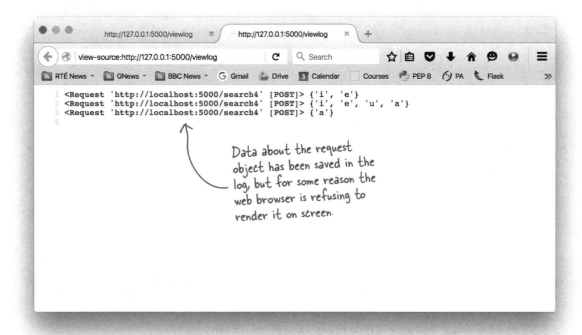

The explanation as to why the request data is not rendering is subtle, and the fact that *Firefox* has highlighted the request data in red helps in understanding what's going on. It appears there's nothing wrong with the actual request data. However, it seems that the data enclosed in angle brackets (< and >) is upsetting the browser. When browsers see an opening angle bracket, they treat everything between that bracket and the matching closing angle bracket as an HTML tag. As `<Request>` is not a valid HTML tag, modern browsers simply ignore it and refuse to render any of the text between the brackets, which is what's happening here. This solves the mystery of the disappearing request data. But we still want to be able to see this data when we view the log using */viewlog*.

What we need to do is somehow tell the browser not to treat the angle brackets surrounding the request object as an HTML tag, but treat them as plain-text instead. As luck would have it, Flask comes with a function that can help.

It's Time to Escape (Your Data)

When HTML was first created, its designers knew that some web page designers would want to display angle brackets (and the other characters that have special meaning to HTML). Consequently, they came up with the concept known as *escaping*: encoding HTML's special characters so that they could appear on a webpage but not be interpreted as HTML. A series of translations were defined, one for each special character. It's a simple idea: a special character such as < is defined as <, while > is defined as >. If you send these translations *instead of* the raw data, your web browser does the right thing: it displays < and > as opposed to ignoring them, and displays all the text between them.

Flask includes a function called escape (which is actually inherited from Jinja2). When provided with some raw data, escape translates the data into its HTML-escaped equivalent. Let's experiment with escape at the Python >>> prompt to get a feel for how it works.

Begin by importing the escape function from the flask module, then call escape with a string containing none of the special characters:

> Geek Bits
>
> Flask's **Markup** object is text that has been marked as being safe within an HTML/XML context. Markup inherits from Python's built-in unicode string, and can be used anywhere you'd use a string.

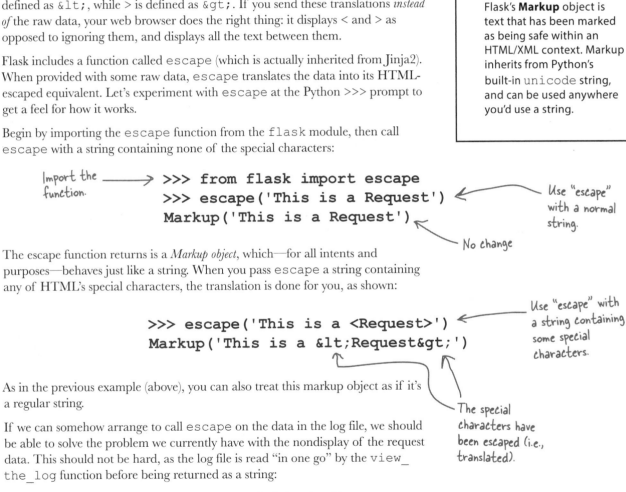

Import the function.

```
>>> from flask import escape
>>> escape('This is a Request')
Markup('This is a Request')
```

Use "escape" with a normal string.

No change

The escape function returns is a *Markup object*, which—for all intents and purposes—behaves just like a string. When you pass escape a string containing any of HTML's special characters, the translation is done for you, as shown:

```
>>> escape('This is a <Request>')
Markup('This is a &lt;Request&gt;')
```

Use "escape" with a string containing some special characters.

The special characters have been escaped (i.e., translated).

As in the previous example (above), you can also treat this markup object as if it's a regular string.

If we can somehow arrange to call escape on the data in the log file, we should be able to solve the problem we currently have with the nondisplay of the request data. This should not be hard, as the log file is read "in one go" by the view_the_log function before being returned as a string:

```
@app.route('/viewlog')
def view_the_log() -> str:
    with open('vsearch.log') as log:
        contents = log.read()
    return contents
```

Here's our log data (as a string).

To solve our problem, all we need to do is call escape on contents.

Viewing the Entire Log in Your Webapp

The change to your code is trivial, but makes a big difference. Add `escape` to the import list for the `flask` module (at the top of your program), then call `escape` on the string returned from calling the `join` method:

```
from flask import Flask, render_template, request, escape

    ...

@app.route('/viewlog')
def view_the_log() -> str:
    with open('vsearch.log') as log:
        contents = log.read()
    return escape(contents)
```

Add to the import list.

Call "escape" on the returned string.

TEST DRIVE

Amend your program to import and call `escape` as shown above, then save your code (so that your webapp reloads). Next, reload the */viewlog* URL in your browser. All of your log data should now appear on screen. Be sure to view the HTML source to confirm that the escaping is working. Here's what we saw when we tested this version of our webapp with *Chrome*:

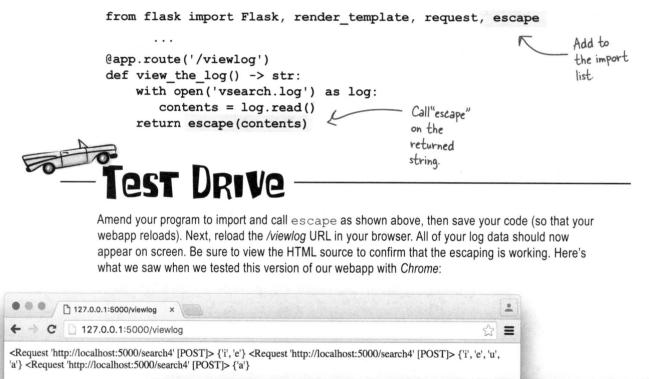

<Request 'http://localhost:5000/search4' [POST]> {'i', 'e'} <Request 'http://localhost:5000/search4' [POST]> {'i', 'e', 'u', 'a'} <Request 'http://localhost:5000/search4' [POST]> {'a'}

All the data from the log file is now appearing...

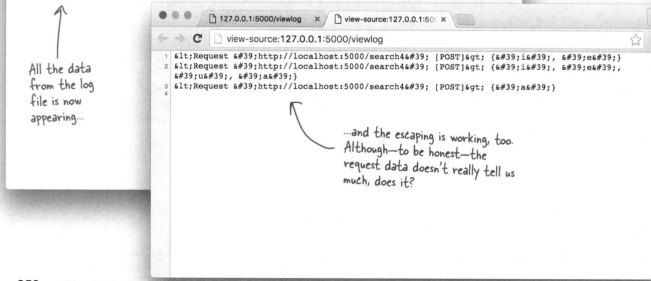

```
1  &lt;Request &#39;http://localhost:5000/search4&#39; [POST]&gt; {&#39;i&#39;, &#39;e&#39;}
2  &lt;Request &#39;http://localhost:5000/search4&#39; [POST]&gt; {&#39;i&#39;, &#39;e&#39;,
   &#39;u&#39;, &#39;a&#39;}
3  &lt;Request &#39;http://localhost:5000/search4&#39; [POST]&gt; {&#39;a&#39;}
4
```

...and the escaping is working, too. Although—to be honest—the request data doesn't really tell us much, does it?

Learning More About the Request Object

The data in the log file relating to the web request isn't really all that useful.
Here's an example of what's currently logged; although each logged result is
different, each logged web request is showing up as *exactly* the same:

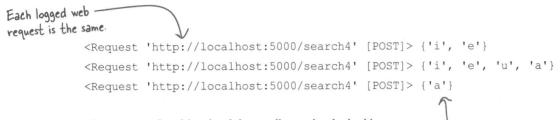

Each logged web
request is the same.

```
<Request 'http://localhost:5000/search4' [POST]> {'i', 'e'}
<Request 'http://localhost:5000/search4' [POST]> {'i', 'e', 'u', 'a'}
<Request 'http://localhost:5000/search4' [POST]> {'a'}
```

Each logged
result is
different.

We're logging the web request at the object level, but really need to be looking
inside the request and logging some of the data it contains. As you saw earlier in
this book, when you need to learn what something in Python contains, you feed it
to the `dir` built-in to see a list of its methods and attributes.

Let's make a small adjustment to the `log_request` function to log the output
from calling `dir` on each request object. It's not a huge change...rather than
passing the raw `req` as the first argument to `print`, let's pass in a stringified
version of the result of calling `dir(req)`. Here's the new version of `log_
request` with the change highlighted:

```
def log_request(req:'flask_request', res:str) -> None:
    with open('vsearch.log', 'a') as log:
        print(str(dir(req)), res, file=log)
```

We call "dir" on "req", which produces a list, and then we
stringify the list by passing the list to "str". The resulting
string is then saved to the log file along with the value of "res".

Exercise

Let's try out this new logging code to see what difference it makes. Perform the following steps:

1. Amend your copy of `log_request` to match ours.
2. Save `vsearch4log.py` in order to restart your webapp.
3. Find and delete your current `vsearch.log` file.
4. Use your browser to enter three new searches.
5. View the newly created log using the */viewlog* URL.

Now: have a good look at what appears in your browser. Does what you now see help at all?

TEST DRIVE

Here's what we saw after we worked through the five steps from the bottom of the last page. We're using *Safari* (although every other browser shows the same thing):

This all looks kinda messy. But look closely: here's the results of one of the searches we performed.

127.0.0.1:5000/viewlog

['__class__', '__delattr__', '__dict__', '__dir__', '__doc__', '__enter__', '__eq__', '__exit__', '__format__', '__ge__', '__getattribute__', '__gt__', '__hash__', '__init__', '__le__', '__lt__', '__module__', '__ne__', '__new__', '__reduce__', '__reduce_ex__', '__repr__', '__setattr__', '__sizeof__', '__str__', '__subclasshook__', '__weakref__', '_get_file_stream', '_get_stream_for_parsing', '_is_old_module', '_load_form_data', '_parse_content_type', '_parsed_content_type', 'accept_charsets', 'accept_encodings', 'accept_languages', 'accept_mimetypes', 'access_route', 'application', 'args', 'authorization', 'base_url', 'blueprint', 'cache_control', 'charset', 'close', 'content_encoding', 'content_length', 'content_md5', 'content_type', 'cookies', 'data', 'date', 'dict_storage_class', 'disable_data_descriptor', 'encoding_errors', 'endpoint', 'environ', 'files', 'form', 'form_data_parser_class', 'from_values', 'full_path', 'get_data', 'get_json', 'headers', 'host', 'host_url', 'if_match', 'if_modified_since', 'if_none_match', 'if_range', 'if_unmodified_since', 'input_stream', 'is_multiprocess', 'is_multithread', 'is_run_once', 'is_secure', 'is_xhr', 'json', 'list_storage_class', 'make_form_data_parser', 'max_content_length', 'max_form_memory_size', 'max_forwards', 'method', 'mimetype', 'mimetype_params', 'module', 'on_json_loading_failed', 'parameter_storage_class', 'path', 'pragma', 'query_string', 'range', 'referrer', 'remote_addr', 'remote_user', 'routing_exception', 'scheme', 'script_root', 'shallow', 'stream', 'trusted_hosts', 'url', 'url_charset', 'url_root', 'url_rule', 'user_agent', 'values', 'view_args', 'want_form_data_parsed' {'x', 'y'} ['__class__', '__delattr__', '__dict__', '__dir__', '__doc__', '__enter__', '__eq__', '__exit__', '__format__', '__ge__', '__getattribute__', '__gt__', '__hash__', '__init__', '__le__', '__lt__', '__module__', '__ne__', '__new__', '__reduce__', '__reduce_ex__', '__repr__', '__setattr__', '__sizeof__', '__str__', '__subclasshook__', '__weakref__', '_get_file_stream', '_get_stream_for_parsing', '_is_old_module', '_load_form_data', '_parse_content_type', '_parsed_content_type', 'accept_charsets', 'accept_encodings', 'accept_languages', 'accept_mimetypes', 'access_route', 'application', 'args', 'authorization', 'base_url', 'blueprint', 'cache_control', 'charset', 'close', 'content_encoding', 'content_length', 'content_md5', 'content_type', 'cookies', 'data', 'date', 'dict_storage_class', 'disable_data_descriptor', 'encoding_errors', 'endpoint', 'environ', 'files', 'form', 'form_data_parser_class', 'from_values', 'full_path', 'get_data', 'get_json', 'headers', 'host', 'host_url', 'if_match', 'if_modified_since', 'if_none_match', 'if_range', 'if_unmodified_since', 'input_stream', 'is_multiprocess', 'is_multithread', 'is_run_once', 'is_secure', 'is_xhr', 'json', 'list_storage_class', 'make_form_data_parser', 'max_content_length', 'max_form_memory_size', 'max_forwards', 'method', 'mimetype', 'mimetype_params', 'module', 'on_json_loading_failed', 'parameter_storage_class', 'path', 'pragma', 'query_string', 'range', 'referrer', 'remote_addr', 'remote_user', 'routing_exception', 'scheme', 'script_root', 'shallow', 'stream', 'trusted_hosts', 'url', 'url_charset', 'url_root', 'url_rule', 'user_agent', 'values', 'view_args', 'want_form_data_parsed'] {'u', 'i', 'e',

What's all this, then?

You can just about pick out the logged results in the above output. The rest of the output is the result of calling `dir` on the request object. As you can see, each request has a lot of methods and attributes associated with it (even when you ignore the *dunders* and *wonders*). It makes no sense to log *all* of these attributes.

We took a look at all of these attributes, and decided that there are three that we think are important enough to log:

> `req.form`: The data posted from the webapp's HTML form.
>
> `req.remote_addr`: The IP address the web browser is running on.
>
> `req.user_agent`: The identity of the browser posting the data.

Let's adjust `log_request` to log these three specific pieces of data, in addition to the results of the call to `search4letters`.

Logging Specific Web Request Attributes

As you now have four data items to log—the form details, the remote IP address, the browser identity, and the results of the call to `search4letters`—a first attempt at amending `log_request` might result in code that looks like this, where each data item is logged with its own `print` call:

```
def log_request(req:'flask_request', res:str) -> None:
    with open('vsearch.log', 'a') as log:
        print(req.form, file=log)
        print(req.remote_addr, file=log)
        print(req.user_agent, file=log)
        print(res, file=log)
```

Log each data item with its own "print" statement.

This code works, but it has a problem in that each `print` call appends a newline character by default, which means there are **four** lines being logged per web request. Here's what the data would look like if the log file used the above code:

The data as entered into the HTML form appears on its own line. BTW: the "ImmutableMultiDict" is a Flask-specific version of Python's dictionary (and it works in the same way).

There's a line of data for each remote IP address.

```
ImmutableMultiDict([('letters', 'aeiou'), ('phrase', 'hitch-hiker')])
127.0.0.1
Mozilla/5.0 (Macintosh; Intel Mac OS X 10_11_3) ... Safari/601.4.4
{'i', 'e'}
ImmutableMultiDict([('letters', 'aeiou'), ('phrase', 'life, the universe, and everything')])
127.0.0.1
Mozilla/5.0 (Macintosh; Intel Mac OS X 10_11_3) ... Safari/601.4.4
{'a', 'e', 'i', 'u'}
ImmutableMultiDict([('letters', 'xyz'), ('phrase', 'galaxy')])
127.0.0.1
Mozilla/5.0 (Macintosh; Intel Mac OS X 10_11_3) ... Safari/601.4.4
{'x', 'y'}
```

The browser is identified on its own line.

The results of the call to "search4letters" are clearly shown (each on its own line).

There's nothing inherently wrong with this as a strategy (as the logged data is easy for us humans to read). However, consider what you'd have to do when reading this data into a program: each logged web request would require **four** reads from the log file—one for each line of logged data. This is in spite of the fact that the four lines of data refer to one *single* web request. As a strategy, this approach seems wasteful. It would be much better if the code only logged **one** line per web request.

Log a Single Line of Delimited Data

A better logging strategy may be to write the four pieces of data as one line, while using an appropriately selected delimiter to separate one data item from the next.

Choosing a delimiter can be tricky, as you don't want to choose a character that might actually occur in the data you're logging. Using the space character as a delimiter is next to useless (as the logged data contains lots of spaces), and even using colon (:), comma (,), and semicolon (;) may be problematic given the data being logged. We checked with the programmers over at *Head First Labs*, and they suggested using a vertical bar (|) as a delimiter: it's easy for us humans to spot, and it's unlikely to be part of the data we log. Let's go with this suggestion and see how we get on.

As you saw earlier, we can adjust `print`'s default behavior by providing additional arguments. In addition to the `file` argument, there's the `end` argument, which allows you to specify an alternate *end-of-line* value over the default newline.

Let's amend `log_request` to use a vertical bar as the end-of-line value, as opposed to the default newline:

Geek Bit

Think of a **delimiter** as a sequence of one or more characters performing the role of a boundary within a line of text. The classic example is the comma character (,) as used in CSV files.

```python
def log_request(req: 'flask_request', res: str) -> None:
    with open('vsearch.log', 'a') as log:
        print(req.form, file=log, end='|')
        print(req.remote_addr, file=log, end='|')
        print(req.user_agent, file=log, end='|')
        print(res, file=log)
```

Each of these "print" statements replaces the default newline with a vertical bar.

This works as expected: each web request now results in a single line of logged data, with a vertical bar delimiting each logged data item. Here's what the data looks like in our log file when we used this amended version of `log_request`:

Each web request is written to its own line (which we've word-wrapped in order to fit on this page).

```
ImmutableMultiDict([('letters', 'aeiou'), ('phrase', 'hitch-hiker')])|127.0.0.1|Mozilla/5.0
(Macintosh; Intel Mac OS X 10_11_2) AppleWebKit/601.3.9 (KHTML, like Gecko) Version/9.0.2
Safari/601.3.9|{'e', 'i'}

ImmutableMultiDict([('letters', 'aeiou'), ('phrase', 'life, the universe, and everything')])|12
7.0.0.1|Mozilla/5.0 (Macintosh; Intel Mac OS X 10_11_2) AppleWebKit/601.3.9 (KHTML, like Gecko)
Version/9.0.2 Safari/601.3.9|{'e', 'u', 'a', 'i'}

ImmutableMultiDict([('letters', 'xyz'), ('phrase', 'galaxy')])|127.0.0.1|Mozilla/5.0
(Macintosh; Intel Mac OS X 10_11_2) AppleWebKit/601.3.9 (KHTML, like Gecko) Version/9.0.2
Safari/601.3.9|{'y', 'x'}
```

Did you spot the vertical bars used as delimiters? There are three bars, which means we have logged four pieces of data per line.

There were three web requests, so we see three lines of data in the log file.

One Final Change to Our Logging Code

Working with overly verbose code is a pet peeve of many Python programmers. Our most recent version of `log_request` works fine, but it's more verbose than it needs to be. Specifically, it feels like overkill to give each item of logged data its own `print` statement.

The `print` function has another optional argument, `sep`, which allows you to specify a separation value to be used when printing multiple values in a single call to `print`. By default, `sep` is set to a single space character, but you can use any value you wish. In the code that follows, the four calls to `print` (from the last page) have been replaced with a single `print` call, which takes advantage of the `sep` argument, setting it to the vertical bar character. In doing so, we negate the need to specify a value for `end` as the `print`'s default end-of-line value, which is why all mentions of `end` have been removed from this code:

Only one "print" call instead of four

```python
def log_request(req: 'flask_request', res: str) -> None:
    with open('vsearch.log', 'a') as log:
        print(req.form, req.remote_addr, req.user_agent, res, file=log, sep='|')
```

Doesn't PEP 8 have something to say about this long line of code?

Yes, this line breaks a PEP 8 guideline.

Some Python programmers frown at this last line of code, as the **PEP 8** standard specifically warns against lines longer than 79 characters. At 80 characters, our line of code is pushing this guideline *a little*, but we think it's a reasonable trade-off given what we're doing here.

Remember: strict adherence to PEP 8 is not an absolute must, as PEP 8 is a *style guide*, not an unbreakable set of rules. We think we're good to go.

Let's see what difference this new code makes. Adjust your `log_request` function to look like this:

```python
def log_request(req: 'flask_request', res: str) -> None:
    with open('vsearch.log', 'a') as log:
        print(req.form, req.remote_addr, req.user_agent, res, file=log, sep='|')
```

Then perform these four steps:

1. Save `vsearch4log.py` (which restarts your webapp).

2. Find and delete your current `vsearch.log` file.

3. Use your browser to enter three new searches.

4. View the newly created log using the */viewlog* URL.

Have another good look at your browser display. Is this better than before?

Test Drive

Having completed the four steps detailed in the above exercise, we ran our latest tests using *Chrome*. Here's what we saw on screen:

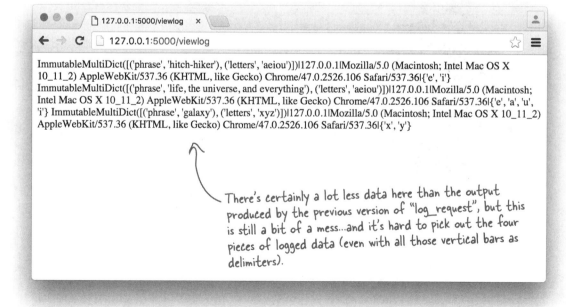

ImmutableMultiDict([('phrase', 'hitch-hiker'), ('letters', 'aeiou')])|127.0.0.1|Mozilla/5.0 (Macintosh; Intel Mac OS X 10_11_2) AppleWebKit/537.36 (KHTML, like Gecko) Chrome/47.0.2526.106 Safari/537.36|{'e', 'i'}
ImmutableMultiDict([('phrase', 'life, the universe, and everything'), ('letters', 'aeiou')])|127.0.0.1|Mozilla/5.0 (Macintosh; Intel Mac OS X 10_11_2) AppleWebKit/537.36 (KHTML, like Gecko) Chrome/47.0.2526.106 Safari/537.36|{'e', 'a', 'u', 'i'} ImmutableMultiDict([('phrase', 'galaxy'), ('letters', 'xyz')])|127.0.0.1|Mozilla/5.0 (Macintosh; Intel Mac OS X 10_11_2) AppleWebKit/537.36 (KHTML, like Gecko) Chrome/47.0.2526.106 Safari/537.36|{'x', 'y'}

There's certainly a lot less data here than the output produced by the previous version of "log_request", but this is still a bit of a mess...and it's hard to pick out the four pieces of logged data (even with all those vertical bars as delimiters).

From Raw Data to Readable Output

The data displayed in the browser window is in its *raw form*. Remember, we perform HTML escaping on the data as read in from the log file but do nothing else before sending the string to the waiting web browser. Modern web browsers will receive the string, remove any unwanted whitespace characters (such as extra spaces, newlines, and so on), then dump the data to the window. This is what's happening during our *Test Drive*. The logged data—all of it—is visible, but it's anything but easy to read. We could consider performing further text manipulations on the raw data (in order to make the output easier to read), but a better approach to producing readable output might be to manipulate the raw data in such a way as to turn it into a table:

```
ImmutableMultiDict([('phrase', 'hitch-hiker'), ('letters', 'aeiou')])|127.0.0.1|Mozilla/5.0
(Macintosh; Intel Mac OS X 10_11_2) AppleWebKit/537.36 (KHTML, like Gecko) Chrome/47.0.2526.106
Safari/537.36|{'e', 'i'} ImmutableMultiDict([('phrase', 'life, the universe, and
everything'), ('letters', 'aeiou')])|127.0.0.1|Mozilla/5.0 (Macintosh; Intel Mac OS X 10_11_2)
AppleWebKit/537.36 (KHTML, like Gecko) Chrome/47.0.2526.106 Safari/537.36|{'e', 'a', 'u',
'i'} ImmutableMultiDict([('phrase', 'galaxy'), ('letters', 'xyz')])|127.0.0.1|Mozilla/5.0
(Macintosh; Intel Mac OS X 10_11_2) AppleWebKit/537.36 (KHTML, like Gecko) Chrome/47.0.2526.106
Safari/537.36|{'x', 'y'}
```

Can we take this (unreadable) raw data...

...and transform it into a table that looks like this?

Form Data	Remote_addr	User_agent	Results
ImmutableMultiDict([('phrase', 'hitch-hiker'), ('letters', 'aeiou')])	127.0.0.1	Mozilla/5.0 (Macintosh; Intel Mac OS X 10_11_2) AppleWebKit/537.36 (KHTML, like Gecko) Chrome/47.0.2526 .106 Safari/537.36	{'e', 'i'}
ImmutableMultiDict([('phrase', 'life, the universe, and everything'), ('letters', 'aeiou')])	127.0.0.1	Mozilla/5.0 (Macintosh; Intel Mac OS X 10_11_2) AppleWebKit/537.36 (KHTML, like Gecko) Chrome/47.0.2526 .106 Safari/537.36	{'e', 'a', 'u', 'i'}
ImmutableMultiDict([('phrase', 'galaxy'), ('letters', 'xyz')])	127.0.0.1	Mozilla/5.0 (Macintosh; Intel Mac OS X 10_11_2) AppleWebKit/537.36 (KHTML, like Gecko) Chrome/47.0.2526 .106 Safari/537.36	{'x', 'y'}

If our webapp could perform this transformation, then *anyone* could view the log data in their web browser and likely make sense of it.

Does This Remind You of Anything?

Take another look at what you are trying to produce. To save on space, we're only showing the top portion of the table shown on the previous page. Does what you're trying to produce here remind you of anything from earlier in this book?

Form Data	Remote_addr	User_agent	Results
ImmutableMultiDict([('phrase', 'hitch-hiker'), ('letters', 'aeiou')])	127.0.0.1	Mozilla/5.0 (Macintosh; Intel Mac OS X 10_11_2) AppleWebKit/537.36 (KHTML, like Gecko) Chrome/47.0.2526 .106 Safari/537.36	{'e', 'i'}

> Correct me if I'm wrong, but is that not a lot like my complex data structure from the end of Chapter 3?

Yes. That does look like something we've seen before.

At the end of Chapter 3, recall that we took the table of data below and transformed it into a complex data structure—a dictionary of dictionaries:

Name	Gender	Occupation	Home Planet
Ford Prefect	Male	Researcher	Betelgeuse Seven
Arthur Dent	Male	Sandwich-Maker	Earth
Tricia McMillan	Female	Mathematician	Earth
Marvin	Unknown	Paranoid Android	Unknown

The shape of this table is similar to what we're hoping to produce above, but is a dictionary of dictionaries the right data structure to use here?

Use a Dict of Dicts...or Something Else?

The table of data from Chapter 3 fit the dictionary of dictionaries model because it allowed you to quickly dip into the data structure and extract specific data. For instance, if you wanted to know Ford Prefect's home planet, all you had to do was this:

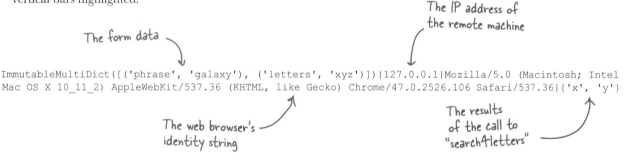

people['Ford']['Home Planet']

Access Ford's data...

...then extract the value associated with the "Home Planet" key.

When it comes to randomly accessing a data structure, nothing beats a dictionary of dictionaries. However, is this what we want for our logged data?

Let's consider what we currently have.

Take a closer look at the logged data

Remember, every logged line contains four pieces of data, each separated by vertical bars: the HTML form's data, the remote IP address, the identity of the web browser, and the results of the call to `search4letters`.

Here's a sample line of data from our `vsearch.log` file with each of the vertical bars highlighted:

The form data

The IP address of the remote machine

```
ImmutableMultiDict([('phrase', 'galaxy'), ('letters', 'xyz')])|127.0.0.1|Mozilla/5.0 (Macintosh; Intel
Mac OS X 10_11_2) AppleWebKit/537.36 (KHTML, like Gecko) Chrome/47.0.2526.106 Safari/537.36|{'x', 'y'}
```

The web browser's identity string

The results of the call to "search4letters"

When the logged data is read from the `vsearch.log` file, it arrives in your code as a *list of strings* thanks to our use of the `readlines` method. Because you probably won't need to randomly access individual data items from the logged data, converting the data to a dictionary of dictionaries seems like a bad move. However, you need to process each line *in order*, as well as process each individual data item within each line *in order*. You already have a list of strings, so you're half-way there, as it's easy to process a list with a `for` loop. However, the line of data is currently one string, and this is the issue. It would be easier to process each line if it were a list of data items, as opposed to one large string. The question is: *is it possible to convert a string to a list?*

What's Joined Together Can Be Split Apart

You already know that you can take a list of strings and convert them to a single string using the "join trick." Let's show this once more at the >>> prompt:

A list of individual strings

```
>>> names = ['Terry', 'John', 'Michael', 'Graham', 'Eric']
>>> pythons = '|'.join(names)
>>> pythons
'Terry|John|Michael|Graham|Eric'
```

The "join trick" in action.

A single string with each string from the "names" list concatenated with the next and delimited by a vertical bar

Thanks to the "join trick," what was a list of strings is now a single string, with each list item separated from the next by a vertical bar (in this case). You can reverse this process using the split method, which comes built in to every Python string:

Take the string and split it into a list using the given delimiter.

```
>>> individuals = pythons.split('|')
>>> individuals
['Terry', 'John', 'Michael', 'Graham', 'Eric']
```

And now we are back to our list of strings.

Getting to a list of lists from a list of strings

Now that you have the split method in your coding arsenal, let's return to the data stored in the log file and consider what needs to happen to it. At the moment, each individual line in the vsearch.log file is a string:

The raw data

```
ImmutableMultiDict([('phrase', 'galaxy'), ('letters', 'xyz')])|127.0.0.1|Mozilla/5.0 (Macintosh; Intel
Mac OS X 10_11_2) AppleWebKit/537.36 (KHTML, like Gecko) Chrome/47.0.2526.106 Safari/537.36|{'x', 'y'}
```

Your code currently reads all the lines from vsearch.log into a list of strings called contents. Shown here are the last three lines of code from the view_the_log function, which read the data from the file and produce the large string:

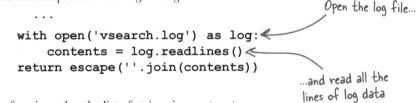

Open the log file...

```
. . .
with open('vsearch.log') as log:
    contents = log.readlines()
return escape(''.join(contents))
```

...and read all the lines of log data into a list called "contents".

The last line of the view_the_log function takes the list of strings in contents and concatenates them into one large string (thanks to join). This single string is then returned to the waiting web browser.

If contents were a list of *lists* instead of a list of *strings*, it would open up the possibility of processing contents *in order* using a for loop. It should then be possible to produce more readable output than what we're currently seeing on screen.

When Should the Conversion Occur?

At the moment, the `view_the_log` function reads all the data from the log file into a list of strings (called `contents`). But we'd rather have the data as a list of lists. The thing is, when's the "best time" to do this conversion? Should we read in all the data into a list of strings, then convert it to a list of lists "as we go," or should we build the list of lists while reading in each line of data?

The data we need is already in "contents", so let's convert that into a list of lists.

I'm not so sure, as that way we'll end up processing the data twice: once when we read it in, and then again when we convert it.

The fact that the data is already in `contents` (thanks to our use of the `readlines` method) shouldn't blind us to the fact that we've already looped through the data *once* at this point. Invoking `readlines` may only be a single call for us, but the interpreter (while executing `readlines`) *is* looping through the data in the file. If we then loop through the data again (to convert the strings to lists), we're **doubling** the amount of looping that's occurring. This isn't a big deal when there's only a handful of log entries...but it might be an issue when the log grows in size. The bottom line is this: *if we can make do by only looping once, then let's do so!*

Processing Data: What We Already Know

Earlier in this chapter, you saw three lines of Python code that processed the lines of data in the `todos.txt` file:

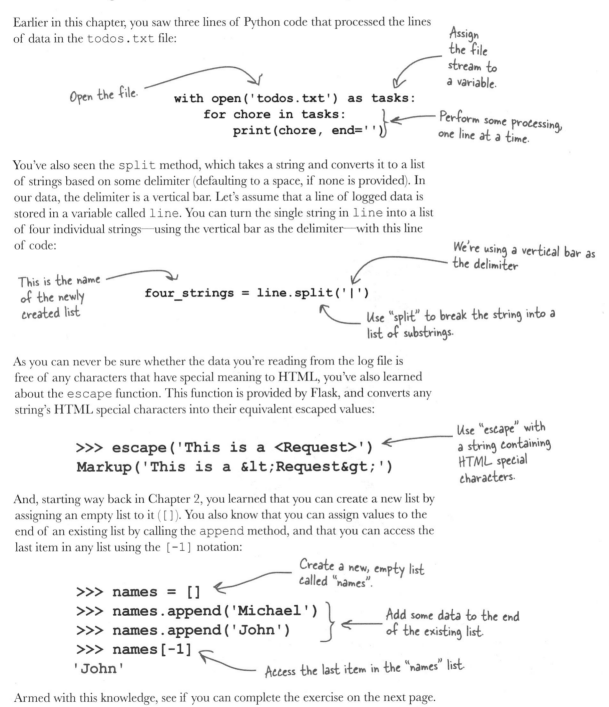

Open the file.

Assign the file stream to a variable.

```
with open('todos.txt') as tasks:
    for chore in tasks:
        print(chore, end='')
```

Perform some processing, one line at a time.

You've also seen the `split` method, which takes a string and converts it to a list of strings based on some delimiter (defaulting to a space, if none is provided). In our data, the delimiter is a vertical bar. Let's assume that a line of logged data is stored in a variable called `line`. You can turn the single string in `line` into a list of four individual strings—using the vertical bar as the delimiter—with this line of code:

This is the name of the newly created list

We're using a vertical bar as the delimiter

```
four_strings = line.split('|')
```

Use "split" to break the string into a list of substrings.

As you can never be sure whether the data you're reading from the log file is free of any characters that have special meaning to HTML, you've also learned about the `escape` function. This function is provided by Flask, and converts any string's HTML special characters into their equivalent escaped values:

```
>>> escape('This is a <Request>')
Markup('This is a &lt;Request&gt;')
```

Use "escape" with a string containing HTML special characters.

And, starting way back in Chapter 2, you learned that you can create a new list by assigning an empty list to it (`[]`). You also know that you can assign values to the end of an existing list by calling the `append` method, and that you can access the last item in any list using the `[-1]` notation:

Create a new, empty list called "names".

```
>>> names = []
>>> names.append('Michael')
>>> names.append('John')
>>> names[-1]
'John'
```

Add some data to the end of the existing list.

Access the last item in the "names" list.

Armed with this knowledge, see if you can complete the exercise on the next page.

Sharpen your pencil

Here is the `view_the_log` function's current code:

```
@app.route('/viewlog')
def view_the_log() -> str:
    with open('vsearch.log') as log:
        contents = log.readlines()
    return escape(''.join(contents))
```

This code reads the data from the log file into a list of strings. Your job is to convert this code to read the data into a list of lists.

Make sure that the data written to the list of lists is properly escaped, as you do not want any HTML special characters sneaking through.

Also, ensure that your new code still returns a string to the waiting web browser.

We've got you started—fill in the missing code:

The first two lines remain unchanged.

```
@app.route('/viewlog')
def view_the_log() -> 'str':
```

....

....

....

....

....

Add your new code here.

....

....

....

....

The function still returns a string.

```
return str(contents)
```

Take your time here. Feel free to experiment at the >>> shell as needed, and don't worry if you get stuck—it's OK to flip the page and look at the solution.

Sharpen your pencil Solution

Here is the `view_the_log` function's code:

```
@app.route('/viewlog')
def view_the_log() -> str:
    with open('vsearch.log') as log:
        contents = log.readlines()
    return escape(''.join(contents))
```

Your job was to convert this code to read the data into a list of lists.

You were to ensure that the data written to the list of lists is properly escaped, as you do not want any HTML special characters sneaking through.

You were also to ensure that your new code still returns a string to the waiting web browser.

We'd started for you, and you were to fill in the missing code:

```
@app.route('/viewlog')
def view_the_log() -> 'str':
```

Create a new, empty list called "contents". →
```
contents = []
```

Open the log file and assign it to a file stream called "log". →
```
with open('vsearch.log') as log:
```

Loop through each line in the "log" file stream. →
```
for line in log:
```

Append a new, empty list to "contents". →
```
contents.append([])
```

Split the line (based on the vertical bar), then process each item in the resulting "split list". →
```
for item in line.split('|'):
```

Did you remember to call "escape"?
```
contents[-1].append(escape(item))
```

Append the escaped data to the end of the list at the end of "contents".

```
return str(contents)
```

Don't worry if this line of code from the above rewrite of the `view_the_log` function has your head spinning:

Read this code from the inside out, and from right to left.

```
contents[-1].append(escape(item))
```

The trick to understanding this (initially daunting) line is to read it from the inside out, and from right to left. You start with the `item` from the enclosing `for` loop, which gets passed to `escape`. The resulting string is then `appended` to the list at the end (`[-1]`) of `contents`. Remember: `contents` is itself a *list of lists*.

TEST DRIVE

Go ahead and change your `view_the_log` function to look like this:

```python
@app.route('/viewlog')
def view_the_log() -> 'str':
    contents = []
    with open('vsearch.log') as log:
        for line in log:
            contents.append([])
            for item in line.split('|'):
                contents[-1].append(escape(item))
    return str(contents)
```

Save your code (which causes your webapp to reload), then reload the *viewlog* URL in your browser. Here's what we saw in ours:

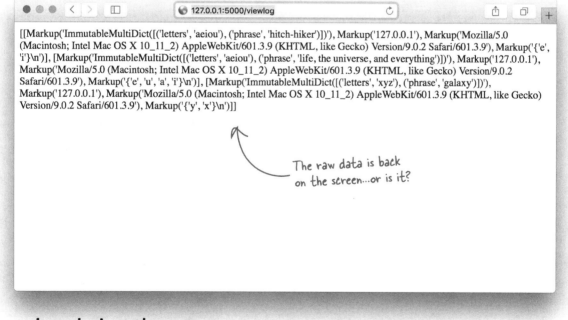

[[Markup('ImmutableMultiDict([('letters', 'aeiou'), ('phrase', 'hitch-hiker')])'), Markup('127.0.0.1'), Markup('Mozilla/5.0 (Macintosh; Intel Mac OS X 10_11_2) AppleWebKit/601.3.9 (KHTML, like Gecko) Version/9.0.2 Safari/601.3.9'), Markup('{'e', 'i'}\n')], [Markup('ImmutableMultiDict([('letters', 'aeiou'), ('phrase', 'life, the universe, and everything')])'), Markup('127.0.0.1'), Markup('Mozilla/5.0 (Macintosh; Intel Mac OS X 10_11_2) AppleWebKit/601.3.9 (KHTML, like Gecko) Version/9.0.2 Safari/601.3.9'), Markup('{'e', 'u', 'a', 'i'}\n')], [Markup('ImmutableMultiDict([('letters', 'xyz'), ('phrase', 'galaxy')])'), Markup('127.0.0.1'), Markup('Mozilla/5.0 (Macintosh; Intel Mac OS X 10_11_2) AppleWebKit/601.3.9 (KHTML, like Gecko) Version/9.0.2 Safari/601.3.9'), Markup('{'y', 'x'}\n')]]

The raw data is back on the screen...or is it?

Take a closer look at the output

At first glance, the output produced by this new version of `view_the_log` looks very similar to what you had before. But it isn't: this new output is a list of lists, not a list of strings. This a crucial change. If you can now arrange to process `contents` using an appropriately designed Jinja2 template, you should be able to get pretty close to the readable output required here.

Generate Readable Output With HTML

Recall that our goal is to produce output that looks better on screen than the raw data from the last page. To that end, HTML comes with a set of tags for defining the content of tables, including: `<table>`, `<th>`, `<tr>`, and `<td>`. With this in mind, let's take another look at the top portion of the table we're hoping to produce once more. It has one row of data for each line in the log, arranged as four columns (each with a descriptive title).

You could put the entire table within an HTML `<table>` tag, with each row of data having its own `<tr>` tag. The descriptive titles each get `<th>` tags, while each piece of raw data gets its own `<td>` tag:

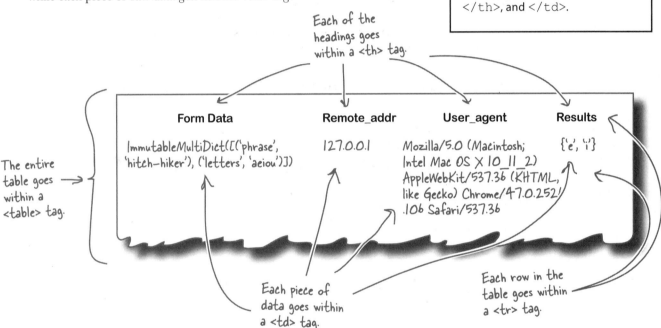

Each of the headings goes within a `<th>` tag.

The entire table goes within a `<table>` tag.

Each piece of data goes within a `<td>` tag.

Each row in the table goes within a `<tr>` tag.

Form Data	Remote_addr	User_agent	Results
ImmutableMultiDict([('phrase', 'hitch-hiker'), ('letters', 'aeiou')])	127.0.0.1	Mozilla/5.0 (Macintosh; Intel Mac OS X 10_11_2) AppleWebKit/537.36 (KHTML, like Gecko) Chrome/47.0.252/.106 Safari/537.36	{'e', 'i'}

Whenever you find yourself needing to generate any HTML (especially a `<table>`), remember Jinja2. The Jinja2 template engine is primarily designed to generate HTML, and the engine contains some basic programming constructs (loosely based on Python syntax) that you can use to "automate" any required display logic you might need.

In the last chapter, you saw how the Jinja2 `{{` and `}}` tags, as well as the `{% block %}` tag, allow you to use variables and blocks of HTML as arguments to templates. It turns out the `{%` and `%}` tags are much more general, and can contain any Jinja2 *statement*, with one of the supported statements being a `for` loop construct. On the next page you'll find a new template that takes advantage of Jinja2's `for` loop to build the readable output from the list of lists contained in `contents`.

Embed Display Logic in Your Template

Below is a new template, called `viewlog.html`, which can be used to transform the raw data from the log file into an HTML table. The template expects the `contents` list of lists to be one of its arguments. We've highlighted the bits of this template we want you to concentrate on. Note that Jinja2's `for` loop construct is very similar to Python's. There are two major differences:

- There's no need for a colon (`:`) at the end of the `for` line (as the `%}` tag acts as a delimiter).

- The loop's suite is terminated with `{% endfor %}`, as Jinja2 doesn't support indentation (so some other mechanism is required).

As you can see, the first `for` loop expects to find its data in a variable called `the_row_titles`, while the second `for` loop expects its data in something called `the_data`. A third `for` loop (embedded in the second) expects its data to be a list of items:

You don't have to create this template yourself. Download it from *http://python.itcarlow.ie/ed2/.*

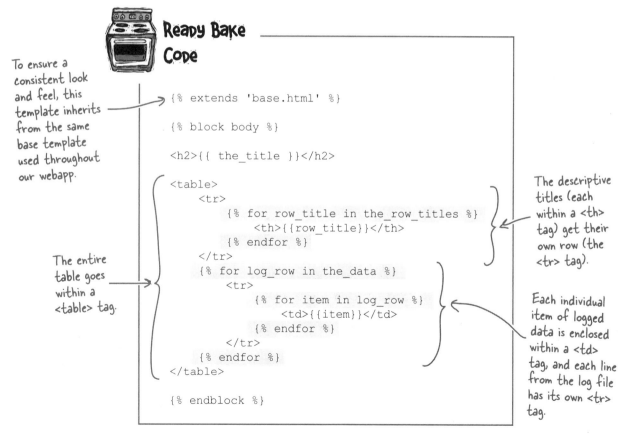

Ready Bake Code

To ensure a consistent look and feel, this template inherits from the same base template used throughout our webapp.

```
{% extends 'base.html' %}

{% block body %}

<h2>{{ the_title }}</h2>

<table>
    <tr>
        {% for row_title in the_row_titles %}
            <th>{{row_title}}</th>
        {% endfor %}
    </tr>
    {% for log_row in the_data %}
        <tr>
            {% for item in log_row %}
                <td>{{item}}</td>
            {% endfor %}
        </tr>
    {% endfor %}
</table>

{% endblock %}
```

The entire table goes within a `<table>` tag.

The descriptive titles (each within a `<th>` tag) get their own row (the `<tr>` tag).

Each individual item of logged data is enclosed within a `<td>` tag, and each line from the log file has its own `<tr>` tag.

Be sure to place this new template in your webapp's `templates` folder prior to use.

Producing Readable Output with Jinja2

As the viewlog.html template inherits from base.html, you need to
remember to provide a value for the the_title argument and provide a list of
column headings (the descriptive titles) in the_row_titles. And don't forget
to assign contents to the_data argument.

The view_the_log function currently looks like this:

We currently return a string to the waiting web browser.

```
@app.route('/viewlog')
def view_the_log() -> 'str':
    contents = []
    with open('vsearch.log') as log:
        for line in log:
            contents.append([])
            for item in line.split('|'):
                contents[-1].append(escape(item))
    return str(contents)
```

You need to call render_template on viewlog.html, and pass it values for
each of the three arguments it expects. Let's create a tuple of descriptive titles and
assign it to the_row_titles, then assign the value of contents to the_
data. We'll also provide an appropriate value for the_title before rendering
the template.

Remember: a tuple is a read-only list.

With all of that in mind, let's amend view_the_log (we've highlighted the
changes):

Change the annotation to indicate that HTML is being returned (instead of a string).

```
@app.route('/viewlog')
def view_the_log() -> 'html':
    contents = []
    with open('vsearch.log') as log:
        for line in log:
            contents.append([])
            for item in line.split('|'):
                contents[-1].append(escape(item))
    titles = ('Form Data', 'Remote_addr', 'User_agent', 'Results')
    return render_template('viewlog.html',
                           the_title='View Log',
                           the_row_titles=titles,
                           the_data=contents,)
```

Create a tuple of descriptive titles.

Call "render_template", providing values for each of the template's arguments.

Go ahead and make these changes to your view_the_log function and then
save them so that Flask restarts your webapp. When you're ready, view the log
within your browser using the *http://127.0.0.1:5000/viewlog* URL.

Test Drive

Here's what we saw when we viewed the log using our updated webapp. The page has the same look and feel as all our other pages, so we are confident that our webapp is using the correct template.

We're pretty pleased with the result (and we hope you are too), as this looks very similar to what we were hoping to achieve: readable output.

127.0.0.1:5000/viewlog

View Log

Form Data	Remote_addr	User_agent	Results
ImmutableMultiDict([('letters', 'aeiou'), ('phrase', 'hitch-hiker')])	127.0.0.1	Mozilla/5.0 (Macintosh; Intel Mac OS X 10_11_2) AppleWebKit/601.3.9 (KHTML, like Gecko) Version/9.0.2 Safari/601.3.9	{'e', 'i'}
ImmutableMultiDict([('letters', 'aeiou'), ('phrase', 'life, the universe, and everything')])	127.0.0.1	Mozilla/5.0 (Macintosh; Intel Mac OS X 10_11_2) AppleWebKit/601.3.9 (KHTML, like Gecko) Version/9.0.2 Safari/601.3.9	{'e', 'u', 'a', 'i'}
ImmutableMultiDict([('letters', 'xyz'), ('phrase', 'galaxy')])	127.0.0.1	Mozilla/5.0 (Macintosh; Intel Mac OS X 10_11_2) AppleWebKit/601.3.9 (KHTML, like Gecko) Version/9.0.2 Safari/601.3.9	{'y', 'x'}

Not only is this output readable, but it looks good, too. ☺

If you view the source of the above page—right-click on the page, then choose the appropriate option from the pop-up menu—you'll see that every single data item from the log is being given its own `<td>` tag, each line of data has its own `<tr>` tag, and the entire table is within a HTML `<table>`.

The Current State of Our Webapp Code

Let's pause for a moment and review our webapp's code. The addition of the logging code (`log_request` and `view_the_log`) has added to our webapp's codebase, but everything still fits on a single page. Here's the code for `vsearch4web.py` displayed in an IDLE edit window (which lets you review the code in all its syntax-highlighted glory):

```
● ● ●    vsearch4web.py - /Users/paul/Desktop/_NewBook/ch06/webapp/vsearch4web.py (3.5.1)

from flask import Flask, render_template, request, escape
from vsearch import search4letters

app = Flask(__name__)

def log_request(req:'flask_request', res:str) -> None:
    with open('vsearch.log', 'a') as log:
        print(req.form, req.remote_addr, req.user_agent, res, file=log, sep='|')

@app.route('/search4', methods=['POST'])
def do_search() -> 'html':
    phrase = request.form['phrase']
    letters = request.form['letters']
    title = 'Here are your results:'
    results = str(search4letters(phrase, letters))
    log_request(request, results)
    return render_template('results.html',
                            the_title=title,
                            the_phrase=phrase,
                            the_letters=letters,
                            the_results=results,)

@app.route('/')
@app.route('/entry')
def entry_page() -> 'html':
    return render_template('entry.html',
                            the_title='Welcome to search4letters on the web!')

@app.route('/viewlog')
def view_the_log() -> 'html':
    contents = []
    with open('vsearch.log') as log:
        for line in log:
            contents.append([])
            for item in line.split('|'):
                contents[-1].append(escape(item))
    titles = ('Form Data', 'Remote_addr', 'User_agent', 'Results')
    return render_template('viewlog.html',
                            the_title='View Log',
                            the_row_titles=titles,
                            the_data=contents,)

if __name__ == '__main__':
    app.run(debug=True)

                                                           Ln: 2   Col: 0
```

Asking Questions of Your Data

Our webapp's functionality is shaping up nicely, but are we any closer to answering the questions posed at the start of this chapter: *How many requests have been responded to? What's the most common list of letters? Which IP addresses are the requests coming from? Which browser is being used the most?*

The last two questions can be somewhat answered by the output displayed by the */viewlog* URL. You can tell where the requests are coming from (the **Remote_addr** column), as well as see which web browser is being used (the **User_agent** column). But, if you want to calculate which of the major browsers is used most by users of your site, that's not so easy. Simply looking at the displayed log data isn't enough; you'll have to perform additional calculations.

The first two questions cannot be easily answered either. It should be clear that further calculations must be performed here, too.

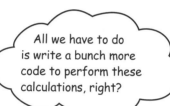

All we have to do is write a bunch more code to perform these calculations, right?

Only write more code when you have to.

If all we had available to us was Python, then, yes, we'd need to write a lot more code to answer these questions (and any others that might arise). After all, it's fun to write Python code, and Python is also great at manipulating data. Writing more code to answer our questions seems like a no-brainer, doesn't it?

Well...other technologies exist that make it easy to answer the sort of questions we're posing without us having to write much more Python code. Specifically, if we could save the log data to a database, we could take advantage of the power of the database's querying technology to answer almost any question that might arise.

In the next chapter, you'll see what's involved in amending your webapp to log its data to a database as opposed to a text file.

Chapter 6's Code

Remember: they both do the same thing, but Python programmers prefer this code over this.

```
with open('todos.txt') as tasks:
    for chore in tasks:
        print(chore, end='')
```

```
tasks = open('todos.txt')
for chore in tasks:
    print(chore, end='')
tasks.close()
```

Here's the code we added to the webapp to support logging our web requests to a text file.

```
    ...

def log_request(req: 'flask_request', res: str) -> None:
    with open('vsearch.log', 'a') as log:
        print(req.form, req.remote_addr, req.user_agent, res, file=log, sep='|')

    ...


@app.route('/viewlog')
def view_the_log() -> 'html':
    contents = []
    with open('vsearch.log') as log:
        for line in log:
            contents.append([])
            for item in line.split('|'):
                contents[-1].append(escape(item))
    titles = ('Form Data', 'Remote_addr', 'User_agent', 'Results')
    return render_template('viewlog.html',
                           the_title='View Log',
                           the_row_titles=titles,
                           the_data=contents,)

    ...
```

We aren't showing all the "vsearch4web.py" code here, just the new stuff. (You'll find the entire program two pages back.)

7 using a database

Putting Python's DB-API to Use

Interesting...according to this, we're much better off storing our data in a database.

Yes. I see that. But...how?

Storing data in a relational database system is handy.

In this chapter, you'll learn how to write code that interacts with the popular **MySQL** database technology, using a generic database API called **DB-API**. The DB-API (which comes standard with every Python install) allows you to write code that is easily transferred from one database product to the next...assuming your database talks SQL. Although we'll be using MySQL, there's nothing stopping you from using your DB-API code with your favorite relational database, whatever it may be. Let's see what's involved in using a relational database with Python. There's not a lot of new Python in this chapter, but using Python to talk to databases is a **big deal**, so it's well worth learning.

Database-Enabling Your Webapp

The plan for this chapter is to get to the point where you can amend your webapp to store its log data in a database, as opposed to a text file, as was the case in the last chapter. The hope is that in doing so, you can then provide answers to the questions posed in the last chapter: *How many requests have been responded to? What's the most common list of letters? Which IP addresses are the requests coming from? Which browser is being used the most?*

To get there, however, we need to decide on a database system to use. There are lots of choices here, and it would be easy to take a dozen pages or so to present a bunch of alternative database technologies while exploring the pluses and minuses of each. But we're not going to do that. Instead, we're going to stick with a popular choice and use *MySQL* as our database technology.

Having selected MySQL, here are the four tasks we'll work through over the next dozen pages:

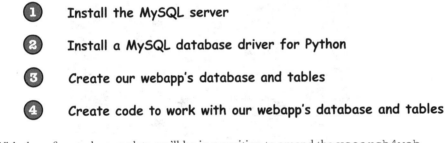

1 **Install the MySQL server**

2 **Install a MySQL database driver for Python**

3 **Create our webapp's database and tables**

4 **Create code to work with our webapp's database and tables**

With these four tasks complete, we'll be in a position to amend the `vsearch4web.py` code to log to MySQL as opposed to a text file. We'll then use SQL to ask and—with luck—answer our questions.

there are no
Dumb Questions

Q: Do we have to use MySQL here?

A: If you want to follow along with the examples in the remainder of this chapter, the answer is yes.

Q: Can I use MariaDB instead of MySQL?

A: Yes. As MariaDB is a clone of MySQL, we have no issue with you using MariaDB as your database system instead of the "official" MySQL. (In fact, over at *Head First Labs*, MariaDB is a favorite among the DevOps team.)

Q: What about PostgreSQL? Can I use that?

A: Emm, eh...yes, subject to the following caveat: if you are already using PostgreSQL (or any other SQL-based database management system), you can try using it in place of MySQL. However, note that this chapter doesn't provide any specific instructions related to PostgreSQL (or anything else), so you may have to experiment on your own when something we show you working with MySQL doesn't work in quite the same way with your chosen database. There's also the standalone, single-user **SQLite,** which comes with Python and lets you work with SQL *without* the need for a separate server. That said, which database technology you use very much depends on what you're trying to do.

Task 1: Install the MySQL Server

If you already have MySQL installed on your computer, feel free to move on to Task 2.

How you go about installing MySQL depends on the operating system you're using. Thankfully, the folks behind MySQL (and its close cousin, MariaDB) do a great job of making the installation process straightforward.

If you're running *Linux*, you should have no trouble finding `mysql-server` (or `mariadb-server`) in your software repositories. Use your software installation utility (`apt`, `aptitude`, `rpm`, `yum`, or whatever) to install MySQL as you would any other package.

If you're running *Mac OS X*, we recommend installing *Homebrew* (find out about Homebrew here: *http://brew.sh*), then using it to install MariaDB, as in our experience this combination works well.

For all other systems (including all the various *Windows* versions), we recommend you install the **Community Edition** of the MySQL server, available from:

http://dev.mysql.com/downloads/mysql/

Or, if you want to go with MariaDB, check out:

https://mariadb.org/download/

Be sure to read the installation documentation associated with whichever version of the server your download and install.

> This is going to be painful, as I've never used MySQL before...

Don't worry if this is new to you.

We don't expect you to be a MySQL whiz-kid while working through this material. We'll provide you with everything you need in order to get each of our examples to work (even if you've never used MySQL before).

If you want to take some time to learn more, we recommended *Lynn Beighley's* excellent *Head First SQL* as a wonderful primer.

☐ Install MySQL on your computer.
☐ Install a MySQL Python driver.
☐ Create the database and tables.
☐ Create code to read/write data.

We'll check off each completed task as we work through them.

Note from Marketing: Of all the MySQL books...in all the world...this is the one we brought to the ~~bar~~ ...eh...office when we first learned MySQL.

Although this is a book about the SQL query language, it uses the MySQL database management system for all its examples. Despite its age, it's still great learning resource.

Introducing Python's DB-API

With the database server installed, let's park it for a bit, while we add support for working with MySQL into Python.

Out of the box, the Python interpreter comes with some support for working with databases, but nothing specific to MySQL. What's provided is a standard database API (application programmer interface) for working with SQL-based databases, known as *DB-API*. What's missing is the **driver** to connect the DB-API up to the actual database technology you're using.

The convention is that programmers use the DB-API when interacting with any underlying database using Python, no matter what that database technology happens to be. They do that because the driver shields programmers from having to understand the nitty-gritty details of interacting with the database's actual API, as the DB-API provides an abstract layer between the two. The idea is that, by programming to the DB-API, you can replace the underlying database technology as needed without having to throw away any existing code.

We'll have more to say about the DB-API later in this chapter. Here's a visualization of what happens when you use Python's DB-API:

☑ Install MySQL on your computer.
☐ Install a MySQL Python driver.
☐ Create the database and tables.
☐ Create code to read/write data.

Geek Bits

Python's DB-API is defined in PEP 0247. That said, don't feel the need to run off and read this PEP, as it's primarily designed to be used as a specification by database driver implementers (as opposed to being a how-to tutorial).

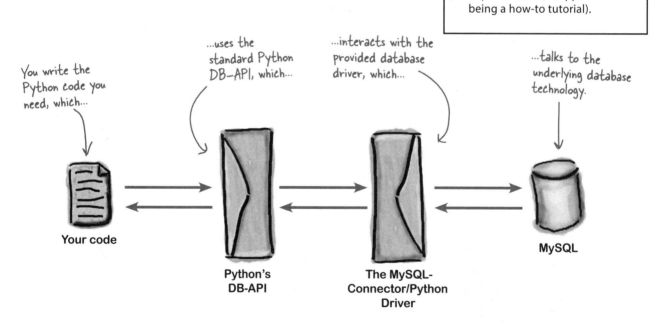

You write the Python code you need, which...

...uses the standard Python DB–API, which...

...interacts with the provided database driver, which...

...talks to the underlying database technology.

Your code

Python's DB-API

The MySQL-Connector/Python Driver

MySQL

Some programmers look at this diagram and conclude that using Python's DB-API must be hugely inefficient. After all, there are *two* layers of technology between your code and the underlying database system. However, using the DB-API allows you to swap out the underlying database as needed, avoiding any database "lock-in," which occurs when you code *directly* to a database. When you also consider that no two SQL dialects are the same, using DB-API helps by providing a higher level of abstraction.

Task 2: Install a MySQL Database Driver for Python

☑ Install MySQL on your computer.
☐ Install a MySQL Python driver.
☐ Create the database and tables.
☐ Create code to read/write data.

Anyone is free to write a database driver (and many people do), but it is typical for each database manufacturer to provide an *official driver* for each of the programming languages they support. *Oracle*, the owner of the MySQL technologies, provides the *MySQL-Connector/Python* driver, and that's what we propose to use in this chapter. There's just one problem: *MySQL-Connector/Python* can't be installed with `pip`.

Does that mean we're out of luck when it comes to using *MySQL-Connector/Python* with Python? No, far from it. The fact that a third-party module doesn't use the `pip` machinery is rarely a show-stopper. All we need to do is install the module "by hand"—it's a small amount of extra work (over using `pip`), but not much.

Let's install the *MySQL-Connector/Python* driver by hand (bearing in mind there are *other* drivers available, such as *PyMySQL*; that said, we prefer *MySQL-Connector/Python*, as it's the officially supported driver provided by the makers of MySQL).

Begin by visiting the *MySQL-Connector/Python* download page: *https://dev.mysql.com/ downloads/connector/python/*. Landing on this web page will likely preselect your operating system from the *Select Platform* drop-down menu. Ignore this, and adjust the selection drop-down to read *Platform Independent*, as shown here:

Then, go ahead and click either of the *Download* buttons (typically, *Windows* users should download the ZIP file, whereas *Linux* and *Mac OS X* users can download the GZ file). Save the downloaded file to your computer, then double-click on the file to expand it within your download location.

Don't worry if your version is different from ours: as long as it is at least this version, all is OK.

Install MySQL-Connector/Python

☑	Install MySQL on your computer.
☐	Install a MySQL Python driver.
☐	Create the database and tables.
☐	Create code to read/write data.

With the driver downloaded and expanded on your computer, open a terminal window in the newly created folder (if you're on *Windows*, open the terminal window with *Run as Administrator*).

On our computer, the created folder is called `mysql-connector-python-2.1.3` and was expanded in our `Downloads` folder. To install the driver into *Windows*, issue this command from within the `mysql-connector-python-2.1.3` folder:

```
py -3 setup.py install
```

On *Linux* or *Mac OS X*, use this command instead:

```
sudo -H python3 setup.py install
```

No matter which operating system you're using, issuing either of the above commands results in a collection of messages appearing on screen, which should look similar to these:

```
running install
Not Installing C Extension
running build
running build_py
running install_lib
running install_egg_info
Removing /Library/Frameworks/Python.framework/Versions/3.5/lib/python3.5/site-packages/
mysql_connector_python-2.1.3-py3.5.egg-info
Writing /Library/Frameworks/Python.framework/Versions/3.5/lib/python3.5/site-packages/
mysql_connector_python-2.1.3-py3.5.egg-info
```

These paths may be different on your computer. Don't worry about it if they are.

When you install a module with `pip`, it runs though this same process, but hides these messages from you. What you're seeing here is the status messages that indicate that the installation is proceeding smoothly. If something goes wrong, the resulting error message should provide enough information to resolve the problem. If all goes well with the installation, the appearance of these messages is confirmation that *MySQL-Connector/Python* is ready to be used.

there are no
Dumb Questions

Q: Should I worry about that "Not Installing C Extension" message?

A: No. Third-party modules sometimes include embedded C code, which can help improve computationally intensive processing. However, not all operating systems come with a preinstalled C compiler, so you have to specifically ask for the C extension support to be enabled when installing a module (should you decide you need it). When you don't ask, the third-party module installation machinery uses (potentially slower) Python code in place of the C code. This allows the module to work on any platform, regardless of the existence of a C compiler. When a third-party module uses Python code *exclusively*, it is referred to as being written in "pure Python." In the example above, we've installed the pure Python version of the *MySQL-Connector/Python* driver.

Task 3: Create Our Webapp's Database and Tables

☑ Install MySQL on your computer.
☑ Install a MySQL Python driver.
☐ Create the database and tables.
☐ Create code to read/write data.

You now have the MySQL database server and the *MySQL-Connector/Python* driver installed on your computer. It's time for Task 3, which involves creating the database and the tables required by our webapp.

To do this, you're going to interact with the MySQL server using its command-line tool, which is a small utility that you start from your terminal window. This tool is known as the MySQL *console*. Here's the command to start the console, logging in as the MySQL database administrator (which uses the `root` user ID):

```
mysql  -u  root  -p
```

If you set an administrator password when you installed the MySQL server, type in that password after pressing the *Enter* key. Alternatively, if you have no password, just press the *Enter* key twice. Either way, you'll be taken to the **console prompt**, which looks like this (on the left) when using MySQL, or like this (on the right) when using MariaDB:

```
mysql>                          MariaDB [None]>
```

Any commands you type at the console prompt are delivered to the MySQL server for execution. Let's start by creating a database for our webapp. Remember: we want to use the database to store logging data, so the database's name should reflect this purpose. Let's call our database `vsearchlogDB`. Here's the console command that creates our database:

```
mysql> create database vsearchlogDB;
```

> Be sure to terminate each command you enter into the MySQL console with a semicolon.

The console responds with a (rather cryptic) status message: `Query OK, 1 row affected (0.00 sec)`. This is the console's way of letting you know that everything is golden.

Let's create a database user ID and password specifically for our webapp to use when interacting with MySQL as opposed to using the `root` user ID all the time (which is regarded as bad practice). This next command creates a new MySQL user called `vsearch`, uses "vsearchpasswd" as the new user's password, and gives the `vsearch` user full rights to the `vsearchlogDB` database:

```
mysql> grant all on vsearchlogDB.* to 'vsearch' identified by 'vsearchpasswd';
```

> You can use a different password if you like. Just remember to use yours as opposed to ours in the examples that follow.

A similar `Query OK` status message should appear, which confirms the creation of this user. Let's now log out of the console using this command:

```
mysql> quit
```

You'll see a friendly `Bye` message from the console before being returned to your operating system.

Decide on a Structure for Your Log Data

Now that you've created a database to use with your webapp, you can create any number of tables within that database (as required by your application). For our purposes, a single table will suffice here, as all we need to store is the data relating to each logged web request.

Recall how we stored this data in a text file in the previous chapter, with each line in the vsearch.log file conforming to a specific format:

...as well as the value of "letters".

We log the value of the "phrase"...

The IP address of the computer that submitted the form data is also logged.

```
ImmutableMultiDict([('phrase', 'galaxy'), ('letters', 'xyz')])|127.0.0.1|Mozilla/5.0 (Macintosh; Intel
Mac OS X 10_11_2) AppleWebKit/537.36 (KHTML, like Gecko) Chrome/47.0.2526.106 Safari/537.36|{'x', 'y'}
```

There's a (rather large) string that describes the web browser being used.

Last—but not least—the actual results produced by searching for "letters" in "phrase" are also logged.

At the very least, the table you create needs five fields: for the phrase, letters, IP address, browser string, and result values. But let's also include two other fields: a unique ID for each logged request, as well as a timestamp that records when the request was logged. As these two latter fields are so common, MySQL provides an easy way to add this data to each logged request, as shown at the bottom of this page.

You can specify the structure of the table you want to create within the console. Before doing so, however, let's log in as our newly created vsearch user using this command (and supplying the correct password after pressing the *Enter* key):

```
mysql -u vsearch -p vsearchlogDB
```

Remember: we set this user's password to "vsearchpasswd".

Here's the SQL statement we used to create the required table (called log). Note that the -> symbol is not part of the SQL statement, as it's added automatically by the console to indicate that it expects more input from you (when your SQL runs to multiple lines). The statement ends (and executes) when you type the terminating semicolon character, and then press the *Enter* key:

This is the console's continuation symbol.

MySQL will automatically provide data for these fields.

These fields will hold the data for each request (as provided in the form data).

```
mysql> create table log (
    -> id int auto_increment primary key,
    -> ts timestamp default current_timestamp,
    -> phrase varchar(128) not null,
    -> letters varchar(32) not null,
    -> ip varchar(16) not null,
    -> browser_string varchar(256) not null,
    -> results varchar(64) not null );
```

☑ Install MySQL on your computer.
☑ Install a MySQL Python driver.
☐ Create the database and tables.
☐ Create code to read/write data.

Confirm Your Table Is Ready for Data

With the table created, we're done with Task 3.

Let's confirm at the console that the table has indeed been created with the structure we require. While still logged into the MySQL console as user `vsearch`, issue the **describe log** command at the prompt:

☑ Install MySQL on your computer.

☑ Install a MySQL Python driver.

☑ Create the database and tables.

☐ Create code to read/write data.

```
mysql> describe log;
+---------------+--------------+------+-----+-------------------+----------------+
| Field         | Type         | Null | Key | Default           | Extra          |
+---------------+--------------+------+-----+-------------------+----------------+
| id            | int(11)      | NO   | PRI | NULL              | auto_increment |
| ts            | timestamp    | NO   |     | CURRENT_TIMESTAMP |                |
| phrase        | varchar(128) | NO   |     | NULL              |                |
| letters       | varchar(32)  | NO   |     | NULL              |                |
| ip            | varchar(16)  | NO   |     | NULL              |                |
| browser_string| varchar(256) | NO   |     | NULL              |                |
| results       | varchar(64)  | NO   |     | NULL              |                |
+---------------+--------------+------+-----+-------------------+----------------+
```

And there it is: proof that the `log` table exists and has a structure that fits with our web application's logging needs. Type **quit** to exit the console (as you are done with it for now).

So now I'm ready to add data to the table, right? My friend who's an SQL expert says I can use a bunch of manual INSERT statements to do that..

Yes, that's one possibility.

There's nothing stopping you from *manually* typing a bunch of SQL INSERT statements into the console to *manually* add data to your newly created table. But remember: we want our webapp to add our web request data to the `log` table **automatically**, and this applies to INSERT statements, too.

To do this, we need to write some Python code to interact with the `log` table. And to do *that*, we need to learn more about Python's DB-API.

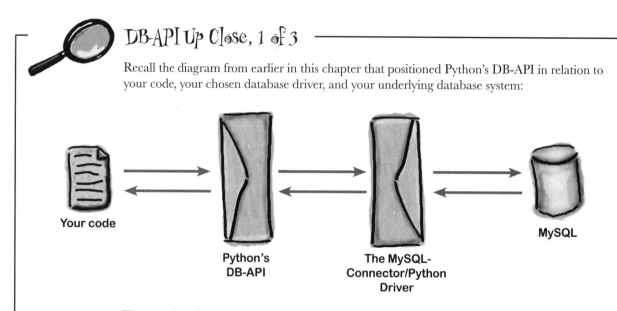

DB-API Up Close, 1 of 3

Recall the diagram from earlier in this chapter that positioned Python's DB-API in relation to your code, your chosen database driver, and your underlying database system:

Your code → **Python's DB-API** → **The MySQL-Connector/Python Driver** → **MySQL**

The promise of using DB-API is that you can replace the driver/database combination with very minor modifications to your Python code, so long as you limit yourself to only using the facilities provided by the DB-API.

Let's review what's involved in programming to this important Python standard. We are going to present six steps here.

DB-API Step 1: Define your connection characteristics

There are four pieces of information you need when connecting to MySQL: (1) the IP address/name of the computer running the MySQL server (known as the *host*), (2) the user ID to use, (3) the password associated with the user ID, and (4) the name of the database the user ID wants to interact with.

The *MySQL-Connector/Python* driver allows you to put these connection characteristics into a Python dictionary for ease of use and ease of reference. Let's do that now by typing the code in this *Up Close* into the >>> prompt. Be sure to follow along on your computer. Here's a dictionary (called dbconfig) that associates the four required "connection keys" with their corresponding values:

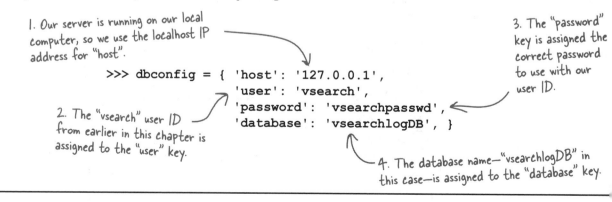

1. Our server is running on our local computer, so we use the localhost IP address for "host".

```
>>> dbconfig = { 'host': '127.0.0.1',
                 'user': 'vsearch',
                 'password': 'vsearchpasswd',
                 'database': 'vsearchlogDB', }
```

2. The "vsearch" user ID from earlier in this chapter is assigned to the "user" key.

3. The "password" key is assigned the correct password to use with our user ID.

4. The database name—"vsearchlogDB" in this case—is assigned to the "database" key.

DB-API Step 2: Import your database driver

With the connection characteristics defined, it's time to `import` our database driver:

>>> **import mysql.connector** ← *Import the driver for the database you are using.*

This import makes the MySQL-specific driver available to the DB-API.

DB-API Step 3: Establish a connection to the server

Let's establish a connection to the server by using the DB-API's `connect` function to establish our connection. Let's save a reference to the connection in a variable called `conn`. Here's the call to `connect`, which establishes the connection to the MySQL database server (and creates `conn`):

>>> **conn = mysql.connector.connect(**dbconfig)**

This call establishes the connection. ↗   ↖ *Pass in the dictionary of connection characteristics.*

Note the strange `**` that precedes the single argument to the `connect` function. (If you're a C/C++ programmer, do **not** read `**` as "a pointer to a pointer," as Python has no notion of pointers.) The `**` notation tells the `connect` function that a dictionary of arguments is being supplied in a single variable (in this case `dbconfig`, the dictionary you just created). On seeing the `**`, the `connect` function expands the single dictionary argument into four individual arguments, which are then used within the `connect` function to establish the connection. (You'll see more of the `**` notation in a later chapter; for now, just use it as is.)

DB-API Step 4: Open a cursor

To send SQL commands to your database (via the just-opened connection) as well as receive results from your database, you need a *cursor*. Think of a cursor as the database equivalent of the *file handle* from the last chapter (which lets you communicate with a disk file once it was opened).

Creating a cursor is straightforward: you do so by calling the `cursor` method included with every connection object. As with the connection above, we save a reference to the created cursor in a variable (which, in a wild fit of imaginative creativity, we've named `cursor`):

>>> **cursor = conn.cursor()** ← *Create a cursor to send commands to the server, and to receive results.*

We are now ready to send SQL commands to the server, and—hopefully—get some results back.

But, before we do that, let's take a moment to review the steps completed so far. We've defined the connection characteristics for the database, imported the driver module, created a connection object, and created a cursor. No matter which database you use, these steps are common to all interactions with MySQL (only the connection characteristics change). Keep this in mind as you interact with your data through the cursor.

 ## DB-API Up Close, 2 of 3

With the cursor created and assigned to a variable, it's time to interact with the data in your database using the SQL query language.

DB-API Step 5: Do the SQL thing!

The `cursor` variable lets you send SQL queries to MySQL, as well as retrieve any results produced by MySQL's processing of the query.

As a general rule, the Python programmers over at *Head First Labs* like to code the SQL they intend to send to the database server in a triple-quoted string, then assign the string to a variable called _SQL. A triple-quoted string is used because SQL queries can often run to multiple lines, and using a triple-quoted string temporarily switches off the Python interpreter's "end-of-line is the end-of-statement" rule. Using _SQL as the variable name is a convention among the *Head First Labs* programmers for defining constant values in Python, but you can use any variable name (and it doesn't have to be all uppercase, nor prefixed within an underscore).

Let's start by asking MySQL for the names of the tables in the database we're connected to. To do this, assign the `show tables` query to the _SQL variable, and then call the `cursor.execute` function, passing _SQL as an argument:

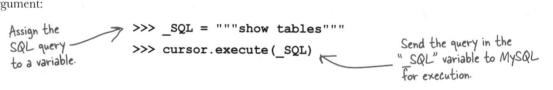

Assign the SQL query to a variable.

```
>>> _SQL = """show tables"""
>>> cursor.execute(_SQL)
```

Send the query in the "_SQL" variable to MySQL for execution.

When you type the above `cursor.execute` command at the >>> prompt, the SQL query is sent to your MySQL server, which proceeds to execute the query (assuming it's valid and correct SQL). However, any results from the query *don't* appear immediately; you have to ask for them.

You can ask for results using one of three cursor methods:

- `cursor.fetchone` retrieves a **single** row of results.

- `cursor.fetchmany` retrieves the **number** of rows you specify.

- `cursor.fetchall` retrieves **all** the rows that make up the results.

For now, let's use the `cursor.fetchall` method to retrieve all the results from the above query, assigning the results to a variable called `res`, then displaying the contents of `res` at the >>> prompt:

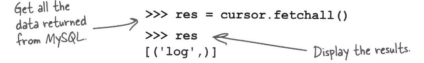

Get all the data returned from MySQL.

```
>>> res = cursor.fetchall()
>>> res
[('log',)]
```

Display the results.

The contents of `res` look a little weird, don't they? You were probably expecting to see a single word here, as we know from earlier that our database (`vsearchlogDB`) contains a single table called `log`. However, what's returned by `cursor.fetchall` is always a *list of tuples*, even when there's only a single piece of data returned (as is the case above). Let's look at another example that returns more data from MySQL.

Our next query, `describe log`, queries for the information about the `log` table as stored in the database. As you'll see below, the information is shown *twice*: once in its raw form (which is a little messy) and then over multiple lines. Recall that the result returned by `cursor.fetchall` is a list of tuples.

Here's `cursor.fetchall` in action once more:

```
>>> _SQL = """describe log"""
>>> cursor.execute(_SQL)
>>> res = cursor.fetchall()
>>> res
[('id', 'int(11)', 'NO', 'PRI', None, 'auto_increment'), ('ts',
'timestamp', 'NO', '', 'CURRENT_TIMESTAMP', ''), ('phrase',
'varchar(128)', 'NO', '', None, ''), ('letters', 'varchar(32)',
'NO', '', None, ''), ('ip', 'varchar(16)', 'NO', '', None, ''),
('browser_string', 'varchar(256)', 'NO', '', None, ''), ('results',
'varchar(64)', 'NO', '', None, '')]
```

Take the SQL query...

...then send it to the server...

...and then access the results.

It looks a little messy, but this is a list of tuples.

```
>>> for row in res:
        print(row)
```

Take each row in the results...

...and display it on its own line.

Each tuple from the list of tuples is now on its own line.

```
('id', 'int(11)', 'NO', 'PRI', None, 'auto_increment')
('ts', 'timestamp', 'NO', '', 'CURRENT_TIMESTAMP', '')
('phrase', 'varchar(128)', 'NO', '', None, '')
('letters', 'varchar(32)', 'NO', '', None, '')
('ip', 'varchar(16)', 'NO', '', None, '')
('browser_string', 'varchar(256)', 'NO', '', None, '')
('results', 'varchar(64)', 'NO', '', None, '')
```

The per-row display above may not look like much of an improvement over the raw output, but compare it to the output displayed by the MySQL console from earlier (shown below). What's shown above is the same data as what's shown below, only now the data is in a Python data structure called `res`:

```
mysql> describe log;
+----------------+--------------+------+-----+-------------------+----------------+
| Field          | Type         | Null | Key | Default           | Extra          |
+----------------+--------------+------+-----+-------------------+----------------+
| id             | int(11)      | NO   | PRI | NULL              | auto_increment |
| ts             | timestamp    | NO   |     | CURRENT_TIMESTAMP |                |
| phrase         | varchar(128) | NO   |     | NULL              |                |
| letters        | varchar(32)  | NO   |     | NULL              |                |
| ip             | varchar(16)  | NO   |     | NULL              |                |
| browser_string | varchar(256) | NO   |     | NULL              |                |
| results        | varchar(64)  | NO   |     | NULL              |                |
+----------------+--------------+------+-----+-------------------+----------------+
```

Look closely. It's the same data.

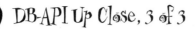

DB-API Up Close, 3 of 3

Let's use an `insert` query to add some sample data to the `log` table.

It's tempting to assign the query shown below (which we've written over multiple lines) to the `_SQL` variable, then call `cursor.execute` to send the query to the server:

```
>>> _SQL = """insert into log
              (phrase, letters, ip, browser_string, results)
              values
              ('hitch-hiker', 'aeiou', '127.0.0.1', 'Firefox', "{'e', 'i'}")"""
>>> cursor.execute(_SQL)
```

Don't get us wrong, what's shown above *does* work. However, *hardcoding* the data values in this way is rarely what you'll want to do, as the data values you store in your table will likely change with every `insert`. Remember: you plan to log the details of each web request to the `log` table, which means these data values *will* change with every request, so hardcoding the data in this way would be a disaster.

To avoid the need to hardcode data (as shown above), Python's DB-API lets you position "data placeholders" in your query string, which are filled in with the actual values when you call `cursor.execute`. In effect, this lets you reuse a query with many different data values, passing the values as arguments to the query just before it's executed. The placeholders in your query are stringed values, and are identified as `%s` in the code below.

Compare these commands below with those shown above:

When composing your query, use DB-API placeholders instead of actual data values.

```
>>> _SQL = """insert into log
              (phrase, letters, ip, browser_string, results)
              values
              (%s, %s, %s, %s, %s)"""
>>> cursor.execute(_SQL, ('hitch-hiker', 'xyz', '127.0.0.1', 'Safari', 'set()'))
```

There are two things to note above. First, instead of hardcoding the actual data values in the SQL query, we used the `%s` placeholder, which tells DB-API to expect a stringed value to be substituted into the query prior to execution. As you can see, there are five `%s` placeholders above, so the second thing to note is that `cursor.execute` call is going to expect five additional parameters when called. The only problem is that `cursor.execute` doesn't accept just *any* number of parameters; it accepts *at most* two.

How can this be?

Looking at the last line of code shown above, it's clear that `cursor.execute` accepts the *five* data values provided to it (without complaint), so what gives?

Take another, closer look at that line of code. See the pair of parentheses around the data values? The use of parentheses turns the five data values into a single tuple (containing the individual data values). In effect, the above line of code supplies two arguments to `cursor.execute`: the placeholder-containing query, as well as a single tuple of data values.

So, when the code on this page executes, data values are inserted into the `log` table, right? Well...not quite.

When you use `cursor.execute` to send data to a database system (using the `insert` query), the data may not be saved to the database immediately. This is because writing to a database is an **expensive** operation (from a processing-cycle perspective), so many database systems cache `inserts`, then apply them all at once later. This can sometimes mean the data you think is in your table isn't there *yet*, which can lead to problems.

For instance, if you use `insert` to send data to a table, then immediately use `select` to read it back, the data may not be available, as it is still in the database system's cache waiting to be written. If this happens, you're out of luck, as the `select` fails to return any data. Eventually, the data is written, so it's not lost, but this default caching behavior may not be what you desire.

If you are happy to take the performance hit associated with a database write, you can force your database system to commit all potentially cached data to your table using the `conn.commit` method. Let's do that now to ensure the two `insert` statements from the previous page are applied to the `log` table. With your data written, you can now use a `select` query to confirm the data values are saved:

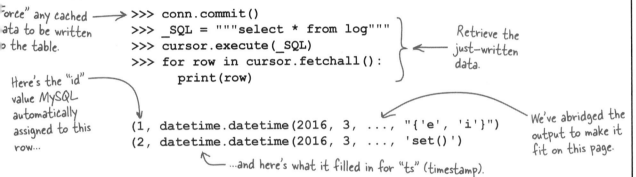

"Force" any cached data to be written to the table.

```
>>> conn.commit()
>>> _SQL = """select * from log"""
>>> cursor.execute(_SQL)
>>> for row in cursor.fetchall():
        print(row)
```
Retrieve the just-written data.

Here's the "id" value MySQL automatically assigned to this row...

```
(1, datetime.datetime(2016, 3, ..., "{'e', 'i'}")
(2, datetime.datetime(2016, 3, ..., 'set()')
```
...and here's what it filled in for "ts" (timestamp).

We've abridged the output to make it fit on this page.

From the above you can see that MySQL has automatically determined the correct values to use for `id` and `ts` when data is inserted into a row. The data returned from the database server is (as before) a list of tuples. Rather than save the results of `cursor.fetchall` to a variable that is then iterated over, we've used `cursor.fetchall` directly in a `for` loop in this code. Also, don't forget: a tuple is an immutable list and, as such, supports the usual square bracket access notation. This means you can index into the `row` variable used within the above `for` loop to pick out individual data items as needed. For instance, `row[2]` picks out the phrase, `row[3]` picks out the letters, and `row[-1]` picks out the results.

DB-API Step 6: Close your cursor and connection

With your data committed to its table, tidy up after yourself by closing the cursor as well as the connection:

```
>>> cursor.close()
True
>>> conn.close()
```
It's always a good idea to tidy up.

Note that the cursor confirms successful closure by returning `True`, while the connection simply shuts down. It's always a good idea to close your cursor and your connection when they're no longer needed, as your database system has a finite set of resources. Over at *Head First Labs*, the programmers like to keep their database cursors and connections open for as long as required, but no longer.

Task 4: Create Code to Work with Our Webapp's Database and Tables

☑ Install MySQL on your computer.

☑ Install a MySQL Python driver.

☑ Create the database and tables.

☑ Create code to read/write data.

With the six *steps* of the DB-API *Up Close* completed, you now have the code needed to interact with the log table, which means you've completed Task 4: *Create code to work with our webapp's database and tables.*

Let's review the code you can use (in its entirety):

Our task list is done!

Define your connection characteristics.

```
dbconfig = { 'host': '127.0.0.1',
             'user': 'vsearch',
             'password': 'vsearchpasswd',
             'database': 'vsearchlogDB', }

import mysql.connector
```

Import the database driver.

Establish a connection and create a cursor.

```
conn = mysql.connector.connect(**dbconfig)

cursor = conn.cursor()

_SQL = """insert into log
            (phrase, letters, ip, browser_string, results)
          values
            (%s, %s, %s, %s, %s)"""
```

Assign a query to a string (note the five placeholder arguments).

```
cursor.execute(_SQL, ('galaxy', 'xyz', '127.0.0.1', 'Opera', "{'x', 'y'}")
```

Force the database to write your data.

```
conn.commit()

_SQL = """select * from log"""

cursor.execute(_SQL)

for row in cursor.fetchall():
    print(row)

cursor.close()

conn.close()
```

Send the query to the server, remembering to provide values for each of the required arguments (in a tuple).

Retrieve the (just written) data from the table, displaying the output row by row.

Tidy up when you're done.

With each of the four tasks now complete, you're ready to adjust your webapp to log the web request data to your MySQL database system as opposed to a text file (as is currently the case). Let's start doing this now.

Database Magnets

Take another look at the `log_request` function from the last chapter.

Recall that this small function accepts two arguments: a web request object, and the results of the vsearch:

```
def log_request(req: 'flask_request', res: str) -> None:
    with open('vsearch.log', 'a') as log:
        print(req.form, req.remote_addr, req.user_agent, res, file=log, sep='|')
```

Your job is to replace this function's suite with code that logs to your database (as opposed to the text file). The `def` line is to remain unchanged. Decide on the magnets you need from those scattered at the bottom on this page, then position them to provide the function's code:

```
def log_request(req: 'flask_request', res: str) -> None:
```

Crikey! What a mess of magnets. Can you help?

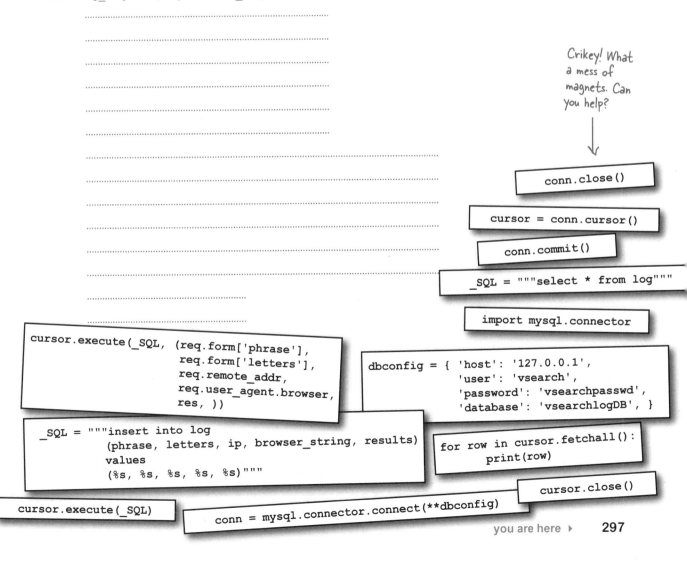

```
conn.close()
```

```
cursor = conn.cursor()
```

```
conn.commit()
```

```
_SQL = """select * from log"""
```

```
import mysql.connector
```

```
cursor.execute(_SQL, (req.form['phrase'],
                      req.form['letters'],
                      req.remote_addr,
                      req.user_agent.browser,
                      res, ))
```

```
dbconfig = { 'host': '127.0.0.1',
             'user': 'vsearch',
             'password': 'vsearchpasswd',
             'database': 'vsearchlogDB', }
```

```
_SQL = """insert into log
          (phrase, letters, ip, browser_string, results)
          values
          (%s, %s, %s, %s, %s)"""
```

```
for row in cursor.fetchall():
    print(row)
```

```
cursor.close()
```

```
cursor.execute(_SQL)
```

```
conn = mysql.connector.connect(**dbconfig)
```

Database Magnets Solution

You were to take another look at the `log_request` function from the last chapter:

```python
def log_request(req: 'flask_request', res: str) -> None:
    with open('vsearch.log', 'a') as log:
        print(req.form, req.remote_addr, req.user_agent, res, file=log, sep='|')
```

Your job was to replace this function's suite with code that logs to your database. The `def` line was to remain unchanged. You were to decide which magnets you needed from those scattered at the bottom on the page.

```python
def log_request(req: 'flask_request', res: str) -> None:
```

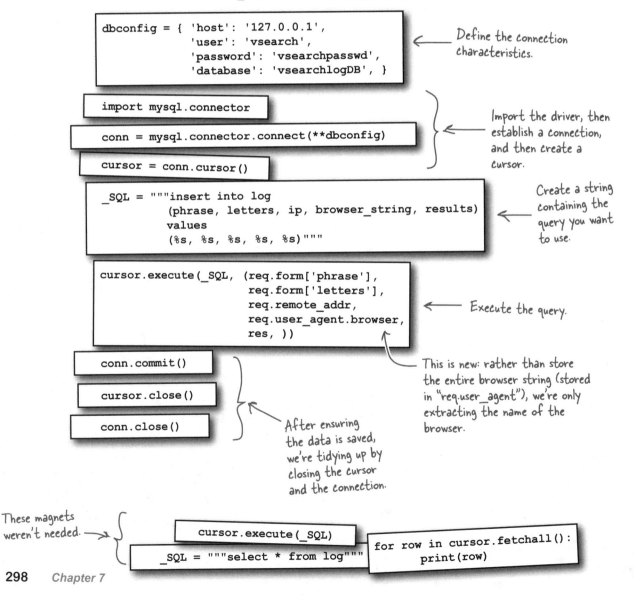

```python
dbconfig = { 'host': '127.0.0.1',
             'user': 'vsearch',
             'password': 'vsearchpasswd',
             'database': 'vsearchlogDB', }
```
← Define the connection characteristics.

```python
import mysql.connector

conn = mysql.connector.connect(**dbconfig)

cursor = conn.cursor()
```
← Import the driver, then establish a connection, and then create a cursor.

```python
_SQL = """insert into log
          (phrase, letters, ip, browser_string, results)
          values
          (%s, %s, %s, %s, %s)"""
```
← Create a string containing the query you want to use.

```python
cursor.execute(_SQL, (req.form['phrase'],
                      req.form['letters'],
                      req.remote_addr,
                      req.user_agent.browser,
                      res, ))
```
← Execute the query.

```python
conn.commit()

cursor.close()

conn.close()
```
After ensuring the data is saved, we're tidying up by closing the cursor and the connection.

This is new: rather than store the entire browser string (stored in "req.user_agent"), we're only extracting the name of the browser.

These magnets weren't needed. →

```python
cursor.execute(_SQL)
```

```python
_SQL = """select * from log"""
```

```python
for row in cursor.fetchall():
    print(row)
```

TEST DRIVE

Change the code in your `vsearch4web.py` file to replace the original `log_request` function's code with that from the last page. When you have saved your code, start up this latest version of your webapp at a command prompt. Recall that on *Windows*, you need to use this command:

```
C:\webapps> py -3 vsearch4web.py
```

While on *Linux* or *Mac OS X*, use this command:

```
$ python3 vsearch4web.py
```

Your webapp should start running at this web address:

http://127.0.0.1:5000/

Use your favorite web browser to perform a few searches to confirm that your webapp runs fine.

There are two points we'd like to make here:

- Your webapp performs exactly as it did before: each search returns a "results page" to the user.

- Your users have no idea that the search data is now being logged to a database table as opposed to a text file.

Regrettably, you can't use the */viewlog* URL to view these latest log entries, as the function associated with that URL (`view_the_log`) only works with the `vsearch.log` text file (not the database). We'll have more to say about fixing this over the page.

For now, let's conclude this *Test Drive* by using the MySQL console to confirm that this newest version of `log_request` is logging data to the `log` table. Open another terminal window and follow along (note: we've reformatted and abridged our output to make it fit on this page):

Log in to the MySQL console.

This query asks to see all the data in the "log" table (your actual data will likely differ).

```
File  Edit  Window  Help   Checking our log DB
$ mysql -u vsearch -p vsearchlogDB
Enter password:

Welcome to MySQL monitor...


mysql> select * from log;
+----+---------------------+----------------------+---------+-----------+----------------+----------------------+
| id | ts                  | phrase               | letters | ip        | browser_string | results              |
+----+---------------------+----------------------+---------+-----------+----------------+----------------------+
|  1 | 2016-03-09 13:40:46 | life, the uni ... ything | aeiou | 127.0.0.1 | firefox        | {'u', 'e', 'i', 'a'} |
|  2 | 2016-03-09 13:42:07 | hitch-hiker          | aeiou   | 127.0.0.1 | safari         | {'i', 'e'}           |
|  3 | 2016-03-09 13:42:15 | galaxy               | xyz     | 127.0.0.1 | chrome         | {'y', 'x'}           |
|  4 | 2016-03-09 13:43:07 | hitch-hiker          | xyz     | 127.0.0.1 | firefox        | set()                |
+----+---------------------+----------------------+---------+-----------+----------------+----------------------+
4 rows in set (0.0 sec)


mysql> quit
Bye
```

Don't forget to quit the console when you're done.

Remember: we're only storing the browser name.

Storing Data Is Only Half the Battle

Having run though the *Test Drive* on the last page, you've now confirmed that your
Python DB-API–compliant code in `log_request` does indeed store the details of
each web request in your `log` table.

Take a look at the most recent version of the `log_request` function once more
(which includes a docstring as its first line of code):

```python
def log_request(req: 'flask_request', res: str) -> None:
    """Log details of the web request and the results."""
    dbconfig = { 'host': '127.0.0.1',
                 'user': 'vsearch',
                 'password': 'vsearchpasswd',
                 'database': 'vsearchlogDB', }

    import mysql.connector

    conn = mysql.connector.connect(**dbconfig)
    cursor = conn.cursor()
    _SQL = """insert into log
              (phrase, letters, ip, browser_string, results)
              values
              (%s, %s, %s, %s, %s)"""
    cursor.execute(_SQL, (req.form['phrase'],
                          req.form['letters'],
                          req.remote_addr,
                          req.user_agent.browser,
                          res, ))
    conn.commit()
    cursor.close()
    conn.close()
```

This new function is a big change

There's a lot more code in the `log_request` function now than when it operated on
a simple text file, but the extra code is needed to interact with MySQL (which you're
going to use to answer questions about your logged data at the end of this chapter), so
this new, bigger, more complex version of `log_request` appears justified.

However, recall that your webapp has another function, called `view_the_log`,
which retrieves the data from the `vsearch.log` log file and displays it in a nicely
formatted web page. We now need to update the `view_the_log` function's code to
retrieve its data from the `log` table in the database, as opposed to the text file.

The question is: what's the best way to do this?

Experienced Python
programmers may
well look at this
function's code and
let out a gasp of
disapproval. You'll
learn why in a few
pages' time.

How Best to Reuse Your Database Code?

You now have code that logs the details of each of your webapp's requests to MySQL. It shouldn't be too much work to do something similar in order to retrieve the data from the `log` table for use in the `view_the_log` function. The question is: what's the best way to do this? We asked three programmers our question...and got three different answers.

Let's quickly cut and paste that code, then change it. Done!

I vote we put that database-handling code into its own function, then call it as needed.

Isn't it clear it's time we considered using classes and objects as the correct way to handle this type of reuse?

In its own way, each of these suggestions is valid, if a little suspect (especially the first one). What may come as a surprise is that, in this case, a Python programmer would be unlikely to embrace any of these proposed solutions *on their own*.

Consider What You're Trying to Reuse

Let's take another look our database code in the `log_request` function.

It should be clear that there are parts of this function we can reuse when writing additional code that interacts with a database system. Thus, we've annotated the function's code to highlight the parts we think are reusable, as opposed to the parts that are specific to the central idea of what the `log_request` function actually does:

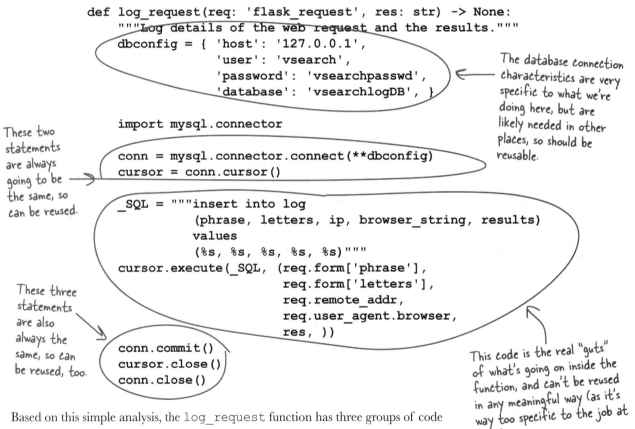

```
def log_request(req: 'flask_request', res: str) -> None:
    """Log details of the web request and the results."""
    dbconfig = { 'host': '127.0.0.1',
                 'user': 'vsearch',
                 'password': 'vsearchpasswd',
                 'database': 'vsearchlogDB', }

    import mysql.connector

    conn = mysql.connector.connect(**dbconfig)
    cursor = conn.cursor()

    _SQL = """insert into log
              (phrase, letters, ip, browser_string, results)
              values
              (%s, %s, %s, %s, %s)"""
    cursor.execute(_SQL, (req.form['phrase'],
                          req.form['letters'],
                          req.remote_addr,
                          req.user_agent.browser,
                          res, ))

    conn.commit()
    cursor.close()
    conn.close()
```

The database connection characteristics are very specific to what we're doing here, but are likely needed in other places, so should be reusable.

These two statements are always going to be the same, so can be reused.

These three statements are also always the same, so can be reused, too.

This code is the real "guts" of what's going on inside the function, and can't be reused in any meaningful way (as it's way too specific to the job at hand).

Based on this simple analysis, the `log_request` function has three groups of code statements:

- statements that can be easily reused (such as the creation of `conn` and `cursor`, as well as the calls to `commit` and `close`);

- statements that are specific to the problem but still need to be reusable (such as the use of the `dbconfig` dictionary); and

- statements that cannot be reused (such as the assignment to `_SQL` and the call to `cursor.execute`). Any further interactions with MySQL are very likely to require a different SQL query, as well as different arguments (if any).

What About That Import?

All this talk of reuse is great... but did you forget to consider reusing that "import" statement?

Nope, we didn't forget.

The `import mysql.connector` statement wasn't forgotten when we considered reusing the `log_request` function's code.

This omission was deliberate on our part, as we wanted to call out this statement for special treatment. The problem isn't that we don't want to reuse that statement; it's that it shouldn't appear in the function's suite!

Be careful when positioning your import statements

We mentioned a few pages back that experienced Python programmers may well look at the `log_request` function's code and let out a gasp of disapproval. This is due to the inclusion of the `import mysql.connector` line of code in the function's suite. And this disapproval is in spite of the fact that our most recent *Test Drive* clearly demonstrated that this code works. So, what's the problem?

The problem has to do with what happens when the interpreter encounters an `import` statement in your code: the imported module is read in full, then executed by the interpreter. This behavior is fine when your `import` statement occurs *outside of a function*, as the imported module is (typically) only read *once*, then executed *once*.

However, when an `import` statement appears *within* a function, it is read *and* executed **every time the function is called**. This is regarded as an extremely wasteful practice (even though, as we've seen, the interpreter won't stop you from putting an `import` statement in a function). Our advice is simple: think carefully about where you position your `import` statements, and don't put any inside a function.

Consider What You're Trying to Do

In addition to looking at the code in `log_request` from a reuse perspective, it's also possible to categorize the function's code based on *when* it runs.

The "guts" of the function is the assignment to the `_SQL` variable and the call to `cursor.execute`. Those two statements most patently represent *what* the function is meant to **do**, which—to be honest—is the most important bit. The function's initial statements define the connection characteristics (in `dbconfig`), then create a connection and cursor. This **setup** code always has to run *before* the guts of the function. The last three statements in the function (the single `commit` and the two `closes`) execute *after* the guts of the function. This is **teardown** code, which performs any required tidying up.

With this *setup, do, teardown* pattern in mind, let's look at the function once more. Note that we've repositioned the `import` statement to execute outside of the `log_request` function's suite (so as to avoid any further disapproving gasps):

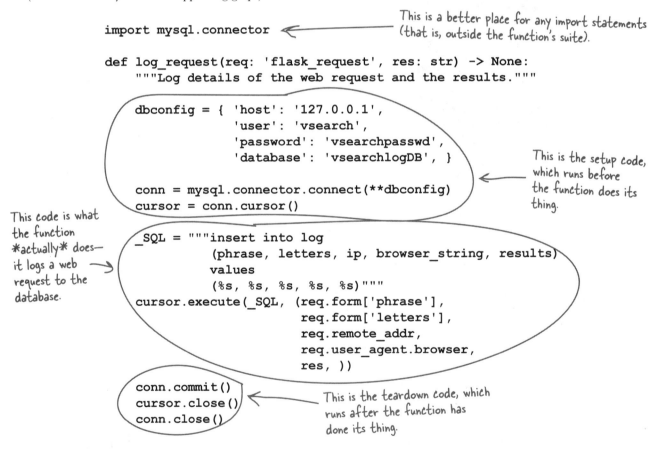

```python
import mysql.connector
```
This is a better place for any import statements (that is, outside the function's suite).

```python
def log_request(req: 'flask_request', res: str) -> None:
    """Log details of the web request and the results."""

    dbconfig = { 'host': '127.0.0.1',
                 'user': 'vsearch',
                 'password': 'vsearchpasswd',
                 'database': 'vsearchlogDB', }

    conn = mysql.connector.connect(**dbconfig)
    cursor = conn.cursor()
```
This is the setup code, which runs before the function does its thing.

```python
    _SQL = """insert into log
              (phrase, letters, ip, browser_string, results)
              values
              (%s, %s, %s, %s, %s)"""
    cursor.execute(_SQL, (req.form['phrase'],
                          req.form['letters'],
                          req.remote_addr,
                          req.user_agent.browser,
                          res, ))
```
This code is what the function *actually* does—it logs a web request to the database.

```python
    conn.commit()
    cursor.close()
    conn.close()
```
This is the teardown code, which runs after the function has done its thing.

Wouldn't it be neat if there were a way to reuse this setup, do, teardown pattern?

You've Seen This Pattern Before

Consider the pattern we just identified: setup code to get ready, followed by code to do what needs to be done, and then teardown code to tidy up. It may not be immediately obvious, but in the previous chapter, you encountered code that conforms to this pattern. Here it is again:

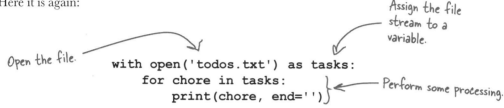

Open the file.

Assign the file stream to a variable.

```
with open('todos.txt') as tasks:
    for chore in tasks:
        print(chore, end='')
```

Perform some processing.

Recall how the `with` statement *manages the context* within which the code in its suite runs. When you're working with files (as in the code above), the `with` statement arranges to open the named file and return a variable representing the file stream. In this example, that's the `tasks` variable; this is the **setup** code. The suite associated with the `with` statement is the **do** code; here that's the `for` loop, which does the actual work (a.k.a. "the important bit"). Finally, when you use `with` to open a file, it comes with the promise that the open file will be closed when the `with`'s suite terminates. This is the **teardown** code.

It would be neat if we could integrate our database programming code into the `with` statement. Ideally, it would be great if we could write code like this, and have the `with` statement take care of all the database setup and teardown details:

We still need to define the connection characteristics.

```
dbconfig = { 'host': '127.0.0.1',
             'user': 'vsearch',
             'password': 'vsearchpasswd',
             'database': 'vsearchlogDB', }
```

This "with" statement works with databases as opposed to disk files, and returns a cursor for us to work with.

The "do code" from the last page remains unchanged.

```
with UseDatabase(dbconfig) as cursor:
    _SQL = """insert into log
              (phrase, letters, ip, browser_string, results)
              values
              (%s, %s, %s, %s, %s)"""
    cursor.execute(_SQL, (req.form['phrase'],
                          req.form['letters'],
                          req.remote_addr,
                          req.user_agent.browser,
                          res, ))
```

Don't try to run this code, as you've yet to write the "UseDatabase" context manager.

The *good news* is that Python provides the **context management protocol**, which enables programmers to hook into the `with` statement as needed. Which brings us to the *bad news*...

The Bad News Isn't Really All That Bad

At the bottom of the last page, we stated that the *good news* is that Python provides a context management protocol that enables programmers to hook into the `with` statement as and when required. If you learn how to do this, you can then create a context manager called `UseDatabase`, which can be used as part of a `with` statement to talk to your database.

The idea is that the setup and teardown "boilerplate" code that you've just written to save your webapp's logging data to a database can be replaced by a single `with` statement that looks like this:

```
    . . .
with UseDatabase(dbconfig) as cursor:
    . . .
```

This "with" statement is similar to the one used with files and the "open" BIF, except that this one works with a database instead.

The *bad news* is that creating a context manager is complicated by the fact that you need to know how to create a Python class in order to successfully hook into the protocol.

Consider that up until this point in this book, you've managed to write a lot of usable code without having to create a class, which is pretty good going, especially when you consider that some programming languages don't let you do *anything* without first creating a class (we're looking at *you*, Java).

However, it's now time to bite the bullet (although, to be honest, creating a class in Python is nothing to be scared of).

As the ability to create a class is generally useful, let's deviate from our current discussion about adding database code to our webapp, and dedicate the next (short) chapter to classes. We'll be showing you just enough to enable you to create the `UseDatabase` context manager. Once that's done, in the chapter after that, we'll return to our database code (and our webapp) and put our newly acquired class-writing abilities to work by writing the `UseDatabase` context manager.

Chapter 7's Code

```
import mysql.connector

def log_request(req: 'flask_request', res: str) -> None:
    """Log details of the web request and the results."""

    dbconfig = { 'host': '127.0.0.1',
                 'user': 'vsearch',
                 'password': 'vsearchpasswd',
                 'database': 'vsearchlogDB', }

    conn = mysql.connector.connect(**dbconfig)
    cursor = conn.cursor()

    _SQL = """insert into log
              (phrase, letters, ip, browser_string, results)
              values
              (%s, %s, %s, %s, %s)"""
    cursor.execute(_SQL, (req.form['phrase'],
                          req.form['letters'],
                          req.remote_addr,
                          req.user_agent.browser,
                          res, ))
    conn.commit()
    cursor.close()
    conn.close()
```

This is the database code that currently runs within your webapp (i.e., the "log_request" function).

```
dbconfig = { 'host': '127.0.0.1',
             'user': 'vsearch',
             'password': 'vsearchpasswd',
             'database': 'vsearchlogDB', }

with UseDatabase(dbconfig) as cursor:
    _SQL = """insert into log
              (phrase, letters, ip, browser_string, results)
              values
              (%s, %s, %s, %s, %s)"""
    cursor.execute(_SQL, (req.form['phrase'],
                          req.form['letters'],
                          req.remote_addr,
                          req.user_agent.browser,
                          res, ))
```

This is the code that we'd like to be able to write in order to do the same thing as our current code (replacing the suite in the "log_request" function). But don't try to run this code yet, as it won't work without the "UseDatabase" context manager.

8 a little bit of class

Abstracting Behavior and State

Well...just lookee here: all of my state, and all of your behavior...

...and it's all in the one place. Fancy that!

Classes let you bundle code behavior and state together.

In this chapter, you're setting your webapp aside while you learn about creating Python **classes.** You're doing this in order to get to the point where you can create a context manager with the help of a Python class. As creating and using classes is such a useful thing to know about anyway, we're dedicating this chapter to them. We won't cover everything about classes, but we'll touch on all the bits you'll need to understand in order to confidently create the context manager your webapp is waiting for. Let's dive in and see what's involved.

Hooking into the "with" Statement

At stated at the end of the last chapter, understanding how to hook your setup and teardown code into Python's `with` statement is straightforward...assuming you know how to create a Python **class**.

Despite being well over halfway through this book, you've managed to get by without having to define a class. You've written useful and reusable code using nothing more than Python's function machinery. There are other ways to write and organize your code, and object orientation is very popular.

You're never forced to program exclusively in the object-oriented paradigm when using Python, and the language is flexible when it comes to how you go about writing your code. But, when it comes to hooking into the `with` statement, doing so through a class is the **recommended approach**, even though the standard library comes with support for doing something similar *without* a class (although the standard library's approach is less widely applicable, so we aren't going to use it here).

So, to hook into the `with` statement, you'll have to create a class. Once you know how to write classes, you can then create one that implements and adheres to the **context management protocol**. This protocol is the mechanism (built into Python) that hooks into the `with` statement.

Let's learn how to create and use classes in Python, before returning to our context management protocol discussion in the next chapter.

> **The context management protocol lets your write a class that hooks into the "with" statement.**

---

there are no Dumb Questions

Q: Exactly what type of programming language is Python: object-oriented, functional, or procedural?

A: That's a great question, which many programmers moving to Python eventually ask. The answer is that Python supports programming paradigms borrowed from all three of these popular approaches, and Python encourages programmers to mix and match as needed. This concept can be hard to get your head around, especially if you come from the perspective where all the code you write has to be in a class that you instantiate objects from (as in other programming languages like, for instance, Java).

Our advice is not to let this worry you: create code in whatever paradigm you're comfortable with, but don't discount the others simply because—as approaches—they appear alien to you.

Q: So...is it wrong to always start by creating a class?

A: No, it isn't, if that's what your application needs. You don't have to put all your code in classes, but if you want to, Python won't get in your way.

So far in this book, we've gotten by without having to create a class, but we're now at the point where it makes sense to use one to solve a specific application issue we're grappling with: how best to share our database processing code within our webapp. We're mixing and matching programming paradigms to solve our current problem, and that's OK.

An Object-Oriented Primer

Before we get going with classes, it's important to note that we don't intend to cover everything there is to know about classes in Python in this chapter. Our intention is merely to show you enough to enable you to confidently create a class that implements the context management protocol.

Therefore, we won't discuss some topics that seasoned practitioners of object-oriented programming (OOP) might expect to see here, such as *inheritance* and *polymorphism* (even though Python provides support for both). That's because we're primarily interested in **encapsulation** when creating a context manager.

If the jargon in that last paragraph has put you in a *blind panic*, don't worry: you can safely read on without knowing what any of that OOP-speak actually means.

On the last page, you learned that you need to create a class in order to hook into the `with` statement. Before getting to the specifics of how to do that, let's look at what constitutes a class in Python, writing an example class as we go. Once you understand how to write a class, we'll return to the problem of hooking into the `with` statement (in the next chapter).

Don't be freaked out by all the buzzwords on this page!

If we were to run a competition to determine the page in this book with this most buzzwords on it, this one would win hands-down. Don't be put off by all the jargon used here, though. If you already know OOP, this should all make sense. **If not, the really important bits are shown below**. Don't worry: all this will become clearer as you work through the example on the next few pages.

A class bundles behavior and state

Using a class lets you bundle **behavior** and **state** together in an object.

When you hear the word *behavior*, think *function*—that is, a chunk of code that does something (or *implements a behavior*, if you prefer).

When you hear the word *state*, think *variables*—that is, a place to store values within a class. When we assert that a class bundles behavior and state *together*, we're simply stating that a class packages functions and variables.

The upshot of all of the above is this: if you know what a function is and what variables are, you're most of the way to understanding what a class is (as well as how to create one).

Classes have methods and attributes

In Python, you define a class behavior by creating a method.

The word *method* is the OOP name given to a function that's defined within a class. Just why methods aren't simply known as *class functions* has been lost in the mists of time, as has the fact that *class variables* aren't referred to as such—they are known by the name *attribute*.

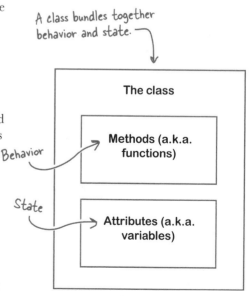

A class bundles together behavior and state.

The class

Behavior → Methods (a.k.a. functions)

State → Attributes (a.k.a. variables)

Creating Objects from Classes

To use a class, you create an object from it (you'll see an example of this below). This is known as **object instantiation**. When you hear the word *instantiate*, think *invoke*; that is, you invoke a class to create an object.

Perhaps surprisingly, you can create a class that has no state or behavior, yet is still a class as far as Python is concerned. In effect, such a class is *empty*. Let's start our class examples with an empty one and take things from there. We'll work at the interpreter's >>> prompt, and you're encouraged to follow along.

We begin by creating an empty class called `CountFromBy`. We do this by prefixing the class name with the `class` keyword, then providing the suite of code that implements the class (after the obligatory colon):

> "pass" is a valid statement (i.e., it is syntactically correct), but it does nothing. Think of it as an empty statement.

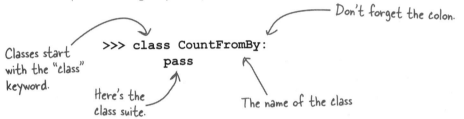

Don't forget the colon.

Classes start with the "class" keyword.

Here's the class suite.

The name of the class

```
>>> class CountFromBy:
        pass
```

Note how this class's suite contains the Python keyword `pass`, which is Python's empty statement (in that it does nothing). You can use `pass` in any place the interpreter expects to find actual code. In this case, we aren't quite ready to fill in the details of the `CountFromBy` class, so we use `pass` to avoid any syntax errors that would normally result when we try to create a class without any code in its suite.

Now that the class exists, let's create two objects from it, one called a and another called b. Note how creating an object from a class looks very much like calling a function:

```
>>> a = CountFromBy()
>>> b = CountFromBy()
```

← These look like function calls, don't they?

Create an object by appending parentheses to the class name, then assign the newly created object to a variable.

---

there are no
Dumb Questions

Q: When I'm looking at someone else's code, how do I know if something like `CountFromBy()` is code that creates an object or code that calls a function? That looks like a function call to me...

A: That's a great question. On the face of things, you don't know. However, there's a well-established convention in the Python programming community to name functions using lowercase letters (with underscores for emphasis), while *CamelCase* (concatenated words, capitalized) is used to name classes. Following this convention, it should be clear that `count_from_by()` is a function call, whereas `CountFromBy()` creates an object. All is fine just so long as everyone follows this convention, and you're **strongly encouraged** to do so, too. However, if you ignore this suggestion, all bets are off, and most Python programmers will likely avoid you and your code.

Objects Share Behavior but Not State

When you create objects from a class, each object shares the class's coded behaviors (the methods defined in the class), but maintains its own copy of any state (the attributes):

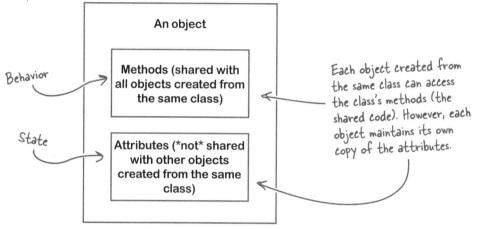

An object

Methods (shared with all objects created from the same class)

Behavior

State

Attributes (*not* shared with other objects created from the same class)

Each object created from the same class can access the class's methods (the shared code). However, each object maintains its own copy of the attributes.

This distinction will make more sense as we flesh out the CountFromBy example.

Defining what we want CountFromBy to do

Let's now define what we want the CountFromBy class to actually do (as an empty class is rarely useful).

Let's make CountFromBy an incrementing counter. By default, the counter will start at 0 and be incremented (on request) by 1. We'll also make it possible to provide an alternative starting value and/or amount to increment by. This means you'll be able to create, for example, a CountFromBy object that starts at 100 and increments by 10.

Let's preview what the CountFromBy class will be able to do (once we have written its code). By understanding how the class will be used, you'll be better equipped to understand the CountFromBy code as we write it. Our first example uses the class defaults: start at 0, and increment by 1 on request by calling the increase method. The newly created object is assigned to a new variable, which we've called c:

Note: this new "CountFromBy" class doesn't exist just yet. You'll create it in a little bit.

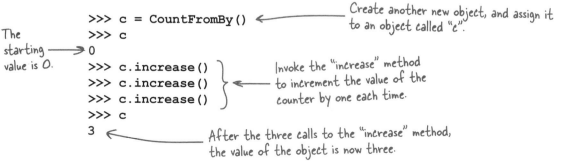

The starting value is 0.

```
>>> c = CountFromBy()
>>> c
0
>>> c.increase()
>>> c.increase()
>>> c.increase()
>>> c
3
```

Create another new object, and assign it to an object called "c".

Invoke the "increase" method to increment the value of the counter by one each time.

After the three calls to the "increase" method, the value of the object is now three.

Doing More with CountFromBy

The example usage of CountFromBy at the bottom of the last page
demonstrated the default behavior: unless specified, the counter maintained by
a CountFromBy object starts at 0 and is incremented by 1. It's also possible to
specify an alternative starting value, as demonstrated in this next example, where
the count starts from 100:

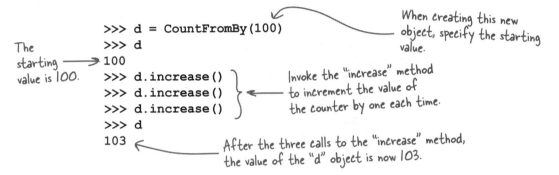

The
starting
value is 100.

```
>>> d = CountFromBy(100)
>>> d
100
>>> d.increase()
>>> d.increase()
>>> d.increase()
>>> d
103
```

When creating this new
object, specify the starting
value.

Invoke the "increase" method
to increment the value of
the counter by one each time.

After the three calls to the "increase" method,
the value of the "d" object is now 103.

As well as specifying the starting value, it's also possible to specify the amount to
increase by, as shown here, where we start at 100 and increment by 10:

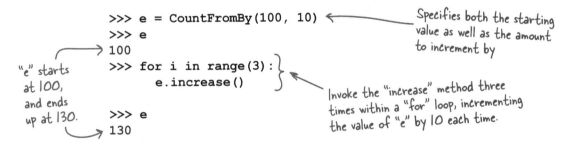

"e" starts
at 100,
and ends
up at 130.

```
>>> e = CountFromBy(100, 10)
>>> e
100
>>> for i in range(3):
        e.increase()
>>> e
130
```

Specifies both the starting
value as well as the amount
to increment by

Invoke the "increase" method three
times within a "for" loop, incrementing
the value of "e" by 10 each time.

In this final example, the counter starts at 0 (the default), but increments by
15. Rather than having to specify (0, 15) as the arguments to the class, this
example uses a keyword argument that allows us to specify the amount to
increment by, while leaving the starting value at the default (0):

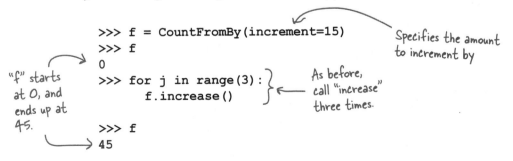

"f" starts
at 0, and
ends up at
45.

```
>>> f = CountFromBy(increment=15)
>>> f
0
>>> for j in range(3):
        f.increase()
>>> f
45
```

Specifies the amount
to increment by

As before,
call "increase"
three times.

It's Worth Repeating Ourselves: Objects Share Behavior but Not State

The previous examples created four new CountFromBy objects: c, d, e, and f, each of which has access to the increase method, which is a behavior that's shared by all objects created from the CountFromBy class. There's only ever one copy of the increase method's code, which all these objects use. However, each object maintains its own attribute values. In these examples, that's the current value of the counter, which is different for each of the objects, as shown here:

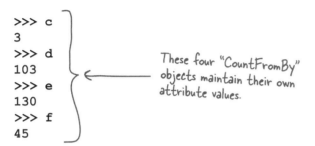

```
>>> c
3
>>> d
103
>>> e
130
>>> f
45
```

These four "CountFromBy" objects maintain their own attribute values.

Here's the key point again: the method code is shared, but the attribute data isn't.

It can be useful to think of a class as a "cookie-cutter template" that is used by a factory to churn out objects that all behave the same, but have their own data.

Class behavior is shared by each of its objects, whereas state is not. Each object maintains its own state.

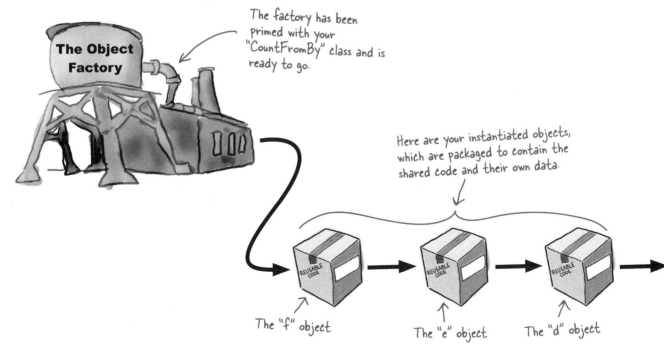

The Object Factory

The factory has been primed with your "CountFromBy" class and is ready to go.

Here are your instantiated objects, which are packaged to contain the shared code and their own data.

The "f" object

The "e" object

The "d" object

Invoking a Method: Understand the Details

We stated earlier that a method is *a function defined within a class*. We also saw examples of a method from `CountFromBy` being invoked. The `increase` method is invoked using the familiar dot notation:

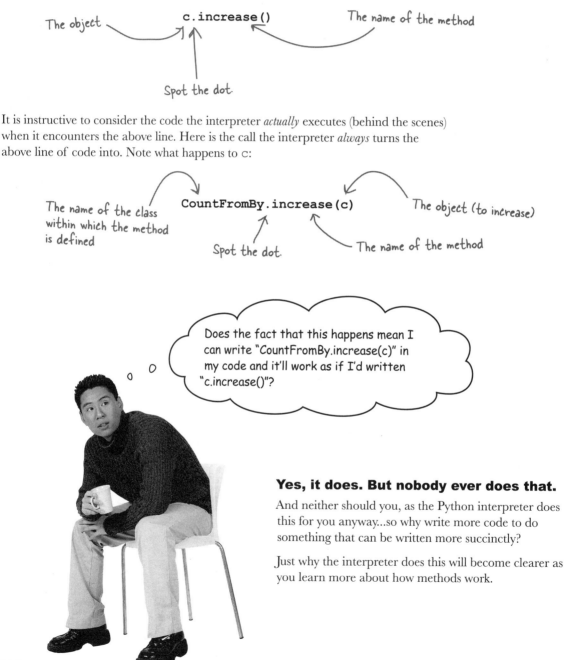

The object ⟶ **`c.increase()`** ⟵ The name of the method

Spot the dot.

It is instructive to consider the code the interpreter *actually* executes (behind the scenes) when it encounters the above line. Here is the call the interpreter *always* turns the above line of code into. Note what happens to c:

The name of the class within which the method is defined ⟶ **`CountFromBy.increase(c)`** ⟵ The object (to increase)

Spot the dot. ⟶ The name of the method

> Does the fact that this happens mean I can write "CountFromBy.increase(c)" in my code and it'll work as if I'd written "c.increase()"?

Yes, it does. But nobody ever does that.

And neither should you, as the Python interpreter does this for you anyway...so why write more code to do something that can be written more succinctly?

Just why the interpreter does this will become clearer as you learn more about how methods work.

Method Invocation: What Actually Happens

At first sight, the interpreter turning `c.increase()` into `CountFromBy.increase(c)` may look a little strange, but understanding that this happens helps explain why every method you write takes *at least* one argument.

It's OK for methods to take more than one argument, but the first argument *always* has to exist in order to take the object as an argument (which, in the example from the last page, is c). In fact, it is a well-established practice in the Python programming community to give each method's first argument a special name: `self`.

When `increase` is invoked as `c.increase()`, you'd imagine the method's `def` line should look like this:

`def increase():`

However, defining a method without the mandatory first argument will cause the interpreter to raise an error when your code runs. Consequently, the `increase` method's `def` line actually needs to be written as follows:

`def increase(self):`

It is regarded as **very bad form** to use something other than the name `self` in your class code, even though the use of `self` does take a bit of getting used to. (Many other programming languages have a similar notion, although they favor the name `this`. Python's `self` is basically the same idea as `this`.)

When you invoke a method on an object, Python arranges for the first argument to be the invoking object instance, which is *always* assigned to each method's `self` argument. This fact alone explains why `self` is so important and also why `self` needs to be the *first argument* to every object method you write. When you invoke a method, you don't need to supply a value for `self`, as the interpreter does this for you:

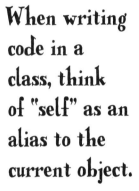

When writing code in a class, think of "self" as an alias to the current object.

What you write: What Python executes:

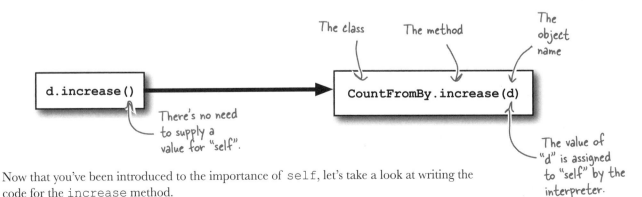

The class   The method   The object name

```
d.increase()              CountFromBy.increase(d)
```

There's no need to supply a value for "self".

The value of "d" is assigned to "self" by the interpreter.

Now that you've been introduced to the importance of `self`, let's take a look at writing the code for the `increase` method.

Adding a Method to a Class

Let's create a new file to save our class code into. Create `countfromby.py`, then add in the class code from earlier in this chapter:

```
class CountFromBy:
    pass
```

We're going to add the `increase` method to this class, and to do so we'll remove the `pass` statement and replace it with `increase`'s method definition. Before doing this, recall how `increase` is invoked:

```
c.increase()
```

Based on this call, you'd be forgiven for assuming the `increase` method takes no arguments, as there's nothing between the parentheses, right? However, this is only half true. As you just learned, the interpreter transforms the above line of code into the following call:

```
CountFromBy.increase(c)
```

The method code we write needs to take this transformation into consideration. With all of the above in mind, here's the `def` line for the `increase` method that we'd use in this class:

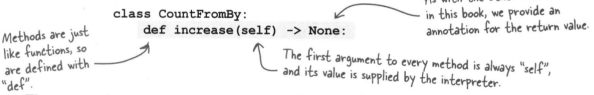

```
class CountFromBy:
    def increase(self) -> None:
```

Methods are just like functions, so are defined with "def".

As with the other functions in this book, we provide an annotation for the return value.

The first argument to every method is always "self", and its value is supplied by the interpreter.

There are no other arguments to the `increase` method, so we do not need to provide anything other than `self` on the `def` line. However, it *is* vitally important that we include `self` here, as forgetting to results in syntax errors.

With the `def` line written, all we need to do now is add some code to `increase`. Let's assume that the class maintains two attributes: `val`, which contains the current value of the current object, and `incr`, which contains the amount to increment `val` by every time `increase` is invoked. Knowing this, you might be tempted to add this **incorrect** line of code to `increase` in an attempt to perform the increment:

```
val += incr
```

But here's the **correct** line of code to add to the `increase` method:

```
class CountFromBy:
    def increase(self) -> None:
        self.val += self.incr
```

Take the object's current value of "val" and increase it by the value of "incr".

Why do you think this line of code is correct, whereas the previous was incorrect?

Are You Serious About "self"?

> Wait a minute...I thought one of Python's big wins was that its code is easy to read. I find that use of "self" anything but easy on the eye, and the fact that it's part of classes (which must get a lot of use) has me thinking: seriously?!?

Don't worry. Getting used to `self` won't take long.

We agree that Python's use of `self` does look a little weird...at first. However, over time, you'll get used to it, so much so that you'll hardly even notice it's there.

If you completely forget about it and fail to add it to your methods, you'll know pretty quickly that something is amiss—the interpreter will display a slew of `TypeErrors` informing you that something is missing, and that something is `self`.

As to whether or not the use of `self` makes Python's class code harder to read...well, we're not so sure. In our mind, every time we see `self` used as the first argument to a function, our brains automatically know that we're looking at a method, *not* a function. This, for us, is a good thing.

Think of it this way: the use of `self` indicates that the code you're reading is a method, as opposed to a function (when `self` is *not* used).

The Importance of "self"

The `increase` method, shown below, prefixes each of the class's attributes with `self` within its suite. You were asked to consider why this might be:

```python
class CountFromBy:
    def increase(self) -> None:
        self.val += self.incr
```

What's the deal with using "self" within the method's suite?

You already know that `self` is assigned the current object by the interpreter when a method is invoked, and that the interpreter expects each method's first argument to take this into account (so that the assignment can occur).

Now, consider what we already know about each object created from a class: it shares the class's method code (a.k.a. behavior) with every other object created from the same class, but maintains its *own copy* of any attribute data (a.k.a. state). It does this by associating the attribute values with the object—that is, with `self`.

Knowing this, consider this version of the `increase` method, which, as we said a couple of pages ago, is **incorrect**:

```python
class CountFromBy:
    def increase(self) -> None:
        val += incr
```

Don't do this—it won't do what you think it should.

On the face of things, that last line of code seems innocent enough, as all it does is increment the current value of `val` by the current value of `incr`. But consider what happens when this `increase` method terminates: `val` and `incr`, which exist *within* `increase`, both go out of scope and consequently are destroyed the moment the method ends.

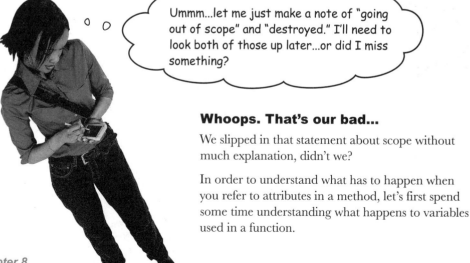

Ummm...let me just make a note of "going out of scope" and "destroyed." I'll need to look both of those up later...or did I miss something?

Whoops. That's our bad...

We slipped in that statement about scope without much explanation, didn't we?

In order to understand what has to happen when you refer to attributes in a method, let's first spend some time understanding what happens to variables used in a function.

Coping with Scoping

To demonstrate what happens to variables used within a function, let's experiment at the >>> prompt. Try out the code below as you read it. We've numbered the annotations 1 through 8 to guide you as you follow along:

1. The "soundbite" function accepts a single argument.

2. A value is assigned to a variable inside the function.

3. The argument is assigned to another variable inside the function.

4. The function's variables are used to display a message.

5. A value is assigned to a variable called "name".

6. The "soundbite" function is invoked.

7. After the function displays the soundbite, the value of "name" is still accessible.

8. But none of the variables used within the function are accessible, as they only exist within the function's suite.

```
Python 3.5.1 Shell
>>>
>>> def soundbite(from_outside):
        insider = 'James'
        outsider = from_outside
        print(from_outside, insider, outsider)

>>> name = 'Bond'
>>> soundbite(name)
Bond James Bond
>>> name
'Bond'
>>> insider
Traceback (most recent call last):
  File "<pyshell#29>", line 1, in <module>
    insider
NameError: name 'insider' is not defined
>>> outsider
Traceback (most recent call last):
  File "<pyshell#30>", line 1, in <module>
    outsider
NameError: name 'outsider' is not defined
>>> from_outside
Traceback (most recent call last):
  File "<pyshell#31>", line 1, in <module>
    from_outside
NameError: name 'from_outside' is not defined
>>>
>>> |
                                    Ln: 83  Col: 4
```

When variables are defined within a function's suite, they exist while the function runs. That is, the variables are "in scope," both visible and usable within the function's suite. However, once the function ends, any variables defined within the function are destroyed—they are "out of scope," and any resources they used are reclaimed by the interpreter.

This is what happens to the three variables used within the soundbite function, as shown above. The moment the function terminates, insider, outsider, and from_outside cease to exist. Any attempt to refer to them outside the suite of function (a.k.a. outside the function's scope) results in a NameError.

Prefix Your Attribute Names with "self"

This function behavior described on the last page is fine when you're dealing with a function that gets invoked, does some work, and then returns a value. You typically don't care what happens to any variables used within a function, as you're usually only interested in the function's return value.

Now that you know what happens to variables when a function ends, it should be clear that this (incorrect) code is likely to cause problems when you attempt to use variables to store and remember attribute values with a class. As methods are functions by another name, neither `val` nor `incr` will survive an invocation of the `increase` method if this is how you code `increase`:

```python
class CountFromBy:
    def increase(self) -> None:
        val += incr
```

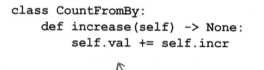 Don't do this, as these variables won't survive once the method ends.

However, with methods, things are *different*. The method uses attribute values that belong to an object, and the object's attributes continue to exist *after* the method terminates. That is, an object's attribute values are **not** destroyed when the method terminates.

In order for an attribute assignment to survive method termination, the attribute value has to be assigned to something that doesn't get destroyed as soon as the method ends. That *something* is the current object invoking the method, which is stored in `self`, which explains why each attribute value needs to be prefixed with `self` in your method code, as shown here:

```python
class CountFromBy:
    def increase(self) -> None:
        self.val += self.incr
```

This is much better, as "val" and "incr" are now associated with the object thanks to the use of "self".

"self" is an alias to the object.

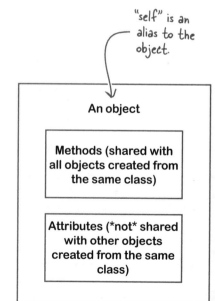

The rule is straightforward: if you need to refer to an attribute in your class, you *must* prefix the attribute name with `self`. The value in `self` as an *alias* that points back to the object invoking the method.

In this context, when you see `self`, think "this object's." So, `self.val` can be read as "this object's `val`."

Initialize (Attribute) Values Before Use

All of the discussion of the importance of `self` sidestepped an important issue: how are attributes assigned a starting value? As it stands, the code in the `increase` method—the correct code, which uses `self`—fails if you execute it. This failure occurs because in Python you can't use a variable before it has been assigned a value, no matter where the variable is used.

To demonstrate the seriousness of this issue, consider this short session at the >>> prompt. Note how the first statement fails to execute when *either* of the variables is undefined:

If you try to execute code that refers to uninitialized variables...

```
>>> val += incr
Traceback (most recent call last):
  File "<pyshell#1>", line 1, in <module>
    val += incr
NameError: name 'val' is not defined
```

...the interpreter complains.

As "val" is undefined, the interpreter refuses to run the line of code.

Assign a value to "val", then try again...
```
>>> val = 0
```

```
>>> val += incr
Traceback (most recent call last):
  File "<pyshell#3>", line 1, in <module>
    val += incr
NameError: name 'incr' is not defined
```

...and the interpreter complains again!

As "incr" is undefined, the interpreter continues to refuse to run the line of code.

Assign a value to "incr", and try again...
```
>>> incr = 1
```

...and it worked this time.
```
>>> val += incr
>>> val
1
>>> incr
1
>>>
```

As both "val" and "incr" have values (i.e., they are initialized), the interpreter is happy to use their values without raising a NameError.

No matter where you use variables in Python, you have to initialize them with a starting value. The question is: *how do we do this for a new object created from a Python class?*

If you know OOP, the word "constructor" may be popping into your brain right about now. In other languages, a constructor is a special method that lets you define what happens when an object is first created, and it usually involves both object instantiation and attribute initialization. In Python, object instantiation is handled automatically by the interpreter, so you don't need to define a constructor to do this. A magic method called `__init__` lets you initialize attributes as needed. Let's take a look at what dunder `init` can do.

Dunder "init" Initializes Attributes

Cast your mind back to the last chapter, when you used the `dir` built-in function to display all the details of Flask's `req` object. Remember this output?

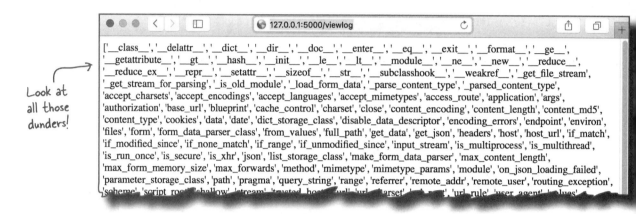

Look at all those dunders!

At the time, we suggested you ignore all those dunders. However, it's now time to reveal their purpose: the dunders provide hooks into every class's standard behavior.

Unless you override it, this standard behavior is implemented in a class called `object`. The `object` class is built into the interpreter, and every other Python class *automatically* inherits from it (including yours). This is OOP-speak for stating that the dunder methods provided by `object` are available to your class to use as is, or to override as needed (by providing your own implementation of them).

You don't have to override any `object` methods if you don't want to. But if, for example, you want to specify what happens when objects created from your class are used with the equality operator (==), then you can write your own code for the `__eq__` method. If you want to specify what happens when objects are used with the greater-than operator (>), you can override the `__ge__` method. And when you want to *initialize* the attributes associated with your object, you can use the `__init__` method.

As the dunders provided by `object` are so useful, they're held in near-mystical reverence by Python programmers. So much so, in fact, that many Python programmers refer to these dunders as *the magic methods* (as they give the appearance of doing what they do "as if by magic").

All of this means that if you provide a method in your class with a `def` line like the one below, the interpreter will call your `__init__` method every time you create a new object from your class. Note the inclusion of `self` as this dunder init's first argument (as per the rule for all methods in all classes):

The standard dunder methods, available to all classes, are known as "the magic methods."

```
def __init__(self):
```

Despite the strange-looking name, dunder "init" is a method like any other. Remember: you must pass "self" as its first argument.

Initializing Attributes with Dunder "init"

Let's add __init__ to our CountFromBy class in order to initialize the objects we create from our class.

For now, let's add an *empty* __init__ method that does nothing but pass (we'll add behavior in just a moment):

```
class CountFromBy:
    def __init__(self) -> None:
        pass
    def increase(self) -> None:
        self.val += self.incr
```

At the moment, this dunder "init" doesn't do anything. However, the use of "self" as its first argument is a BIG CLUE that dunder "init" is a method.

We know from the code already in increase that we can access attributes in our class by prefixing their names with self. This means we can use self.val and self.incr to refer to our attributes within __init__, too. However, we want to use __init__ to *initialize* our class's attributes (val and incr). The question is: where do these initialization values come from and how do their values get into __init__?

Pass any amount of argument data to dunder "init"

As __init__ is a method, and methods are functions in disguise, you can pass as many argument values as you like to __init__ (or any method, for that matter). All you have to do is give your arguments names. Let's give the argument that we'll use to initialize self.val the name v, and use the name i for self.incr.

Let's add v and i to the def line of our __init__ method, then use the values in dunder init's suite to initialize our class attributes, as follows:

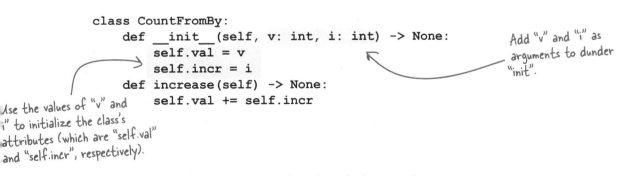

```
class CountFromBy:
    def __init__(self, v: int, i: int) -> None:
        self.val = v
        self.incr = i
    def increase(self) -> None:
        self.val += self.incr
```

Add "v" and "i" as arguments to dunder "init".

Use the values of "v" and "i" to initialize the class's attributes (which are "self.val" and "self.incr", respectively).

If we can now somehow arrange for v and i to acquire values, the latest version of __init__ will initialize our class's attributes. Which raises yet another question: how do we get values into v and i? To help answer this question, we need to try out this version of our class and see what happens. Let's do that now.

TEST DRIVE

Using the edit window in IDLE, take a moment to update the code in your `countfromby.py` file to look like that shown below. When you're done, press F5 to start creating objects at IDLE's >>> prompt:

Press F5 to try out the "CountFromBy" class in IDLE's shell.

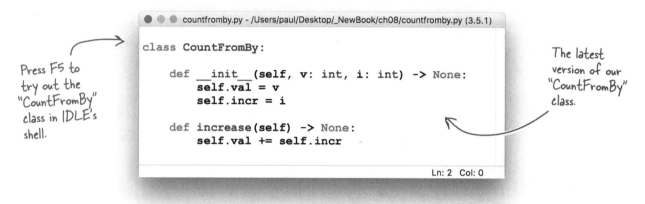

The latest version of our "CountFromBy" class.

```
countfromby.py - /Users/paul/Desktop/_NewBook/ch08/countfromby.py (3.5.1)

class CountFromBy:

    def __init__(self, v: int, i: int) -> None:
        self.val = v
        self.incr = i

    def increase(self) -> None:
        self.val += self.incr

                                                          Ln: 2  Col: 0
```

Pressing F5 executes the code in the edit window, which imports the `CountFromBy` class into the interpreter. Look at what happens when we try to create a new object from our `CountFromBy` class:

Create a new object (called "g") from the class...but when you do this, you get an error!

```
                                 Python 3.5.1 Shell
Python 3.5.1 (v3.5.1:37a07cee5969, Dec  5 2015, 21:12:44)
[GCC 4.2.1 (Apple Inc. build 5666) (dot 3)] on darwin
Type "copyright", "credits" or "license()" for more information.
>>>
======== RESTART: /Users/paul/Desktop/_NewBook/ch07/countfromby.py ========
>>>
>>> g = CountFromBy()
Traceback (most recent call last):
  File "<pyshell#1>", line 1, in <module>
    g = CountFromBy()
TypeError: __init__() missing 2 required positional arguments: 'v' and 'i'
>>>
>>> |
                                                          Ln: 13  Col: 4
```

This may not have been what you were expecting to see. But take a look at the error message (which is classed as a `TypeError`), paying particular attention to the message on the `TypeError` line. The interpreter is telling us that the `__init__` method expected to receive two argument values, `v` and `i`, but received something else (in this case, nothing). We provided no arguments to the class, but this error message tells us that any arguments provided to the class (when creating a new object) are passed to the `__init__` method.

Bearing this in mind, let's have another go at creating a `CountFromBy` object.

Let's return to the >>> prompt, and create another object (called h) that takes two integer values as arguments for v and i:

No "TypeError" this time

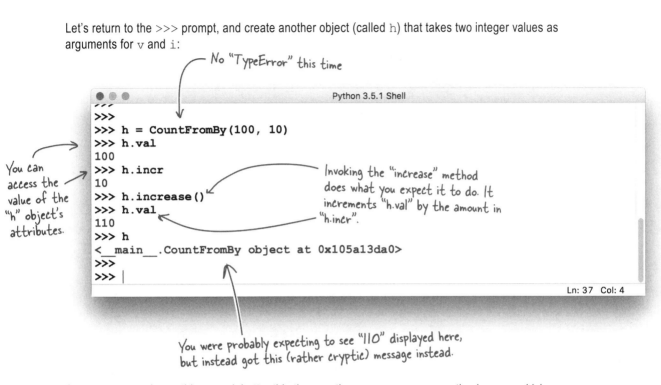

You can access the value of the "h" object's attributes.

Invoking the "increase" method does what you expect it to do. It increments "h.val" by the amount in "h.incr".

```
Python 3.5.1 Shell
>>>
>>> h = CountFromBy(100, 10)
>>> h.val
100
>>> h.incr
10
>>> h.increase()
>>> h.val
110
>>> h
<__main__.CountFromBy object at 0x105a13da0>
>>>
>>> |
                                          Ln: 37  Col: 4
```

You were probably expecting to see "110" displayed here, but instead got this (rather cryptic) message instead.

As you can see above, things work better this time, as the TypeError exception is gone, which means the h object was created successfully. You can access the values of h's attributes using h.val and h.incr, as well as call the object's increase method. Only when you try to access the value of h do things get strange again.

What have we learned from this Test Drive?

Here are the main takeaways from this *Test Drive*:

- When you're creating objects, any argument values provided to the class are passed to the __init__ method, as was the case with 100 and 10 above. (Note that v and i cease to exist as soon as dunder init ends, but we aren't worried, as their values are safely stored in the object's self.val and self.incr attributes, respectively.)

- We can access the attribute values by combining the object's name with the attribute name. Note how we used h.val and h.incr to do this. (For those readers coming to Python from a "stricter" OOP language, note that we did this without having to create *getters* or *setters*.)

- When we use the object name on its own (as in the last interaction with the shell above), the interpreter spits back a cryptic message. Just what this is (and why this happens) will be discussed next.

Understanding CountFromBy's Representation

When we typed the name of the object into the shell in an attempt to display its current value, the interpreter produced this output:

<__main__.CountFromBy object at 0x105a13da0>

Don't worry if you have a different value here. All will become clear before the end of this page.

We described the above output as "strange," and on first glance, it would certainly appear to be. To understand what this output means, let's return to IDLE's shell and create yet another object from CountFromBy, which due to our deeply ingrained unwillingness to rock the boat, we're calling j.

In the session below, note how the strange message displayed for j is made up of values that are produced when we call certain built-in functions (BIFs). Follow along with the session first, then read on for an explanation of what these BIFs do:

```
Python 3.5.1 Shell
>>>
>>> j = CountFromBy(100, 10)
>>> j
<__main__.CountFromBy object at 0x1035be278>
>>>
>>> type(j)
<class '__main__.CountFromBy'>
>>>
>>> id(j)
4351320696
>>>
>>> hex(id(j))
'0x1035be278'
>>>
>>>
                                              Ln: 21  Col: 4
```

The output for "j" is made up of values produced by some of Python's BIFs.

The type BIF displays information on the class the object was created from, reporting (above) that j is a CountFromBy object.

The id BIF displays information on an object's memory address (which is a unique identifier used by the interpreter to keep track of your objects). What you see on your screen is likely different from what is reported above.

The memory address displayed as part of j's output is the value of id converted to a hexadecimal number (which is what the hex BIF does). So, the entire message displayed for j is a combination of type's output, as well as id's (converted to hexadecimal).

A reasonable question is: *why does this happen?*

In the absence of you telling the interpreter how you want to represent your objects, the interpreter has to do *something*, so it does what's shown above. Thankfully, you can override this default behavior by coding your own __repr__ magic method.

Override dunder "repr" to specify how your objects are represented by the interpreter.

Defining CountFromBy's Representation

As well as being a magic method, the __repr__ functionality is also available as a built-in function called repr. Here's part of what the help BIF displays when you ask it to tell you what repr does: "Return the canonical string representation of the object." In other words, the help BIF is telling you that repr (and by extension, __repr__) needs to return a stringified version of an object.

What this "stringified version of an object" looks like depends on what each individual object does. You can control what happens for *your* objects by writing a __repr__ method for your class. Let's do this now for the CountFromBy class.

Begin by adding a new def line to the CountFromBy class for dunder repr, which takes no arguments other than the required self (remember: it's a method). As is our practice, let's also add an annotation that lets readers of our code know this method returns a string:

```
def __repr__(self) -> str:
```

Like every other method we'll write, this one has to take into account that the interpreter always provides a value for the first argument.

This lets users of this method know that this function intends to return a string. Remember: using annotations in your code is optional, but helpful.

With the def line written, all that remains is to write the code that returns a string representation of a CountFromBy object. For our purposes, all we want to do here is take the value in self.val, which is an integer, and convert it to a string.

Thanks to the str BIF, doing so is straightforward:

```
def __repr__(self) -> str:
    return str(self.val)
```

Take the value in "self.val", turn it into a string, and then return it to this method's caller.

When you add this short function to your class, the interpreter uses it whenever it needs to display a CountFromBy object at the >>> prompt. The print BIF also uses dunder repr to display objects.

Before making this change and taking the updated code for a spin, let's return briefly to another issue that surfaced during the last *Test Drive*.

Providing Sensible Defaults for CountFromBy

Let's remind ourselves of the current version of the CountFromBy class's __init__ method:

```
        ...
    def __init__(self, v: int, i: int) -> None:
        self.val = v
        self.incr = i
        ...
```

This version of the dunder "init" method expects two argument values to be provided every time it is invoked.

Recall that when we tried to create a new object from this class without passing values for v and i, we got a TypeError:

```
>>> g = CountFromBy()
Traceback (most recent call last):
  File "<pyshell#1>", line 1, in <module>
    g = CountFromBy()
TypeError: __init__() missing 2 required positional arguments: 'v' and 'i'
>>>
>>>
```

Yikes! Not good.

Earlier in this chapter, we specified that we wanted the CountFromBy class to support the following default behavior: the counter will start at 0 and be incremented (on request) by 1. You already know how to provide default values to function arguments, and the same goes for methods, too—assign the default values on the def line:

```
        ...
    def __init__(self, v: int=0, i: int=1) -> None:
        self.val = v
        self.incr = i
        ...
```

As methods are functions, they support the use of default values for arguments (although we're scoring a B— here for our use of single-character variable names: "v" is the value, whereas "i" is the incrementing value).

If you make this small (but important) change to your CountFromBy code, then save the file (before pressing F5 once more), you'll see that objects can now be created with this default behavior:

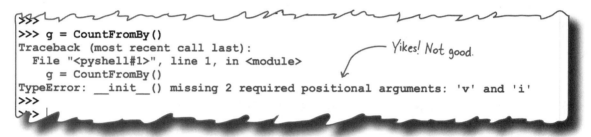

```
>>>
>>>
>>> i = CountFromBy()
>>> i.val
0
>>> i.incr
1
>>> i.increase()
>>> i.val
1
>>>
>>>
```
Python 3.5.1 Shell

We haven't specified values to use when initializing the object, so the class provides the default values as specified in dunder "init".

This all works as expected, with the "increase" method incremented "i.val" by one each time it's invoked. This is the default behavior.

Ln: 50 Col: 4

TEST DRIVE

Make sure your class code (in `countfromby.py`) is the same as ours below. With your class code loaded into IDLE's edit window, press F5 to take your latest version of the `CountFromBy` class for a spin:

This is the "CountFromBy" class with the code for dunder "repr" added.

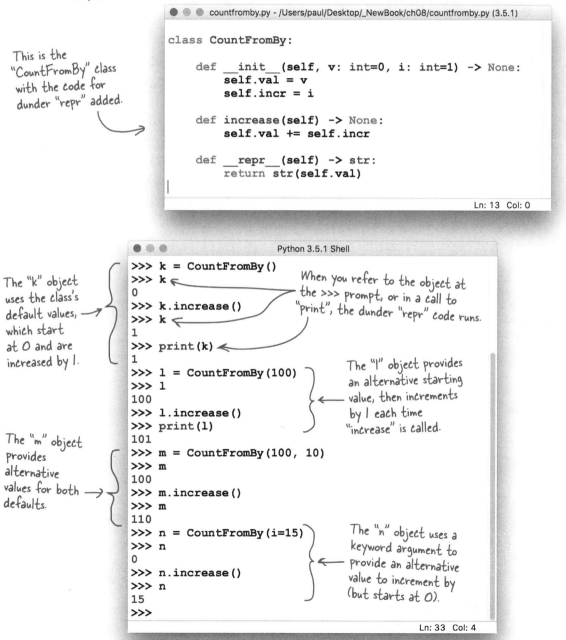

```
countfromby.py - /Users/paul/Desktop/_NewBook/ch08/countfromby.py (3.5.1)

class CountFromBy:

    def __init__(self, v: int=0, i: int=1) -> None:
        self.val = v
        self.incr = i

    def increase(self) -> None:
        self.val += self.incr

    def __repr__(self) -> str:
        return str(self.val)
```
Ln: 13 Col: 0

The "k" object uses the class's default values, which start at 0 and are increased by 1.

```
Python 3.5.1 Shell
>>> k = CountFromBy()
>>> k
0
>>> k.increase()
>>> k
1
>>> print(k)
1
>>> l = CountFromBy(100)
>>> l
100
>>> l.increase()
>>> print(l)
101
>>> m = CountFromBy(100, 10)
>>> m
100
>>> m.increase()
>>> m
110
>>> n = CountFromBy(i=15)
>>> n
0
>>> n.increase()
>>> n
15
>>>
```
Ln: 33 Col: 4

When you refer to the object at the >>> prompt, or in a call to "print", the dunder "repr" code runs.

The "l" object provides an alternative starting value, then increments by 1 each time "increase" is called.

The "m" object provides alternative values for both defaults.

The "n" object uses a keyword argument to provide an alternative value to increment by (but starts at 0).

Classes: What We Know

With the `CountFromBy` class behaving as specified earlier in this chapter, let's review what we now know about classes in Python:

> ## BULLET POINTS
>
> - Python classes let you share **behavior** (a.k.a. methods) and **state** (a.k.a. attributes).
>
> - If you remember that methods are **functions**, and attributes are **variables**, you won't go far wrong.
>
> - The `class` keyword introduces a new class in your code.
>
> - Creating a new object from a class looks very like a function call. Remember: to create an object called `mycount` from a class called `CountFromBy`, you'd use this line of code:
>
>   ```
>   mycount = CountFromBy()
>   ```
>
> - When an object is created from a class, the object **shares** the class's code with every other object created from the class. However, each object maintains its **own copy** of the attributes.
>
> - You add behaviors to a class by creating **methods**. A method is a function defined within a class.
>
> - To add an **attribute** to a class, create a variable.
>
> - Every method is passed an **alias** to the current object as its first argument. Python convention insists that this first argument is called `self`.
>
> - Within a method's suite, referrals to attributes are prefixed with `self`, ensuring the attribute's value **survives** after the method code ends.
>
> - The `__init__` method is one of the many **magic methods** provided with all Python classes.
>
> - Attribute values are initialized by the `__init__` method (a.k.a. dunder `init`). This method lets you assign starting values to your attributes when a new object is created. Dunder `init` receives a **copy** of any values passed to the class when an object is created. For example, the values `100` and `10` are passed into `__init__` when this object is created:
>
>   ```
>   mycount2 = CountFromBy(100, 10)
>   ```
>
> - Another magic method is `__repr__`, which allows you to control how an object appears when displayed at the >>> prompt, as well as when used with the `print` BIF.

> This is all fine and dandy...but remind me: what was the point of learning all this class stuff?

We wanted to create a context manager.

We know it's been a while, but the reason we started down this path was to learn enough about classes to enable us to create code that hooks into Python's **context management protocol**. If we can hook into the protocol, we can use our webapp's database code with Python's `with` statement, as doing so should make it easier to share the database code, as well as reuse it. Now that you know a bit about classes, you're ready to get hooked into the context management protocol (in the next chapter).

Chapter 8's Code

This is the code in the "countfromby. py" file.

```python
class CountFromBy:

    def __init__(self, v: int=0, i: int=1) -> None:
        self.val = v
        self.incr = i

    def increase(self) -> None:
        self.val += self.incr

    def __repr__(self) -> str:
        return str(self.val)
```

9 the context management protocol

Hooking into Python's with Statement

Yes, indeed...for a small fee, we can certainly manage the context within which your code runs.

It's time to take what you've just learned and put it to work.

Chapter 7 discussed using a **relational database** with Python, while Chapter 8 provided an introduction to using **classes** in your Python code. In this chapter, both of these techniques are combined to produce a **context manager** that lets us extend the `with` statement to work with relational database systems. In this chapter, you'll hook into the `with` statement by creating a new class, which conforms to Python's **context management protocol**.

What's the Best Way to Share Our Webapp's Database Code?

During Chapter 7 you created database code in your `log_request` function that worked, but you had to pause to consider how best to share it. Recall the suggestions from the end of Chapter 7:

Let's quickly cut and paste that code, then change it. Done!

I vote we put that database-handling code into its own function, then call it as needed.

Isn't it clear it's time we considered using classes and objects as the correct way to handle this type of reuse?

At the time, we proposed that each of these suggestions was valid, but believed Python programmers would be unlikely to embrace any of these proposed solutions *on their own*. We decided that a better strategy was to hook into the context management protocol using the `with` statement, but in order to do that, you needed to learn a bit about classes. They were the subject of the last chapter. Now that you know how to create a class, it's time to return to the task at hand: creating a context manager to share your webapp's database code.

Consider What You're Trying to Do, Revisited

Below is our database management code from Chapter 7. This code is currently part of our Flask webapp. Recall how this code connected to our MySQL database, saved the details of the web request to the `log` table, committed any *unsaved* data, and then disconnected from the database:

```python
import mysql.connector

def log_request(req: 'flask_request', res: str) -> None:
    """Log details of the web request and the results."""

    dbconfig = { 'host': '127.0.0.1',
                 'user': 'vsearch',
                 'password': 'vsearchpasswd',
                 'database': 'vsearchlogDB', }

    conn = mysql.connector.connect(**dbconfig)
    cursor = conn.cursor()

    _SQL = """insert into log
              (phrase, letters, ip, browser_string, results)
              values
              (%s, %s, %s, %s, %s)"""
    cursor.execute(_SQL, (req.form['phrase'],
                          req.form['letters'],
                          req.remote_addr,
                          req.user_agent.browser,
                          res, ))

    conn.commit()
    cursor.close()
    conn.close()
```

This dictionary details the database connection characteristics.

This bit uses the credentials to connect to the database, then creates a cursor.

This is the code that does the actual work: it adds the request data to the "log" database table.

Finally, this code tears down the database connection.

How best to create a context manager?

Before getting to the point where you can transform the above code into something that can be used as part of a `with` statement, let's discuss how this is achieved by conforming to the context management protocol. Although there is support for creating simple context managers in the standard library (using the `contextlib` module), creating a class that conforms to the protocol is regarded as the correct approach when you're using `with` to control some external object, such as a database connection (as is the case here).

With that in mind, let's take a look at what's meant by "conforming to the context management protocol."

Managing Context with Methods

The context management protocol sounds intimidating and scary, but it's actually quite simple. It dictates that any class you create must define at least two magic methods: `__enter__` and `__exit__`. This is the protocol. When you adhere to the protocol, your class can hook into the `with` statement.

Dunder "enter" performs setup

When an object is used with a `with` statement, the interpreter invokes the object's `__enter__` method *before* the `with` statement's suite starts. This provides an opportunity for you to perform any required setup code within dunder `enter`.

The protocol further states that dunder `enter` can (but doesn't have to) return a value to the `with` statement (you'll see why this is important in a little bit).

Dunder "exit" does teardown

As soon as the `with` statement's suite ends, the interpreter *always* invokes the object's `__exit__` method. This occurs *after* the `with`'s suite terminates, and it provides an opportunity for you to perform any required teardown.

As the code in the `with` statement's suite may fail (and raise an exception), dunder `exit` has to be ready to handle this if it happens. We'll return to this issue when we create the code for our dunder `exit` method later in this chapter.

If you create a class that defines `__enter__` and `__exit__`, the class is automatically regarded as a context manager by the interpreter and can, as a consequence, hook into (and be used with) `with`. In other words, such a class *conforms* to the context management protocol, and *implements* a context manager.

(As you know) dunder "init" initializes

In addition to dunder `enter` and dunder `exit`, you can add other methods to your class as needed, including defining your own `__init__` method. As you know from the last chapter, defining dunder init lets you perform additional object initialization. Dunder init runs *before* __enter__ (that is, *before your context manager's setup code executes*).

It's not an absolute requirement to define `__init__` for your context manager (as `__enter__` and `__exit__` are all you really need), but it can sometimes be useful to do so, as it lets you separate any initialization activity from any setup activity. When we create a context manager for use with our database connections (later in this chapter), we define `__init__` to initialize our database connection credentials. Doing so isn't absolutely necessary, but we think it helps to keep things nice and tidy, and makes our context manager class code easier to read and understand.

> A protocol is an agreed procedure (or set of rules) that is to be adhered to.

> If your class defines dunder "enter" and dunder "exit", it's a context manager.

You've Already Seen a Context Manager in Action

You first encountered a `with` statement back in Chapter 6 when you used one to ensure a previously opened file was *automatically* closed once its associated `with` statement terminated. Recall how this code opened the `todos.txt` file, then read and displayed each line in the file one by one, before automatically closing the file (thanks to the fact that `open` is a context manager):

Your first-ever "with" statement (borrowed from Chapter 6).

```
with open('todos.txt') as tasks:
    for chore in tasks:
        print(chore, end='')
```

Let's take another look at this `with` statement, highlighting where dunder `enter`, dunder `exit`, and dunder `init` are invoked. We've numbered each of the annotations to help you understand the order the dunders execute in. Note that we don't see the initialization, setup, or teardown code here; we just know (and trust) that those methods run "behind the scenes" when needed:

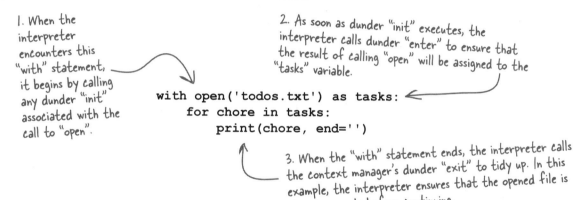

1. When the interpreter encounters this "with" statement, it begins by calling any dunder "init" associated with the call to "open".

2. As soon as dunder "init" executes, the interpreter calls dunder "enter" to ensure that the result of calling "open" will be assigned to the "tasks" variable.

```
with open('todos.txt') as tasks:
    for chore in tasks:
        print(chore, end='')
```

3. When the "with" statement ends, the interpreter calls the context manager's dunder "exit" to tidy up. In this example, the interpreter ensures that the opened file is closed properly before continuing.

What's required from you

Before we get to creating our very own context manager (with the help of a new class), let's review what the context management protocol expects you to provide in order to hook into the `with` statement. You must create a class that provides:

1. an `__init__` method to perform initialization (if needed);

2. an `__enter__` method to do any setup; and

3. an `__exit__` method to do any teardown (a.k.a. tidying-up).

Armed with this knowledge, let's now create a context manager class, writing these methods one by one, while borrowing from our existing database code as needed.

Create a New Context Manager Class

To get going, we need to give our new class a name. Additionally, let's put our new class code into its own file, so that we can easily reuse it (remember: when you put Python code in a separate file it becomes a module, which can be imported into other Python programs as required).

Let's call our new file DBcm.py (short for *database context manager*), and let's call our new class UseDatabase. Be sure to create the DBcm.py file in the same folder that currently contains your webapp code, as it's your webapp that's going to import the UseDatabase class (once you've written it, that is).

Using your favorite editor (or IDLE), create a new edit window, and then save the new, empty file as DBcm.py. We know that in order for our class to conform to the context management protocol it has to:

1. provide an __init__ method that performs initialization;

2. provide an __enter__ method that includes any setup code; and

3. provide an __exit__ method that includes any teardown code.

For now, let's add three "empty" definitions for each of these required methods to our class code. An empty method contains a single pass statement. Here's the code so far:

> **Remember: use CamelCase when naming a class in Python.**

This is what our "DBcm.py" file looks like in IDLE. At the moment, it's made up from a single "import" statement, together with a class called "UseDatabase" that contains three "empty" methods.

```
● ● ●   DBcm.py - /Users/paul/Desktop/_NewBook/ch09/webapp/DBcm.py (3.5.1)
import mysql.connector


class UseDatabase:

    def __init__(self):
        pass

    def __enter__(self):
        pass

    def __exit__(self):
        pass

                                                    Ln: 14  Col: 0
```

Note how at the top of the DBCm.py file we've included an import statement, which includes the *MySQL Connector* functionality (which our new class depends on).

All we have to do now is move the relevant bits from the log_request function into the correct method within the UseDatabase class. Well...when we say *we*, we actually mean **you**. It's time to roll up your sleeves and write some method code.

Initialize the Class with the Database Config

Let's remind ourselves of how we intend to use the `UseDatabase` context manager.
Here's the code from the last chapter, rewritten to use a `with` statement, which itself
uses the `UseDatabase` context manager that you're about to write:

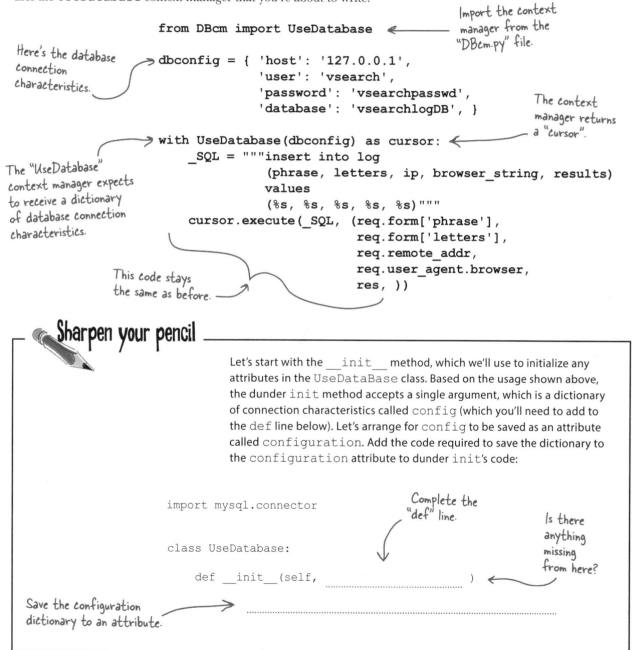

```
from DBcm import UseDatabase
```
Import the context manager from the "DBcm.py" file.

Here's the database connection characteristics.
```
dbconfig = { 'host': '127.0.0.1',
             'user': 'vsearch',
             'password': 'vsearchpasswd',
             'database': 'vsearchlogDB', }
```

The "UseDatabase" context manager expects to receive a dictionary of database connection characteristics.

The context manager returns a "cursor".

```
with UseDatabase(dbconfig) as cursor:
    _SQL = """insert into log
              (phrase, letters, ip, browser_string, results)
              values
              (%s, %s, %s, %s, %s)"""
    cursor.execute(_SQL, (req.form['phrase'],
                          req.form['letters'],
                          req.remote_addr,
                          req.user_agent.browser,
                          res, ))
```

This code stays the same as before.

Sharpen your pencil

Let's start with the `__init__` method, which we'll use to initialize any
attributes in the `UseDataBase` class. Based on the usage shown above,
the dunder `init` method accepts a single argument, which is a dictionary
of connection characteristics called `config` (which you'll need to add to
the `def` line below). Let's arrange for `config` to be saved as an attribute
called `configuration`. Add the code required to save the dictionary to
the `configuration` attribute to dunder `init`'s code:

```
import mysql.connector


class UseDatabase:

    def __init__(self, ............................... )
```

Complete the "def" line.

Is there anything missing from here?

Save the configuration dictionary to an attribute. ....

Sharpen your pencil
Solution

You started with the __init__ method, which was to initialize any attributes in the UseDataBase class. The dunder init method accepts a single argument, which is a dictionary of connection characteristics called config (which you needed to add to the def line below). You were to arrange for config to be saved to an attribute called configuration. You were to add the code required to save the dictionary to the configuration attribute in dunder init's code:

```
import mysql.connector

class UseDatabase:

    def __init__(self,    config: dict    ) -> None :
        self.configuration = config
```

Dunder "init" accepts a single dictionary, which we're calling "config".

The value of the "config" argument is assigned to an attribute called "configuration". Did you remember to prefix the attribute with "self"?

The (optional) "None" annotation confirms that this method has no return value (which is nice to know), and the colon terminates the "def" line.

Your context manager begins to take shape

With the dunder init method written, you can move on to coding the dunder enter method (__enter__). Before you do, make sure the code you've written so far matches ours, which is shown below in IDLE:

Make sure your dunder "init" matches ours.

```
● ● ●   DBcm.py - /Users/paul/Desktop/_NewBook/ch09/webapp/DBcm.py (3.5.1)
import mysql.connector


class UseDatabase:

    def __init__(self, config: dict) -> None:
        self.configuration = config

    def __enter__(self):
        pass

    def __exit__(self):
        pass
                                                    Ln: 14  Col: 0
```

Perform Setup with Dunder "enter"

The dunder enter method provides a place for you to execute the setup code that
needs to be executed *before* the suite in your with statement runs. Recall the code from
the log_request function that handles this setup:

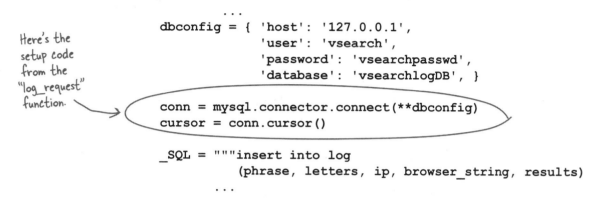

Here's the setup code from the "log_request" function.

```
        ...
dbconfig = { 'host': '127.0.0.1',
             'user': 'vsearch',
             'password': 'vsearchpasswd',
             'database': 'vsearchlogDB', }

conn = mysql.connector.connect(**dbconfig)
cursor = conn.cursor()

_SQL = """insert into log
            (phrase, letters, ip, browser_string, results)
        ...
```

This setup code uses the connection characteristics dictionary to connect to MySQL,
then creates a database cursor on the connection (which we'll need to send commands
to the database from our Python code). As this setup code is something you'll do every
time you write code to talk to your database, let's do this work in your context manager
class instead so that you can more easily reuse it.

Sharpen your pencil

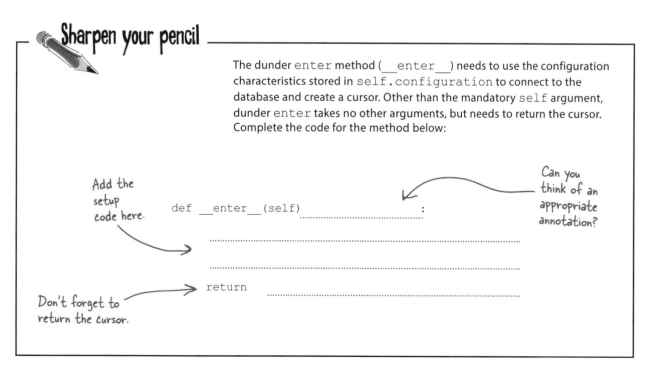

The dunder enter method (__enter__) needs to use the configuration
characteristics stored in self.configuration to connect to the
database and create a cursor. Other than the mandatory self argument,
dunder enter takes no other arguments, but needs to return the cursor.
Complete the code for the method below:

Can you think of an appropriate annotation?

Add the setup code here.

```
def __enter__(self)                              :

    ........................................................................

    ........................................................................

    return ...........................................................
```

Don't forget to return the cursor.

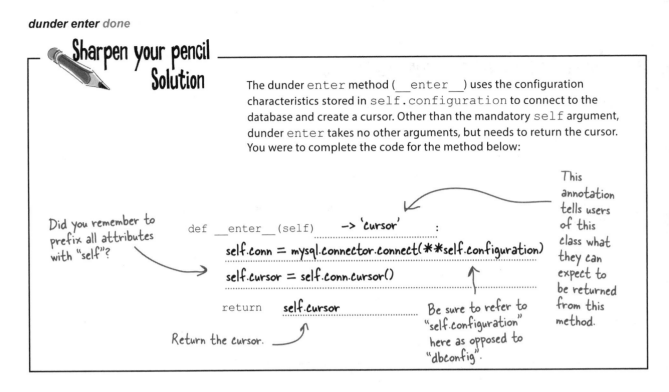

Sharpen your pencil Solution

The dunder enter method (__enter__) uses the configuration characteristics stored in self.configuration to connect to the database and create a cursor. Other than the mandatory self argument, dunder enter takes no other arguments, but needs to return the cursor. You were to complete the code for the method below:

This annotation tells users of this class what they can expect to be returned from this method.

Did you remember to prefix all attributes with "self"?

```
def __enter__(self) -> 'cursor':
    self.conn = mysql.connector.connect(**self.configuration)
    self.cursor = self.conn.cursor()
    return self.cursor
```

Return the cursor.

Be sure to refer to "self.configuration" here as opposed to "dbconfig".

Don't forget to prefix all attributes with "self"

You may be surprised that we designated conn and cursor as attributes in dunder enter (by prefixing each with self). We did this in order to ensure both conn and cursor survive when the method ends, as both variables are needed in the __exit__ method. To ensure this happens, we added the self prefix to both the conn and cursor variables; doing so adds them to the class's attribute list.

Before you get to writing dunder exit, confirm that your code matches ours:

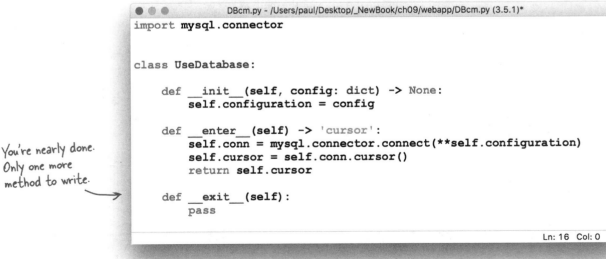

You're nearly done. Only one more method to write.

```
DBcm.py - /Users/paul/Desktop/_NewBook/ch09/webapp/DBcm.py (3.5.1)*
import mysql.connector


class UseDatabase:

    def __init__(self, config: dict) -> None:
        self.configuration = config

    def __enter__(self) -> 'cursor':
        self.conn = mysql.connector.connect(**self.configuration)
        self.cursor = self.conn.cursor()
        return self.cursor

    def __exit__(self):
        pass
```
Ln: 16 Col: 0

Perform Teardown with Dunder "exit"

The dunder `exit` method provides a place for you to execute the teardown code that needs to be run when your `with` statement terminates. Recall the code from the `log_request` function that handles teardown:

```
          . . .
cursor.execute(_SQL, (req.form['phrase'],
                      req.form['letters'],
                      req.remote_addr,
                      req.user_agent.browser,
                      res, ))
conn.commit()
cursor.close()
conn.close()
```

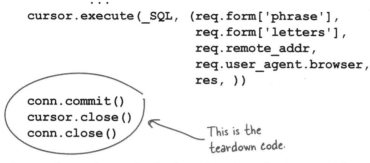 This is the
teardown code.

The teardown code commits any data to the database, then closes the cursor and the connection. This teardown happens *every* time you interact with the database, so let's add this code to your context manager class by moving these three lines into dunder `exit`.

Before you do this, however, you need to know that there's a complication with dunder `exit`, which has to do with handling any exceptions that might occur within the `with`'s suite. When something goes wrong, the interpreter *always* notifies `__exit__` by passing three arguments into the method: `exec_type`, `exc_value`, and `exc_trace`. Your `def` line needs to take this into account, which is why we've added the three arguments to the code below. Having said that, we're going to *ignore* this exception-handling mechanism for now, but will return to it in a later chapter when we discuss what can go wrong and how you can handle it (so stay tuned).

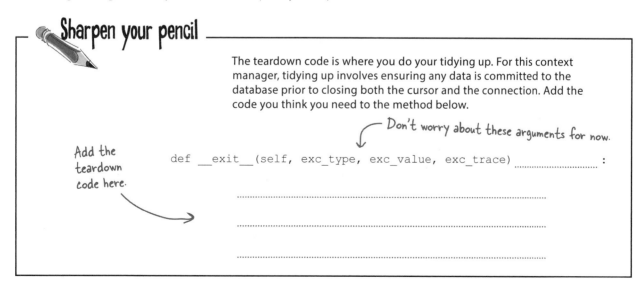

Sharpen your pencil

The teardown code is where you do your tidying up. For this context manager, tidying up involves ensuring any data is committed to the database prior to closing both the cursor and the connection. Add the code you think you need to the method below.

Don't worry about these arguments for now.

Add the teardown code here.

```
def __exit__(self, exc_type, exc_value, exc_trace) ................ :
         .......................................................................
         .......................................................................
         .......................................................................
```

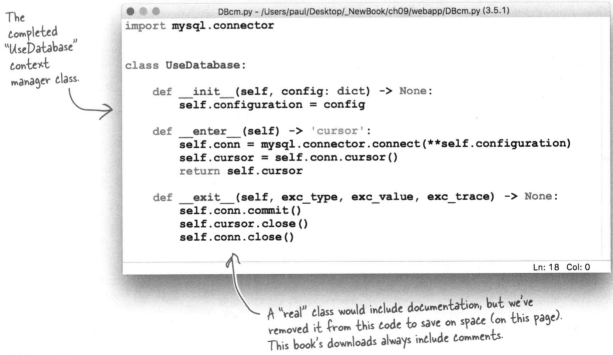

Sharpen your pencil
Solution

The teardown code is where you do your tidying up. For this context manager, tidying up involves ensuring any data is committed to the database prior to closing both the cursor and the connection. You were to add the code you think you need to the method below.

Don't worry about these arguments for now.

```
def __exit__(self, exc_type, exc_value, exc_trace) -> None :
```

This annotation confirms that this method has no return value; such annotations are optional but are good practice..

```
    self.conn.commit()
    self.cursor.close()
    self.conn.close()
```

The previously saved attributes are used to commit unsaved data, as well as close the cursor and connection. As always, remember to prefix your attribute names with "self".

Your context manager is ready for testing

With the dunder `exit` code written, it's now time to test your context manager prior to integrating it into your webapp code. As has been our custom, we'll first test this new code at Python's shell prompt (the >>>). Before doing this, perform one last check to ensure your code is the same as ours:

The completed "UseDatabase" context manager class.

```
DBcm.py - /Users/paul/Desktop/_NewBook/ch09/webapp/DBcm.py (3.5.1)
import mysql.connector


class UseDatabase:

    def __init__(self, config: dict) -> None:
        self.configuration = config

    def __enter__(self) -> 'cursor':
        self.conn = mysql.connector.connect(**self.configuration)
        self.cursor = self.conn.cursor()
        return self.cursor

    def __exit__(self, exc_type, exc_value, exc_trace) -> None:
        self.conn.commit()
        self.cursor.close()
        self.conn.close()
```

`Ln: 18  Col: 0`

A "real" class would include documentation, but we've removed it from this code to save on space (on this page). This book's downloads always include comments.

Test Drive

Import the context manager class from the "DBcm.py" module file.

With the code for `DBcm.py` in an IDLE edit window, press F5 to test your context manager:

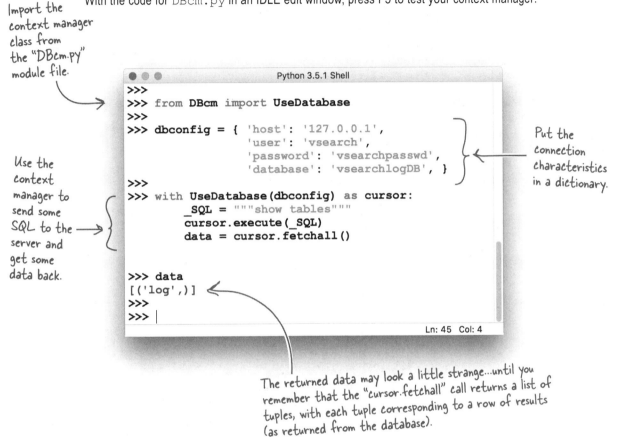

Use the context manager to send some SQL to the server and get some data back.

Put the connection characteristics in a dictionary.

The returned data may look a little strange...until you remember that the "cursor.fetchall" call returns a list of tuples, with each tuple corresponding to a row of results (as returned from the database).

There's not much code here, is there?

Hopefully, you're looking at the code above and deciding there's not an awful lot to it. As you've successfully moved some of your database handling code into the `UseDatabase` class, the initialization, setup, and teardown are now handled "behind the scenes" by your context manager. All you have to do is provide the connection characteristics and the SQL query you wish to execute—the context manager does all the rest. Your setup and teardown code is reused as part of the context manager. It's also clearer what the "meat" of this code is: getting data from the database and processing it. The context manager hides the details of connecting/disconnecting to/ from the database (which are always going to be the same), thereby leaving you free to concentrate on what you're trying to do with your data.

Let's update your webapp to use your context manager.

Reconsidering Your Webapp Code, 1 of 2

It's been quite a while since you've considered your webapp's code.

The last time you worked on it (in Chapter 7), you updated the `log_request` function to save the webapp's web request to the MySQL database. The reason we started down the path to learning about classes (in Chapter 8) was to determine the best way to share the database code you added to `log_request`. We now know that the best way (for this situation) is to use the just-written `UseDatabase` context manager class.

In addition to amending `log_request` to use the context manager, the other function in the code that we need to amend work with the data in the database is called `view_the_log` (which currently works with the `vsearch.log` text file). Before we get to amending both of these functions, let's remind ourselves of the current state of the webapp's code (on this page and the next). We've highlighted the bits that need to be worked on:

> Your webapp's code is in the "vsearch4web.py" file in your "webapp" folder.

```python
from flask import Flask, render_template, request, escape
from vsearch import search4letters

import mysql.connector          ← We need to
                                   import "DBcm"
app = Flask(__name__)              here instead.


def log_request(req: 'flask_request', res: str) -> None:
    """Log details of the web request and the results."""
    dbconfig = {'host': '127.0.0.1',
                'user': 'vsearch',
                'password': 'vsearchpasswd',
                'database': 'vsearchlogDB', }

    conn = mysql.connector.connect(**dbconfig)
    cursor = conn.cursor()
    _SQL = """insert into log
            (phrase, letters, ip, browser_string, results)
            values
            (%s, %s, %s, %s, %s)"""
    cursor.execute(_SQL, (req.form['phrase'],
                          req.form['letters'],
                          req.remote_addr,
                          req.user_agent.browser,
                          res, ))
    conn.commit()
    cursor.close()
    conn.close()
```

This code has to be amended to use the "UseDatabase" context manager.

Reconsidering Your Webapp Code, 2 of 2

```python
@app.route('/search4', methods=['POST'])
def do_search() -> 'html':
    """Extract the posted data; perform the search; return results."""
    phrase = request.form['phrase']
    letters = request.form['letters']
    title = 'Here are your results:'
    results = str(search4letters(phrase, letters))
    log_request(request, results)
    return render_template('results.html',
                           the_title=title,
                           the_phrase=phrase,
                           the_letters=letters,
                           the_results=results,)


@app.route('/')
@app.route('/entry')
def entry_page() -> 'html':
    """Display this webapp's HTML form."""
    return render_template('entry.html',
                           the_title='Welcome to search4letters on the web!')


@app.route('/viewlog')
def view_the_log() -> 'html':
    """Display the contents of the log file as a HTML table."""
    contents = []
    with open('vsearch.log') as log:
        for line in log:
            contents.append([])
            for item in line.split('|'):
                contents[-1].append(escape(item))
    titles = ('Form Data', 'Remote_addr', 'User_agent', 'Results')
    return render_template('viewlog.html',
                           the_title='View Log',
                           the_row_titles=titles,
                           the_data=contents,)


if __name__ == '__main__':
    app.run(debug=True)
```

This code needs to be amended to use the data in the database via the "UseDatabase" context manager.

Recalling the "log_request" Function

When it comes to amending the `log_request` function to use the `UseDatabase` context manager, a lot of the work has already been done for you (as we showed you the code we were shooting for earlier).

Take a look at `log_request` once more. At the moment, the database connection characteristics dictionary (`dbconfig` in the code) is defined within `log_request`. As you'll want to use this dictionary in the other function you have to amend (`view_the_log`), let's move it out of the `log_request`'s function so that you can share it with other functions as needed:

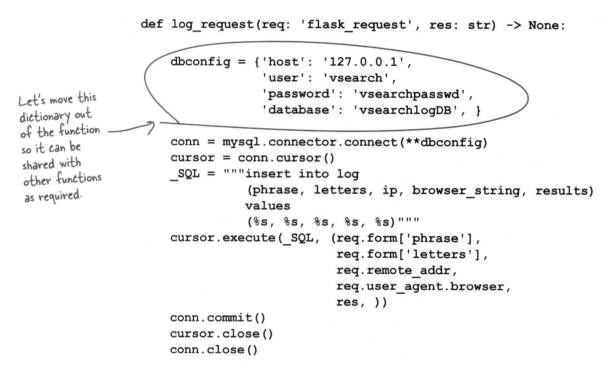

```
def log_request(req: 'flask_request', res: str) -> None:

    dbconfig = {'host': '127.0.0.1',
                'user': 'vsearch',
                'password': 'vsearchpasswd',
                'database': 'vsearchlogDB', }

    conn = mysql.connector.connect(**dbconfig)
    cursor = conn.cursor()
    _SQL = """insert into log
                (phrase, letters, ip, browser_string, results)
                values
                (%s, %s, %s, %s, %s)"""
    cursor.execute(_SQL, (req.form['phrase'],
                          req.form['letters'],
                          req.remote_addr,
                          req.user_agent.browser,
                          res, ))
    conn.commit()
    cursor.close()
    conn.close()
```

Let's move this dictionary out of the function so it can be shared with other functions as required.

Rather than move `dbconfig` into our webapp's global space, it would be useful if we could somehow add it to our webapp's internal configuration.

As luck would have it, Flask (like many other web frameworks) comes with a built-in configuration mechanism: a dictionary (which Flask calls `app.config`) allows you to adjust some of your webapp's internal settings. As `app.config` is a regular Python dictionary, you can add your own keys and values to it as needed, which is what you'll do for the data in `dbconfig`.

The rest of `log_request`'s code can then be amended to use `UseDatabase`.

Let's make these changes now.

Amending the "log_request" Function

Now that we've applied the changes to our webapp, our code looks like this:

We changed the old "import" statement to this updated one.

We added the connection characteristics dictionary to the webapp's configuration.

We adjusted the code to use "UseDatabase", being sure to pass in the database configuration from "app.config".

```
vsearch4web.py - /Users/paul/Desktop/_NewBook/ch09/webapp/vsearch4web.py (3.5.1)
from flask import Flask, render_template, request, escape
from vsearch import search4letters

from DBcm import UseDatabase

app = Flask(__name__)

app.config['dbconfig'] = {'host': '127.0.0.1',
                          'user': 'vsearch',
                          'password': 'vsearchpasswd',
                          'database': 'vsearchlogDB', }


def log_request(req: 'flask_request', res: str) -> None:
    """Log details of the web request and the results."""

    with UseDatabase(app.config['dbconfig']) as cursor:
        _SQL = """insert into log
                      (phrase, letters, ip, browser_string, results)
                      values
                      (%s, %s, %s, %s, %s)"""
        cursor.execute(_SQL, (req.form['phrase'],
                              req.form['letters'],
                              req.remote_addr,
                              req.user_agent.browser,
                              res, ))
```
Ln: 10 Col: 0

Near the top of the file, we've replaced the `import mysql.connector` statement with an `import` statement that grabs `UseDatabase` from our `DBcm` module. The `DBcm.py` file itself includes the `import mysql.connector` statement in its code, hence the removal of `import mysql.connector` from this file (as we don't want to import it twice).

We've also moved the database connection characteristics dictionary into our webapp's configuration. And we've amended `log_request`'s code to use our context manager.

After all your work on classes and context managers, you should be able to read and understand the code shown above.

Let's now move onto amending the `view_the_log` function. Make sure your webapp code is amended to be exactly like ours above before turning the page.

Recalling the "view_the_log" Function

Let's take a long, hard look at the code in view_the_log, as it's been quite a while
since you've considered it in detail. To recap, the current version of this function
extracts the logged data from the vsearch.log text file, turns it into a list of lists
(called contents), and then sends the data to a template called viewlog.html:

Grab each line of
data from the file,
and then transform
it into a list of
escaped items, which
are appended to the
"contents" list.

```python
@app.route('/viewlog')
def view_the_log() -> 'html':

    contents = []
    with open('vsearch.log') as log:
        for line in log:
            contents.append([])
            for item in line.split('|'):
                contents[-1].append(escape(item))

    titles = ('Form Data', 'Remote_addr', 'User_agent', 'Results')
    return render_template('viewlog.html',
                           the_title='View Log',
                           the_row_titles=titles,
                           the_data=contents,)
```

The processed log
data is sent to the
template for display.

Here's what the output looks like when the viewlog.html template is rendered with
the data from the contents list of lists. This functionality is currently available to
your webapp via the */viewlog* URL:

The data from
"contents" is displayed
in the form. Note
how the form
data ("phrase" and
"letters") is presented
in a single column.

Form Data	Remote_addr	User_agent	Results
ImmutableMultiDict([('letters', 'aeiou'), ('phrase', 'hitch-hiker')])	127.0.0.1	Mozilla/5.0 (Macintosh; Intel Mac OS X 10_11_2) AppleWebKit/601.3.9 (KHTML, like Gecko) Version/9.0.2 Safari/601.3.9	{'e', 'i'}
ImmutableMultiDict([('letters', 'aeiou'), ('phrase', 'life, the	127.0.0.1	Mozilla/5.0 (Macintosh; Intel Mac OS X 10_11_2) AppleWeb	{'e', 'u',

View Log (displayed at 127.0.0.1:5000/viewlog)

It's Not Just the Code That Changes

Before diving in and changing the code in `view_the_log` to use your context manager, let's pause to consider the data as stored in the `log` table in your database. When you tested your initial `log_request` code in Chapter 7, you were able to log into the MySQL console, then check that the data was saved. Recall this MySQL console session from earlier:

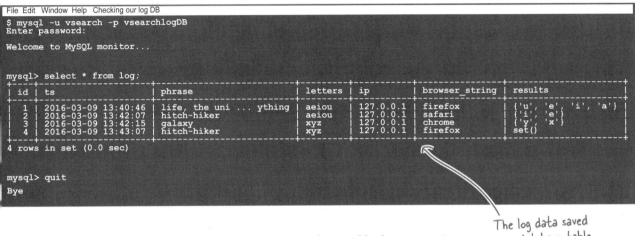

The log data saved in a database table

If you consider the above data in relation to what's currently stored in the `vsearch.log` file, it's clear that some of the processing `view_the_log` does is no longer needed, as the data is now stored in a table. Here's a snippet of what the log data looks like in the `vsearch.log` file:

```
ImmutableMultiDict([('phrase', 'galaxy'), ('letters', 'xyz')])|127.0.0.1|Mozilla/5.0 (Macintosh; Intel
Mac OS X 10_11_2) AppleWebKit/537.36 (KHTML, like Gecko) Chrome/47.0.2526.106 Safari/537.36|{'x', 'y'}
```

Some of the code currently in `view_the_log` is only there because the log data is currently stored as a collection of long strings (delimited by vertical bars) in the `vsearch.log` file. That format worked, but we did need to write extra code to make sense of it.

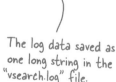

The log data saved as one long string in the "vsearch.log" file.

This is not the case with data in the `log` table, as it is "structured by default." This should mean you don't need to perform any additional processing within `view_the_log`: all you have to do is extract the data from the table, which—happily—is returned to you as a list of tuples (thanks to DB-API's `fetchall` method).

On top of this, the data in the `log` table separates the value for `phrase` from the value for `letters`. If you make a small change to your template-rendering code, the output produced can display five columns of data (as opposed to the current four), making what the browser displays even more useful and easier to read.

Amending the "view_the_log" Function

Based on everything discussed on the last few pages, you've two things to do to amend your current `view_the_log` code:

1.   Grab the log data from the database table (as opposed to the file).

2.   Adjust the `titles` list to support five columns (as opposed to four).

If you're scratching your head and wondering why this small list of amendments doesn't include adjusting the `viewlog.html` template, wonder no more: you don't need to make any changes to *that* file, as the current template quite happily processes any number of titles and any amount of data you send to it.

Here's the `view_the_log` function's current code, which you are about to amend:

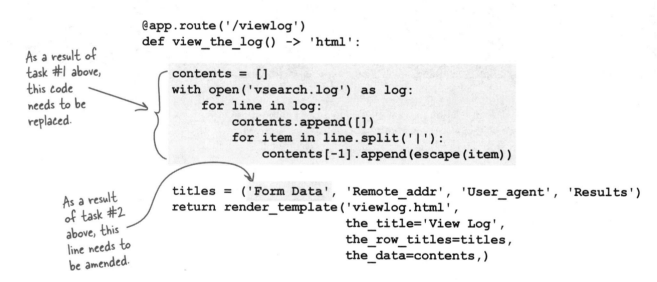

As a result of task #1 above, this code needs to be replaced.

As a result of task #2 above, this line needs to be amended.

```
@app.route('/viewlog')
def view_the_log() -> 'html':

    contents = []
    with open('vsearch.log') as log:
        for line in log:
            contents.append([])
            for item in line.split('|'):
                contents[-1].append(escape(item))
    titles = ('Form Data', 'Remote_addr', 'User_agent', 'Results')
    return render_template('viewlog.html',
                            the_title='View Log',
                            the_row_titles=titles,
                            the_data=contents,)
```

Here's the SQL query you'll need

Ahead of the next exercise (where you'll update the `view_the_log` function), here's an SQL query that, when executed, returns all the logged data stored in the webapp's MySQL database. The data is returned to your Python code from the database as a list of tuples. You'll need to use this query in the exercise on the next page:

```
select phrase, letters, ip, browser_string, results
from log
```

Sharpen your pencil

Here's the `view_the_log` function, which has to be amended to use the data in the `log` table. Your job is to provide the missing code. Be sure to read the annotations for hints on what you need to do:

```
@app.route('/viewlog')
def view_the_log() -> 'html':

    with ........................................................................... :

        _SQL = """select phrase, letters, ip, browser_string, results
                    from log"""

        ...................................................................
        ...................................................................

        titles = ( .................. , .................. , 'Remote_addr', 'User_agent', 'Results')

        return render_template('viewlog.html',
                                    the_title='View Log',
                                    the_row_titles=titles,
                                    the_data=contents,)
```

Use your context manager here, and don't forget the cursor.

Send the query to the server, then fetch the results.

Which column titles are missing from here?

I'm just going to make a note of what's going on here. Not only is my new code shorter than what I had before, it's easier for me to understand and read, too.

Yep—that was our goal all along.

By moving the log data into a MySQL database, you've removed the requirement to create, and then process, a custom text-based file format.

Also, by reusing your context manager, you've simplified your interactions with MySQL when working in Python. What's not to like?

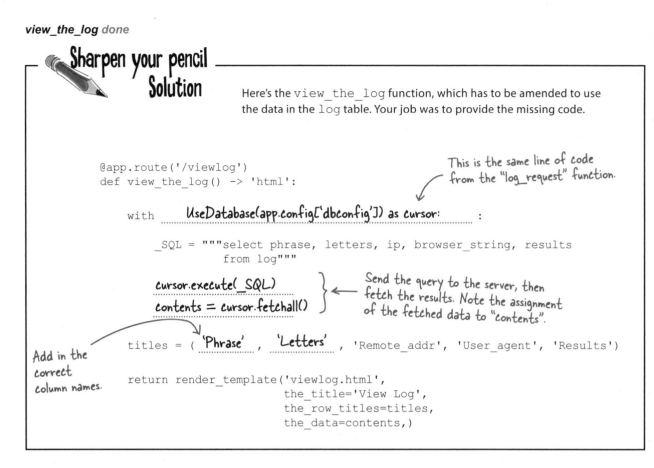

Sharpen your pencil
Solution

Here's the `view_the_log` function, which has to be amended to use the data in the `log` table. Your job was to provide the missing code.

```
@app.route('/viewlog')
def view_the_log() -> 'html':
```

with ___UseDatabase(app.config['dbconfig']) as cursor:___ :

This is the same line of code from the "log_request" function.

```
    _SQL = """select phrase, letters, ip, browser_string, results
              from log"""
```

___cursor.execute(_SQL)___

___contents = cursor.fetchall()___

Send the query to the server, then fetch the results. Note the assignment of the fetched data to "contents".

```
    titles = ( 'Phrase' , 'Letters' , 'Remote_addr', 'User_agent', 'Results')
```

Add in the correct column names.

```
    return render_template('viewlog.html',
                            the_title='View Log',
                            the_row_titles=titles,
                            the_data=contents,)
```

It's nearly time for one last Test Drive

Before taking this new version of your webapp for a spin, take a moment to confirm that your view_the_log function is the same as ours:

```
                    vsearch4web.py - /Users/paul/Desktop/_NewBook/ch09/webapp/vsearch4web.py (3.5.1)
@app.route('/viewlog')
def view_the_log() -> 'html':
    """Display the contents of the log file as a HTML table."""
    with UseDatabase(app.config['dbconfig']) as cursor:
        _SQL = """select phrase, letters, ip, browser_string, results
                  from log"""
        cursor.execute(_SQL)
        contents = cursor.fetchall()
    titles = ('Phrase', 'Letters', 'Remote_addr', 'User_agent', 'Results')
    return render_template('viewlog.html',
                            the_title='View Log',
                            the_row_titles=titles,
                            the_data=contents,)
                                                                        Ln: 1  Col: 0
```

Test Drive

It's time to take your database-ready webapp for a spin.

Be sure the DBcm.py file is in the same folder as your vsearch4web.py file, then start your webapp in the usual way on your operating system:

- Use python3 vsearch4web.py on *Linux/Mac OS X*
- Use py -3 vsearch4web.py on *Windows*.

Use your browser to go to your webapp's home page (running at *http://127.0.0.1:5000*), then enter a handful of searches. Once you've confirmed that the search feature is working, use the */viewlog* URL to view the contents of your log in your browser window.

Although the searches you enter will very likely differ from ours, here's what we saw in our browser window, which confirms that everything is working as expected:

⬤ ⬤ ⬤ ⟨ ⟩ ▢   🌐 127.0.0.1:5000/viewlog   ↻   ⬆ ⬜ +

View Log

Phrase	Letters	Remote_addr	User_agent	Results
life, the universe, and everything	aeiou	127.0.0.1	firefox	{'u', 'e', 'i', 'a'}
hitch-hiker	aeiou	127.0.0.1	safari	{'i', 'e'}
galaxy	xyz	127.0.0.1	chrome	{'y', 'x'}
hitch-hiker	xyz	127.0.0.1	firefox	set()
lightning in a bottle	aeiou	127.0.0.1	firefox	{'i', 'a', 'o', 'e'}
testing the database-enabled webapp	aeiou	127.0.0.1	firefox	{'e', 'a', 'i'}

This browser output confirms the logged data is being read from the MySQL database when the */viewlog* URL is accessed. This means the code in view_the_log is working—which, incidentally, confirms the log_request function is working as expected, too, as it's putting the log data in the database as a result of every successful search.

Only if you feel the need, take a few moments to log into your MySQL database using the MySQL console to confirm that the data is safely stored in your database server. (Or just trust us: based on what our webapp is displaying above, it is.)

All That Remains...

It's now time to return to the questions first posed in Chapter 7:

- *How many requests have been responded to?*
- *What's the most common list of letters?*
- *Which IP addresses are the requests coming from?*
- *Which browser is being used the most?*

Although it *is* possible to write Python code to answer these questions, we aren't going to in this case, even though we've just spent this and the previous two chapters looking at how Python and databases work together. In our opinion, creating Python code to answer these types of questions is nearly always a bad move...

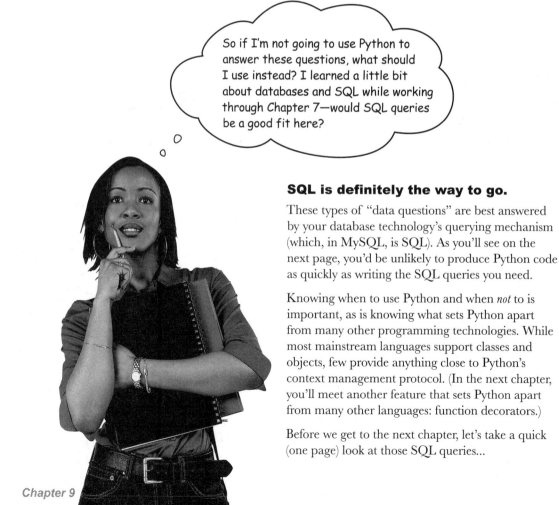

So if I'm not going to use Python to answer these questions, what should I use instead? I learned a little bit about databases and SQL while working through Chapter 7—would SQL queries be a good fit here?

SQL is definitely the way to go.

These types of "data questions" are best answered by your database technology's querying mechanism (which, in MySQL, is SQL). As you'll see on the next page, you'd be unlikely to produce Python code as quickly as writing the SQL queries you need.

Knowing when to use Python and when *not* to is important, as is knowing what sets Python apart from many other programming technologies. While most mainstream languages support classes and objects, few provide anything close to Python's context management protocol. (In the next chapter, you'll meet another feature that sets Python apart from many other languages: function decorators.)

Before we get to the next chapter, let's take a quick (one page) look at those SQL queries...

Answering the Data Questions

Let's take the questions first posed in Chapter 7 one by one, answering each with the help of some database queries written in SQL.

How many requests have been responded to?

If you're already a SQL dude (or dudette), you may be scoffing at this question, seeing as it doesn't really get much simpler. You already know that this most basic of SQL queries displays all the data in a database table:

```
select * from log;
```

To transform this query into one that reports how many rows of data a table has, pass the * into the SQL function count, as follows:

```
select count(*) from log;
```
⟵ *We're *not* showing you the answers here. If you want to see them, you'll have to run these queries yourself in the MySQL console (see Chapter 7 for a refresh).*

What's the most common list of letters?

The SQL query that answers this question looks a little scary, but isn't really. Here it is:

```
select count(letters) as 'count', letters
from log
group by letters
order by count desc
limit 1;
```

As suggested in Chapter 7, we always recommend this book when someone's first learning SQL (as well as updating previous knowledge that might be a bit rusty).

Which IP addresses are the requests coming from?

The SQL dudes/dudettes out there are probably thinking "that's almost too easy":

```
select distinct ip from log;
```

Which browser is being used the most?

The SQL query that answers this question is a slight variation on the query that answered the second question:

```
select browser_string, count(browser_string) as 'count'
from log
group by browser_string
order by count desc
limit 1;
```

So there you have it: all your pressing questions answered with a few simple SQL queries. Go ahead and try them at your mysql> prompt before starting in on the next chapter.

Chapter 9's Code, 1 of 2

This is the context manager code in "DBcm.py".

```python
import mysql.connector

class UseDatabase:

    def __init__(self, config: dict) -> None:
        self.configuration = config

    def __enter__(self) -> 'cursor':
        self.conn = mysql.connector.connect(**self.configuration)
        self.cursor = self.conn.cursor()
        return self.cursor

    def __exit__(self, exc_type, exc_value, exc_trace) -> None:
        self.conn.commit()
        self.cursor.close()
        self.conn.close()
```

This is the first half of the webapp code in "vsearch4web.py".

```python
from flask import Flask, render_template, request, escape
from vsearch import search4letters

from DBcm import UseDatabase

app = Flask(__name__)

app.config['dbconfig'] = {'host': '127.0.0.1',
                          'user': 'vsearch',
                          'password': 'vsearchpasswd',
                          'database': 'vsearchlogDB', }

def log_request(req: 'flask_request', res: str) -> None:
    with UseDatabase(app.config['dbconfig']) as cursor:
        _SQL = """insert into log
                    (phrase, letters, ip, browser_string, results)
                    values
                    (%s, %s, %s, %s, %s)"""
        cursor.execute(_SQL, (req.form['phrase'],
                              req.form['letters'],
                              req.remote_addr,
                              req.user_agent.browser,
                              res, ))
```

Chapter 9's Code, 2 of 2

This is the second half of the webapp code in "vsearch4web.py".

```python
@app.route('/search4', methods=['POST'])
def do_search() -> 'html':
    phrase = request.form['phrase']
    letters = request.form['letters']
    title = 'Here are your results:'
    results = str(search4letters(phrase, letters))
    log_request(request, results)
    return render_template('results.html',
                           the_title=title,
                           the_phrase=phrase,
                           the_letters=letters,
                           the_results=results,)


@app.route('/')
@app.route('/entry')
def entry_page() -> 'html':
    return render_template('entry.html',
                           the_title='Welcome to search4letters on the web!')


@app.route('/viewlog')
def view_the_log() -> 'html':
    with UseDatabase(app.config['dbconfig']) as cursor:
        _SQL = """select phrase, letters, ip, browser_string, results
                    from log"""
        cursor.execute(_SQL)
        contents = cursor.fetchall()
    titles = ('Phrase', 'Letters', 'Remote_addr', 'User_agent', 'Results')
    return render_template('viewlog.html',
                           the_title='View Log',
                           the_row_titles=titles,
                           the_data=contents,)


if __name__ == '__main__':
    app.run(debug=True)
```

10 function decorators

✳ *Wrapping Functions* ✳

As soon as I get done here, my plan is to decorate Dad's walls with my dirty fingers...

When it comes to augmenting your code, Chapter 9's context management protocol is not the only game in town.

Python also lets you use function **decorators**, a technique whereby you can add code to an existing function *without* having to change any of the existing function's code. If you think this sounds like some sort of black art, don't despair: it's nothing of the sort. However, as coding techniques go, creating a function decorator is often considered to be on the harder side by many Python programmers, and thus is not used as often as it should be. In this chapter, our plan is to show you that, despite being an advanced technique, creating and using your own decorators is not that hard.

Your Webapp Is Working Well, But...

You've shown the latest version of your webapp to a colleague, and they're impressed by what you've done. However, they pose an interesting question: *is it wise to let any web user view the log page?*

The point they're making is that anybody who is aware of the */viewlog* URL can use it to view the logged data whether they have your permission or not. In fact, at the moment, every one of your webapp's URLs are public, so any web user can access any of them.

Depending on what you're trying to do with your webapp, this may or may not be an issue. However, it is common for websites to require users to authenticate before certain content is made available to them. It's probably a good idea to be prudent when it comes to providing access to the */viewlog* URL. The question is: *how do you restrict access to certain pages in your webapp?*

Only authenticated users gain access

You typically need to provide an **ID** and **password** when you access a website that serves restricted content. If your ID/password combination match, access is granted, as you've been authenticated. Once you're authenticated, the system knows to let you access the restricted content. Maintaining this state (whether authenticated or not) seems like it might be as simple as setting a switch to `True` (access allowed; you are logged in) or `False` (access forbidden; you are *not* logged in).

> That sounds straightforward to me. A simple HTML form can ask for the user's credentials, and then a boolean on the server can be set to "True" or "False" as needed, right?

It's a bit more complicated than that.

There's a twist here (due to the way the Web works) which makes this idea a tad more complicated than it at first appears. Let's explore what this complication is first (and see how to deal with it) before solving our restricted access issue.

The Web Is Stateless

In its most basic form, a web server appears incredibly silly: each and every request that a web server processes is treated as an independent request, having nothing whatsoever to do with what came before, nor what comes after.

This means that sending three quick requests to a web server from your computer appears as three independent *individual* requests. This is in spite of the fact that the three requests originated from the same web browser running on the same computer, which is using the same unchanging IP address (which the web server sees as part of the request).

As stated at the top of the page: it's as if the web server is being silly. Even though we assume the three requests sent from our computer are related, the web server doesn't see things this way: *every web request is independent of what came before it, as well as what comes after.*

> When running as a web server, I pride myself in responding quickly...and forgetting fast. I'm stateless...

HTTP is to blame...

The reason web servers behave in this way is due to the protocol that underpins the Web, and which is used by both the web server and your web browser: HTTP (the HyperText Transfer Protocol).

HTTP dictates that web servers must work as described above, and the reason for this has to do with performance: if the amount of work a web server needs to do is minimized, it's possible to scale web servers to handle many, many requests. Higher performance is achieved at the expense of requiring the web server to maintain information on how a series of requests may be related. This information—known as **state** in HTTP (and not related to OOP in any way)—is of no interest to the web server, as every request is treated as an independent entity. In a way, the web server is optimized to respond quickly, but forget fast, and is said to operate in a **stateless** manner.

Which is all well and good until such time as your webapp needs to remember something.

> Isn't that what variables are for: remembering stuff in code? Surely this is a no-brainer?

If only the Web were that simple.

When your code is running as part of a web server, its behavior can differ from when you run it on your computer. Let's explore this issue in more detail.

Your Web Server (Not Your Computer) Runs Your Code

When Flask runs your webapp on your computer, it keeps your code in memory at all times. With this in mind, recall these two lines from the bottom of your webapp's code, which we initially discussed at the end of Chapter 5:

```
if __name__ == '__main__':
    app.run(debug=True)
```

> This line of code does NOT execute when this code is imported.

This `if` statement checks to see whether the interpreter is executing the code directly or whether the code is being imported (by the interpreter or by something like *PythonAnywhere*). When Flask executes on your computer, your webapp's code runs directly, resulting in this `app.run` line executing. However, when a web server is configured to execute your code your webapp's code is *imported*, and the `app.run` line does **not** run.

Why? Because the web server runs your webapp code *as it sees fit*. This can involve the web server importing your webapp's code, then calling its functions as needed, keeping your webapp's code in memory at all times. Or the web server may decide to load/unload your webapp code as needed, the assumption being that, during periods of inactivity, the web server will only load and run the code it needs. It's this second mode of operation—where the web server loads your code as and when it needs it—that can lead to problems with storing your webapp's state in variables. For instance, consider what would happen if you were to add this line of code to your webapp:

```
logged_in = False
if __name__ == '__main__':
    app.run(debug=True)
```

> The "logged_in" variable could be used to indicate whether a user of your webapp is logged in or not.

The idea here is that other parts of your webapp can refer to the variable `logged_in` in order to determine whether a user is authenticated. Additionally, your code can change this variable's value as needed (based on, say, a successful login). As the `logged_in` variable is *global* in nature, all of your webapp's code can access and set its value. This seems like a reasonable approach, but has *two* problems.

Firstly, your web server can unload your webapp's running code at any time (and without warning), so any values associated with global variables are likely **lost**, and are going to be reset to their starting value when your code is next imported. If a previously loaded function sets `logged_in` to `True`, your reimported code helpfully resets `logged_in` to `False`, and confusion reigns...

Secondly, as it stands, there's only a *single copy* of the global `logged_in` variable in your running code, which is fine if all you ever plan to have is a single user of your webapp (good luck with that). If you have two or more users each accessing and/or changing the value of `logged_in`, not only will confusion reign, but frustration will make a guest appearance, too. As a general rule of thumb, storing your webapp's state in a global variable is a bad idea.

Don't store your webapp's state in global variables.

It's Time for a Bit of a Session

As a result of what we learned on the last page, we need two things:

- A way to store variables without resorting to using globals
- A way to keep one webapp user's data from interferring with another's

Most webapp development frameworks (including Flask) provide for both of these requirements using a single technology: the **session**.

Think of a session as a layer of state spread on top of the stateless Web.

By adding a small piece of identification data to your browser (a *cookie*), and linking this to a small piece of identification data on the web server (the *session ID*), Flask uses its session technology to keep everything straight. Not only can you store state in your webapp that persists over time, but each user of your webapp gets their own copy of the state. Confusion and frustration are no more.

To demonstrate how Flask's session mechanism works, let's take a look at a very small webapp that is saved to a file called `quick_session.py`. Take a moment to read the code first, paying particular attention to the highlighted parts. We'll discuss what's going on after you've had a chance to read this code:

Ready Bake Code

Be sure to add "session" to your list of imports.

This is the "quick_session.py" code.

Your secret key should be hard to guess.

Manipulate the data in "session" as required.

```python
from flask import Flask, session

app = Flask(__name__)

app.secret_key = 'YouWillNeverGuess'

@app.route('/setuser/<user>')
def setuser(user: str) -> str:
    session['user'] = user
    return 'User value set to: ' + session['user']


@app.route('/getuser')
def getuser() -> str:
    return 'User value is currently set to: ' + session['user']


if __name__ == '__main__':
    app.run(debug=True)
```

Flask's Session Technology Adds State

In order to use Flask's session technology, you first have to import `session` from the `flask` module, which the `quick_session.py` webapp you just saw does on its very first line. Think of `session` as a global Python dictionary within which you store your webapp's state (albeit a dictionary with some added superpowers):

```
from flask import Flask, session
...
```

Start by importing "session".

Even though your webapp is still running on the stateless Web, this single import gives your webapp the ability to remember state.

Flask ensures that any data stored in `session` exists for the entire time your webapp runs (no matter how many times your web server loads and reloads your webapp code). Additionally, any data stored in `session` is keyed by a unique browser cookie, which ensures your session data is kept away from that of every other user of your webapp.

Find out more about Flask sessions here: http://flask.pocoo.org/docs/0.11/api/#sessions

Just how Flask does all of this is not important: the fact that it does *is*. To enable all this extra goodness, you need to seed Flask's cookie generation technology with a "secret key," which is used by Flask to encrypt your cookie, protecting it from any prying eyes. Here's how `quick_session.py` does this:

```
...
app = Flask(__name__)

app.secret_key = 'YouWillNeverGuess'
...
```

Create a new Flask webapp in the usual way.

Seed Flask's cookie-generation technology with a secret key. (Note: any string will do here. Although, like any other password you use, it should be hard to guess.)

Flask's documentation suggests picking a secret key that is hard to guess, but any stringed value works here. Flask uses the string to encrypt your cookie prior to transmitting it to your browser.

Once `session` is imported and the secret key set, you can use `session` in your code as you would any other Python dictionary. Within `quick_session.py`, the */setuser* URL (and its associated `setuser` function) assigns a user-supplied value to the `user` key in `session`, then returns the value to your browser:

The value of the "user" variable is assigned to the "user" key in the "session" dictionary.

```
...
@app.route('/setuser/<user>')
def setuser(user: str) -> str:
    session['user'] = user
    return 'User value set to: ' + session['user']
...
```

The URL expects to be provided with a value to assign to the "user" variable (you'll see how this works in a little bit).

Now that we've set some session data, let's look at the code that accesses it.

Dictionary Lookup Retrieves State

Now that a value is associated with the user key in session, it's not hard to access the data associated with user when you need it.

The second URL in the quick_session.py webapp, */getuser*, is associated with the getuser function. When invoked, this function accesses the value associated with the user key and returns it to the waiting web browser as part of the stringed message. The getuser function is shown below, together with this webapp's *dunder name equals dunder main* test (first discussed near the end of Chapter 5):

```
    . . .
@app.route('/getuser')
def getuser() -> str:
    return 'User value is currently set to: ' + session['user']


if __name__ == '__main__':
    app.run(debug=True)
```

As is the custom with all Flask apps, we control when "app.run" executes using this well-established Python idiom.

Accessing the data in "session" is not hard. It's a dictionary lookup.

Time for a Test Drive?

It's nearly time to take the quick_session.py webapp for a spin. However, before we do, let's think a bit about what it is we want to test.

For starters, we want to check that the webapp is storing and retrieving the session data provided to it. On top of that, we want to ensure that more than one user can interact with the webapp without stepping on any other user's toes: the session data from one user shouldn't impact the data of any other.

To perform these tests, we're going to simulate multiple users by running multiple browsers. Although the browsers are all running on one computer, as far as the web server is concerned, they are all independent, individual connections: the Web is stateless, after all. If we were to repeat these tests on three physically different computers on three different networks, the results would be the same, as all web servers see each request in isolation, no matter where the request originates. Recall that the session technology in Flask layers a stateful technology on top of the stateless Web.

To start this webapp, use this command within a terminal on *Linux* or *Mac OS X*:

```
$ python3 quick_session.py
```

or use this command at a command prompt on *Windows*:

```
C:\> py -3 quick_session.py
```

TEST DRIVE, 1 OF 2

With the `quick_session.py` webapp up and running, let's open a Chrome browser and use it to set a value for the `user` key in `session`. We do this by typing */setuser/Alice* into the location bar, which instructs the webapp to use the value `Alice` for `user`:

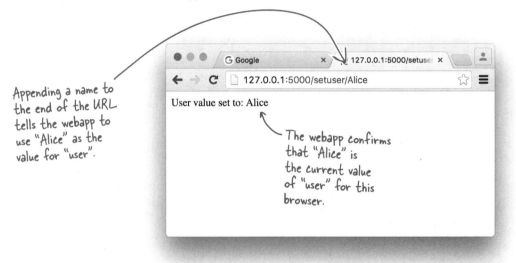

Appending a name to the end of the URL tells the webapp to use "Alice" as the value for "user".

The webapp confirms that "Alice" is the current value of "user" for this browser.

Next, let's open up the Opera browser and use it to set the value of `user` to `Bob` (if you don't have access to Opera, use whichever browser is handy, as long as it's not Chrome):

User value set to: Bob

Confirmation that "user" has been set to "Bob" by the webapp

As with Chrome, we append a name to the URL to set the value of "user". In this case, we append the name "Bob".

When we opened up Safari (or you can use Edge if you are on Windows), we used the webapp's other URL, */getuser*, to retrieve the current value of user from the webapp. However, when we did this, we're greeted with a rather intimidating error message:

The "/getuser" URL lets you check the current value of "user".

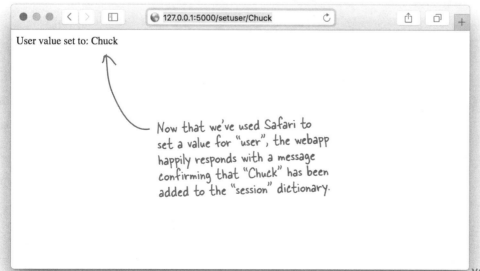

```
127.0.0.1:5000/getuser
```

builtins.KeyError

KeyError: 'user'

Traceback (most recent call last)

File "/Library/Frameworks/Python.framework/Versions/3.5/lib/python3.5/site-packages/flask/app.py", line *1836*, in __call__

   return self.wsgi_app(environ, start_response)

File "/Library/Frameworks/Python.framework/Versions/3.5/lib/python3.5/site-packages/flask/app.py", line *1820*, in wsgi_app

  response = self.make_response(self.handle_exception(e))

File "/Library/Frameworks/Python.framework/Versions/3.5/lib/python3.5/site-packages/flask/app.py", line *1403*, in handle_exception

Yikes! That's quite the error message, isn't it? The important bit is at the top: we have a "KeyError", as we haven't used Safari to set a value for "user" yet. (Remember: we set a "user" value using Chrome and Opera, not Safari.)

Let's use Safari to set the value of user to Chuck:

```
127.0.0.1:5000/setuser/Chuck
```

User value set to: Chuck

Now that we've used Safari to set a value for "user", the webapp happily responds with a message confirming that "Chuck" has been added to the "session" dictionary.

TEST DRIVE, 2 OF 2

Now that we've used the three browsers to set values for `user`, let's confirm that the webapp (thanks to our use of `session`) is stopping each browser's value of `user` from interfering with any other browser's data. Even though we've just used Safari to set the value of `user` to Chuck, let's see what its value is in Opera by using the */getuser* URL:

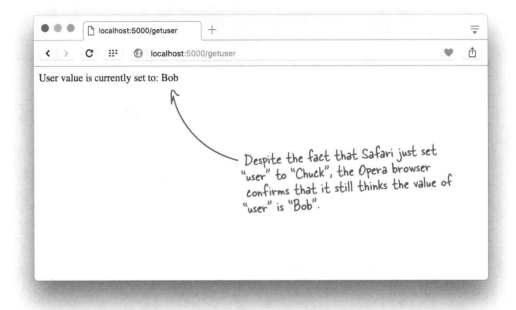

User value is currently set to: Bob

Despite the fact that Safari just set "user" to "Chuck", the Opera browser confirms that it still thinks the value of "user" is "Bob".

Having confirmed that Opera is showing `user`'s value as `Bob`, let's return to the Chrome browser window and issue the */getuser* URL there. As expected, Chrome confirms that, as far as it's concerned, the value of `user` is `Alice`:

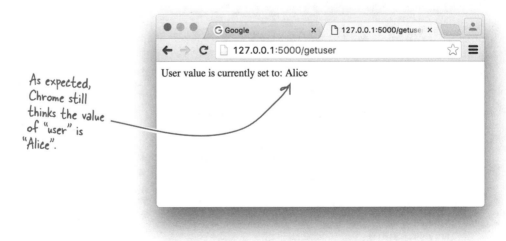

User value is currently set to: Alice

As expected, Chrome still thinks the value of "user" is "Alice".

We've just used Opera and Chrome to access the value of user using the */getuser* URL, which just leaves Safari. Here's what we see when we issue */getuser* in Safari, which doesn't produce an error message this time, as user has a value associated with it now (so, no more KeyError):

User value is currently set to: Chuck

Sure enough, Safari confirms that—as far as it's concerned—the value of "user" is still "Chuck".

So...each browser maintains its own copy of the "user" value, right?

No, not quite—it all happens in the webapp.

The use of the session dictionary in the webapp enables the behavior you're seeing here. By automatically setting a unique cookie within each browser, the webapp (thanks to session) maintains a browser-identifiable value of user for *each* browser.

From the webapp's perspective, it's as if there are multiple values of user in the session dictionary (keyed by cookie). From each browser's perspective, it's as if there is only ever one value of user (the one associated with their individual, unique cookie).

Managing Logins with Sessions

Based on our work with quick_session.py, we know we can store browser-specific state in session. No matter how many browsers interact with our webapp, each browser's server-side data (a.k.a. *state*) is managed for us by Flask whenever session is used.

Let's use this new know-how to return to the problem of controlling web access to specific pages within the vsearch4web.py webapp. Recall that we want to get to the point where we can restrict who has access to the */viewlog* URL.

Rather than experimenting on our working vsearch4web.py code, let's put that code to one side for now and work with some other code, which we'll experiment with in order to work out what we need to do. We'll return to the vsearch4web.py code once we've worked out the best way to approach this. We can then confidently amend the vsearch4web.py code to restrict access to */viewlog*.

Here's the code to yet another Flask-based webapp. As before, take some time to read this code prior to our discussion of it. This is simple_webapp.py:

 Ready Bake Code

```python
from flask import Flask

app = Flask(__name__)

@app.route('/')
def hello() -> str:
    return 'Hello from the simple webapp.'

@app.route('/page1')
def page1() -> str:
    return 'This is page 1.'

@app.route('/page2')
def page2() -> str:
    return 'This is page 2.'

@app.route('/page3')
def page3() -> str:
    return 'This is page 3.'

if __name__ == '__main__':
    app.run(debug=True)
```

This is "simple_webapp.py". At this stage in this book, you should have no difficulty reading this code and understanding what this webapp does.

Let's Do Login

The `simple_webapp.py` code is straightforward: all of the URLs are public in that they can be accessed by anyone using a browser.

In addition to the default / URL (which results in the `hello` function executing), there are three other URLs, */page1*, */page2*, and */page3* (which invoke similarly named functions when accessed). All of the webapp's URLs return a specific message to the browser.

As webapps go, this one is really just a shell, but will do for our purposes. We'd like to get to the point where */page1*, */page2*, and */page3* are only visible to logged-in users, but restricted to everyone else. We're going to use Flask's `session` technology to enable this functionality.

Let's begin by providing a really simple */login* URL. For now, we're not going to worry about providing an HTML form that asks for a login ID and password. All we're going to do here is create some code that adjusts `session` to indicate that a successful login has occurred.

Sharpen your pencil

Let's write the code for the */login* URL below. In the space shown, provide code that adjusts `session` by setting a value for the `logged_in` key to `True`. Additionally, have the URL's function return the "You are now logged in" message to the waiting browser:

Add the new code here.

```
@app.route('/login')
def do_login() -> str:

    ............................................................................................
    return
        ........................................................................................
```

In addition to creating the code for the */login* URL, you'll need to make two other changes to the code to enable sessions. Detail what you think these changes are here:

1 ....

2 ....

Sharpen your pencil
Solution

You were to write the code for the */login* URL below. You were to provide code that adjusts `session` by setting a value for the `logged_in` key to `True`. Additionally, you were to have the URL's function return the "You are now logged in" message to the waiting browser:

Set the "logged_in" key in the "session" dictionary to "True".

```
@app.route('/login')
def do_login() -> str:
    session['logged_in'] = True
    return 'You are now logged in.'
```

Return this message to the waiting browser.

In addition to creating the code for the */login* URL, you needed to make two other changes to the code to enable sessions. You were to detail what you think these changes were:

1 We need to add 'session' to the import line at the top of the code.

2 We need to set a value for this webapp's secret key.

Let's not forget to do these.

Amend the webapp's code to handle logins

We're going to hold off on testing this new code until we've added another two URLs: */logout* and */status*. Before you move on, make sure your copy of `simple_webapp.py` has been amended to include the changes shown below. Note: we're not showing all of the webapp's code here, just the new bits (which are highlighted):

```
from flask import Flask, session

app = Flask(__name__)

    ...

@app.route('/login')
def do_login() -> str:
    session['logged_in'] = True
    return 'You are now logged in.'


app.secret_key = 'YouWillNeverGuessMySecretKey'

if __name__ == '__main__':
    app.run(debug=True)
```

Remember to import "session".

Add the code for the "/login" URL.

Set a value for this webapp's secret key (which enables the use of sessions).

Let's Do Logout and Status Checking

Adding the code for the */logout* and */status* URLs is our next task.

When it comes to logging out, one strategy is to set the `session` dictionary's `logged_in` key to `False`. Another strategy is to *remove* the `logged_in` key from `session` altogether. We're going to go with the second option; the reason why will become clear after we code the */status* URL.

✎ Sharpen your pencil

Let's write the code for the */logout* URL, which needs to remove the `logged_in` key from the `session` dictionary, then return the "You are now logged out" message to the waiting browser. Add your code into the spaces below:

Add the logout code here.

Hint: if you've forgotten how to remove a key from a dictionary, type "dir(dict)" at the >>> prompt for a list of available dictionary methods.

```
@app.route('/logout')
def do_logout() -> str:

    .................................................
    return .................................................
```

With */logout* written, we now turn our attention to */status*, which returns one of two messages to the waiting web browser.

The message "You are currently logged in" is returned when `logged_in` exists as a value in the `session` dictionary (and, by definition, is set to `True`).

The message "You are NOT logged in" is returned when the `session` dictionary doesn't have a `logged_in` key. Note that we can't check `logged_in` for `False`, as the */logout* URL removes the key from the `session` dictionary as opposed to changing its value. (We haven't forgotten that we still need to explain why we're doing things this way, and we'll get to the explanation in a while. For now, trust that this is the way you have to code this functionality.)

Let's write the code for the */status* URL in the space below:

Check if the "logged_in" key exists in the "session" dictionary, then return the appropriate message.

Put your status-checking code here.

```
@app.route('/status')
def check_status() -> str:
    if  .................................................
        return .................................................
    return .................................................
```

Sharpen your pencil
Solution

You were to write the code for the */logout* URL, which needed to remove the `logged_in` key from the `session` dictionary, then return the "You are now logged out" message to the waiting browser:

Use the "pop" method to remove the "logged_in" key from the "session" dictionary.

```
@app.route('/logout')
def do_logout() -> str:
```
session.pop('logged_in')

```
        return
```
'You are now logged out.'

With */logout* written, you were to turn your attention to the */status* URL, which returns one of two messages to the waiting web browser.

The message "You are currently logged in" is returned when `logged_in` exists as a value in the `session` dictionary (and, by definition, is set to `True`).

The message "You are NOT logged in" is returned when the `session` dictionary doesn't have a `logged_in` key.

You were to write the code for */status* in the space below:

Does the "logged_in" key exist in the "session" dictionary?

```
@app.route('/status')
def check_status() -> str:
    if
```
'logged_in' in session:

```
            return
```
'You are currently logged in.' ← *If yes, return this message.*

```
    return
```
'You are NOT logged in.' ← *If no, return this message.*

Amend the webapp's code once more

We're still holding off on testing this new version of the webapp, but here (on the right) is a highlighted version of the code you need to add to your copy of `simple_webapp.py`.

Make sure you've amended your code to match ours before getting to the next *Test Drive*, which is coming up right after we make good on an earlier promise.

Two new URL routes

```
. . .

@app.route('/logout')
def do_logout() -> str:
    session.pop('logged_in')
    return 'You are now logged out.'


@app.route('/status')
def check_status() -> str:
    if 'logged_in' in session:
        return 'You are currently logged in.'
    return 'You are NOT logged in.'

app.secret_key = 'YouWillNeverGuessMySecretKey'

if __name__ == '__main__':
    app.run(debug=True)
```

Why Not Check for False?

When you coded the */login* URL, you set the `logged_in` key to `True` in the `session` dictionary (which indicated that the browser was logged into the webapp). However, when you coded the */logout* URL, the code didn't set the value associated with the `logged_in` key to `False`, as we preferred instead to remove all trace of the `logged_in` key from the `session` dictionary. In the code that handled the */status* URL, we checked the "login status" by determining whether or not the `logged_in` key existed in the `session` dictionary; we didn't check whether `logged_in` is `False` (or `True`, for that matter). Which begs the question: *why does the webapp not use* `False` *to indicate "not logged in"?*

The answer is subtle, but important, and it has to do with the way dictionaries work in Python. To illustrate the issue, let's experiment at the >>> prompt and simulate what can happen to the `session` dictionary when used by the webapp. Be sure to follow along with this session, and carefully read each of the annotations:

```
Python 3.5.1 Shell
>>>
>>> session = dict()                         ◀─── Create a new, empty
>>>                                               dictionary called "session".
>>> if session['logged_in']:
        print('Found it.')              ◀─── Try to check for the existence of a
                                             "logged_in" value using an "if" statement.
Traceback (most recent call last):
  File "<pyshell#47>", line 1, in <module>   Whoops! The "logged_in" key doesn't
    if session['logged_in']:              ◀── exist yet, so we get a "KeyError", and
KeyError: 'logged_in'                        our code has crashed as a result.
>>>
>>> if 'logged_in' in session:               However, if we check for existence using
        print('Found it.')              ◀─── "in", our code doesn't crash (there's no
                                             "KeyError") even though the key has no value.
>>> session['logged_in'] = True         ◀─── Let's assign a value to the "logged_in" key.
>>>
>>> if 'logged_in' in session:
        print('Found it.')                   Checking for existence with "in" still works,
                                      ◀───── although this time around we get a positive
                                             result (as the key exists and has a value).
Found it.
>>>                                          Checking with an "if" statement works too
>>> if session['logged_in']:         ◀───── (now that the key has a value associated
        print('Found it.')                   with it). However, if the key is removed from
                                             the dictionary (using the "pop" method) this
Found it.                                    code is once again vulnerable to "KeyError".
>>> |
                                 Ln: 115  Col: 4
```

The above experimentation shows that it is **not** possible to check a dictionary for a key's value until a key/value pairing exists. Trying to do so results in an `KeyError`. As it's a good idea to avoid errors like this, the `simple_webapp.py` code checks for the existence of the `logged_in` key as proof that the browser's logged in, as opposed to checking the key's actual value, thus avoiding the possibility of a `KeyError`.

TEST DRIVE

Let's take the `simple_webapp.py` webapp for a spin to see how well the */login*, */logout*, and */status* URLs perform. As with the last *Test Drive*, we're going to test this webapp using more than one browser in order to confirm that each browser maintains its own "login state" on the server. Let's start the webapp from our operating system's terminal:

On Linux and Mac OS X: **python3 simple_webapp.py**

On Windows: **py -3 simple_webapp.py**

Let's fire up Opera and check its initial login status by accessing the */status* URL. As expected, the browser is not logged in:

> Access the "/status" URL to determine whether the browser is logged in or not.

| ● ● ● | 🗋 127.0.0.1:5000/status | + | ≡ |

< > C ⠿ 🌐 127.0.0.1:5000/status ♥ 🔼

You are NOT logged in.

> As you've only just started the webapp, and this is your first interaction with it, this message confirms exactly what you'd expect: that you are not logged in.

Let's simulate logging in, by accessing the */login* URL. The message changes to confirm that the login was successful:

> Accessing "/login" does exactly what is expected of it. The browser is now logged into the webapp.

| ● ● ● | 🗋 127.0.0.1:5000/login | + | ≡ |

< > C ⠿ 🌐 127.0.0.1:5000/login ♥ 🔼

You are now logged in.

Now that you are logged in, let's confirm the status change by accessing the *status* URL within Opera. Doing so confirms that the user of the Opera browser is logged in. If you use Chrome to check the status, too, you'll see that the user of Chrome isn't logged in, which is exactly what we want (as each user of the webapp—each browser—has its own state maintained by the webapp):

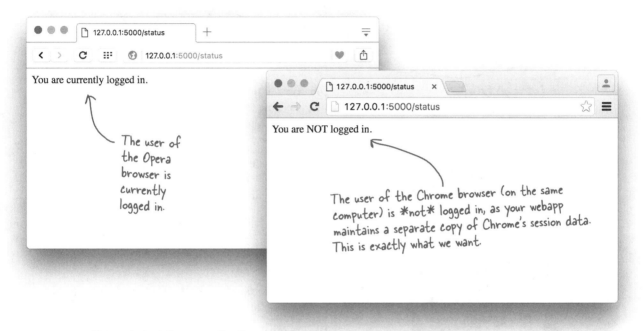

To conclude, let's access the *logout* URL within Opera to tell the webapp that we are logging out of the session:

Although we haven't asked any of our browser's users for a login ID or password, the */login*, */logout*, and */status* URLs allow us to simulate what would happen to the webapp's `session` dictionary if we were to create the required HTML form, then hook up the form's data to a backend "credentials" database. The details of how this might happen are very much application-specific, but the basic mechanism (i.e., manipulating `session`) is the same no matter what a specific webapp might want to do.

Are we now ready to restrict access to the */page1*, */page2*, and */page3* URLs?

Can We Now Restrict Access to URLs?

Take a look at this login code, guys. I think it's pretty clear what I need to do...

Jim: Hey, Frank...what are you stuck on?

Frank: I need to come up with a way to restrict access to the */page1*, */page2*, and */page3* URLs...

Joe: It can't be that hard, can it? You've already got the code you need in the function that handles */status*...

Frank: ...and it knows if a user's browser is logged in or not, right?

Joe: Yeah, it does. So, all you have to do is copy and paste that checking code from the function that handles */status* into each of the URLs you want to restrict, and then you're home and dry!

Jim: Oh, man! Copy and paste...the web developer's *Achilles' heel*. You really don't want to copy and paste code like that... it can only lead to problems down the road.

Frank: Of course! CS 101... I'll create a function with the code from */status*, then call *that* function as needed within the functions that handle the */page1*, */page2*, and */page3* URLs. Problem solved.

Joe: I like that idea...and I think it'll work. (I knew there was a reason we sat through all those *boring* CS lectures.)

Jim: Hang on...not so fast. What you're suggesting with a function is much better than your copy-and-paste idea, but I'm still not convinced it's the best way to go here.

Frank and **Joe** (together, and incredulously): *What's not to like?!?!?*

Jim: It bugs me that you're planning to add code to the functions that handle the */page1*, */page2*, and */page3* URLs that has nothing to do with what those functions actually *do*. Granted, you need to check whether a user is logged in before granting access, but adding a function call to do this to every URL doesn't sit quite right with me...

Frank: So what's your big idea, then?

Jim: If it were me, I'd create, then use, a decorator.

Joe: Of course! That's an even better idea. Let's do that.

Copy-and-Paste Is Rarely a Good Idea

Let's convince ourselves that the ideas suggested on the last page are *not* the best way to approach the problem at hand—namely, how best to restrict access to specific web pages.

The first suggestion was to copy and paste some of the code from the function that handles the */status* URL (namely, the `check_status` function). Here's the code in question:

This is the code to copy and paste. ➔

```
@app.route('/status')
def check_status() -> str:
    if 'logged_in' in session:
        return 'You are currently logged in.'
    return 'You are NOT logged in.'
```

⬅ *This code returns a different message based on whether or not the user's browser is logged in.*

Here's what the `page1` function currently looks like:

```
@app.route('/page1')
def page1() -> str:
    return 'This is page 1.'
```

⬅ *This is the page-specific functionality.*

If we copy and paste the highlighted code from `check_status` into `page1`, the latter's code would end up looking like this:

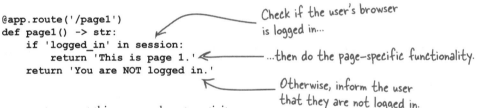

```
@app.route('/page1')
def page1() -> str:
    if 'logged_in' in session:
        return 'This is page 1.'
    return 'You are NOT logged in.'
```

Check if the user's browser is logged in...

...then do the page-specific functionality.

Otherwise, inform the user that they are not logged in.

The above code works, but if you were to repeat this copy-and-paste activity for the */page2* and */page3* URLs (as well as any other URLs you were to add to your webapp), you'd quickly create a *maintenance nightmare*, especially when you consider all the edits you'd have to make should you decide to change how your login-checking code works (by, maybe, checking a submitted user ID and password against data stored in a database).

Put shared code into its own function

When you have code that you need to use in many different places, the classic solution to the maintenance problem inherent in any copy-and-paste "quick fix" is to put the shared code into a function, which is then invoked as needed.

As such a strategy solves the maintenance problem (as the shared code exists in only one place as opposed to being copied and pasted willy-nilly), let's see what creating a login-checking function does for our webapp.

Creating a Function Helps, But...

Let's create a new function called `check_logged_in`, which, when invoked, returns `True` if the user's browser is currently logged in, and `False` otherwise.

It's not a big job (most of the code is already in `check_status`); here's how we'd write this new function:

```
def check_logged_in() -> bool:
    if 'logged_in' in session:
        return True
    return False
```

Rather than returning a message, this code returns a boolean based on whether or not the user's browser is logged in.

With this function written, let's use it in the `page1` function instead of that copied and pasted code:

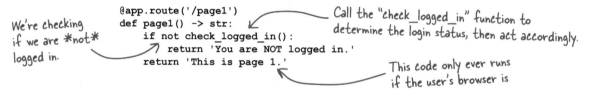

We're checking if we are *not* logged in.

```
@app.route('/page1')
def page1() -> str:
    if not check_logged_in():
        return 'You are NOT logged in.'
    return 'This is page 1.'
```

Call the "check_logged_in" function to determine the login status, then act accordingly.

This code only ever runs if the user's browser is logged in.

This strategy is a bit better than copy-and-paste, as you can now change how the login process works by making changes to the `check_logged_in` function. However, to use the `check_logged_in` function you still have to make similar changes to the `page2` and `page3` functions (as well as to any new URLs you create), and you do that by copying and pasting this new code from `page1` into the other functions... In fact, if you compare what you did to the `page1` function on this page with what you did to `page1` on the last page, it's roughly the same amount of work, and it's *still* copy-and-paste! Additionally, with *both* of these "solutions," the added code is **obscuring** what `page1` actually does.

It would be nice if you could somehow check if the user's browser is logged in *without* having to amend *any* of your existing function's code (so as not to obscure anything). That way, the code in each of your webapp's functions can remain *directly* related to what each function does, and the login status-checking code won't get in the way. If only there was a way to do this?

As we learned from our three friendly developers—Frank, Joe, and Jim—a few pages back, Python includes a language feature that can help here, and it goes by the name **decorator**. A decorator allows you to augment an existing function with extra code, and it does this by letting you change the behavior of the existing function *without* having to change its code.

If you're reading that last sentence and saying: *"What?!?!?"*, don't worry: it does sound strange the first time you hear it. After all, how can you possibly change how a function works without changing the function's code? Does it even make sense to try?

Let's find out by learning about decorators.

You've Been Using Decorators All Along

You've been *using* decorators for as long as you've written webapps with Flask, which you started back in Chapter 5.

Here's the earliest version of the `hello_flask.py` webapp from that chapter, which highlights the use of a decorator called `@app.route`, which comes with Flask. The `@app.route` decorator is applied to an existing function (`hello` in this code), and the decorator augments the function it precedes by arranging to call `hello` whenever the webapp processes the `/` URL. Decorators are easy to spot; they're prefixed with the `@` symbol:

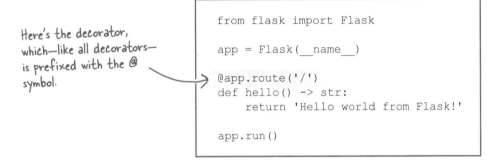

Here's the decorator, which—like all decorators—is prefixed with the @ symbol.

```
from flask import Flask

app = Flask(__name__)

@app.route('/')
def hello() -> str:
    return 'Hello world from Flask!'

app.run()
```

Note how, as a user of the `@app.route` decorator, you have no idea how the decorator works its magic. All you're concerned with is that the decorator does what it promises: links a given URL with a function. All of the nitty-gritty, behind-the-scenes details of how the decorator works are hidden from you.

When you decide to create a decorator, you need to peek under the covers and (much like when you created a context manager in the last chapter) hook into Python's decorator machinery. There are four things that you need to know and understand to write a decorator:

1 **How to create a function**

2 **How to pass a function as an argument to a function**

3 **How to return a function from a function**

4 **How to process any number and type of function arguments**

You've been successfully creating and using your own functions since Chapter 4, which means this list of "four things to know" is really only three. Let's take some time to work through items 2 through 4 from this list as we progress toward writing a decorator of our own.

Pass a Function to a Function

It's been a while, but way back in Chapter 2 we introduced the notion that *everything is an object* in Python. Although it may sound counterintuitive, the "everything" includes functions, which means functions are objects, too.

Clearly, when you invoke a function, it runs. However, like everything else in Python, functions are objects, and have an object ID: think of functions as "function objects."

Take a quick look at the short IDLE session below. A string is assigned to a variable called `msg`, and then its object ID is reported through a call to the `id` built-in function (BIF). A small function, called `hello`, is then defined. The `hello` function is then passed to the `id` BIF that reports the function's object ID. The `type` BIF then confirms that `msg` is a string and `hello` is a function, and finally `hello` is invoked and prints the current value of `msg` on screen:

> ☐ Pass a function to a function.
> ☐ Return a function from a function.
> ☐ Process any number/ type of arguments.

We'll check off each completed topic as we work through this material.

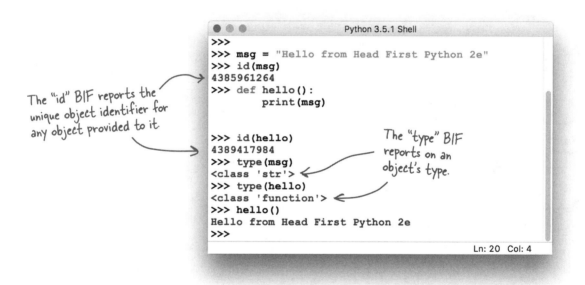

The "id" BIF reports the unique object identifier for any object provided to it.

```
●●●                    Python 3.5.1 Shell
>>>
>>> msg = "Hello from Head First Python 2e"
>>> id(msg)
4385961264
>>> def hello():
        print(msg)


>>> id(hello)
4389417984
>>> type(msg)
<class 'str'>
>>> type(hello)
<class 'function'>
>>> hello()
Hello from Head First Python 2e
>>>
                                         Ln: 20  Col: 4
```

The "type" BIF reports on an object's type.

We were a little devious in not drawing your attention to this before we had you look at the above IDLE session, but...did you notice *how* we passed `hello` to the `id` and `type` BIFs? We didn't invoke `hello`; we passed its *name* to each of the functions as an argument. In doing so, we passed a function to a function.

Functions can take a function as an argument

The calls to `id` and `type` above demonstrate that some of Python's built-in functions accept a function as an argument (or to be more precise: *a function object*). What a function does with the argument is up to the function. Neither `id` nor `type` invokes the function, although it could have. Let's see how that works.

Invoking a Passed Function

When a function object is passed as an argument to a function, the receiving function can *invoke* the passed-in function object.

Here's a small function (called `apply`) that takes two arguments: a function object and a value. The `apply` function invokes the function object and passes the value to the invoked function as an argument, returning the results of invoking the function on the value to the calling code:

The "apply" function accepts a function object as an argument. The "object" annotation helps to confirm our intention here (and the use of the argument name "func" is a common convention).

```
func.py - /Users/paul/Documents/func.py (3.5.1)

def apply(func: object, value: object) -> object:
    return func(value)

                                        Ln: 6  Col: 0
```

Any value (of any type) can be passed as the second argument. Again, the annotations hint at what's allowed as an argument type here: any object.

The function (passed as an argument) is invoked, with the "value" passed to it as its only argument. The result of this function call is returned from the "apply" function.

Note how `apply`'s annotations hint that it accepts any function object together with any value, then returns anything (which is all very *generic*). A quick test of `apply` at the >>> prompt confirms that `apply` works as expected:

The "apply" function runs a bunch of BIFs against some values (and works as expected).

```
Python 3.5.1 Shell

>>>
>>> apply(print, 42)
42
>>> apply(id, 42)
4297539264
>>> apply(type, 42)
<class 'int'>
>>> apply(len, 'Marvin')
6
>>> apply(type, apply)
<class 'function'>
>>>

                                        Ln: 110  Col: 4
```

The "apply" function takes any object for "value". In this example, it takes itself as "value" and confirms that it's a function.

In each of these examples, the first argument to "apply" is assigned to the "func" argument (above).

If you're reading this page and wondering when you'd ever need to do something like this, don't fret: we'll get to that when we write our decorator. For now, concentrate on understanding that it's possible to pass a function object to a function, which the latter can then invoke.

Functions Can Be Nested Inside Functions

Usually, when you create a function, you take some existing code and make it reusable by giving it a name, and using the existing code as the function's suite. This is the most common function use case. However, what sometimes comes as a surprise is that, in Python, the code in a function's suite can be *any* code, including code that defines another function (often referred to as a *nested* or *inner* function). Even more surprising is that the nested function can be *returned* from the outer, enclosing function; in effect, what gets returned is a *function object*. Let's look at a few examples that demonstrate these other, less common function use cases.

First up is an example that shows a function (called `inner`) nested inside another function (called `outer`). It is not possible to invoke `inner` from anywhere other than within `outer`'s suite, as `inner` is local in scope to `outer`:

☑	Pass a function to a function.
☐	Return a function from a function.
☐	Process any number/ type of arguments.

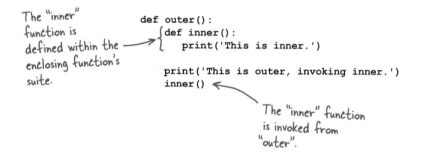

The "inner" function is defined within the enclosing function's suite.

```
def outer():
    def inner():
        print('This is inner.')

    print('This is outer, invoking inner.')
    inner()
```

The "inner" function is invoked from "outer".

When `outer` is invoked, it runs all the code in its suite: `inner` is defined, the call to the `print` BIF in `outer` is executed, and then the `inner` function is invoked (which calls the `print` BIF within `inner`). Here's what appears on screen:

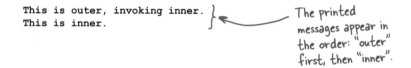

```
This is outer, invoking inner.
This is inner.
```

The printed messages appear in the order: "outer" first, then "inner".

When would you ever use this?

Looking at this simple example, you might find it hard to think of a situation where creating a function inside another function would be useful. However, when a function is complex and contains many lines of code, abstracting some of the function's code into a nested function often makes sense (and can make the enclosing function's code easier to read).

A more common usage of this technique arranges for the enclosing function to return the nested function as its value, using the `return` statement. This is what allows you to create a decorator.

So, let's see what happens when we return a function from a function.

Return a Function from a Function

☑ Pass a function to a function.

☐ Return a function from a function.

☐ Process any number/ type of arguments.

Our second example is very similar to the first, but for the fact that the `outer` function no longer invokes `inner`, but instead returns it. Take a look at the code:

The "inner" function is still defined within "outer".

```
def outer():
    def inner():
        print('This is inner.')

    print('This is outer, returning inner.')
    return inner
```

The "return" statement does not invoke "inner"; instead, it returns the "inner" function object to the calling code.

Let's see what this new version of the `outer` function does, by returning to the IDLE shell and taking `outer` for a spin.

Note how we assign the result of invoking `outer` to a variable, called `i` in this example. We then use `i` as if it were a function object—first checking its type by invoking the `type` BIF, then invoking `i` as we would any other function (by appending parentheses). When we invoke `i`, the `inner` function executes. In effect, `i` is now an *alias* for the `inner` function as created inside `outer`:

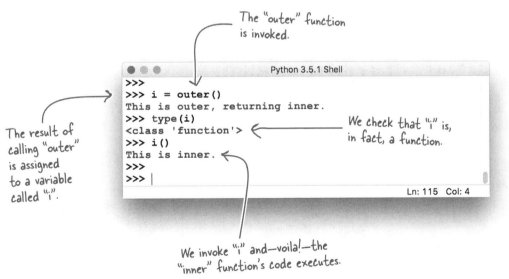

The "outer" function is invoked.

The result of calling "outer" is assigned to a variable called "i".

We check that "i" is, in fact, a function.

We invoke "i" and—voila!—the "inner" function's code executes.

So far, so good. You can now *return* a function from a function, as well as *send* a function to a function. You're nearly ready to put all this together in your quest to create a decorator. There's just one more thing you need to understand: creating a function that can handle any number and type of arguments. Let's look at how to do this now.

Accepting a List of Arguments

Imagine you have a requirement to create a function (which we'll call `myfunc` in this example) that can be called with any number of arguments. For example, you might call `myfunc` like this:

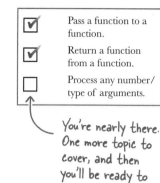

☑	Pass a function to a function.
☑	Return a function from a function.
☐	Process any number/ type of arguments.

You're nearly there. One more topic to cover, and then you'll be ready to create a decorator.

$$myfunc(10)$$

One argument

or you might call `myfunc` like this:

No arguments

$$myfunc()$$

or you might call `myfunc` like this:

$$myfunc(10, 20, 30, 40, 50, 60, 70)$$

Many arguments (which, in this example, are all numbers, but could be anything: numbers, strings, booleans, list.

In fact, you might call `myfunc` with *any* number of arguments, with the proviso that you don't know ahead of time how many arguments are going to be provided.

As it isn't possible to define three distinct versions of `myfunc` to handle each of the three above invocations, the question becomes: *is it possible to accept any number of arguments in a function?*

Use * to accept an arbitrary list of arguments

Python provides a special notation that allows you to specify that a function can take any number of arguments (where "any number" means "zero or more"). This notation uses the * character to represent *any number*, and is combined with an argument name (by convention, `args` is used) to specify that a function can accept an arbitrary list of arguments (even though `*args` is technically a tuple).

Here's a version of `myfunc` that uses this notation to accept any number of arguments when invoked. If any arguments are provided, `myfunc` prints their values to the screen:

Think of * as meaning "expand to a list of values."

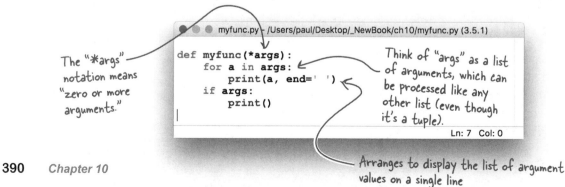

myfunc.py - /Users/paul/Desktop/_NewBook/ch10/myfunc.py (3.5.1)

```
def myfunc(*args):
    for a in args:
        print(a, end=' ')
    if args:
        print()
```

Ln: 7 Col: 0

The "*args" notation means "zero or more arguments."

Think of "args" as a list of arguments, which can be processed like any other list (even though it's a tuple).

Arranges to display the list of argument values on a single line

Processing a List of Arguments

Now that `myfunc` exists, let's see if it can handle the example invocations from the last page, namely:

```
myfunc(10)
myfunc()
myfunc(10, 20, 30, 40, 50, 60, 70)
```

<table>
<tr><td>☑</td><td>Pass a function to a function.</td></tr>
<tr><td>☑</td><td>Return a function from a function.</td></tr>
<tr><td>☐</td><td>Process any number/ type of arguments.</td></tr>
</table>

Here's another IDLE session that confirms that `myfunc` is up to the task. No matter how many arguments we supply (including *none*), `myfunc` processes them accordingly:

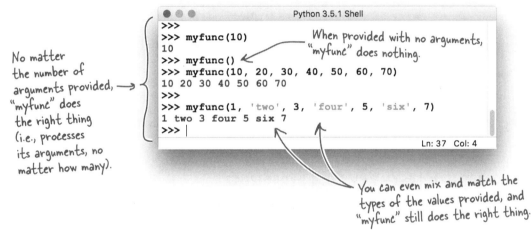

No matter the number of arguments provided, → "myfunc" does the right thing (i.e., processes its arguments, no matter how many).

When provided with no arguments, "myfunc" does nothing.

You can even mix and match the types of the values provided, and "myfunc" still does the right thing.

* works on the way in, too

If you provide a list to `myfunc` as an argument, the list (despite potentially containing many values) is treated as one item (i.e., it's *one* list). To instruct the interpreter to **expand** the list to behave as if each of the list's items were an *individual* argument, prefix the list's name with the * character when invoking the function.

Another short IDLE session demonstrates the difference using * can have:

The list is processed as a single argument to the function.

```
>>>
>>> values = [1, 2, 3, 5, 7, 11]
>>>
>>> myfunc(values)
[1, 2, 3, 5, 7, 11]
>>>
>>> myfunc(*values)
1 2 3 5 7 11
>>>
>>>
```

A list of six integers

When a list is prefixed with "*", it expands to a list of individual arguments.

Accepting a Dictionary of Arguments

When it comes to sending values into functions, it's also possible to provide the names of the arguments together with their associated values, then rely on the interpreter to match things up accordingly.

You first saw this technique in Chapter 4 with the `search4letters` function, which—you may recall—expects two argument values, one for `phrase` and another for `letters`. When keyword arguments are used, the order in which the arguments are provided to the `search4letters` function doesn't matter:

☑ Pass a function to a function.

☑ Return a function from a function.

☐ Process any number/ type of arguments.

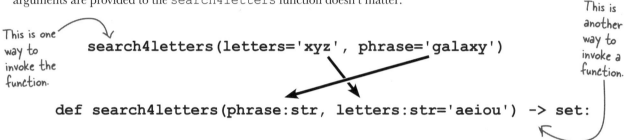

This is one way to invoke the function.

```
search4letters(letters='xyz', phrase='galaxy')
```

This is another way to invoke a function.

```
def search4letters(phrase:str, letters:str='aeiou') -> set:
```

Like with lists, it's also possible arrange for a function to accept an arbitrary number of keyword arguments—that is, keys with values assigned to them (as with `phrase` and `letters` in the above example).

Use ** to accept arbitrary keyword arguments

In addition to the `*` notation, Python also provides `**`, which expands to a collection of keyword arguments. Where `*` uses `args` as its variable name (by convention), `**` uses `kwargs`, which is short for "keyword arguments." (Note: you can use names other than `args` and `kwargs` within this context, but very few Python programmers do.)

Let's look at another function, called `myfunc2`, which accepts any number of keyword arguments:

Think of ** as meaning "expand to a dictionary of keys and values."

```
● ● ●  myfunc.py - /Users/paul/Desktop/_NewBook/ch10/myfunc.py (3.5.1)

def myfunc(*args):
    for a in args:
        print(a, end=' ')
    if args:
        print()

def myfunc2(**kwargs):
    for k, v in kwargs.items():
        print(k, v, sep='->', end=' ')
    if kwargs:
        print()
|
                                              Ln: 13  Col: 0
```

The "**" tells the function to expect keyword arguments.

Take each key and value pairing in the dictionary, and display it on screen.

Within the function, "kwargs" behaves just like any other dictionary.

Processing a Dictionary of Arguments

☑ Pass a function to a function.

☑ Return a function from a function.

☐ Process any number/ type of arguments.

The code within myfunc2's suite takes the dictionary of arguments and processes them, displaying all the key/value pairings on a single line.

Here's another IDLE session that demonstrates myfunc2 in action. No matter how many key/value pairings are provided (including none), myfunc2 does the right thing:

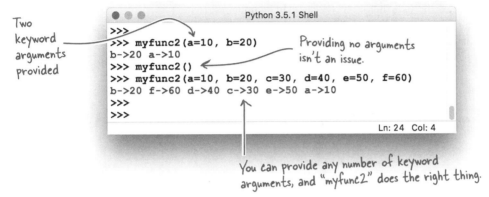

Two keyword arguments provided

Providing no arguments isn't an issue.

You can provide any number of keyword arguments, and "myfunc2" does the right thing.

** works on the way in, too

You probably guessed this was coming, didn't you? As with *args, when you use **kwargs it's also possible to use ** when invoking the myfunc2 function. Rather than demonstrate how this works with myfunc2, we're going to remind you of a prior usage of this technique from earlier in this book. Back in Chapter 7, when you learned how to use Python's DB-API, you defined a dictionary of connection characteristics as follows:

A dictionary of key/value pairings

```python
dbconfig = { 'host': '127.0.0.1',
             'user': 'vsearch',
             'password': 'vsearchpasswd',
             'database': 'vsearchlogDB', }
```

When it came time to establish a connection to your waiting MySQL (or MariaDB) database server, you used the dbconfig dictionary as follows. Notice anything about the way the dbconfig argument is specified?

Does this look familiar?

```python
conn = mysql.connector.connect(**dbconfig)
```

By prefixing the dbconfig argument with **, we tell the interpreter to treat the single dictionary as a collection of keys and their associated values. In effect, it's as if you invoked connect with four individual keyword arguments, like this:

```python
conn = mysql.connector.connect('host'='127.0.0.1', 'user'='vsearch',
                    'password'='vsearchpasswd', 'database'='vsearchlogDB')
```

Accepting Any Number and Type of Function Arguments

☑ Pass a function to a function.

☑ Return a function from a function.

☐ Process any number/ type of arguments.

When creating your own functions, it's neat that Python lets you accept a list of arguments (using *), in addition to any number of keyword arguments (using **). What's even neater is that you can combine the two techniques, which lets you create a function that can accept any number and type of arguments.

Here's a third version of myfunc (which goes by the shockingly imaginative name of myfunc3). This function accepts any list of arguments, any number of keyword arguments, or a combination of both:

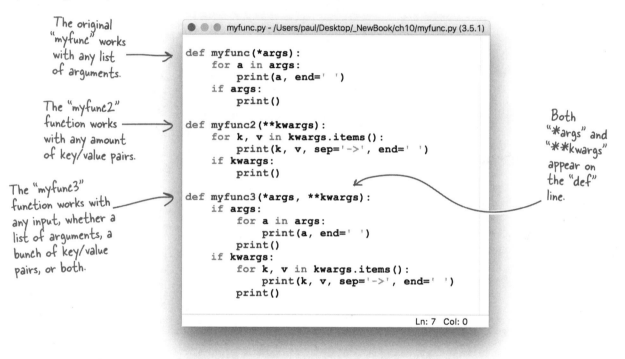

The original "myfunc" works with any list of arguments.

The "myfunc2" function works with any amount of key/value pairs.

The "myfunc3" function works with any input, whether a list of arguments, a bunch of key/value pairs, or both.

```
myfunc.py - /Users/paul/Desktop/_NewBook/ch10/myfunc.py (3.5.1)

def myfunc(*args):
    for a in args:
        print(a, end=' ')
    if args:
        print()

def myfunc2(**kwargs):
    for k, v in kwargs.items():
        print(k, v, sep='->', end=' ')
    if kwargs:
        print()

def myfunc3(*args, **kwargs):
    if args:
        for a in args:
            print(a, end=' ')
        print()
    if kwargs:
        for k, v in kwargs.items():
            print(k, v, sep='->', end=' ')
        print()

                                    Ln: 7  Col: 0
```

Both "*args" and "**kwargs" appear on the "def" line.

This short IDLE session showcases myfunc3:

Works with no arguments

Works with a combination of a list and keyword arguments

```
                        Python 3.5.1 Shell
>>>
>>> myfunc3()
>>> myfunc3(1, 2, 3)          ← Works with a list
1 2 3
>>> myfunc3(a=10, b=20, c=30)  ← Works with
a->10 b->20 c->30              keyword
>>> myfunc3(1, 2, 3, a=10, b=20, c=30)  arguments
1 2 3
a->10 b->20 c->30
>>> |
                                    Ln: 68  Col: 4
```

A Recipe for Creating a Function Decorator

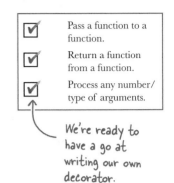

☑	Pass a function to a function.
☑	Return a function from a function.
☑	Process any number/ type of arguments.

We're ready to have a go at writing our own decorator.

With three items marked in the checklist on the right, you now have an understanding of the Python language features that allow you to create a decorator. All you need to know now is how you take these features and combine them to create the decorator you need.

Just like when you created your own context manager (in the last chapter), creating a decorator conforms to a set of rules or *recipe*. Recall that a decorator allows you to augment an existing function with extra code, without requiring you to change the existing function's code (which, we'll admit, still sounds freaky).

To create a function decorator, you need to know that:

 A decorator is a function

In fact, as far as the interpreter is concerned, your decorator is *just another function*, albeit one that manipulates an existing function. Let's refer to this existing function as *the decorated function* from here on in. Having made it this far in this book, you know that creating a function is easy: use Python's `def` keyword.

 A decorator takes the decorated function as an argument

A decorator needs to accept the decorated function as an argument. To do this, you simply pass the decorated function as a *function object* to your decorator. Now that you've worked through the last 10 pages, you know that this too is easy: you arrive at a function object by referring to the function *without* parentheses (i.e., using just the function's name).

③ A decorator returns a new function

A decorator returns a new function as its return value. Much like when `outer` returned `inner` (a few pages back), your decorator is going to do something similar, except that the function it returns needs to *invoke* the decorated function. Doing this is—*dare we say it?*—easy but for one small complication, which is what Step 4 is all about.

 A decorator maintains the decorated function's signature

A decorator needs to ensure that the function it returns takes the same number and type of arguments as expected by the decorated function. The number and type of any function's arguments is known as its **signature** (as each function's `def` line is unique).

It's time to grab a pencil and put this information to work creating your first decorator.

Recap: We Need to Restrict Access to Certain URLs

OK. I think I'm getting most of this. But remind me...why am I doing this again?

We're trying to avoid copying and pasting all that login-status-checking code.

We've been working with the simple_webapp.py code, and we need our decorator to check to see whether the user's browser is logged in or not. If it is logged in, restricted web pages are visible. If the browser isn't logged in, the webapp should advise the user to log in prior to viewing any restricted pages. We'll create a decorator to handle this logic. Recall the check_status function, which demonstrates the logic we want our decorator to mimic:

Remember: this code returns a different message based on whether or not the user's browser is logged in.

We want to avoid copying and pasting this code.

```
@app.route('/status')
def check_status() -> str:
    if 'logged_in' in session:
        return 'You are currently logged in.'
    return 'You are NOT logged in.'
```

Creating a Function Decorator

To comply with item 1 in our list, you had to create a new function. Remember:

 A decorator is a function

In fact, as far as the interpreter is concerned, your decorator is *just another function*, albeit one that manipulates an existing function. Let's refer to this existing function as *the decorated function* from here on in. You know that creating a function is easy: use Python's `def` keyword.

Complying with item 2 involves ensuring your decorator accepts a function object as an argument. Again, remember:

 A decorator takes the decorated function as an argument

Your decorator needs to accept the decorated function as an argument. To do this, you simply pass the decorated function as a *function object* to your decorator. You arrive at a function object by referring to the function *without* parentheses (i.e., using the function's name).

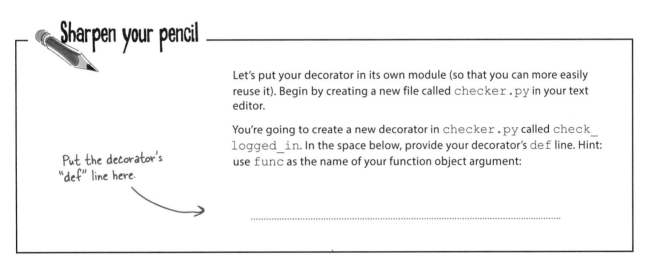

Sharpen your pencil

Let's put your decorator in its own module (so that you can more easily reuse it). Begin by creating a new file called `checker.py` in your text editor.

You're going to create a new decorator in `checker.py` called `check_logged_in`. In the space below, provide your decorator's `def` line. Hint: use `func` as the name of your function object argument:

Put the decorator's "def" line here.

....

there are no Dumb Questions

Q: Does it matter where on my system I create `checker.py`?

A: Yes. Our plan is to import `checker.py` into webapps that need it, so you need to ensure that the interpreter can find it when your code includes the `import checker` line. For now, put `checker.py` in the same folder as `simple_webapp.py`.

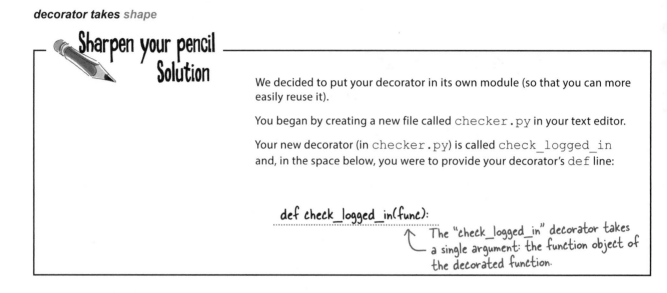

That's almost too easy, isn't it?

Remember: a decorator is *just another function*, which takes a function object as an argument (`func` in the above `def` line).

Let's move on to the next item in our "create a decorator" recipe, which is a little more involved (but not by much). Recall what you need your decorator to do:

③ **A decorator returns a new function**

Your decorator returns a new function as its return value. Just like when `outer` returned `inner` (a few pages back), your decorator is going to do something similar, except that the function it returns needs to *invoke* the decorated function.

Earlier in this chapter, you met the `outer` function, which, when invoked, returned the `inner` function. Here's `outer`'s code once more:

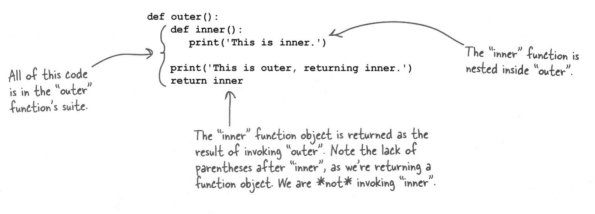

Sharpen your pencil

Now that you've written your decorator's `def` line, let's add some code to its suite. You need to do four things here.

1. Define a nested function called `wrapper` that is returned by `check_logged_in`. (You could use any function name here, but, as you'll see in a bit, `wrapper` is a pretty good choice.)

2. Within `wrapper`, add some of the code from your existing `check_status` function that implements one of two behaviors based on whether the user's browser is logged in or not. To save you the page-flip, here's the `check_status` code once more (with the important bits highlighted):

```
@app.route('/status')
def check_status() -> str:
    if 'logged_in' in session:
        return 'You are currently logged in.'
    return 'You are NOT logged in.'
```

3. As per item 3 of our decorator-creating recipe, you need to adjust the nested function's code so that it invokes the decorated function (as opposed to returning the "You are currently logged in" message).

4. With the nested function written, you need to return its function object from `check_logged_in`.

Add the required code to `check_logged_in`'s suite in the spaces provided below:

```
def check_logged_in(func):
```

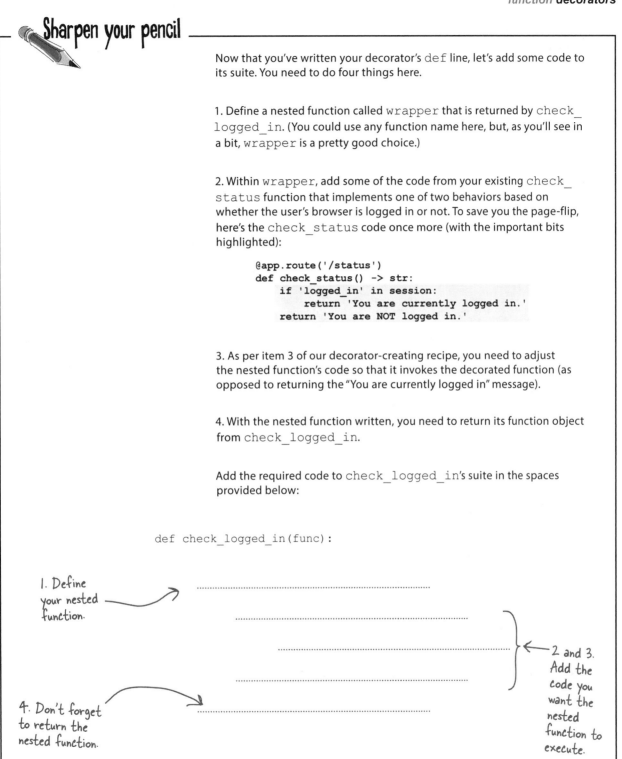

1. Define your nested function.

....

....

.... ⎫
                                                              ⎬ ← 2 and 3.
.... ⎭   Add the
                                                                      code you
                                                                      want the
4. Don't forget to return the nested function.
....   nested
                                                                      function to
                                                                      execute.

Sharpen your pencil
Solution

With your decorator's `def` line written, you were to add some code to its suite. You needed to do four things:

1. Define a nested function called `wrapper` that is returned by `check_logged_in`.

2. Within `wrapper`, add some of the code from your existing `check_status` function that implements one of two behaviors based on whether the user's browser is logged in or not.

3. As per item 3 of our decorator-creating recipe, adjust the nested function's code so that it invokes the decorated function (as opposed to returning the "You are currently logged in" message).

4. With the nested function written, return its function object from `check_logged_in`.

You were to add the required code to `check_logged_in`'s suite in the spaces provided:

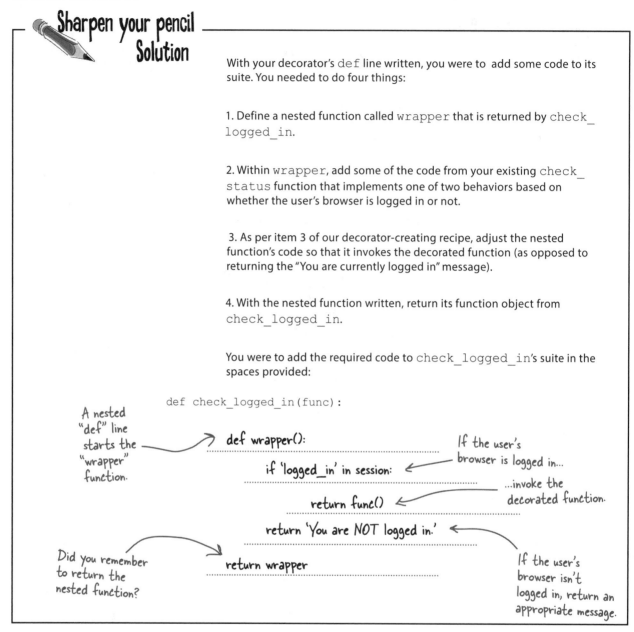

```
def check_logged_in(func):
```

A nested "def" line starts the "wrapper" function.

```
    def wrapper():
```
If the user's browser is logged in...
```
        if 'logged_in' in session:
```
...invoke the decorated function.
```
            return func()
```
If the user's browser isn't logged in, return an appropriate message.
```
        return 'You are NOT logged in.'
```
Did you remember to return the nested function?
```
    return wrapper
```

Can you see why the nested function is called "wrapper"?

If you take a moment to study the decorator's code (so far), you'll see that the nested function not only invokes the decorated function (stored in `func`), but also augments it by *wrapping* extra code around the call. In this case, the extra code is checking to see if the `logged_in` key exists within your webapp's `session`. Critically, if the user's browser is *not* logged in, the decorated function is *never* invoked by `wrapper`.

The Final Step: Handling Arguments

We are nearly there—the "guts" of the decorator's code is in place. What remains is to ensure the decorator handles the decorated function's arguments properly, no matter what they might be. Recall item 4 from the recipe:

 A decorator maintains the decorated function's signature
Your decorator needs to ensure that the function it returns takes the same number and type of arguments as expected by the decorated function.

When a decorator is applied to an existing function, any calls to the existing function are **replaced** by calls to the function returned by the decorator. As you saw in the solution on the previous page, to comply with item 3 of our decorator-creation recipe, we return a wrapped version of the existing function, which implements extra code as needed. This wrapped version *decorates* the existing function.

But there's a problem with this, as doing the wrapping on its own is not enough; the *calling characteristics* of the decorated function need to be maintained, too. This means, for instance, that if your existing function accepts two arguments, your wrapped function also has to accept two arguments. If you could know ahead of time how many arguments to expect, then you could plan accordingly. Unfortunately, you can't know this ahead of time because your decorator can be applied to any existing function, which could have—quite literally—any number and type of arguments.

What to do? The solution is to go "generic," and arrange for the `wrapper` function to support any number and type of arguments. You already know how to do this, as you've already seen what `*args` and `**kwargs` can do.

Remember: `*args` and `**kwargs` support any number and type of arguments.

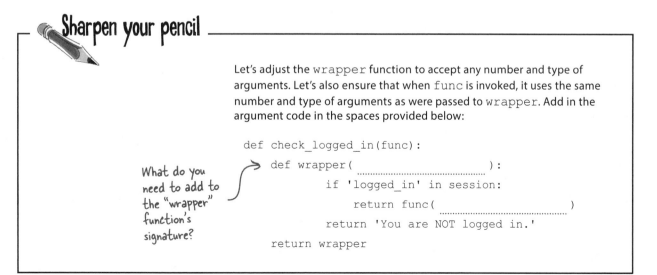

Sharpen your pencil

Let's adjust the `wrapper` function to accept any number and type of arguments. Let's also ensure that when `func` is invoked, it uses the same number and type of arguments as were passed to `wrapper`. Add in the argument code in the spaces provided below:

```
def check_logged_in(func):
    def wrapper(........................................):
        if 'logged_in' in session:
            return func(........................................)
        return 'You are NOT logged in.'
    return wrapper
```

What do you need to add to the "wrapper" function's signature?

Sharpen your pencil
Solution

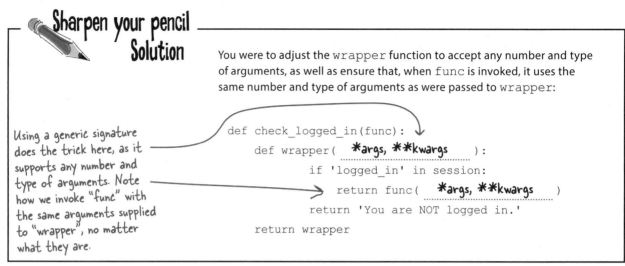

You were to adjust the `wrapper` function to accept any number and type of arguments, as well as ensure that, when `func` is invoked, it uses the same number and type of arguments as were passed to `wrapper`:

Using a generic signature does the trick here, as it supports any number and type of arguments. Note how we invoke "func" with the same arguments supplied to "wrapper", no matter what they are.

```
def check_logged_in(func):
    def wrapper(  *args, **kwargs  ):
        if 'logged_in' in session:
            return func(  *args, **kwargs  )
        return 'You are NOT logged in.'
    return wrapper
```

We're done...or are we?

If you check our decorator-creating recipe, you'd be forgiven for believing that we're done. We are...almost. There are two issues that we still need to deal with: one has to do with all decorators, whereas the other has to do with this specific one.

Let's get the specific issue out of the way first. As the `check_logged_in` decorator is in its own module, we need to ensure that any modules its code refers to are also imported into `checker.py`. The `check_logged_in` decorator uses `session`, which has to be imported from Flask to avoid errors. Handling this is straightforward, as all you need to do is add this `import` statement to the top of `checker.py`:

```
from flask import session
```

The other issue, which affects *all* decorators, has to do with how functions identify themselves to the interpreter. When decorated, and if due care is not taken, a function can forget its identity, which can lead to problems. The reason why this happens is very technical and a little exotic, and it requires a knowledge of Python's internals that most people don't need (or want) to know. Consequently, Python's standard library comes with a module that handles these details for you (so you need never worry about them). All you have to do is remember to import the required module (`functools`), then call a single function (`wraps`).

Perhaps somewhat ironically, the `wraps` function is implemented as a decorator, so you don't actually call it, but rather use it to decorate your `wrapper` function *inside* your own decorator. We've already gone ahead and done this for you, and you'll find the code to the completed `check_logged_in` decorator at the top of the next page.

When creating your own decorators, always import, then use, the "functools" module's "wraps" function.

Your Decorator in All Its Glory

Before continuing, make sure your decorator code *exactly* matches ours:

Be sure to import "session" from the "flask" module.

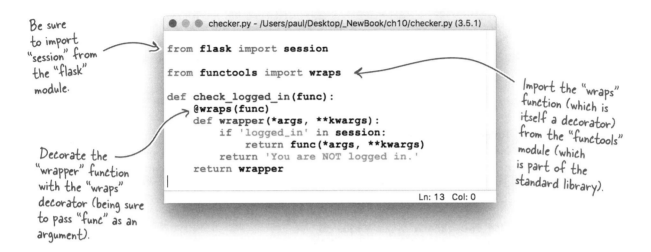

```
checker.py - /Users/paul/Desktop/_NewBook/ch10/checker.py (3.5.1)

from flask import session

from functools import wraps

def check_logged_in(func):
    @wraps(func)
    def wrapper(*args, **kwargs):
        if 'logged_in' in session:
            return func(*args, **kwargs)
        return 'You are NOT logged in.'
    return wrapper
                                              Ln: 13  Col: 0
```

Import the "wraps" function (which is itself a decorator) from the "functools" module (which is part of the standard library).

Decorate the "wrapper" function with the "wraps" decorator (being sure to pass "func" as an argument).

Now that the `checker.py` module contains a completed `check_logged_in` function, let's put it to use within `simple_webapp.py`. Here is the current version of the code to this webapp (which we're showing here over two columns):

```
from flask import Flask, session

app = Flask(__name__)

@app.route('/')
def hello() -> str:
    return 'Hello from the simple webapp.'

@app.route('/page1')
def page1() -> str:
    return 'This is page 1.'

@app.route('/page2')
def page2() -> str:
    return 'This is page 2.'

@app.route('/page3')
def page3() -> str:
    return 'This is page 3.'

@app.route('/login')
def do_login() -> str:
    session['logged_in'] = True
    return 'You are now logged in.'
```

```
@app.route('/logout')
def do_logout() -> str:
    session.pop('logged_in')
    return 'You are now logged out.'

@app.route('/status')
def check_status() -> str:
    if 'logged_in' in session:
        return 'You are currently logged in.'
    return 'You are NOT logged in.'

app.secret_key = 'YouWillNeverGuess...'

if __name__ == '__main__':
    app.run(debug=True)
```

> Recall that our goal here is to restrict access to the */page1*, */page2*, and */page3* URLs, which are currently accessible to any user's browser (based on this code).

Putting Your Decorator to Work

Adjusting the `simple_webapp.py` code to use the `check_logged_in` decorator is not difficult. Here's a list of what needs to happen:

 Import the decorator
The `check_logged_in` decorator needs to be imported from the `checker.py` module. Adding the required `import` statement to the top of our webapp's code does the trick here.

 Remove any unnecessary code
Now that the `check_logged_in` decorator exists, we no longer have any need for the `check_status` function, so it can be removed from `simple_webapp.py`.

 Use the decorator as required
To use the `check_logged_in` decorator, apply it to any of our webapp's functions using the @ syntax.

Here's the code to `simple_webapp.py` once more, with the three changes listed above applied. Note how the */page1*, */page2*, and */page3* URLs now have two decorators associated with them: `@app.route` (which comes with Flask), and `@check_logged_in` (which you've just created):

Apply a decorator to an existing function using the @ syntax.

```
from flask import Flask, session

from checker import check_logged_in

app = Flask(__name__)

@app.route('/')
def hello() -> str:
    return 'Hello from the simple webapp.'

@app.route('/page1')
@check_logged_in
def page1() -> str:
    return 'This is page 1.'

@app.route('/page2')
@check_logged_in
def page2() -> str:
    return 'This is page 2.'
```

```
@app.route('/page3')
@check_logged_in
def page3() -> str:
    return 'This is page 3.'

@app.route('/login')
def do_login() -> str:
    session['logged_in'] = True
    return 'You are now logged in.'

@app.route('/logout')
def do_logout() -> str:
    session.pop('logged_in')
    return 'You are now logged out.'

app.secret_key = 'YouWillNeverGuess...'

if __name__ == '__main__':
    app.run(debug=True)
```

Don't forget to apply these highlighted edits to your webapp *before* continuing

Test Drive

To convince ourselves that our login-checking decorator is working as required, let's take the decorator-enabled version of `simple_webapp.py` for a spin.

With the webapp running, use a browser to try to access */page1* prior to logging in. After logging in, try to access */page1* again and then, after logging out, try to access the restricted content once more. Let's see what happens:

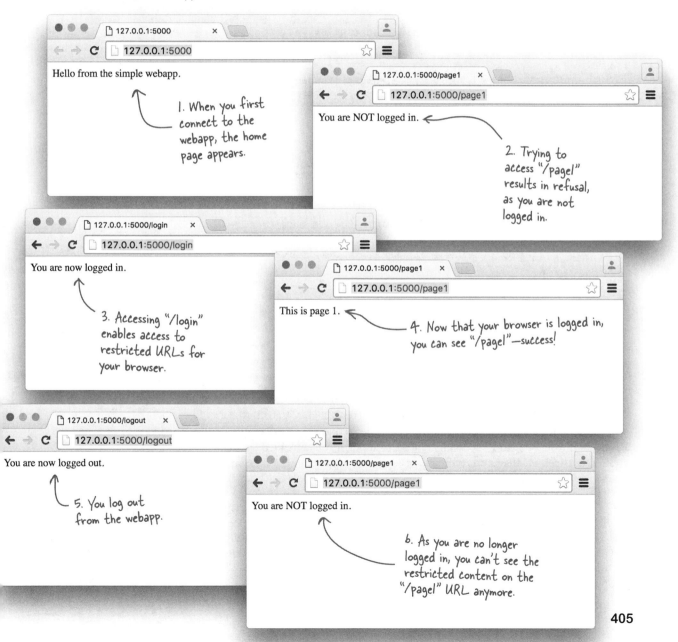

405

The Beauty of Decorators

Take another look at the code for your `check_logged_in` decorator. Note how it abstracts the logic used to check if a user's browser is logged in, putting this (potentially complex) code in one place—*inside* the decorator—and then making it available throughout your code, thanks to the `@check_logged_in` decorator syntax:

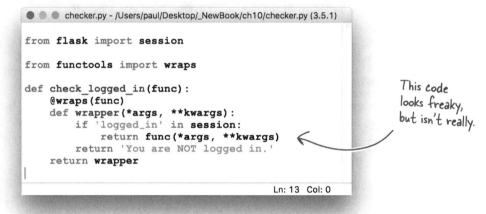

```
● ● ●   checker.py - /Users/paul/Desktop/_NewBook/ch10/checker.py (3.5.1)

from flask import session

from functools import wraps

def check_logged_in(func):
    @wraps(func)
    def wrapper(*args, **kwargs):
        if 'logged_in' in session:
            return func(*args, **kwargs)
        return 'You are NOT logged in.'
    return wrapper
|
                                              Ln: 13  Col: 0
```

This code looks freaky, but isn't really.

Abstracting code in a decorator makes the code that uses it easier to read. Consider this usage of our decorator on the */page2* URL:

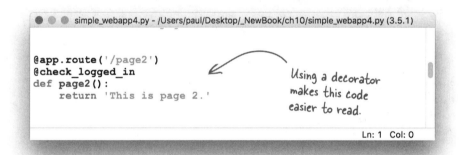

```
● ● ●   simple_webapp4.py - /Users/paul/Desktop/_NewBook/ch10/simple_webapp4.py (3.5.1)

@app.route('/page2')
@check_logged_in
def page2():
    return 'This is page 2.'

                                              Ln: 1  Col: 0
```

Using a decorator makes this code easier to read.

Note how the `page2` function's code is only concerned with what it needs to do: display the */page2* content. In this example, the `page2` code is a single, simple statement; it would be harder to read and understand if it *also* contained the logic required to check whether a user's browser is logged in or not. Using a decorator to separate out the login-checking code is a big win.

This "logic abstraction" is one of the reasons the use of decorators is popular in Python. Another is that, if you think about it, in creating the `check_logged_in` decorator, you've managed to write code that *augments an existing function with extra code, by changing the behavior of the existing function without changing its code*. When it was first introduced earlier in this chapter, this idea was described as "freaky." But, now that you've done it, there's really nothing to it, is there?

Decorators aren't freaky; they're fun.

Creating More Decorators

With the process of creating the `check_logged_in` decorator behind you, you can use its code as the basis of any new decorators you create from here on in.

To make your life easier, here's a generic code template (in the file `tmpl_decorator.py`) that you can use as the basis of any new decorators you write:

```
tmpl_decorator.py - /Users/paul/Desktop/_NewBook/ch10/tmpl_decorator.py (3.5.1)

from functools import wraps

def decorator_name(func):
    @wraps(func)
    def wrapper(*args, **kwargs):
        # 1. Code to execute BEFORE calling the decorated function.

        # 2. Call the decorated function as required, returning its
        #     results if needed.
        return func(*args, **kwargs)

        # 3. Code to execute INSTEAD of calling the decorated function.
    return wrapper

                                                            Ln: 15  Col: 0
```

Replace these comments with your new decorator's code.

This code template can be adjusted as needed to suit your needs. All you need to do is give your new decorator an appropriate name, then replace the three comments in the template with your decorator's specific code.

If it makes sense for your new decorator to invoke the decorated function without returning its results, that's fine. After all, what you put in your `wrapper` function is your code, and you are free to do whatever you want to.

there are no
Dumb Questions

Q: Aren't decorators just like the last chapter's context manager in that they both let me wrap code with additional functionality?

A: That's a great question. The answer is: yes *and* no. Yes, both decorators and context managers augment existing code with additional logic. But no, they are not the same. Decorators are specifically concerned with augmenting existing functions with additional functionality, whereas context mangers are more interested in ensuring your code executes within a specific context, arranging for code to run before a `with` statement as well as ensuring that code **always** executes after a `with` statement. You can do something similar with decorators, but most Python programmers would regard you as a little mad if you were to attempt this. Also, note that your decorator code is under no obligation to do anything after it invokes the decorated function (as is the case with the `check_logged_in` decorator, which does nothing). This decorator behavior is very different from the protocol that context managers are expected to adhere to.

Back to Restricting Access to /viewlog

Ah ha! Now that I can restrict pages for "simple_webapp.py" I can do much the same thing for "vsearch4web.py", too, right?

It's not a case of "much the same": it's EXACTLY the same. It's the same code; just reuse the decorator, do_login, and do_logout functions.

Now that you've created a mechanism that lets you restrict access to certain URLs in simple_webapp.py, it's a no-brainer to apply the same mechanism to any other webapp.

This includes vsearch4web.py, where you had a requirement to restrict access to the */viewlog* URL. All you need to do is copy the do_login and do_logout functions from simple_webapp.py into vsearch4web.py, import the checker.py module, and then decorate the view_the_log function with check_logged_in. Granted, you may want to add some sophistication to do_login and do_logout (by, perhaps, checking user credentials against those stored in a database), but—as regards restricting access to certain URLs—the check_logged_in decorator does most of the heavy lifting for you.

What's Next?

Rather than spend a bunch of pages doing to `vsearch4web.py` what you've just spent a chunk of time doing to `simple_webapp.py`, we're going to leave adjusting `vsearch4web.py` for you to do *on your own*. At the start of the next chapter, we'll present an updated version of the `vsearch4web.py` webapp for you to compare with yours, as our updated code is used to frame the discussion in the next chapter.

To date, all of the code in this book has been written under the assumption that nothing bad ever happens, and nothing ever goes wrong. This was a deliberate strategy on our part, as we wanted to ensure you had a good grasp of Python before getting into topics such as error correction, error avoidance, error detection, exception handling, and the like.

We have now reached the point where we can no longer follow this strategy. The environments within which our code runs are real, and things can (and do) go wrong. Some things are fixable (or avoidable), and some aren't. If at all possible, you'll want your code to handle most error situations, only resulting in a crash when something truly exceptional happens that is beyond your control. In the next chapter, we look at various strategies for deciding what's a reasonable thing to do when stuff goes wrong.

Prior to that, though, here's a quick review of this chapter's key points.

BULLET POINTS

- When you need to store server-side state within a Flask webapp, use the ***session*** dictionary (and don't forget to set a hard-to-guess ***secret_key***).

- You can pass a function as an argument to another function. Using the function's name (without the parentheses) gives you a **function object**, which can be manipulated like any other variable.

- When you use a function object as an argument to a function, you can have the receiving function **invoke** the passed-in function object by appending parentheses.

- A function can be **nested** inside an enclosing function's suite (and is only visible within the enclosing scope).

- In addition to accepting a function object as an argument, functions can **return** a nested function as a return value.

- `*args` is shorthand for "expand to a list of items."

- `**kwargs` is shorthand for "expand to a dictionary of keys and values." When you see "kw," think "keywords."

- Both `*` and `**` can also be used "on the way in," in that a list or keyword collection can be passed into a function as a single (expandable) argument.

- Using (`*args`, `**kwargs`) as a **function signature** lets you create functions that accept any number and type of arguments.

- Using the new function features from this chapter, you learned how to create a **function decorator**, which changes the behavior of an existing function without the need to change the function's actual code. This sounds freaky, but is quite a bit of fun (and is very useful, too).

Chapter 10's Code, 1 of 2

This is "quick_session.py".

```python
from flask import Flask, session

app = Flask(__name__)

app.secret_key = 'YouWillNeverGuess'


@app.route('/setuser/<user>')
def setuser(user: str) -> str:
    session['user'] = user
    return 'User value set to: ' + session['user']


@app.route('/getuser')
def getuser() -> str:
    return 'User value is currently set to: ' + session['user']


if __name__ == '__main__':
    app.run(debug=True)
```

```python
from flask import session

from functools import wraps

def check_logged_in(func):
    @wraps(func)
    def wrapper(*args, **kwargs):
        if 'logged_in' in session:
            return func(*args, **kwargs)
        return 'You are NOT logged in.'
    return wrapper
```

This is "checker.py", which contains the code to this chapter's decorator: "check_logged_in".

This is "tmpl_decorator.py", which is a handy decorator-creating template for you to reuse as you see fit.

```python
from functools import wraps

def decorator_name(func):
    @wraps(func)
    def wrapper(*args, **kwargs):
        # 1. Code to execute BEFORE calling the decorated function.

        # 2. Call the decorated function as required, returning its
        #    results if needed.
        return func(*args, **kwargs)

        # 3. Code to execute INSTEAD of calling the decorated function.
    return wrapper
```

Chapter 10's Code, 2 of 2

```
from flask import Flask, session

from checker import check_logged_in

app = Flask(__name__)


@app.route('/')
def hello() -> str:
    return 'Hello from the simple webapp.'


@app.route('/page1')
@check_logged_in
def page1() -> str:
    return 'This is page 1.'


@app.route('/page2')
@check_logged_in
def page2() -> str:
    return 'This is page 2.'


@app.route('/page3')
@check_logged_in
def page3() -> str:
    return 'This is page 3.'


@app.route('/login')
def do_login() -> str:
    session['logged_in'] = True
    return 'You are now logged in.'


@app.route('/logout')
def do_logout() -> str:
    session.pop('logged_in')
    return 'You are now logged out.'


app.secret_key = 'YouWillNeverGuessMySecretKey'

if __name__ == '__main__':
    app.run(debug=True)
```

This is "simple_webapp.py", which pulls all of this chapter's code together. When you need to restrict access to specific URLs, base your strategy on this webapp's mechanism.

We think the use of decorators makes this webapp's code easy to read and understand. Don't you? ☺

11 exception handling

What to Do When Things Go Wrong

I've tested this rope to destruction...what can possibly go wrong?

Things go wrong, all the time—no matter how good your code is.

You've successfully executed all of the examples in this book, and you're likely confident all of the code presented thus far works. But does this mean the code is robust? Probably not. Writing code based on the assumption that nothing bad ever happens is (at best) naive. At worst, it's dangerous, as unforeseen things do (and will) happen. It's much better if you're wary while coding, as opposed to trusting. Care is needed to ensure your code does what you want it to, as well as reacts properly when things go south. In this chapter, you'll not only see what can go wrong, but also learn what to do when (and, oftentimes, before) things do.

♪Long Exercise

We're starting this chapter by diving right in. Presented below is the latest code to the `vsearch4web.py` webapp. As you'll see, we've updated this code to use the `check_logged_in` decorator from the last chapter to control when the information presented by the */viewlog* URL is (and isn't) visible to users.

Take as long as you need to read this code, then use a pencil to circle and annotate the parts you think might cause problems when operating within a production environment. Highlight *everything* that you think might cause an issue, not just potential runtime issues or errors.

```python
from flask import Flask, render_template, request, escape, session
from vsearch import search4letters

from DBcm import UseDatabase
from checker import check_logged_in


app = Flask(__name__)

app.config['dbconfig'] = {'host': '127.0.0.1',
                          'user': 'vsearch',
                          'password': 'vsearchpasswd',
                          'database': 'vsearchlogDB', }

@app.route('/login')
def do_login() -> str:
    session['logged_in'] = True
    return 'You are now logged in.'

@app.route('/logout')
def do_logout() -> str:
    session.pop('logged_in')
    return 'You are now logged out.'

def log_request(req: 'flask_request', res: str) -> None:
    with UseDatabase(app.config['dbconfig']) as cursor:
        _SQL = """insert into log
                    (phrase, letters, ip, browser_string, results)
                    values
                    (%s, %s, %s, %s, %s)"""
        cursor.execute(_SQL, (req.form['phrase'],
                              req.form['letters'],
                              req.remote_addr,
                              req.user_agent.browser,
                              res, ))
```

```
@app.route('/search4', methods=['POST'])
def do_search() -> 'html':
    phrase = request.form['phrase']
    letters = request.form['letters']
    title = 'Here are your results:'
    results = str(search4letters(phrase, letters))
    log_request(request, results)
    return render_template('results.html',
                           the_title=title,
                           the_phrase=phrase,
                           the_letters=letters,
                           the_results=results,)


@app.route('/')
@app.route('/entry')
def entry_page() -> 'html':
    return render_template('entry.html',
                           the_title='Welcome to search4letters on the web!')


@app.route('/viewlog')
@check_logged_in
def view_the_log() -> 'html':
    with UseDatabase(app.config['dbconfig']) as cursor:
        _SQL = """select phrase, letters, ip, browser_string, results
                    from log"""
        cursor.execute(_SQL)
        contents = cursor.fetchall()
    titles = ('Phrase', 'Letters', 'Remote_addr', 'User_agent', 'Results')
    return render_template('viewlog.html',
                           the_title='View Log',
                           the_row_titles=titles,
                           the_data=contents,)


app.secret_key = 'YouWillNeverGuessMySecretKey'

if __name__ == '__main__':
    app.run(debug=True)
```

Long Exercise Solution

You were to take as long as you needed to read the code shown below (which is an updated version of the `vsearch4web.py` webapp). Then, using a pencil, you were to circle and annotate the parts you thought might cause problems when operating within a production environment. You were to highlight everything you thought might cause an issue, not just potential runtime issues or errors. (We've numbered our annotations for ease of reference.)

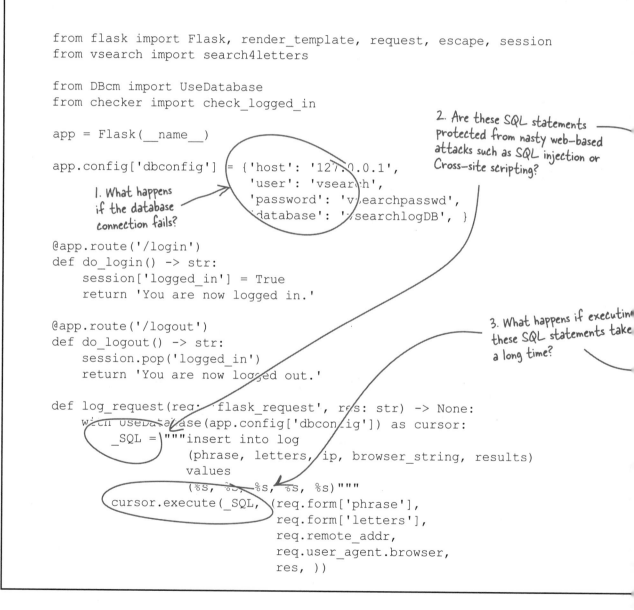

```python
from flask import Flask, render_template, request, escape, session
from vsearch import search4letters

from DBcm import UseDatabase
from checker import check_logged_in

app = Flask(__name__)

app.config['dbconfig'] = {'host': '127.0.0.1',
                          'user': 'vsearch',
                          'password': 'vsearchpasswd',
                          'database': 'vsearchlogDB', }

@app.route('/login')
def do_login() -> str:
    session['logged_in'] = True
    return 'You are now logged in.'

@app.route('/logout')
def do_logout() -> str:
    session.pop('logged_in')
    return 'You are now logged out.'

def log_request(req: 'flask_request', res: str) -> None:
    with UseDatabase(app.config['dbconfig']) as cursor:
        _SQL = """insert into log
                  (phrase, letters, ip, browser_string, results)
                  values
                  (%s, %s, %s, %s, %s)"""
        cursor.execute(_SQL, (req.form['phrase'],
                              req.form['letters'],
                              req.remote_addr,
                              req.user_agent.browser,
                              res, ))
```

Annotations:

1. What happens if the database connection fails?

2. Are these SQL statements protected from nasty web-based attacks such as SQL injection or Cross-site scripting?

3. What happens if executing these SQL statements take a long time?

```
@app.route('/search4', methods=['POST'])
def do_search() -> 'html':
    phrase = request.form['phrase']
    letters = request.form['letters']
    title = 'Here are your results:'
    results = str(search4letters(phrase, letters))
    log_request(request, results)
    return render_template('results.html',
                            the_title=title,
                            the_phrase=phrase,
                            the_letters=letters,
                            the_results=results,)
```

4. What happens if this call fails?

```
@app.route('/')
@app.route('/entry')
def entry_page() -> 'html':
    return render_template('entry.html',
                            the_title='Welcome to search4letters on the web!')


@app.route('/viewlog')
@check_logged_in
def view_the_log() -> 'html':
    with UseDatabase(app.config['dbconfig']) as cursor:
        _SQL = """select phrase, letters, ip, browser_string, results
                  from log"""
        cursor.execute(_SQL)
        contents = cursor.fetchall()
    titles = ('Phrase', 'Letters', 'Remote_addr', 'User_agent', 'Results')
    return render_template('viewlog.html',
                            the_title='View Log',
                            the_row_titles=titles,
                            the_data=contents,)


app.secret_key = 'YouWillNeverGuessMySecretKey'

if __name__ == '__main__':
    app.run(debug=True)
```

Databases Aren't Always Available

We've identified four potential issues with the `vsearch4web.py` code, and we concede that there may be many more, but we'll worry about these four issues for now. Let's consider each of the four issues in more detail (which we do here and on the next few pages, by simply describing the problems; *we'll work on solutions later in this chapter*). First up is worrying about the backend database:

 What happens if the database connection fails?
Our webapp blissfully assumes that the backend database is always operational and available, but it may not be (for any number of reasons). At the moment, it is unclear what happens when the database is down, as our code does not consider this eventuality.

Let's see what happens if we temporarily switch *off* the backend database. As you can see below, our webapp loads fine, but as soon as we do anything, an intimidating error message appears:

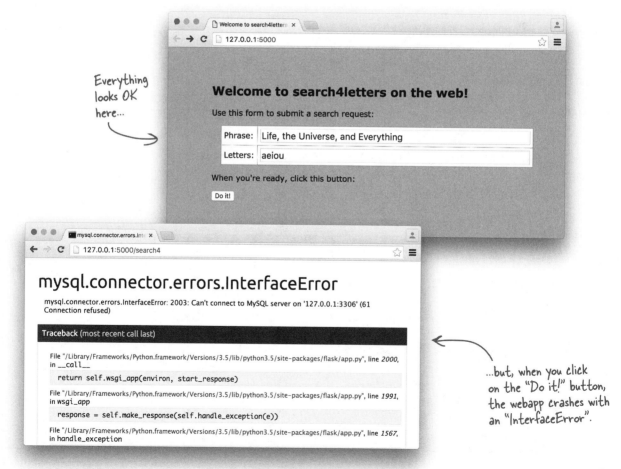

Everything looks OK here...

...but, when you click on the "Do it!" button, the webapp crashes with an "InterfaceError".

Web Attacks Are a Real Pain

As well as worrying about issues with your backend database, you also need to
worry about nasty individuals trying to do nasty things to your webapp, which
brings us to the second issue:

 Is our webapp protected from web attacks?
The phrases *SQL injection (SQLi)* and *Cross-site scripting (XSS)* should
strike fear in the heart of every web developer. The former allows
attackers to exploit your backend database, while the latter allows them
to exploit your website. There are other web exploits that you'll need to
worry about, but these are the "big two."

As with the first issue, let's see what happens when we try to simulate these exploits
against our webapp. As you can see, it appears we're ready for both of them:

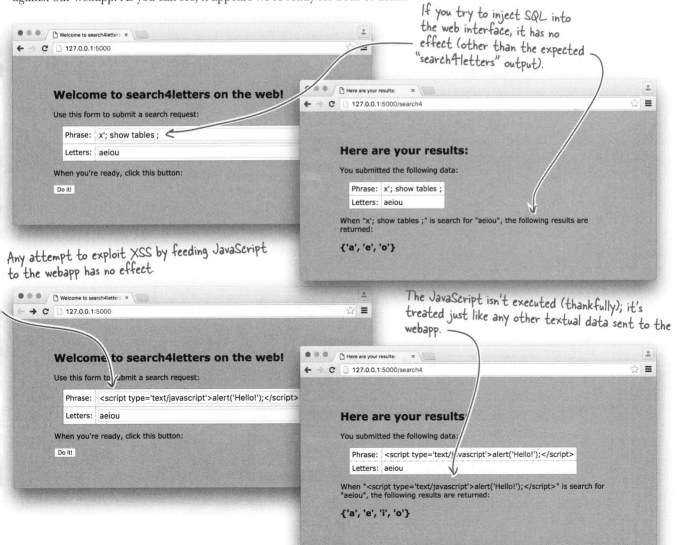

If you try to inject SQL into the web interface, it has no effect (other than the expected "search4letters" output).

Any attempt to exploit XSS by feeding JavaScript to the webapp has no effect.

The JavaScript isn't executed (thankfully); it's treated just like any other textual data sent to the webapp.

Input-Output Is (Sometimes) Slow

At the moment, our webapp communicates with our backend database in an almost instantaneous manner, and users of our webapp notice little or no delay as the webapp interacts with the database. But imagine if the interactions with the backend database took some time, perhaps seconds:

 What happens if something takes a long time?
Perhaps the backend database is on another machine, in another building, on another continent...what would happen then?

Communications with the backend database may take time. In fact, whenever your code has to interact with something that's external to it (for example: a file, a database, a network, or whatever), the interaction can take any amount of time, the determination of which is usually beyond your control. Despite this lack of control, you do have to be cognizant that some operations may be lengthy.

To demonstrate this issue, let's add an *artificial* delay to our webapp (using the `sleep` function, which is part of the standard library's `time` module). Add this line of code to the top of your webapp (near the other `import` statements):

```
from time import sleep
```

With the above `import` statement inserted, edit the `log_request` function and insert this line of code before the `with` statement:

```
sleep(15)
```

If you restart your webapp, then initiate a search, there's a very distinct delay while your web browser waits for your webapp to catch up. As web delays go, 15 seconds will feel like a lifetime, which will prompt most users of your webapp to believe something has *crashed*:

After clicking on the "Do it!" button, your web browser waits...and waits... and waits...and waits...

> ● ● ●   Welcome to search4letters   +
>
> ‹ › ✕ ⠿   🌐 127.0.0.1:5000   ♥ ↥ ▭
>
> ## Welcome to search4letters on the web!
>
> Use this form to submit a search request:
>
> | Phrase: | This search takes 15 seconds |
> | Letters: | aeiou |
>
> When you're ready, click this button:
>
> Do it!
>
> Waiting for 127.0.0.1...

Your Function Calls Can Fail

The final issue identified during this chapter's opening exercise relates to the
function call to `log_request` within the `do_search` function:

 What happens if a function call fails?
There's never a guarantee that a function call will succeed, especially if
the function in question interacts with something external to your code.

We've already seen what can happen when the backend database is unavailable—
the webapp crashes with an `InterfaceError`:

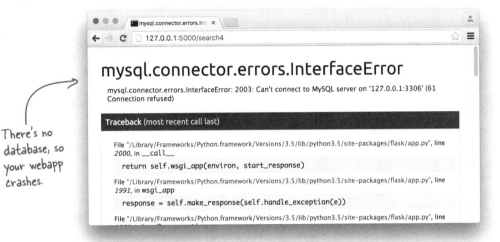

There's no
database, so
your webapp
crashes.

Other problems can surface, too. To simulate another error, find the **sleep(15)**
line you added from the Issue 3 discussion, and replace it with a single statement:
raise. When executed by the interpreter, `raise` forces a runtime error. If you
try your webapp again, a *different* error occurs this time:

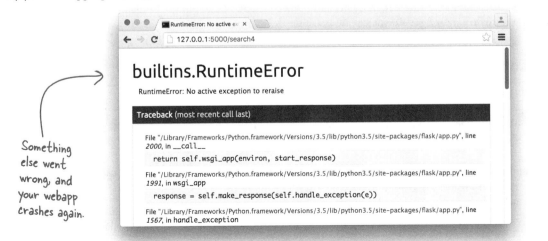

Something
else went
wrong, and
your webapp
crashes again.

Before flipping the
page, remove that
call to "raise" from
your code to ensure
the webapp starts
working again.

Considering the Identified Problems

We've identified four issues with the `vsearch4web.py` code. Let's revisit each and consider our next steps.

1. Your database connection fails

Errors occur whenever an external system your code relies on is unavailable. The interpreter reported an `InterfaceError` when this happened. It's possible to spot, then react to, these types of errors using Python's built-in exception-handling mechanism. If you can spot when an error occurs, you're then in a position to do something about it.

2. Your application is subjected to an attack

Although a case can be made that worrying about attacks on your application is only of concern to web developers, developing practices that improve the robustness of the code you write are always worth considering. With `vsearch4web.py`, dealing with the "big two" web attack vectors, *SQL injection (SQLi)* and *Cross-site scripting (XSS)*, appears to be well in hand. This is more of a happy accident than by design on your part, as the Jinja2 library is built to guard against *XSS* by default, escaping any potentially problematic strings (recall that the JavaScript we tried to trick our webapp into executing had no effect). As regards *SQLi*, our use of DB-API's parameterized SQL strings (with all those ? placeholders) ensures—again, thanks to the way these modules were designed—that your code is protected from this entire class of attack.

Geek Bits

If you want to know more about *SQLi* and *XSS*, Wikipedia is a great place to start. See *https://en.wikipedia.org/wiki/SQL_injection* and *https://en.wikipedia.org/wiki/Cross-site_scripting*, respectively. And remember, there are all kinds of other types of attack that can cause problems for your app; these are just the two biggies.

3. Your code takes a long time to execute

If your code takes a long time to execute, you have to consider the impact on your user's experience. If your user doesn't notice, then you're likely OK. However, if your user has to wait, you may have to do something about it (otherwise, your user may decide the wait isn't worth it, and go elsewhere).

4. Your function call fails

It's not just external systems that generate exceptions in the interpreter—your code can raise exceptions, too. When this happens, you need to be ready to spot the exception, then recover as needed. The mechanism you use to enable this behavior is the same one hinted at in the discussion of issue 1, above.

So...where do we *start* when dealing with these four issues? It's possible to use the same mechanism to deal with issues 1 and 4, so that's where we'll begin.

Always Try to Execute Error-Prone Code

When something goes wrong with your code, Python raises a runtime **exception**. Think of an exception as a controlled program crash triggered by the interpreter.

As you've seen with issues 1 and 4, exceptions can be raised under many different circumstances. In fact, the interpreter comes with a whole host of built-in exception types, of which `RuntimeError` (from issue 4) is only one example. As well as the built-in exception types, it's possible to define your own custom exceptions, and you've seen an example of this too: the `InterfaceError` exception (from issue 1) is defined by the *MySQL Connector* module.

For a complete list of the built-in exceptions, see https://docs.python.org/3/library/exceptions.html.

To spot (and, hopefully, recover from) a runtime exception, deploy Python's `try` statement, which can help you manage exceptions as they occur at runtime.

To see `try` in action, let's first consider a snippet of code that might fail when executed. Here are three innocent-looking, but potentially problematic, lines of code for you to consider:

```
try_examples.py - /Users/paul/Desktop/_NewBo...
with open('myfile.txt') as fh:
    file_data = fh.read()
print(file_data)

                                  Ln: 5  Col: 0
```

There's nothing weird or wonderful going on here: the named file is opened, and its data is obtained and then displayed on screen.

There's nothing wrong with these three lines of code and—as currently written—they will execute. However, this code might fail if it can't access `myfile.txt`. Perhaps the file is missing, or your code doesn't have the necessary file-reading permissions. When the code fails, an exception is raised:

When a runtime error occurs, Python displays a "traceback", which details what went wrong, and where. In this case, the interpreter thinks the problem is on line 2.

```
                        Python 3.5.1 Shell
>>>
========= RESTART: /Users/paul/Desktop/_NewBook/ch11/try_examples.py =========
Traceback (most recent call last):
  File "/Users/paul/Desktop/_NewBook/ch11/try_examples.py", line 2, in <module>
    with open('myfile.txt') as fh:
FileNotFoundError: [Errno 2] No such file or directory: 'myfile.txt'
>>>
>>>
                                                        Ln: 119  Col: 4
```

Whoops!

Let's start learning what `try` can do by adjusting the above code snippet to protect against this `FileNotFoundError` exception.

Despite being ugly to look at, the traceback message is useful.

Catching an Error Is Not Enough

When a runtime error occurs, an exception is **raised**. If you *ignore* a raised exception it is referred to as **uncaught**, and the interpreter will terminate your code, then display a runtime error message (as shown in the example from the bottom of the last page). That said, raised exceptions can also be **caught** (i.e., dealt with) with the `try` statement. Note that it's not enough to catch runtime errors, you *also* have to decide what you're going to do next.

Perhaps you'll decide to deliberately ignore the raised exception, and keep going...with your fingers firmly crossed. Or maybe you'll try to run some other code in place of the code that crashed, and keep going. Or perhaps the best thing to do is to log the error before terminating your application as cleanly as possible. Whatever you decide to do, the `try` statement can help.

In its most basic form, the `try` statement allows you to react whenever the execution of your code results in a raised exception. To protect code with `try`, put the code within `try`'s suite. If an exception occurs, the code in the `try`'s suite terminates, and then the code in the `try`'s `except` suite runs. The `except` suite is where you define what you want to happen next.

Let's update the code snippet from the last page to display a short message whenever the `FileNotFoundError` exception is raised. The code on the left is what you had previously, while the code on the right has been amended to take advantage of what `try` and `except` have to offer:

> When a runtime error is raised, it can be caught or uncaught: "try" lets you catch a raised error, and "except" lets you do something about it.

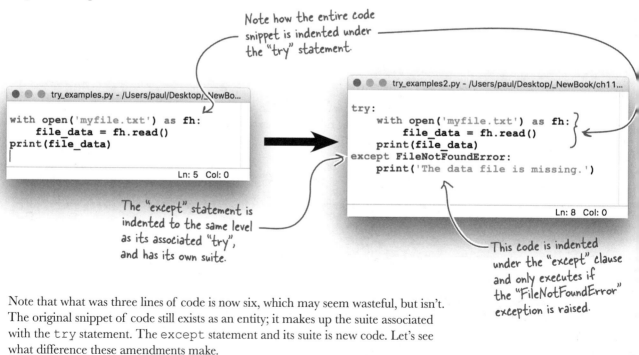

Note how the entire code snippet is indented under the "try" statement.

```
try_examples.py - /Users/paul/Desktop/_NewBo...

with open('myfile.txt') as fh:
    file_data = fh.read()
print(file_data)

                                    Ln: 5  Col: 0
```

The "except" statement is indented to the same level as its associated "try", and has its own suite.

```
try_examples2.py - /Users/paul/Desktop/_NewBook/ch11...

try:
    with open('myfile.txt') as fh:
        file_data = fh.read()
    print(file_data)
except FileNotFoundError:
    print('The data file is missing.')

                                          Ln: 8  Col: 0
```

This code is indented under the "except" clause and only executes if the "FileNotFoundError" exception is raised.

Note that what was three lines of code is now six, which may seem wasteful, but isn't. The original snippet of code still exists as an entity; it makes up the suite associated with the `try` statement. The `except` statement and its suite is new code. Let's see what difference these amendments make.

TEST DRIVE

Let's take the `try...except` version of your code snippet for a spin. If `myfile.txt` exists and is readable by your code, its contents will appear on screen. If not, a run-time exception is raised. We already know that `myfile.txt` does not exist, but now, instead of seeing the ugly traceback message from earlier, the exception-handling code fires and we're presented with a friendlier message (even though our code snippet *still* crashed):

The first time you ran the code snippet, the interpreter generated this ugly traceback.

```
● ● ●                          Python 3.5.1 Shell
>>>
========= RESTART: /Users/paul/Desktop/_NewBook/ch11/try_examples.py =========
Traceback (most recent call last):
  File "/Users/paul/Desktop/_NewBook/ch11/try_examples.py", line 2, in <module>
    with open('myfile.txt') as fh:
FileNotFoundError: [Errno 2] No such file or directory: 'myfile.txt'
>>>
>>>
========= RESTART: /Users/paul/Desktop/_NewBook/ch11/try_examples2.py ========
The data file is missing.
>>>
                                                                    Ln: 17  Col: 4
```

The new version of the code produces a much friendlier messages thanks to "try" and "except".

There can be more than one exception raised...

This new behavior is better, but what happens if `myfile.txt` exists but your code does not have permission to read from it? To see what happens, we created the file, then set its permissions to simulate this eventuality. Rerunning the new code produces this output:

Yikes! We're back to seeing an ugly traceback message, as a "PermissionError" was raised.

```
● ● ●                          Python 3.5.1 Shell
>>>
========= RESTART: /Users/paul/Desktop/_NewBook/ch11/try_examples2.py ========
The data file is missing.
>>>
========= RESTART: /Users/paul/Desktop/_NewBook/ch11/try_examples2.py ========
Traceback (most recent call last):
  File "/Users/paul/Desktop/_NewBook/ch11/try_examples2.py", line 3, in <module>
    with open('myfile.txt') as fh:
PermissionError: [Errno 13] Permission denied: 'myfile.txt'
>>>
>>>
                                                                    Ln: 24  Col: 4
```

try Once, but except Many Times

To protect against another exception being raised, simply add another `except` suite to your `try` statement, identifying the exception you're interested in and providing whatever code you deem necessary in the new `except`'s suite. Here's another updated version of the code that handles the `PermissionError` exception (should it be raised):

In addition to "FileNotFoundError" exceptions, this code also handles a "PermissionError".

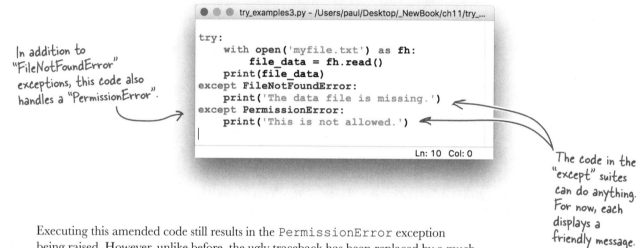

```
try:
    with open('myfile.txt') as fh:
        file_data = fh.read()
    print(file_data)
except FileNotFoundError:
    print('The data file is missing.')
except PermissionError:
    print('This is not allowed.')
```

The code in the "except" suites can do anything. For now, each displays a friendly message.

Executing this amended code still results in the `PermissionError` exception being raised. However, unlike before, the ugly traceback has been replaced by a much friendlier message:

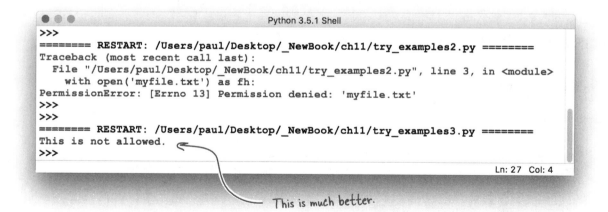

```
>>>
======= RESTART: /Users/paul/Desktop/_NewBook/ch11/try_examples2.py =======
Traceback (most recent call last):
  File "/Users/paul/Desktop/_NewBook/ch11/try_examples2.py", line 3, in <module>
    with open('myfile.txt') as fh:
PermissionError: [Errno 13] Permission denied: 'myfile.txt'
>>>
>>>
======= RESTART: /Users/paul/Desktop/_NewBook/ch11/try_examples3.py =======
This is not allowed.
>>>
```

This is much better.

This is looking good: you've managed to adjust what happens whenever the file you're hoping to work with isn't there (it doesn't exist), or is inaccessible (you don't have the correct permissions). But what happens if an exception is raised that you weren't expecting?

A Lot of Things Can Go Wrong

Before answering the question posed at the bottom of the last page—*what happens if an exception is raised that you weren't expecting?*—take a look at some of Python 3's built-in exceptions (which are copied directly from the Python documentation). Don't be surprised if you're struck by just how many there are:

```
       . . .
     Exception
          +-- StopIteration
          +-- StopAsyncIteration
          +-- ArithmeticError
          |    +-- FloatingPointError
          |    +-- OverflowError
          |    +-- ZeroDivisionError
          +-- AssertionError
          +-- AttributeError
          +-- BufferError
          +-- EOFError
          +-- ImportError
          +-- LookupError
          |    +-- IndexError
          |    +-- KeyError
          +-- MemoryError
          +-- NameError
          |    +-- UnboundLocalError
          +-- OSError
          |    +-- BlockingIOError
          |    +-- ChildProcessError
          |    +-- ConnectionError
          |    |    +-- BrokenPipeError
          |    |    +-- ConnectionAbortedError
          |    |    +-- ConnectionRefusedError
          |    |    +-- ConnectionResetError
          |    +-- FileExistsError
          |    +-- FileNotFoundError
          |    +-- InterruptedError
          |    +-- IsADirectoryError
          |    +-- NotADirectoryError
          |    +-- PermissionError
          |    +-- ProcessLookupError
          |    +-- TimeoutError
               . . .
```

All the built-in exceptions inherit from a class called "Exception".

There are an awful lot of these, aren't there?

Here's the two exceptions that our code currently handles.

It would be crazy to try to write a separate except suite for each of these runtime exceptions, as some of them may never occur. That said, some *might* occur, so you do need to worry about them a little bit. Rather than try to handle each exception *individually*, Python lets you define a **catch-all** except suite, which fires whenever a runtime exception occurs that you haven't specifically identified.

The Catch-All Exception Handler

Let's see what happens when some other error occurs. To simulate just such an occurrence, we've changed `myfile.txt` from a file into a folder. Let's see what happens when we run the code now:

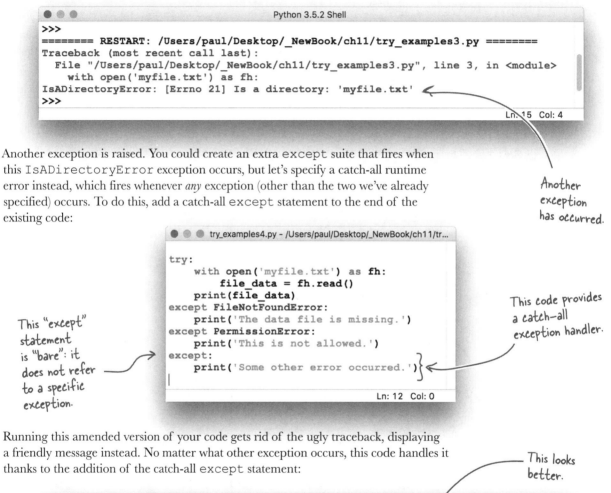

```
● ● ●                     Python 3.5.2 Shell
>>>
======== RESTART: /Users/paul/Desktop/_NewBook/ch11/try_examples3.py ========
Traceback (most recent call last):
  File "/Users/paul/Desktop/_NewBook/ch11/try_examples3.py", line 3, in <module>
    with open('myfile.txt') as fh:
IsADirectoryError: [Errno 21] Is a directory: 'myfile.txt'
>>>
                                                              Ln: 15  Col: 4
```

Another exception has occurred.

Another exception is raised. You could create an extra `except` suite that fires when this `IsADirectoryError` exception occurs, but let's specify a catch-all runtime error instead, which fires whenever *any* exception (other than the two we've already specified) occurs. To do this, add a catch-all `except` statement to the end of the existing code:

```
● ● ●    try_examples4.py - /Users/paul/Desktop/_NewBook/ch11/tr...
try:
    with open('myfile.txt') as fh:
        file_data = fh.read()
    print(file_data)
except FileNotFoundError:
    print('The data file is missing.')
except PermissionError:
    print('This is not allowed.')
except:
    print('Some other error occurred.')
|
                                             Ln: 12  Col: 0
```

This "except" statement is "bare": it does not refer to a specific exception.

This code provides a catch-all exception handler.

Running this amended version of your code gets rid of the ugly traceback, displaying a friendly message instead. No matter what other exception occurs, this code handles it thanks to the addition of the catch-all `except` statement:

This looks better.

```
● ● ●                     Python 3.5.2 Shell
>>>
======== RESTART: /Users/paul/Desktop/_NewBook/ch11/try_examples3.py ========
Traceback (most recent call last):
  File "/Users/paul/Desktop/_NewBook/ch11/try_examples3.py", line 3, in <module>
    with open('myfile.txt') as fh:
IsADirectoryError: [Errno 21] Is a directory: 'myfile.txt'
>>>
======== RESTART: /Users/paul/Desktop/_NewBook/ch11/try_examples4.py ========
Some other error occurred.
>>>
                                                              Ln: 16  Col: 4
```

Haven't We Just Lost Something?

OK. I get what's going on here. But does this code not now hide the fact that we just had an "IsADirectoryError"? Isn't it important to know exactly which error you've encountered?

Ah, yes...good catch.

This latest code has tidied up the output (in that the ugly traceback is gone), but you've also lost some important information: you no longer know what the *specific* issue with your code was.

Knowing what exception was raised is often important, so Python lets you get at the data associated with the most-recent exception information *as it's being handled*. There are two ways to do this: using the facilities of the `sys` module, and using an extension to the `try/except` syntax.

Let's look at both of these techniques.

---

there are no
Dumb Questions

Q: Is it possible to create a catch-all exception handler that does nothing?

A: Yes. It is often tempting to add this `except` suite to the bottom of a `try` statement:

```
except:
        pass
```

Please try not to do this. This `except` suite implements a catch-all that *ignores* any other exception (presumedly in the misguided hope that if something is ignored it might go away). This is a dangerous practice, as—at the very least—an unexpected exception should result in an error message appearing on screen. So, be sure to always write error-checking code that handles exceptions, as opposed to ignores them.

Learning About Exceptions from "sys"

The standard library comes with a module called `sys` that provides access to the interpreters, *internals* (a set of variables and functions available at runtime).

One such function is `exc_info`, which provides information on the exception currently being handled. When invoked, `exc_info` returns a three-valued tuple where the first value indicates the exception's **type**, the second details the exception's **value**, and the third contains a **traceback object** that provides access to the traceback message (should you need it). When there is no currently available exception, `exc_info` returns the Python null value for each of the tuple values, which looks like this: (None, None, None).

Knowing all of this, let's experiment at the >>> shell. In the IDLE session that follows, we've written some code that's always going to fail (as dividing by zero is *never* a good idea). A catch-all `except` suite uses the `sys.exc_info` function to extract and display data relating to the currently firing exception:

> To learn more about "sys", see https://docs.python.org/3/library/sys.html.

```
Python 3.5.2 Shell
>>>
=========================== RESTART: Shell ===========================
>>>
>>> import sys            ← ——— Be sure to import the "sys" module.
>>>
>>> try:
        1/0  ←            Dividing by zero is *never* a good idea...and when your code
except:                   divides by zero an exception occurs
        err = sys.exc_info() ←    Let's extract and display the data associated
        for e in err:             with the currently occurring exception.
            print(e)  ←

<class 'ZeroDivisionError'>              Here's the data associated with the
division by zero             ←          exception, which confirms that we
<traceback object at 0x105b22188>       have an issue with divide-by-zero.
>>> |
                                                          Ln: 117  Col: 4
```

It's possible to delve deeper into the traceback object to learn more about what just happened, but this already feels like too much work, doesn't it? All we really want to know is what *type* of exception occurred.

To make this (and your life) easier, Python extends the `try/except` syntax to make it convenient to get at the information returned by the `sys.exc_info` function, and it does this without you having to remember to import the `sys` module, or wrangle with the tuple returned by that function.

Recall from a few pages back that the interpreter arranges exceptions in a hierarchy, with each exception inheriting from one called `Exception`. Let's take advantage of this hierarchical arrangement as we rewrite our catch-all exception handler.

> Recall the exception hierarchy from earlier.

```
...
Exception
    +-- StopIteration
    +-- StopAsyncIteration
    +-- ArithmeticError
    |    +-- FloatingPointError
    |    +-- OverflowError
    |    +-- ZeroDivisionError
    +-- AssertionError
    +-- AttributeError
    +-- BufferError
    +-- EOFError
    ...
```

The Catch-All Exception Handler, Revisited

Consider your current code, which explicitly identifies the two exceptions you want to handle (`FileNotFoundError` and `PermissionError`), as well as provides a generic catch-all `except` suite (to handle everything else):

This code works, but doesn't really tell you much when some unexpected exception occurs.

Note how, when referring to a *specific* exception, we've identified the exception by name after the `except` keyword. As well as identifying specific exceptions after `except`, it's also possible to identify *classes* of exceptions using any of the names in the hierarchy.

Recall that all the exceptions inherit from "Exception".

```
        ...
Exception
    +-- StopIteration
    +-- StopAsyncIteration
    +-- ArithmeticError
    |       +-- FloatingPointError
    |       +-- OverflowError
    |       +-- ZeroDivisionError
    +-- AssertionError
    +-- AttributeError
    +-- BufferError
    +-- EOFError
        ...
```

For instance, if you're only interested in knowing that an arithmetic error has occurred (as opposed to—specifically—a divide-by-zero error), you could specify `except ArithmeticError`, which would then catch a `FloatingPointError`, an `OverflowError`, and a `ZeroDivisionError` should they occur. Similarly, if you specify `except Exception`, you'll catch *any* error.

But how does this help...surely you're already catching all errors with a "bare" `except` statement? It's true: you are. But you can extend the `except Exception` statement with the `as` keyword, which allows you to assign the current exception object to a variable (with `err` being a very popular name in this situation) and create more informative error message. Take a look at another version of the code, which uses `except Exception as`:

Unlike the "bare" except catch-all shown above, this one arranges for the exception object to be assigned to the "err" variable.

The value of "err" is then used as part of the friendly message (as it's always a good idea to report all exceptions).

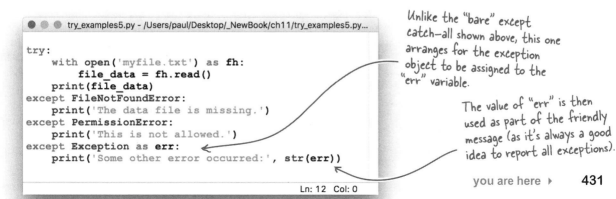

TEST DRIVE

With this—the last of the changes to your `try`/`except` code—applied, let's confirm that everything is working as expected before returning to `vsearch4web.py` and applying what you now know about exceptions to your webapp.

Let's start with confirming that the code displays the correct message when the file is missing:

```
                          Python 3.5.2 Shell
>>>
======== RESTART: /Users/paul/Desktop/_NewBook/ch11/try_examples5.py ========
The data file is missing.
>>>
                                                           Ln: 7  Col: 4
```

"myfile.txt" doesn't exist.

If the file exists, but you don't have permission to access it, a different exception is raised:

```
                          Python 3.5.2 Shell
>>>
======== RESTART: /Users/paul/Desktop/_NewBook/ch11/try_examples5.py ========
The data file is missing.
>>>
======== RESTART: /Users/paul/Desktop/_NewBook/ch11/try_examples5.py ========
This is not allowed.
>>> |
                                                           Ln: 10  Col: 4
```

The file exists, but you can't read it.

Any other exception is handled by the catch-all, which displays a friendly message:

```
                          Python 3.5.2 Shell
>>>
======== RESTART: /Users/paul/Desktop/_NewBook/ch11/try_examples5.py ========
The data file is missing.
>>>
======== RESTART: /Users/paul/Desktop/_NewBook/ch11/try_examples5.py ========
This is not allowed.
>>>
======== RESTART: /Users/paul/Desktop/_NewBook/ch11/try_examples5.py ========
Some other error occurred: [Errno 21] Is a directory: 'myfile.txt'
>>>
                                                           Ln: 23  Col: 4
```

Some other exception has occurred. In this case, what you thought was a file is in fact a folder.

Finally, if all is OK, the `try` suite runs without error, and the file's contents appear on screen:

```
                          Python 3.5.2 Shell
>>>
======== RESTART: /Users/paul/Desktop/_NewBook/ch11/try_examples5.py ========
The data file is missing.
>>>
======== RESTART: /Users/paul/Desktop/_NewBook/ch11/try_examples5.py ========
This is not allowed.
>>>
======== RESTART: /Users/paul/Desktop/_NewBook/ch11/try_examples5.py ========
Some other error occurred: [Errno 21] Is a directory: 'myfile.txt'
>>>
======== RESTART: /Users/paul/Desktop/_NewBook/ch11/try_examples5.py ========
Empty (well... except for this line).

>>>
                                                           Ln: 27  Col: 4
```

Success! No exceptions occur, so the "try" suite runs to completion.

Getting Back to Our Webapp Code

Recall from the start of this chapter that we identified an issue with the call to
`log_request` within `vsearch4web.py`'s `do_search` function. Specifically,
we're concerned about what to do when the call to `log_request` fails:

```
    . . .
@app.route('/search4', methods=['POST'])
def do_search() -> 'html':
    phrase = request.form['phrase']
    letters = request.form['letters']
    title = 'Here are your results:'
    results = str(searchfiles(phrase, letters))
    log_request(request, results)
    return render_template('results.html',
                            the_title=title,
                            the_phrase=phrase,
                            the_letters=letters,
                            the_results=results,)

    . . .
```

4. What happens if this call fails?

Based on our investigations, we learned that this call might fail if the backend
database is unavailable, or if some other error occurs. When an error (of any
type) occurs, the webapp responds with an unfriendly error page, which is likely to
confuse (rather than enlighten) your webapp's users:

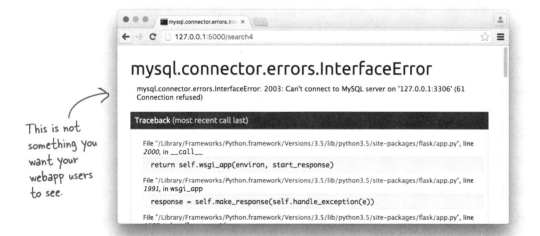

This is not something you want your webapp users to see.

Although it is important to us, the logging of each web request is not something
that our webapp users really care about; all they want to see is the results of their
search. Consequently, let's adjust the webapp's code so that it deals with errors
within `log_request` by handling any raised exceptions *silently*.

Silently Handling Exceptions

Seriously? You're planning to handle exceptions raised by "log_request" silently? Isn't that just another variant of ignoring exceptions and hoping they'll go away?

No: "silently" does not mean "ignore."

When we suggest handling exceptions *silently* in this context, we're referring to handling any exceptions raised in such a way that your webapp users don't notice. At the moment, your users *do* notice, as the webapp crashes with a confusing and—let's be honest—*scary* error page.

Your webapp users don't need to worry about log_request failing, but you do. So let's adjust your code so that exceptions raised by log_request aren't noticed by your users (i.e., they are silenced), but *are* noticed by you.

---

there are no Dumb Questions

Q: Doesn't all this try/except stuff just make my code harder to read and understand?

A: It's true that the example code in this chapter started out as three easy-to-understand lines of Python code, and then we added seven lines of code, which—on the face of things—have nothing to do with what the first three lines of code are doing. However, it is important to protect code that can potentially raise an exception, and try/except is generally regarded as the best way to do this. Over time, your brain will learn to spot the important stuff (the code actually doing the work) that lives in the try suite, and filter out the except suites that are there to handle exceptions. When trying to understand code that uses try/except, always read the try suite first to learn what the code does, then look at the except suites if you need to understand what happens when things go wrong.

Sharpen your pencil

Let's add some `try`/`except` code to `do_search`'s invocation of the `log_request` function. To keep things straightforward, let's add a catch-all exception handler around the call to `log_request`, which, when it fires, displays a helpful message on standard output (using a call to the `print` BIF). In defining a catch-all exception handler, you can suppress your webapp's standard exception-handling behavior, which currently displays the unfriendly error page.

Here's `log_request`'s code as it's currently written:

```
@app.route('/search4', methods=['POST'])
def do_search() -> 'html':
    phrase = request.form['phrase']
    letters = request.form['letters']
    title = 'Here are your results:'
    results = str(search4letters(phrase, letters))
    log_request(request, results)
    return render_template('results.html',
                           the_title=title,
                           the_phrase=phrase,
                           the_letters=letters,
                           the_results=results,)
```

This line of code needs to be protected in case it fails (raising a runtime error).

In the spaces below, provide the code that implements a catch-all exception handler around the call to `log_request`:

```
@app.route('/search4', methods=['POST'])
def do_search() -> 'html':
    phrase = request.form['phrase']
    letters = request.form['letters']
    title = 'Here are your results:'
    results = str(search4letters(phrase, letters))

    ...................................

                ...........................................................................

    ...........................................................................

                ...........................................................................

    return render_template('results.html',
                           the_title=title,
                           the_phrase=phrase,
                           the_letters=letters,
                           the_results=results,)
```

Don't forget to call "log_request" as part of the code you add.

Sharpen your pencil
Solution

The plan was to add some `try`/`except` code to `do_search`'s invocation of the `log_request` function. To keep things straightforward, we decided to add a catch-all exception handler around the call to `log_request`, which, when it fires, displays a helpful message on standard output (using a call to the `print` BIF).

Here's `log_request`'s code as currently written:

```
@app.route('/search4', methods=['POST'])
def do_search() -> 'html':
    phrase = request.form['phrase']
    letters = request.form['letters']
    title = 'Here are your results:'
    results = str(search4letters(phrase, letters))
    log_request(request, results)
    return render_template('results.html',
                            the_title=title,
                            the_phrase=phrase,
                            the_letters=letters,
                            the_results=results,)
```

In the spaces below, you were to provide the code that implements a catch-all exception handler around the call to `log_request`:

```
@app.route('/search4', methods=['POST'])
def do_search() -> 'html':
    phrase = request.form['phrase']
    letters = request.form['letters']
    title = 'Here are your results:'
    results = str(search4letters(phrase, letters))
    try:
        log_request(request, results)
    except Exception as err:
        print('***** Logging failed with this error:', str(err))
    return render_template('results.html',
                            the_title=title,
                            the_phrase=phrase,
                            the_letters=letters,
                            the_results=results,)
```

The call to "log_request" is moved into the suite associated with a new "try" statement.

This is the catch-all.

When a runtime error occurs, this message is displayed on screen for the admin only. Your user sees nothing.

(Extended) Test Drive, 1 of 3

With the catch-all exception-handling code added to `vsearch4web.py`, let's take your webapp for an extended spin (over the next few pages) to see the difference this new code makes. Previously, when something went wrong, your user was greeted with an unfriendly error page. Now, however, the error is handled "silently" by the catch-all code. If you haven't done so already, run `vsearch4web.py`, then use any browser to surf to your webapp's home page:

```
$ python3 vsearch4web.py
 * Running on http://127.0.0.1:5000/ (Press CTRL+C to quit)
 * Restarting with fsevents reloader
 * Debugger is active!
 * Debugger pin code: 184-855-980
```

Your webapp is up and running, waiting to hear fom a browser...

Go ahead and surf on over to your webapp's home page.

Welcome to search4letters on the web!

Use this form to submit a search request:

| Phrase: | |
| Letters: | aeiou |

When you're ready, click this button:

Do it!

On the terminal that's running your code, you should see something like this:

```
    ...
 * Debugger pin code: 184-855-980
127.0.0.1 - - [14/Jul/2016 10:54:31] "GET / HTTP/1.1" 200 -
127.0.0.1 - - [14/Jul/2016 10:54:31] "GET /static/hf.css HTTP/1.1" 200 -
127.0.0.1 - - [14/Jul/2016 10:54:32] "GET /favicon.ico HTTP/1.1" 404 -
```

These 200s confirm that your webapp is up and running (and serving up its home page). All is good at this point.

BTW: Don't worry about this 404...we haven't defined a "favicon.ico" file for our webapp (so it gets reported as not found when your browser asks for it).

(Extended) Test Drive, 2 of 3

In order to simulate an error, we've switched off our backend database, which should result in an error occurring whenever the webapp tries to interact with the database. As our code silently catches all errors generated by `log_request`, the webapp user isn't aware that the logging hasn't occurred. The catch-all code has arranged to generate a message on screen describing the problem. Sure enough, when you enter a phrase and click on the "Do it!" button, the webapp displays the results of your search in the browser, whereas the webapp's terminal screen displays the "silenced" error message. Note that, despite the runtime error, the webapp continues to execute and successfully services the call to */search*:

Welcome to search4letters on the web!

Use this form to submit a search request:

Phrase:	Testing out catch all code
Letters:	testing

When you're ready, click this button:

[Do it!]

Here are your results:

You submitted the following data:

Phrase:	Testing out catch all code
Letters:	testing

When "Testing out catch all code" is search for "testing", the following results are returned:

{'e', 'n', 'g', 's', 't', 'i'}

```
...
127.0.0.1 - - [14/Jul/2016 10:54:32] "GET /favicon.ico HTTP/1.1" 404 -
***** Logging failed with this error: 2003: Can't connect to MySQL server on '127.0.0.1:3306'
(61 Connection refused)
127.0.0.1 - - [14/Jul/2016 10:55:55] "POST /search4 HTTP/1.1" 200 -
```

This message is generated by your catch-all exception-handling code. The webapp user doesn't see it.

Even though an error occurred, the webapp didn't crash. In other words, the search worked (but the webapp user isn't aware that the logging failed).

(Extended) Test Drive, 3 of 3

In fact, no matter what error occurs when `log_request` runs, the catch-all code handles it.

We restarted our backend database, then tried to connect with an incorrect username. You can raise this error by changing the `dbconfig` dictionary in `vsearch4web.py` to use `vsearchwrong` as the value for `user`:

```
        ...
app.config['dbconfig'] = {'host': '127.0.0.1',
                          'user': 'vsearchwrong',   ←
                          'password': 'vsearchpasswd',
                          'database': 'vsearchlogDB', }
        ....
```

When your webapp reloads and you perform a search, you'll see a message like this in your terminal:

```
    ...
***** Logging failed with this error: 1045 (28000): Access denied for user 'vsearchwrong'@
'localhost' (using password: YES)
```

Change the value for user back to `vsearch`, and then let's try to access a nonexistent table, by changing the name of the table in the SQL query used in the `log_request` function to be `logwrong` (instead of `log`):

```
def log_request(req: 'flask_request', res: str) -> None:
    with UseDatabase(app.config['dbconfig']) as cursor:
        _SQL = """insert into logwrong    ←
                    (phrase, letters, ip, browser_string, results)
                    values
                    (%s, %s, %s, %s, %s)"""
        ...
```

When your webapp reloads and you perform a search, you'll see a message like this in your terminal:

```
    ...
***** Logging failed with this error: 1146 (42S02): Table 'vsearchlogdb.logwrong' doesn't exist
```

Change the name of the table back to `log` and then, as a final example, let's add a `raise` statement to the `log_request` function (just before the `with` statement), which generates a custom exception:

```
def log_request(req: 'flask_request', res: str) -> None:
    raise Exception("Something awful just happened.")   ←
    with UseDatabase(app.config['dbconfig']) as cursor:
        ...
```

When your webapp reloads one last time, and you perform one last search, you'll see the following message in your terminal:

```
    ...
***** Logging failed with this error: Something awful just happened.   ←
```

Handling Other Database Errors

The `log_request` function makes use of the `UseDatabase` context manager (as provided by the `DBcm` module). Now that you've protected the call to `log_request`, you can rest easy, safe in the knowledge that any issues relating to problems with the database will be caught (and handled) by your catch-all exception-handling code.

However, the `log_request` function isn't the only place where your webapp interacts with the database. The `view_the_log` function grabs the logging data from the database prior to displaying it on screen.

All of this code needs to be protected, too.

Recall the code for the `view_the_log` function:

```
    . . .
@app.route('/viewlog')
@check_logged_in
def view_the_log() -> 'html':
    with UseDatabase(app.config['dbconfig']) as cursor:
        _SQL = """select phrase, letters, ip, browser_string, results
                    from log"""
        cursor.execute(_SQL)
        contents = cursor.fetchall()
    titles = ('Phrase', 'Letters', 'Remote_addr', 'User_agent', 'Results')
    return render_template('viewlog.html',
                            the_title='View Log',
                            the_row_titles=titles,
                            the_data=contents,)
    . . .
```

This code can fail, too, as it interacts with the backend database. However, unlike `log_request`, the `view_the_log` function is not called from the code in `vsearch4web.py`; it's invoked by Flask on your behalf. This means you can't write code to protect the invocation of `view_the_log`, as it's the Flask framework that calls the function, not you.

If you can't protect the invocation of `view_the_log`, the next best thing is to protect the code in its suite, specifically the use of the `UseDatabase` context manager. Before considering how to do this, let's consider what can go wrong:

- The backend database may be unavailable.

- You may not be able to log in to a working database.

- After a successful login, your database query might fail.

- Something else (unexpected) might happen.

This list of problems is similar to those you had to worry about with `log_request`.

Does "More Errors" Mean "More excepts"?

Knowing what we now know about `try/except`, we could add some code to the `view_the_log` function to protect the use of the `UseDatabase` context manager:

```
        ...
@app.route('/viewlog')
@check_logged_in
def view_the_log() -> 'html':
    try:
        with UseDatabase(app.config['dbconfig']) as cursor:
            ...

    except Exception as err:
        print('Something went wrong:', str(err))
```

Another catch-all exception handler

The rest of the function's code goes here.

This catch-all strategy certainly works (after all, that's what you used with `log_request`). However, things can get complicated if you decide to do something other than implement a catch-all exception handler. What if you decide you need to react to a specific database error, such as "Database not found"? Recall from the beginning of this chapter that MySQL reports an `InterfaceError` exception when this happens:

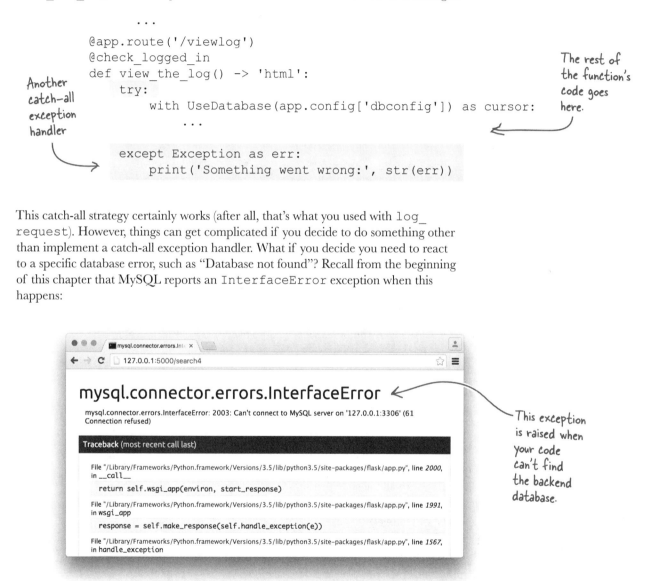

This exception is raised when your code can't find the backend database.

You could add an `except` statement that targets the `InterfaceError` exception, but to do this your code also has to import the `mysql.connector` module, which defines this particular exception.

On the face of things, this doesn't seem like a big deal. But it is.

Avoid Tightly Coupled Code

Let's assume you've decided to create an except statement that protects against your backend database being unavailable. You could adjust the code in view_the_log to look something like this:

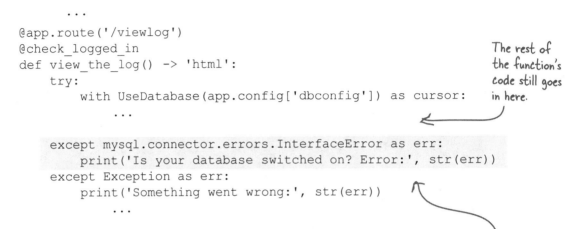

```
    ...
@app.route('/viewlog')
@check_logged_in
def view_the_log() -> 'html':
    try:
        with UseDatabase(app.config['dbconfig']) as cursor:
            ...

    except mysql.connector.errors.InterfaceError as err:
        print('Is your database switched on? Error:', str(err))
    except Exception as err:
        print('Something went wrong:', str(err))
        ...
```

The rest of the function's code still goes in here.

Add another "except" statement to handle a specific exception

If you also remember to add import mysql.connector to the top of your code, this additional except statement works. When your backend database can't be found, this additional code allows your webapp to remind you to check that your database is switched on.

This new code works, and you can see what's going on here...what's not to like?

The issue with approaching the problem in this way is that the code in vsearch4web.py is now very **tightly coupled** to the *MySQL* database, and specifically the use of the *MySQL Connector* module. Prior to adding this second except statement, your vsearch4web.py code interacted with your backend database via the DBcm module (developed earlier in this book). Specifically, the UseDatabase context manager provides a convenient **abstraction** that decouples the code in vsearch4web.py from the backend database. If, at some time in the future, you needed to replace *MySQL* with *PostgreSQL*, the only changes you'd need to make would be to the DBcm module, *not* to all the code that uses UseDatabase. However, when you create code like that shown above, you tightly bind (i.e., couple) your webapp code to the MySQL backend database because of that import mysql.connector statement, in addition to your new except statement's reference to mysql.connector.errors.InterfaceError.

If you need to write code that tightly couples to your backend database, always consider putting that code in the DBcm module. This way, your webapp can be written to use the generic interface provided by DBcm, as opposed to a specific interface that targets (and locks you into) a specific backend database.

Let's now consider what moving the above except code into DBcm does for our webapp.

The DBcm Module, Revisited

You last looked at DBcm in Chapter 9, when you created that module in order to provide a hook into the with statement when working with a *MySQL* database. Back then, we sidestepped any discussion of error handling (by conveniently ignoring the issue). Now that you've seen what the sys.exc_info function does, you should have a better idea of what the arguments to UseDatabase's __exit__ method mean:

This is the context manager code in "DBcm.py".

```
import mysql.connector

class UseDatabase:

    def __init__(self, config: dict) -> None:
        self.configuration = config

    def __enter__(self) -> 'cursor':
        self.conn = mysql.connector.connect(**self.configuration)
        self.cursor = self.conn.cursor()
        return self.cursor

    def __exit__(self, exc_type, exc_value, exc_trace) -> None:
        self.conn.commit()
        self.cursor.close()
        self.conn.close()
```

Now that you've seen "exc_info", it should be clear what these method arguments refer to: exception data.

Recall that UseDatabase implements three methods:

* __init__ provides a configuration opportunity *prior* to with executing,

* __enter__ executes as the with statement *starts*, and

* __exit__ is guaranteed to execute whenever the with's suite *terminates*.

At least, that's the expected behavior whenever everything goes to plan. When things go wrong, this behavior **changes**.

For instance, if an exception is raised while __enter__ is executing, the with statement terminates, and any subsequent processing of __exit__ is *cancelled*. This makes sense: if __enter__ runs into trouble, __exit__ can no longer assume that the execution context is initialized and configured correctly (so it's prudent not to run the __exit__ method's code).

The big issue with the __enter__ method's code is that the backend database may not be available, so let's take some time to adjust __enter__ for this possibility, generating a custom exception when the database connection cannot be established. Once we've done this, we'll adjust view_the_log to check for our custom exception instead of the highly database-specific mysql.connector.errors.InterfaceError.

Creating Custom Exceptions

Creating your own custom exceptions couldn't be any easier: decide on an appropriate name, then define an empty class that inherits from Python's built-in `Exception` class. Once you've defined a custom exception, it can be raised with the `raise` keyword. And once an exception is raised, it's caught (and dealt with) by `try`/`except`.

A quick trip to IDLE's >>> prompt demonstrates custom exceptions in action. In this example, we're creating a custom exception called `ConnectionError`, which we then raise (with `raise`), before catching with `try`/`except`. Read the annotations in numbered order, and (if you're following along) enter the code we've typed at the >>> prompt:

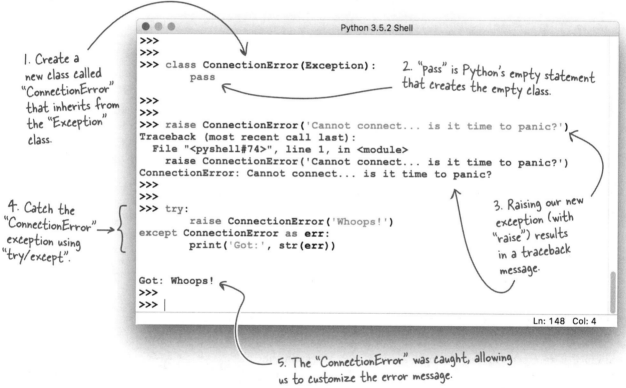

1. Create a new class called "ConnectionError" that inherits from the "Exception" class.

2. "pass" is Python's empty statement that creates the empty class.

3. Raising our new exception (with "raise") results in a traceback message.

4. Catch the "ConnectionError" exception using "try/except".

5. The "ConnectionError" was caught, allowing us to customize the error message.

The empty class isn't quite empty...

In describing the `ConnectionError` class as "empty," we told a little lie. Granted, the use of `pass` ensures that there's no *new* code associated with the `ConnectionError` class, but the fact that `ConnectionError` **inherits** from Python's built-in `Exception` class means that all of the attributes and behaviors of `Exception` are available in `ConnectionError` too (making it anything but empty). This explains why `ConnectionError` works just as you'd expect it to with `raise` and `try`/`except`.

Sharpen your pencil

Let's adjust the DBcm module to raise a custom ConnectionError whenever a connection to the backend database fails.

1

Here's the current code to DBcm.py. In the spaces provided, add in the code required to raise a ConnectionError.

Define your custom exception.

```
import mysql.connector
```

....

....

```
class UseDatabase:

    def __init__(self, config: dict) -> None:
        self.configuration = config

    def __enter__(self) -> 'cursor':
```

Add code to "raise" a "ConnnectionError".

```
            ...........................
            self.conn = mysql.connector.connect(**self.configuration)
            self.cursor = self.conn.cursor()
            return self.cursor
```

....

....

```
    def __exit__(self, exc_type, exc_value, exc_trace) -> None:
        self.conn.commit()
        self.cursor.close()
        self.conn.close()
```

2

With the code in the DBcm module amended, use your pencil to detail any changes you'd make to this code from vsearch4web.py in order to take advantage of the newly defined ConnectionError exception:

Use your pencil to show the changes you'd make to this code now that the "ConnectionError" exception exists.

```
from DBcm import UseDatabase
import mysql.connector

    ...
                                    the_row_titles=titles,
                                    the_data=contents,)
    except mysql.connector.errors.InterfaceError as err:
        print('Is your database switched on? Error:', str(err))
    except Exception as err:
        print('Something went wrong:', str(err))
    return 'Error'
```

Sharpen your pencil
Solution

You were to adjust the DBcm module to `raise` a custom
1 `ConnectionError` whenever a connection to the backend database
fails. You were to adjust the current code to DBcm.py to add in the code
required to `raise` a `ConnectionError`.

Define the
custom exception
as an "empty"
class that
inherits from
"Exception".

```
import mysql.connector

class ConnectionError(Exception):

    pass

class UseDatabase:

    def __init__(self, config: dict) -> None:
        self.configuration = config

    def __enter__(self) -> 'cursor':

        try:

            self.conn = mysql.connector.connect(**self.configuration)
            self.cursor = self.conn.cursor()
            return self.cursor
        except mysql.connector.errors.InterfaceError as err:

            raise ConnectionError(err)

    def __exit__(self, exc_type, exc_value, exc_trace) -> None:
        self.conn.commit()
        self.cursor.close()
        self.conn.close()
```

A new "try/
except"
construct
protects the
database
connection code.

Within the "DBcm.py" code,
refer to the backend
database-specific exceptions
by their full name.

Raise the custom
exception.

You don't need
to import
"mysql.connector"
anymore (as
"DBcm" does
this for you).

With the code in the DBcm module amended, you were to detail any
2 changes you'd make to this code from `vsearch4web.py` in order to
take advantage of the newly defined `ConnectionError` exception:

```
from DBcm import UseDatabase, ConnectionError
import mysql.connector

        ...

                            the_row_titles=titles,
        ConnectionError     the_data=contents,)
except mysql.connector.errors.InterfaceError as err:
    print('Is your database switched on? Error:', str(err))
except Exception as err:
    print('Something went wrong:', str(err))
return 'Error'
```

Be sure to
import the
"ConnectionError"
exception from
"DBcm".

Change the first
"except" statement
to look for a
"ConnectionError"
as opposed to an
"InterfaceError".

TEST DRIVE

Let's see what difference this new code makes. Recall that you've moved the MySQL-specific exception-handling code from vsearch4web.py into DBcm.py (and replaced it with code that looks for your custom ConnectionError exception). Has this made any difference?

Here are the messages that the previous version of vsearch4web.py generated whenever the backend database couldn't be found:

```
...
Is your database switched on? Error: 2003: Can't connect to MySQL server on '127.0.0.1:3306'
(61 Connection refused)
127.0.0.1 - - [16/Jul/2016 21:21:51] "GET /viewlog HTTP/1.1" 200 -
```

And here are the messages that the most recent version of vsearch4web.py generates whenever the backend database can't be found:

```
...
Is your database switched on? Error: 2003: Can't connect to MySQL server on '127.0.0.1:3306'
(61 Connection refused)
127.0.0.1 - - [16/Jul/2016 21:22:58] "GET /viewlog HTTP/1.1" 200 -
```

You're trying to trick me, aren't you? These error messages are the same!

Yes. On the face of things, these are the same.

However, although the output from the current and previous versions of vsearch4web.py appears identical, behind the scenes things are *very different*.

If you decide to change the backend database from *MySQL* to *PostgreSQL*, you no longer have to worry about changing any of the code in vsearch4web.py, as all of your database-specific code resides in DBcm.py. As long as the changes you make to DBcm.py maintain the same *interface* as previous versions of the module, you can change SQL databases as often as you like. This may not seem like a big deal now, but if vsearch4web.py grows to hundreds, thousands, or tens of thousands of lines of code, its really is a big deal.

What Else Can Go Wrong with "DBcm"?

Even if your backend database is up and running, things can still go wrong.

For example, the credentials used to access the database may be incorrect. If they are, the __enter__ method will fail again, this time with a mysql. connector.errors.ProgrammingError.

Or, the suite of code associated with your UseDatabase context manager may raise an exception, as there's never a guarantee that it executes correctly. A mysql.connector.errors.ProgrammingError is *also* raised whenever your database query (the SQL you're executing) contains an error.

The error message associated with an SQL query error is different than the message associated with the credentials error, but the exception raised is the same: mysql.connector.errors.ProgrammingError. Unlike with credentials errors, errors in your SQL results in an exception being raised while the with statement is executing. This means that you'll need to consider protecting against this exception in more than one place. The question is: where?

To answer this question, let's take another look at DBcm's code:

```python
import mysql.connector

class ConnectionError(Exception):
    pass

class UseDatabase:
    def __init__(self, config: dict):
        self.configuration = config

    def __enter__(self) -> 'cursor':
        try:
            self.conn = mysql.connector.connect(**self.configuration)
            self.cursor = self.conn.cursor()
            return self.cursor
        except mysql.connector.errors.InterfaceError as err:
            raise ConnectionError(err)

    def __exit__(self, exc_type, exc_value, exc_traceback):
        self.conn.commit()
        self.cursor.close()
        self.conn.close()
```

This code can raise a "ProgrammingError" exception.

But what about exceptions that occur within the "with" suite? These happen *after* the "__enter__" method ends but *before* the "__exit__" method starts.

You might be tempted to suggest that exceptions raised within the with suite should be handled with a try/except statement *within* the with, but such a strategy gets you right back to writing tightly coupled code. But consider this: when an exception is raised within with's suite and *not* caught, the with statement arranges to pass details of the uncaught exception into your context manager's __exit__ method, where you have the option of doing something about it.

Creating More Custom Exceptions

Let's extend DBcm.py to report two additional, custom exceptions.

The first is called CredentialsError and is raised when a ProgrammingError occurs within the __enter__ method. The second is called SQLError and is raised when a ProgrammingError is reported to the __exit__ method.

Defining these new exceptions is easy: add two new, empty exception classes to the top of DBcm.py:

```
import mysql.connector

class ConnectionError(Exception):
    pass

class CredentialsError(Exception):
    pass

class SQLError(Exception):
    pass

class UseDatabase:
    def __init__(self, configuration: dict):
        self.config = configuration
        . . .
```

Two additional classes define your two new exceptions.

A CredentialsError can occur during __enter__, so let's adjust that method's code to reflect this. Recall that an incorrect MySQL username or password results in a ProgrammingError being raised:

Add this code to the "__enter__" method to deal with any login issues.

```
        . . .
        try:
            self.conn = mysql.connector.connect(**self.config)
            self.cursor = self.conn.cursor()
            return self.cursor
        except mysql.connector.errors.InterfaceError as err:
            raise ConnectionError(err)
        except mysql.connector.errors.ProgrammingError as err:
            raise CredentialsError(err)

    def __exit__(self, exc_type, exc_value, exc_traceback):
        self.conn.commit()
        self.cursor.close()
        self.conn.close()
```

These code changes adjust DBcm.py to raise a CredentialsError exception when you provide either an incorrect username or password from your code to your backend database (MySQL). Adjusting vsearch4web.py's code is your next task.

Are Your Database Credentials Correct?

With these latest changes made to DBcm.py, let's now adjust the code in
vsearch4web.py, paying particular attention to the view_the_log function.
However, before doing anything else, add CredentialsError to the list of
imports from DBcm at the top of your vsearch4web.py code:

Be sure to import your new exception.

```
...
from DBcm import UseDatabase, ConnectionError, CredentialsError
...
```

With the import line amended, you next need to add a new except
suite to the view_the_log function. As when you added support for a
ConnectionError, this is a straightforward edit:

```
@app.route('/viewlog')
@check_logged_in
def view_the_log() -> 'html':
    try:
        with UseDatabase(app.config['dbconfig']) as cursor:
            _SQL = """select phrase, letters, ip, browser_string, results
                      from log"""
            cursor.execute(_SQL)
            contents = cursor.fetchall()
        titles = ('Phrase', 'Letters', 'Remote_addr', 'User_agent', 'Results')
        return render_template('viewlog.html',
                               the_title='View Log',
                               the_row_titles=titles,
                               the_data=contents,)
    except ConnectionError as err:
        print('Is your database switched on? Error:', str(err))
    except CredentialsError as err:
        print('User-id/Password issues. Error:', str(err))
    except Exception as err:
        print('Something went wrong:', str(err))
    return 'Error'
```

Add this code to "view_the_log" to catch when your code uses the wrong username or password with MySQL.

There's really nothing new here, as all you're doing is repeating what you did
for ConnectionError. Sure enough, if you try to connect to your backend
database with an incorrect username (or password), your webapp now displays an
appropriate message, like this:

```
...
User-id/Password issues. Error: 1045 (28000): Access denied for user 'vsearcherror'@'localhost'
(using password: YES)
127.0.0.1 - - [25/Jul/2016 16:29:37] "GET /viewlog HTTP/1.1" 200 -
```

Now that your code knows all about "CredentialsError", you generate an exception-specific error message.

Handling SQLError Is Different

Both `ConnectionError` and `CredentialsError` are raised due to problems with the `__enter__` method's code executing. When either exception is raised, the corresponding `with` statement's suite is **not** executed.

If all is well, your `with` suite executes as normal.

Recall this `with` statement from the `log_request` function, which uses the `UseDatabase` context manager (provided by DBcm) to insert data into the backend database:

```
with UseDatabase(app.config['dbconfig']) as cursor:
    _SQL = """insert into log
                (phrase, letters, ip, browser_string, results)
                values
                (%s, %s, %s, %s, %s)"""
    cursor.execute(_SQL, (req.form['phrase'],
                          req.form['letters'],
                          req.remote_addr,
                          req.user_agent.browser,
                          res, ))
```

need to worry out what happens something goes rong with this ode)i.e., the code ithin the "with" uite).

If (for some reason) your SQL query contains an error, the *MySQL Connector* module generates a `ProgrammingError`, just like the one raised during your context manager's `__enter__` method. However, as this exception occurs *within* your context manager (i.e., within the `with` statement) and is *not* caught there, the exception is passed back to the `__exit__` method as three arguments: the *type* of the exception, the *value* of the exception, and the *traceback* associated with the exception.

If you take a quick look at DBcm's existing code for `__exit__`, you'll see that the three arguments are ready and waiting to be used:

The three exception arguments are ready for use.

```
def __exit__(self, exc_type, exc_value, exc_traceback):
    self.conn.commit()
    self.cursor.close()
    self.conn.close()
```

When an exception is raised within the `with` suite and not caught, the context manager terminates the `with` suite's code, and jumps to the `__exit__` method, which then executes. Knowing this, you can write code that checks for exceptions of interest to your application. However, if no exception is raised, the three arguments (`exc_type`, `exc_value`, and `exc_traceback`) are all set to `None`. Otherwise, they are populated with details of the raised exception.

Let's exploit this behavior to raise an `SQLError` whenever something goes wrong within the `UseDatabase` context manager's `with` suite.

"None" is Python's null value.

Be Careful with Code Positioning

To check whether an uncaught exception has occurred within your code's `with` statement, check the `exc_type` argument to the `__exit__` method within `__exit__`'s suite, being careful to consider exactly where you add your new code.

> You're not about to tell me that it makes a difference where I put my "exc_type" checking code, are you?

Yes, it does make a difference.

To understand why, consider that your context manager's `__exit__` method provides a place where you can put code that is **guaranteed** to execute *after* your `with` suite ends. That behavior is part of the context manager protocol, after all.

This behavior needs to hold even when exceptions are raised within your context manager's `with` suite. Which means that if you plan to add code to the `__exit__` method, it's best to put it *after* any existing code in `__exit__`, as that way you'll still guarantee the method's existing code executes (and preserve the semantics of the context manager protocol).

Let's take another look at the existing code in the `__exit__` method in light of this code placement discussion. Consider that any code we add needs to raise an SQLError exception if `exc_type` indicates a `ProgrammingError` has occurred:

```
def __exit__(self, exc_type, exc_value, exc_traceback):
    self.conn.commit()
    self.cursor.close()
    self.conn.close()
```

If you add code in here, and that code raises an exception, the three existing lines of code won't be executed.

Adding code *after* the three existing lines of code ensures "__exit__" does its thing *before* any passed-in exception is dealt with.

Raising an SQLError

At this stage, you've already added the SQLError exception class to the top of the DBcm.py file:

```
import mysql.connector

class ConnectionError(Exception):
    pass

class CredentialsError(Exception):
    pass

class SQLError(Exception):
    pass

class UseDatabase:
    def __init__(self, config: dict):
        self.configuration = config
        ...
```

Here's where you added in the "SQLError" exception.

With the SQLError exception class defined, all you need to do now is add some code to the __exit__ method to check whether exc_type is the exception you're interested in, and if it is, raise an SQLError. This is so straightforward that we are resisting the usual *Head First* urge to turn creating the required code into an exercise, as no one wants to insult anyone's intelligence at this stage in this book. So, here's the code you need to append to the __exit__ method:

If a "ProgrammingError" occurs, raise an "SQLError".

```
def __exit__(self, exc_type, exc_value, exc_traceback):
    self.conn.commit()
    self.cursor.close()
    self.conn.close()
    if exc_type is mysql.connector.errors.ProgrammingError:
        raise SQLError(exc_value)
```

If you want to be **extra safe**, and do something sensible with any other, unexpected exception sent to __exit__, you can add an elif suite to the end of the __exit__ method that reraises the unexpected exception to the calling code:

```
    ...
    self.conn.close()
    if exc_type is mysql.connector.errors.ProgrammingError:
        raise SQLError(exc_value)
    elif exc_type:
        raise exc_type(exc_value)
```

This "elif" raises any other exception that might occur.

Test Drive

With support for the `SQLError` exception added to `DBcm.py`, add another `except` suite to your `view_the_log` function to catch any `SQLError`s that occur:

```
        ...
    except ConnectionError as err:
        print('Is your database switched on? Error:', str(err))
    except CredentialsError as err:
        print('User-id/Password issues. Error:', str(err))
    except SQLError as err:
        print('Is your query correct? Error:', str(err))
    except Exception as err:
        print('Something went wrong:', str(err))
    return 'Error'
```

Add this code into the "view_the_log" function within your "vsearch4web.py" webapp.

Once you save `vsearch4web.py`, your webapp should reload and be ready for testing. If you try to execute an SQL query that contains errors, the exception is handled by the above code:

```
    ...
Is your query correct? Error: 1146 (42S02): Table 'vsearchlogdb.logerror' doesn't exist
127.0.0.1 - - [25/Jul/2016 21:38:25] "GET /viewlog HTTP/1.1" 200 -
```

No more generic "ProgrammingError" exceptions from MySQL Connector, as your custom exception-handling code catches these errors now.

Equally, if something unexpected happens, your webapp's catch-all code kicks into gear, displaying an appropriate message:

```
    ...
Something went wrong: Some unknown exception.
127.0.0.1 - - [25/Jul/2016 21:43:14] "GET /viewlog HTTP/1.1" 200 -
```

If something unexpected happens, your code handles it.

With exception-handling code added to your webapp, no matter what runtime error occurs, your webapp continues to function without displaying a scary or confusing error page to your users.

And the really nice thing about this is that this code takes the generic "ProgrammingError" exception provided by the MySQL Connector module and turns it into two custom exceptions that have specific meaning for our webapp.

Yes, it does. And this is very powerful.

A Quick Recap: Adding Robustness

Let's take a minute to remind ourselves of what we set out to do in this chapter. In attempting to make our webapp code more robust, we had to answer four questions relating to four identified issues. Let's review each question and note how we did:

 What happens if the database connection fails?
You created a new exception called `ConnectionError` that is raised whenever your backend database can't be found. You then used `try/except` to handle a `ConnectionError` were it to occur.

 Is our webapp protected from web attacks?
It was a "happy accident," but your choice of *Flask* plus *Jinja2*, together with Python's DB-API specification, protects your webapp from the most notorious of web attacks. So, yes, your webapp is protected from *some* web attacks (but not all).

 What happens if something takes a long time?
We still haven't answered this question, other than to demonstrate what happens when your webapp takes 15 seconds to respond to a user request: your web user has to wait (or, more likely, your web user gets fed up waiting and leaves).

 What happens if a function call fails?
You used `try/except` to protect the function call, which allowed you to control what the user of your webapp sees when something goes wrong.

What happens if something takes a long time?

When you did the initial exercise at the start of this chapter, this question resulted from our examination of the `cursor.execute` calls that occurred in the `log_request` and `view_the_log` functions. Although you've already worked with both of these functions in answering questions 1 and 4, above, you're not done with them quite yet.

Both `log_request` and `view_the_log` use the `UseDatabase` context manager to execute an SQL query. The `log_request` function **writes** the details of the submitted search to the backend database, whereas the `view_the_log` function **reads** from the database.

The question is: *what do you do if this write or read takes a long time?*

Well, as with a lot of things in the programming world, it depends.

How to Deal with Wait? It Depends...

How you decide to deal with code that makes your users wait—either on a read, or on a write—can get complex. So we're going to pause this discussion and defer a solution until the next, short chapter.

In fact, the next chapter is so short that it doesn't warrant its own chapter number (as you'll see), but the material it presents is complex enough to justify splitting it off from this chapter's main discussion, which presented Python's `try/except` mechanism. So, let's hang on for a bit before putting to rest issue 3: *what happens if something takes a long time?*

You do realize you're asking us to wait to deal with code that waits?

Yes. The irony is not lost on us.

We're asking you to *wait* to learn how to handle "waits" in your code.

But you've already learned a lot in this chapter, and we think it's important to take a bit of time to let the `try/except` material sink into your brain.

So, we'd like you to pause, and take a short break...after you've cast your eye over the code seen thus far in this chapter.

Chapter 11's Code, 1 of 3

This is "try_example.py".

```python
try:
    with open('myfile.txt') as fh:
        file_data = fh.read()
    print(file_data)
except FileNotFoundError:
    print('The data file is missing.')
except PermissionError:
    print('This is not allowed.')
except Exception as err:
    print('Some other error occurred:', str(err))
```

```python
import mysql.connector

class ConnectionError(Exception):
    pass

class CredentialsError(Exception):
    pass

class SQLError(Exception):
    pass

class UseDatabase:
    def __init__(self, config: dict):
        self.configuration = config

    def __enter__(self) -> 'cursor':
        try:
            self.conn = mysql.connector.connect(**self.configuration)
            self.cursor = self.conn.cursor()
            return self.cursor
        except mysql.connector.errors.InterfaceError as err:
            raise ConnectionError(err)
        except mysql.connector.errors.ProgrammingError as err:
            raise CredentialsError(err)

    def __exit__(self, exc_type, exc_value, exc_traceback):
        self.conn.commit()
        self.cursor.close()
        self.conn.close()
        if exc_type is mysql.connector.errors.ProgrammingError:
            raise SQLError(exc_value)
        elif exc_type:
            raise exc_type(exc_value)
```

This is the exception-savvy version of "DBcm.py".

Chapter 11's Code, 2 of 3

This is the version of "vsearch4web.py" that makes your users wait...

```python
from flask import Flask, render_template, request, escape, session
from flask import copy_current_request_context

from vsearch import search4letters

from DBcm import UseDatabase, ConnectionError, CredentialsError, SQLError
from checker import check_logged_in

from time import sleep

app = Flask(__name__)

app.config['dbconfig'] = {'host': '127.0.0.1',
                          'user': 'vsearch',
                          'password': 'vsearchpasswd',
                          'database': 'vsearchlogDB', }

@app.route('/login')
def do_login() -> str:
    session['logged_in'] = True
    return 'You are now logged in.'

@app.route('/logout')
def do_logout() -> str:
    session.pop('logged_in')
    return 'You are now logged out.'

@app.route('/search4', methods=['POST'])
def do_search() -> 'html':

    @copy_current_request_context
    def log_request(req: 'flask_request', res: str) -> None:
        sleep(15)   # This makes log_request really slow...
        with UseDatabase(app.config['dbconfig']) as cursor:
            _SQL = """insert into log
                        (phrase, letters, ip, browser_string, results)
                        values
                        (%s, %s, %s, %s, %s)"""
            cursor.execute(_SQL, (req.form['phrase'],
                                  req.form['letters'],
                                  req.remote_addr,
                                  req.user_agent.browser,
                                  res, ))

    phrase = request.form['phrase']
    letters = request.form['letters']
    title = 'Here are your results:'
```

It's probably a good idea to protect this "with" statement in much the same way as you protected the "with" statement in "view_the_log" (on the next page).

The rest of "do_search" is at the top of the next page. ⟶

Chapter 11's Code, 3 of 3

```python
        results = str(search4letters(phrase, letters))
        try:
            log_request(request, results))
        except Exception as err:
            print('***** Logging failed with this error:', str(err))
        return render_template('results.html',
                            the_title=title,
                            the_phrase=phrase,
                            the_letters=letters,
                            the_results=results,)

@app.route('/')
@app.route('/entry')
def entry_page() -> 'html':
    return render_template('entry.html',
                        the_title='Welcome to search4letters on the web!')


@app.route('/viewlog')
@check_logged_in
def view_the_log() -> 'html':
    try:
        with UseDatabase(app.config['dbconfig']) as cursor:
            _SQL = """select phrase, letters, ip, browser_string, results
                    from log"""
            cursor.execute(_SQL)
            contents = cursor.fetchall()
        # raise Exception("Some unknown exception.")
        titles = ('Phrase', 'Letters', 'Remote_addr', 'User_agent', 'Results')
        return render_template('viewlog.html',
                            the_title='View Log',
                            the_row_titles=titles,
                            the_data=contents,)
    except ConnectionError as err:
        print('Is your database switched on? Error:', str(err))
    except CredentialsError as err:
        print('User-id/Password issues. Error:', str(err))
    except SQLError as err:
        print('Is your query correct? Error:', str(err))
    except Exception as err:
        print('Something went wrong:', str(err))
    return 'Error'


app.secret_key = 'YouWillNeverGuessMySecretKey'

if __name__ == '__main__':
    app.run(debug=True)
```

This is the rest of the "do_search" function.

11¾ a little bit of threading

Dealing with Waiting

Your code can sometimes take a long time to execute.

Depending on who notices, this may or may not be an issue. If some code takes 30 seconds to do its thing "behind the scenes," the wait may not be an issue. However, if your user is waiting for your application to respond, and it takes 30 seconds, everyone notices. What you should do to fix this problem depends on what you're trying to do (and who's doing the waiting). In this short chapter, we'll briefly discuss some options, then look at one solution to the issue at hand: *what happens if something takes too long?*

Waiting: What to Do?

When you write code that has the potential to make your users wait, you need to think carefully about what it is you are trying to do. Let's consider some points of view.

Listen, dude, if you have to wait, there's nothing else for it: you wait...

Maybe how you wait is different when you're writing than when you're reading?

Like everything else, it all depends on what you're trying to do, and the user experience you're shooting for...

Maybe it is the case that waiting for a write is *different* from waiting for a read, especially as it relates to how your webapp works?

Let's take another look at the SQL queries in `log_request` and `view_the_log` to see how you're using them.

How Are You Querying Your Database?

In the `log_request` function, we are using an SQL `INSERT` to add details of
the request to our backend database. When `log_request` is called, it **waits**
while the `INSERT` is executed by `cursor.execute`:

```
def log_request(req: 'flask_request', res: str) -> None:
    with UseDatabase(app.config['dbconfig']) as cursor:
        _SQL = """insert into log
                    (phrase, letters, ip, browser_string, results)
                    values
                    (%s, %s, %s, %s, %s)"""
        cursor.execute(_SQL, (req.form['phrase'],
                              req.form['letters'],
                              req.remote_addr,
                              req.user_agent.browser,
                              res, ))
```

At this point, the webapp "blocks" while it waits for the backend database to do its thing.

Geek Bits

Code that waits for something external to complete is referred to as "blocking code," in that the execution of your program is **blocked** from continuing until the wait is over. As a general rule, blocking code that takes a noticeable length of time is bad.

The same holds for the `view_the_log` function, which also **waits** whenever
the SQL `SELECT` query is executed:

```
@app.route('/viewlog')
@check_logged_in
def view_the_log() -> 'html':
    try:
        with UseDatabase(app.config['dbconfig']) as cursor:
            _SQL = """select phrase, letters, ip, browser_string, results
                        from log"""
            cursor.execute(_SQL)
            contents = cursor.fetchall()
        titles = ('Phrase', 'Letters', 'Remote_addr', 'User_agent', 'Results')
        return render_template('viewlog.html',
                               the_title='View Log',
                               the_row_titles=titles,
                               the_data=contents,)
    except ConnectionError as err:
        ...
```

Your webapp "blocks" here, too, while it waits for the database.

To save on space, we're not showing all of the code for "view_the_log". The exception-handling code still goes here.

Both functions block. However, look closely at what happens *after* the call
to `cursor.execute` in both functions. In `log_request`, the `cursor.
execute` call is the last thing that function does, whereas in `view_the_log`,
the results of `cursor.execute` are used by the rest of the function.

Let's consider the implications of this difference.

Database INSERTs and SELECTs Are Different

If you're reading the title to this page and thinking "Of course they are!", be assured that (this late in this book) we haven't lost our marbles.

Yes: an SQL INSERT is *different* from an SQL SELECT, but, as it relates to your use of both queries in your webapp, it turns out that the INSERT in log_request doesn't need to block, whereas the SELECT in view_the_log does, which makes the queries *very* different.

This is a key observation.

If the SELECT in view_the_log doesn't wait for the data to return from the backend database, the code that follows cursor.execute will likely fail (as it'll have no data to work with). The view_the_log function **must** block, as it has to wait for data *before* proceeding.

When your webapp calls log_request, it wants the function to log the details of the current web request to the database. The calling code doesn't really care *when* this happens, just that it does. The log_request function returns no value, nor data; the calling code isn't waiting for a response. All the calling code cares about is that the web request is logged *eventually*.

Which begs the question: why does log_request force its callers to wait?

> Are you about to suggest that the "log_request" code could somehow run concurrently with the webapp's code?

Yes. That's our madcap idea.

When users of your webapp enter a new search, they couldn't care less that the request details are logged to some backend database, so let's not make them wait while your webapp does that work.

Instead, let's arrange for some other process to do the logging *eventually* and independently of the webapp's main function (which is to allow your users to perform searches).

Doing More Than One Thing at Once

Here's the plan: you're going to arrange for the `log_request` function to execute independently of your main webapp. To do this, you're going to adjust your webapp's code so each call to `log_request` runs concurrently. This will mean that your webapp no longer has to wait for `log_request` to complete before servicing another request from another user (i.e., no more delays).

If `log_request` takes an instant, a few seconds, a minute, or even hours to execute, your webapp doesn't care (and neither does your user). What you care about is that the code eventually executes.

Concurrent code: you have options

When it comes to arranging for some of your application's code to run concurrently, Python has a few options. As well as lots of support from third-party modules, the standard library comes with some built-in goodies that can help here.

One of the most well known is the `threading` library, which provides a high-level interface to the threading implementation provided by the operating system hosting your webapp. To use the library, all you need to do is `import` the `Thread` class from the `threading` module near the top of your program code:

```
from threading import Thread
```

Go ahead and add this line of code near the top of your `vsearch4web.py` file.

Now the fun starts.

To create a new thread, you create a `Thread` object, assigning the name of the function you want the thread to execute to a named argument called `target`, and providing any arguments as a tuple to another named argument called `args`. The created `Thread` object is then assigned to a variable of your choosing.

As an example, let's assume that you have a function called `execute_slowly`, which takes three arguments, which we'll assume are three numbers. The code that invokes `execute_slowly` has assigned the three values to variables called `glacial`, `plodding`, and `leaden`. Here's how `execute_slowly` is invoked normally (i.e., without our worrying about concurrent execution):

```
execute_slowly(glacial, plodding, leaden)
```

If `execute_slowly` takes 30 seconds to do what it has to do, the calling code blocks and waits for 30 seconds before doing anything else. Bummer.

> For the full list of (and all the details about) Python's standard library concurrency options, see https://docs.python.org/3/library/concurrency.html.

Don't Get Bummed Out: Use Threads

In the big scheme of things, waiting 30 seconds for the `execute_slowly` function to complete doesn't sound like the end of the world. But, if your user is sitting and waiting, they'll be wondering what's gone wrong.

If your application can continue to run while `execute_slowly` goes about its business, you can create a `Thread` to run `execute_slowly` concurrently. Here's the normal function call once more, together with the code that turns the function call into a request for threaded execution:

The original function call

```
execute_slowly(glacial, plodding, leaden)
```

Import the required module and class near the top of your code...

```
from threading import Thread

    . . .

t = Thread(target=execute_slowly, args=(glacial, plodding, leaden))
```

...then create a new "Thread" object, which identifies the target function to execute as well as any argument values.

Granted, this use of `Thread` looks a little strange, but it's not really. The key to understanding what's going on here is to note that the `Thread` object has been assigned to a variable (t in this example), and that the `execute_slowly` function has yet to execute.

Assigning the `Thread` object to t *prepares* it for execution. To ask Python's threading technology to run `execute_slowly`, start the thread like this:

```
t.start()
```

When you call "start", the function associated with the "t" thread is scheduled for execution by the "threading" module.

At this point, the code that called `t.start` continues to run. The 30-second wait that results from running `execute_slowly` has no effect on the calling code, as `execute_slowly`'s execution is handled by Python's `threading` module, not by you. The threading module conspires with the Python interpreter to run `execute_slowly` *eventually*.

Sharpen your pencil

When it comes to calling `log_request` in your webapp code, there's only one place you need to look: in the `do_search` function. Recall that you've already put your call to `log_request` inside a `try/except` to guard against unexpected runtime errors.

Note, too, that we've added a 15-second delay—using `sleep(15)`—to our `log_request` code (making it slow). Here's the current code to `do_search`:

Here's how you currently invoke "log_request".

```
@app.route('/search4', methods=['POST'])
def do_search() -> 'html':
    phrase = request.form['phrase']
    letters = request.form['letters']
    title = 'Here are your results:'
    results = str(search4letters(phrase, letters))
    try:
        log_request(request, results)
    except Exception as err:
        print('***** Logging failed with this error:',
str(err))
    return render_template('results.html',
                           the_title=title,
                           the_phrase=phrase,
                           the_letters=letters,
                           the_results=results,)
```

We are going to assume that you have already added `from threading import Thread` to the top of your webapp's code.

Grab your pencil, and in the space provided below, write the code you'd insert into `do_search` instead of the standard call to `log_request`.

Remember: you are to use a `Thread` object to run `log_request`, just like we did with the `execute_slowly` example from the last page.

Add the threading code you'd use to eventually execute "log_request".

....

....

....

Sharpen your pencil
Solution

When it comes to calling `log_request` in your webapp code, there's only one place you need to look: in the `do_search` function. Recall that you've already put your call to `log_request` inside a `try`/`except` to guard against unexpected run-time errors.

Note, too, that we've added a 15 second delay - using `sleep(15)` - to our `log_request` code (making it slow). Here's the current code to `do_search`:

Here's how you currently invoke "log_request".

```
@app.route('/search4', methods=['POST'])
def do_search() -> 'html':
    phrase = request.form['phrase']
    letters = request.form['letters']
    title = 'Here are your results:'
    results = str(search4letters(phrase, letters))
    try:
        log_request(request, results)
    except Exception as err:
        print('***** Logging failed with this error:',
str(err))
    return render_template('results.html',
                                the_title=title,
                                the_phrase=phrase,
                                the_letters=letters,
                                the_results=results,)
```

We assumed that you had already added `from threading import Thread` to the top of your webapp's code.

In the space provided below, you were to write the code you'd insert into `do_search` instead of the standard call to `log_request`.

You were to use a `Thread` object to run `log_request`, just like we did with the recent `execute_slowly` example.

We're keeping the "try" statement (for now).

```
try:
```

```
t = Thread(target=log_request, args=(request, results))
```

The "except" suite is unchanged, so we aren't showing it here.

```
    t.start()
except ...
```

Just like the earlier example, identify the target function to run, supply any arguments it needs, and don't forget to schedule your thread to run.

TEST DRIVE

With these edits applied to `vsearch4web.py`, you are ready for another test run. What you're expecting to see here is next-to-no wait when you enter a search into your webapp's search page (as the `log_request` code is being run concurrently by the `threading` module).

Go ahead and give it a go.

Sure enough, the instant you click on the "Do it!" button, your webapp returns with your results. The assumption is that the `threading` module is now executing `log_request`, and waiting however long it takes to run that function's code to completion (approximately 15 seconds).

You're just about to give yourself a pat on the back (for a job well done) when, out of nowhere and after about 15 seconds, your webapp's terminal window erupts with error messages, not unlike these:

ake
look
t this
essage.

The last request was a success.

```
    ...
127.0.0.1 - - [29/Jul/2016 19:43:31] "POST /search4 HTTP/1.1" 200 -
Exception in thread Thread-6:
Traceback (most recent call last):
  File "vsearch4web.not.slow.with.threads.but.broken.py", line 42, in log_request
    cursor.execute(_SQL, (req.form['phrase'],
  File "/Library/Frameworks/Python.framework/Versions/3.5/lib/python3.5/site-packages/
werkzeug/local.py", line 343, in __getattr__
    ...
    raise RuntimeError(_request_ctx_err_msg)
RuntimeError: Working outside of request context.
```

Whoops! An uncaught exception.

Lots (!!)
more
traceback
messages
here

```
This typically means that you attempted to use functionality that needed
an active HTTP request.  Consult the documentation on testing for
information about how to avoid this problem.

During handling of the above exception, another exception occurred:

Traceback (most recent call last):
  File "/Library/Frameworks/Python.framework/Versions/3.5/lib/python3.5/threading.py",
line 914, in _bootstrap_inner
    self.run()
    ...
RuntimeError: Working outside of request context.
```

And another one...yikes!

```
This typically means that you attempted to use functionality that needed
an active HTTP request.  Consult the documentation on testing for
information about how to avoid this problem.
```

If you check your backend database, you'll learn that the details of your web request were **not** logged. Based on the messages above, it appears the `threading` module isn't at all happy with your code. A lot of the second group of traceback messages refer to `threading.py`, whereas the first group of traceback messages refer to code in the `werkzeug` and `flask` folders. What's clear is that adding in the threading code has resulted in a **huge mess**. What's going on?

First Things First: Don't Panic

Your first instinct may be to back out the code you added to run `log_request` in its own thread (and get yourself back to a known good state). But let's not panic, and let's **not** do that. Instead, let's take a look at that descriptive paragraph that appeared twice in the traceback messages:

```
    . . .
    This typically means that you attempted to use functionality that needed
    an active HTTP request.  Consult the documentation on testing for
    information about how to avoid this problem.
    . . .
```

This message is coming from Flask, not from the `threading` module. We know this because the `threading` module couldn't care less about what you use it for, and definitely has no interest in what you're trying to do with HTTP.

Let's take another look at the code that schedules the thread for execution, which we know takes 15 seconds to run, as that's how long `log_request` takes. While you're looking at this code, think about what happens during that 15 seconds:

```python
@app.route('/search4', methods=['POST'])
def do_search() -> 'html':
    phrase = request.form['phrase']
    letters = request.form['letters']
    title = 'Here are your results:'
    results = str(search4letters(phrase, letters))
    try:
        t = Thread(target=log_request, args=(request, results))
        t.start()
    except Exception as err:
        print('***** Logging failed with this error:', str(err))
    return render_template('results.html',
                            the_title=title,
                            the_phrase=phrase,
                            the_letters=letters,
                            the_results=results,)
```

What happens while this thread takes 15 seconds to execute?

The instant the thread is scheduled for execution, the calling code (the `do_search` function) continues to execute. The `render_template` function executes (in the blink of an eye), and then the `do_search` function *ends*.

When `do_search` ends, all of the data associated with the function (its *context*) is reclaimed by the interpreter. The variables `request`, `phrase`, `letters`, `title`, and `results` cease to be. However, the `request` and `results` variables are passed as arguments to `log_request`, which tries to access them 15 seconds later. Unfortunately, at that point in time, the variables no longer exist, as `do_search` has ended. Bummer.

Don't Get Bummed Out: Flask Can Help

Based on what you've just learned, it appears the `log_request` function (when executed within a thread) can no longer "see" its argument data. This is due to the fact that the interpreter has long since cleaned up after itself, and reclaimed the memory used by these variables (as `do_search` has ended). Specifically, the `request` object is no longer active, and when `log_request` goes looking for it, it can't be found.

So, what can be done? Don't fret: help is at hand.

I'm just going to pencil you in for next week, when I know you're going to ask me to rewrite the "log_request" function. OK?

There's really no need for a rewrite.

At first glance, it might appear that you'd need to rewrite `log_request` to somehow rely less on its arguments... assuming that's even possible. But it turns out that Flask comes with a decorator that can help here.

The decorator, `copy_current_request_context`, ensures that the HTTP request that is active when a function is called *remains* active even when the function is subsequently executed in a thread. To use it, you need to add `copy_current_request_context` to the list of imports at the top of your webapp's code.

As with any other decorator, you apply it to an existing function using the usual @ syntax. However, there is a caveat: the function being decorated has to be defined *within* the function that calls it; the decorated function must be nested inside its caller (as an inner function).

Exercise

Here's what we want you to do (after updating the list of imports from Flask):

1. Take the `log_request` function and nest it inside the `do_search` function.
2. Decorate `log_request` with `@copy_current_request_context`.
3. Confirm that the runtime errors from the last *Test Drive* have gone away.

EXERCISE SOLUTION

We asked you to do three things:

1. Take the `log_request` function and nest it inside the `do_search` function.
2. Decorate `log_request` with `@copy_current_request_context`.
3. Confirm that the runtime errors from the last *Test Drive* have gone away.

Here's what our `do_search` code looks like after we perform tasks 1 and 2 (note: we'll discuss task 3 over the page):

```
@app.route('/search4', methods=['POST'])
def do_search() -> 'html':

    @copy_current_request_context
    def log_request(req: 'flask_request', res: str) -> None:
        sleep(15)  # This makes log_request really slow...
        with UseDatabase(app.config['dbconfig']) as cursor:
            _SQL = """insert into log
                        (phrase, letters, ip, browser_string, results)
                        values
                        (%s, %s, %s, %s, %s)"""
            cursor.execute(_SQL, (req.form['phrase'],
                                  req.form['letters'],
                                  req.remote_addr,
                                  req.user_agent.browser,
                                  res, ))

    phrase = request.form['phrase']
    letters = request.form['letters']
    title = 'Here are your results:'
    results = str(search4letters(phrase, letters))
    try:
        t = Thread(target=log_request, args=(request, results))
        t.start()
    except Exception as err:
        print('***** Logging failed with this error:', str(err))
    return render_template('results.html',
                            the_title=title,
                            the_phrase=phrase,
                            the_letters=letters,
                            the_results=results,)
```

Task 2. The decorator has been applied to "log_request".

Task 1. The "log_request" function is now defined (nested) inside the "do_search" function.

All of the rest of this code remains unchanged.

---

there are no
Dumb Questions

Q: Does it still make sense to protect the threaded invocation of `log_request` with try/except?

A: Not if you are hoping to react to a runtime issue with `log_request`, as the try/except will have ended before the thread starts. However, your system may fail trying to create a new thread, so we figure it can't hurt to leave try/except in `do_search`.

TEST DRIVE

Task 3: Taking this latest version of `vsearch4web.py` for a spin confirms that the runtime errors from the last *Test Drive* are a thing of the past. Your webapp's terminal window confirms that all is well:

```
    . . .
127.0.0.1 - - [30/Jul/2016 20:42:46] "GET / HTTP/1.1" 200 -
127.0.0.1 - - [30/Jul/2016 20:43:10] "POST /search4 HTTP/1.1" 200 -
127.0.0.1 - - [30/Jul/2016 20:43:14] "GET /login HTTP/1.1" 200 -
127.0.0.1 - - [30/Jul/2016 20:43:17] "GET /viewlog HTTP/1.1" 200 -
127.0.0.1 - - [30/Jul/2016 20:43:37] "GET /viewlog HTTP/1.1" 200 -
```

No more scary runtime exceptions. All those 200s mean all is well with your webapp. And, 15 seconds after you submit a new search, your webapp eventually logs the details to your backend database WITHOUT requiring your webapp user to wait. ☺

According to this card, I get to ask one last question. Is there any downside to defining "log_request" within "do_search"?

No. Not in this case.

For this webapp, the `log_request` function was only ever called by `do_search`, so nesting `log_request`'s within `do_search` isn't an issue.

If you later decide to invoke `log_request` from some other function, you may have an issue (and you'll have to rethink things). But, for now, you're golden.

Is Your Webapp Robust Now?

Here are the four questions posed at the start of Chapter 11:

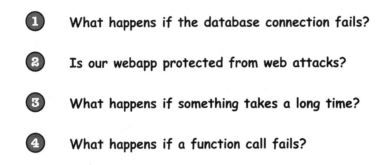

1 **What happens if the database connection fails?**

2 **Is our webapp protected from web attacks?**

3 **What happens if something takes a long time?**

4 **What happens if a function call fails?**

Your webapp now handles a number of runtime exceptions, thanks to your use of `try/except` and some custom exceptions that you can `raise` and catch as required.

When you know something can go wrong at runtime, fortify your code against any exceptions that might occur. This improves the overall robustness of your application, which is a good thing.

Note that there are other areas where robustness could be improved. You spent a lot of time adding `try/except` code to `view_the_log`'s code, which took advantage of the `UseDatabase` context manager. `UseDatabase` is *also* used within `log_request`, and should probably be protected, too (and doing so is left as a homework exercise for you).

Your webapp is more responsive due to your use of threading to handle a task that has to be performed eventually, but not right away. This is a good design strategy, although you do need to be careful not to go overboard with threads: the threading example in this chapter is very straightforward. However, it is very easy to create threading code that nobody can understand, and which will drive you mad when you have to debug it. **Use threads with care.**

In answering question 3—*what happens if something takes a long time?*—the use of threads improved the performance of the database write, but not the database read. It is a case of just having to wait for the data to arrive after the read, no matter now long it takes, as the webapp wasn't able to proceed without the data.

To make the database read go faster (assuming it's actually slow in the first place), you may have to look at using an alternative (faster) database setup. But that's a worry for another day that we won't concern ourselves with further in this book.

However, having said that, in the next and last chapter, we do indeed consider performance, but we'll be doing so while discussing a topic everyone understands, and which we've already discussed in this book: looping.

Chapter 11¾'s Code, 1 of 2

This is the latest and greatest version of "vsearch4web.py".

```python
from flask import Flask, render_template, request, escape, session
from flask import copy_current_request_context
from vsearch import search4letters

from DBcm import UseDatabase, ConnectionError, CredentialsError, SQLError
from checker import check_logged_in

from threading import Thread
from time import sleep

app = Flask(__name__)

app.config['dbconfig'] = {'host': '127.0.0.1',
                          'user': 'vsearch',
                          'password': 'vsearchpasswd',
                          'database': 'vsearchlogDB', }

@app.route('/login')
def do_login() -> str:
    session['logged_in'] = True
    return 'You are now logged in.'

@app.route('/logout')
def do_logout() -> str:
    session.pop('logged_in')
    return 'You are now logged out.'

@app.route('/search4', methods=['POST'])
def do_search() -> 'html':

    @copy_current_request_context
    def log_request(req: 'flask_request', res: str) -> None:
        sleep(15)   # This makes log_request really slow...
        with UseDatabase(app.config['dbconfig']) as cursor:
            _SQL = """insert into log
                        (phrase, letters, ip, browser_string, results)
                        values
                        (%s, %s, %s, %s, %s)"""
            cursor.execute(_SQL, (req.form['phrase'],
                                  req.form['letters'],
                                  req.remote_addr,
                                  req.user_agent.browser,
                                  res, ))

    phrase = request.form['phrase']
    letters = request.form['letters']
    title = 'Here are your results:'
```

The rest of "do_search" is at the top of the next page. ——→

Chapter 11¾'s Code, 2 of 2

```
        results = str(search4letters(phrase, letters))
        try:
            t = Thread(target=log_request, args=(request, results))
            t.start()
        except Exception as err:
            print('***** Logging failed with this error:', str(err))
        return render_template('results.html',
                               the_title=title,
                               the_phrase=phrase,
                               the_letters=letters,
                               the_results=results,)


@app.route('/')
@app.route('/entry')
def entry_page() -> 'html':
    return render_template('entry.html',
                           the_title='Welcome to search4letters on the web!')


@app.route('/viewlog')
@check_logged_in
def view_the_log() -> 'html':
    try:
        with UseDatabase(app.config['dbconfig']) as cursor:
            _SQL = """select phrase, letters, ip, browser_string, results
                    from log"""
            cursor.execute(_SQL)
            contents = cursor.fetchall()
        # raise Exception("Some unknown exception.")
        titles = ('Phrase', 'Letters', 'Remote_addr', 'User_agent', 'Results')
        return render_template('viewlog.html',
                               the_title='View Log',
                               the_row_titles=titles,
                               the_data=contents,)
    except ConnectionError as err:
        print('Is your database switched on? Error:', str(err))
    except CredentialsError as err:
        print('User-id/Password issues. Error:', str(err))
    except SQLError as err:
        print('Is your query correct? Error:', str(err))
    except Exception as err:
        print('Something went wrong:', str(err))
    return 'Error'


app.secret_key = 'YouWillNeverGuessMySecretKey'


if __name__ == '__main__':
    app.run(debug=True)
```

This is the rest of the "do_search" function.

12 advanced iteration

Looping Like Crazy

> I've just had the most wonderful idea: what if I could make my loops go faster?

It's often amazing how much time our programs spend in loops.

This isn't a surprise, as most programs exist to perform something quickly a whole heap of times. When it comes to optimizing loops, there are two approaches: (1) improve the loop syntax (to make it easier to specify a loop), and (2) improve how loops execute (to make them go faster). Early in the lifetime of Python 2 (that is, a *long, long* time ago), the language designers added a single language feature that implements both approaches, and it goes by a rather strange name: **comprehension**. But don't let the strange name put you off: by the time you've worked through this chapter, you'll be wondering how you managed to live without comprehensions for so long.

Bahamas Buzzers Have Places to Go

We've places to go, people to see...

To learn what loop comprehensions can do for you, you're going to take a look at some "real" data.

Operating out of Nassau on New Providence Island, *Bahamas Buzzers* provides island-hopping flights to some of the larger island airports. The airline has pioneered just-in-time flight scheduling: based on the previous day's demand, the airline predicts (which is just a fancy term for "guesses") how many flights they need the next day. At the end of each day, the *BB Head Office* generates the next day's flight schedule, which ends up in a text-based CSV (*comma-separated value*) file.

Here's what tomorrow's CSV file contains:

The header tells us to expect two columns of data: one representing times, the other destinations.

```
TIME,DESTINATION
09:35,FREEPORT
17:00,FREEPORT
09:55,WEST END
19:00,WEST END
10:45,TREASURE CAY
12:00,TREASURE CAY
11:45,ROCK SOUND
17:55,ROCK SOUND
```

The rest of the CSV file contains the actual flight data.

This is a standard CSV file, with the first line given over to header information. It all looks OK except for the fact that everything's UPPERCASE (which is a little "old school").

Head Office calls this CSV file `buzzers.csv`.

If you were asked to read the data from the CSV file and display it on screen, you'd use a `with` statement. Here's what we did at IDLE's >>> prompt, after using Python's `os` module to change into the folder that contains the file:

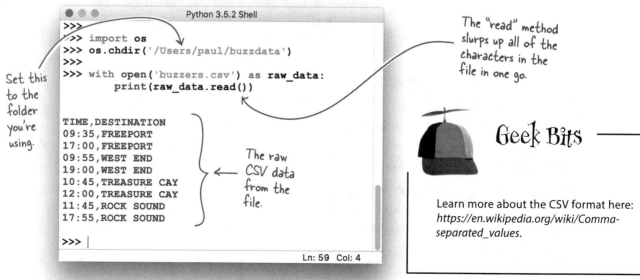

Set this to the folder you're using.

```
>>>
>>> import os
>>> os.chdir('/Users/paul/buzzdata')
>>>
>>> with open('buzzers.csv') as raw_data:
        print(raw_data.read())

TIME,DESTINATION
09:35,FREEPORT
17:00,FREEPORT
09:55,WEST END
19:00,WEST END
10:45,TREASURE CAY
12:00,TREASURE CAY
11:45,ROCK SOUND
17:55,ROCK SOUND

>>>
```

Ln: 59 Col: 4

The "read" method slurps up all of the characters in the file in one go.

The raw CSV data from the file.

Geek Bits

Learn more about the CSV format here: *https://en.wikipedia.org/wiki/Comma-separated_values*.

Reading CSV Data As Lists

The CSV data, in its raw form, is not very useful. It would be more useful if you could read and break apart each line at the comma, making it easier to get at the data.

Although it is possible to do this "breaking apart" with hand-crafted Python code (taking advantage of the string object's `split` method), working with CSV data is such a common activity that the *standard library* comes with a module named `csv` that can help.

Here's another small `for` loop that demonstrates the `csv` module in action. Unlike the last example, where you used the `read` method to grab the entire contents of the file *in one go*, in the code that follows, `csv.reader` is used to read the CSV file *one line at a time* within the `for` loop. On each iteration, the `for` loop assigns each line of CSV data to a variable (called `line`), which is then displayed on screen:

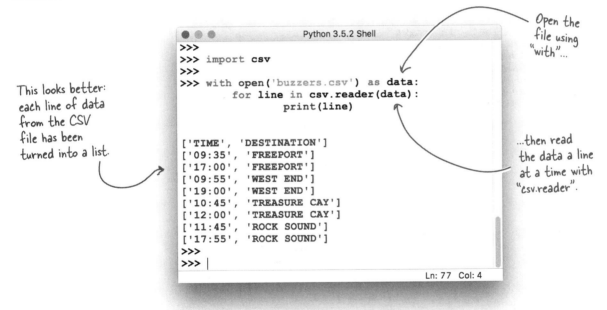

Open the file using "with"...

This looks better: each line of data from the CSV file has been turned into a list.

...then read the data a line at a time with "csv.reader".

The `csv` module is doing quite a bit of work here. Each line of raw data is being read from the file, then "magically" turned into a two-item list.

In addition to the header information (from the first line of the file) being returned as a list, each individual flight time and destination pair also gets its own list. Take note of the *type* of the individual data items returned: everything is a string, even though the first item in each list (clearly) represents a time.

The `csv` module has a few more tricks up its sleeve. Another interesting function is `csv.DictReader`. Let's see what that does for you.

Reading CSV Data As Dictionaries

Here's code similar to the last example, but for the fact that this new code uses `csv.DictReader` as opposed to `csv.reader`. When `DictReader` is used, the data from the CSV file is returned as a collection of dictionaries, with the keys for each dictionary taken from the CSV file's header line, and the values taken from each of the subsequent lines. Here's the code:

Using "csv.DictReader" is a simple change, but it makes a big difference. What was lines of lists (last time) are now lines of dictionaries.

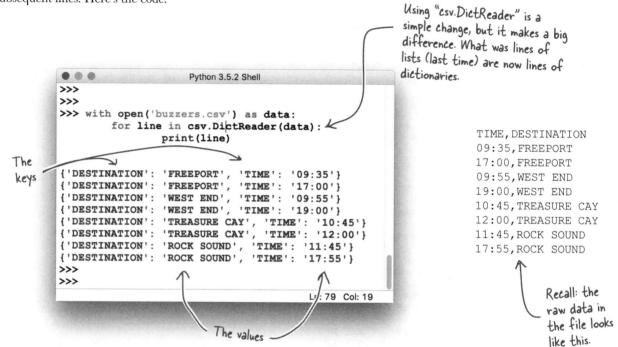

The keys

The values

TIME,DESTINATION
09:35,FREEPORT
17:00,FREEPORT
09:55,WEST END
19:00,WEST END
10:45,TREASURE CAY
12:00,TREASURE CAY
11:45,ROCK SOUND
17:55,ROCK SOUND

Recall: the raw data in the file looks like this.

There is no doubt that this is powerful stuff: with a single call to `DictReader`, the `csv` module has transformed the raw data in your CSV file into a collection of Python dictionaries.

But imagine you've been tasked with converting the raw data in the CSV file based on the following requirements:

1   **Convert the flight times from 24-hour format to AM/PM format**

2   **Convert the destinations from UPPERCASE to Titlecase**

In and of themselves, these are not difficult tasks. However, when you consider the raw data as a collection of lists or a collection of dictionaries, they can be. So, let's write a custom `for` loop to read the data into a single dictionary that can then be used to perform these conversions with a lot less fuss.

Let's Back Up a Little Bit

Rather than use `csv.reader` or `csv.DictReader`, let's roll our own code to convert the raw data in the CSV file into a *single* dictionary, which we can then manipulate to perform the required conversions.

We've had a chat with the *Head Office* folks over at *Bahamas Buzzers*, and they've told us they're very happy with the conversions we have in mind, but would still like the data kept in its "raw form," as that's how their antiquated departures board expects its data to arrive: 24-hour format for flight times, and all UPPERCASE for destinations.

You could perform conversions on the raw data in your single dictionary, but let's ensure that the conversions are performed on *copies* of the data, not the actual raw data as read in. Although it's not totally clear at the moment, the noises coming out of *Head Office* seem to indicate that whatever code you create may have to interface with some existing systems. So, rather than face the prospect of converting the data back into its raw form, let's read it into a single dictionary as is, then convert to copies as required (while leaving the raw data in the original dictionary *untouched*).

It's not an awful lot of work (over and above what you had to do with the `csv` module) to read the raw data into a dictionary. In the code below, the file is opened, and the first line is read and ignored (as we don't need the header info). A `for` loop then reads each line of raw data, splitting it in two at the comma, with the flight time being used as your dictionary *key*, and the destination used as your dictionary *value*.

The raw data

↓

```
TIME,DESTINATION
09:35,FREEPORT
17:00,FREEPORT
09:55,WEST END
19:00,WEST END
10:45,TREASURE CAY
12:00,TREASURE CAY
11:45,ROCK SOUND
17:55,ROCK SOUND
```

↑

Can you break each line in two, using the comma as the delimiter?

Open the file as before.

Create a new, empty dictionary called "flights".

Process each line.

Ignore the header info.

Break apart the line at the comma, which returns two values: the key (flight time) and value (destination).

Assign destination to flight time.

```
●  ●  ●              Python 3.5.2 Shell
>>>
>>> with open('buzzers.csv') as data:
        ignore = data.readline()
        flights = {}
        for line in data:
            k, v = line.split(',')
            flights[k] = v

>>> flights
{'12:00': 'TREASURE CAY\n', '09:35': 'FREEPORT\n', '
17:00': 'FREEPORT\n', '19:00': 'WEST END\n', '17:55'
: 'ROCK SOUND\n', '10:45': 'TREASURE CAY\n', '09:55'
: 'WEST END\n', '11:45': 'ROCK SOUND\n'}
>>>
>>> import pprint
>>> pprint.pprint(flights)
{'09:35': 'FREEPORT\n',
 '09:55': 'WEST END\n',
 '10:45': 'TREASURE CAY\n',
 '11:45': 'ROCK SOUND\n',
 '12:00': 'TREASURE CAY\n',
 '17:00': 'FREEPORT\n',
 '17:55': 'ROCK SOUND\n',
 '19:00': 'WEST END\n'}
>>> |
                                      Ln: 486  Col: 4
```

Display the contents of the dictionary, which looks a little messed up until...

...the "pretty-printing" library produces more human-friendly output.

The inclusion of the newline character looks a little strange, doesn't it?

Stripping, Then Splitting, Your Raw Data

The latest `with` statement used the `split` method (included with all string objects) to break the line of raw data in two. What's returned is a list of strings, which the code individually assigns to the k and v variables. This multivariable assignment is possible due to the fact that you have a tuple of variables on the left of the assignment operator, as well as code that produces a list of values on the right of the operator (remember: tuples are *immutable* lists):

A tuple of variables on the left

```
...
k, v = line.split(',')
...
```

Code that produces a list of values on the right

Another string method, `strip`, removes whitespace from the beginning and end of an existing string. Let's use it to remove the unwanted trailing newline from the raw data *before* preforming the `split`.

Here's one final version of our data-reading code. We create a dictionary called `flights`, which uses the flight times as keys and the destinations (without the newline) as values:

Geek Bits

Whitespace: the following characters are considered whitespace in strings: *space*, \t, \n, and \r.

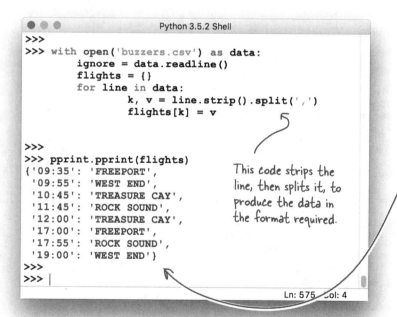

```
Python 3.5.2 Shell
>>>
>>> with open('buzzers.csv') as data:
        ignore = data.readline()
        flights = {}
        for line in data:
                k, v = line.strip().split(',')
                flights[k] = v


>>>
>>> pprint.pprint(flights)
{'09:35': 'FREEPORT',
 '09:55': 'WEST END',
 '10:45': 'TREASURE CAY',
 '11:45': 'ROCK SOUND',
 '12:00': 'TREASURE CAY',
 '17:00': 'FREEPORT',
 '17:55': 'ROCK SOUND',
 '19:00': 'WEST END'}
>>>
>>> |
                                  Ln: 575  Col: 4
```

This code strips the line, then splits it, to produce the data in the format required.

You may not have spotted this, but the order of the rows in the dictionary different from what's in the data file. This happens because dictionaries do NOT maintain insertion order. Don't worry about this for now.

```
TIME,DESTINATION
09:35,FREEPORT
17:00,FREEPORT
09:55,WEST END
19:00,WEST END
10:45,TREASURE CAY
12:00,TREASURE CAY
11:45,ROCK SOUND
17:55,ROCK SOUND
```

What if you switched the order of the methods in your code, like so:

```
line.split(',').strip()
```

What do you think would happen?

When you string methods together like this, it's called a "method chain."

Be Careful When Chaining Method Calls

Some programmers don't like the fact that Python's method calls can be chained together (as `strip` and `split` were in the last example), because such chains can be hard to read the first time you see them. However, method chaining is popular among Python programmers, so you'll likely run across code that uses this technique "in the wild." Care is needed, however, as the order of the method calls is *not* interchangeable.

As an example of what can go wrong, consider this code (which is very similar to what came before). Whereas before the order was `strip`, then `split`, this code calls `split` first, then tries to call `strip`. Look what happens:

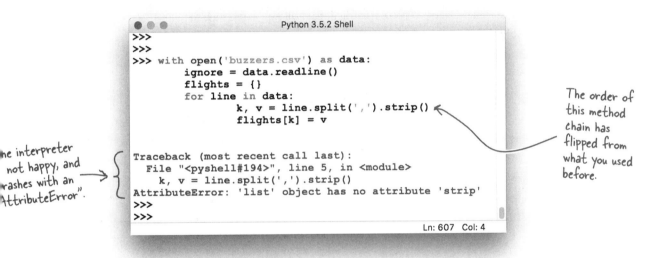

```
● ● ●                    Python 3.5.2 Shell
>>>
>>>
>>> with open('buzzers.csv') as data:
        ignore = data.readline()
        flights = {}
        for line in data:
                k, v = line.split(',').strip()
                flights[k] = v


Traceback (most recent call last):
  File "<pyshell#194>", line 5, in <module>
    k, v = line.split(',').strip()
AttributeError: 'list' object has no attribute 'strip'
>>>
>>>
                                                Ln: 607  Col: 4
```

The order of this method chain has flipped from what you used before.

The interpreter is not happy, and crashes with an "AttributeError".

To understand what's going on here, consider the *type* of the data to the right of the assignment operator as the above method chain executes.

Before anything happens, `line` is a string. Calling `split` on a string returns a list of strings, using the argument to `split` as a delimiter. What started out as a *string* (`line`) has dynamically morphed into a *list*, which then has another method invoked against it. In this example, the next method is `strip`, which expects to be invoked on a string, *not* a list, so the interpreter raises an `AttributeError`, as lists don't have a method called `strip`.

The method chain from the previous page does not suffer from this issue:

```
    . . .
line.strip().split(',')
    . . .
```

With this code, the interpreter starts out with a string (in `line`), which has any leading/trailing whitespace removed by `strip` (yielding another string), which is then `split` into a list of strings based on the comma delimiter. There's no `AttributeError`, as the method chain doesn't violate any typing rules.

Transforming Data into the Format You Need

Now that the data is in the `flights` dictionary, let's consider the data manipulations *BB Head Office* has asked you to perform.

The first is to perform the two conversions identified earlier in this chapter, creating a new dictionary in the process:

 Convert the flight times from 24-hour format to AM/PM format

 Convert the destinations from UPPERCASE to Titlecase

Applying these two transformations to the `flights` dictionary allows you to turn the dictionary on the left into the one on the right:

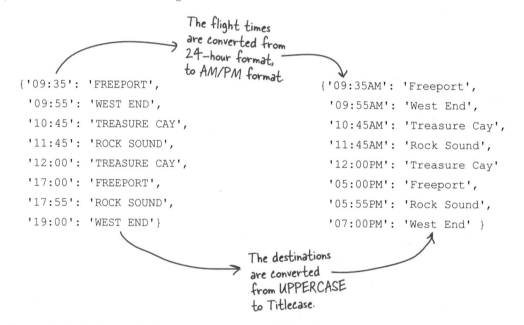

The flight times are converted from 24-hour format, to AM/PM format.

```
{'09:35': 'FREEPORT',              {'09:35AM': 'Freeport',
 '09:55': 'WEST END',               '09:55AM': 'West End',
 '10:45': 'TREASURE CAY',           '10:45AM': 'Treasure Cay',
 '11:45': 'ROCK SOUND',             '11:45AM': 'Rock Sound',
 '12:00': 'TREASURE CAY',           '12:00PM': 'Treasure Cay'
 '17:00': 'FREEPORT',               '05:00PM': 'Freeport',
 '17:55': 'ROCK SOUND',             '05:55PM': 'Rock Sound',
 '19:00': 'WEST END'}               '07:00PM': 'West End' }
```

The destinations are converted from UPPERCASE to Titlecase.

Note that the data in both dictionaries has the same meaning, it's just the representation that's changed. *Head Office* needs the second dictionary, as they feel that its data is more universally understandable, as well as friendlier; *Head Office* thinks all-UPPERCASE is akin to shouting.

At the moment, the data in both dictionaries has a single line for each flight time/destination combination. Although *Head Office* will be happy when you've transformed the dictionary on the left into the dictionary on the right, they've also suggested that it would be really useful if the data could be presented with single destinations as keys and a list of flight times as values—that is, a single row of data for each destination. Let's look at how *that* dictionary would appear before embarking on coding the required manipulations.

Transforming into a Dictionary Of Lists

Once the data in `flights` has been transformed, *Head Office* wants you to perform this second manipulation (discussed at the bottom of the last page):

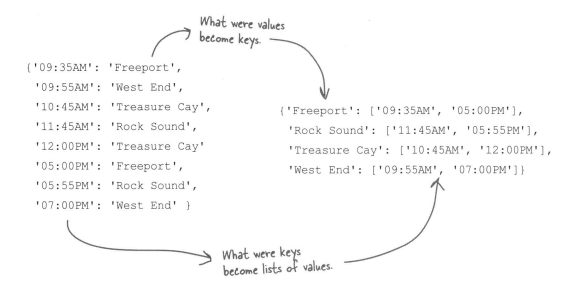

What were values become keys.

```
{'09:35AM': 'Freeport',
 '09:55AM': 'West End',
 '10:45AM': 'Treasure Cay',
 '11:45AM': 'Rock Sound',
 '12:00PM': 'Treasure Cay'
 '05:00PM': 'Freeport',
 '05:55PM': 'Rock Sound',
 '07:00PM': 'West End' }
```

```
{'Freeport': ['09:35AM', '05:00PM'],
 'Rock Sound': ['11:45AM', '05:55PM'],
 'Treasure Cay': ['10:45AM', '12:00PM'],
 'West End': ['09:55AM', '07:00PM']}
```

What were keys become lists of values.

Think about the data wrangling that's needed here...

There's a bit of work required to get from the raw data in the CSV file to the dictionary of lists shown above on the right. Take a moment to think about how you'd go about doing this using the Python you already know.

If you're like most programmers, it won't take you long to work out that the `for` loop is your friend here. As Python's main looping mechanism, `for` has already helped you extract the raw data from the CSV file and populate the `flights` dictionary:

This is a classic use of "for", and a hugely popular programming idiom in Python.

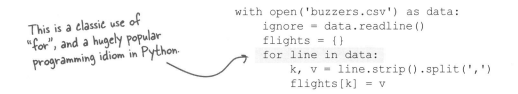

```python
with open('buzzers.csv') as data:
    ignore = data.readline()
    flights = {}
    for line in data:
        k, v = line.strip().split(',')
        flights[k] = v
```

It's tempting to suggest that this code be amended to perform the transformations to the raw data as it is read from the CSV file—that is, *prior* to adding rows of data to `flights`. But recall the *Head Office's* request that the raw data remain untouched in `flights`: any transformations need to be applied to a **copy** of the data. This makes things more complex, but not by much.

Let's Do the Basic Conversions

At the moment, the `flights` dictionary contains flight times in 24-hour format as its keys, with UPPERCASE strings representing destinations as its values. You have two initial conversions to perform:

 Convert the flight times from 24-hour format to AM/PM format

 Convert the destinations from UPPERCASE to Titlecase

Conversion #2 is easy, so let's do that one first. Once data is in a string, simply call the string's `title` method, as this IDLE session demonstrates:

The "title" method returns a copy of the data in "s".

```
>>> s = "I DID NOT MEAN TO SHOUT."
>>> print(s)
I DID NOT MEAN TO SHOUT.
>>> t = s.title()
>>> print(t)
I Did Not Mean To Shout.
```

This is much friendlier than before.

Conversion #1 involves a bit more work.

If you think about it for a minute, things get quite involved when it comes to converting `19:00` into `7:00PM`. However, this is only the case when you look at the `19:00` data as a string. You'd need to write a lot of code to do the conversion.

If you instead consider that `19:00` is a time, you can take advantage of the `datetime` module that is included as part of Python's *standard library*. This module's `datetime` class can take a string (like `19:00`) and convert it to its equivalent AM/PM format using two prebuilt functions and what's known as *string format specifiers*. Here's a small function, called `convert2ampm`, which uses the facilities of the `datetime` module to perform the conversion you need:

For more on string format specifiers, see https://docs. python.org/3/ library/datetime. html#strftime-and strptime-behavior.

Ready Bake Code

```python
from datetime import datetime

def convert2ampm(time24: str) -> str:
    return datetime.strptime(time24, '%H:%M').strftime('%I:%M%p')
```

Given a time in 24-hour format (as a string), this method chain converts it into a string in AM/PM format.

Sharpen your pencil

Let's put the conversion techniques from the last page to work.

Below is the code that reads the raw data from the CSV file, populating the flights dictionary as it goes. The convert2ampm function is also shown.

Your job is to write a for loop that takes the data in flights and converts the keys to AM/PM format, and the values to *Titlecase*. A new dictionary, called flights2, is created to hold the converted data. Use your pencil to add the for loop code in the space provided.

Hint: when processing a dictionary with a for loop, recall that the items method returns the key and value for each row (as a tuple) on each iteration.

Define the conversion function.

```python
from datetime import datetime
import pprint


def convert2ampm(time24: str) -> str:
    return datetime.strptime(time24, '%H:%M').strftime('%I:%M%p')
```

Grab the data from the file.

```python
with open('buzzers.csv') as data:
    ignore = data.readline()
    flights = {}
    for line in data:
        k, v = line.strip().split(',')
        flights[k] = v
```

Pretty-print the "flights" dictionary prior to performing the conversions.

```python
pprint.pprint(flights)
print()

flights2 = {}
```

The new dictionary, called "flights2", starts out empty.

Add your "for" loop here.

....

....

```python
pprint.pprint(flights2)
```

Pretty-print the "flights2" dictionary to confirm that the conversions are working.

Sharpen your pencil
Solution

Your job was to write a `for` loop that takes the data in `flights` and
converts the keys to AM/PM format, and the values to *Titlecase*. You were
to create a new dictionary, called `flights2`, to hold the converted data,
and you were to add the `for` loop code in the space provided.

*We saved all
of this code
in a file called
"do_convert.py".*

```python
from datetime import datetime
import pprint


def convert2ampm(time24: str) -> str:
    return datetime.strptime(time24, '%H:%M').strftime('%I:%M%p')


with open('buzzers.csv') as data:
    ignore = data.readline()
    flights = {}
    for line in data:
        k, v = line.strip().split(',')
        flights[k] = v

pprint.pprint(flights)
print()

flights2 = {}
```

*The "items"
method returns
each row from
the "flights"
dictionary.*

```python
for k, v in flights.items():

    flights2[convert2ampm(k)] = v.title()

pprint.pprint(flights2)
```

*On each iteration, the
key (in "k") is converted
to AM/PM format,
then used as the new
dictionary's key.*

*The value (in "v") is
converted to Titlecase,
then assigned to the
converted key.*

TEST DRIVE

If you execute the above program, two dictionaries are displayed on screen (which we're showing
below, side by side). The conversions work, although the ordering in each dictionary differs, as the
interpreter does **not** maintain *insertion order* when you populate a new dictionary with data:

*This is
"flights".*

```
{'09:35': 'FREEPORT',
 '09:55': 'WEST END',
 '10:45': 'TREASURE CAY',
 '11:45': 'ROCK SOUND',
 '12:00': 'TREASURE CAY',
 '17:00': 'FREEPORT',
 '17:55': 'ROCK SOUND',
 '19:00': 'WEST END'}
```

```
{'05:00PM': 'Freeport',
 '05:55PM': 'Rock Sound',
 '07:00PM': 'West End',
 '09:35AM': 'Freeport',
 '09:55AM': 'West End',
 '10:45AM': 'Treasure Cay',
 '11:45AM': 'Rock Sound',
 '12:00PM': 'Treasure Cay'}
```

*This is
"flights2".*

*The raw data is
transformed.*

Did You Spot the Pattern in Your Code?

Take another look at the program you've just executed. There's a very common programming pattern used *twice* in this code. Can you spot it?

```python
from datetime import datetime
import pprint

def convert2ampm(time24: str) -> str:
    return datetime.strptime(time24, '%H:%M').strftime('%I:%M%p')

with open('buzzers.csv') as data:
    ignore = data.readline()
    flights = {}
    for line in data:
        k, v = line.strip().split(',')
        flights[k] = v

pprint.pprint(flights)
print()

flights2 = {}
for k, v in flights.items():
    flights2[convert2ampm(k)] = v.title()

pprint.pprint(flights2)
```

If you answered: "the `for` loop," you're only half-right. The `for` loop *is* part of the pattern, but take another look at the code that *surrounds* it. Spot anything else?

```python
from datetime import datetime
import pprint

def convert2ampm(time24: str) -> str:
    return datetime.strptime(time24, '%H:%M').strftime('%I:%M%p')

with open('buzzers.csv') as data:
    ignore = data.readline()
    flights = {}
    for line in data:
        k, v = line.strip().split(',')
        flights[k] = v

pprint.pprint(flights)
print()

flights2 = {}
for k, v in flights.items():
    flights2[convert2ampm(k)] = v.title()

pprint.pprint(flights2)
```

Each of the "for" loops is preceded by the creation of a new, empty data structure (e.g., a dictionary).

Each of the "for" loop's suites contains code that adds data to the new data structure, based on the processing of some existing data.

Spotting the Pattern with Lists

The examples on the last page highlighted the programming pattern as it relates to dictionaries: start with a new, empty dictionary, then use a `for` loop to process an existing dictionary, generating data for a new dictionary as you go:

The new, initially empty, dictionary

The existing dictionary

```
flights2 = {}
for k, v in flights.items():
    flights2[convert2ampm(k)] = v.title()
```

A regular "for" loop processes the existing data.

The existing data is used to generate keys and values, which are inserted into the new dictionary.

This pattern also makes an appearance with lists, where it is easier to spot. Take a look at this IDLE session, where the keys (i.e., the flight times) and the values (i.e., the destinations) are extracted from the `flights` dictionary as lists, then converted into new lists using the programming pattern (numbered 1 through 4 in the annotations):

1. Start with a new, empty list.

2. Iterate through each of the flight times.

3. Append the converted data to the new list.

4. View the new list's data.

1. Start with a new, empty list.

2. Iterate through each of the destinations

3. Append the converted data to the new list.

4. View the new list's data.

```
Python 3.5.2 Shell
>>>
>>>
>>> flight_times = []
>>> for ft in flights.keys():
        flight_times.append(convert2ampm(ft))

>>> print(flight_times)
['05:00PM', '09:55AM', '11:45AM', '10:45AM', '07:00PM', '05:55PM',
'12:00PM', '09:35AM']
>>>
>>> destinations = []
>>> for dest in flights.values():
        destinations.append(dest.title())

>>> print(destinations)
['Freeport', 'West End', 'Rock Sound', 'Treasure Cay', 'West End',
'Rock Sound', 'Treasure Cay', 'Freeport']
>>>
>>> |
                                              Ln: 154  Col: 4
```

This pattern is used so often that Python provides a convenient shorthand notation for it called the **comprehension**. Let's see what's involved in creating a comprehension.

Converting Patterns into Comprehensions

Let's take the most recent `for` loop that processed the destinations as our example. Here it is again:

```
destinations = []
for dest in flights.values():
    destinations.append(dest.title())
```

1. Start with a new, empty list.

2. Iterate through each of the destinations.

3. Append the converted data to the new list.

Python's built-in **comprehension** feature lets you rework the above three lines of code as a single line.

To convert the above three lines into a comprehension, we're going to step through the process, building up to the complete comprehension.

Begin by starting with a new, empty list, which is assigned to a new variable (which we're calling `more_dests` in this example):

```
more_dests = []
```

1. Start with a new, empty list (and give it a name).

Specify how the existing data (in `flights` in this example) is to be iterated over using the familiar `for` notation, and place this code within the new list's square brackets (note the *absence* of the colon at the end of the `for` code):

```
more_dests = [for dest in flights.values()]
```

2. Iterate through each of the destinations.

Note that there's NO colon here.

To complete the comprehension, specify the transformation to be applied to the data (in `dest`), and put this transformation *before* the `for` keyword (note the *absence* of the call to `append`, which is assumed by the comprehension):

```
more_dests = [dest.title() for dest in flights.values()]
```

3. Append the converted data to the new list, without actually calling "append".

And that's it. The single line of code at the bottom of this page is functionally equivalent to the three lines of code at the top. Go ahead and run this line of code at your >>> prompt to convince yourself that the `more_dests` list contains the same data as the `destinations` list.

Take a Closer Look at the Comprehension

Let's look at the comprehension in a little more detail. Here's the original three lines of code as well as the single-line comprehension that performs the same task.

Remember: both versions produce new lists (destinations and more_dests) that have exactly the same data:

```
destinations = []
for dest in flights.values():
        destinations.append(dest.title())
```

```
more_dests = [dest.title() for dest in flights.values()]
```

It's also possible to pick out the parts of the original three lines of code and see where they've been used in the comprehension:

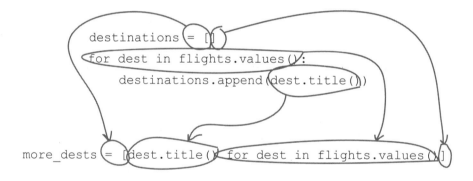

If you spot this pattern in other code, you can easily turn it into a comprehension. For example, here's some code from earlier (which produces the list of AM/PM flight times) reworked as a comprehension:

```
flight_times = []
for ft in flights.keys():
        flight_times.append(convert2ampm(ft))
```

These do the
same thing.

```
fts2 = [convert2ampm(ft) for ft in flights.keys()]
```

What's the Big Deal?

> These comprehensions look hard to understand. I'm pretty happy using a "for" loop when I need to do something like this. Is learning how to write comprehensions really worth the effort?

Yes. We think it's well worth the effort.

There are two main reasons why taking the time to understand comprehensions pays off.

Firstly, as well as requiring less code (which means comprehensions are easier on your fingers), the Python interpreter is optimized to run comprehensions as quickly as possible. This means comprehensions execute *faster* than the equivalent `for` loop code.

Secondly, comprehensions can be used in places where `for` loops can't. In fact, you've already seen this, as all the comprehensions presented so far in this chapter have appeared to the *right* of the assignment operator, which is something a regular `for` loop can't do. This can be surprisingly useful (as you'll see as this chapter progresses).

Comprehensions aren't just for lists

The comprehensions you've seen so far have created new lists, so each is known as a **list comprehension** (or *listcomp* for short). If your comprehension creates a new dictionary, it's known as a **dictionary comprehension** (*dictcomp*). And, so as not to leave any data structure out, you can also specify a **set comprehension** (*setcomp*).

There's no such thing as a *tuple comprehension*; we'll explain why later in this chapter.

First, though, let's take a look at a dictionary comprehension.

Specifying a Dictionary Comprehension

Recall the code from earlier in this chapter that read the raw data from the CSV file into a dictionary called `flights`. This data was then transformed into a new dictionary called `flights2`, which is keyed by AM/PM flight times and uses "titlecased" destinations as values:

```
        . . .

    flights2 = {}
    for k, v in flights.items():
        flights2[convert2ampm(k)] = v.title()

        . . .
```

This code conforms to the "comprehension pattern."

Let's rework these three lines of code as a dictionary comprehension.

Start by assigning a new, empty dictionary to a variable (which we are calling `more_flights`):

```
        more_flights = {}
```

1. Start with a new, empty dictionary.

Specify how the existing data (in `flights`) is to be iterated over using the `for` loop notation (being sure not to include the usual trailing colon):

```
    more_flights = {for k, v in flights.items()}
```

2. Iterate through each of the keys and values from the existing data.

Note that there's NO colon here.

To complete the dictcomp, specify how the new dictionary's keys and values relate to each other. The `for` loop at the top of the page produces the key by converting it to an AM/PM flight time using the `convert2ampm` function, while the associated value is turned into titlecase thanks to the string's `title` method. An equivalent dictcomp can do the same thing and, as with listcomps, this relationship is specified to the *left* of the dictcomp's `for` keyword. Note the inclusion of the colon separating the new key from the new value:

```
    more_flights = {convert2ampm(k): v.title() for k, v in flights.items()}
```

3. Associate the converted key with its "titlecased" value (and note the use of the colon here).

And there it is: your first dictionary comprehension. Go ahead and take it for a spin to confirm that it works.

Extend Comprehensions with Filters

Let's imagine you need only the converted flight data for *Freeport*.

Reverting to the original `for` loop, you'd likely extend the code to include an `if` statement that filters based on the current value in `v` (the destination), producing code like this:

```
just_freeport = {}
for k, v in flights.items():
    if v == 'FREEPORT':
        just_freeport[convert2ampm(k)] = v.title()
```

The flight data is only converted and added to the "just_freeport" dictionary if it relates to the Freeport destination.

```
TIME,DESTINATION
09:35,FREEPORT
17:00,FREEPORT
09:55,WEST END
19:00,WEST END
10:45,TREASURE CAY
12:00,TREASURE CAY
11:45,ROCK SOUND
17:55,ROCK SOUND
```

The raw data

If you execute the above loop code at the >>> prompt, you'll end up with just two rows of data (representing the two scheduled flights to *Freeport* as contained in the raw data file). This shouldn't be surprising, as using an `if` in this way to filter data is a standard technique. It turns out that such filters can be used with comprehensions, too. Simply take the `if` statement (minus the colon) and tack it onto the end of your comprehension. Here's the dictcomp from the bottom of the last page:

```
more_flights = {convert2ampm(k): v.title() for k, v in flights.items()}
```

And here's a version of the same dictcomp with the filter added:

```
just_freeport2 = {convert2ampm(k): v.title() for k, v in flights.items() if v == 'FREEPORT'}
```

The flight data is only converted and added to the "just_freeport2" dictionary if it relates to the Freeport destination.

If you execute this filtered dictcomp at your >>> prompt, the data in the newly created `just_freeport2` dictionary is identical to the data in `just_freeport`. Both `just_freeport` and `just_freeport2`'s data is a **copy** of the original data in the `flights` dictionary.

Granted, the line of code that produces `just_freeport2` looks intimidating. Many programmers new to Python complain that comprehensions are **hard to read**. However, recall that Python's usual end-of-line-means-end-of-statement rule is switched off whenever code appears between a bracket pair, so you can rewrite any comprehension over multiple lines to make it easier to read, like so:

```
just_freeport3 = {convert2ampm(k): v.title()
                  for k, v in flights.items()
                  if v == 'FREEPORT'}
```

You'll need to get used to reading those one-line comprehensions. That said, Python programmers are increasingly writing longer comprehensions over multiple lines (so you'll see this syntax, too).

Recall What You Set Out to Do

Now that you've seen what comprehensions can do for you, let's revisit the required dictionary manipulations from earlier in this chapter to see how we're doing. Here's the first requirement:

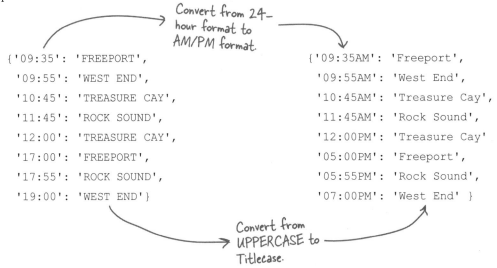

Given the data in the `flights` dictionary, you've seen that the following dictionary comprehension performs the above conversions *in one line of code*, assigning the copied data to a new dictionary called `fts` here:

```
fts = {convert2ampm(k): v.title() for k, v in flights.items()}
```

The second manipulation (listing flight times per destination) is a little more involved. There's a bit more work to do due to the fact that the data manipulations are more complex:

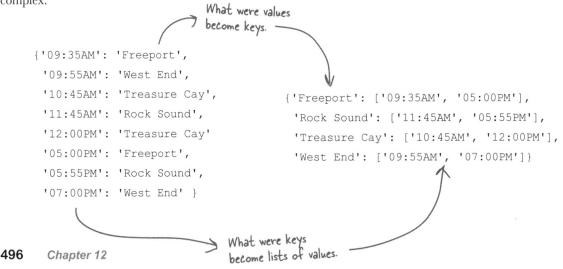

Sharpen your pencil

Before starting to work on the second manipulation, let's pause for a bit to see how well the comprehension material is seeping into your brain.

You've been tasked with transforming the three `for` loops on this page into comprehensions. As you do, don't forget to test your code in IDLE (before flipping the page and peeking at our solutions). In fact, before you try to write the comprehensions, execute these loops and see what they do. Write your comprehension solutions in the spaces provided.

1
```
data = [ 1, 2, 3, 4, 5, 6, 7, 8 ]
evens = []
for num in data:
        if not num % 2:
                evens.append(num)
```

The % operator is Python's modulo operator, which works as follows: given two numbers, divide the first by the second, then return the remainder.

....

....

2
```
data = [ 1, 'one', 2, 'two', 3, 'three', 4, 'four' ]
words = []
for num in data:
        if isinstance(num, str):
                words.append(num)
```

The "isinstance" BIF checks to see whether a variable refers to an object of a certain type.

....

....

3
```
data = list('So long and thanks for all the fish'.split())
title = []
for word in data:
        title.append(word.title())
```

....

....

Sharpen your pencil
Solution

You were to grab your pencil, and pop your thinking cap on. For each of these three `for` loops, you were tasked with transforming them into comprehensions, being sure to test your code in IDLE.

1
```
data = [ 1, 2, 3, 4, 5, 6, 7, 8 ]
evens = []
for num in data:
        if not num % 2:
                evens.append(num)
```
These four lines of loop code (which populate "evens") become one line of comprehension.

evens = [num for num in data if not num % 2]

2
```
data = [ 1, 'one', 2, 'two', 3, 'three', 4, 'four' ]
words = []
for num in data:
        if isinstance(num, str):
                words.append(num)
```
Again, this four-line loop is reworked as a one-line comprehension.

words = [num for num in data if isinstance(num, str)]

3
```
data = list('So long and thanks for all the fish'.split())
title = []
for word in data:
        title.append(word.title())
```
You should find this one the easiest of the three (as it contains no filter).

title = [word.title() for word in data]

Deal with Complexity the Python Way

With your comprehension practice session behind you, let's experiment at the >>> prompt to work out what has to happen to the data in the `fts` dictionary in order to transform it into what's required.

Before writing any code, take another look at the required transformation. Notice how the keys in the new dictionary (on the right) are a list of unique destinations taken from the values in the `fts` dictionary (on the left):

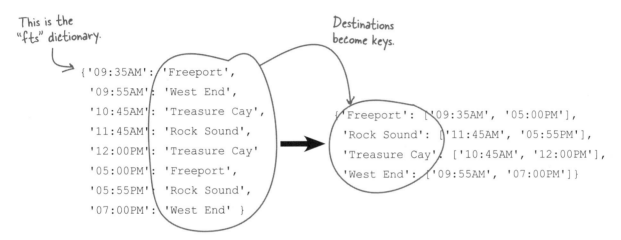

This is the "fts" dictionary.

Destinations become keys.

```
{'09:35AM': 'Freeport',
 '09:55AM': 'West End',
 '10:45AM': 'Treasure Cay',
 '11:45AM': 'Rock Sound',
 '12:00PM': 'Treasure Cay'
 '05:00PM': 'Freeport',
 '05:55PM': 'Rock Sound',
 '07:00PM': 'West End' }
```

```
{'Freeport': ['09:35AM', '05:00PM'],
 'Rock Sound': ['11:45AM', '05:55PM'],
 'Treasure Cay': ['10:45AM', '12:00PM'],
 'West End': ['09:55AM', '07:00PM']}
```

It turns out that producing those four unique destinations is very straightforward. Given that you have the data on the left in a dictionary called `fts`, you can access all of the values using `fts.values`, then feed that to the `set` BIF to remove duplicates. Let's store the unique destinations in a variable called `dests`:

Grab all of the values in "fts", then feed them to the "set" BIF. This gets you the data you need.

```
>>> dests = set(fts.values())
>>> print(dests)
{'Freeport', 'West End', 'Rock Sound', 'Treasure Cay'}
```

Here are the four unique destinations, which you can use as the new dictionary's keys.

Now that you have a way to get the unique destinations, it's time to grab the flight times associated with those destinations. This data is also in the `fts` dictionary.

Before turning the page, have a think about how you'd go about extracting the flight times given each unique destination.

In fact, don't worry about extracting all the flight times for *every* destination; just work out how to do it for *West End* first.

Extract a Single Destination's Flight Times

Let's start by extracting the flight time data for a single destination, namely *West End*.
Here's the data you need to extract:

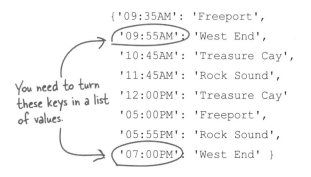

```
{'09:35AM': 'Freeport',
 '09:55AM': 'West End',
 '10:45AM': 'Treasure Cay',
 '11:45AM': 'Rock Sound',
 '12:00PM': 'Treasure Cay'
 '05:00PM': 'Freeport',
 '05:55PM': 'Rock Sound',
 '07:00PM': 'West End' }
```

You need to turn these keys in a list of values.

As before, pull up the >>> prompt and get to work. Given the `fts` dictionary, you can
extract the *West End* flight times using code like this:

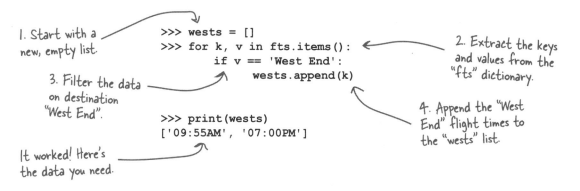

```
>>> wests = []
>>> for k, v in fts.items():
        if v == 'West End':
            wests.append(k)

>>> print(wests)
['09:55AM', '07:00PM']
```

1. Start with a new, empty list.

2. Extract the keys and values from the "fts" dictionary.

3. Filter the data on destination "West End".

4. Append the "West End" flight times to the "wests" list.

It worked! Here's the data you need.

On seeing this code, you should hear little alarm bells ringing in your brain, as this
`for` loop is surely a candidate for reworking as a list comprehension, right?

What was four lines of code is now one, thanks to your use of a listcomp.

That `for` loop becomes this equivalent listcomp:

```
>>> wests2 = [k for k, v in fts.items() if v == 'West End']

>>> print(wests2)
['09:55AM', '07:00PM']
```

It also worked! Here's the data you need.

**Now that you know how to extract this data for one
specific destination, let's do it for all the destinations.**

Extract Flight Times for All Destinations

You now have this code, which extracts the set of unique destinations:

```
dests = set(fts.values())
```
← The unique destinations

And you also have this listcomp, which extracts the list of flight times for a given destination (in this example, that destination is *West End*):

```
wests2 = [k for k, v in fts.items() if v == 'West End']
```
← The flight times for the "West End" destination

To extract the list of flights times for *all* of the destinations, you need to combine these two statements (within a `for` loop).

In the code that follows, we've dispensed with the need for the `dests` and `west2` variables, preferring to use the code *directly* as part of the `for` loop. We no longer hardcode *West End*, as the current destination is in `dest` (within the listcomp):

The unique destinations

```
>>> for dest in set(fts.values()):
        print(dest, '->', [k for k, v in fts.items() if v == dest])
```

The flight times for the destination referred to by the current value of "dest".

```
Treasure Cay -> ['10:45AM', '12:00PM']
West End -> ['07:00PM', '09:55AM']
Rock Sound -> ['05:55PM', '11:45AM']
Freeport -> ['09:35AM', '05:00PM']
```

The fact that we've just written a `for` loop that appears to conform to our comprehension pattern starts our brain's little bell ringing again. Let's try to suppress that ringing for now, as the code you've just experimented with at your >>> prompt *displays* the data we need...but what you really need is to *store* the data in a new dictionary. Let's create a new dictionary (called `when`) to hold this newly extracted data. Head back to your >>> prompt and adjust the above `for` loop to use `when`:

art with w, empty ionary.

2. Extract the unique set of destinations.

```
>>> when = {}
>>> for dest in set(fts.values()):
        when[dest] = [k for k, v in fts.items() if v == dest]
```

3. Update the "when" dictionary with the flight times.

```
>>> pprint.pprint(when)
{'Freeport': ['09:35AM', '05:00PM'],
 'Rock Sound': ['05:55PM', '11:45AM'],
 'Treasure Cay': ['10:45AM', '12:00PM'],
 'West End': ['07:00PM', '09:55AM']}
```

Here it is: the data you need, in a dictionary called "when".

If you're like us, your little brain bell (that you've been trying to suppress) is likely ringing loudly and driving you crazy as you look at this code.

That Feeling You Get...

...when a single line of code starts to look like *magic*.

Switch off your brain bell, then take another look at the code that makes up your most recent `for` loop:

```
when = {}
for dest in set(fts.values()):
    when[dest] = [k for k, v in fts.items() if v == dest]
```

This code conforms to the pattern that makes it a potential target for reworking as a comprehension. Here's the above `for` loop code reworked as a dictcomp that extracts a *copy* of the data you need into a new dictionary called `when2`:

```
when2 = {dest: [k for k, v in fts.items() if v == dest] for dest in set(fts.values())}
```

It looks like *magic*, doesn't it?

This is the most complex comprehension you've seen so far, due mainly to the fact that the *outer* dictcomp contains an *inner* listcomp. That said, this dictcomp showcases one of the features that set comprehensions apart from the equivalent `for` loop code: you can put a comprehension almost anywhere in your code. The same does not hold for `for` loops, which can only appear as statements in your code (that is, not as part of expressions).

Of course, that's not to say you should *always* do something like this:

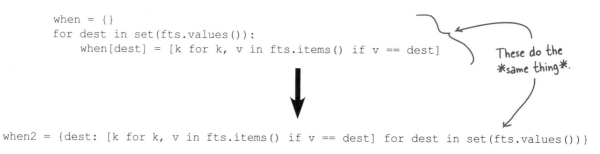

```
when = {}
for dest in set(fts.values()):
    when[dest] = [k for k, v in fts.items() if v == dest]
```

These do the
same thing.

```
when2 = {dest: [k for k, v in fts.items() if v == dest] for dest in set(fts.values())}
```

Be warned: a dictionary comprehension containing an embedded list comprehension is hard to read *the first time you see it*.

However, with repeated exposure, comprehensions do get easier to read and understand, and—as stated earlier in this chapter—Python programmers use them *a lot*. Whether you use comprehensions is up to you. If you are happier with the `for` loop code, use that. If you like the look of comprehensions, use them...just don't feel you *have* to.

Test Drive

Before moving on, let's put all of this comprehension code into our do_convert.py file. We can then run the code in this file (using IDLE) to see that the conversions and transformations that are required by *Bahamas Buzzers* are occurring as required. Confirm that your code is the same as ours, then execute the code to confirm that everything is working to specification.

```
● ● ●                do_convert.py - /Users/paul/Desktop/_NewBook/ch12/do_convert.py (3.5.2)
|
from datetime import datetime
import pprint

def convert2ampm(time24: str) -> str:
    return datetime.strptime(time24, '%H:%M').strftime('%I:%M%p')

with open('buzzers.csv') as data:
    ignore = data.readline()
    flights = {}
    for line in data:
        k, v = line.strip().split(',')
        flights[k] = v

pprint.pprint(flights)
print()

fts = {convert2ampm(k): v.title() for k, v in flights.items()}

pprint.pprint(fts)
print()

when = {dest: [k for k, v in fts.items() if v == dest] for dest in set(fts.values())}

pprint.pprint(when)
print()
```

```
● ● ●                        Python 3.5.2 Shell
/ch12/do_convert.py ===========
{'09:35': 'FREEPORT',
 '09:55': 'WEST END',
 '10:45': 'TREASURE CAY',
 '11:45': 'ROCK SOUND',
 '12:00': 'TREASURE CAY',
 '17:00': 'FREEPORT',
 '17:55': 'ROCK SOUND',
 '19:00': 'WEST END'}

{'05:00PM': 'Freeport',
 '05:55PM': 'Rock Sound',
 '07:00PM': 'West End',
 '09:35AM': 'Freeport',
 '09:55AM': 'West End',
 '10:45AM': 'Treasure Cay',
 '11:45AM': 'Rock Sound',
 '12:00PM': 'Treasure Cay'}

{'Freeport': ['05:00PM', '09:35AM'],
 'Rock Sound': ['05:55PM', '11:45AM'],
 'Treasure Cay': ['10:45AM', '12:00PM'],
 'West End': ['07:00PM', '09:55AM']}

>>>
```

Ln: 1 Col: 0

Ln: 214 Col: 4

1. The original, raw data, as read in from the CSV data file. This is "flights".

2. The raw data, copied and transformed into AM/PM format and Titlecase. This is "fts".

3. The list of flight times per destination (extracted from "fts"). This is "when".

We're flying now!

there are no
Dumb Questions

Q: So...let me get this straight: a comprehension is just syntactic shorthand for a standard looping construct?

A: Yes, specifically the `for` loop. A standard `for` loop and its equivalent comprehension do the same thing. It's just that the comprehension tends to execute considerably faster.

Q: When will I know when to use a list comprehension?

A: There are no hard and fast rules here. Typically, if you are producing a new list from an existing one, have a good look at your loop code. Ask yourself if the loop is a candidate for conversion to an equivalent comprehension. If the new list is "temporary" (that is, used once, then thrown away), ask yourself if an *embedded* list comprehension would be better for the task at hand. As a general rule, you should avoid introducing temporary variables into your code, especially if they're only used once. Ask yourself if a comprehension can be used instead.

Q: Can I avoid comprehensions altogether?

A: Yes, you can. However, they tend to see quite a bit of use within the wider Python community, so unless your plan is to never look at anyone else's code, we'd suggest taking the time to become familiar with Python's comprehension technology. Once you get used to seeing them, you'll wonder how you ever lived without them. Did we mention that they are *fast*?

Q: Yes, I get that, but is speed such a big deal nowadays? My laptop is super-fast and it runs my `for` loops quick enough.

A: That's an interesting observation. It's true that today we have computers that are vastly more powerful than anything that's come before. It's also true that we spend a lot less time trying to eke out every last CPU cycle from our code (because, let's face it: we don't have to anymore). However, when presented with a technology that offers a performance boost, why not use it? It's a small bit of effort for a big return in performance.

> I find a really strong cup of coffee (with a little something in it) helps me get my head around most comprehensions. By the way, do they work with sets and tuples?

That's a great question.

And the answer is: yes and no.

Yes, it is possible to create and use a *set comprehension* (although, to be honest, you will encounter them only very rarely).

And, no, there's no such thing as a "tuple comprehension." We'll get to *why* this is after we've shown you set comprehensions in action.

The Set Comprehension in Action

A set comprehensions (or *setcomp* for short) allows you to create a new set in one line of code, using a construct that's very similar to the list comprehension syntax.

What sets a setcomp apart from a listcomp is that the set comprehension is surrounded by curly braces (unlike the square brackets around a listcomp). This can be confusing, as dictcomps are surrounded by curly braces, too. (One wonders what came over the Python core developers when they decided to do this.)

A literal set is surrounded by curly braces, as are literal dictionaries. To tell them apart, look for the colon character used as a delimiter in dictionaries, as the colon has no meaning in sets. The same advice applies to quickly determining whether a curly-braced comprehension is a dictcomp or a setcomp: look for the colon. If it's there, you're looking at a dictcomp. If not, it's a setcomp.

Here's a quick set comprehension example (which hearkens back to an earlier example in this book). Given a set of letters (in `vowels`), and a string (in `message`), the `for` loop as well as its equivalent setcomp produce the same result— a set of the vowels found in `message`:

```
vowels = {'a', 'e', 'i', 'o', 'u'}
message = "Don't forget to pack your towel."

found = set()
for v in vowels:
    if v in message:
        found.add(v)
```

The setcomp follows the same pattern as the listcomp.

```
found2 = { v for v in vowels if v in message  }
```

Note the use of curly braces here, as this comprehension produces a set when executed by the interpreter

Take a few moments to experiment with the code on this page at your >>> prompt. Because you already know what listcomps and dictcomps can do, getting your head around set comprehensions isn't that tricky. There's really nothing more to them than what's on this page.

How to Spot a Comprehension

As you become more familiar with the look of comprehension code, they become easier to spot and understand. Here's a good general rule for spotting list comprehensions:

If you spot code surrounded by [and], then you are looking at a list comprehension.

This rule can be generalized as follows:

If you spot code surrounded by brackets (curly or square), then you are likely looking at a comprehension.

Why the use of the word "likely"?

In addition to code being surrounded by [ ], comprehensions can also, as you've seen, be surrounded by { }. When code is surrounded by [and], you are looking at a **list** comprehension. When code is surrounded by { and }, you are looking at either a **set** or a **dictionary** comprehension. A dictcomp is easy to spot thanks to its use of the colon character as a delimiter.

However, code can also appear between (and), which is a *special case*, even though you'd be forgiven for suggesting that code surrounded by parentheses must surely be a *tuple comprehension*. You'd be forgiven, but wrong: "tuple comprehensions" don't exist, even though you can put code between (and). After the "fun" you've been having with comprehensions so far in this chapter, you may be thinking: *could this get any weirder?*

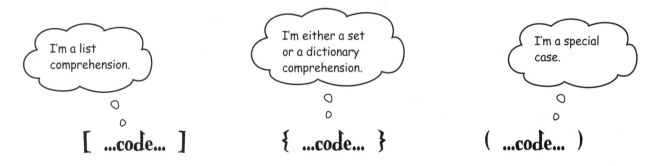

Let's conclude this chapter (and this book) by exploring what's going on with code that appears between (and). It's not a "tuple comprehension," but it is obviously allowed, so what is it?

What About "Tuple Comprehensions"?

Python's four built-in data structures (tuples, lists, sets, and dictionaries) can be put to many uses. However, all but tuples can be created via a comprehension.

Why is this?

It turns out that the idea of a "tuple comprehension" doesn't really make sense. Recall that tuples are *immutable*: once a tuple is created, it cannot be changed. This also means that it's not possible to generate a tuple's values in code, as this short IDLE session shows:

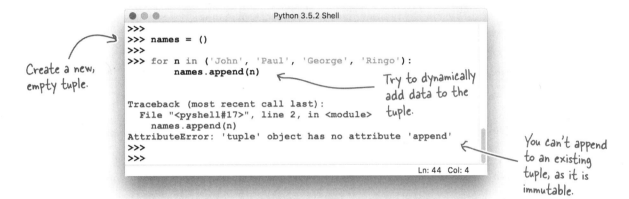

Create a new, empty tuple.

Try to dynamically add data to the tuple.

You can't append to an existing tuple, as it is immutable.

There's nothing weird or wonderful going on here, as this is the behavior expected from tuples: once one exists, it *cannot* be changed. This fact alone should be enough to rule out using a tuple within any sort of comprehension. But take a look at this interaction at the >>> prompt. The second loop differs from the first in the smallest of ways: the square brackets around the listcomp (in the first loop) have been replaced with parentheses (in the second):

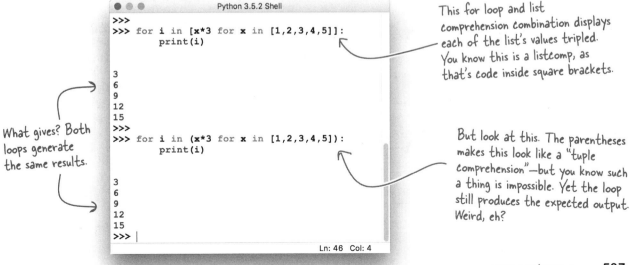

This for loop and list comprehension combination displays each of the list's values tripled. You know this is a listcomp, as that's code inside square brackets.

What gives? Both loops generate the same results.

But look at this. The parentheses makes this look like a "tuple comprehension"—but you know such a thing is impossible. Yet the loop still produces the expected output. Weird, eh?

Parentheses Around Code == Generator

When you come across something that looks like a listcomp but is surrounded by parentheses, you're looking at a **generator**:

This looks like a listcomp, but isn't: it's a generator.

```
for i in (x*3 for x in [1, 2, 3, 4, 5]):
    print(i)
```

A generator can be used anywhere a listcomp is used, and produces the same results.

As you saw at the bottom of the last page, when you replace a listcomp's surrounding square brackets with parentheses, the results are the same; that is, the generator and the listcomp produce the same data.

However, they do not execute in the same way.

If you're scratching your head at the previous sentence, consider this: when a listcomp executes, it produces **all** of its data prior to any other processing occurring. Taken in the context of the example at the top of this page, the for loop doesn't start processing *any* of the data produced by the listcomp until the listcomp is done. This means that a listcomp that takes a long time to produce data delays any other code from running *until the listcomp concludes*.

With a small list of data items (as shown above), this is not a big issue.

But imagine your listcomp is required to work with a list that produces 10 million items of data. You've now got two issues: (1) you have to wait for the listcomp to process those 10 million data items *before doing anything else*, and (2) you have to worry that the computer running your listcomp has enough RAM to hold all that data in memory while the listcomp executes (**10 million** individual pieces of data). If your listcomp runs out of memory, the interpreter terminates (and your program is toast).

Generators produce data items one at a time...

When you replace your listcomp's square brackets with parentheses, the listcomp becomes a **generator**, and your code behaves differently.

Unlike a listcomp, which must conclude before any other code can execute, a generator releases data as soon as the data is produced by the generator's code. This means if you generate 10 million data items, the interpreter only needs enough memory to hold **one** data item (at a time), and any code that's waiting to consume the data items produced by the generator executes immediately; that is, *there's no waiting*.

There's nothing quite like an example to understand the difference using a generator can make, so let's perform a simple task twice: once with a listcomp, then again with a generator.

Listcomps and generators produce the same results, but operate in a very different way.

Using a Listcomp to Process URLs

To demonstrate the difference using a generator can make, let's perform a task using a listcomp (before rewriting the task as a generator).

As has been our practice throughout this book, let's experiment with some code at the >>> prompt that uses the requests library (which lets you programmatically interact with the Web). Here's a small interactive session that imports the requests library, defines a three-item tuple (called urls), and then combines a for loop with a listcomp to request each URL's landing page, before processing the web response returned.

To understand what's going on here, you need to follow along on your computer.

> Download "requests" from PyPI using the "pip" command.

Define a tuple of URLs. Feel free to substitute your own URLs here. Just be sure to define at least three.

The "for" loop contains a listcomp, which, for each of the URLs in "urls", gets the website's landing page.

```
Python 3.5.2 Shell
>>>
>>> import requests
>>>
>>> urls = ('http://headfirstlabs.com', 'http://oreilly.com', 'http://twitter.com')
>>>
>>> for resp in [requests.get(url) for url in urls]:
        print(len(resp.content), '->', resp.status_code, '->', resp.url)


31590 -> 200 -> http://headfirstlabs.com/
78722 -> 200 -> http://www.oreilly.com/
128244 -> 200 -> https://twitter.com/
>>> |
                                                          Ln: 106  Col: 4
```

Nothing weird or wonderful here. The output produced is exactly what's expected.

With each response received, display the size of the returned landing page (in bytes), the HTTP status code, and the URL used.

If you're following along on your computer, you will experience a noticeable delay between entering the for loop code and seeing the results. When the results appear, they are displayed in one go (all at once). This is because the listcomp works through each of the URLs in the urls tuple before making any results available to the for loop. The outcome? You have to wait for your output.

Note that there's *nothing* wrong with this code: it does what you want it to, and the output is correct. However, let's rework this listcomp as a generator to see the difference it makes. As mentioned above, be sure to follow along on your computer as you work through the next page (so you can see what happens).

Using a Generator to Process URLs

Here's the example from the last page reworked as a generator. Doing so is easy;
simply replace the listcomp's square brackets with parentheses:

```
●●●                                    *Python 3.5.2 Shell*
>>>
>>>            An important change: replace
>>>            the square brackets with
>>>            parentheses.
>>>
>>> for resp in (requests.get(url) for url in urls):
        print(len(resp.content), '->', resp.status_code, '->', resp.url)

                                                            Ln: 151  Col: 1
```

A short moment after entering the above `for` loop, the first result appears:

```
●●●                                    *Python 3.5.2 Shell*
>>>
>>>
>>> for resp in (requests.get(url) for url in urls):
        print(len(resp.content), '->', resp.status_code, '->', resp.url)

31590 -> 200 -> http://headfirstlabs.com/   ←── The first URL's response
|
                                                            Ln: 153  Col: 0
```

Then, a moment later, the next line of results appear:

```
●●●                                    *Python 3.5.2 Shell*
>>>
>>> for resp in (requests.get(url) for url in urls):
        print(len(resp.content), '->', resp.status_code, '->', resp.url)

31590 -> 200 -> http://headfirstlabs.com/
78722 -> 200 -> http://www.oreilly.com/  ←── The second URL's response
                                                            Ln: 154  Col: 0
```

Then—finally—a few moments later, the last results line appears (and the `for` loop ends):

```
●●●                                    Python 3.5.2 Shell
>>> for resp in (requests.get(url) for url in urls):
        print(len(resp.content), '->', resp.status_code, '->', resp.url)

31590 -> 200 -> http://headfirstlabs.com/
78722 -> 200 -> http://www.oreilly.com/
128244 -> 200 -> https://twitter.com/   ←── The third, and final, URL's response
>>> |
                                                            Ln: 156  Col: 4
```

Using a Generator: What Just Happened?

If you compare the results produced by your listcomp to those produced by your generator, they are *identical*. However, the behavior of your code isn't.

The listcomp **waits** for all of its data to be produced before feeding any data to the waiting `for` loop, whereas the generator **releases** data as soon as it becomes available. This means the `for` loop that uses the generator is much more responsive, as opposed to the listcomp (which makes you wait).

If you're thinking this isn't really that big a deal, imagine if the URLs tuple was defined with one hundred, one thousand, or one million URLs. Further, imagine that the code processing the response is feeding the processed data to another process (perhaps a waiting database). As the number of URLs increases, the listcomp's behavior becomes worse compared to that of the generator.

So...does this mean I should always use a generator over a listcomp?

No. We wouldn't say that.

Don't misunderstand: the fact that generators exist is *great*, but this doesn't mean you'll want to replace all of your listcomps with an equivalent generator. Like a lot of things in programming, which approach you use depends on what you're trying to do.

If you can afford to wait, then listcomps are fine; otherwise, consider using a generator.

One interesting usage of generators is to embed them within a function. Let's take a look at encapsulating your just-created generator in a function.

Define What Your Function Needs to Do

Let's imagine that you want to take your requests generator and turn it into a function. You've decided to package the generator within a small module you're writing, and you want other programmers to be able to use it without having to know or understand generators.

Here's your generator code once more:

```
import requests
urls = ('http://headfirstlabs.com', 'http://oreilly.com', 'http://twitter.com')
for resp in (requests.get(url) for url in urls):
    print(len(resp.content), '->', resp.status_code, '->', resp.url)
```

Import any required libraries.

Define a tuple of URLs.

Process the generated data.

The generator (remember: looks like a listcomp, but is surrounded by parentheses)

Let's create a function that encapsulates this code. The function, which is called gen_from_urls, takes a single argument (a tuple of URLs), and returns a tuple of results for each URL. The returned tuple contains three values: the length of the URL's content, the HTTP status code, and the URL the response came from.

Assuming gen_from_urls exists, you want other programmers to be able to execute your function as part of a for loop, like this:

```
from url_utils import gen_from_urls
urls = ('http://headfirstlabs.com', 'http://oreilly.com', 'http://twitter.com')
for resp_len, status, url in gen_from_urls(urls):
    print(resp_len, status, url)
```

Import the function from your module.

Define a tuple of URLs.

Process the data.

Call the function on each iteration of the "for" loop.

Although this new code does not look all that different from the code at the top of the page, note that programmers using gen_from_urls have no clue (nor do they need to know) that you're using requests to talk to the Web. Nor do they need to know that you're using a generator. All of your implementation details and choices are hidden behind that easy-to-understand function call.

Let's see what's involved in writing gen_from_urls so that it can generate the data you need.

Yield to the Power of Generator Functions

Now that you know what the `gen_from_urls` function needs to do, let's go about writing it. Begin by creating a new file called `url_utils.py`. Edit this file, then add `import requests` as its first line of code.

The function's `def` line is straightforward, as it takes a single tuple on the way in, and returns a tuple on output (note how we've included type annotations to make this explicit for users of our generator function). Go ahead and add the function's `def` line to the file, like so:

```
import requests

def gen_from_urls(urls: tuple) -> tuple:
```

After importing "requests", define your new function.

The function's suite is the generator from the last page, and the `for` line is a simple copy-and-paste:

```
import requests

def gen_from_urls(urls: tuple) -> tuple:
    for resp in (requests.get(url) for url in urls):
```

Add in your "for" loop line with the generator.

The next line of code needs to "return" the result of that GET request as performed by the `requests.get` function. Although it's tempting to add the following line as the `for`'s suite, **please don't do this**:

```
    return len(resp.content), resp.status_code, resp.url
```

When a function executes a `return` statement, the function *terminates*. You don't want this to happen here, as the `gen_from_urls` function is being called as part of a `for` loop, which is expecting a *different* tuple of results *each time the function's called*.

But, if you can't execute `return`, what are you to do?

Use `yield` instead. The `yield` keyword was added to Python to support the creation of **generator functions**, and you can use it anywhere a `return` is used. When you do, your function morphs into a generator function that can be "called" from any iterator, which, in this case, is from within your `for` loop:

```
import requests

def gen_from_urls(urls: tuple) -> tuple:
    for resp in (requests.get(url) for url in urls):
        yield len(resp.content), resp.status_code, resp.url
```

Use "yield" to return each line of results from the GET response to the waiting "for" loop. Remember: DON'T use "return".

Let's take a closer look at what's going on here.

Tracing Your Generator Function, 1 of 2

To understand what happens when your generator function runs, let's trace the execution of the following code:

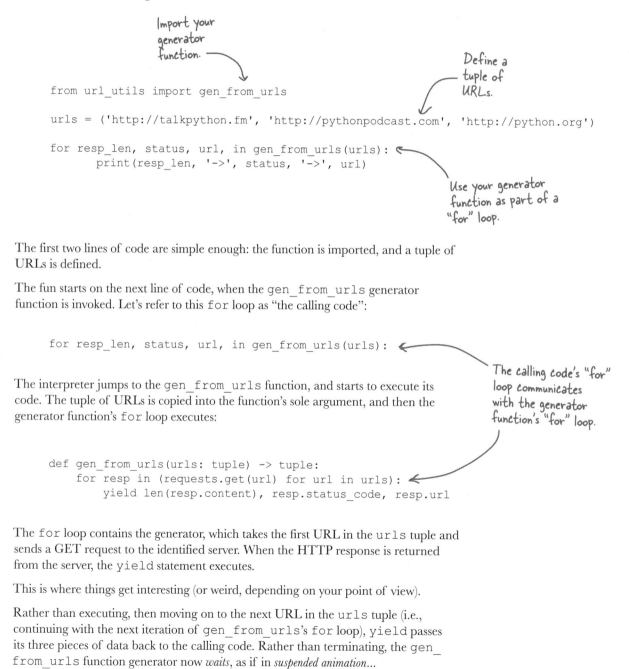

Import your generator function.

Define a tuple of URLs.

```
from url_utils import gen_from_urls

urls = ('http://talkpython.fm', 'http://pythonpodcast.com', 'http://python.org')

for resp_len, status, url, in gen_from_urls(urls):
    print(resp_len, '->', status, '->', url)
```

Use your generator function as part of a "for" loop.

The first two lines of code are simple enough: the function is imported, and a tuple of URLs is defined.

The fun starts on the next line of code, when the gen_from_urls generator function is invoked. Let's refer to this for loop as "the calling code":

```
for resp_len, status, url, in gen_from_urls(urls):
```

The interpreter jumps to the gen_from_urls function, and starts to execute its code. The tuple of URLs is copied into the function's sole argument, and then the generator function's for loop executes:

```
def gen_from_urls(urls: tuple) -> tuple:
    for resp in (requests.get(url) for url in urls):
        yield len(resp.content), resp.status_code, resp.url
```

The calling code's "for" loop communicates with the generator function's "for" loop.

The for loop contains the generator, which takes the first URL in the urls tuple and sends a GET request to the identified server. When the HTTP response is returned from the server, the yield statement executes.

This is where things get interesting (or weird, depending on your point of view).

Rather than executing, then moving on to the next URL in the urls tuple (i.e., continuing with the next iteration of gen_from_urls's for loop), yield passes its three pieces of data back to the calling code. Rather than terminating, the gen_from_urls function generator now *waits*, as if in *suspended animation*...

Tracing Your Generator Function, 2 of 2

When the data (as passed back by `yield`) arrives at the calling code, the `for` loop's suite executes. As the suite contains a single call to the `print` BIF, that line of code executes and displays the results from the first URL on screen:

```
print(resp_len, '->', status, '->', url)

34591 -> 200 -> https://talkpython.fm/
```

The calling code's `for` loop then iterates, calling `gen_from_urls` again...sort of.

This is *almost* what happens. What actually happens is that `gen_from_urls` is awakened from its suspended animation, then continues to run. The `for` loop within `gen_from_urls` iterates, takes the next URL from the `urls` tuple, and contacts the server associated with the URL. When the HTTP response is returned from the server, the `yield` statement executes, passing its three pieces of data back to the calling code (which the function accesses via the `resp` object):

```
yield len(resp.content), resp.status_code, resp.url
```

The three yielded pieces of data are taken from the "resp" object returned by the "requests" library's "get" method.

As before, rather than terminating, the `gen_from_urls` generator function now *waits* once more, as if in *suspended animation*...

When the data (as passed back by `yield`) arrives at the calling code, the `for` loop's suite executes `print` once more, displaying the second set of results on screen:

```
34591 -> 200 -> https://talkpython.fm/
19468 -> 200 -> http://pythonpodcast.com/
```

The calling code's `for` loop iterates, "calling" `gen_from_urls` once more, which results in your generator function awakening again. The `yield` statement is executed, results are returned to the calling code, and the display updates again:

```
34591 -> 200 -> https://talkpython.fm/
19468 -> 200 -> http://pythonpodcast.com/
47413 -> 200 -> https://www.python.org/
```

At this point, you've exhausted your tuple of URLs, so the generator function and the calling code's `for` loop both terminate. It's as if the two pieces of code were taking turns to execute, passing data between themselves on each turn.

Let's see this in action at the >>> prompt. It's now time for one last *Test Drive*.

TEST DRIVE

In this, the last *Test Drive* in this book, let's take your generator function for a spin. As has been our practice all along, load your code into an IDLE edit window, then press F5 to exercise the function at the >>> prompt. Follow along with our session (below):

Here's the "gen_from_urls" generator function in the "url_utils.py" module.

```
url_utils.py - /Users/paul/Desktop/_NewBook/ch12/url_utils.py (3.5.2)

import requests

def gen_from_urls(urls: tuple) -> tuple:
    for resp in (requests.get(url) for url in urls):
        yield len(resp.content), resp.status_code, resp.url

                                                              Ln: 8  Col: 0
```

The first example below shows gen_from_urls being called as part of a for loop. As expected, the output is the same as that obtained a few pages back.

The second example below shows gen_from_urls being used as part of a dictcomp. Note how the new dictionary only needs to store the URL (as a key) and the size of the landing page (as the value). The HTTP status code is *not* needed in this example, so we tell the interpreter to ignore it using Python's **default variable name** (which is a single underscore character):

```
Python 3.5.2 Shell
>>>
>>>
>>> for resp_len, status, url in gen_from_urls(urls):
        print(resp_len, '->', status, '->', url)


31590 -> 200 -> http://headfirstlabs.com/
78722 -> 200 -> http://www.oreilly.com/
128244 -> 200 -> https://twitter.com/
>>>
>>> urls_res = {url: size for size, _, url in gen_from_urls(urls)}
>>>
>>> import pprint
>>>
>>> pprint.pprint(urls_res)
{'http://headfirstlabs.com/': 31590,
 'http://www.oreilly.com/': 78722,
 'https://twitter.com/': 128244}
>>>
>>>
                                                              Ln: 271  Col: 0
```

Each line of results appears, after a short pause, as the data is generated by the function.

Pass the tuple of URLs to the generator function.

This dictcomp associates the URL with the length of its landing page.

The underscore tells the code to ignore the yielded HTTP status code value.

Pretty-printing the "url_res" dictionary confirms that the generator function can be used within a dictcomp (as well as within a "for" loop).

Concluding Remarks

The use of comprehensions and generator functions is often regarded as an advanced topic in the Python world. However, this is mainly due to the fact that these features are missing from other mainstream programming languages, which means that programmers moving to Python sometimes struggle with them (as they have no existing point of reference).

That said, over at *Head First Labs*, the Python programming team *loves* comprehensions and generators, and believes that with repeated exposure, specifying the looping constructs that use them becomes second nature. They can't imagine having to do without them.

Even if you find the comprehension and generator syntax weird, our advice is to stick with them. Even if you dismiss the fact that they are more performant than the equivalent `for` loop, the fact that you can use comprehensions and generators in places where you cannot use a `for` loop is reason enough to take a serious look at these Python features. Over time, and as you become more familiar with their syntax, opportunities to exploit comprehensions and generators will present themselves as naturally as those that tell your programming brain to use a function here, a loop there, a class over here, and so on. Here's a review of what you were introduced to in this chapter:

BULLET POINTS

- When it comes to working with data in files, Python has options. As well as the standard `open` BIF, you can use the facilities of the standard library's `csv` module to work with CSV-formatted data.

- Method **chains** allow you to perform processing on data in one line of code. The `string.strip().split()` chain is seen a lot in Python code.

- Take care with how you order your method chains. Specifically, pay attention to the type of data returned from each method (and ensure type compatibility is maintained).

- A `for` loop used to transform data from one format to another can be reworked as a **comprehension**.

- Comprehensions can be written to process existing lists, dictionaries, and sets, with list comprehensions being the most popular variant "in the wild." Seasoned Python programmers refer to these constructs as *listcomps*, *dictcomps*, and *setcomps*.

- A **listcomp** is code surrounded by square brackets, while a **dictcomp** is code surrounded by curly braces (with colon delimiters). A **setcomp** is also code surrounded by curly braces (but without the dictcomp's colon).

- There's no such thing as a "tuple comprehension," as tuples are immutable (so it makes no sense to try to dynamically create one).

- If you spot comprehension code surrounded by parentheses, you're looking at a **generator** (which can be turned into a function that itself uses `yield` to generate data as needed).

As this chapter concludes (and, by definition, the core content of this book), we have one final question to ask you. Take a deep breath, then flip the page.

One Final Question

OK. Here goes, our final question to you: *at this stage in this book, do you even notice Python's use of significant whitespace?*

The most common complaint heard from programmers new to Python is its use of whitespace to signify blocks of code (instead of, for instance, curly braces). But, after a while, your brain tends not to notice anymore.

This is not an accident: Python's use of significant whitespace was intentional on the part of the language's creator.

It was deliberately done this way, because **code is read more than it's written**. This means code that conforms to a consistent and well-known look and feel is easier to read. This also means that Python code written 10 years ago by a complete stranger is still readable by you *today* because of Python's use of whitespace.

This is a big win for the Python community, which makes it a big win for *you*, too.

Chapter 12's Code

This is "do_convert.py".

```python
from datetime import datetime
import pprint

def convert2ampm(time24: str) -> str:
    return datetime.strptime(time24, '%H:%M').strftime('%I:%M%p')

with open('buzzers.csv') as data:
    ignore = data.readline()
    flights = {}
    for line in data:
        k, v = line.strip().split(',')
        flights[k] = v

pprint.pprint(flights)
print()

fts = {convert2ampm(k): v.title() for k, v in flights.items()}

pprint.pprint(fts)
print()

when = {dest: [k for k, v in fts.items() if v == dest] for dest in set(fts.values())}

pprint.pprint(when)
print()
```

This is "url_utils.py".

```python
import requests

def gen_from_urls(urls: tuple) -> tuple:
    for resp in (requests.get(url) for url in urls):
        yield len(resp.content), resp.status_code, resp.url
```

It's Time to Go...

You're on your way!

We're sad to see you leave, but nothing would make us happier than you taking what you've learned about Python in this book and *putting it to use*. You're at the start of your Python journey, and there's always more to learn. Of course, you're not quite done with this book just yet. There's the five (yes: five!) appendixes to work through. We promise they're not that long, and are well worth the effort. And, of course, there's the index—let's not forget about the index!

We hope you've had as much fun learning about Python as we've had writing this book for you. It's been a blast. Enjoy!

appendix a: installation

Installing Python

Doris, I've got great news: the latest Python installers are a breeze to work with.

First things first: let's get Python installed on your computer.

Whether you're running on *Windows*, *Mac OS X*, or *Linux*, Python's got you covered. How you install it on each of these platforms is specific to how things work on each of these operating systems (we know...a shocker, eh?), and the Python community works hard to provide installers that target all the popular systems. In this short appendix, you'll be guided through installing Python on your computer.

Install Python 3 on Windows

Unless you (or someone else) has installed the Python interpreter onto your Windows PC, it is unlikely to be preinstalled. Even if it is, let's install the latest and greatest version of Python 3 into your *Windows* computer now.

If you already have a version of Python 3 installed, it'll be upgraded. If you have Python 2 installed, Python 3 will install alongside it (but won't interfere with your Python 2 in any way). And if you don't have any version of Python yet, well, you soon will!

Download, then install

Point your browser to *www.python.org*, and then click the *Downloads* tab.

Two large buttons will appear, offering the choice of the latest version of Python 3 or Python 2. *Click on the Python 3 button.* Go ahead and save the file for download when prompted. After a little while, the download will complete. Locate the downloaded file in your *Downloads* folder (or wherever you saved it), then double-click on the file to start the install.

A standard *Windows* installation process begins. By and large, you can click on *Next* at each of the prompts, except for this one (shown below), where you'll want to pause to make a configuration change to ensure *Add Python 3.5 to Path* is selected; this ensures *Windows* can find the interpreter whenever it needs to:

Note: As this book hurtles toward its date with the printing press, the next version of Python 3 (release 3.6) is due out. As this won't be until the end of 2016 (a mere handful of weeks *after* this book publishes), we're showing 3.5 in these screenshots. Don't worry about matching the version we have here. Go ahead and download/install the latest.

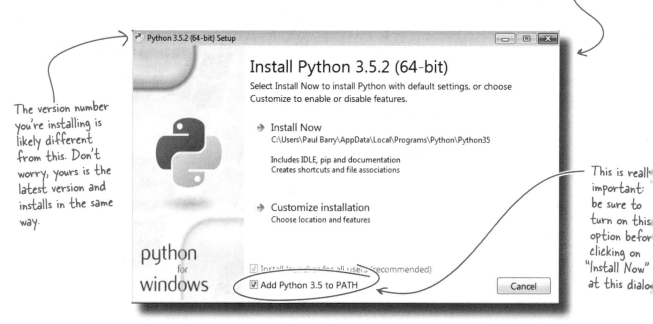

The version number you're installing is likely different from this. Don't worry, yours is the latest version and installs in the same way.

This is really important: be sure to turn on this option before clicking on "Install Now" at this dialog.

Check Python 3 on Windows

Now that the Python interpreter is installed on your *Windows* machine, let's run a few checks to confirm all is OK.

For starters, you should have a new group on your *Start* menu under *All Programs*. We've included what it looks like on one of the *Head First Labs'* *Windows 7* machines. Yours should look similar. If it doesn't, you may need to redo the installation. Windows 8 users (or higher) should also have a new group similar to this.

Let's examine the items in the Python 3.5 group from the bottom up.

The Python installer adds a new group to your All Programs list.

The *Python 3.5 Modules Docs* option provides access to all of the documentation included with all of the installed modules that are available within your Python system. You'll be learning lots about modules as you work through this book, so you don't need to worry about doing anything with this option right now.

The *Python 3.5 Manuals* option opens the entire set of Python language documentation in the standard *Windows* help utility. This material is a copy of the Python 3 documentation available on the Web.

The *Python 3.5* option fires up a text-based interactive command prompt, >>>, which is used to experiment with code as you write it. We'll have more to say about the >>> prompt starting from Chapter 1. If you have clicked on this option to try it out and are now at a loss as to what to do, type `quit()` to escape back to *Windows*.

The final option, *IDLE (Python 3.5)*, runs the Python integrated development environment, which is called *IDLE*. This is a very simple IDE that provides access to Python's >>> prompt, a passable text editor, the Python debugger, and the Python documentation. We'll be using *IDLE* a lot in this book, starting in Chapter 1.

It's Python 3 on Windows, sort of...

Python's heritage is on Unix and Unix-like systems, and this can sometimes come through when you're working in *Windows*. For instance, some software that is assumed to exist by Python isn't always available by default on *Windows*, so to get the most out of Python, programmers on *Windows* often have to install a few extra bits and pieces. Let's take a moment to install one such bonus piece to demonstrate how these missing bits can be added when needed.

Add to Python 3 on Windows

Sometimes programmers using the *Windows* version of Python feel like they are being short-changed: some of the features assumed (by Python) on those other platforms are "missing" from *Windows*.

Thankfully, some enterprising programmers have written third-party modules that can be installed *into* Python, thus providing the missing functionality. Installing any of these modules involves only a little bit of work at the *Windows* command prompt.

As an example, let's add Python's implementation of the popular `readline` functionality to your *Windows* version of Python. The `pyreadline` module provides a Python version of `readline`, effectively plugging this particular hole in any default *Windows* installation.

Open up a *Windows* command prompt and follow along. Here, we're going to use a software installation tool (included in Python 3.5) to install the `pyreadline` module. The tool is called `pip`, short for "Python Index Project," named after the work that spawned `pip`'s creation.

At the *Windows* command prompt, type **pip install pyreadline**:

Geek Bits

The `readline` library implements a set of functions that provide interactive text-editing facilities (typically at command lines). The `pyreadline` module provides a Python interface to `readline`.

This is what you need to type into the command prompt.

```
File Edit Window Help InstallingPyReadLine
Microsoft Windows [Version 6.1.7601]
Copyright (c) 2009 Microsoft Corporation. All rights reserved.
C:\Users\Head First>
C:\Users\Head First> pip install pyreadline
Downloading/unpacking pyreadline
    . . .
    . . .
    . . .
Successfully installed pyreadline
Cleaning up...
C:\Users\Head First>
```

You'll see lots of messages here.

If you see this message, all is OK.

Make sure you are connected to the Internet before issuing this comm

And with that, `pyreadline` is installed and ready to go on *Windows*.

You can now flip back to Chapter 1 to get started with some sample Python code.

Install Python 3 on Mac OS X (macOS)

Python 2 comes preinstalled on *Mac OS X* by default. But this is no use to us, as we want to use Python 3 instead. Thankfully, when you visit the Python website (*http://www.python.org*), it is smart enough to work out that you're using a Mac. Hover your mouse over the *Download* tab, then click the 3.5.x button to download the Mac installer for Python. Select the latest version of Python 3, download its package, and then install in the usual "Mac way."

A standard Mac OS X installation program for Python 3.5.2 and above. If you have a more recent release than what we're showing here, that's fine—install away!

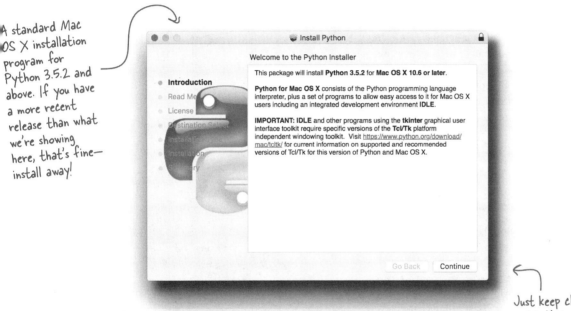

Just keep clicking until it's installed.

Using a package manager

On Macs, it is also possible to use one of the popular open source *package managers*, namely *Homebrew* or *MacPorts*. If you have never used either of these package managers, feel free to skip this little section and jump over to the top of the next page. If, however, you are already using either of these package managers, here are the commands you need to install Python 3 on your Mac from inside a terminal window:

- On *Homebrew*, type **brew install python3**.

- On *MacPorts* type **port install python3**.

And that's it: you're golden. Python 3 is ready for action on *Mac OS X*—let's take a look at what gets installed.

Check and Configure Python 3 on Mac OS X

To see if the install succeeded on *Mac OS X*, click on the *Applications* icon on your dock, then look for the *Python 3* folder.

Click on the *Python 3* folder and you'll see a bunch of icons (below).

The Python 3 folder on Mac OS X

The first option, *IDLE*, is by far the most useful, and it is how you will interact with Python 3 most of the time while learning the language. Choosing this option opens Python's integrated development environment called *IDLE*. This is a very simple IDE that provides access to Python's >>> interactive prompt, a passable text editor, the Python debugger, and the Python documentation. We'll be using *IDLE* a lot in this book.

The *Python Documentation.html* option opens a local copy of Python's entire documentation in HTML within your default browser (without requiring you to be online).

The *Python Launcher* option is automatically run by *Mac OS X* whenever you double-click on an executable file containing Python code. Although this may be useful for some, at *Head First Labs* we rarely use it, but it's still nice to know it's there if we ever do need it.

The last option, *Update Shell Profile.command*, updates the configuration files on *Mac OS X* to ensure the location of the Python interpreter and its associated utilities are correctly added to your operating system's path. You can click on this option now to run this command, then forget about ever having to run it again—once is enough.

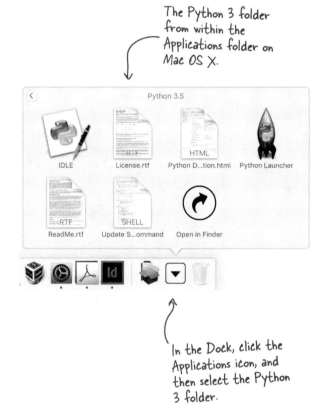

The Python 3 folder from within the Applications folder on Mac OS X.

In the Dock, click the Applications icon, and then select the Python 3 folder.

You're ready to run on Mac OS X

And with that, you're all set on *Mac OS X*.

You can now skip back to Chapter 1 and get started.

Install Python 3 on Linux

If you are running a recent distribution of your favorite *Linux*, the *really great news* is that you most likely have Python 2 *and* Python 3 already installed.

Here's a quick way to ask the Python interpreter to fess up its currently installed version number; open up a command line and type:

```
$ python3 -V
3.5.2
```

Be careful: that's an UPPERCASE "V".

How cool is that? Our Linux has the latest Python 3 installed.

If, after you issue this command, *Linux* complains that it can't find `python3`, you need to install a copy. How you do this depends on the *Linux* distribution you are running.

If your *Linux* is one based on the popular *Debian* or *Ubuntu* distribution (as is the one we use at *Head First Labs*), you can use the `apt-get` utility to install Python 3. Here's the command to use:

```
$ sudo apt-get install python3 idle3
```

If you are running a *yum*-based or *rpm*-based distribution, use the equivalent command for those systems. Or fire up your favorite *Linux* GUI and use your distribution's GUI-based package manager to select `python3` *and* `idle3` for installation. On many *Linux* systems, the *Synaptic Package Manager* is a popular choice here, as are any number of GUI-based software installers.

After installing Python 3, use the command from the top of this page to check that all is OK.

No matter which distribution you use, the `python3` command gives you access to the Python interpreter at the command line, whereas the `idle3` command gives you access to the GUI-based integrated development environment called *IDLE*. This is a very simple IDE that provides access to Python's >>> interactive prompt, a passable text editor, the Python debugger, and the Python documentation.

We'll be using the >>> prompt and *IDLE* a lot in this book, starting in Chapter 1, which you can flip back to now.

Be sure to select the "python3" and "idle3" packages for installation on Linux.

appendix b: pythonanywhere

Deploying Your Webapp

I can deploy my webapp to the cloud in about 10 minutes?!?!? I don't believe it...

At the end of Chapter 5, we claimed that deploying your webapp to the cloud was only 10 minutes away.

It's now time to make good on that promise. In this appendix, we are going to take you through the process of deploying your webapp on *PythonAnywhere*, going from zero to deployed in about 10 minutes. *PythonAnywhere* is a favorite among the Python programming community, and it's not hard to see why: it works exactly as you'd expect it to, has great support for Python (and Flask), and—best of all—you can get started hosting your webapp at no cost. Let's check out *PythonAnywhere*.

Step 0: A Little Prep

At the moment, you have your webapp code on your computer in a folder called webapp, which contains the vsearch4web.py file and the static and templates folders (as shown below). To prepare all this stuff for deployment, create a ZIP archive file of everything in your webapp folder, and call the archive file webapp.zip:

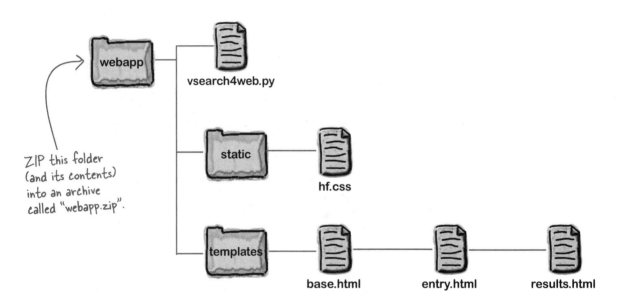

ZIP this folder (and its contents) into an archive called "webapp.zip".

In addition to webapp.zip, you also need to upload and install the vsearch module from Chapter 4. For now, all you need to do is locate the distribution file that you created back then. On our computer, the archive file is called vsearch-1.0.tar.gz and it's stored in our mymodules/vsearch/dist folder (on *Windows*, the file is likely called vsearch-1.0.zip).

Recall from Chapter 4 that Python's "setuptools" module creates ZIPs on Windows, and .tar.gz files on everything else.

You don't need to do anything with either archive file right now. Just make a note of where both archive files are on your computer so that they are easy to find when you upload them to *PythonAnywhere*. Feel free to grab a pencil and scribble down each archive file's location here:

webapp.zip

vsearch-1.0.tar.gz

This is "vsearch.zip" instead if you're on Windows.

Step 1: Sign Up for PythonAnywhere

This step couldn't be any easier. Surf over to *pythonanywhere.com*, then click on the **Pricing & signup** link:

— Start here.

Click on the big, blue button to create a *Beginner account*, then fill in the details on the signup form:

— Fill in this form.

This is the
"free signup" option.

If all is well, the PythonAnywhere dashboard appears. Note: you are both registered *and* signed in at this point:

The
PythonAnywhere
dashboard. Note
the five tabs
available to you.

Step 2: Upload Your Files to the Cloud

Click on the **Files** tab to view the folders and files available to you:

Click here.

Here are your folders.

Here are the files in your home folder.

Use the *Upload a file* option to locate and upload the two archive files from **Step 0**:

Use this option to upload each of your archive files.

You're going to click this link in a moment.

When you're done uploading, both archive files should appear on the list of files in your home folder.

You're now ready to extract and install these two uploaded archive files, and you'll do that during **Step 3**. To get ready, click the *Open a bash console here* link at the top right of the above page. This opens up a terminal window in your browser window (on *PythonAnywhere*).

Step 3: Extract and Install Your Code

When you click the *Open a bash console here* link, *PythonAnywhere* responds by replacing the *Files* dashboard with a browser-based Linux console (command prompt). You're going to issue a few commands to extract and install the vsearch module as well as your webapp's code within this console. Begin by installing vsearch into Python as a "private module" (i.e., just for your use) using this command (be sure to use vsearch-1.0.zip if you're on *Windows*):

```
python3 -m pip install vsearch-1.0.tar.gz --user
```

"--user" ensures the "vsearch" module is installed for your use only. PythonAnywhere does not allow you to install a module for everyone's use (just your own).

Run the command.

Success!

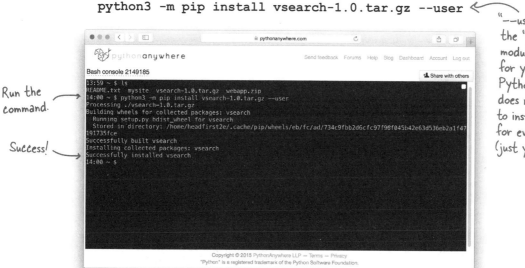

With the vsearch module successfully installed, it's time to turn your attention to your webapp's code, which has to be installed into the mysite folder (which already exists on your *PythonAnywhere* home folder). To do this, you need to issue two commands:

Unpack your webapp's code...

```
unzip webapp.zip
mv webapp/* mysite
```

...then move the code into the "mysite" folder.

You should see messages similar to these.

Step 4: Create a Starter Webapp, 1 of 2

With **Step 3** done, return to the *PythonAnywhere* dashboard and select the **Web** tab, where *PythonAnywhere* invites you to create a new starter webapp. You'll do this, then swap out the starter's webapp code for your own. Note that each *Beginner account* gets one webapp for free; if you want more, you'll have to upgrade to a paid account. Luckily—for now—you only need the one, so let's keep going by clicking *Add a new web app*:

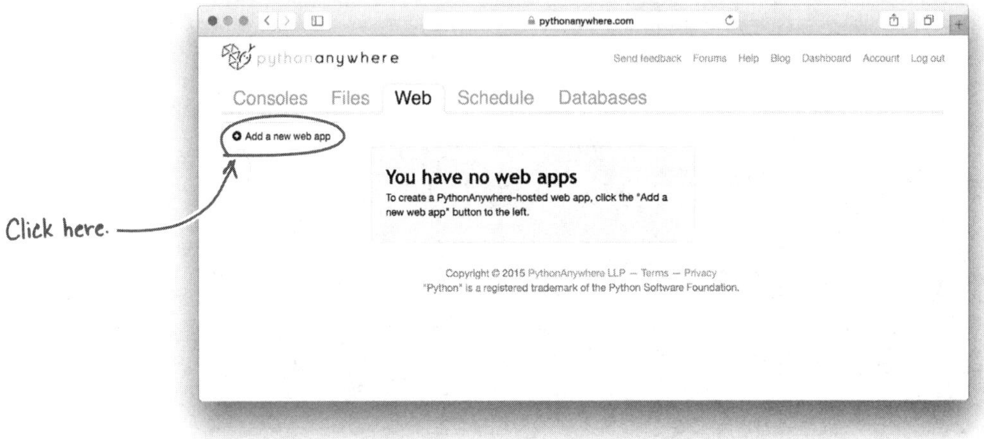

Click here.

As you are using a free account, your webapp is going to run on the site name shown on the next screen. Click the *Next* button to proceed with *PythonAnywhere's* suggested site name:

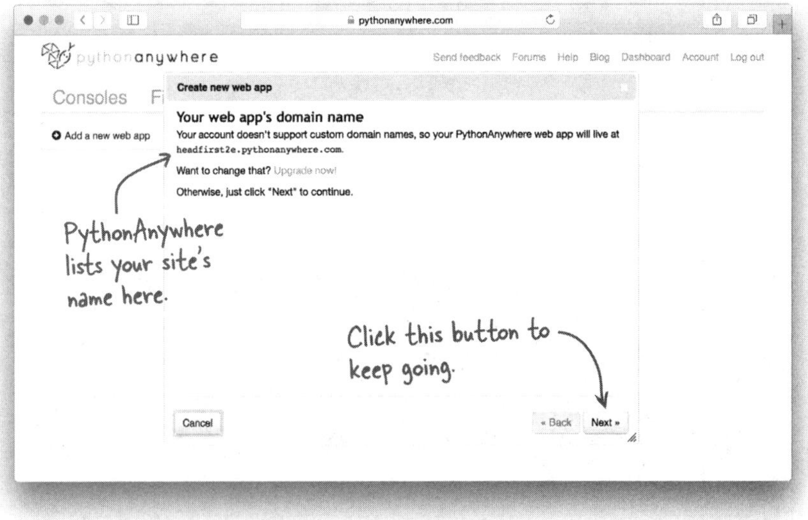

PythonAnywhere lists your site's name here.

Click this button to keep going.

Click *Next* to continue with this step.

Step 4: Create a Starter Webapp, 2 of 2

PythonAnywhere supports more than one Python web framework, so the next screen offers you a choice among the many supported systems. Pick Flask, then select the version of Flask and Python you wish to deploy to. As of this writing, Python 3.4 and Flask 0.10.1 are the most up-to-date versions supported by *PythonAnywhere*, so go with that combination unless a newer combination is offered (in which case, pick the newer one instead):

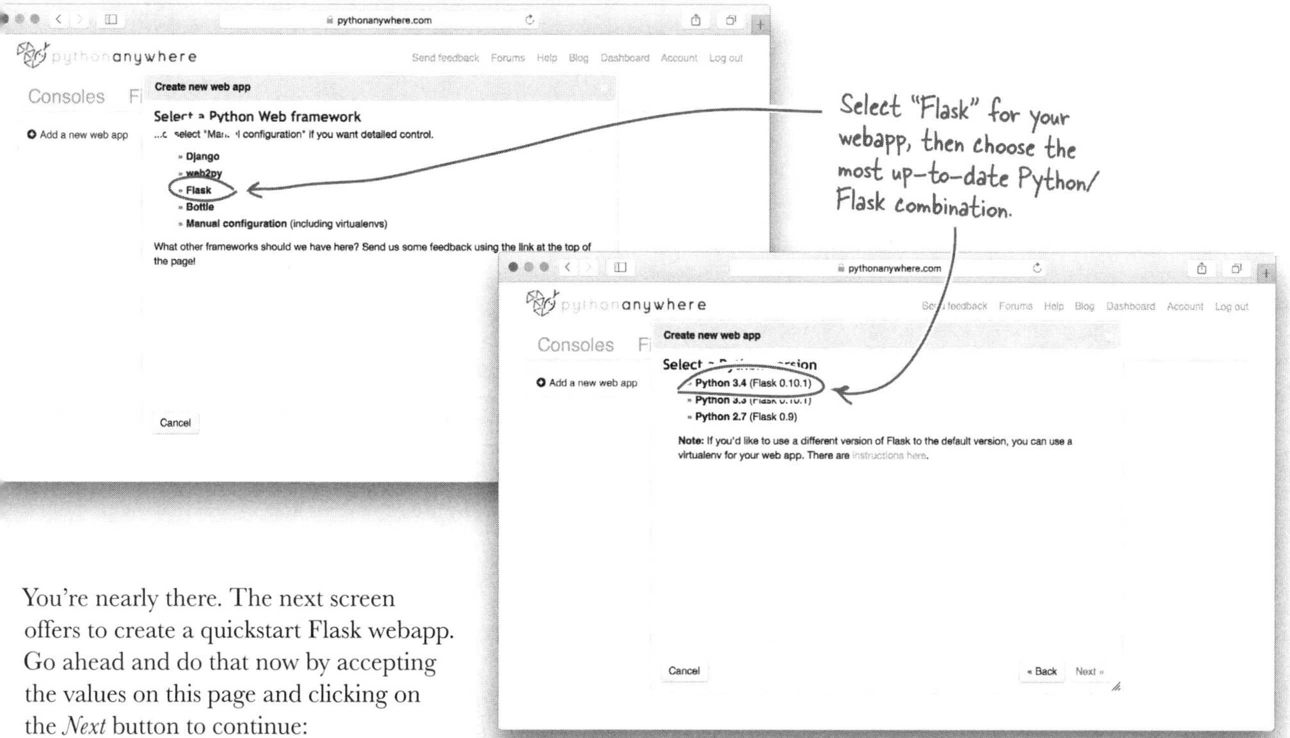

Select "Flask" for your webapp, then choose the most up-to-date Python/ Flask combination.

You're nearly there. The next screen offers to create a quickstart Flask webapp. Go ahead and do that now by accepting the values on this page and clicking on the *Next* button to continue:

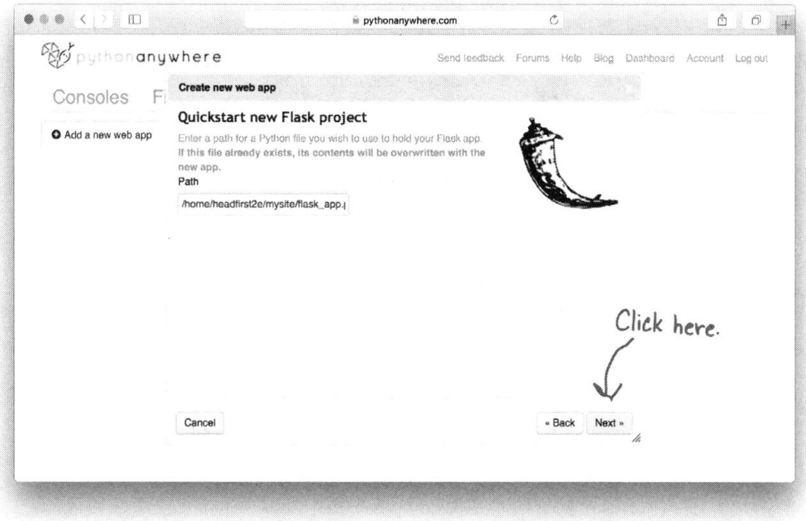

You don't need to click "Next" here. As soon as you choose the combination you want, this screen appears.

Click here.

Step 5: Configure Your Webapp

With **Step 4** complete, you are presented with the **Web** dashboard. Don't be tempted to click that big, green button just yet—you haven't told *PythonAnywhere* about your code yet, so hold off on running anything for now. Instead, click in the long link to the right of the *WSGI configuration file* label:

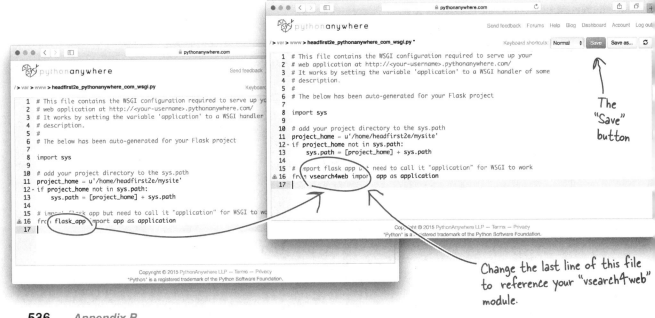

It's tempting, but DON'T click this button just yet.

Click this link instead.

Clicking that long link loads your newly created Flask webapp's configuration file into *PythonAnywhere's* web-based text editor. At the end of Chapter 5, we told you that *PythonAnywhere* imports your webapp code before invoking app.run() for you. This is the file that supports that behavior. However, it needs to be told to reference *your* code, not the code in the starter app, so you need to edit the last line of this file (as shown below), and then click *Save*:

The "Save" button

Change the last line of this file to reference your "vsearch4web" module.

Step 6: Take Your Cloud-Based Webapp for a Spin!

Be sure to save your changed configuration file, then return to the **Web** tab on the dashboard. It is now time to click on that big, tempting, green button. Go for it!

After but a brief moment, your webapp appears in your browser, and it works exactly as it did when you ran it locally, only now anybody with an Internet connection and a web browser can use it too:

Anyone can use this web address to interact with your webapp.

We're looking good for input and output in the cloud.

And with that, you're done. The webapp you developed in Chapter 5 has been deployed to *PythonAnywhere's* cloud (in less than 10 minutes). There's lots more to *PythonAnywhere* than what's shown in this short appendix, so feel free to explore and experiment. At some point, remember to return the *PythonAnywhere* dashboard and log out. Note that, despite your logging out, your webapp keeps running in the cloud until you tell it otherwise. That's pretty cool, isn't it?

appendix c: top ten things we didn't cover

There's Always More to Learn

I think we have a problem here. There are a whole bunch of things they didn't cover.

It was never our intention to try to cover everything.

This book's goal was always to show you enough Python to get you up to speed as quickly as possible. There's a lot more we could've covered, but didn't. In this appendix, we discuss the top 10 things that—given another 600 pages or so—we would've eventually gotten around to. Not all of the 10 things will interest you, but quickly flip through them just in case we've hit on your sweet spot, or provided an answer to that nagging question. All the programming technologies in this appendix come baked in to Python and its interpreter.

1. What About Python 2?

As of this book's publication date (late 2016) there are two mainstream flavors of Python in widespread use. You already know quite a bit about **Python 3**, as that's the flavor you've used throughout this book.

All new language developments and enhancements are being applied to Python 3, which is on a 12- to 18-month minor release cycle. Release 3.6 is due before 2016 ends, and you can expect 3.7 to arrive late in 2017 or early in 2018.

Python 2 has been "stuck" at release 2.7 for some time now. This has to do with the fact that the *Python core developers* (the people who guide the development of Python) decided that Python 3 was the future, and that Python 2 should quietly go away. There were solid technical reasons for this approach, but no one really expected things to take so long. After all, Python 3—the future of the language—first appeared in late 2008.

An entire book could be written on what's happened since late 2008 until now. Suffice it to say, Python 2 stubbornly refused to go away. There was (and still is) a huge installed base of Python 2 code and developers, with some domains dragging their heels when it comes to upgrading. There's a very simple reason for why this is: Python 3 introduced a handful of enhancements that broke backward compatibility. Put another way: there's lots of Python 2 code that will not run *unchanged* in Python 3 (even though, at a first glance, it can be hard to tell Python 2 code from Python 3 code). Also, many programmers simply believed Python 2 was "good enough," and didn't upgrade.

Recently (over the last year), there's been a sea change. The switching rate from 2 to 3 appears to be increasing. Some very popular third-party modules have released Python 3–compatible versions, and this is having a positive effect on Python 3 adoption. Additionally, the *Python core developers* keep adding extra goodness to Python 3, making it a more attractive programming language over time. The practice of "backporting" the cool new features from 3 to 2 has stopped with 2.7, and although bug and security fixes are still being applied, the *Python core developers* have announced that this activity will stop in 2020. The clock is ticking for Python 2.

Here's the common advice offered when you're trying to decide whether 3 or 2 is right for you:

> I'm just some of the Python 2 code that's out there. There's lots and lots of code like me.

If you're starting a new project, use Python 3.

You need to resist the urge to create more legacy code in Python 2, especially if you're starting with a blank slate. If you have to maintain some existing Python 2 code, what you know about 3 carries over: you'll certainly be able to read the code and understand it (it's still Python, regardless of the major version number). If there are technical reasons why the code has to remain running in Python 2, then so be it. If, however, the code can be ported to Python 3 without too much fuss, then we believe the gain is worth the pain, as Python 3 *is* the better language, and *is* the future.

2. Virtual Programming Environments

Let's imagine you have two clients, one with Python code that relies on one version of a third-party module, and another that relies on a *different* version of the same third-party module for their code. And, of course, you're the poor soul who has to maintain both projects' code.

Doing so on one computer can be problematic, as the Python interpreter doesn't support the installation of different versions of third-party modules.

That said, help is at hand thanks to Python's notion of virtual environments.

A **virtual environment** lets you create a new, clean Python environment within which you can run your code. You can install third-party modules into one virtual environment without impacting another, and you can have as many virtual environments as you like on your computer, switching between them by *activating* the one you want to work on. As each virtual environment can maintain its own copy of whatever third-party modules you wish to install, you can use two different virtual environments, one for each of your client projects discussed above.

Before doing so, however, you have to make a choice: use the virtual environment technology, called `venv`, that ships with Python 3's *standard library*, or install the `virtualenv` module from PyPI (which does the same thing as `venv`, but has more bells and whistles). It's best if you make an informed choice.

To learn more about `venv`, check out its documentation page:

```
https://docs.python.org/3/library/venv.html
```

To find out what `virtualenv` offers over and above `venv`, start here:

```
https://pypi.org/project/virtualenv/
```

Whether you use virtual environments for your projects is a personal choice. Some programmers swear by them, refusing to write any Python code unless it's within a virtual environment. This may be a bit of an extreme stance, but to each their own.

We chose not to cover virtual environments in the main body of this book. We feel virtual environments are—if you need them—a total godsend, but we don't yet believe every Python programmer needs to use one for everything they do.

We recommend you slowly back away from people who say that you aren't a proper Python programmer *unless* you use `virtualenv`.

I'm pretty sure I've solved my multiple third-party module problem... all I had to do was read all of these.

All he had to do was use a virtual environment.

3. More on Object Orientation

If you've read through this entire book, by now you'll (hopefully) appreciate what's meant by this phrase: "In Python, everything's an object."

Python's use of objects is great. It generally means that things work the way you expect them to. However, the fact that everything's an object does **not** mean that everything has to belong to a class, especially when it comes to your code.

In this book, we didn't learn how to create our own class until we needed one in order to create a custom context manager. Even then, we only learned as much as was needed, and nothing more. If you've come to Python from a programming language that insists all your code resides in a class (with *Java* being the classic example), the way we've gone about things in this book may be disconcerting. Don't let this worry you, as Python is much less strict than *Java* (for instance) when it comes to how you go about writing your programs.

If you decide to create a bunch of functions to do the work you need to do, then have at it. If your brain thinks in a more functional way, Python can help here too with the comprehension syntax, tipping its hat to the world of functional programming. And if you can't get away from the fact that your code needs to reside in a class, Python has full-featured object-oriented-programming syntax built right in.

If you do end up spending a lot of time creating classes, check out the following:

*   @staticmethod: A decorator that lets you create a static function within a class (which does not receive self as its first argument).

*   @classmethod: A decorator that lets you create a class method that expects a class as its first object (usually referred to as cls), not self.

*   @property: A decorator that allows you to redesignate and use a method as if it were an attribute.

*   __slots__: A class directive that (when used) can greatly improve the memory efficiency of the objects created from your class (at the expense of some flexibility).

To learn more about any of these, consult the Python docs (*https://docs.python.org/3/*). Or check out some of our favorite Python books (discussed in the next appendix).

> OK, chaps...let's think about this for a moment. Does that code really need to be in a class?

4. Formats for Strings and the Like

The recurring example application used in this book displayed its output in a web browser. This allowed us to defer any output formatting to HTML (specifically, we used the *Jinja2* module included with *Flask*). In doing so, we sidestepped one area where Python shines: text-based string formatting.

Let's say you have a string that needs to contain values that won't be known until your code runs. You want to create a message (msg) that contains the values so you can perform some later processing (perhaps you're going to print the message on screen, include the message within an HTML page you're creating with *Jinja2*, or tweet the message to your 3 million followers). The values your code generates at runtime are in two variables: price (the price of the item in question) and tag (a catchy marketing tagline). You have a few options here:

- Build the message you need using concatenation (the + operator).
- Use old-style string formats (using the % syntax).
- Take advantage of every string's format method to build your message.

Here's a short >>> session showing each of these techniques in action (bearing in mind that you, having worked through this book, already concur with what the generated message is telling you):

```
Python 3.5.2 Shell
>>>
>>> price = 49.99
>>> tag = 'is a real bargain!'
>>>
>>> msg = 'At ' + str(price) + ', Head First Python ' + tag
>>> msg
'At 49.99, Head First Python is a real bargain!'
>>>
>>> msg = 'At %2.2f, Head First Python %s' % (price, tag)
>>> msg
'At 49.99, Head First Python is a real bargain!'
>>>
>>> msg = 'At {}, Head First Python {}'.format(price, tag)
>>> msg
'At 49.99, Head First Python is a real bargain!'
>>> |
                                              Ln: 115  Col: 4
```

You already knew this, right? ☺

> The %s and %f format specifiers are as old as the hills...but, hey, like me, they still work.

Which of these techniques you use is a personal preference, although there's a bit of a push on to encourage the use of the format method over the other two (see *PEP 3101* at *https://www.python.org/dev/peps/pep-3101/*). You'll find code in the wild that uses one technique over the other, and sometimes (and not at all helpfully) mixes all three. To learn more, start here:

https://docs.python.org/3/library/string.html#formatspec

5. Getting Things Sorted

Python has wonderful built-in sorting capabilities. Some of the built-in data structures (lists, for example) contain `sort` methods that can be used to perform in-place ordering of your data. However, it is the `sorted` BIF that makes Python truly special (as this BIF works with *any* of the built-in data structures).

In the IDLE session below, we first define a small dictionary (`product`), which we then process with a succession of `for` loops. The `sorted` BIF is exploited to control the order in which each `for` loop receives the dictionary's data. Follow along on your computer while you read the annotations:

BIF is short for "built-in function."

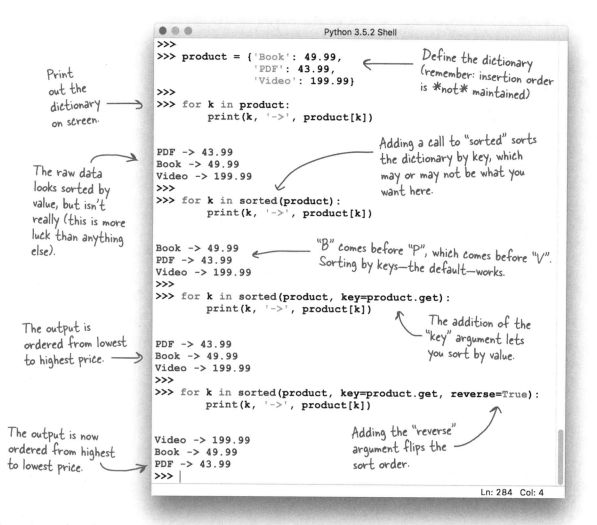

Print out the dictionary on screen.

Define the dictionary (remember: insertion order is *not* maintained)

The raw data looks sorted by value, but isn't really (this is more luck than anything else).

Adding a call to "sorted" sorts the dictionary by key, which may or may not be what you want here.

"B" comes before "P", which comes before "V". Sorting by keys—the default—works.

The output is ordered from lowest to highest price.

The addition of the "key" argument lets you sort by value.

The output is now ordered from highest to lowest price.

Adding the "reverse" argument flips the sort order.

```
Python 3.5.2 Shell
>>>
>>> product = {'Book': 49.99,
               'PDF': 43.99,
               'Video': 199.99}
>>>
>>> for k in product:
        print(k, '->', product[k])

PDF -> 43.99
Book -> 49.99
Video -> 199.99
>>>
>>> for k in sorted(product):
        print(k, '->', product[k])

Book -> 49.99
PDF -> 43.99
Video -> 199.99
>>>
>>> for k in sorted(product, key=product.get):
        print(k, '->', product[k])

PDF -> 43.99
Book -> 49.99
Video -> 199.99
>>>
>>> for k in sorted(product, key=product.get, reverse=True):
        print(k, '->', product[k])

Video -> 199.99
Book -> 49.99
PDF -> 43.99
>>> |
                                        Ln: 284  Col: 4
```

Learn more about how to sort with Python from this wonderful *HOWTO*:

https://docs.python.org/3/howto/sorting.html#sortinghowto

6. More from the Standard Library

Python's *standard library* is full of goodness. It's always a worthy exercise to take 20 minutes every once in a while to review what's available, starting here:

https://docs.python.org/3/library/index.html

If what you need is in the *standard library*, don't waste your precious time rewriting it. Use (and/or extend) what's already available. In addition to the Python docs, *Doug Hellmann* has ported his popular *Module of the Week* material over to Python 3. Find Doug's excellent material here:

https://pymotw.com/3/

We've reviewed a few of our favorite *standard library* modules below. Note that we can't stress enough how important it is to know what's in the *standard library*, as well as what all the provided modules can do for you.

collections

This module provides importable data structures, over and above the built-in list, tuple, dictionary, and set. There's lots to like in this module. Here's an abbreviated list of what's in collections:

- OrderedDict: A dictionary that maintains insertion order.

- Counter: A class that makes counting things almost too easy.

- ChainMap: Combines one or more dictionaries and makes them appear as one.

> Yes, yes...I get the joke, and it's very droll: "batteries included," right?

itertools

You already know Python's for loop is great, and when reworked as a comprehension, looping is crazy cool. This module, itertools, provides a large collection of tools for building custom iterations. This module has a lot to offer, but be sure to also check out product, permutations, and combinations (and once you do, sit back and thank your lucky stars you didn't have to write any of that code).

functools

The functools library provides a collection of higher-order functions (functions that take function objects as arguments). Our favorite is partial, which lets you "freeze" argument values to an existing function, then invoke the function with a new name of your choosing. You won't know what you're missing until you try it.

7. Running Your Code Concurrently

In Chapter 11¾, you used a thread to solve a waiting problem. Threads are not the only game in town when it comes to running code concurrently within your programs, although, to be honest, threads are the most used and abused of all of the available techniques. In this book, we deliberately kept our use of threads as simple as possible.

There are other technologies available to you when you find yourself in a situation where your code has to do more than one thing at once. Not every program needs these types of services, but it is nice to know that Python has a bunch of choices in this area should the need arise.

In addition to the `threading` module, here are some modules worth checking out (and we also refer you back one page to #6, as *Doug Hellmann* has some great posts on some of these modules):

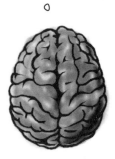

You do realize there's only one of me, right? Yet you expect me to perform and understand multiple computer tasks at once?!?!?

- `multiprocessing`: This module allows you to spawn multiple Python processes, which—if you have more than one CPU core—can spread your computational load across many CPUs.

- `asyncio`: Lets you specify concurrency via the creation and specification of coroutines. This is a relatively new addition to Python 3, so—for many programmers—it's a very new idea (and the jury is still out).

- `concurrent.futures`: Lets you manage and run a collection of tasks concurrently.

Which of these is right for you is a question you'll be able to answer once you've tried each of them with some of your code.

New keywords: async and await

The `async` and `await` keywords were added in Python 3.5, and provide a standard way to create coroutines.

The `async` keyword can be used in front of the existing `for`, `with`, and `def` keywords (with the `def` usage receiving the most attention to date). The `await` keyword can be used in front of (almost) any other code. As of the end of 2016, `async` and `await` are very new, and Python programmers the world over are only just beginning to explore what they can do with them.

The Python docs have been updated with information on these new keywords, but, for our money, you'll find the best descriptions of their use (and the craziness that using them induces) by searching *YouTube* for anything on the topic by *David Beazley*. **Be warned**: David's talks are always excellent, but do tend to lean toward the more advanced topics in the Python language ecosystem.

David's talks on Python's *GIL* are regarded as classics by many, and his books are great too; more on this in *Appendix E*.

Geek Bits

"GIL" stands for "Global Interpreter Lock". The GIL is an internal mechanism used by the interpreter to ensure stability. Its continued use within the interpreter is the subject of much discussion and debate within the Python community.

8. GUIs with Tkinter (and Fun with Turtles)

Python comes with a complete library called `tkinter` (the *Tk interface*) for building cross-platform GUIs. You may not realize it, but you've been using an application from the very first chapter of this book that is built with `tkinter`: IDLE.

What's neat about `tkinter` is that it comes preinstalled (and ready for use) with every Python installation that includes IDLE (i.e., nearly all of them). Despite this, `tkinter` doesn't receive the use (and love) it deserves, as many believe it to be unnecessarily clunky (compared to some third-party alternatives). Nevertheless, and as IDLE demonstrates, it is possible to produce useful and usable programs with `tkinter`. (Did we mention that `tkinter` comes preinstalled and ready for use?)

One such usage is the `turtle` module (which is also part of the *standard library*). To quote the Python docs: *Turtle graphics is a popular way for introducing programming to kids. It was part of the original Logo programming language developed by Wally Feurzig and Seymour Papert in 1966.* Programmers (i.e., mainly kids, but fun for newbies, too) can use commands like `left`, `right`, `pendown`, `penup`, and so on to draw on a GUI canvas (provided by `tkinter`).

Here's a small program, which has been adapted ever so slightly from the example that comes with the `turtle` docs:

As well as showing "turtle" in action, this small program also demonstrates the use of Python's "while" loop and "break" statement. They work exactly as you'd expect them to, but don't see nearly as much action as the "for" loop and comprehensions.

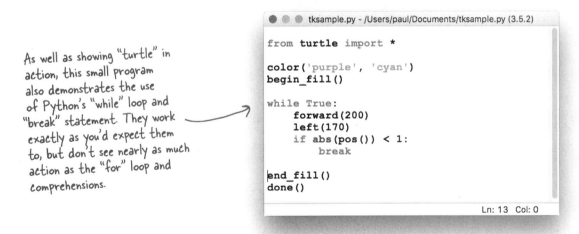

```
tksample.py - /Users/paul/Documents/tksample.py (3.5.2)

from turtle import *

color('purple', 'cyan')
begin_fill()

while True:
    forward(200)
    left(170)
    if abs(pos()) < 1:
        break

end_fill()
done()
                                          Ln: 13   Col: 0
```

And when this small `turtle` program is executed, a thing of beauty is drawn and appears on screen:

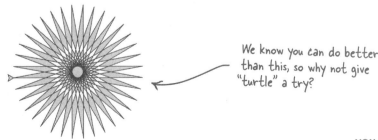

We know you can do better than this, so why not give "turtle" a try?

9. It's Not Over 'Til It's Tested

This book has barely mentioned automated testing, aside from a passing nod to the py.test tool for checking conformance to *PEP 8* (at the end of Chapter 4). This is not because we think automated testing isn't important. **We think automated testing is very important**. It is such an important topic that entire books are dedicated to it.

That said, in this book, we avoided automated testing tools on purpose. This has nothing to do with how we feel about automated testing (it really *is* very important). However, when you are first learning to program in a new programming language, introducing automated testing can confuse more than it clarifies, as the creation of tests assumes a good understanding of the thing being tested, and if that "thing" happens to be a new programming language that you're learning...well, you can see where we're going with this, can't you? It's a bit like the chicken and the egg. Which comes first: learning to code, or learning how to test the code you're learning?

Of course, now that you're a bona-fide Python programmer, you can take the time to understand how Python's *standard library* makes it easy to test your code. There are two modules to look at (and consider):

Hey, don't look at me... I didn't put that there.

- doctest: This module lets you embed your tests in your module's docstrings, which isn't as weird as it sounds and *is* very useful.

- unittest: You may have already used a "unittest" library with another programming language, and Python comes with its very own version (which works exactly as you'd expect it to).

The doctest module is adored by those who use it. The unittest module works like most other "unittest" libraries in other languages, and a lot of Python programmers complain that it's not *pythonic* enough. This has led to the creation of the hugely popular py.test (which we talk more about in the next appendix).

Don't you dare flip on over to the next page before you've thought about how you'd use Python's automated testing tools to check the correctness of the code you write.

10. Debug, Debug, Debug

You'd be forgiven for thinking that the vast majority of Python programmers revert to adding `print` calls to their code when something goes wrong. And you wouldn't be far off: it's a popular debugging technique.

Another is experimenting at the >>> prompt, which—if you think about it—is very like a debugging session *without* the usual debugging chores of watching traces and setting up breakpoints. It is impossible to quantify how productive the >>> prompt makes Python programmers. All we know is this: if a future release of Python decides to remove the interactive prompt, things will get ugly.

If you have code that's not doing what you think it should, and the addition of `print` calls as well as experimenting at the >>> prompt have left you none the wiser, consider using Python's included debugger: `pdb`.

It's possible to run the `pdb` debugger directly from your operating system's terminal window, using a command like this (where `myprog.py` is the program you need to fix):

```
python3 -m pdb myprog.py
```

> As always, Windows users need to use "py -3" instead of "python3". (That's "py", space, then minus 3).

It's also possible to interact with `pdb` from the >>> prompt, which is as close an instantiation of "the best of both worlds" as we think you'll ever come across. The details of how this works, as well as a discussion of all the usual debugger commands (set a breakpoint, skip, run, etc.) are in the docs:

https://docs.python.org/3/library/pdb.html

The `pdb` technology is not an "also ran," nor was it an afterthought; it's a wonderfully feature-full debugger for Python (and it comes built-in).

You can learn all about traces and breakpoints by working through the "pdb" docs.

> Make sure a working understanding of Python's "pdb" debugger is part of your toolkit.

appendix d: top ten projects not covered

Even More Tools, Libraries, and Modules

No matter the job at hand, the most important thing I do is to make sure I'm using the right tools.

We know what you're thinking as you read this appendix's title.

Why on Earth didn't they make the title of the last appendix: *The Top Twenty Things We Didn't Cover*? Why *another* 10? In the last appendix, we limited our discussion to stuff that comes baked in to Python (part of the language's "batteries included"). In this appendix, we cast the net much further afield, discussing a whole host of technologies that are available to you *because* Python exists. There's lots of good stuff here and—just like with the last appendix—a quick perusal won't hurt you *one single bit*.

1. Alternatives to >>>

Throughout this book we've happily worked at Python's built-in >>> prompt, either from within a terminal window or from within IDLE. In doing so, we hope we've demonstrated just how effective using the >>> prompt can be when you're experimenting with ideas, exploring libraries, and trying out code.

There are lots of alternatives to the built-in >>> prompt, but the one that gets the most attention is called ipython, and if you find yourself wishing you could do more at the >>> prompt, ipython is worth a look. It is very popular with many Python programmers, but is *especially* popular within the scientific community.

To give you an idea of what ipython can do compared to the plain ol' >>> prompt, consider this short interactive ipython session:

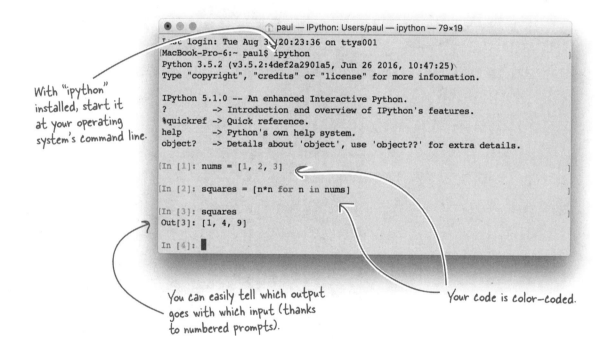

With "ipython" installed, start it at your operating system's command line.

You can easily tell which output goes with which input (thanks to numbered prompts).

Your code is color-coded.

Find out more about ipython at *https://ipython.org*.

There are other >>> alternatives, but the only other one that's a match (in our view) for what ipython has to offer is ptpython (more information can be found here: *https://pypi.org/project/ptpython/*). If you like working within a text-based terminal window, but are looking for something a bit more "full screen" than ipython, take a look at ptpython. You won't be disappointed.

— Pssst! Since discovering "ptpython", Paul has used it every day.

As with all third-party modules, you can use "pip" to install both "ipython" and "ptpython".

2. Alternatives to IDLE

We're not afraid to state this: we have a soft spot for *IDLE*. We really like the fact that Python not only comes with a capable >>> prompt, but also ships with a passable cross-platform GUI-based editor and debugger. There are few other mainstream programming languages that provide anything similar as part of their default install.

Regrettably, *IDLE* gets a fair amount of flack in the Python community, as it stacks up poorly against some of the more capable "professional" offerings. We think this is an *unfair* comparison, as *IDLE* was never designed to compete in that space. *IDLE*'s main goal is to get new users up and going as quickly as possible, and it does this *in spades*. Consequently, we feel *IDLE* should be celebrated more in the Python community.

IDLE aside, if you need a more professional IDE, you have choices. The most popular in the Python space include:

- *Eclipse*: ***https://www.eclipse.org***
- *PyCharm*: ***https://www.jetbrains.com/pycharm/***
- *WingWare*: ***https://wingware.com***

Eclipse is a completely open source technology, so won't cost you more than the download. If you're already an *Eclipse* fan, its support for Python is very good. But, if you aren't currently using *Eclipse*, we wouldn't recommend its use to you, due to the existence of *PyCharm* and *WingWare*.

Both *PyCharm* and *WingWare* are commercial products, with "community versions" available for download at no cost (but with some restrictions). Unlike *Eclipse*, which targets many programming languages, both *PyCharm* and *WingWare* target Python programmers specifically and, like all IDEs, have great support for project work, links to source code management tools (like *git*), support for teams, links to the Python docs, and so on. We encourage you to try both, then make your choice.

If IDEs aren't for you, fear not: all of the world's major text editors offer excellent language support to Python programmers.

> Well, WingWare, between the two of us, we have the Python IDE world covered.

> I'll drink to that!

Mr. PyCharm   Mr. WingWare

What does Paul use?

Paul's text editor of choice is `vim` (Paul uses *MacVim* on his development machines). When working on Python projects, Paul supplements his use of `vim` with `ptpython` (when experimenting with code snippets), and he's also a fan of *IDLE*. Paul uses *git* for local version control.

For what it's worth, Paul doesn't use a full-featured IDE, but his students love *PyCharm*. Paul also uses (and recommends) *Jupyter Notebook*, which is discussed next.

3. Jupyter Notebook: The Web-Based IDE

In item #1, we drew your attention to `ipython` (which is an excellent >>> alternative). From the same project team comes *Jupyter Notebook* (previously known as *iPython Notebook*).

The next generation of Jupyter Notebook is called Jupyter Lab, and it was in "alpha" as work on this book was concluding. Keep an eye out for the Jupyter Lab project: it's going to be something rather special.

Jupyter Notebook can be described as the power of `ipython` in an interactive web page (which goes by the generic name of "notebook"). What's amazing about *Jupyter Notebook* is that your code is editable and runnable from within the notebook, and—if you feel the need—you can add text and graphics, too.

Here's some code from Chapter 12 running within a *Jupyter Notebook*. Note how we've added textual descriptions to the notebook to indicate what's going on:

```
● ● ●    ○ Home              ×  ○ Appendix D           ×

←  →  C   ⓘ localhost:8888/notebooks/Appendix%20D.ipynb#Playing-with-the-url_utils.py        ☆  ⋮

     ○ Jupyter   Appendix D (autosaved)                                                    🐍

     File   Edit   View   Insert   Cell   Kernel   Help                        ✎ | Python 3 ○

     💾  +  ✂  🗐  🗋  ↑  ↓  ▶  ■  C   Code         ⇕  ⌨  CellToolbar


              Playing with the code from url_utils.py

              Define the <b>``gen_from_urls``</b> generator function:

     In [1]:  import requests

              def gen_from_urls(urls: tuple) -> tuple:
                  for resp in (requests.get(url) for url in urls):
                      yield len(resp.content), resp.status_code, resp.url

              Let's specify three URLs to work with:

     In [2]:  urls = ('http://jupyter.org/', 'http://ipython.org/', 'http://pydata.org/')

              Use the generator function with a for loop:

     In [3]:  for _, status, _ in gen_from_urls(urls):
                  print(status)

              200
              200
              200
```

Learn more about *Jupyter Notebook* from its website (*http://jupyter.org*), and use `pip` to install it onto your computer, then start exploring. You will be glad you did. *Jupyter Notebook* is a *killer* Python application.

4. Doing Data Science

When it comes to Python adoption and usage, there's one domain that continues to experience explosive growth: the world of **data science**.

This is not an accident. The tools available to data scientists using Python are world class (and the envy of many other programming communities). What's great for non–data scientists is that the tools favored by the data folks have wide applicability outside the *Big Data* landscape.

Entire books have been (and continue to be) written about using Python within the *data science* space. Although you may think this advice biased, the books on this subject from *O'Reilly Media* are excellent (and plentiful). *O'Reilly Media* has made a business out of spotting where the technology industry is heading, then ensuring there's plenty of great, high-quality learning material available to those wanting to learn more.

Note from Marketing: This means they got our memo. ☺

Here's just a selection of some of the libraries and modules available to you if you do data science (or any other science calculations, for that matter). If *data science* isn't your thing, check out this stuff anyway—there's lots to like here:

- `bokeh`: A set of technologies for publishing interactive graphics on web pages.

- `matplotlib/seaborn`: A comprehensive set of graphing modules (which integrates with `ipython` and *Jupyter Notebook*).

- `numpy`: Among other things, allows you to efficiently store and manipulate multidimensional data. If you're a fan of matrices, you'll love `numpy`.

- `scipy`: A set of scientific modules optimized for numerical data analysis, which complements and expands upon what's provided by `numpy`.

- `pandas`: If you are coming to Python from the *R* language, then you'll feel right at home with `pandas`, which provides optimized analysis data structures and tools (and is built on top of `numpy` and `matplotlib`). The need to use `pandas` is what brings a lot of data folk to the community (and long may this continue). `pandas` is another *killer* Python application.

- `scikit-learn`: A set of machine learning algorithms and technologies implemented in Python.

Note: most of these libraries and modules are `pip`-installable.

The best place to start learning about the intersection of Python and *data science* is the *PyData* website: *http://pydata.org*. Click on *Downloads*, then marvel at what's available (all as open source). Have fun!

Sacrebleu! They dare to ask me how I know my soup recipe's the best?!? Why...I ran a quick pandas data analysis, then published it in a Jupyter Notebook. Voilà—now everyone knows.

5. Web Development Technologies

Python is very strong in the web space, but *Flask* (with *Jinja2*) isn't the only game in town when it comes to building server-side webapps (even though *Flask* is a very popular choice, especially if your needs are modest).

The best-known technology for building webapps with Python is *Django*. It wasn't used in this book due to the fact that (unlike *Flask*) you have to learn and understand quite a bit before you create your first *Django* webapp (so, for a book like this, which concentrates on teaching the basics of Python *well*, Django is a poor fit). That said, there's a reason *Django* is so popular among Python programmers: it's really, really good.

If you class yourself as a "web developer," you should take the time to (at the very least) work through *Django*'s tutorial. In doing so, you'll be better informed as to whether you'll stick with *Flask* or move to *Django*.

If you do move to *Django*, you'll be in very good company: *Django* is such a large community within the wider Python community that it's able to sustain its own conference: *DjangoCon*. To date, *DjangoCon* has occurred in the US, Europe, and Australia. Here are some links to learn more:

- Djanjo's landing page (which has a link to the tutorial):
  https://www.djangoproject.com

- DjangoCon US:
  https://djangocon.us

- DjangoCon Europe:
  https://djangocon.eu

- DjangoCon Australia:
  http://djangocon.com.au

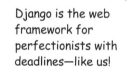

Django is the web framework for perfectionists with deadlines—like us!

But wait, there's more

As well as *Flask* and *Django*, there are other web frameworks (and we know we'll neglect to mention somebody's favorite). Those we hear the most about include: *Pyramid*, *TurboGears*, *web2py*, *CherryPy*, and *Bottle*. Find a more complete list on the Python wiki:

https://wiki.python.org/moin/WebFrameworks

6. Working with Web Data

In Chapter 12, we briefly used the `requests` library to demonstrate just how cool our generator was (compared to its equivalent comprehension). Our decision to use `requests` was no accident. If you ask most Python developers working with the Web what their favorite PyPI module is, the majority responds with one word: "requests."

The `requests` module lets you work with HTTP and web services via a simple, yet powerful, Python API. Even if your day job doesn't involve working directly with the Web, you'll learn a lot just from looking at the code for `requests` (the entire `requests` project is regarded as a master class in how to do things the Python way).

Find out more about `requests` here:

> *http://docs.python-requests.org/en/master/*

PyPI: The Python Package Index lives at https://pypi.org/.

Scrape that web data!

As the Web is primarily a text-based platform, Python has always worked well in that space, and the *standard library* has modules for working with JSON, HTML, XML, and the other similar text-based formats, as well as all the relevant Internet protocols. See the following sections of the Python docs for a list of modules that come with the *standard library* and are of most interest to web/Internet programmers:

- Internet Data Handling:
  > *https://docs.python.org/3/library/netdata.html*

- Structured Markup Processing Tools:
  > *https://docs.python.org/3/library/markup.html*

- Internet Protocols and Support:
  > *https://docs.python.org/3/library/internet.html*

If you find yourself having to work with data that's only available to you via a static web page, you'll likely want to *scrape* that data (for a quick scraping primer, see *https://en.wikipedia.org/wiki/Web_scraping*). Python has two third-party modules that will save you lots of time:

- *Beautiful Soup*:
  > *https://www.crummy.com/software/BeautifulSoup/*

- *Scrapy*:
  > *http://scrapy.org*

Try both, see which one solves your problem best, and then get on with whatever else needs doing.

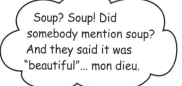

Soup? Soup! Did somebody mention soup? And they said it was "beautiful"... mon dieu.

7. More Data Sources

To keep things as real as possible (while trying to keep it simple), we used *MySQL* as our database backend in this book. If you spend a lot of time working with SQL (regardless of the database vendor you favor), then stop whatever you're doing and take two minutes to use `pip` to install `sqlalchemy`—it may be your best two-minute installation *ever*.

The `sqlalchemy` module is to SQL geeks what `requests` is to web geeks: indispensable. The *SQL Alchemy* project provides a high-level, Python-inspired set of technologies for working with tabular data (as stored in the likes of *MySQL*, *PostgreSQL*, *Oracle*, *SQL Server*, and so on). If you liked what we did with the DBcm module, you're going to love *SQL Alchemy*, which bills itself as *the* database toolkit for Python.

Find out more about the project at:

> ### *http://www.sqlalchemy.org*

There's more to querying data than SQL

Not all the data you'll ever need is in an SQL database, so there will be times when *SQL Alchemy* won't do. NoSQL database backends are now accepted as a valid addition to any data center, with *MongoDB* serving as the classic example as well as the most popular choice (even though there are many).

If you end up working with data that's being presented to you as JSON, or in a nontabular (yet structured) format, *MongoDB* (or something similar) may be just what you're looking for. Find out more about *MongoDB* here:

> ### *https://www.mongodb.com*

And check out the Python support for programming *MongoDB* using the `pymongo` database driver from the *PyMongo* documentation page:

> ### *https://api.mongodb.com/python/current/*

No matter where our data is—in an SQL or NoSQL data store—Python and its third-party modules do the trick.

8. Programming Tools

No matter how good you think your code is, bugs happen.

When they do, Python has lots to help you: the >>> prompt, the pdb debugger, *IDLE*, print statements, unittest, and doctest. When these options aren't enough, there are some third-party modules that might help.

Sometimes, you'll make a classic mistake that everyone else has made before you. Or perhaps you've forgotten to import some required module, and the problem doesn't crop up until you're showing off how great your code is to a room full of strangers (whoops).

To help avoid this type of thing, get *PyLint*, Python's code analysis tool:

https://www.pylint.org

PyLint takes your code and tells you what might be wrong with it *before* you run it for the first time.

If you use *PyLint* on your code before you run it in front of a room full of strangers, it may very well prevent blushing. *PyLint* might also hurt your feelings, as no one likes to be told their code is not up to scratch. But the pain is worth the gain (or maybe that should be: *the pain is better than the public embarrassment*).

More help with testing, too

In *Appendix C*, #9, we discussed the built-in support Python provides for automated testing. There are other such tools, too, and you already know that py.test is one of them (as we used it earlier in this book to check our code for *PEP 8* compliance).

Testing frameworks are like web frameworks: everyone has their favorite. That said, more Python programmers than not favor py.test, so we'd encourage you to take a closer look:

http://doc.pytest.org/en/latest/

I think someone's a little confused. I was told to "clean up the lint"...but I think they meant for me to use PyLint to clean up your code. What a mess...if only you'd written a py.test first, eh?

9. Kivy: Our Pick for "Coolest Project Ever"

One area where Python is not as strong as it could be is in the world of mobile touch devices. There are a lot of reasons why this is (which we aren't going to get into here). Suffice it to say, at the time of publication, it is still a challenge to create an *Android* or *iOS* app with Python alone.

One project is attempting to make progress in this area: *Kivy*.

Kivy is a Python library that allows for the development of applications that use multitouch interfaces. Pop on over to the *Kivy* landing page to see what's on offer:

https://kivy.org

Once there, click on the *Gallery* link and sit back for a moment while the page loads. If a project grabs your eye, click on the graphic for more information and a demo. While you view the demo, keep the following in mind: *everything you are looking at was coded with Python*. The *Blog* link has some excellent material, too.

What's really cool is that your *Kivy* user interface code is written once, then deployed on any supported platform *unchanged*.

If you are looking around for a Python project to contribute to, consider donating your time to *Kivy*: it's a great project, has a great team working on it, and is technically challenging. If nothing else, you won't be bored.

A snapshot of Kivy's landing page form 2016 showing one of their deployments: a fully immersive touch interface experience.

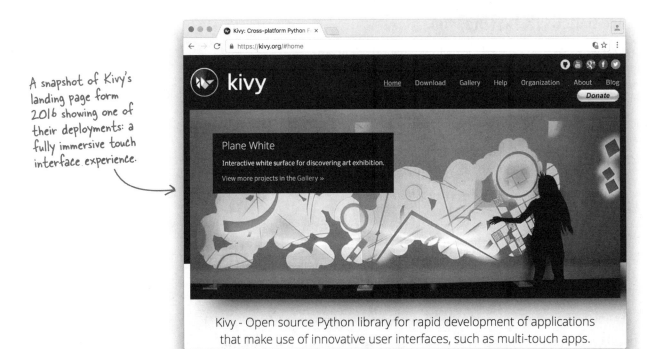

Kivy - Open source Python library for rapid development of applications that make use of innovative user interfaces, such as multi-touch apps.

10. Alternative Implementations

You already know from item #1 in *Appendix C* that there's more than one Python language release (Python 2 *and* Python 3). This means that there's *at least* two Python interpreters: one that runs Python 2 code, and one that runs Python 3 code (which is the one we've used throughout this book). When you download and install one of the Python interpreters from the Python website (like you did in *Appendix A*), the interpreter is referred to as the *CPython reference implementation*. *CPython* is the version of Python distributed by the *Python core developers*, and takes its name from the fact that it's written in portable C code: it's designed to be easily ported to other computing platforms. As you saw in *Appendix A*, you can download installers for *Windows* and *Mac OS X*, as well as find the interpreter preinstalled within your favorite Linux distribution. All of these interpreters are based on *CPython*.

Python is open source, so anyone is free to take *CPython* and change it in any way they wish. Developers can also take the Python language and implement their own interpreter for it in whichever programming language they wish, using whichever compiler techniques they like, running on whatever platform they're using. Although doing all of this is not for the faint of heart, plenty of developers do this (some of them describe it as "fun"). Here are short descriptions and links to some of the more active projects:

- *PyPy* (pronounced "pie-pie") is a experimental compiler testbed for Python 2 (with Python 3 support on the way). *PyPy* takes your Python code and runs it through a just-in-time compilation process, producing a final product that runs faster than *CPython* in many instances. Find out more here:

  ### *http://pypy.org*

- *IronPython* is a version of Python 2 for the *.NET* platform:

  ### *http://ironpython.net*

- *Jython* is a version of Python 2 that runs on *Java's JVM*:

  ### *http://www.jython.org*

- *MicroPython* is a port of Python 3 for use on the *pyboard* microcontroller, which is no bigger than your two thumbs side by side, and may well be the coolest little thing you've ever seen. Take a look:

  ### *http://micropython.org*

I'm open source and written in C. You'll find me everywhere!

Despite all these alternative Python interpreters, the majority of Python programmers remain happy with *CPython*. Increasingly, more developers are choosing Python 3.

appendix e: getting involved

The Python Community

No, no...there's no one else here. They've all gone to PyCon.

Python is much more than a great programming language.

It's a great community, too. The Python Community is welcoming, diverse, open, friendly, sharing, and giving. We're just amazed that no one, to date, has thought to put that on a greeting card! Seriously, though, there's more to programming in Python than the language. An entire ecosystem has grown up around Python, in the form of excellent books, blogs, websites, conferences, meetups, user groups, and personalities. In this appendix, we take a survey of the Python community and see what it has to offer. Don't just sit around programming on your own: **get involved**!

BDFL: Benevolent Dictator for Life

Guido van Rossum is a Dutch programmer whose gift to the world is the Python programming language (which he started as a "hobby" in the last 1980s). The ongoing development and direction of the language is set by the *Python core developers*, of which Guido is but one (albeit a very important one). Guido's title of *Benevolent Dictator for Life* is in recognition of the central role he continues to play in the day-to-day life of Python. If you see the letters BDFL in relation to Python, that's a reference to Guido.

Guido is on the record as stating that the name "Python" is a nod (and a wink) toward the British television comedy troupe *Monty Python's Flying Circus*, which helps explain the use of the name spam for many of the variables referred to in the Python docs.

Despite Guido's leading role, he does **not** own Python: nobody does. However, the interests of the language are protected by the PSF.

PSF: The Python Software Foundation

The PSF is a nonprofit organization that looks after the interests of Python, and is run by a nominated/elected board of directors. The PSF promotes and sponsors the continued development of the language. This is from the PSF's mission statement:

> *The mission of the Python Software Foundation is to promote, protect, and advance the Python programming language, and to support and facilitate the growth of a diverse and international community of Python programmers.*

Anyone can join the PSF and get involved. See the PSF website for details:

Have your say: join the PSF.

> *https://www.python.org/psf/*

One of the PSF's major activities is involvement in (and the underwriting of) the annual Python conference: *PyCon*.

PyCon: The Python Conference

Anyone can attend (and speak at) PyCon. In 2016, Portland, Oregon, hosted the conference, with thousands of Python developers in attendance (the previous two PyCons were held in Montreal, Canada). PyCon is the largest Python conference, but not the only one. You'll find Python conferences across the globe, ranging in size from small, regional conferences (tens of attendees), through national conferences (hundreds of attendees), up to the likes of *EuroPython* (thousands of attendees).

To see if there's a PyCon near you, search for the word "PyCon" together with the name of your nearest city (or the country you live in). Chances are, you'll be pleasantly surprised by what you find. Attending a local PyCon is a great way to meet and interact with like-minded developers. Many of the talks and sessions at the various PyCons are recorded: pop over to *YouTube* and type "PyCon" for an idea of what's available to view.

Get involved: attend PyCon.

A Tolerant Community: Respect for Diversity

Of all the programming conferences that exist today, PyCon was one of the first to introduce and insist on a *Code of Conduct*. You can read the 2016 Code of Conduct here:

https://us.pycon.org/2016/about/code-of-conduct/

Such a development is a *very good thing*. More and more, the smaller regional PyCons are adopting the Code of Conduct, too, which is also very welcome. A community grows to be strong and inclusive when there are clear guidelines about what's acceptable and what isn't, and the Code of Conduct helps to make sure all the world's PyCons are as welcoming as they can be.

In addition to striving to ensure everyone is welcome, a number of initiatives attempt to increase the representation of specific groups within the Python community, especially where—traditionally—such groups have been underrepresented. The best-known of these is *PyLadies*, which was established per their mission to help "more women become active participants and leaders in the Python open source community." If you're lucky, there's a *PyLadies* "chapter" near you: find out by starting your search from the *PyLadies* website:

http://www.pyladies.com

Just like the Python community, *PyLadies* started out small, but has very quickly grown to have global reach (which is truly inspirational).

Come for the language, stay for the community

Many programmers new to Python comment on how inclusive the Python community is. A lot of this attitude stems from Guido's guiding hand and example: firm, yet benevolent. There are other leading lights, too, and plenty of inspirational stories.

It doesn't get much more inspirational than *Naomi Ceder's* talk at *EuroPython* (which was repeated at other regional conferences, including *PyCon Ireland*). Here's a link to Naomi's talk, which we encourage you to watch:

https://www.youtube.com/watch?v=cCCiA-IlVco

Naomi's talk surveys a life in Python, and discusses how the community supports diversity, and how there's always more work for everyone to do.

One way to learn more about a community is to listen to some of the podcasts generated by its participants. We discuss two Python podcasts next.

> Encourage and support diversity within the Python community.

Python Podcasts

There are podcasts on *everything* these days. Within the Python community, there are two we feel are well worth subscribing and listening to. Whether it's something to listen to while driving, cycling, running, or chilling out, these podcasts are both deserving of your attention:

- *Talk Python to Me*: **https://talkpython.fm**
- *Podcast.__init__*: **http://pythonpodcast.com**

Follow both of these podcasts on *Twitter*, tell your friends about them, and give the producers of these podcasts your full support. Both *Talk Python To Me* and *Podcast.__init__* are produced by regular members of the Python community for the benefit of all of us (and *not* for profit).

Python Newsletters

If podcasts aren't your thing, but you still want to keep up with what's happening in the Python world, there are three weekly newsletters that can help:

- Pycoder's Weekly: **http://pycoders.com**
- Python Weekly: **http://www.pythonweekly.com**
- Import Python: **http://importpython.com/newsletter**

These curated newsletters provide links to all types of material: blogs, vlogs, articles, books, videos, talks, new modules, and projects. And their weekly announcements arrive right to your email inbox. So, go ahead and sign up.

As well as a foundation, multiple conferences, subgroups like *PyLadies*, codes of conduct, recognition of diversity, podcasts, and newsletters, Python also has its very own notion of *Zen*.

There's nothing quite like working out to the Python-related podcasts.

Reciting the Zen of Python helps me get in the zone...

The Zen of Python

Many moons ago, Tim Peters (one of Python's early leading lights) sat down and wondered: *what is it that makes Python Python?*

The answer came to Tim as *The Zen of Python*, which you can read by starting any version of the interpreter and typing the following incantation into the >>> prompt:

```
import this
```

We've done this for you, and shown the output of the above line of code in the screenshot at the bottom of this page. Be sure to read *The Zen of Python* at least once a month.

Many have tried to compress *The Zen of Python* into something a little easier to digest. None other than xkcd has given it a go. If you're connected to the Internet, type this line of code into your >>> prompt to see (quite literally) how xkcd got on:

```
import antigravity
```

Code is read more than it's written...

```
● ● ●                    Python 3.5.2 Shell
>>>
>>> import this
The Zen of Python, by Tim Peters

Beautiful is better than ugly.
Explicit is better than implicit.
Simple is better than complex.
Complex is better than complicated.
Flat is better than nested.
Sparse is better than dense.
Readability counts.
Special cases aren't special enough to break the rules.
Although practicality beats purity.
Errors should never pass silently.
Unless explicitly silenced.
In the face of ambiguity, refuse the temptation to guess.
There should be one-- and preferably only one --obvious way to do it.
Although that way may not be obvious at first unless you're Dutch.
Now is better than never.
Although never is often better than *right* now.
If the implementation is hard to explain, it's a bad idea.
If the implementation is easy to explain, it may be a good idea.
Namespaces are one honking great idea -- let's do more of those!
>>>
                                                    Ln: 28  Col: 4
```

Remember: read this *at least* once a month.

Which Book Should I Read Next?

Our Favorite Python Books

As Python has grown in popularity, the number of books devoted to the language has blossomed. Of all the books out there, there are two we regard as indispensable.

We mentioned David Beazley's work in an earlier appendix. In this book, David teams up with Brian K. Jones to document a wonderful collection of Python coding recipes. If you find yourself wondering how you do something in Python, wonder no more: look up the answer in Python Cookbook.

If deep-dives are more your thing, read this excellent book. There's a lot in here, but it's all good (and you'll be a better Python programmer for the experience).

Index

Symbols

>>>. *See* Python Shell

<> (angle brackets) 256–257

= (assignment operator) 13, 55, 72–74

\ (backslash) 77

^ (caret) 192

: (colon). *See* colon (:)

, (comma) 54, 123, 134

+ (concatenation operator) 543

{} (curly braces). *See* curly braces {}

-= (decrement operator) 106

/ (forward slash) 207

+= (increment operator) 106, 318

* (multiplication operator) 87

* notation 390–391

** notation 392–393

() (parentheses). *See* parentheses ()

[] (square brackets). *See* square brackets []

@ symbol 207

symbol 147

% syntax 214, 543

| (vertical bar) 262

A

Alt-P key combination (Linux/Windows) 31, 118

angle brackets 256–257

annotations (function) 162–163

append method 58–59, 72, 270

app.run() function 207, 211, 217

apt-get utility 527

*args keyword 390, 401

arguments
  about 147, 154–155
  adding multiple 165
  any number and type of 394
  by-address argument passing 184, 186–187
  by-reference argument passing 184, 186–187
  by-value argument passing 184–185, 187
  dictionary of 392–393
  function decorators 223, 390–395, 401
  interpreter processing 148
  list of 390
  methods and 317, 319–320, 322
  positional versus keyword assignment 171
  specifying default values for 170

arrays. *See* lists

arrow symbol 162–163

assignment operator 13, 55, 72–74

assignment statements 13–14

associative arrays. *See* dictionaries

asterisks 390–393

asyncio module 546

async keyword 546

AttributeError exception 483

attributes (state)
  about 49
  classes and 311–312, 322
  dictionary lookup retrieves 369
  displaying 30
  Flask's session technology and 368
  initializing values 323–325

Learn from experts.
Find the answers you need.

Sign up for a **10-day free trial** to get **unlimited access** to all of the content on Safari, including Learning Paths, interactive tutorials, and curated playlists that draw from thousands of ebooks and training videos on a wide range of topics, including data, design, DevOps, management, business—and much more.

Start your free trial at:
oreilly.com/safari

(No credit card required.)